INTERDISCIPLINARY PERSP_____ ___.____ LAW AND INTERNA_____ RELATIONS

The State of the Art

Interdisciplinary Perspectives on International Law and International Relations: The State of the Art brings together the most influential contemporary writers in the fields of international law and international relations to take stock of what we know about the making, interpretation, and enforcement of international law. The contributions to this volume critically explore what recent interdisciplinary work reveals about the design and workings of international institutions, the various roles played by international and domestic courts, and the factors that enhance compliance with international law. The volume also explores how interdisciplinary work has advanced theoretical understandings of the causes and consequences of the increased legalization of international affairs.

Jeffrey L. Dunoff is the Laura H. Carnell Professor of Law at Temple University Beasley School of Law, where he directs the Institute for International Law and Public Policy. Dunoff has previously served as the Nomura Visiting Professor at Harvard Law School, as a senior visiting research scholar and a visiting professor at Princeton University, and as a visiting Fellow at the Lauterpacht Research Centre for International Law at Cambridge University. His scholarship focuses on public international law; international regulatory regimes; and interdisciplinary approaches to international law. He is co-author (with Steven Ratner and David Wippman) of a leading textbook, *International Law: Actors, Norms, Process,* and his writings have appeared in the *American Journal of International Law, European Journal of International Law, Journal of International Economic Law,* and other publications.

Mark A. Pollack is professor of Political Science and Jean Monnet Chair *ad personam* at Temple University. He previously served as associate professor at the University of Wisconsin–Madison and as visiting professor at the European University Institute in Florence, Italy. His research focuses on the role of international institutions and international law in regional and global governance, with specific projects examining the delegation of powers to international organizations, institutions and policy-making in the European Union, and the global regulation of genetically modified foods. Pollack is the author of *The Engines of European Integration: Delegation, Agency, and Agenda Setting in the EU* and co-author (with Gregory C. Shaffer) of *When Cooperation Fails: The Law and Politics of Genetically Modified Foods.* He is also co-editor of seven books, as well as many articles and book chapters.

Interdisciplinary Perspectives on International Law and International Relations

THE STATE OF THE ART

Edited by

JEFFREY L. DUNOFF

Temple University

MARK A. POLLACK

Temple University

CAMBRIDGE
UNIVERSITY PRESS

CAMBRIDGE UNIVERSITY PRESS
Cambridge, New York, Melbourne, Madrid, Cape Town,
Singapore, São Paulo, Delhi, Mexico City

Cambridge University Press
32 Avenue of the Americas, New York, NY 10013-2473, USA

www.cambridge.org
Information on this title: www.cambridge.org/9781107684027

First published 2013

Printed in the United States of America

A catalog record for this publication is available from the British Library.

Library of Congress Cataloging in Publication Data

Interdisciplinary Perspectives on International Law and International Relations : The State of the Art /
[edited by] Jeffrey L. Dunoff, Temple University, Mark A. Pollack, Temple University.
    pages cm
Includes bibliographical references and index.
ISBN 978-1-107-02074-0 (hardback) – ISBN 978-1-107-68402-7 (paperback)
1. International law.   2. Effectiveness and validity of law.   3. International relations.   I. Dunoff, Jeffrey
L., 1960– editor of compilation.   II. Pollack, Mark A., 1966– editor of compilation.
KZ3410.I5759   2013
341–dc23   2012020053

ISBN 978-1-107-02074-0 Hardback
ISBN 978-1-107-68402-7 Paperback

Contents

Contributors

Kenneth W. Abbott is Professor of Law and Professor of Global Studies, Willard H. Pedrick Distinguished Research Scholar, and Senior Sustainability Scholar at Arizona State University. His research focuses on public and private institutions in international law and governance, in fields including sustainable development, global health, and economic relations.

Karen J. Alter is Professor of Political Science and Law at Northwestern University and a permanent visiting professor at the iCourts Center for Excellence, University of Copenhagen Faculty of Law. Her latest book, *The New Terrain of International Law: Courts, Politics, Rights*, is forthcoming from Princeton University Press in 2013.

Timm Betz is a graduate student at the University of Michigan, Ann Arbor. His research interests cover international political economy and the design of international institutions.

Daniel Bodansky is the Lincoln Professor of Law, Ethics and Sustainability, Sandra Day O'Connor College of Law, Arizona State University. He is the author of *The Art and Craft of International Environmental Law* (2010), which won the 2011 Sprout Award from the International Studies Association.

Rachel Brewster is a Professor of Law at Duke University and co-director of Duke's Center for International and Comparative Law. She received her BA and JD from the University of Virginia and her PhD in Political Science from the University of North Carolina at Chapel Hill.

Jutta Brunnée is Associate Dean of Law (Graduate) and Professor of Law and Metcalf Chair in Environmental Law, University of Toronto. Her academic interests are in the areas of public international law and international environmental law. She is co-author of *Legitimacy and Legality in International Law: An Interactional Account* (Cambridge University Press, 2010), which was awarded the American

Society of International Law's 2011 Certificate of Merit for preeminent contribution to creative scholarship. She serves on the Board of Editors of the *American Journal of International Law*.

Lisa Conant is an Associate Professor of Political Science at the University of Denver and author of *Justice Contained: Law and Politics in the European Union*. Her current research focuses on the European Court of Human Rights and the state of human rights protection in contemporary Europe.

Manfred Elsig is Assistant Professor of International Relations at the World Trade Institute of the University of Bern. His research focuses on the politics of international trade and on international organizations. He is the co-editor of *Governing the World Trade Organization: Past, Present and Beyond Doha* (Cambridge University Press, 2011) and *The EU's Foreign Economic Policies: A Principal-Agent Perspective* (Routledge, 2011).

Laurence R. Helfer is Harry R. Chadwick, Sr., Professor of Law and co-director of the Center for International and Comparative Law at Duke University School of Law. Helfer has authored more than sixty publications on his diverse research interests, which include human rights, international adjudication, and interdisciplinary analysis of international institutions.

Ian Johnstone is a Professor of International Law at the Fletcher School of Law and Diplomacy, Tufts University. From 1991 to 1992 and then 1994 to 2000, he worked for the United Nations, including five years in the Executive Office of the Secretary-General. His most recent book is *The Power of Deliberation: International Law, Politics and Organizations* (Oxford University Press, 2011).

Barbara Koremenos is an Associate Professor of Political Science at the University of Michigan. She has published in both political science and law journals, including *American Political Science Review, International Organization, Journal of Legal Studies,* and *Law and Contemporary Problems*. Koremenos received a National Science Foundation CAREER Award for her research; she was the first award winner to study international relations and law.

Lisa L. Martin received her PhD from Harvard University in 1989 and is now Professor of Political Science at the University of Wisconsin–Madison. Her research is focused on the role of institutions in world politics. She has published two books with Princeton University Press. Her research has also been published in *International Organization, World Politics, International Security,* and *International Studies Quarterly*.

Andrew Moravcsik is Professor of Politics and Director of the European Union Program at Princeton University's Woodrow Wilson School. From 1992 to 2004, he held similar positions at Harvard University. He has authored more than 125 scholarly publications, including four books, on European integration, transatlantic relations, international organization and politics, defense-industrial globalization, and global human rights.

Abraham L. Newman is an Associate Professor at the Edmund Walsh School of Foreign Service at Georgetown University. His work on international regulatory politics has appeared in journals such as *International Organization*, the *Journal of European Public Policy*, and the *Review of International Political Economy*. He co-edited with John Zysman *How Revolutionary Was the Digital Revolution? National Responses, Market Transitions, and Global Technology* (Stanford University Press, 2006) and is the author of *Protectors of Privacy: Regulating Personal Data in the Global Economy* (Cornell University Press, 2008).

Joost Pauwelyn is Professor of International Law at the Graduate Institute of International and Development Studies in Geneva, Switzerland, and Co-Director of the Institute's Centre for Trade and Economic Integration (CTEI). He is also Senior Advisor with the law firm of King & Spalding LLC. Previously, he was a tenured professor at Duke Law School and served as legal officer at the World Trade Organization.

Steven R. Ratner is the Bruno Simma Collegiate Professor of Law at the University of Michigan Law School. His research focuses on a range of challenges facing governments and international institutions, including regulation of warfare, territorial disputes, counterterrorism strategies, corporate and state duties regarding foreign investment, accountability for human rights violations, and global justice.

Kal Raustiala is a Professor at UCLA Law School, Director of the Ronald W. Burkle Center for International Relations, and Associate Vice Provost for International Studies at UCLA. He has been a Visiting Professor at Harvard Law School, Columbia Law School, Princeton University, and the University of Chicago Law School, and he serves on the editorial boards of *International Organization* and the *American Journal of International Law*. His most recent book is *Does the Constitution Follow the Flag? The Evolution of Territoriality in American Law* (Oxford University Press, 2009).

Gregory Shaffer is the Melvin C. Steen Professor of Law at the University of Minnesota Law School. His publications include *Dispute Settlement at the WTO: The Developing Country Experience* (with Ricardo Melendez-Ortiz, Cambridge University Press, 2010), *When Cooperation Fails: The International Law and Politics of Genetically Modified Foods* (with Mark Pollack, Oxford University Press, 2009), *Defending Interests: Public-Private Partnerships in WTO Litigation* (Brookings Institution Press, 2003), and more than sixty articles and book chapters on international trade law, global governance, and globalization's impact on domestic regulation.

Anne-Marie Slaughter is the Bert G. Kerstetter '66 University Professor of Politics and International Affairs at Princeton University. She served as the Director of Policy Planning at the U.S. Department of State from 2010 to 2011 and as President of the American Society of International Law from 2004 to 2006.

Duncan Snidal is Professor of International Relations at Nuffield College, University of Oxford. His research focuses on international institutions, including international organizations, international law, public-private regulatory partnerships, and the design of international institutions. Snidal is co-editor of the journal *International Theory* and of *The Oxford Handbook of International Relations*.

Peter J. Spiro is Charles Weiner Professor of Law at Temple University Beasley School of Law. He is the author of *Beyond Citizenship: American Identity after Globalization* (Oxford University Press, 2008).

Richard H. Steinberg writes and teaches in the areas of international law and international relations at the UCLA School of Law, where he also serves as Director of the Sanela Diana Jenkins Human Rights Law Project. His most recent books are *Assessing the Legacy of the ICTY* (Martinus Nijhoff, 2011); *International Institutions* (co-edited, SAGE, 2009); *International Law and International Relations* (co-edited, Cambridge University Press, 2007); and *The Evolution of the Trade Regime: Economics, Law, and Politics of the GATT/WTO* (co-authored, Princeton University Press, 2006).

Alexander Thompson is Associate Professor of Political Science at Ohio State University. He is the author of *Channels of Power: The UN Security Council and U.S. Statecraft in Iraq* (Cornell University Press, 2010) and numerous articles on the politics of international law and organizations.

Stephen J. Toope is President and Vice-Chancellor of the University of British Columbia and Professor of International Law. His academic interests include public international law, legal theory, human rights, and international dispute resolution. Professor Toope earned his PhD from Trinity College, Cambridge, England (1987); his degrees in common law (LLB) and civil law (BCL) with honors from McGill University (1983); and graduated magna cum laude with his AB in History and Literature from Harvard University (1979). He was Law Clerk to Chief Justice Dickson of the Supreme Court of Canada.

Joel P. Trachtman is Professor of International Law at the Fletcher School of Law and Diplomacy, Tufts University. He has also served as academic dean and as interim dean. His research and teaching focus on international economic law and economic analysis of international law. His latest book is *The Future of International Law: Global Government* (Cambridge University Press, 2012).

Erik Voeten is the Peter F. Krogh Associate Professor of Geopolitics and Justice in World Affairs at Georgetown University's Edmund A. Walsh School of Foreign Service and Government Department. His research examines the role of international institutions and law in international affairs and has been published in leading journals such as the *American Political Science Review, International Organization, International Studies Quarterly,* the *Journal of Legal Studies,* and the *Chicago Journal of International Law.*

Jana von Stein is an Assistant Professor of Political Science and a Faculty Associate at the Center of Political Studies, both at the University of Michigan. She is interested in how international law reflects and affects governments' interests, particularly in human rights and environmental affairs. She has published in the *American Political Science Review,* the *Journal of Conflict Resolution, Civil Wars,* and *The ISA Compendium.*

David Zaring is Assistant Professor of Law at the Wharton School of the University of Pennsylvania. He writes at the intersection of financial regulation, international law, and domestic administration. He has written more than thirty articles, including publications in the NYU, Michigan, Virginia, and UCLA law reviews, and a number of international law journals.

Acknowledgments

This volume reflects the contributions and advice of many colleagues and friends who share our interest in understanding the role of international law in international relations. We have been fortunate to work with an extraordinary group of scholars, and to have enjoyed significant support from the university at which we work.

We were extremely fortunate to receive a major grant to support interdisciplinary research from the Temple University Office of the Provost. This support enabled us to host two workshops at Temple University in spring 2011. These workshops afforded an opportunity for authors to present their papers and receive sustained feedback from one another, as well as from an outstanding group of expert commentators, including Paul Berman, Harlan Cohen, John Crook, Lori Damrosch, Meg deGuzman, Andrew Guzman, Oona Hathaway, Duncan Hollis, Ian Hurd, Leslie Johns, Claire Kelly, Robert Keohane, Peter Lindseth, Ralf Michaels, Jide Nzelibe, Tonya Putnam, Jaya Ramji-Nogales, Cesare Romano, Beth Simmons, and Pierre-Hugues Verdier. We thank each of these individuals for their thoughtful comments and many constructive suggestions.

We are also grateful to Temple Law School, and particularly to Dean JoAnne Epps, for supporting this project. We also wish to thank Debbie Feldman, Dorothy Lee, Dimitri Ferrell, and Joel Houkom for their efforts in ensuring the success of the workshops. We also thank Temple law students Alex Varghese and Keith Greenwald and Temple political science students Gorana Draguljic and Danielle Scherer for their useful research, and Erica Maier, Joel Houkom and Shannon Crocker for their assistance with the preparation of the volume.

Thanks are also due to John Berger, Rebecca McCary, and the editorial team at Cambridge University Press for their support and guidance through the editorial and publishing processes.

Finally, and most important, we thank our families – Theresa, Elizabeth, and Joel, and Rita, Cameron, and Fiona – for their unstinting support. This book is dedicated to them.

PART I

Introduction: Setting the Stage

International Law and International Relations:

Introducing an Interdisciplinary Dialogue

Jeffrey L. Dunoff and Mark A. Pollack

A casual observer might expect that international lawyers and international relations scholars would share overlapping research interests and scholarly agendas. In fact, for several decades prior to the Second World War, practitioners in both fields pursued common interests in the making, interpretation, and enforcement of international law. As a matter of disciplinary history, however, World War II served as a watershed event, largely discrediting international law among political scientists as "realist" theorists rejected the notion that international law could serve as a meaningful constraint on states' pursuit of the national interest. Over the next four decades, international relations (IR) and international law (IL) scholarship developed along separate and rarely intersecting tracks. Legal scholars sought to emphasize law's autonomy from politics, and focused on identifying, criticizing, or justifying specific legal rules and decision-making processes. For their part, political scientists seldom referenced international law as such, even when their topics of interest, such as international cooperation and international regimes, overlapped in clear ways with international law.

The mutual neglect among international law and politics began to ebb only with the end of the Cold War and the increased salience of international rules and institutions. In 1989, legal scholar Kenneth Abbott published a manifesto calling for interdisciplinary scholarship on international law and encouraging legal scholars to draw upon recent political science scholarship. Over the next decade, a growing number of legal scholars began to ask new questions about the design and workings of international law, drawing on both theories of international relations and on qualitative and quantitative methods imported from political science. By the early 2000s, political scientists in turn "rediscovered" international law, a development marked most clearly by the publication of a special issue of *International Organization*, the leading journal in the field, devoted to understanding the causes and consequences of the "legalization" of international politics.

One decade later, we see a wealth of cross-disciplinary scholarship, in which political scientists are applying new tools to the study of legal phenomena, legal scholars continue to import insights from political scientists, and a growing number of scholars engage in genuinely interdisciplinary analysis. Yet, the interdisciplinary nature of this scholarship and its fragmentation by issue areas – such as trade, human rights, criminal, and humanitarian law – have meant that few scholars have paused to take stock of what we have learned over the past two decades, aggregate empirical findings across disciplines and issue areas, draw lessons, and chart an agenda for future research.

This volume aims to fill this scholarly void. Our goal is not to celebrate uncritically the rise of international law and international relations (IL/IR) as an approach, but to assess critically the value-added (if any) of IL/IR to our understanding of international law, as well as to identify IL/IR's lacunae, biases, and blind spots. In doing so, we are particularly interested in two potential sources of value-added: conceptual and empirical. In conceptual terms, we detail the ways in which concepts from the various strands of international relations theory have been imported and adapted to the study of international law, and we explore whether they add analytical leverage to existing theories of IL. We also review and evaluate the "new empiricism," a large body of scholarship that uses systematic qualitative and quantitative data about international law and state behavior to test propositions about the making, interpretation, and enforcement of international law. The contributions to this volume will highlight both of these developments, exploring not only how scholars have *theorized* international legal issues but also the *empirical evidence* that IL/IR scholarship has brought to bear on these questions over the past two decades.

The remainder of this introductory chapter sets the stage for these explorations. We begin with a brief overview of IL/IR's emergence as an interdisciplinary field of study. In this context, we offer some reflections on the "terms of trade" between the two disciplines found in seminal IL/IR scholarship. We suggest that those terms have been largely unidirectional, with political science/IR providing much of the theoretical content and (to a lesser extent) epistemological and methodological guidance of IL/IR scholarship, and with IL *as a discipline*[1] contributing primarily a deep knowledge of legal doctrine, institutional design and processes, and dispute settlement mechanisms.

We next examine some of the interdisciplinary tensions sparked by IL/IR scholarship. Like virtually all efforts to bridge distinct disciplinary traditions, IL/IR writings have sparked a sustained backlash, particularly among some international lawyers. We examine three sources of these disciplinary tensions: different substantive

---

[1] Here, we distinguish IL as a discipline from individual legal scholars, many of whom have formal IR training and have been among the pioneers and leaders in the field. Our claim is not that the legal scholars have played a small role in IL/IR, but that both legal and political science scholars have drawn primarily upon the tools of IR in such scholarship.

theories and ideas about the nature and role of theory, different epistemologies, and different conceptions of international law associated with the two disciplines. Consideration of the issues that underlie disciplinary tensions sheds light on the promise and the limits of interdisciplinary work, and identifies key issues to be addressed in future research.

In the final part of this introduction, we provide an overview of the volume's organization and contents.

I. THE RISE, FALL, AND REBIRTH OF IL/IR SCHOLARSHIP

As this volume takes stock of a large body of interdisciplinary IL/IR research, it is useful to begin with a brief discussion of the historic split and recent rapprochement between the disciplines of international law and international relations. Although some readers will be familiar with this trajectory, it provides a valuable backdrop to our discussion of the canonical calls for IL/IR research. Our analysis of these important works, in turn, sets the stage for our discussion of the disciplinary tensions associated with IL/IR writings.

A. *The Birth of International Relations and the Disciplinary Break*

Although the discipline of international law is hundreds of years old, the academic field of international relations is of much more recent vintage. The birth of IR as a distinct academic field is often linked to the establishment, in 1919, of the world's first chair for the study of international politics at the University College of Wales, Aberystwyth (Schmidt 2002). At this time and into the inter-war era, the disciplines of international law and international relations overlapped substantially. Leading voices in both fields argued that the spread of democracy and development of international institutions could replace war and power politics with something akin to the rule of law. However, this era of disciplinary convergence ended with the cataclysm of World War II. The war prompted many leading political scientists to reject the "idealism" associated with inter-war scholarship (Kennan 1951: 95; Carr 2001). These so-called realists argued that, in the absence of centralized enforcement mechanisms, international agreements could not meaningfully constrain state action, particularly as states generally retained the ability to auto-interpret and apply treaty provisions (Morgenthau 1948).

Hence, during the early postwar years, political science was prominently marked by influential and sustained critiques of international law, resulting in the marginalization of the study of international law within the discipline, particularly in the United States.[2] These tendencies were reinforced by a "neorealist" (or "structural

---

[2] The disciplinary estrangement was not as pronounced in the United Kingdom, where an influential "English school" highlighted law's importance in international affairs (Bull 1977).

realist") literature that viewed international outcomes as a product of the distribution of capabilities and power across states (Waltz 1979). The neorealist approach was widely understood to leave "no room whatsoever for international law" (Slaughter Burley 1993: 217; but see Steinberg 2013) and strengthened the dominant realist claims that international law is inconsequential and epiphenomenal.

Realism's hostility to international law had two important consequences. First, it led to a decades-long mutual estrangement between the two disciplines, as a generation or more of political scientists accepted and taught as conventional wisdom that international law could not significantly impact international affairs. Second, realism's prominence would eventually spark a series of theoretical moves and empirical inquiries in both disciplines that had the effect of reconceptualizing the relationship between international politics and international law. These developments have been ably described elsewhere (Slaughter Burley 1993; Keohane 1997); for current purposes, a thumbnail history will suffice.

B. *International Law: Responding to the Realist Challenge*

Realism posed a powerful challenge to international lawyers' self-understanding of their field. In response, some scholars retreated to ever more technical analysis of legal texts and doctrines. But others addressed directly the realist challenge by seeking to demonstrate international law's practical relevance to the world of international affairs. In so doing, these scholars reconceived, in various ways, the relationship between international law and politics. As Slaughter explains, these efforts involved three central analytic moves: "First, all [the efforts] sought to relate law more closely to politics. . . . Second, as part of this mission, all redefined the form of law, moving in some measure from rules to process. Third, all reassessed the primary functions of law. Whereas rules guide and constrain behavior, . . . processes perform a wider range of functions: communication, reassurance, monitoring and routinization" (Slaughter Burley 1993: 209).

One of the most influential and enduring of these responses was originally known as "policy oriented jurisprudence" but today is more commonly called the "New Haven School." Pioneered by the interdisciplinary team of Myres McDougal and Harold Lasswell, the New Haven School understands law as an ongoing process of authoritative and controlling decision. Decisions are "authoritative" insofar as they are in conformity with community values and expectations; they are "controlling" insofar as they are supported by sufficient bases of power to secure consequential control. These scholars view international law as purposive: it is designed to promote a world public order dedicated to the promotion of human dignity. New Haven scholars shared the political realists' insight that understanding state power is critical to understanding state behavior. However, they rejected claims that power was the only or predominant value that international actors pursue; they also seek wealth, enlightenment, well-being, skill, respect, affection, and rectitude. Hence, the New

Haven scholars emphasized the importance and efficacy of the international legal system, understood in terms of "the realization of values rather than the restraint of behavior" (Falk 1970).

Other international legal scholars similarly generated new understandings of international law that focused less on how or whether rules constrain states in the absence of coercive enforcement mechanisms and more on the various ways that law empowers states and facilitates pursuit of national and collective interests. For example, Louis Henkin (1979) argued that international law provides the "submerged" rules of international relations, creates "justified expectations," and facilitates cooperation in the pursuit of common objectives, whereas Abram Chayes and others in the "international legal process" school produced materials demonstrating international law's effects in specific circumstances, such as the Cuban Missile Crisis (Chayes 1974; Chayes, Ehrlich & Lowenfeld 1968). In these and other efforts, lawyers self-consciously responded to the realist critique of international law's relevancy by attempting to demonstrate law's connections to and influence on international affairs.

C. Political Science: Developing Alternatives to Realism

Realist claims also triggered a series of developments in political science. One important development came from political scientists who studied "international organizations." As detailed by Kratochwil and Ruggie (1986: 755), scholars in this field shifted their attentions from the formal arrangements and objectives of international bodies to actual decision-making processes. Over time, this focus became more generalized to overall patterns of influence that shaped organizational outcomes. The next critical analytic move in this development was to reconceive the field of "international organizations" as the study of "international regimes," understood as "principles, norms, rules and decision-making procedures around which actor expectations converge in a given issue-area" (Krasner 1982: 185). In detailing the various ways that international regimes condition and constrain state behavior, this approach challenged important realist claims. Regime theory attracted a number of young scholars, and, by the 1970s and 1980s, it was "one of the most vibrant and exciting areas of general international relations theory" (Slaughter Burley 1993: 218).

Roughly contemporaneously, Robert Keohane and others began to draw on rational choice premises to develop a "functional" theory of international regimes that understood regimes as a product of states' rational pursuit of their own self-interests (Keohane 1984). Keohane argued that regimes enhance the likelihood of state cooperation by reducing transaction costs, generating information, reducing uncertainty, and increasing expectations of compliance.

Another important perspective with roots in the early regimes literature came to be known as constructivism. Kratochwil and Ruggie's (1986) focus on the intersubjective understandings associated with the rise and evolution of international regimes invited approaches that were more sociological and contextual, and less materialistic and strategic. These authors, and other constructivists, view international law as a reflection of social purpose. International legal rules thus shape understandings of interests, perceptions of legitimate behavior, and the nature of justificatory discourse in international affairs (Ruggie 1998; Wendt 1999; Brunnée and Toope 2000; Reus-Smit 2004).

Finally, by the early 1990s, liberalism had emerged as a distinctive and coherent theory of international relations. Liberalism emphasizes the primacy of societal actors, argues that states represent a subset of domestic society, and claims that the configuration of independent state preferences determines state behavior (Moravcsik 1997). This approach focuses "on the demands of individual social groups, and their relative power in society, as a fundamental force driving state policy," and, ultimately, world order (Moravcsik 2013).

Each of these theoretical approaches is analyzed in more detail in the individual contributions to Part II of the volume. For now, the critical point is that a series of analytic developments and intellectual dynamics internal to each field created the conceptual tools and scholarly space for researchers in each discipline to draw upon insights associated with the other. At roughly the same time, external events – in particular, the end of the Cold War and the apparent revitalization of many international legal norms and institutions – raised numerous research questions of interest to scholars from both fields, resulting in several high-visibility calls for interdisciplinary IL/IR research. As these seminal papers provide useful insights into the underlying assumptions, characteristic modes of thought, and dominant lines of inquiry of the newly emerging IL/IR field, we examine them in some detail.

D. *The Canonical Calls for IL/IR Research*

For current purposes, the rebirth of IL/IR scholarship begins with publication of Kenneth Abbott's *Modern International Relations Theory: A Prospectus* (Abbott 1989). This seminal piece opens with a description of the "estrangement" between IL and IR, and argues that the ascendance of regime theory and related theories of international cooperation "offers a long-overdue opportunity to re-integrate IL and IR" (338). Abbott urges international lawyers to become "functionalists" rather than "formalists," and argues that IR provides conceptual approaches and tools for doing so. Deliberately designed to "inform (and entice)" IL scholars, the article provides clear and concise explanations of key IR concepts, including a variety of collective action problems and theories of economic and political market failures.

Four years later, Anne-Marie Slaughter Burley published "International Law and International Relations Theory: A Dual Agenda" in the *American Journal of International Law*, perhaps the field's preeminent journal. "Dual Agenda" reviews in considerable detail the postwar trajectory summarized above. The article then details an "institutionalist" agenda focused upon "the study of improved institutional design for maximally effective international organizations, compliance with international obligations, and international ethics" (Slaughter Burley 1993: 206). Significantly, "Dual Agenda" then takes a step that *Prospectus* does not; it serves as both an introduction to, and a critique of, IR approaches. The paper argues that "[i]nstitutionalism, however formulated, remains theoretically inadequate in many ways" (225), including by its inability to analyze either domestic state–society relations or transnational relations among non-state actors. Given the rise of many areas where non-state actors are critical, including international human rights law, transnational litigation and arbitration, and the regulation of transnational business, Slaughter urges use of an alternative framework.

"Dual Agenda" argues that liberalism takes account of many factors excluded by institutionalism, including the role of non-state actors, and political and economic ideologies. The paper sets out the core assumptions of liberal theory and argues that liberal approaches can inform a rich IL/IR research agenda. Slaughter Burley optimistically concludes that "[t]he prospects for genuine interdisciplinary collaboration, to the benefit of both disciplines, have never been better" (1993: 238).

On the IR side, the key publication marking the arrival of IL/IR scholarship was a special symposium issue of *International Organization* devoted to "Legalization and World Politics." The symposium was rooted in, and justified by, the empirical claim that international affairs were undergoing a strong, albeit uneven, "move to law," and the contributions to this volume seek to generate "a better understanding of this variation in the use and consequences of law in international politics." Unlike the seminal articles in legal journals, the Legalization symposium is not an explicit call for others to engage in interdisciplinary work. However, the prominence of the authors and journal clearly communicated the message that international legal phenomena were worthy of sustained scholarly attention by political scientists.

For current purposes, two elements of these groundbreaking contributions stand out. First, although virtually all of the early articles purport to call for a wide-ranging encounter between, if not synthesis of, IL and IR, in at least one important respect the papers misrepresent themselves. In fact, virtually all of the early papers emphasize some elements of modern IR theory and pointedly ignore or underplay others. Specifically, the canonical works reviewed above are, without exception, strongly rationalist in their orientation. This rationalist focus led to a corresponding underemphasis on alternative approaches, notably constructivism. The failure to meaningfully engage constructivist approaches represents a missed opportunity; these approaches would, in time, contribute significantly to the IR/IL literature.[3] Moreover, the rationalist approaches largely rest on highly instrumental conceptions of international law that triggered a backlash among many international lawyers, as

---

[3] Indeed, the authors of the canonical calls subsequently highlighted the contributions of constructivist approaches (Slaughter 2000; Abbott 2004–2005).

discussed more fully in Section II.C. below, which explores competing conceptions of international law at play in both disciplines.

Second, virtually all of the early IL/IR writings urge the application of methods or theoretical approaches from one discipline to questions posed by the other discipline. Although in principle either of the two disciplines could be the source of the theory or methods, in practice international law and international relations have not been similarly situated. Rather, the intellectual terms of trade have been highly asymmetrical, with most IL/IR writings involving the application of international relations theories and methods to the study of international legal phenomena.

For example, although Abbott's *Prospectus* claims that "IL and IR have much to contribute to each other," it quickly becomes clear that the two disciplines' respective contributions are quite distinct: "The opportunity to integrate IL and IR stems . . . from the analytical approaches, insights and techniques of modern IR theory, which can readily be applied to a variety of legal norms and institutions. . . . For its part, IL can offer modern IR scholars an immense reservoir of information about legal rules and institutions, the raw material for growth and application of the theory" (1989: 339–40). Slaughter's paper presents much the same argument. Although calling for a "dual agenda" might imply that each discipline should contribute to the other, Slaughter is clear that she is presenting a dual agenda for lawyers, based on both institutionalist and liberal IR theory (Slaughter 1993: 206–07).

The Legalization volume follows a similar path. The volume's organizers claim that their framework is "able to unite perspectives developed by political scientists and international legal scholars and engage in a genuinely collaborative venture" (Abbott *et al.* 2000: 387). Yet, once again, to be "collaborative" is not necessarily to contribute equally. The Legalization issue's introduction notes that international law has "chronicled and categorized th[e] 'move to law' but has largely failed to evaluate or challenge it." The authors claim that "approaches from political science should be more helpful in explaining the puzzle of uneven legalization" (Abbott *et al.* 2000: 388), and the paper thereafter focuses on political science explanations of international legalization.

In short, in each of these canonical statements – and, to a large extent, in the subsequent literature – the intellectual terms of trade have been highly unequal, consisting primarily of the application of the theories and methods of political science as a *discipline* to the study of international law as a *subject*.[4] The contributions to this volume can be read, in part, as an inquiry into whether better integration of the various contributions of IL and IR is desirable, or possible. For current purposes,

---

4 For a recent example, see Hafner-Burton, Victor, and Lupu (2012), who argue that "[l]arge gains from collaboration are most likely where the research tools from political science can be combined with the important substantive and procedural expertise of international lawyers. . . . "

however, we note that the asymmetrical terms of trade have given rise to significant interdisciplinary tensions, the topic to which we now turn.

II. INTERDISCIPLINARY TENSIONS

Despite the contributions made by IL/IR research, efforts to bridge the disciplines have generated considerable frictions and some degree of backlash from legal scholars who fear an imperialist invasion of the legal realm by political scientists armed with theories, epistemologies, and conceptions of law that are fundamentally foreign to those of most legal scholars (see, e.g., Byers 1997; Koskenniemi 2000, 2009*a*, 2009*b*; Klabbers 2004–2005, 2009).[5] This rejection of IR by legal scholars, in turn, is matched by a widespread ignorance of legal theory and epistemology among political science and IR scholars, who often proceed without any discussion of international legal theories or methods (Klabbers 2009: 122). These tensions have not only acted as a substantial barrier to genuinely interdisciplinary inquiry, but also limited the influence of IL/IR insights on mainstream scholarship in both professions.

In our view, each of these purported disciplinary divides is at the very least exaggerated, and each one masks considerable diversity within each discipline, as well as commonalities and points of tangency across disciplines. Nevertheless, each contains a kernel of truth, and we therefore devote this section to brief discussions of the substance and nature of theories, the epistemological commitments, and the conceptions of law that inform the work of scholars in each discipline. Critically examining the concerns that underlie disciplinary tensions can point the way toward more productive collaborations across the disciplines and permit a better understanding of the possibilities and limits of IL/IR work.

A. *Theoretical Differences*

Some of the tensions generated by IL/IR scholarship arise out of the different substantive theories that each discipline brings to bear on the study of international law. Theoretical differences, to the extent that they exist, can and often do provide an incentive for IL/IR scholarship; yet, these theoretical differences can also act as potential *obstacles* to interdisciplinary dialogue, particularly if and insofar as

---

[5] This sentiment has been expressed most memorably by Jan Klabbers (2009: 120), for whom "[i]nterdisciplinary scholarship is always, and inevitably, about subjection. Interdisciplinary scholarship is, more often than not, about imposing the vocabulary, methods, theories and idiosyncracies of discipline A on the work of discipline B. Interdisciplinary scholarship, in a word, is about power, and when it comes to links between international legal scholarship and international relations scholarship, the power balance tilts strongly in favor of the latter." Although we agree with Klabbers about the general direction of influence from IL to IR, we disagree about the extent or the inevitability of IL's "subjection" to IR. See Section II.C below.

practitioners in each discipline are ignorant of or caricature the aims and the substance of theories from the other. Unfortunately, such mischaracterizations of both IR and IL theories have been commonplace.

In the legal discipline, a number of eminent scholars associate IR theory explicitly with realist, statist, and/or rationalist assumptions, and reject the entire IL/IR enterprise on that basis (see, e.g., Klabbers 2004–2005; Koskenniemi 2009*a*, 2009*b*). This association of IR theory with realism and rationalism is understandable, particularly insofar as some of the most influential and widely cited IL/IR writings associate IR theory with state-centric, rational choice approaches (e.g., Abbott 1989) or assert positions that draw on realist traditions that are deeply skeptical of the role of law in international politics (e.g., Goldsmith and Posner 2005).[6] To associate IR exclusively with rationalism, statism, or realism, however, is misleading and ignores the increasing diversity of IR theory and its applications to IL in recent years. Indeed, much of the most influential scholarship in IL/IR has been institutionalist, open to and theorizing explicitly about the prospect that international norms, rules, and institutions can help states cooperate under anarchy (Keohane 1984; Abbott *et al.* 2000; Koremenos, Lipson, and Snidal 2001; Koremenos 2013). Furthermore, while much of this scholarship has indeed been statist in its assumptions, liberal IR theory has opened the "black box" of the state, analyzing both how domestic politics and law shape states' preferences toward international law, as well as how international law is "internalized" within domestic legal and political orders (Moravcsik 2013; Trachtman 2013). Finally, constructivist scholars have increasingly broken the rationalist "lock" on IR approaches to international law, theorizing about alternative logics through which law can both express intersubjectively shared norms and influence states through processes of socialization and acculturation (Reus-Smit 2004; Goodman and Jinks 2004; Brunnée and Toope 2013).

Of course, this theoretical diversity can give rise to what David Lake (2011) has recently called the "ism wars," in which gladiatorial combat among would-be hegemonic theoretical approaches impedes rather than advances our understanding of concrete empirical phenomena, including the making, interpretation of, and compliance with international law. Increasingly, however, IR and IL scholars have called for approaches that are more problem-driven, less theory-driven, and more open to considering that the realities of international law and international politics may reflect power-politics considerations associated with realism, functional concerns associated with institutionalism, domestic/international interactions associated with liberalism, *and* normative or ideational processes emphasized by constructivists. This realization has led to influential calls for "eclectic theorizing," so that we might better "understand inherently complex social and political processes" (Katzenstein and Okawara 2001: 167; see also Katzenstein and Sil 2008; Sil and Katzenstein 2011; and

---

[6] On the latter point, however, see Hathaway and Lavinbuk (2006), arguing that a commitment to rationalism need not entail a rejection of the causal impact, or the moral force, of international law.

Nau 2011). Reflecting the same thinking, Abbott (2004–2005), whose 1989 manifesto associated IL/IR with the rational choice institutionalism of that era, has called for a "richer institutionalism" capable of incorporating insights from all four theoretical traditions.

In both structure and content, this volume similarly emphasizes the theoretical diversity of contemporary IR, as well as the possibility for dialogue among theoretical traditions, each of which may identify causal factors and processes through which international law is made, interpreted, and implemented (or not implemented) by states. In any event, the diversity of contemporary IR theory – and the increased use of eclectic theorizing – fatally undermines the notion that using IR theory commits legal scholars to a single, alien theoretical perspective that is uniformly hostile to international law.

On the IR side, caricature and ignorance of international legal scholarship is, if anything, more widespread. It appears that many political scientists are concerned that legal scholarship is overtly normative and fails to generate predictive, testable hypotheses; is highly formalistic, overly technical, and inaccessible to those who lack legal training; and ignores issues of fundamental interest to IR scholars, such as the role of power asymmetries in producing international outcomes. In this view, the discipline of international law may appear as a sort of theoretical *tabula rasa*, waiting to be written on by IR scholars.

However, just as some international lawyers hold outdated views of IR theory, many IR scholars hold a mistaken and outmoded view of contemporary IL theory. To be sure, during the late nineteenth and early twentieth centuries, legal scholarship did indeed focus primarily on the identification, analysis, and critique of legal doctrine. At the turn of the century, the distinguished international law jurist Lassa Oppenheim could confidently declare that "the first and chief task [of the science of international law] is the exposition of the existing rules of international law" (Oppenheim 1908). In both its domestic and international law versions, this classic form of scholarship is characterized by careful and sustained attention to constitutions, statutes, judicial opinions, and other legal texts.

In addition to its *descriptive* goals, classic doctrinal scholarship typically has a *prescriptive* dimension. Thus, doctrinal description is often accompanied by doctrinal critique and proposed reforms addressed to judges, legislators, and other legal actors. The prescriptive dimension is perhaps accentuated in international legal scholarship, as international law treats "the teachings of the most highly qualified publicists" as a means of determining the content of the law.[7] Thus, international lawyers have tended to self-identify as part of an "invisible college" dedicated to advancing an international order governed by the rule of law (Schachter 1977).

Although doctrinal scholars do indeed engage in a very different type of theory than do their IR counterparts, the reality is that legal scholars are no longer centrally

---

[7] ICJ Statute, art. 38.

preoccupied with doctrinal analysis. As early as the 1920s and 1930s, the legal realists powerfully challenged the view that legal doctrine could generate determinative outcomes in specific legal disputes (Schlegel 1995). By the 1940s and 1950s, the realist challenge prompted the rise of a legal process school that viewed the legal system primarily as a structure of decision-making processes and only secondarily as a collection of substantive rules, rights, and duties. Doctrinal scholarship in international law came under pressure as well, from both the legal realists and, as explained earlier, the political science realists. The postwar era saw international legal theorists move away from conceptions of international law as a set of rules and toward conceptualizing international law in terms of process rather than doctrine (Nourse and Shaffer 2009; Dunoff and Pollack 2012). This strong interest in questions of process still marks contemporary international law.

Moreover, the past few decades, in particular, have seen dramatic changes in the nature and substance of international legal theory. In the 1970s and 1980s, in particular, new forms of interdisciplinary scholarship began to emerge in the leading law schools. By the 1990s, international law was characterized by a variety of theoretical approaches, including legal positivism, the New Haven School, international legal process, critical legal studies, feminist, and law and economics, in addition to IL/IR (Dunoff and Pollack 2012). More recent approaches, such as global administrative law, international constitutionalism, and global legal pluralism, further complicate – and enrich – the theoretical landscape of IL scholarship (Dunoff 2010).

For these reasons, we reject efforts to construct or reify a disciplinary divide between IR and IL theories, depicting the former as purely realist, statist, or rationalist and the latter as formal, doctrinal, and lacking insight into the basic features of international politics. This is not to say, of course, that the constellations of IR and IL theories are symmetrical or address identical questions. *Ceteris paribus*, international relations theories are more likely to problematize the problem of cooperation under anarchy, highlight the role of state power and the substantial difficulties of securing compliance with international law, and question the effectiveness of international norms and institutions. Similarly, international legal theories are generally more attentive to questions of legal process, the interpretive methodologies used by judges and other actors, the allocation of decision-making authority among different institutions, and the normative underpinnings and consequences of international law. However, both IR and IL are theoretically plural – and increasingly so – thus raising points of tangency and the prospect of theoretical dialogue across disciplinary boundaries. Furthermore, the asymmetries we do observe between IL and IR theories raise the prospect that theories from one discipline can and should inform those from the other, prompting IL theorists to focus on collective action problems, distributive conflicts, and compliance mechanisms, and challenging IR theorists to think more systematically about legal processes, argumentative strategies, and normative commitments that are not reducible to instrumental political action (Dunoff and Pollack 2012).

B. *Epistemological Differences*

A more serious potential divide between political science and law, already hinted at in the previous section, is epistemological, relating to the aims of scholarship and the means whereby scholars establish the validity of their theories and learn about the empirical world. The term epistemology itself, Colin Wight argues, has been subject to multiple different uses in IR alone, but "[t]he main problems with which epistemology is concerned include: the definition of knowledge and related concepts; the sources and criteria of knowledge; [and] the kinds of knowledge [that are] possible" (Wight 2002: 35). As such, epistemological questions are logically prior to the more frequently discussed issue of research methodology, such as the contentious debate over the use of qualitative and quantitative methods.

Within IR, and political science more broadly, it has become common to argue that the modal approach is *positivist*, in the scientific rather than the legal sense of that term. Although definitions of positivism have also proliferated in political science, we would follow Hollis and Smith (1990: 12), who associate positivism with "the stress . . . on experience (on observation and testing) as the only way to justify claims to knowledge of the world, and hence on methods of verification as the key to the meaning of scientific statements."

To be sure, political science is not monolithic in its commitment to positivism, either today or in the past. Looking back at the development of the field, Wight (2002: 26) refers to early IR as "a science with no philosophy," that is to say, a field characterized by a vague commitment to international relations as a "science," but without a clear set of epistemological standards for what constituted scientific study. With the behavioral revolution of the 1950s and the 1960s, however, IR in the United States embraced a positivist epistemology in which the empirical testing of general causal claims became the central aim of most of the leading scholars in the field. Perhaps the strongest statement of this position came with the publication of King, Keohane, and Verba's *Designing Social Inquiry* (1994), which put forward a single, unified logic of inference to guide both quantitative and qualitative work in the social sciences.

This embrace of positivism has not, of course, been universal, but has met "sustained resistance" within IR, first in the 1960s from scholars like Hedley Bull (1969) and Stanley Hoffmann (1961), who argued for a more humanistic, classical approach, and later from a wide range of "postpositivist" scholars from critical theory, feminist theory, and postmodernism (Lapid 1989; Wight 2002: 33–35). These scholars challenged mainstream claims about IR as a neutral science, in favor of a critical approach devoted not to theory testing but to deconstructing existing theories and promoting human emancipation (Cox 1981; Ashley 1984; Hollis and Smith 1990; Wyn Jones 2001).

The field of international relations, then, is not epistemologically monolithic, yet there is a more widespread epistemological consensus within the field on positivism, broadly construed, than on any substantive theory of international politics. The field's mainstream, including most of the key journals in the United States, accepts the key tenets of positivism, as do many leading constructivists, who follow Alexander Wendt's embrace of positivism and of a scientific constructivism committed to testing theoretical propositions systematically against empirical evidence (Wendt 1999; Fearon and Wendt 2002; Checkel 2003; Risse 2004: 160).

By contrast with political science, legal scholarship appears both more diverse and less systematically self-aware on the question of epistemology. In a provocative essay, comparative law scholar Geoffrey Samuel (2009: 432) asks, "Should social scientists take law, as it has been constructed by history, seriously as a modern intellectual discipline?" Samuel generally argues that we should not do so, largely on epistemological grounds. The social sciences, Samuel argues, generally pursue a broadly positivist "enquiry paradigm," which judges the validity of scientific claims against "external" sources of evidence, and such an approach has made some degree of headway in the legal community in the form of legal realism and sociolegal scholarship, particularly in the Anglo-Saxon world. By contrast, he continues, much legal scholarship – particularly but not only in countries with a civil law tradition – adopts an "authority" paradigm, in which the legal text is taken as authoritative and the study of law is explicitly "internal" to these legal sources. By contrast with the "externalist" epistemology of the social sciences, Samuel argues, doctrinal, formalist, or "black-letter" legal approaches determine the validity of legal claims internally, with respect to the law itself.

To his credit, Samuel does not present a monolithic view of law as a uniformly internalist discipline. "Nevertheless," he argues, "if one looks at the current literature on bookshop and library shelves, in both the civil law and common law countries, a considerable proportion is devoted largely to descriptive work on various areas of the law" (Samuel 2009: 433), and this internalist scholarship, he continues, has little to offer empirically oriented social scientists. In part for this reason, some scholars claim that, although law is a powerful *professional* discipline, it has historically been a relatively weak *academic* discipline (Balkin 1996; Ulen 2004).

Some legal scholars respond that the criticism of legal scholarship as being insufficiently positivist misses the mark because this critique misunderstands the purpose of legal scholarship. They argue that legal scholarship's purpose is not to generate empirically testable causal claims. As Jack Goldsmith and Adrian Vermeule (2002: 153–154) note, positivist critics

> overlook that legal scholarship frequently pursues doctrinal, interpretive, and normative purposes rather than empirical ones. Legal scholars often are just playing a different game than the empiricists play, which means that no amount of insistence on the empiricists' rules can indict legal scholarship – any more than strict adherence to the rules of baseball supports an indictment of cricket. [Positivist critics] miss this point because their empirical methodology blinds them to legal scholarship's internal perspective. [The critics'] external perspective – if valid – might

cause legal scholars to see their practices in a new and interesting light. But in many domains of legal scholarship, it provides no basis for persuading insiders to accept [the critics'] methodological counsels.

We should not accept too readily Goldsmith and Vermeule's critique of social scientific, positivist epistemology. Although Goldsmith and Vermeule are clearly correct that it would be inappropriate to apply a positivist or "externalist" epistemology and methodology to a purely doctrinal or normative legal analysis that relies exclusively on a reading of sources internal to the law, social science critics are also correct that legal scholars may and sometimes do smuggle empirical claims into normative or doctrinal analyses, and to the extent that they do so, these claims should not escape systematic empirical testing. In the IL/IR literature, for example, Goldsmith and Posner (2005) combine the use of game theory, empirical case studies, and normative arguments about the moral force (or lack of force) of international law in innovative and provocative ways; however, insofar as these authors make empirical claims about the causal force (or lack of force) of international law, their empirical analysis arguably falls short from the perspective of positivist epistemology, with little effort to explain and justify case selection, document data collection and sources, or control for competing explanations of their data. Our point here is not that IL/IR scholarship is methodologically lacking, or that it must all embrace positivist epistemological standards, but rather that legal scholars, to the extent that they do make empirical claims, should not receive an epistemological "pass" by virtue of their professional affiliation. And, indeed, as the chapters of this book demonstrate, IL/IR scholarship by legal scholars has demonstrated an impressive and increasing methodological rigor over time, even according to the demanding and contentious standards of inference put forward by positivist social scientists (see also the excellent review of empirical IL scholarship in Ginsburg and Shaffer 2012).

However we may assess individual works of scholarship, it does seem clear that some part of the opposition to IL/IR on the part of legal scholars results from a resistance to the imposition of positivist, "externalist" social science epistemology on legal scholarship that arguably pursues different aims and adopts a different, "internalist" epistemology. Here again, however, it is important not to reify disciplinary boundaries, for two reasons. First, the positivist/postpositivist and internalist/externalist divides do not map neatly onto monolithic political science and legal disciplines. Rather, there exists a sizable group of positivists, broadly conceived, on both sides of the purported disciplinary divide, thus raising the prospect of a common explanatory project and common epistemological standards for such scholars. Indeed, as the chapters in Parts III, IV, and V of this volume demonstrate, international lawyers increasingly address questions of institutional design, international judicial behavior, and enforcement and compliance, generating empirical findings and conceptual analyses that can be used to inform and enrich research in these areas. By the same token, scholars of a critical or postpositivist bent similarly straddle disciplinary boundaries, asking similar questions about the implicit norms and hidden power relations to be found in the corpus of international law. This phenomenon has led Klabbers (2009: 124) to claim that, "interdisciplinary work owes more to background sensibilities than to common objects of study, because only those background sensibilities (the methodological and epistemological assumptions) facilitate communications between people trained and well versed in distinct disciplines."

Second, even assuming that a sharp distinction can be drawn between positivist and postpositivist, internalist and externalist, and positive and normative scholarship, scholars with different epistemological commitments might yet have something to teach each other. As Beth Simmons and Andrew Breidenbach point out, "lawyers and legal scholars can focus [empirical social scientists] on questions that actually need answering, can help us understand why things are the way they are and what possibilities there are for the future, and are the conduits by which data and doctrine are translated into policy" (Simmons and Breidenbach 2011: 221). More generally, we would argue, even internalist doctrinal scholarship can serve as an important corrective to rational choice scholarship that fails to recognize the constraining effects of legal process and discourse on international judges (see, e.g., Mattli and Slaughter 1995) and other actors, or to constructivist scholarship that emphasizes norms without interrogating the specifically legal aspects of those norms (Finnemore 2000; Brunnée and Toope 2000, 2010).

C. Competing Conceptions of International Law

A final set of interdisciplinary tensions arise out of the different conceptions of international law that are implicit or explicit in IL and IR scholarship. To be sure, neither all IR nor all IL scholars utilize the same conception of law. However, in the dominant rationalist strands of IR theory, law is frequently understood in highly instrumental terms. Thus, realism, institutionalism, and liberalism all assume that international actors behave purposively, pursuing their interests and goals via means–ends rationality, subject to limitations in decision-making ability and external constraints. Under these rationalist perspectives, law is understood as a set of rules used to alter behavior by modifying the costs and benefits associated with different actions. Rationalist approaches highlight the material, reputational, and other "sanctions" associated with noncompliance – and, in particular, on how these sanctions influence behavior – and predict that states will contract into and comply with international law when, and only when, the benefits exceed the costs (Goldsmith and Posner 2005; Thompson 2013).

Not surprisingly, legal theorists have long debated the necessity and centrality of sanctions in legal systems. The nineteenth-century theorist John Austin famously defined law as the command of a sovereign, backed by the threat of coercive force.

For Austin, the concept of sanctions was "the *key* to the science[] of jurispru-dence," and, until the 1960s, the notion of sanctions was central to virtually every other theory of law as well (Shapiro 2006). Contemporary legal theory, however, largely rejects sanctions-centered accounts of law. H. L. A. Hart famously criticized such accounts for being unable to distinguish "law" from an outlaw's commands – both are "orders backed by threats." Hart argued that "law" has not only an exter-nal, but also an internal aspect, which he called "the internal point of view."[8] From this internal perspective, "law is not simply sanction-threatening, -directing, or -predicting, but is obligation-imposing" (Shapiro 2006). Building on Hart's insight, many legal theorists argue that law's impact on behavior cannot be satisfactorily described in purely behavioral terms. In short, modern jurisprudence has generally coalesced around the claim that descriptions and explanations that fail to account for the obligation-creating aspect of law – its normativity – are seriously deficient.

In a move that evokes Hart's critique of Austin, a number of international lawyers have criticized rationalist IR approaches to international law for overemphasizing the role of sanctions and ignoring "the very essence of law," its normativity (Byers 1997: 205). One version of this critique comes from international lawyers who iden-tify IR with "a more or less realist version of international relations scholarship" (Klabbers 2004–2005: 38), which is often associated with claims that, given the lack of coercive enforcement mechanisms, much international law has little indepen-dent impact on behavior. It follows that law is largely powerless to resolve collective action problems, and, more controversially, that states do not – and should not – feel any legal or moral obligation to follow international law when instrumental calculations reveal that noncompliance would better advance state interests (Gold-smith and Posner, 2005). Some lawyers complain that this IR perspective reduces "law" to "an irrelevant decoration" (Koskenniemi 2009*b*: 410). Moreover, even IR approaches that allow a greater role for international law, such as institutional-ism and liberalism, are similarly viewed as denying law's autonomy and normative significance. Koskenniemi, for example, argues that IR approaches entail a form of "managerialism" that views formal legal doctrine "as an obstacle [to] effective action" (Koskenniemi 2009*a*: 15) and urges deformalized norms and processes designed to maximize actor utility. Hence, critics charge that the "dual agenda" threatens to produce a "thoroughly function-dependent, non-autonomous law" (Koskenniemi 2001: 487).

A stronger version of this critique goes even further and stresses not simply that IR approaches deny law's normativity, but that they substitute another form of nor-mativity in its place – with undesirable political consequences. Draining law of its normative force and viewing it as entirely instrumental is understood as under-mining law's ability to restrain powerful international actors. In thus "liberat[ing]"

---

[8] Note that the meaning of the term "internal" in Hart's analysis differs from the meaning of the term as used in the context of contrasting doctrinal scholarship with positivist scholarship above.

governments "from whatever constraints (valid) legal rules might exert over them," critics argue that IR approaches serve to reinforce, rather than address, existing power asymmetries. The status quo bias built into IR's technocratic conceptualization of the international legal order has even led some to go so far as to suggest, in an unfortunate turn of phrase, that IL/IR is "an American crusade," an academic project promoted by U.S.-based academics that "cannot but buttress the justification of American hegemony in the world" (Koskenniemi 2000: 30).

Several of these criticisms fall well wide of the mark. As we have already argued, Klabbers misstates the degree of theoretical and epistemological uniformity, and the influence of realism, in contemporary IR. Indeed, the IL/IR literature that is the subject of this volume often focuses on identifying the causal mechanisms through which international norms and processes influence (or fail to influence) state behavior. Second, some rationalist IR approaches do acknowledge law's normativity. For example, the canonical Legalization volume identifies "obligation" as one of the three hallmarks of "legalization," and follows Hart in claiming that "[l]egal obligations are different in kind from obligations resulting from coercion, comity, or morality alone" (Abbott *et al.* 2000: 408). Moreover, as we discuss below, many of the contributions to this volume suggest ways that IR approaches can account for law's normativity. Finally, nothing in IL/IR approaches necessarily legitimates or reinforces existing power asymmetries or entails a commitment to U.S. hegemony. To the contrary, IL/IR approaches are better understood as raising a set of questions and a process of inquiry regarding international legal phenomena than as offering a list of settled conclusions – and, in any event, a number of IL/IR works are explicitly or implicitly critical of U.S. policies across a variety of issue areas.

Nevertheless, the tensions that critics identify between instrumentalist conceptions of international law and those that emphasize law's normativity highlight an exceedingly important fault line – even if it has received surprisingly little attention in the literature. Given the trajectories of both disciplines outlined above, it should not surprise us that scholars from different traditions rely upon competing conceptions of international law. A central question facing IL/IR scholars is how to navigate this fault line. The critics' writings suggest that, at a minimum, the competing conceptions of international law that characterize the two disciplines have limited the audience for, and the influence of, IL/IR work, at least among the "invisible college of international lawyers." More important, to the extent that the lawyers' critique is accurate, then dominant IR approaches have failed to account adequately for a central feature of law. Thus, both for strategic and conceptual reasons, addressing the tensions associated with the competing conceptions of international law remains a critical undertaking.

Significantly, a number of the chapters in this volume attempt precisely this task. Some attempt to do so by generating new understandings of international law that draw from both traditions. So, by way of example, Kenneth Abbott and Duncan Snidal's chapter attempts to build a theoretical account of legalization that explicitly takes account of both "the interest-based mechanisms so prominent in rationalist analyses" and "the normative channels more prominent in legal and constructivist approaches." The chapter conceptualizes legalization as "a distinct form of politics" that is characterized by "the interaction of positive and normative factors – interests and values – over time." Other chapters attempt to bridge disciplinary divides by building positive models that account for law's normative dimensions. For example, Steven Ratner's chapter (Chapter 23) constructs a theoretical model identifying a series of independent variables that bear on whether and when a "normative intermediary" invokes legal arguments when attempting to persuade an actor to comply with international norms, and Joost Pauwelyn and Manfred Elsig's chapter (Chapter 18) attempts to identify the causal factors that drive variation in interpretative strategies across international courts. These chapters, along with other contributions to the volume, impressively demonstrate that creative scholars can employ a variety of conceptual and methodological moves designed to address the disciplinary tensions associated with competing conceptions of international law in play in IL and IR scholarship.

III. AN OVERVIEW OF THE VOLUME

Previous surveys of IL/IR scholarship have been organized primarily by issue area (Biersteker *et al.* 2006; Armstrong, Farrell, and Lambert 2007). This can be a constructive approach, as it permits us to identify concrete contributions that IL/IR writings have made to our understanding of specific topics, such as human rights or international trade. Yet, in our view, one cost of pigeonholing research into issue-specific academic silos has been a failure to aggregate findings across issue areas so as to gain a "big picture" of the contribution of IL/IR as a whole. For this reason, we adopt a different approach. In keeping with our aspiration to overcome the divisions of the literature along disciplinary and issue area boundaries, this introductory section is followed by four cross-cutting thematic sections on theorizing international law (Part II), the making or designing of international law (Part III), interpretation and adjudication (Part IV), and compliance and enforcement (Part V). As we shall see, each of these four thematic areas has been the subject of significant developments over the past two decades.

In addition to this introductory chapter, the first section includes a chapter by Kenneth Abbott and Duncan Snidal (Chapter 2) that explores the processes of international legalization. Their essay conceptualizes legalization as "a distinct form of politics, because it is shaped and often constrained by the existing body of law." As noted above, this chapter seeks to bring together the rationalist perspectives associated with IR and the normative perspective associated with IL to develop a rich and nuanced account of the dynamics of legalization.

Part II of the volume focuses on theory and, in particular, on the development and application to international law of four leading theoretical traditions in IR:

realism, institutionalism/rational design, liberalism, and constructivism. Richard Steinberg's chapter (Chapter 6) memorably describes why realism is the theoretical approach that international lawyers love to hate. More important, Steinberg explains how lawyers, in particular, have often misunderstood realist claims and why realism remains a useful tool for positive analysis of international law. His chapter describes how realist premises can be combined with insights from other approaches to constitute a research program in international law with substantial explanatory and predictive power.

Barbara Korememos's chapter (Chapter 3) provides a synoptic overview of rational choice institutionalism, with a particular focus on the question of rational design. As Koremenos notes, the theoretical framework of rational design draws from institutionalist theories of IR, but shares with international legal scholarship a desire to catalogue and explain states' choices about the design of international legal agreements and institutions.

Andrew Moravcsik's chapter (Chapter 4) provides both a distillation and an extension of liberal approaches to international relations. Departing from past descriptions of this approach, this chapter highlights liberalism's utility in understanding all stages of the international legal process, not simply preference formation, and it theorizes a liberal approach to the dynamic aspects of international legal development. Jutta Brunnée and Stephen Toope (Chapter 5) discuss the fourth great theoretical tradition, constructivism. As the authors note, constructivists' study of intersubjectively shared norms and of the potentially constitutive role they can play in socializing states theorizes an aspect of international law about which other IR theories are largely silent, and one that finds resonance in many strands of international legal theory. In each case, our authors clearly set out key assumptions underlying their theory, candidly assess the strengths and weaknesses of their approach, and evaluate how the encounter with international law has influenced theoretical developments in IR and enriched our understanding of IL.

Part III addresses the making of international law. International legal scholars have long been concerned with the question – simultaneously analytical, empirical, and normative – of how to design international law to maximize its effectiveness, however defined. In recent years, IL/IR scholars have addressed the same question, bringing to bear the theoretical and methodological tools of political science on the related question of institutional design. International law-making, therefore, is an area where research agendas at least partially overlap, and in which IR methods fruitfully address issues of long-standing concern to international lawyers.

This section opens with a chapter by Larry Helfer (Chapter 7) that provides a useful typology of flexibility mechanisms, an overview of IL/IR research into these mechanisms, and a detailed discussion of "exit" and "escape" clauses, two of the most important and interesting flexibility mechanisms states use when designing international rules and institutions. Helfer's chapter highlights the various ways that states use institutional design to achieve joint gains, addresses whether flexibilities help or hinder cooperation, and emphasizes the interplay between formal and informal flexibility mechanisms. Gregory Shaffer and Mark Pollack's chapter (Chapter 8) on the limits of formality in international law-making addresses similar themes, exploring why states might choose to adopt hard or soft legal provisions, the advantages and disadvantages of each in terms of law-making and subsequent compliance and effectiveness, and the interaction of hard and soft law in practice.

Three of the chapters in this section address important shifts in international affairs and the international legal order that impact the actors and the fora involved in international law-making. Peter Spiro's chapter (Chapter 9) addresses the rise of nongovernmental (NGO) actors as participants in the law-making process. Spiro argues that both IL and IR scholars have emphasized NGO activity vis-à-vis the state and have undertheorized the exercise of NGO power through and against other actors, including international organizations, firms, and other NGOs. Abraham Newman and David Zaring's chapter (Chapter 10) focuses on regulatory networks. Their chapter reviews how IL and IR scholarship on networks has diverged in recent years, with IR scholars often focusing on the power relationships embedded in network architectures, and IL scholars focusing on variation in legal structures and implementation strategies, and on issues of legitimacy. The chapter outlines a research agenda that integrates both perspectives and that systematically explores how networks induce domestic actors to comply with their mandates and thereby serve as an innovative international governance mechanism. Ian Johnstone's contribution (Chapter 11) explores the important but understudied phenomenon of law-making by international organizations. This chapter examines the complexities embedded in the concepts of "delegation" and "law-making," and develops a pluralist account of the different types of law that IOs produce. Johnstone then explores how well various strands of IL/IR theory explain the phenomena of delegated law-making by IOs.

The proliferation of law-making fora and international regimes have given rise in recent years to widespread concerns over "forum shopping" and significant theoretical work analyzing the phenomenon of "legal fragmentation" or "regime complexity." Kal Raustiala's chapter (Chapter 12) provides an overview of IL and IR literature exploring how the increased density of international norms and institutions creates both conflict and cooperation among legal regimes. The chapter describes how complexity and fragmentation impact world politics and explores the distributional implications of fragmentation.

The increasing reach, density, and salience of international norms has given rise to concerns over international law's legitimacy. Daniel Bodansky's chapter (Chapter 13) surveys IL/IR scholarship and distinguishes between normative and descriptive conceptions of legitimacy that are often conflated in the literature. Bodansky argues that the treatment of legitimacy contrasts sharply with many of the other topics considered in the volume, where IL has been the consumer of theoretical approaches produced by IR scholars. In the case of legitimacy, IL has been the more theoretically active of the two disciplines, developing theories of legitimacy based on different conceptions of law, including the concept of "interactional law," global constitutionalism, and global administrative law.

Part IV addresses the interpretation and application of international law. The significant increase in and/or strengthening of a growing number of international courts and tribunals – and the dramatic growth in international adjudication – have greatly increased the frequency and salience of legal interpretation. At the same time, international law is interpreted and applied in a variety of nonjudicial settings, including innovative "noncompliance" mechanisms, administrative fora, and a variety of overtly political settings.

IL/IR scholarship has used multiple theoretical lenses, and both quantitative and qualitative case study analyses, to study the delegation of authority to international courts and tribunals, as well as the judicial behavior of those bodies. The contributions to Part IV survey and extend this rich body of writings. This section opens with a chapter by Karen Alter (Chapter 14) that details the multiple roles that international courts and tribunals play in the global legal and political system, which she labels as dispute resolution, enforcement, administrative review, and constitutional review. By carefully disentangling and analyzing these various roles, Alter's chapter enables scholars to more precisely identify and evaluate the utility of international courts in contemporary international affairs. Barbara Koremenos and Timm Betz's chapter (Chapter 15) on the design of international courts builds upon and extends earlier work in rational design. Koremenos and Betz start from the premise that the inclusion of dispute settlement provisions is a deliberate design feature intended to address specific cooperation problems. They demonstrate that international treaties vary dramatically in their dispute settlement systems, and seek to explain states' design choices in terms of variables such as commitment problems, enforcement problems, and uncertainty. They argue further that, even when rarely invoked, dispute settlement provisions can facilitate cooperation, both by screening states at the stage of treaty ratification and by providing potential enforcement, which will limit cases of defection.

Lisa Conant's chapter (Chapter 16) reviews the literature on domestic courts' use of international law. The chapter identifies points of tangency between IL scholarship, which often revolves around the normative question of whether domestic courts should act as agents of the international legal order or whether they should prioritize domestic values and constituencies, and IR scholarship, which develops positive theories designed to explain and predict the actions of national courts. She examines different theoretical accounts, including socialization theories, liberal theories that emphasize domestic institutions, and realist accounts, in exploring whether we should expect to see greater convergence or divergence in domestic courts' use and interpretation of international law. In the next chapter (Chapter 17), Erik Voeten surveys the IL/IR literature on judicial independence. Are international judges simply "diplomats in robes"? And, if not, what are the institutional and ideational factors that provide judges with greater or lesser degrees of independence? His chapter reviews how rational institutionalism and neofunctionalist approaches treat various potential control mechanisms that states can use to constrain judicial behavior, and underlines the challenges of empirical testing of such propositions. Voeten explores whether there is an optimal level of judicial independence, and thoughtfully examines whether "the judicialization of politics is met by an increased politicization of the judiciary."

All of these chapters fit comfortably into the dominant strand of IL/IR scholarship on international tribunals, which generally emphasizes causal explanations of judicial behavior with respect to state interests, but devotes far less attention to the practice of legal interpretation as a deliberative, norm-driven enterprise. Joost Pauwelyn and Manfred Elsig's chapter (Chapter 18) represents an important extension of this dominant strand of scholarship. Their chapter categorizes and analyzes the interpretive approaches employed by different international tribunals and is an important example of how IL/IR scholars can use political science methods in ways that take seriously questions of interpretative strategy that preoccupy international lawyers.

Part V groups together a set of chapters that examines the compliance with, and enforcement and effectiveness of, international law. Until recently, state compliance with international law was a neglected subject, with legal scholars largely assuming the efficacy of international law and political scientists assuming its ineffectiveness. Early contributions to the IL/IR literature were structured around the so-called management/enforcement debate, which was itself structured largely along disciplinary lines, with legal scholars emphasizing the significance of management as an ongoing legal process and political scientists emphasizing the importance of enforcement in an anarchical, collective action setting. Since then, scholarly inquiry has largely moved on from this overarching debate to more fine-grained questions about the measurement and determinants of state compliance with international law.

This part opens with Jana von Stein's sweeping overview of the compliance literature (Chapter 19). Building on her previous work on the topic, von Stein's chapter identifies a number of hypothesized instrumental or normative mechanisms that might serve as "the engines of compliance" and surveys the empirical literature, noting what she calls the quantification of compliance studies, with its attendant strengths and weaknesses. Next, a series of chapters focus on particular mechanisms that might explain the variable propensity of states to honor their international commitments. Rachel Brewster's chapter (Chapter 21) focuses on reputation as a potential cause of compliance, noting the often unrecognized scope conditions under which a concern for reputation does – or does not – promote compliance with international law. In addition to reviewing the literature, Brewster develops a counterintuitive account of how the addition of formal dispute settlement systems might *reduce* the reputational costs associated with noncompliance. Alexander Thompson (Chapter 20) similarly points out the challenges of enforcing international law through military, economic, and diplomatic sanctions, underlining the collective action problems associated with the application of sanctions for noncompliance and exploring mechanisms whereby this "sanctioners' dilemma" might be mitigated. Joel Trachtman (Chapter 22) addresses the ways that domestic political and legal processes may induce compliance with international legal norms. Building upon "second image reversed" theories, Trachtman develops an innovative model of adherence to, and compliance with, international law that focuses on the causal influence of domestic voting and lobbying patterns.

Another underexplored and undertheorized area, in both literatures, is the role of persuasion in securing compliance with international law. Most efforts to persuade actors to comply with international law, like most efforts to persuade actors to persuade with domestic law, are made outside of courthouses and formal legal processes and take place among national governments, transnational and transgovernmental networks, subsidiary treaty bodies, and in various bilateral and multilateral fora that are widely studied by IR scholars. This is an arena in which political scientists might indeed have a comparative advantage, yet the IL/IR literature to date has focused little attention to legal persuasion, perhaps because it involves difficult methodological and empirical questions. However, Steve Ratner's contribution to this volume (Chapter 23) illustrates one way that IL/IR research can engage these issues. Drawing on his work with the Organization for Security and Cooperation in Europe (OSCE) High Commissioner on National Minorities and the International Committee of the Red Cross, Ratner constructs a theoretical model designed to explain the persuasive and rhetorical strategies that international actors use in nonjudicial settings to promote legal compliance. The chapter implicitly invites scholars to apply Ratner's model to other international organizations that devote substantial energies to promoting compliance with international legal norms.

In the final contribution to this section of the volume, Lisa Martin (Chapter 24) provocatively asks whether political scientists, in the pursuit of an interdisciplinary dialogue with international lawyers, have mistakenly focused on compliance, rather than effectiveness, as the object of their studies. The chapter explores whether the focus on compliance has led scholars to mistakenly overestimate the impact of institutional participation on state behavior and to underestimate the impact of international institutions on states that are not in compliance with international norms. Martin concludes by making a case for a research program that focuses on analyzing the effectiveness of international law in addressing problems of international cooperation.

The final section includes two chapters. In the first, Anne-Marie Slaughter (Chapter 25) looks back on the development of IL/IR scholarship in the two decades since her seminal article, reflects on the utility of IL/IR insights from the perspective of a practicing government official, and identifies a series of pressing topics in the development of international law, noting that, in each of these areas, the distinctive insights of international lawyers will be vital to a complete understanding.

In the final chapter of the volume (Chapter 26), we attempt to distill lessons from our authors' analyses, identifying for each of our four themes the theoretical and empirical advances of the past two decades and the lessons learned, as well as the systematic weaknesses and blind spots of the IL/IR literature, and we identify a promising agenda, or agendas, for future research.

Taken as a whole, the essays in this volume provide a comprehensive overview of IL/IR's distinctive contributions and address the central questions of contemporary IL/IR research. Despite differences in subject matter and analytical approach, our contributors share a deep interest in mining interdisciplinary work to better understand the workings of contemporary international law. Collectively and separately, the chapters highlight current research frontiers concerning the making, interpretation and enforcement of international law. Our hope is that this volume will advance an ongoing research project that has already done much to expand and deepen our understanding of the role of international law in international relations.

REFERENCES

Abbott, Kenneth W. (1989). "Modern International Relations Theory: A Prospectus for International Lawyers," *Yale Journal of International Law*, Vol. 14, No. 2, pp. 335–411.
────── (2004–05). "Toward a Richer Institutionalism for International Law and Policy," *Journal of International Law and International Relations*, Vol. 1, Nos. 1–2, pp. 9–34.
Abbott, Kenneth W., and Duncan Snidal (2000). "Hard and Soft Law in International Governance," *International Organization*, Vol. 54, No. 3, pp. 421–56.
────── (2013). "Law, Legalization and Politics: An Agenda for the Next Generation of IL/IR Scholars," in Jeffrey L. Dunoff and Mark A. Pollack (eds.), *Interdisciplinary Perspectives on International Law and International Relations: The State of the Art* (New York: Cambridge University Press), pp. 33–56.
Abbott, Kenneth W., Robert O. Keohane, Andrew Moravcsik, Anne-Marie Slaughter, and Duncan Snidal (2000). "The Concept of Legalization," *International Organization*, Vol. 54, No. 3, pp. 401–19.
Alter, Karen J. (2013). "The Multiple Roles of International Courts and Tribunals: Enforcement, Dispute Settlement, Constitutional and Administrative Review," in Jeffrey L. Dunoff and Mark A. Pollack (eds.), *Interdisciplinary Perspectives on International Law and International Relations: The State of the Art* (New York: Cambridge University Press), pp. 345–70.
Armstrong, David, Theo Farrell, and Hélène Lambert (2007). *International Law and International Relations* (Cambridge: Cambridge University Press).
Ashley, Richard K. (1984). "The Poverty of Neorealism," *International Organization*, Vol. 38, No. 2, pp. 225–86.
Balkin, J. M. (1996). "Interdisciplinarity as Colonization," *Washington and Lee Law Review*, Vol. 53, No. 3, pp. 949–70.
Biersteker, Thomas J., Peter J. Spiro, Chandra Lekha Sriram, and Veronica I. Raffo (eds.) (2006). *International Law and International Relations: Bridging Theory and Practice* (Abingdon: Routledge).
Bodansky, Daniel (2013). "Legitimacy: Concepts and Conceptions/Normative and Descriptive," in Jeffrey L. Dunoff and Mark A. Pollack (eds.), *Interdisciplinary Perspectives on*

International Law and International Relations: The State of the Art (New York: Cambridge University Press), pp. 321–41.

Brewster, Rachel (2013). "Reputation in International Relations and International Law Theory," in Jeffrey L. Dunoff and Mark A. Pollack (eds.), *Interdisciplinary Perspectives on International Law and International Relations: The State of the Art* (New York: Cambridge University Press), pp. 524–43.

Brady, Henry E., and David Collier (eds.) (2004). *Rethinking Social Inquiry: Diverse Tools, Shared Standards* (Lanham, MD: Rowman & Littlefield Publishers).

Brunnée, Jutta, and Stephen J. Toope (2000). "International Law and Constructivism: Elements of an Interactional Theory of International Law," *Columbia Journal of Transnational Law*, Vol. 39, No. 1, pp. 19–74.

_____ (2010). *Legitimacy and Legality in International Law: An Interactional Account* (New York: Cambridge University Press).

_____ (2013). "Constructivism and International Law," in Jeffrey L. Dunoff and Mark A. Pollack (eds.), *Interdisciplinary Perspectives on International Law and International Relations: The State of the Art* (New York: Cambridge University Press), pp. 119–45.

Bull, Hedley (1969). "International Theory: The Case for a Classical Approach," in Klaus Knorr and James Rosenau (eds.), *Contending Approaches to International Politics* (Princeton, NJ: Princeton University Press), pp. 20–38.

_____ (1977). *The Anarchical Society: A Study of Order in World Politics* (London: Palgrave Macmillan).

Burley, Anne-Marie, and Walter Mattli (1993). "Europe before the Court: A Political Theory of Legal Integration," *International Organization*, Vol. 47, No. 1, pp. 41–76.

Byers, Michael (1997). "Taking the Law out of International Law: A Critique of the 'Iterative Perspective,'" *Harvard International Law Journal*, Vol. 38, No. 1, 201–05.

Carr, E. H. (2001). *The Twenty Years' Crisis 1919–1939: An Introduction to the Study of International Relations* (London: Palgrave).

Chayes, Abram (1974). *The Cuban Missile Crisis: International Crises and the Role of Law* (New York: Oxford University Press).

Chayes, Abram, Thomas Ehrlich, and Andreas F. Lowenfeld (1968). *International Legal Process: Materials for an Introductory Course* (Boston: Little, Brown and Co.).

Checkel, Jeffrey T. (2003). "'Going Native' in Europe? Theorizing Social Interaction in European Institutions," *Comparative Political Studies*, Vol. 36, Nos. 1–2, pp. 209–231.

Conant, Lisa. (2013). "Whose Agents? The Interpretation of International Law in National Courts," in Jeffrey L. Dunoff and Mark A. Pollack (eds.), *Interdisciplinary Perspectives on International Law and International Relations: The State of the Art* (New York: Cambridge University Press), pp. 394–420.

Cox, Robert W. (1981). "Social Forces, States and World Orders: Beyond International Relations Theory," *Millennium*, Vol. 10, No. 2, pp. 126–55.

Dunoff, Jeffrey L. (2010). "International Law in Perplexing Times," *Maryland Journal of International Law*, Vol. 25, No. 1, pp. 11–36.

Dunoff, Jeffrey L., and Mark A. Pollack (2012). "What Can International Relations Learn from International Law?" (April 9, 2012). Temple University Legal Studies Research Paper No. 2012-14. Available at SSRN: http://ssrn.com/abstract=2037299 or http://dx.doi.org/10.2139/ssrn.2037299.

Falk, Richard A. (1970). *The Status of Law in International Society* (Princeton, NJ: Princeton University Press).

Fearon, James, and Alexander Wendt (2002). "Rationalism v. Constructivism: A Skeptical View," in Walter Carlsnaes, Thomas Risse, and Beth A. Simmons (eds.), *Handbook of International Relations* (Thousand Oaks, CA: Sage Publications), pp. 52–72.

Finnemore, Martha (2000). "Are Legal Norms Distinctive?," *New York University Journal of International Law and Politics*, Vol. 32, No. 3, pp. 699–705.

Finnemore, Martha, and Stephen J. Toope. (2001). "Alternatives to 'Legalization': Richer Views of Law and Politics," *International Organization*, Vol. 55, No. 3, pp. 743–58.

Ginsburg, Tom, and Gregory C. Shaffer (2012). "The Empirical Turn in International Legal Scholarship," *American Journal of International Law*, Vol. 106, No. 1, pp. 1–46.

Goldsmith, Jack L., and Eric A. Posner (2005). *The Limits of International Law* (New York: Oxford University Press).

Goldsmith, Jack, and Adrian Vermeule (2002). "Empirical Methodology and Legal Scholarship," *University of Chicago Law Review*, Vol. 69, No. 1, pp. 153–67.

Goodman, Ryan, and Derek Jinks (2004). "How to Influence States: Socialization and International Human Rights Law," *Duke Law Journal*, Vol. 54, No. 3, pp. 621–703.

Hafner-Burton, Emilie M., David Victor, and Yonatan Lupu (2012). "Political Science Research on International Law: The State of the Field," *American Journal of International Law*, Vol. 106, No. 1, pp. 47–97.

Hart, H. L. A. (1961). *The Concept of Law* (Oxford: Oxford University Press).

Hathaway, Oona A., and Ariel N. Lavinbuk (2006). "Book Review: Rationalism and Revisionism in International Law," *Harvard Law Review*, Vol. 119, No. 5, pp. 1404–43.

Helfer, Laurence R. (2013). "Flexibility in International Agreements," in Jeffrey L. Dunoff and Mark A. Pollack (eds.), *Interdisciplinary Perspectives on International Law and International Relations: The State of the Art* (New York: Cambridge University Press), pp. 175–96.

Henkin, Louis (1979). *How Nations Behave: Law and Foreign Policy*, 2nd ed. (New York: Columbia University Press).

Hoffmann, Stanley H. (1961). "International Relations: The Long Road to Theory," in James N. Rosenau (ed.), *International Politics and Foreign Policy* (New York: The Free Press of Glencoe), pp. 421–37.

Hollis, Martin, and Steve Smith (1990). *Explaining and Understanding International Relations* (New York: Oxford University Press).

Johnstone Ian (2013). "Lawmaking by International Organizations: Perspectives from IL/IR Theory," in Jeffrey L. Dunoff and Mark A. Pollack (eds.), *Interdisciplinary Perspectives on International Law and International Relations: The State of the Art* (New York: Cambridge University Press), pp. 266–92.

Katzenstein, Peter J., and Nobuo Okawara (2001). "Japan, Asian-Pacific Security, and the Case for Analytical Eclecticism," *International Security*, Vol. 26, No. 3, pp. 153–85.

Katzenstein, Peter, and Rudra Sil (2008). "Eclectic Theorizing in the Study and Practice of International Relations," in Christian Reus-Smit and Duncan Snidal (eds.), *The Oxford Handbook of International Relations* (New York: Oxford University Press), pp. 109–30.

Kennan, George F. (1951). *American Diplomacy: 1900–1950* (Chicago: University of Chicago Press).

Keohane, Robert O. (1984). *After Hegemony: Cooperation and Discord in World Political Economy* (Princeton, NJ: Princeton University Press).

———— (1997). "International Relations and International Law: Two Optics," *Harvard International Law Journal*, Vol. 38, No. 2, pp. 487–502.

———— (1998). "When Does International Law Come Home?," *Houston Law Review*, Vol. 35, No. 3, pp. 699–713.

Keohane, Robert O., Andrew Moravcsik, and Anne-Marie Slaughter (2000). "Legalized Dispute Resolution: Interstate and Transnational," *International Organization*, Vol. 54, No. 3, pp. 457–88.

King, Gary, Robert O. Keohane, and Sidney Verba (1994). *Designing Social Inquiry: Scientific Inference in Qualitative Research* (Princeton, NJ: Princeton University Press).

Klabbers, Jan (2004–2005). "The Relative Autonomy of International Law or the Forgotten Politics of Interdisciplinarity," *Journal of International Law & International Relations*, Vol. 1, Nos. 1–2, pp. 35–48.

_____ (2009). "The Bridge Crack'd: A Critical Look at Interdisciplinary Relations," *International Relations*, Vol. 23, No. 1, pp. 119–25.

Koremenos, Barbara (2013). "Institutionalism and International Law," in Jeffrey L. Dunoff and Mark A. Pollack (eds.), *Interdisciplinary Perspectives on International Law and International Relations: The State of the Art* (New York: Cambridge University Press), pp. 59–82.

Koremenos, Barbara, and Timm Betz (2013). "The Design of Dispute Settlement Procedures in International Agreements," in Jeffrey L. Dunoff and Mark A. Pollack (eds.), *Interdisciplinary Perspectives on International Law and International Relations: The State of the Art* (New York: Cambridge University Press), pp. 371–93.

Koremenos, Barbara, Charles Lipson, and Duncan Snidal (2001). "The Rational Design of International Institutions," *International Organization*, Vol. 55, No. 4, pp. 761–99.

Koskenniemi, Martti (2000). "Carl Schmitt, Hans Morgenthau, and the Image of Law in International Relations," in Michael Byers (ed.), *The Role of Law in International Politics: Essays in International Relations and International Law* (New York: Oxford University Press), pp.17–34.

_____ (2001). *The Gentle Civilizer of Nations: The Rise and Fall of International Law 1870–1960* (Cambridge: Cambridge University Press).

_____ (2009a). "The Politics of International Law – 20 Years Later," *European Journal of International Law*, Vol. 20, No. 1, pp. 7–19.

_____ (2009b). "Miserable Comforters: International Relations as New Natural Law," *European Journal of International Relations*, Vol. 15, No. 3, pp. 395–422.

Krasner, Stephen D. (1982). "Structural Causes and Regime Consequences: Regimes as Intervening Variables," *International Organization*, Vol. 36, No. 2, pp. 185–205.

Kratochwil, Friedrich, and John Gerard Ruggie (1986). "International Organization: A State of the Art on an Art of the State," *International Organization*, Vol. 40, No. 4, pp. 753–75.

Lake, David A. (2011). "Why 'isms' are Evil: Theory, Epistemology, and Academic Sects as Impediments to Understanding and Progress," *International Studies Quarterly*, Vol. 55, No. 2, pp. 465–80.

Lapid, Yosef (1989). "The Third Debate: On the Prospects of International Theory in a Post-Positivist Era," *International Studies Quarterly*, Vol. 33, No. 3, pp. 235–54.

Martin, Lisa L. (2013). "Against Compliance," in Jeffrey L. Dunoff and Mark A. Pollack (eds.), *Interdisciplinary Perspectives on International Law and International Relations: The State of the Art* (New York: Cambridge University Press), pp. 591–610.

Mattli, Walter, and Anne-Marie Slaughter (1995). "Law and Politics in the European Union: A Reply to Garrett," *International Organization*, Vol. 49, No. 1, pp. 183–90.

Moravcsik, Andrew (1997). "Taking Preferences Seriously: A Liberal Theory of International Politics," *International Organization*, Vol. 51, No. 4, pp. 513–53.

_____ (2013). "Liberal Theories of International Law," in Jeffrey L. Dunoff and Mark A. Pollack (eds.), *Interdisciplinary Perspectives on International Law and International Relations: The State of the Art* (New York: Cambridge University Press), pp. 83–118.

Morgenthau, Hans (1948). *Politics among Nations: The Struggle for Power and Peace* (New York: Knopf).

Nau, Henry R. (2011). "No Alternative to 'Isms,'" *International Studies Quarterly*, Vol. 55, No. 2, pp. 487–91.

Newman, Abraham, and David Zaring (2013). "Regulatory Networks: Power, Legitimacy, and Compliance," in Jeffrey L. Dunoff and Mark A. Pollack (eds.), *Interdisciplinary Perspectives on International Law and International Relations: The State of the Art* (New York: Cambridge University Press), pp. 244–65.

Nourse, Victoria, and Gregory Shaffer (2009). "Varieties of New Legal Realism: Can a New World Order Prompt a New Legal Theory?," *Cornell Law Review*, Vol. 95, No. 1, pp. 61–138.

Oppenheim, Lassa (1908). "The Science of International Law: Its Task and Method," *American Journal of International Law*, Vol. 2, No. 2, pp. 313–56.

Pauwelyn, Joost, and Manfred Elsig (2013). "The Politics of Treaty Interpretation: Variations and Explanations Across International Tribunals," in Jeffrey L. Dunoff and Mark A. Pollack (eds.), *Interdisciplinary Perspectives on International Law and International Relations: The State of the Art* (New York: Cambridge University Press), pp. 445–73.

Ratner, Steven R. (2013). "Persuading to Comply: On the Deployment and Avoidance of Legal Argumentation," in Jeffrey L. Dunoff and Mark A. Pollack (eds.), *Interdisciplinary Perspectives on International Law and International Relations: The State of the Art* (New York: Cambridge University Press), pp. 568–90.

Raustiala, Kal (2013). "Institutional Proliferation and the International Legal Order," in Jeffrey L. Dunoff and Mark A. Pollack (eds.), *Interdisciplinary Perspectives on International Law and International Relations: The State of the Art* (New York: Cambridge University Press), pp. 293–320.

Reus-Smit, Christian (2004) (ed.). *The Politics of International Law* (New York: Cambridge University Press).

Risse, Thomas (2004). "Social Constructivism and European Integration," in Antje Wiener and Thomas Diez (eds.), *European Integration Theory* (New York: Oxford University Press), pp. 159–76.

Ruggie, John Gerard (1998). "What Makes the World Hang Together? Neo-utilitarianism and the Social Constructivist Challenge," *International Organization*, Vol. 52, No. 4, pp. 855–85.

Samuel, Geoffrey (2009). "Interdisciplinarity and the Authority Paradigm: Should Law Be Taken Seriously by Scientists and Social Scientists?" *Journal of Law and Society*, Vol. 36, No. 4, pp. 431–59.

Schachter, Oscar (1977). "The Invisible College of International Lawyers," *Northwestern University Law Review*, Vol. 72, No. 2, pp. 217–26.

Schlegel, John Henry (1995). *American Legal Realism & Empirical Social Science* (Chapel Hill: University of North Carolina Press).

Schmidt, Brian C. (2002). "On the History and Historiography of International Relations," in Walter Carlsnaes, Thomas Risse, and Beth A. Simmons (eds.), *Handbook of International Relations* (Thousand Oaks, CA: Sage Publications), pp. 3–22.

Shaffer, Gregory C., and Mark A. Pollack (2013). "Hard Law and Soft Law," in Jeffrey L. Dunoff and Mark A. Pollack (eds.), *Interdisciplinary Perspectives on International Law and International Relations: The State of the Art* (New York: Cambridge University Press), pp. 197–222.

Shapiro, Scott J. (2006). "What Is the Internal Point of View?," *Fordham Law Review*, Vol. 75, No. 3, pp. 1157–70.

Sil, Rudra, and Peter J. Katzenstein (2011). "De-Centering, Not Discarding, the 'Isms': Some Friendly Amendments," *International Studies Quarterly*, Vol. 55, No. 2, pp. 481–85.

Simmons, Beth A., and Andrew B. Breidenbach (2011). "The Empirical Turn in International Economic Law," *Minnesota Journal of International Law*, Vol. 20, No. 2, pp. 198–222.

Slaughter, Anne-Marie (2000). "International Law and International Relations," *Recueil des Cours 285* (Boston: Martinus Nijhoff).

———— (2013). "International Law and International Relations Theory: Twenty Years Later," in Jeffrey L. Dunoff and Mark A. Pollack (eds.), *Interdisciplinary Perspectives on International Law and International Relations: The State of the Art* (New York: Cambridge University Press), pp. 613–25.

Slaughter Burley, Anne-Marie (1993). "International Law and International Relations Theory: A Dual Agenda," *American Journal of International Law*, Vol. 87, No. 2, pp. 205–39.

Spiro, Peter J. (2013). "Nongovernmental Organizations in International Relations (Theory)," in Jeffrey L. Dunoff and Mark A. Pollack (eds.), *Interdisciplinary Perspectives on International Law and International Relations: The State of the Art* (New York: Cambridge University Press), pp. 223–43.

Steinberg, Richard (2013). "Wanted – Dead or Alive: Realist Approaches to International Law," in Jeffrey L. Dunoff and Mark A. Pollack (eds.), *Interdisciplinary Perspectives on International Law and International Relations: The State of the Art* (New York: Cambridge University Press), pp. 146–72.

Thompson, Alexander (2013). "Coercive Enforcement in International Law," in Jeffrey L. Dunoff and Mark A. Pollack (eds.), *Interdisciplinary Perspectives on International Law and International Relations: The State of the Art* (New York: Cambridge University Press), pp. 502–23.

Trachtman, Joel P. (2013). "Open Economy Law," in Jeffrey L. Dunoff and Mark A. Pollack (eds.), *Interdisciplinary Perspectives on International Law and International Relations: The State of the Art* (New York: Cambridge University Press), pp. 544–67.

Ulen, Thomas S. (2004). "The Unexpected Guest: Law and Economics, Law and Other Cognate Disciplines, and the Future of Legal Scholarship," *Chicago-Kent Law Review*, Vol. 79, No. 2, pp. 403–29.

Voeten, Erik (2013). "International Judicial Independence," in Jeffrey L. Dunoff and Mark A. Pollack (eds.), *Interdisciplinary Perspectives on International Law and International Relations: The State of the Art* (New York: Cambridge University Press), pp. 421–44.

von Stein, Jana (2013). "The Engines of Compliance," in Jeffrey L. Dunoff and Mark A. Pollack (eds.), *Interdisciplinary Perspectives on International Law and International Relations: The State of the Art* (New York: Cambridge University Press), pp. 477–501.

Waltz, Kenneth N. (1979). *Theory of International Politics* (New York: McGraw-Hill).

Wendt, Alexander (1999). *Social Theory of International Politics* (New York: Cambridge University Press).

Wight, Colin (2002). "Philosophy of Social Science and International Relations," in Walter Carlsnaes, Thomas Risse, and Beth A. Simmons (eds.), *Handbook of International Relations* (Thousand Paks, CA: Sage Publications), pp. 23–51.

Wyn Jones, Richard (2001) (ed.). *Critical Theory & World Politics* (Boulder, CO: Lynne Reinner Publishers).

2

Law, Legalization, and Politics:

An Agenda for the Next Generation of IL/IR Scholars

Kenneth W. Abbott and Duncan Snidal

I. FRAMING THE AGENDA

The intersection of international law and international relations (IL/IR) has developed into a sophisticated intellectual enterprise, as the papers in this volume attest. Although IL/IR continues to make important contributions to both disciplines, however, there remains room for further advances, in part by rebalancing the exchange between the two disciplines. This chapter suggests a research agenda for the field as it moves into its next generation. Our argument turns on a series of conceptual pairings: IL and IR, law at a point in time and law over time, values and interests (and with them constructivist and rationalist analyses), and especially law and politics. Our approach seeks to avoid privileging either side of these pairings, which are sometimes presented as (false) dichotomies; in fact, we argue that the vitality of the IL/IR nexus lies in its ability to bring together these elements and exploit the synergies and tensions among them.

A. International Law/International Relations

Much of the initial work in IL/IR (including our own) was oriented toward understanding IL from an IR perspective as "another" international institution. As a result, IL/IR scholarship has been somewhat one-sided, with IR (often wielded by lawyers) used to explain IL – mainly at a high level of generality – but with far less feedback from IL to IR. It is now time to reverse the gunsights: to ask what IL can contribute to IR, and what IL/IR has to offer traditional IL scholars and practitioners. We urge IL/IR scholars to engage more concretely with the practices of international law, a process which has already begun in this volume. Doing so, we suggest, will especially enrich rationalist/positivist IR analyses of law and legalization.

Thanks to Jutta Brunnée, Jeff Dunoff, Karolina Milewicz, Mark Pollack, Nicole de Silva and Stephen Toope for valuable comments.

B. *Law at a Point in Time and Law over Time*

To separately analyze the static and dynamic features of legal processes, we distinguish between "law" and "legalization." "Law" refers to the legal system and the body of legal rules, procedures, discourses, and institutions existing at a point in time; "legalization" refers to the process of adding to, changing, or subtracting from the body of law and the legal system over time. (This distinction was elided in the Legalization volume of *International Organization* [Abbott *et al.* 2000], which used the term to denote the degree to which institutional arrangements partake of the characteristics of law.) Thus, legalization is the dynamic process through which law changes and develops, whereas law consists of the rules and institutions that result from the cumulation of legalization at any point in time.

Studying the interaction of law and legalization – combining the static and dynamic perspectives – can reveal new insights. To take one significant example, although compliance has been a major emphasis of IL/IR scholarship, Howse and Teitel (2010) argue that compliance is too narrow a focus because it ignores interpretation and the normative impact of IL. Similarly, in the next section, we show how viewing legalization as a process opens up a broader perspective on the impact of law: even if law, or norms short of law, does not immediately have strong impacts on behavior, it may initiate processes of legalization that will move in the desired direction. (Of course, mere "law on the books" is insufficient to demonstrate impact; compliance, or movement toward compliance, remains a significant criterion.)

C. *Values and Interests*

The logic of legalization is closely connected to, but not identical with, that of law, as legalization is a highly political process, as well as a legal one – a natural subject for IL/IR scholars. Some actors in legalization are driven by normative values, others by interests, still others by both; these motivations often influence their strategies. Actors in legalization understand, moreover, that law – the product of legalization – operates not only through the interest-based mechanisms prominent in rationalist analyses, but also through the normative channels prominent in legal and constructivist approaches. By bringing values/interests considerations and rationalist/normative approaches together with static/dynamic views of law and legalization, we can better understand how law (IL) and politics (IR) work together, in practice and in theory.

D. *Law and Politics*

The relationship between law and politics is central to the IL/IR nexus. This is a long-standing issue within legal theory: much legal literature is devoted to maintaining the distinctiveness of law and its separation from politics. That is true even for positivistic IL, where distinctiveness is often expressed in the notion that law is defined by its structure and form, although politics may affect its content (e.g., Hart 1994; Raz 1994). In this view, law is relatively robust, able to maintain its separation from politics. Other scholars, such as Fuller (1964) and Brunnée and Toope (2010), discussed below, see an even deeper separation between the two spheres.

Our view is more complex, emphasizing both the separation of and the intertwined relations among law, legalization, and politics. We begin from the notion that law at a point in time serves to remove issues (albeit incompletely and temporarily) from the realm of ordinary politics. In the ideal characterization of a legal system, once issues are subject to law, they are decided (ideally) according to established legal principles, discourses, and rules, overseen (ideally) by impartial judges or other legal authorities, who (ideally) interpret and apply what has been to a large extent politically decided (i.e., the content of the law). When there are multiple possible interpretations, one is chosen as a matter of law, not of politics.

Of course, politics often intrudes into this ideal – as when judges' personal biases (e.g., based on nationality) affect their judgment (Posner and de Figueredo 2005) or when judicial decisions are made in anticipation of political ramifications (e.g., Garrett and Weingast 1993). In addition, many areas of law are unsettled; battles over interpretation, implementation, enforcement, and amendment or repeal begin as soon as legal rules are created. These political battles, however, are distinctive, as they are constituted and shaped by the existing legal rules, institutions, and procedures. The precise form of legalized politics is likely to vary according to the nature of the existing arrangements – the politics surrounding an International Court of Justice ruling differ from those surrounding an International Criminal Court decision, a treaty, or a customary rule of law – yet the nature of these diverse politics remains poorly understood. This constitutes a significant and challenging research agenda.

Even the ideal characterization of law, moreover, recognizes that the content of law is predominantly political and therefore recognizes implicitly that legalization is political.[1] But legalization entails distinctive politics, shaped and constrained by law and legal institutions. For example, political actors who seek a new legal rule to advance their values and interests must follow established legal procedures for creating it and must do so with the recognition that the new rule will have ramifications for existing rules. To be sure, existing institutions likewise condition the creation of political institutions (e.g., intergovernmental organizations [IGOs]), just as existing norms affect the emergence of nonlegal norms. But the distinctive properties of law (e.g., consistency, obligation) have a special impact. In the extreme case, "constitutional" laws take some political alternatives almost completely off the table. Even these effects are bounded, however: when the stakes are high, constitutional rules

---

[1] Many disparate theories recognize this point, from the law and economics view that law derives from economic incentives, to the critical view that law reflects the interests of the powerful, to the feminist view that law is an instrument of subordination. The distinctiveness of law, however, is that its operation is insulated from its sources.

may be repoliticized, as with abortion in the United States, and even constitutional rules may be amended, although typically under extraordinary procedures.

In sum, although law (at a point in time) is significantly insulated from ordinary politics, it is never (except in its idealization) completely separate from politics; law remains subject to distinctive forms of legalized politics and can always be changed by politics over time. Although legalization (over time) is always political, it always occurs in the context of, and is shaped by, the existing body of law. Thus, law provides boundaries for politics yet is itself bounded by politics; politics changes those boundaries, yet is itself bounded by law. As legalization progresses, we move closer to (but never reach) the ideal type: law plays a more important role and politics a lesser and different one. Because law, legalization, and politics are intertwined in complex ways, neither law nor politics can be said to come first – they come together and coevolve over time.

The interrelation between law and politics is especially salient at the international level because IL is not a highly developed legal system. Although some rules command general respect (e.g., rules related to state sovereignty, much maritime law), many others are open to broad political influence, especially given the relative lack of authoritative institutions to interpret or apply them (or to produce more authoritative law). The heavy reliance on "soft law" – using quasi-legal forms to gain some benefits of law while admitting more extensive politics and (sometimes) as a strategy of legalization – reflects the close connection between international law and politics. The IL/IR nexus is particularly important, then, because international law is neither wholly reducible to politics nor wholly autonomous of politics. The relationship of international law and politics becomes a central feature of the international system to be explained.

The first half of this chapter addresses these issues in general terms; the second half suggests specific IL/IR research agendas. The next section, "Will the 'Ism' Wars Never End?," begins by critiquing the continuing tendency of scholars to divide into theoretical camps. This happens both when lawyers seek to separate law from politics and when IR scholars attempt to reduce law to politics. Consistent with our commitment to bring together analytical concepts often seen as in opposition, we critique such extreme positions as inherently incomplete ways to understand law and legalization. Section III, "Dynamics of Legalization," examines the relations between law and legalization in terms of the interaction of positive and normative factors – interests and values – at points in time and over time. We present a simple model to explicate the relationships between law and legalization and law and politics. Section IV, "Opportunities for International Law/International Relations Scholarship," identifies specific IL/IR topics – both static and dynamic – that are ripe for further research, including issues of legal design. Section V, "Middle-Range Theorizing," considers how to bring abstract theoretical approaches to bear on concrete legal practices, allowing IR to engage IL in greater depth. It suggests that middle-range theorizing, by focusing on problem structure and social mechanisms, can produce concrete yet generalizable understandings of how law works in international relations. The final section is a brief conclusion.

II. WILL THE "ISM" WARS NEVER END?

The study of international law and legalization in IR began as the "ism" wars between rationalists (who emphasize the "logic of consequences") and constructivists (who emphasize the "logic of appropriateness") were subsiding. To be sure, many IR scholars continue to emphasize one or the other approach, but scholars on both sides increasingly recognize their complementarity, and a number have begun explicitly to combine them.[2] Law and legalization provide natural subject matters for this effort, because each involves both rationalist and normative processes and effects, as discussed in the following section, "Dynamics of Legalization." Indeed, we argue that the study of law and legalization demands recognition of these theoretical complementarities. This was reflected in the Legalization volume: although its participants came largely (although not exclusively) from the rationalist perspective, its "concept of legalization" included the normative idea of "obligation" as the first of three central elements (Abbott *et al.* 2000).

Sadly, the ism wars have reawakened in two related settings. One is within the legal community, between rationalist and constructivist legal scholars; the other is between IL and IR scholars, with the former protesting against trespassing by the latter. These divisions do not characterize all scholarship at the IL/IR frontier, but they do raise important issues.

Among legal scholars, on one side of the divide are purely interest-based approaches that explain international law in terms of equilibrium outcomes among rational state actors – often by making very strong (implicit) assumptions about the rational capacities of states. Drawing heavily on arguments from rationalist IR theory, Goldsmith and Posner (2005) argue that international law operates strictly through self-interest, with law itself playing a modest supporting role at best. In such a view, "international law per se has no moral force" (Posner and Sykes 2011: 246). Although these rationalists recognize that there may be moral or domestic political arguments for complying with international norms, they do not see international law itself as providing any justification outside of welfare considerations. International law is simply a means for states to achieve efficiency gains – an expression of pure instrumental rationality.

Guzman's (2008) reputational theory provides a richer and more optimistic account. Guzman takes a contractarian approach based on the "the Three Rs of compliance: reciprocity, retaliation, and reputation," all of which fall under the biggest R of all: rationalism. He emphasizes reputational arguments, using them to

---

[2] Examples include Keck and Sikkink (1998), Abbott and Snidal (1998), Checkel (1998), Fearon and Wendt (2002), Abbott (2005), and Snidal (2012).

explain a wide range of legal phenomena, including customary law, soft law, treaty design, and compliance. But reputation remains an open-ended concept that raises many questions, such as whether reputations relate to cooperation or keeping agreements (Helfer 2005; Kydd 2009), whether they are general or issue-specific (Downs and Jones 2002; Guzman 2008), and whether they pertain to states or governments (Brewster 2010). Similarly, Brewster (2013) makes clear that the impact of reputation is contingent on institutional elements, including dispute resolution design. Guzman himself recognizes that reputation has limited force and that "there are problems it cannot solve" (Guzman 2009: 337). Even though Guzman assigns some importance to international law, at the end of the day, law plays only a supporting role to power and interest. If we wish to understand the efficacy of international law on its own terms, a purely rationalist account remains incomplete.

On the other side of the divide are efforts to assert the independent importance of international law by emphasizing legal obligation. Brunnée and Toope (2010) offer an exemplary analysis. They (2010: 90–91) argue that "purely rationalist accounts miss an important part of the compliance picture precisely because they discount obligation." Although we agree with much of Brunnée and Toope's critique of rationalism, by focusing on a narrow slice of rationalist theory, they overstate their critique and miss important complementarities. For example, the Legalization volume likewise emphasized obligation as the most important legal dimension. However, its conception of obligation was quite thin, amounting to the notion – widely shared by natural law and contract theory proponents – that promises imply obligations (as captured in *pacta sunt servanda*), which are significantly strengthened by being seen as legal obligations.[3] The Legalization volume did not explore the sources of the binding quality of law, leaving an important gap to be filled.

To fill that gap, Brunnée and Toope developed an interactional theory of law, based on Fuller's approach, which argues that only rules that meet eight criteria (generality, promulgation, not retroactive, clarity, noncontradiction, realistic, constant, and congruent with action) can attain legitimacy as law and create legal obligation. In their theory, moreover, the development of legal obligation depends equally on continuing practice within the legal community that upholds and develops the rules, thereby creating and maintaining a shared understanding of legality over time.

The interactional theory is a valuable contribution, but it errs in setting aside broader sources of obligation and legitimacy, such as consent, coercion, or substantive properties (e.g., fairness). Fuller's criteria, even combined with legal practices, lack sufficient content to warrant the legitimizing role Brunnée and Toope attribute to them:[4] they may be necessary but are not sufficient. Broad criteria of legal form

---

[3] The decision not to unpack obligation can be justified as an effort to capture this important element without engaging the complex (endless?) philosophical and jurisprudential issues involved. For a critique of the conception of obligation in the Legalization volume, see Finnemore and Toope (2001).

[4] This harkens back to the Hart-Fuller debate as to whether rules are a matter of efficiency or morality. Brunnée and Toope's effort to resuscitate procedure-based morality is insufficient, especially for their "extrapolation" of Fuller to the "admittedly weak rule-of-law tradition" of international relations.

and professional practices *may* produce legal rules that are normatively attractive (according to external moral criteria), but might also lead to normatively unattractive rules. This difference becomes apparent when, for example, Brunnée and Toope explain the legitimacy of tax rules by adding the conditions that "tax law is seen to be fair" and applied "in an equitable manner." By positing certain criteria and practices as sufficient conditions for legal obligation independent of any other considerations, they replicate the error that proponents of a single "logic" (appropriateness *or* consequences) make: ignoring not only the importance of the other logic but especially how the two work together. This misses the richness of law in uniting interests and values.

A purely interactional approach also provides an incomplete account of law and its origins. Brunnée and Toope (2010: 48) recognize the value of formal rules in crystallizing practice, but argue that new treaty rules "are not interactional law, but may become so over time if they meet the criteria of legality and become the object of a practice of legality." In many cases, however, treaties have relatively rapid legal effect: states rely on them before interaction can be demonstrated. Indeed, formal agreement is often the most effective way to create the expectations on which interactions can develop. Where issues are complex and collective action problems severe, accentuated by high risk and uncertainty (e.g., security dilemmas), the shared expectations necessary for legal interaction might never arise without prior agreement. Thus, a focus on interactions to the exclusion of formal arrangements – or other ways of "creating" law – is as problematic as a focus on formal arrangements to the exclusion of informal practices. In most cases, as we argue below, expectations and legal rules coevolve over time.

One reason Brunnée and Toope prefer the interactional approach is that legal practices provide greater protection than formal law "against the undermining of law by power and politics." Although law can (incompletely) remove issues from direct political contestation and exercises of power at a point in time, law is never independent of politics or power over time. Legalization is inevitably political, as proponents and opponents pursue disparate values and interests. The resulting law is always to some extent "victor's law," reflecting the values and interests of those who were best positioned to affect its development. Only by engaging these considerations directly can we fully appreciate how law operates.

In the final analysis, the central difference between the Legalization project and Brunnée and Toope is one of purpose. The Legalization project understands law as a distinctive institutional form, but one that shares common elements with other institutional arrangements. It views international law as important not only because it is (incompletely) isolated from other institutions and politics, but also because of the special ways it is connected to them. It is ultimately about law as the "continuation of political intercourse, with the addition of other means" (Abbott *et al.* 2000: 419) – including political decisions to depoliticize certain issues through legalization.

By contrast, Brunnée and Toope seek to establish the distinctiveness and (relative) autonomy of law and its community of practice. They aim to insulate legal analysis from politics – and (to a lesser extent) from economics, history, and even sociology. In no small part, their agenda is to make international law as a discipline safe from external intrusions; fortunately, they do not go as far as Klabbers (2005: 36), who argues that "international lawyers should jealously guard the relative autonomy of their discipline." That attitude has implications that extend beyond the usual academic turf battles. It raises an important normative question: why should we trust the members of this legal community as guardians of the public interest? Substitute a different technocratic group – say, "economists" rather than "lawyers" – and many would be concerned about the normative implications. Especially if "interaction" is a substantively empty shell of professional practices, constrained only by broad criteria of legal form, we must worry about who might fill it and about the legitimacy of their choices. Law (and legalization) not only *are* political, they *should* be political, at least at certain stages.

Because it is more complex, our critique of Brunnée and Toope's procedural legalism has been more extended than our critique of rationalism. But our bottom line is the same. Each approach misses important considerations and loses the intellectual advantage of fully bringing together IR and IL perspectives. To be sure, scholars must come at these issues from some perspective and are unlikely to abandon deeply held theoretical paradigms (Nau 2011). Yet important gains can be made by seriously engaging the insights of other approaches. Thus, we critique rationalists who ignore constructivist insights and constructivists who ignore rationalist insights. We similarly critique IR scholars (and IL scholars enchanted with IR) for not taking law seriously enough, and IL scholars for not taking politics seriously enough. The two disciplines, like law and politics themselves, are intertwined: international law and legalization cannot be understood in isolation.

III. DYNAMICS OF LEGALIZATION

Understanding change and development in legal rules, institutions, and procedures, and in the international legal system as a whole, is a singularly important task. Unfortunately, it is easier to call for a dynamic theory than to produce one. Most rationalist scholars address this problem through equilibrium analysis and comparative statics. Those are useful forms of analysis, but the "dynamics" are mainly "hand-waving" about adjustment to equilibrium and equilibrium adjustment, with the sources of change left exogenous (e.g., shifts in technology). Constructivists often criticize rationalists for being static (especially for accepting fixed preferences), but many constructivist mechanisms (e.g., habit, routine, socialization) themselves predict constancy rather than change.

A valuable way to bring together rationalist and constructivist approaches to law is to examine their interplay in the dynamics of legalization. The logics of appropriateness and consequences engage different motivations for law and legalization, which we label "values" and "interests," respectively, building on Abbott and Snidal (2002).

Examining the interrelations between these motivations over time helps us understand each of them better, offering insights as to how law operates and legalization proceeds.

Our basic assumption is that diverse public and private actors use international legalization as a strategy to pursue their values and interests, and that law provides an important part of the institutional backdrop for this quest. Although most actors are motivated by both values and interests, for purposes of exposition we begin by viewing them as distinct actor types.

Importantly, we define actor types not by the ends they pursue, but by the logics underlying their behavior. Interest actors are the rational, strategic actors of the "logic of consequences," whose actions are guided by a desire to maximize preferences. Those preferences may include normative values, but interest actors pursue even those in characteristic strategic ways. Value actors are the sociological and normative actors of the "logic of appropriateness," whose actions are guided by principled beliefs. However, value actors (at least the activists particularly relevant to the creation and implementation of international law) are goal-driven, in that they wish to see their values disseminated and adopted by others; for this reason, entrepreneurial value actors also act instrumentally to promote their values. Conversely, interest actors must adjust their strategies to mobilize value actors.

Although their similarities are striking, the two actor types operate differently. Interest actors interact through side-payments and bargaining, and make trades across issues to achieve joint gains. Interactions on issues such as trade and finance are often dominated by such actions, as may be security. Value actors are guided by principles: their concern with normative consistency makes them reluctant to trade off particular values. Some may refuse to compromise under any circumstances; others are more willing to do so (Büthe 2010: 12). Strategies of persuasion and shaming play important roles in the interactions of value actors. Areas such as human rights and environmental protection are often characterized by such actions.

Whether one or the other actor type dominates particular issue areas is an empirical issue. We have offered the standard view, but Chwieroth (2010) suggests that some global finance actors are driven by values, whereas Hafner-Burton (2009) argues that some state action on human rights is best explained by interests. This suggests the possibility that the same actors (e.g., states) might operate on a different basis in different issue areas (e.g., finance vs. human rights). The association of particular groups with the two actor types is ultimately an empirical question. Usually nongovernmental organizations (NGOs) are seen primarily as value actors and business groups primarily as interest actors, but there are variations within each group. The key point is that there exists a variety of actors whose motives are distinct, although often mixed, and whose relative prevalence may vary across issues and social groups.

To the extent that actors of each type recognize the existence of actors of the other type (and of mixed types), each will use both consequentialist and normative strategies to achieve its goals. Law and legalization both offer such opportunities, as they include features that mobilize interests (coordinating on equilibria, affecting reputations, authorizing sanctions) and that activate values (obligation). Legal rules can be framed both to convey normative power ("thou shalt not kill") and to affect interests ("and you'll go to jail for 20 years if you do"). Rules of one type may also support or modify rules of the other type. For example, a legal system may punish violations of certain legal procedures as harshly as the underlying crimes to create incentives that uphold the value of following the law. In contrast, where rules have little normative content (e.g., commercial contracts), the legal system may allow relatively easy violation (e.g., efficient breach). Finally, the normative power of law is reinforced by its consequentialist impact in meeting actors' objectives, whether values or interests.

Legalization strategies vary according to the actors they target. Efforts to change the behavior of interest actors tend to focus on hard law, which can modify incentives directly. However, even soft law provides information that coordinates actors, changing their behavior. Soft law is even more effective, however, when the targets are value actors, as its normative quality may persuade them to act in desired ways. Again, the separation of value and interest actors is an analytic artifice; real actors combine these elements.

Thus, at a point in time, both types of actors will seek to affect both types of actors through the application or creation of international law. We depict this in Figure 2.1, where arrows 1 and 2 represent the motives leading both value and interest actors to pursue legalization and arrows 3 and 4 reflect their expectations that the resulting law will affect both values and interests. The effects on different actor types will differ, however: (pure) interest actors' preferences may stay the same, but their choice of strategies will be altered by the external impact of law (e.g., sanctions, reputation, coordination); in contrast, although legalization may have similar effects on value actors, it also directly changes their values.

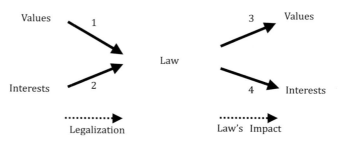

FIGURE 2.1. Values and Interests in Legalization and Law

These effects are hard to distinguish empirically because many actors are mixes of values and interests. This is especially difficult for international law, because states are composite actors whose perspectives are shaped by complex societies of value, interest, and mixed actors (Moravscik 2012).

Values and interests are even more intertwined in the dynamic interplay between legalization and law. Figure 2.2 shows how law at time 0 (LAW_0) shapes the values and interests of actors, whose legalization strategies in turn affect law at time 1 (LAW_1), and so on. (The dashed lines at the bottom of Figure 2.2 show periods of legalization, although the political interactions around law are continuous.) Constructivists correctly argue that interests are constituted over time by ideas (values); we would add that through legalization, past interests (one's own and those of others) play a role in shaping both current interests and current values.

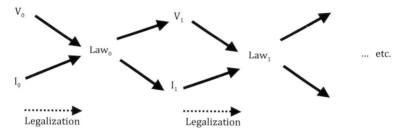

FIGURE 2.2. Values, Interests, and Legalization over Time

Law has impact through a variety of mechanisms. Some are purely rationalistic, as when law identifies mutually beneficial equilibria, especially as asset-specific investments around those equilibria make them stronger and more robust over time. Other mechanisms are sociological, as when actors become socialized or acculturated to legal practices (Finnemore and Sikkink 1998). Still others entail normative learning, as when actors come to value the normative quality of rules that may have been adopted for interest reasons. Over time, these mechanisms may interact in important ways: prohibitions against murder and unprovoked military attack may have arisen for pure interest reasons, taken deeper hold for sociological reasons, and ultimately come to have an independent normative force as basic values.

Just as legalization changes law, so law provides a (relatively) stable environment for legalization. From an interest perspective, law is an equilibrium institution that creates expectations that guide and shape behavior; from a values perspective, law represents norms and practices to which actors increasingly become socialized and habituated. Law, interests, and values are mutually reinforcing.

In this sense, law promotes stability rather than change. Actors who value and benefit from law will arrange their affairs around it, and their investments (in terms of both interests and values) will further strengthen law. Moreover, legalization is more likely to be successful if it is consistent with existing law, rather than working against prevailing interests and values. This explains why law often has a conservative bias, lagging rather than leading social values. It also explains why legal change is difficult, but equally why actors seeking change will pursue legalization to embed their changes in stable law.

Conversely, law operates as a ratchet that consolidates changes made through legalization. A liberal optimist might see an impetus in favor of expanding legalization – arguing that, just as the rule of law has been a progressive force domestically, the same has been true internationally over the last fifty years. But the law–legalization interaction is not teleological, neither inevitable nor necessarily desirable: legalization is a matter of ongoing political choices, and the results may or may not be desirable from any particular normative perspective. Nevertheless, since the law–legalization dynamic is driven by interest and value actors, the impetus of legalization is likely to be in the (progressive?) direction they advocate.

Finally, the law–legalization nexus elucidates the relationships between politics and law. Although the incremental process of legalization (e.g., from LAW_0 to LAW_1) is contested at every step, law (LAW_0 or LAW_1) is at least partially and temporarily insulated from ordinary politics and provides the legal basis upon which actors proceed. For both value and interest reasons – whether legal rules have inherent normative value or represent incentive-compatible equilibria – legal rules and procedures constitute the agreed basis from which to contest other issues. Even actors who want change (except perhaps revolutionaries) need and want a stable framework from which to proceed. The boundaries are always fuzzier in the world than in the model, but it is still a reasonable approximation that, at points in time, law defines the boundaries of politics, whereas, over time, the politics of legalization define the boundaries of law.

IV. OPPORTUNITIES FOR IL/IR SCHOLARSHIP

Here, we identify three areas for IL/IR research that engage the themes discussed above: first, a substantial agenda stemming from ongoing work; second, new forms of cooperation within the "penumbra" of international law; and third, opportunities to connect IL/IR with the practices and concerns of international lawyers in ways that will feed back productively to the theoretical enterprise.

A. *Unfinished Business*

Even where IL/IR scholarship has been productive, existing analytical frameworks leave open significant research agendas.

1. Legalization

The Legalization volume did more than demonstrate "that international legal phenomena were worthy of sustained scholarly attention by political scientists" (Dunoff and Pollack 2013). It argued that law is not a binary phenomenon and introduced a framework for understanding variations in the form and degree to which particular norms and institutions take on legal character. For example, scholars have found that strong obligation, precision, and delegation (the three elements of the framework) in the structure of public–private partnerships are significant factors in effectiveness, especially in terms of service provision (Liese and Beisheim 2011). Nonetheless, the Legalization framework remains underutilized. Treating Legalization as an independent variable, scholars and policy-makers would benefit from more extensive studies comparing the success of hard law and soft law in producing implementation, compliance, and effective outcomes (Shaffer and Pollack 2013). More broadly, the thrust of the Legalization project is the need to compare the impact of varied forms and levels of legalization, not simply of hard and soft law. This provides a valuable opportunity to explore the causal pathways by which different forms of law affect behavior. Do softer forms of law rely primarily on normative influences and harder forms on rationalist ones? Does stronger delegation to legal institutions lead to greater influence on behavior? How do state and non-state norm entrepreneurs utilize harder and softer forms of law? How do different forms of law influence non-state actors? Current evidence on such questions is surprisingly sparse and sometimes inconsistent. In addition, scholars could explore whether (and how) legal arrangements having similar levels of obligation, precision, and delegation, but differing on Brunnée and Toope's legal practice criteria or other characteristics, have different effects on behavior. The Legalization framework was intentionally kept spare to facilitate this kind of analysis.

Treating legalization as the dependent variable, why do different forms and levels of legalization emerge in different issue areas, on different issues, and in different fora? Explanations might lie in "issue structure" (discussed below), related political configurations, or the politics of international negotiations. Abbott and Snidal (2000) suggest that different types of actors (e.g., advocacy NGOs, national officials, IGO secretariats) may prefer different levels of legalization, depending on the situation. That point could be extended to interest and value actors, whose preferences for forms of law may vary.

Similarly, it would be valuable to explore how and why distinct forms of law have developed over time in different issue areas and institutional settings. More generally, the Legalization project was animated by the observation that legalization in international relations appeared to be increasing, albeit unevenly. Yet, this trend has not been fully documented or explained, nor have cases of legal stasis or weakening been systematically identified or explained.

Combining the Legalization framework with the dynamic model discussed above opens other research questions. Is soft law a crucial stage in the development of international law, operating at time LAW_0 to modify interests and values so that harder law can be adopted at time LAW_1? Under what conditions are one or more soft-law stages necessary to achieve hard law? Under what conditions can norm entrepreneurs successfully move international norms from soft to hard? What pathways and sequences are most effective in hardening international law (Abbott and Snidal 2004)?

2. International Legal Design

A parallel literature on rational institutional design (Koremenos, Lipson, and Snidal, 2001) developed contemporaneously with the Legalization project. The Rational Design project started from the premise that states purposively design institutions to advance their goals; it argued that designs vary across dimensions, including membership, centralization, and scope, depending on the contextual details of particular cooperation problems (such as uncertainty, numbers of actors, and distributional issues). Work on principal–agent relations has proceeded in a similar vein (Hawkins *et al.* 2006). Although much of this analysis focuses on political institutions, the underlying ideas are closely related to rationalistic approaches to law. A large body of work in IR and IL now explicitly or implicitly combines these approaches (e.g., Guzman 2005, 2008; Helfer 2006; Shaffer and Pollack 2010; Thompson 2010; Alter 2013; Koremenos 2013; Koremenos and Betz 2013). As IL scholarship has traditionally been much more concerned with explicit design proposals than has IR scholarship, the synergy between them offers a valuable way to enhance that tradition.

But international *legal* design is not the same as rational design. The Rational Design project deliberately wore its rationalism on its sleeve to see how well rational choice approaches could explain the design of international institutions. Legal design, by contrast, must deliberately bring together rational and normative elements, in terms of both actors' motivations and law's power, if not its very status as law. International legal design therefore constitutes an ambitious research agenda.

Normative and procedural properties like those highlighted by Brunnée and Toope (2010) provide important positive and normative guidance to legal design, along with the instrumental considerations of Rational Design. The need to combine approaches presents interesting tensions. However, the ultimate goal of IR/IL should not be to advance a single theory or to pursue a (probably elusive) synthesis of theories, but to understand IL as an important international phenomenon. Thus, the study of legal design presents a strong imperative to incorporate concrete understandings of the practices of international law. An important corollary is that, because IL scholarship is typically more concrete and less theoretical than was Rational Design, joint IL/IR research should be "closer to the ground," better able to offer practical legal design suggestions to address specific problems.

3. Implementation and Compliance

There has been an outpouring of IL/IR scholarship on compliance with international law (von Stein 2013). Yet compliance is not the sine qua non of law. An emphasis on compliance tends to reinforce the traditional view of law as commands backed by sanctions, while overlooking law's aspirational, expressive, constitutive, and learning elements. To the extent that compliance is defined as following a rule when it is against one's immediate interests, moreover, research may overlook impacts on and through values. And, to the extent that research focuses on compliance by states, it overlooks impacts on other actors. In sum, although further compliance research is undoubtedly necessary, studies that trace the other manifold effects of law are equally important (Martin 2013).

As part of considering law's impact on non-state actors, it is important to examine how legal obligations are implemented below the national level, drawing on liberal IR theory (Moravcsik 2013) and comparative politics. The true targets of many international rules are private actors; in most cases, moreover, the degree to which domestic society, not simply national elites, is socialized to international rules strongly influences compliance. However, few international legal arrangements effectively constrain even national decisions; far fewer project international norms into subnational or societal decision-making (Abbott and McElwee 2010).

In addition, implementation of some international norms may burden particular domestic groups – typically disadvantaged groups. Avoiding such outcomes requires communication pathways through which local concerns can be transmitted upward to influence international norms. Formal procedures for civil society input into international decision making represent one important pathway (Abbott and Gartner, forthcoming). In most regimes, however, channels of upward communication are weak if not nonexistent.

B. *The Penumbra of International Law*

A substantial penumbra of nonlegal norms – along with organizations devoted to their interpretation and implementation – has grown up around the core of international law. These soft normative systems are an important object of study. Some are alternatives – even "antagonists" – to law, but many are complementary (Shaffer and Pollack 2013). Nonlegal normative systems also interact with international law in many ways, including adoption, imitation, and competition. Most broadly, the very nature of international law is better understood in relation to the larger universe of normative systems.

1. Soft Law

The most established part of the penumbra is soft law adopted by states and IGOs (Abbott and Snidal 2000; Shelton 2000). As suggested above, however, there remain significant open issues regarding the origins, development, and impact of varied forms of soft law. Of particular interest would be studies of the interactions between law and politics in areas addressed by soft law and in the process of moving from soft to hard(er) law.

A prominent addition to the penumbra is the system of "bottom-up" commitments, exemplified by the 2009 Copenhagen Accord on climate change. In such arrangements, political negotiations lead each participating state to make an individual commitment – e.g., a certain reduction in carbon emissions – attuned to its unique situation (Bodansky 2011). These are not treaty commitments, although they may have legal status as unilateral declarations. International institutions and peer and domestic pressures then encourage participants to fulfill their commitments.

The bottom-up approach, like other forms of soft law, facilitates agreement and helps states avoid "one-size-fits-all" treaties. Yet, the Copenhagen Accord suggests that it may do so at the expense of depth of cooperation, a problem usually associated with hard law (Downs, Rocke, and Barsoom 1996). In addition, individualized commitments increase the fragmentation of international law and its penumbra, already a significant concern (Benvenisti and Downs 2007). The widespread interest in bottom-up commitments makes it important to develop legal and political techniques capable of tying together decentralized commitments, moving them to stronger forms of law, and using the power of law to ratchet up their substantive content (Falkner, Stephan, and Vogler 2010).

2. Regulatory Standard Setting

Dunoff and Pollack (2013) note that much IL/IR scholarship has been state-centric; although liberal theory opens the "black box of the state," it focuses primarily on domestic politics. But the past twenty years have seen an explosion of transnational, non-state rule making. We call this "regulatory standard setting" (RSS), because it deals with issues traditionally addressed through mandatory state regulation (such as the environmental and human rights behavior of business), yet its norms are not legally binding, are created by non-state actors, and apply to private actors rather than to states – features typical of the less-demanding governance of technical standards (Abbott and Snidal 2009*a*, *b*; 2010).

Regulatory standard setting includes industry self-regulation, NGO codes of conduct, and hybrid business–NGO codes, with more or less elaborate and robust mechanisms for implementation, monitoring, and enforcement. Public–private partnerships involving states, IGOs, or substate governments (Betsill and Bulkeley 2006), along with private actors, also engage in RSS. Some IGOs have adopted RSS techniques to bypass states and address private actors directly; others convene, promote, and steer RSS schemes to further public regulatory goals, a process we call "orchestration" (Abbott *et al.*, 2012). Beyond rule making, moreover, private and public-private organizations engage in operational activities, such as knowledge dissemination and financing, which facilitate implementation of international norms (Abbott 2012).

The relationships between RSS and international law are numerous and complex. Many RSS schemes were created because a demand for regulation had not been satisfied (in the eyes of advocates) by states or international law. Although RSS does not immediately engage the coercive power of the state, it often relies on the "shadow" of state regulation as an incentive for norm adherence and compliance. Regulatory standard setting schemes frequently adopt legal rules as the foundation of their norms, along with public rule-making procedures, to reduce transactions costs and gain legitimacy. One can analyze RSS schemes in terms of Legalization, examining the authority (obligation) and framing (precision) of their norms, and their mechanisms for norm elaboration, implementation, monitoring, and enforcement (delegation) (cf. Liese and Beisheim 2011). Regulatory standard setting also relies on normative as well as interest-based strategies. Yet scholarly analysis of these relationships remains in its infancy (Eberlein *et al.* 2012).

C. *International Law/International Relations for Lawyers*

Taken together, these areas suggest a core agenda for the next generation of IL/IR scholarship: to address more concretely the unique structures and practices of international law. These clearly include the practices Brunnée and Toope identify as constituting the "internal morality" of law, but just as clearly go beyond them. This agenda takes what might be called a "soft external" perspective: it accepts that internal understandings of law, embodied in legal practices, are valuable on their own terms, but argues that internal understandings must be supplemented by external perspectives.

A significant example of such research is that by Pauwelyn and Elsig (2013), which examines the legal, normative, and political factors that give international tribunals "interpretation space" and lead them to employ different interpretive approaches. One natural follow-up would be to examine finer-grained strategies of opinion writing, such as the manipulation of precedents. Another would be to examine legal argumentation in judicial and nonjudicial fora (e.g., in diplomatic correspondence); Ratner (2013) makes a significant contribution here. Much important recent research examines the structure and operation of courts and tribunals (e.g., Alter 2013; Conant 2013; Koremenos and Betz 2013; Voeten 2013), which should be extended to other institutions performing legal functions. Some papers in this volume redirect attention to customary international law, but this, too, remains understudied.

Such topics require significant legal expertise to investigate; they are part of the internal understanding of law. As such, they provide excellent opportunities to rebalance the "terms of trade" between IR and IL. Yet, advances in these areas will also pose new questions for IR, generating ongoing cross-fertilization.

V. MIDDLE-RANGE THEORIZING

Although we urge IL/IR scholars to analyze the concrete practices of international law, the promise of IL/IR is intimately tied to its ability to theorize, and most IR theory is at a high level of generality. How can IL/IR bridge this gap?

The *wrong* approach would be to focus only on specific treaties, regimes, or issue areas: for example, why particular environmental agreements contain certain flexibility provisions, or how particular human rights instruments influence behavior in certain contexts. To be sure, that approach produces concrete, problem-driven results. It is also tempting, because most legal scholars specialize in substantive fields. However, such studies lose theoretical value as their focus narrows to specific legal instruments, issues, or outcomes. Their "explanations" cannot easily be transferred to similar phenomena in other areas and often fail to draw on explanations of such phenomena. In short, they do not constitute "proper explanations" (Hedström and Swedberg 1996: 282).

Instead, IL/IR scholars should develop middle-range generalizations regarding specific legal features. Helfer's (2013) analysis of flexibility provisions, which covers a range of agreements, and the Continent of International Law (COIL) project described in Koremenos (2013), are excellent examples. Over time, such research builds up a "toolbox" of explanations that can be widely applied, gradually increasing the field's stock of understanding. The chapters in this volume make significant contributions of this kind, but case-specific investigations remain all too common in IL scholarship as a whole.

One way to balance context specificity with generalizability is to develop theoretical "modules" that apply in multiple contexts (Elster 1989). These are the building blocks of *middle-range theory*: neither grand social theory nor mere descriptions or casual working hypotheses. Two types of theoretical modules seem especially relevant for IL/IR.

The first is problem structure. Hafner-Burton, Victor, and Lupu (2012) identify two broad classes of problem structures: strategic contexts and information/uncertainty problems. *Strategic contexts* are patterns of incentives facing interdependent actors that underlie concrete issues in multiple issue areas. For example, regulatory rules, including RSS, typically address prisoners' dilemma–type problems; technical standards typically address coordination problems. The resolution of problems like these requires characteristic rules and institutions. Most problem structure research has been rationalist, so analysis from a normative perspective may identify additional responses to cooperation problems. For example, a significant literature – not always sufficiently linked to law – identifies how "taboos" and other norms help states resolve cooperation problems in high-stakes areas such as arms control (Price 1995; Tannenwald 1999). The role of legalization in the evolution of such norms has yet to be properly analyzed.

One rich structure that involves both strategic incentives and information is the credible commitment problem. Commitments must be credible if one party must perform on an agreement that entails a specific investment in reliance on future action by others. Credible commitment problems arise across issue areas, among many types of actors, and in connection with material, political, and other types of commitments. Varied institutional arrangements are used to address such problems, but establishing commitments in legal form lends them special seriousness. As "contracts," legal commitments engage actors' reputations in a rationalist sense (Guzman 2008) and expose them to legal sanctions; as "covenants," they engage domestic and international reputations in a moral and social sense based on the legitimacy of law and the value of upholding it (Abbott and Snidal 2000). Law also limits opportunities to escape commitments by constraining the permissible scope of interpretation and discourse.

The second type of theoretical module is the "social mechanism." Social mechanisms fill in our understanding of causal processes by identifying pathways through which causal factors lead to outcomes (Hedström and Swedberg, 1996; Hedström and Ylikoski, 2010). They specify the micro-level elements – including actors, activities, and relationships – through which causal factors operate, thereby providing more complete explanations than merely showing that certain factors lead to certain results. For example, one or more social mechanisms might be used to explain how widespread noncompliance with a legal rule was transformed into widespread compliance. The analysis might first detail how the original state of noncompliance – or some crisis in the regime (Mattli and Woods 2009) – motivated activists, government officials, judges, or other actors to seek to improve compliance and then identify the actions they took to produce the new state of affairs (Coleman 1986).

As in this example, IL/IR has most often deployed social mechanism analyses to explain compliance. The chapters in this volume elucidate several relevant rationalist mechanisms, including concern for state reputation (Brewster 2013), concern over possible sanctions (Thompson 2013), and domestic political processes (Trachtman 2013). Social mechanisms can also be normative, as when actors are motivated to seek compliance based on "logic of appropriateness" responses to obligations viewed as legitimate and persuade governmental officials to comply based on normative arguments. Both types of mechanisms have much in common with international legal process scholarship (Koh 1997).

Yet social mechanisms are challenging analytical tools. They are often difficult to identify and analyze in practice. They require the development of "stylized facts," so that detailed descriptions do not obscure analytical insights. They may be complex: in the compliance setting, for example, multiple distinct mechanisms may be at work. Nonetheless, social mechanisms, like problem structures, produce explanations that are clear, well-grounded, and generalizable. Both can be major elements in the increasingly sophisticated science of IL/IR.

VI. CONCLUSION

The field of IL/IR has come of age. The scope and quality of interdisciplinary scholarship on international law today was virtually unimaginable when one of us began writing on these issues in the 1980s. Our understanding of legal phenomena, from international tribunals to soft law to flexibility provisions, has increased exponentially.

The study of IL/IR has also opened up many new questions. We have outlined some particularly fruitful lines of inquiry going forward. We should explore not only law as it is, but also the process of legalization through which law continually changes. For a full understanding of these phenomena, it is essential to combine the strengths of IR and IL, for law, legalization, and related norms are shaped by, and shape, politics in diverse and multifaceted ways.

The field of IL/IR could make particularly valuable contributions by enhancing its focus on the internal understandings and practices of law, legal actors, and legal institutions. Yet, IL/IR's signal contribution is its ability to theorize and thereby to make generalizable contributions to our understanding of legal phenomena. Combining these goals requires middle-range theorizing, neither as issue-specific as much IL scholarship nor as abstract as much IR theory.

It is likewise essential to draw on the range of theoretical perspectives within each discipline, both for explanatory analysis and for international legal design. Law and legalization involve values and interests; they operate through instrumental and normative channels; they involve power as well as rational design; they are shaped by and shape the behavior of private actors as well as states.

To be sure, there are significant tensions in all these avenues of inquiry: between law and politics, static and dynamic analysis, internal and external perspectives, the logics of consequences and appropriateness, theory and design. Over the last twenty years, however, these tensions have been – most of the time, at least – creative and constructive. We expect that they will continue to be productive influences in the future.

REFERENCES

Abbott, Kenneth W. (2005). "Toward a Richer Institutionalism for International Law and Policy," *Journal of International Law and International Relations*, Vol. 1, No. 1–2, pp. 9–34.

_____ (2012). "The Transnational Regime Complex for Climate Change," *Environment and Planning C: Government and Policy*, Vol. 30, No. 4, pp. 571–90.

Abbott, Kenneth W., and David Gartner (forthcoming). "Reimagining Participation in International Institutions," *Journal of International Law & International Relations*.

Abbott, Kenneth W., and Pamela McElwee (2010). "Global Institutions as Constraints on Local Conservation Decisions," working paper.

Abbott, Kenneth W., and Duncan Snidal (1998). "Why States Act through Formal International Organizations," *Journal of Conflict Resolution*, Vol. 42, No. 1, pp. 3–32.

_____ (2000). "Hard and Soft Law in International Governance," *International Organization*, Vol. 54, No. 3, pp. 421–56.

_____ (2002). "Values and Interests: International Legalization in the Fight against Corruption," *Journal of Legal Studies*, Vol. 31, No. S1, pp. 141–78.

———— (2004). "Pathways to International Cooperation," in Eyal Benvenisti and Moshe Hirsch (eds.), *The Impact of International Law on International Cooperation* (Cambridge: Cambridge University Press), pp. 50–84.

———— (2009a). "The Governance Triangle: Regulatory Standards Institutions and the Shadow of the State," in Walter Mattli and Ngaire Woods (eds.), *The Politics of Global Regulation* (Princeton, Princeton University Press), pp. 44–88.

———— (2009b). "Strengthening International Regulation through Transnational New Governance: Overcoming the Orchestration Deficit," *Vanderbilt Journal of Transnational Law*, Vol. 42, No. 2, pp. 501–78.

———— (2010). "International Regulation without International Government: Improving IO Performance through Orchestration," *Review of International Organizations*, Vol. 5, No. 3, pp. 315–44.

Abbott, Kenneth W., Robert O. Keohane, Andrew Moravcsik, Anne-Marie Slaughter, and Duncan Snidal (2000). "The Concept of Legalization," *International Organization*, Vol. 54, No. 3, pp. 401–19.

Abbott, Kenneth W., Philipp Genschel, Duncan Snidal, and Bernhard Zangl (2012). "International Organizations as Orchestrators," paper presented at Conference on International Organizations as Orchestrators, Center for Advanced Studies, Ludwig-Maximilians-Universtät, Munich, May 20–22.

Alter, Karen J. (2013). "The Multiple Roles of International Courts and Tribunals: Enforcement, Dispute Settlement, Constitutional and Administrative Review," in Jeffrey L. Dunoff and Mark A. Pollack (eds.), *Interdisciplinary Perspectives on International Law and International Relations: The State of the Art* (New York: Cambridge University Press), pp. 345–70.

Benvenisti, Eyal, and George W. Downs (2007). "The Empire's New Clothes: Political Economy and the Fragmentation of International Law," *Stanford Law Review*, Vol. 60, No. 2, pp. 595–632.

Betsill, Michele M., and Harriet Bulkeley (2006). "Cities and the Multilevel Governance of Global Climate Change," *Global Governance*, Vol. 12, No. 2, pp. 141–59.

Bodansky, Daniel (2011). "A Tale of Two Architectures: The Once and Future UN Climate Change Regime," *Arizona State Law Journal*, Vol. 43, pp. 697–713.

Brewster, Rachel (2010). "The Limits of Reputation on Compliance," *International Theory*, Vol. 1, No. 2, pp. 323–33.

———— (2013). "Reputation in International Relations and International Law Theory," in Jeffrey L. Dunoff and Mark A. Pollack (eds.), *Interdisciplinary Perspectives on International Law and International Relations: The State of the Art* (New York: Cambridge University Press), pp. 524–43.

Brunnée, Jutta, and Stephen J. Toope (2010). *Legitimacy and Legality in International Law: An Interactional Account* (Cambridge: Cambridge University Press).

Büthe, Tim (2010). "Global Private Politics: A Research Agenda," *Business and Politics*, Vol. 12, No. 3, Article 12.

Checkel, Jeffrey T. (1998). "The Constructivist Turn in International Relations Theory," *World Politics*, Vol. 50, No. 2, pp. 324–48.

Chwieroth, Jeffrey M. (2010). *Capital Ideas: The IMF and the Rise of Financial Liberalization* (Princeton: Princeton University Press).

Coleman, James S. (1986). "Social Theory, Social Research, and a Theory of Action," *American Journal of Sociology*, Vol. 91, No. 6, pp. 1309–35.

Conant, Lisa (2013). "Whose Agents? The Interpretation of International Law in National Courts," in Jeffrey L. Dunoff and Mark A. Pollack (eds.), *Interdisciplinary Perspectives on*

International Law and International Relations: The State of the Art (New York: Cambridge University Press), pp. 394–420.

Downs, George W., and Jones, Michael A. (2002). "Reputation, Compliance and International Law," *Journal of Legal Studies*, Vol. 31, No. S1, pp. S95–S114.

Downs, George W., David M. Rocke, and Peter N. Barsoom (1996). "Is the Good News about Compliance Good News about Cooperation?," *International Organization*, Vol. 50, No. 3, pp. 379–406.

Dunoff, Jeffrey L., and Mark Pollack (2013). "International Law and International Relations: Introducing an Interdisciplinary Dialogue," in Jeffrey L. Dunoff and Mark A. Pollack (eds.), *Interdisciplinary Perspectives on International Law and International Relations: The State of the Art* (New York: Cambridge University Press), pp. 3–32.

Eberlein, Burkard, Kenneth W. Abbott, Julia Black, Errol Meidinger, and Stepan Wood (2012). "Interactions in Transnational Business Governance: Mapping and Conceptualizing a Terrain," paper presented at Workshop on Interactions in Transnational Business Governance (TBG): Assessing Impacts on Regulatory Capacity and Performance, Hertie School of Governance, Berlin, May 16.

Elster, Jon (1989). *Nuts and Bolts for the Social Sciences* (Cambridge: Cambridge University Press).

Falkner, Robert, Hannes Stephan, and John Vogler (2010). "International Climate Policy after Copenhagen: Towards a 'Building Blocks' Approach," *Global Policy*, Vol. 1, No. 3, pp. 252–62.

Fearon, James and Alexander Wendt (2002). "Constructivism v. Rationalism: A Skeptical View," in Walter Carlsnaes, Thomas Risse, and Beth Simmons (eds.), *Handbook of International Relations* (London: Sage), pp. 52–72.

Finnemore, Martha, and Katherine Sikkink (1998). "International Norm Dynamics and Political Change," *International Organization*, Vol. 52, No. 4, pp. 887–917.

Finnemore, Martha, and Stephen Toope (2001). "Alternatives to 'Legalization': Richer Views of Law and Politics," *International Organization*, Vol. 55, No. 3, pp. 743–58.

Fuller, Lon (1964). *The Morality of Law* (New Haven: Yale University Press).

Garrett, Geoffrey, and Barry Weingast (1993). "Ideas, Interests, and Institutions: Constructing the European Community's Internal Market," In Judith Goldstein & Robert Keohane (eds.), *Ideas and Foreign Policy* (Ithaca, NY: Cornell University Press), pp. 173–206.

Goldsmith, Jack L., and Eric A. Posner (2005). *The Limits of International Law* (New York: Oxford University Press).

Guzman, Andrew (2005). "The Design of International Agreements," *European Journal of International Law*, Vol. 16, No. 4, pp. 579–612.

———— (2008). *How International Law Works: A Rational Choice Theory* (New York: Oxford University Press).

———— (2009). "How International Law Works: A Response to Commentators," *International Theory*, Vol. 1, No. 2, pp 335–43.

Hafner-Burton, Emilie (2009). *Forced to Be Good: Why Trade Agreements Boost Human Rights* (Ithaca: Cornell University Press).

Hafner-Burton, Emilie, David Victor, and Yonatan Lupu (2012). "Political Science Research on International Law: The State of the Field," *American Journal of International Law*, Vol. 106, No. 1, pp. 47–97.

Hart, Herbert L. A. (1994). *The Concept of Law* (2nd ed. P. A. Bulloch and J. Raz, eds.) (Oxford: Clarendon Press).

Hawkins, Darren G., David A. Lake, Daniel L. Nielson, and Michael J. Tierney, eds. (2006). *Delegation and Agency in International Organizations* (Cambridge: Cambridge University Press).

Hedström, Peter, and Petri Ylikoski (2010). "Causal Mechanisms in the Social Sciences," *Annual Review of Sociology*, Vol. 36, pp. 49–67.

Hedström, Peter, and Richard Swedberg (1996). "Social Mechanisms," *Acta Sociologica*, Vol. 39, No. 3, pp. 281–308.

Helfer, Laurence R. (2005). "Exiting Treaties," *Virginia Law Review*, Vol. 91, No. 7, pp. 1579–1648.

Helfer, Laurence R. (2006). "Not Fully Committed? Reservations, Risk, and Treaty Design," *Yale Journal of International Law*, Vol. 31, No. 2, pp. 367–82.

———— (2013). "Flexibility in International Agreements," in Jeffrey L. Dunoff and Mark A. Pollack (eds.), *Interdisciplinary Perspectives on International Law and International Relations: The State of the Art* (New York: Cambridge University Press), pp. 175–96.

Howse, Robert, and Ruti Teitl (2010). "Beyond Compliance: Rethinking Why International Law Matters," *Global Policy*, Vol. 1, No. 2, pp. 127–35.

Keck, Margaret E., and Kathryn Sikkink (1998). *Activists beyond Borders: Advocacy Networks in International Politics* (Ithaca: Cornell University Press).

Klabbers, Jan (2005). "The Relative Autonomy of International Law or the Forgotten Politics of Interdisciplinarity," *Journal of International Law and International Relations*, Vol. 1, No. 1–2, pp. 35–48.

Koh, Harold (1997). "Why Do Nations Obey International Law?," *Yale Law Journal*, Vol. 106, No. 8, pp. 2599–2659.

Koremenos, Barbara (2013). "Institutionalism and International Law," in Jeffrey L. Dunoff and Mark A. Pollack (eds.), *Interdisciplinary Perspectives on International Law and International Relations: The State of the Art* (New York: Cambridge University Press), pp. 59–82.

Koremenos, Barbara, and Timm Betz (2013). "The Design of Dispute Settlement Procedures in International Agreements," in Jeffrey L. Dunoff and Mark A. Pollack (eds.), *Interdisciplinary Perspectives on International Law and International Relations: The State of the Art* (New York: Cambridge University Press), pp. 371–93.

Koremenos, Barbara, Charles Lipson, and Duncan Snidal (2001). "The Rational Design of International Institutions," *International Organization*, Vol. 55, No. 4, pp. 761–99.

Kydd, Andrew (2009). "Reputation and Cooperation: Guzman on International Law," *International Theory*, Vol. 1, No. 2, pp. 295–305.

Liese, Andrea, and Marianne Beisheim (2011). "Transnational Public-Private Partnerships and the Provision of Collective Goods in Developing Countries," in Thomas Risse (ed.), *Governance without a State?: Policies and Politics in Areas of Limited Statehood* (New York: Columbia University Press), pp. 115–43.

Martin, Lisa L. (2013). "Against Compliance," in Jeffrey L. Dunoff and Mark A. Pollack (eds.), *Interdisciplinary Perspectives on International Law and International Relations: The State of the Art* (New York: Cambridge University Press), pp. 591–610.

Mattli, Walter, and Ngaire Woods (2009). "In Whose Benefit? Explaining Regulatory Change in Global Politics," in Walter Mattli and Ngaire Woods (eds.), *The Politics of Global Regulation* (Princeton: Princeton University Press), pp. 1–43.

Moravcsik, Andrew (2013). "Liberal Theories of International Law," in Jeffrey L. Dunoff and Mark A. Pollack (eds.), *Interdisciplinary Perspectives on International Law and International Relations: The State of the Art* (New York: Cambridge University Press), pp. 83–118.

Nau, Henry (2011). "No Alternative to 'Isms,'" *International Studies Quarterly*, Vol. 55, No. 2, pp. 487–91.

Pauwelyn, Joost, and Manfred Elsig (2013). "The Politics of Treaty Interpretation: Variations and Explanations Across International Tribunals," in Jeffrey L. Dunoff and Mark A. Pollack (eds.), *Interdisciplinary Perspectives on International Law and International Relations: The State of the Art* (New York: Cambridge University Press), pp. 445–73.

Posner, Eric A., and Miguel F. P. de Figueiredo (2005). "Is the International Court of Justice Biased?," *Journal of Legal Studies*, Vol. 34, No. 2, pp. 599–630.

Posner, Eric A., and Alan O. Sykes (2011). "Efficient Breach of International Law: Optimal Remedies, 'Legalized Noncompliance,' and Related Issues," *Michigan Law Review*, Vol. 110, No. 2, pp. 243–94.

Price, Richard (1995). "A Genealogy of the Chemical Weapons Taboo," *International Organization*, Vol. 49, No. 1, pp. 73–103.

Ratner, Steven R. (2013). "Persuading to Comply: On the Deployment and Avoidance of Legal Argumentation," in Jeffrey L. Dunoff and Mark A. Pollack (eds.), *Interdisciplinary Perspectives on International Law and International Relations: The State of the Art* (New York: Cambridge University Press), pp. 568–90.

Raz, Joseph (1994). "Authority, Law and Morality," in J. Raz (ed.), *Ethics in the Public Domain: Essays in the Morality of Law and Politics* (Oxford: Clarendon Press), pp. 194–221.

Shelton, Dinah, ed. (2000). *Commitment and Compliance: The Role of Non-Binding Norms in the International Legal System* (Oxford: Oxford University Press).

Shaffer, Gregory, and Mark Pollack (2010). "Hard vs. Soft: Alternatives, Complements and Antagonists in International Governance," *Minnesota Law Review*, Vol. 94, No. x, pp. 706–99.

———— (2013). "Hard Law and Soft Law," in Jeffrey L. Dunoff and Mark A. Pollack (eds.), *Interdisciplinary Perspectives on International Law and International Relations: The State of the Art* (New York: Cambridge University Press), pp. 197–222.

Snidal, Duncan (2012). "Rational Choice and International Relations," in Walter Carlsnaes, Thomas Risse, and Beth Simmons (eds.), *Handbook of International Relations*, 2nd ed. (London: Sage), pp. 85–111.

Tannenwald, Nina (1999). "The Nuclear Taboo: The United States and the Normative Basis of Nuclear Non-Use," *International Organization*, Vol. 53, No. 3, p. 433–68.

Thompson, Alexander (2010). "Rational Design in Motion: Uncertainty and Flexibility in the Global Climate Regime," *European Journal of International Relations*, Vol. 16, No. 2, pp. 269–96.

———— (2013). "Coercive Enforcement in International Law," in Jeffrey L. Dunoff and Mark A. Pollack (eds.), *Interdisciplinary Perspectives on International Law and International Relations: The State of the Art* (New York: Cambridge University Press), pp. 502–23.

Trachtman, Joel P. (2013). "Open Economy Law," in Jeffrey L. Dunoff and Mark A. Pollack (eds.), *Interdisciplinary Perspectives on International Law and International Relations: The State of the Art* (New York: Cambridge University Press), pp. 544–67.

Voeten, Erik (2013). "International Judicial Independence," in Jeffrey L. Dunoff and Mark A. Pollack (eds.), *Interdisciplinary Perspectives on International Law and International Relations: The State of the Art* (New York: Cambridge University Press), pp. 421–44.

von Stein, Jana. (2013). "The Engines of Compliance," in Jeffrey L. Dunoff and Mark A. Pollack (eds.), *Interdisciplinary Perspectives on International Law and International Relations: The State of the Art* (New York: Cambridge University Press), pp. 477–501.

PART II

Theorizing International Law

3

Institutionalism and International Law

Barbara Koremenos

In a major, theoretically oriented political science department in the mid-1990s, a young scholar proposed a dissertation topic that would focus on a detail of international law. In response, a very prominent international relations (IR) professor told the student that such a dissertation would probably yield no interviews, let alone any job offers. Such was the state of the discipline just a mere decade and a half ago – IR scholarship had "evolved" to the point at which international law was foreign! Although this advice went unheeded, it contained a profoundly important kernel of wisdom: if IR scholars were going to take international law (IL) seriously, they needed to be shown that a detail of international law could matter for something really important. Guess what? It turns out the details of international law matter for the things IR scholars care about: when and how international cooperation occurs and is maintained.

Contemporary international cooperation scholars for quite some time ignored international law. The early institutionalist literature, starting with and building on Krasner (1982) and Keohane (1984), still had to fight the uphill battle of whether international institutions matter, given the more fundamental debate over the possibility of cooperation. Prominent realists argued that concerns of states about relative gains and their position in the international system greatly inhibit the prospects for international cooperation (Grieco 1988; Mearsheimer 1994). The institutionalist literature, by contrast, emphasized the possibility to realize absolute gains from cooperation; that is, cooperation could be framed as a positive sum, rather than a zero sum, game. Keohane's *After Hegemony* (1984), for instance, takes Waltz's realist assumptions as a given and shows that cooperation can be maintained through

I owe a great debt to Jeff Dunoff and Mark Pollack. The conference leading to this volume sparked many ideas, thanks to the engagement of the other participants. I thank my advanced undergraduate seminar participants from Spring 2010 for their wonderful work and comments. Many of the author's insights in this chapter derive from research supported by the National Science Foundation under Grant No. 0801581. And, finally, I thank my research assistant Timm Betz for his vitally important role in every aspect of this chapter.

international institutions even in the absence of a hegemon providing goods. Institutions, from this vantage point, facilitate and stabilize cooperation. In particular, institutions reduce transaction costs and provide an arena for regular communication, thereby fostering interdependencies and opportunities for (informational) exchange. And, by collecting and disseminating information, information asymmetries and uncertainties, often inherently hostile to cooperation, are resolved. These mechanisms help to maintain cooperation even in the adverse circumstances of an anarchic international environment.

Embedding their work in explicit game-theoretic terms, Axelrod (1984) and Oye (1986) suggest devices such as lengthening the shadow of the future, practicing reciprocity, and improving recognition capabilities in order to improve the prospects of cooperation – all of these being functions commonly ascribed to international institutions. Yet, although within this literature a consensus emerged that institutions do matter in fostering and maintaining cooperation (Axelrod and Keohane 1985), until the late 1990s, very little attention was paid to the question of how exactly institutions performed these tasks. Rather, analyses remained overly abstract, rigorous case studies were rare, quantitative studies were practically nonexistent, and questions of institutional design were largely neglected.

Things have changed. To some extent, the year 2000 was a theoretical turning point, with two special issues of *International Organization* devoted exclusively to the details of international law (Goldstein *et al.* 2000; Koremenos, Lipson, and Snidal 2001). And, importantly, more theoretically informed case studies appeared, as did the collection of large datasets on the details of international law that allowed for rigorous quantitative analyses. Moreover, the theoretical and empirical work informed each other, generating a well-developed research program in international institutions focusing on the specific mechanisms through which institutions function. Finally, the presumption in the institutionalist literature that international institutions can matter made it amenable for connections to law scholars, much more so than the other paradigms in the field of IR. Therefore, it is not surprising that large parts of IR as a field were shaped by institutionalists and lawyers, and, more significantly, by the discourse between them.

In what follows, I examine theoretical developments over the past two decades and describe what we have learned from the institutionalist literature. The emphasis in this review is put on the *design* of international institutions, given its direct connection to international law, but international adjudication and issues of compliance are discussed as well. This organization, mirroring the organization of this volume, underscores that an institutionalist approach is able to address the three big topics in the IL and IR literature within a unified framework: the making, interpretation, and enforcement of international agreements. Moreover, on the topic of law-making, institutionalism – and rational design especially – provides for a unified theoretical approach across issue areas; this contrasts starkly with Simmons' (2010) comment on the compartmentalization of compliance research, which tends to develop theories that are specific to distinct issue areas and hence are not generalizable. In the final section, I sketch an agenda for the future of institutionalist theories.

I. INTERNATIONAL LAW-MAKING

A. *Legalization*

In the early 2000s, attention was shifted from the possibility of cooperation to an examination of specific institutional details: why are agreements designed the way they are? The special issue of Goldstein *et al.* (2000) is concerned with Legalization as a particular kind of institutional design – one that imposes international legal constraints on states. The authors make great advances in variable conceptualization, defining three dimensions of Legalization – precision, obligation, and delegation – and make these dimensions come to life by giving numerous empirical examples from well-known agreements. They define as "highly legalized" those agreements that score high on each of the three dimensions (Goldstein *et al.* 2000: 402). One of the most widely used concepts to come out of the Legalization issue is the distinction between *hard* and *soft law*. The former is understood as "legally binding obligations that are precise (or can be made precise through adjudication or the issuance of detailed regulations) and that delegate authority for interpreting and implementing the law" (Abbott and Snidal 2000: 421), whereas the realm of soft law begins once an institution is weakened on any of the three dimensions. The main question in this (political science–oriented) literature then is under which conditions states would choose hard law over soft law. It is important to realize that, in IL, the distinction and, hence, the questions pursued are quite different. Here, *soft law* refers to a type of norm that is not legally binding, yet exerts some form of a compliance pull;[1] Shaffer and Pollack (2013) review the different perspectives on hard and soft law in the law and social science literatures (see also Raustiala 2005: 582).

As the Legalization volume is the first political science work to address the subject of the design of international law, and its main objective is to serve as a springboard for more refined theoretical and empirical work, its theoretical articles are framed in general terms. The case studies in the volume focus almost exclusively on describing the level of Legalization in a few prominent agreements and the consequences of that Legalization for the implementation of the agreements. This, then, is no substantive departure from most work on international institutional design at that time.

---

[1] The Legalization dimension of obligation by itself has some correspondence to the IL definition of soft law, but this dimension is the least theorized and least clearly defined of the three, perhaps reflecting that the authors come from both the IR and IL community and have very differing conceptions of the concept of obligation. See Koremenos (2011) for a detailed discussion of these points.

B. *Rational Design*

Rational design (Koremenos *et al.* 2001) as well as its follow-up, the Continent of International Law (COIL) (Koremenos, forthcoming), builds directly on the early institutionalist literature (e.g., Keohane 1984; Oye 1986). States are assumed to behave as rational actors, the main theoretical underpinning is grounded in a game-theoretic perspective, and cooperation is assumed to be at least potentially beneficial.[2] However, unlike the earlier institutionalist literature, rational design is not concerned with the questions of whether cooperation is possible or whether institutions matter. Instead, rational design asks what forms of institutionalized cooperation emerge. In other words, institutions and their specific attributes become part of the game, and rational design sets out to explain why states choose a specific design among the many options they have available.

The basic theoretical premise of rational design is that international agreement design and comparison across agreements begins by understanding the underlying "cooperation problem(s)" that the agreements are trying to solve. Some issues, like trying to ban chemical weapons or trying to encourage the rights of women, pose huge information obstacles: how can one country know what other countries are doing? This cooperation problem, which is labeled "uncertainty about behavior," is then linked to an institutional design solution, like centralized monitoring. By deriving the design of international institutions from underlying cooperation problems, rational design moves away from the abstract nature of the early institutionalist literature. Instead of broad and general claims, nuanced, empirically testable hypotheses are derived. The focus on cooperation problems further deviates from the extant literature by breaking with the paradigm of viewing the world solely in terms of two-by-two games such as "prisoners' dilemma," "chicken," or "battle of the sexes."

The literature affiliated with rational design thus links design features, like the incidence of dispute resolution mechanisms, to underlying incentives to defect (i.e., enforcement problems; Koremenos 2007) or particular flexibility mechanisms, like limited duration or escape clauses, to various types of uncertainty about the state of the world (Koremenos 2001, 2005; Rosendorff and Milner 2001). Perhaps not surprisingly, given the vast resources spent on international negotiations by many states, the extant evidence strongly supports the main conjectures from rational design: states respond in a systematic fashion to the cooperation problems they face by crafting appropriate institutions.

Raustiala (2005), coming from the IL perspective, can be viewed as a complement to both the legalization and the rational design frameworks. Raustiala distinguishes

---

[2] This approach is not at odds with the realist critique that cooperation is hard to achieve if states are risk averse and worry about their place in the international system. Even if this is the case, states can attempt to design institutions that address this concern specifically. This is underscored by the identification of distribution problems as one of the main problems characterizing international institutions – see, for instance, Koremenos's (2002) analysis of the International Coffee Agreements.

between legality (whether an agreement is legally binding), substance (the degree to which an agreement deviates from the status quo), and structure (monitoring and punishment provisions). In particular, Raustiala considers how these three categories relate to one another and assesses the implications for the effectiveness of international institutions.

However, rational design is different from Raustiala's theory on two dimensions. First, rational design links agreement design explicitly to underlying cooperation problems and identifies the conditions that are conducive to certain design features. These conditions are outside the agreement itself and are instead a function of the underlying situation structure. Second, rational design considers a wide range of design elements, not just those addressing noncompliance. Design features are grouped under five headings: membership rules, scope of issues covered, centralization of tasks, rules for controlling the institution, and flexibility of arrangements.

Rational design handily integrates a broad range of earlier work on international institutions. Distribution problems, for instance, can be seen as a tribute to realist debates. The same holds for power asymmetries among states, acknowledging realist arguments about the role of power in the international system. For instance, following realist arguments, one would expect that agreements involving the United States tend to be more asymmetric (e.g., weighted voting rules) than agreements not involving the United States. Data from COIL, which features a random sample of international agreements, supports this notion. That is, the political aspect of international institutions is recognized explicitly (Krasner 1991) – anarchy matters, and power asymmetries can explain why more powerful actors get more favorable terms. However, rational design also acknowledges the legal aspect and lawlike character of international institutions: states design the characteristics of their agreements carefully because smart, detailed institutional design helps them overcome cooperation problems, and thus international law matters for future behavior.

COIL also adds and/or codes cooperation problems in a way that specifically incorporates themes typically found in liberal approaches (e.g., Moravcsik 2008, 2010), thereby preempting critiques that regard them as missing in rational design.[3] Domestic commitment problems, for instance, feature prominently in liberal arguments; as Moravcsik (2000: 220) argues, international human rights agreements are "a tactic used by governments to 'lock in' and consolidate democratic institutions, thereby enhancing their credibility and stability [...]." This motivation for forming and joining international agreements is incorporated into COIL's theoretical framework. In fact, in this regard, COIL moves beyond liberalism because it draws further implications relating commitment problems to institutional design and evaluates these empirically. Another prominent theme in liberal approaches is the two-level

---

[3] The COIL identifies twelve distinct and recurrent cooperation problems that countries potentially face alone or in various combinations. Distinct combinations call for different nuanced agreement design solutions.

game (Putnam 1988), which highlight the presence of differentiated "state" actors on the international and domestic scenes, and, in particular, that governments may have incomplete control over domestic agents. For instance, firms affected by environmental agreements or labor standards will have incentives different from those of the government. COIL not only acknowledges the existence of such two-level problems in its coding of underlying cooperation problems but also allows its implications to be systematically tested.

COIL also forms links to the third main theory of IR, constructivism, by adding norm exportation and reinforcement, a "predominantly" constructivist topic of inquiry (Finnemore and Sikkink 1998), to its list of potential cooperation problems. Koremenos (forthcoming) finds that not only a large majority of human rights agreements, but also a fair share of environmental and disarmament agreements, are concerned with *norm exportation*. Norm exportation is of clear relevance to states and deliberately incorporated into international agreements – yet, this is not acknowledged in much of the institutionalist literature. In particular, the question of how norms are exported through international agreements, and what roles the "sending" and "receiving" side play, merits further inquiry, and constructivists may have much to say in this regard.

Aside from establishing connections to and expanding on the other main IR theories, characterizing international agreements through the underlying cooperation problems facilitates comparisons across issue areas; in fact, rational design aims to overcome arguments based on a posited distinctiveness of issue areas. Instead, rational design seeks to explain *why* issue areas are similar and distinct by reference to the underlying cooperation problems. Human rights agreements, for instance, are often viewed as inherently different from most other agreements. As Koremenos and Hong (2011) show, the issue area of human rights agreements is indeed both similar to and different from other issue areas. A main difference comes to life by looking at distinct combinations of cooperation problems. Unlike technical standards or territorial disputes, which tend to be characterized both by coordination and distribution problems, human rights agreements typically are characterized by distribution problems in the absence of coordination problems. This constellation of cooperation problems makes imprecise language, as well as reservations, valuable institutional solutions, whereas the resulting agreement would be badly flawed if incorporated in an agreement addressing technical standards or territory.

Using cooperation problems to explain agreement design has also made its way into the law literature. Carneiro (2007), for instance, focuses on uncertainty and distribution problems to explain flexibility in arms trade treaties. Uncertainty led participants to such treaties to seek finite agreements, whereas distribution problems caused by a large number of participants increased renegotiation costs, hence inducing states to conclude infinite agreements. This closely follows, in both language and theoretical content, Koremenos (2005) and therefore provides a direct link between the IL and IR literatures. Helfer (2006) and Swaine (2006) provide accounts of reservations as flexibility devices in treaties from the perspective of IL.

Whereas scholars of international conflict long had access to excellent datasets, the literature on international institutions long suffered from the absence of comparable data collections. This made empirical testing of theoretical conjectures excessively difficult and, in many cases, impossible. Leeds' dataset on alliances and Mitchell's on international environmental agreements were major advances in this respect (Leeds *et al.* 2002; Mitchell 2002–12). A more recent advance is Haftel and Thompson's (2006) paper on the independence of international institutions. They develop a theoretical argument, as well as an empirical measure of the independence of international institutions, and propose a coding rule that is applicable to a vast range of settings, allowing for comparisons on a large scale. This measure of institutional independence is based on numerous design features, such as decision-making procedures and the design of dispute settlement mechanisms, and subjected to several theoretically informed empirical tests. COIL has similar purposes, and, responding to Duffield's (2003: 416) critique that rational design obscured parallels to other branches of the literature through "an excessive degree of generality," provides clear definitions and operationalizations for hundreds of variables. This wealth of data should be seen as invitation to other researchers to follow Haftel and Thompson in carefully testing theoretical arguments, potentially by synthesizing variables into broader concepts that are of relevance to the study of international law.

C. How to Build on Rational Design?

1. The Lifecycle of Agreements

Rational design and the institutionalist literature open up a promising line for future research: examining the interdependencies between negotiations, agreement design, and agreement outcomes. Thompson (2010) introduces negotiations into the framework. Examining the link between uncertainty and flexibility, he proposes that not only equilibrium outcomes (the institutional arrangements), but also the process of institutional design (the negotiations) can be understood and explained in terms of (a refined version of) rational design. This is a welcome addition to existing scholarship, in that it incorporates the negotiation phase of international agreements explicitly into the analysis. While Fearon (1998) emphasized the link between bargaining and enforcement more than a decade ago, empirical research rarely considered this explicitly. It may be well worth pursuing even more research with respect to the negotiation process; as Odell (2010) points out, the field in particular lacks answers to the question of how negotiations take place within international institutions, once these are established.

A step in this direction is made by Kay and Ackrill (2009), who examine the development of international trade cooperation with respect to agricultural products. The article traces the institutional development in this issue area and emphasizes how previously negotiated outcomes affected future negotiation rounds and, hence, institutional design. Expanding on the rational design framework, this suggests that states try to incorporate new information obtained from previous cooperative endeavors into the design choices for future institutions.

Duffield (2003: 414) raises the concern that the rational design literature neglects the evolutionary processes leading to institutional outcomes. Constructivism's close attention to the role of negotiations, deliberations, and persuasion (Risse and Kleine 2010) may provide important insights for rational design. Brunnée and Toope (2013), for instance, emphasize the importance that *norm creation* and *norm application* meet "specific criteria of legality" for international law to create legal obligation. Based on these insights, the process and outcome of negotiations will be of crucial importance to the functioning, and hence effectiveness, of an institution.

Turning to the other end of an agreement's lifecycle, this agenda connects rational design to the literatures on interpretation and enforcement, respectively, in an important way: if states design international agreements purposefully, the arising agreements should generate state behavior and outcomes that match the predictions of rational design. If agreement outcomes do not, states must have created dysfunctional institutions; alternatively, the scholar is forced to come up with a rational explanation for why the institution fails to work as predicted. Linking agreement outcomes and agreement design in such a fashion then either provides additional support for the rational design framework, should the agreement function as predicted, or it generates new puzzles and, once the puzzles are resolved, new insights into the design of international institutions.

Still, one must be careful about drawing conclusions from the actual use of agreement design provisions. If the design provision is a renegotiation provision, put in place at least in part to solve uncertainty about future bargaining power, we would indeed expect states to renegotiate the agreement – that is, to see the agreement provision employed. Such is the case in the series of international coffee agreements: the 1962 distribution of quotas was altered in 1968, 1976, and 1983[4] (Koremenos 2002). But if the design provision is a withdrawal clause, its very incorporation into the agreement might make withdrawal less likely, since optimally designed withdrawal notice and waiting periods preclude opportunistic withdrawal (see Koremenos and Nau 2010). In the case of renegotiation provisions, their regular use is part of the institutional equilibrium; in the case of withdrawal provisions, their much less frequent use is itself the equilibrium because the inclusion of withdrawal provisions alters the relative incentives to withdraw from a treaty while at the same time making states more comfortable subjecting themselves to an international commitment.

---

[4] From 1989 on, the provisions regulating exports and imports were suspended.

In *How International Law Works*, Guzman (2008) nicely demonstrates the nexus between design and compliance; his work underscores the promises of an integrated approach. Building on the early institutionalist literature, Guzman argues that reciprocity, retaliation, and, most important, reputation (the "3 Rs") explain why states comply with their commitments and, hence, agreements become enforceable. Guzman uses these factors to explain treaty design as well. One central argument in the book is that, because enforcement through retaliation and sanctioning is costly (but see Thompson 2009, 2013, for a critique), states try to reduce instances of violations by softening their agreements, for example, through weak monitoring provisions, escape and exit clauses, and reservations. Thus, like the rational design literature, Guzman is concerned with questions of institutional design, grounding his argument in an explicit framework of rational actors. Yet, the book also differs in important respects; rather than linking the institutional design to the specific strategic problems faced by states, Guzman frames his arguments in more general terms (thereby teasing out few if any empirically testable hypotheses). The reputation of a state, for instance, helps states to make more credible, hence deeper, commitments, but it does not depend much on the institution in question. In fact, Guzman argues that reputation may carry over from other institutions and even other issue areas. This, in turn, opens up questions that go well beyond the rational design literature, such as the scope for states to acquire and strategically manipulate their reputational capital.

2. Institutional Interdependencies

Another important topic is constituted by interdependencies across institutions, or what IR scholars have referred to as *regime complexity* (see, e.g., Raustiala and Victor 2004; Alter and Meunier 2009; Raustiala 2013). Verdier (2008) examines the coexistence of bilateral and multilateral institutions in the area of nuclear proliferation agreements. Multilateral agreements have the advantage of being negotiated once and generally on the same terms for all participants.[5] Yet, this advantage of uniformity also causes them to be inefficient. The necessity to accommodate all participants requires the inclusion of large incentives, so that even those states least inclined to comply with the agreement are willing to participate. This implies that most states will have an excess incentive to participate because they would have been willing to settle on less favorable terms. This problem is better addressed in bilateral agreements, which can be tailored to match each participant's incentives. Bilateral and multilateral agreements are hence used complementarily, as

---

[5] Exceptions to the uniformity of commitments include the Nuclear Nonproliferation Treaty, which features distinct obligations for nuclear weapon and nonnuclear weapon states, and environmental treaties such as the Kyoto Protocol, which incorporate the notion of "common but differentiated responsibility" with different obligations for different classes of states. Such differentiated responsibilities are themselves a form of flexibility in international agreements.

Verdier argues. For states with low costs of compliance, no additional incentives are needed for participation, and hence a multilateral agreement will be sufficient to induce compliance. For states with higher costs of compliance, bilateral agreements are crafted, providing additional incentives for cooperation tailored to the specific dyad.

Verdier's framework is unambiguously colored by the conditions prevailing in the nuclear proliferation setting: two powerful actors, the United States and the Soviet Union, attempt to elicit cooperation from other actors. This justifies the emphasis on the costs of providing incentives to participants, since these costs had to be borne mainly by one of the two superpowers. However, a similar argument can be made in a more decentralized context as well, as shown by Rixen (2010). Rixen examines the choice between bilateralism and multilateralism in the realm of international cooperation on taxation. Here, states face a coordination game, a problem that is easier to solve in a bilateral than in a multilateral context. At the same time, multilateral institutions benefit from economies of scale when it comes to information dissemination and may serve as focal points for bilateral negotiations. Hence, Rixen argues, states create binding bilateral agreements – since they are easier to negotiate – while using the Organization for Economic Cooperation and Development (OECD)'s model convention on international taxation as a nonbinding focal point for these negotiations. Rixen's model not only provides an explanation for the choice between bilateralism and multilateralism; it also provides a rationale for the coexistence of institutions with different membership rules and degrees of obligation, and it moreover hints at the importance of acknowledging institutional interdependencies that go beyond issue linkages across and within institutions. Some IL literature presents a contrasting account, such as that of Blum (2008), who argues that the choice between bilateralism and multilateralism reflects bureaucratic and political preferences.

3. Domestic Factors and Agreement Design

Bringing the importance of domestic institutions into the picture, Baccini (2010) provides another interesting extension of rational design. Baccini examines flexibility measures in European Union (EU) trade agreements. Starting from the premise that uncertainty should lead to the incorporation of flexibility arrangements, Baccini acknowledges that flexibility measures may also present an opportunity to suspend obligations intentionally by exploiting information asymmetries: claiming exceptional domestic circumstances, a government can try to obtain more favorable terms in an agreement by invoking escape clauses. Foreseeing this, governments will be reluctant to include flexibility arrangements in their agreements when it is difficult to gather information on the domestic politics of the other parties to an agreement. Hence, domestic political and economic transparency become important determinants of the decision to include flexibility measures. This combination of rational design with domestic institutional factors promises to be a fruitful avenue for further research: given that agreement outcomes are hardly separable from domestic politics (see also the discussion of Morrow [2007] and Simmons [2009] in Section III.A), the stage of agreement design should be expected to follow these same imperatives, too. These arguments suggest the importance of domestic institutions for the functioning and, hence, the design of international institutions.

At this point, a clear distinction should be drawn between attempts to refer to domestic institutional factors as explanations for the design of international agreements and attempts to use domestic institutional factors as an explanation for state preferences. Although amenable to the former, rational design is agnostic, and critics might say outright ignorant, about the latter. States (understood as the government actors negotiating the agreement) are assumed to have an interest in cooperation; why this is so is outside the scope of rational design. To reiterate what was said previously, instead of asking why states cooperate, the relevant question in the rational design framework is why states cooperate the way that they do. This distinguishes rational design in particular from liberal approaches, with their heavy focus on domestic institutions and for which, as Moravcsik (2010) puts it, "What matters most is what states want, not how they get it." Rational design is not at odds with any of the core assumptions of liberal theory; some of them are, however, irrelevant from the rational design perspective. While liberal theory is particularly concerned with the *formation* of state preferences, rational design assumes as given a set of preferences, taking these as a starting point for theorizing. The other main assumptions are consistent with each other. Both rational design and liberalism are based on the assumption that states act instrumentally to achieve their goals, and both acknowledge the role of interdependencies of preferences, except that rational design reframes the latter as "cooperation problems," which can be linked to various underlying constellations of preferences. Rational design, therefore, may be seen as both a subset and an extension of liberal theory: as a subset, in that it abstracts from the process of preference formation; as an extension, in that it is much more concerned with the question of how specifically states manage globalization instrumentally (i.e., which institutions they form toward this goal).

This, of course, does not render liberalism and rational design two mutually exclusive approaches; quite the contrary, the discussion should highlight that the two approaches are interested in two distinct sets of questions and could well benefit from each other, as long as this does not come at the cost of the respective approaches' analytical clarity. For instance, liberalism could benefit from paying more attention to how different institutional design elements have different implications for societal actors, and hence should lead to different domestic coalitions in favor of or opposed to specific forms of international cooperation. Rational design, on the other hand, could benefit from a more detailed account of state preferences when states have multiple equilibrium institutions to choose from – when multiple equilibria exist, their different distributional

Barbara Koremenos

TABLE 3.1. *Regression results. dependent variable: complexity of cooperation problem*

	Coefficient	std. error	p-value	95% Confidence interval
average polity score	−0.016	0.013	0.221	[−0.041, 0.009]
Security	−0.354	0.255	0.169	[−0.859, 0.152]
Economics	−0.66	0.196	0.001	[−1.047, −0.273]
Environment	−0.488	0.228	0.034	[−0.938, −0.038]
Constant	2.211	0.185	0.000	[1.845, 2.577]

Note: Standard errors heteroskedasticity-consistent. N = 145.
Source: All data in the following from the Continent of International Law (Koremenos, forthcoming).

consequences for domestic actors may help to determine which outcome will prevail.

Table 3.1 provides a specific example of how liberal theory may be incorporated into rational design. If democratic societies develop broader and more complex relationships, both within the state and across states (Moravcsik 2008), one might expect this to be reflected in the agreements such regime types conclude. Specifically, one would conjecture that more democratic states conclude agreements that address more complex cooperation problems. The data to test this conjecture are obtained from COIL; a crucial point to note is that the complexity variable does not describe the complexity of the agreement content, but rather the complexity of the cooperation problem(s) that states are trying to solve.[6] Relying on the average polity score of the parties to an agreement as a measure of democracy among the participants,[7] Table 3.1 shows that there is no clear relationship between domestic institutions and the complexity of an agreement; the coefficient on the average polity score is small and statistically indistinguishable from zero. Noting also that the coefficient is estimated quite precisely, this suggests that domestic institutions have little, if any, influence, on the types of cooperation problems that states are trying to solve. Of course, this is only preliminary evidence and should by no means be taken as a "test" of liberal theory; rather, it is a simple illustration for the kind of research that the recently collected data on international institutions allow us to pursue.

II. INTERNATIONAL DELEGATION AND ADJUDICATION

An important branch in the literature on international agreements is concerned with the interpretation of law and the extent to which adjudication and delegation in international agreements occur (for a more detailed discussion, see Koremenos and Betz 2013). Parts of this literature go back to Chayes and Chayes' (1993) argument

---

[6] See Koremenos (forthcoming) for a detailed description of the coding of the complexity variable.
[7] Using the median or standard deviation does not change the results substantively.

that states may violate commitments not only because they lack the capabilities for compliance, but also because they simply misinterpreted ambiguous provisions in an agreement. If this is the case, absent some mechanism of adjudication among the disagreeing parties, the institution may break down: an action by one side is (potentially mistakenly) viewed as a breach of commitment by the other and, in turn, triggers retaliation. This, of course, is an unfortunate outcome, since cooperation (which must have been valuable to both sides since otherwise there should not have been an agreement in the first place) breaks down, thus creating an inefficient outcome.

Adjudication may help address this problem. By channeling disputes over the interpretation of agreement language into (often formalized) institutionalized procedures, an unwarranted breakdown of cooperation may be prevented, thus creating more robust forms of cooperation in the presence of "noise," like uncertainties about the behavior of other actors. The presence of adjudication can also be linked to the enforcement phase: being identified as being in violation of an agreement's terms by an authorized, independent body is assumed to inflict an increased reputational cost on the violator, thus preempting violations in the first place (Abbott and Snidal 2000; Simmons 2002; but see Brewster 2013, arguing that, in terms of reputational costs, complying with a court's order can help mitigate the reputational harms associated with a judicial finding that a state has violated its obligations). Additionally, having an external body render a decision about compliance may make it more palatable to domestic audiences, thereby increasing the chance that the body's ruling will be followed and cooperation will ensue (Simmons 2002; Allee and Huth 2006). Similar findings emerge in McLaughlin Mitchell and Hensel (2007). Employing a selection model, they find compliance will be higher when an authoritative third party is involved than when solutions are reached less formally between the parties. As Simmons (2010: 283) states: "These findings illuminate how the legal context potentially shapes the meaning of actions: deferring to legal authority signals a law-abiding character, whereas deferring to an adversary signals nothing but weakness."

Some anecdotal evidence that adjudication leads to more robust cooperation is presented by Rosendorff (2005) in the context of the World Trade Organization's (WTO) dispute settlement procedure. Ghosh (2010) examines explicitly how the Trade Policy Review Mechanism, a highly institutionalized part of the WTO, functions to increase transparency and to provide information to the WTO's members, thus fostering monitoring capabilities. This, then, shows how delegating certain functions in agreements may help to stabilize cooperation by making it more difficult to renege on commitments; recalling Keohane's (1984) argument about the role of international institutions in resolving information asymmetries, Ghosh's paper thus highlights an important function of delegated bodies, substantiating the earlier abstract claims with a specific example and a vast range of data.

Within rational design as well as other institutionalist frameworks (see Bradley and Kelly 2008), adjudication is often treated as a form of delegation. Koremenos

(2007) asks when and why states delegate to third parties and what the consequences of such delegation are. Theoretically, this literature is mainly concerned with the role of principal–agent problems and the concept of state sovereignty: delegating decision-making or interpretative authorities to third parties is assumed to constrain states in their freedom; put differently, delegation is a costly endeavor for states and thus should be expected only when prescribed by the cooperation problems at hand (Koremenos [2007] provides empirical support for this conjecture; see also Koremenos and Betz [2013]).

The vast bulk of research, however, is concerned with the consequences of delegation and the role of power asymmetries. This is, to a large extent, due to the fact that, to date, empirical research on adjudication focuses on the WTO's dispute settlement mechanism (Guzman and Simmons 2002). The focus on power asymmetries is spurred by the observation that developing countries tend to be underrepresented in the dispute resolutions taking place (Busch and Reinhardt 2003; Smith 2004). Sattler and Bernauer (2010) point out another shortcoming of the WTO's dispute settlement mechanism: dyads with large power asymmetries tend to settle disputes outside the WTO's formal procedures, arguably to the disadvantage of the weaker participant, who then cannot rely on the legalized, power-balancing procedures of the WTO (but see Koremenos and Betz [2013], for a discussion of this assertion).

In the perspective of the institutionalist literature, such findings are important because they indicate that a higher degree of institutionalization can be problematic: if taking advantage of highly complicated, institutionalized procedures is too costly for some countries to afford participating in them, the outcomes generated by such institutions will be biased systematically against the weaker parties in the international system – thus supporting realist suspicions that international institutions are merely epiphenomenal of state power. However, there is also some more optimistic evidence in favor of institutionalism: as Davis and Bermeo (2009) argue, the high costs of participation in dispute settlement may deter some countries from initiating disputes; yet, they argue that the main barrier to participation are the high, one-time start-up costs – once these are paid, dispute initiation is facilitated even for weak countries. Hence, over time, we should expect to see a more balanced pattern of participation, as more countries overcome these initial capacity constraints.

Two topics are still relatively neglected in the institutionalist political science literature. One such topic surrounds those factors that influence the interpretation of law. Additional theorizing on the outcomes of dispute settlement procedures would greatly complement existing research on the question of whether dispute settlement procedures are delegated (see also Pauwelyn and Elsig 2013).[8] The second topic

---

[8] In terms of political factors that influence the outcome of dispute settlement, see Busch and Reinhardt (2007), who look at the participation of third parties in WTO dispute settlement and how such third-party involvement affects the settlement of disputes.

deserving further research is the specific design of delegated dispute settlement procedures and how it affects the outcomes of disputes; Alter (2013) provides a welcome attempt to assess such design features, such as private party access, and their implications (see also Koremenos and Betz 2013).

Overall, this literature on delegation, especially of adjudication, deepens the connections between IR and IL in an important respect: it emphasizes the precise design features through which institutions function and affect state behavior. Perhaps most important, this raises hopes for a closer collaboration between the two disciplines in the future.

III. COMPLIANCE AND ENFORCEMENT

A. (Why) Do States Comply with International Law?

A third branch of the institutionalist literature is concerned with questions of compliance and enforcement. (For a more comprehensive review than that provided here, see Simmons [2010] and the chapters by Thompson [2013] and von Stein [2013].) This literature is still tied closely to the older question of whether institutions matter. It has been argued that states negotiate and agree on institutions, but then these institutions do little to induce compliance – violations occur just as states please (and not simply because of incapacities, imprecise treaty language, or temporal changes in preferences, as argued by Chayes and Chayes [1993]). An even more severe problem, both theoretically and for any empirical evaluation, is posed by selection problems: plausibly, only those states willing to follow an agreement's prescribed behavior sign onto them (Downs, Rocke, and Barsoom 1996). Put differently, international law may have little independent effect on state behavior. Institutionalist arguments, on the other hand, are based on reputation, retaliation, or reciprocity (Guzman's "3 Rs") to explain compliance with international law; Levit (2004) goes even further, arguing that specific design features of soft-law regimes explain compliance, rather than state interests.

This theoretical dispute was soon picked up empirically. Examining compliance with the International Monetary Fund (IMF) Articles of Agreement, Simmons (2000) argues that there is, indeed, an independent effect of treaty commitments on state behavior and that compliance is, to a large extent, induced by reputational concerns. However, referring to the argument of Downs, Rocke, and Barsoom (1996) about the inherent selection problems in studies on treaty effectiveness, von Stein (2005) counters Simmon's (2000) findings, arguing instead that the IMF Articles of Agreement mainly screen states, but do little to constrain them. Von Stein's results were, in turn, criticized on methodological grounds by Simmons and Hopkins (2005), defending Simmon's earlier paper and arguing that screening and constraining functions of treaties need not be mutually exclusive.

In any event, substantial evidence on the constraining effects of treaties is reported for many other issue areas. Simmons (2009), for instance, documents how the ratification of human rights treaties changes state–society relations, mobilizing and empowering domestic interest groups; these, in turn, may press for changes in state behavior (a similar argument is made by Hafner-Burton and Tsutsui 2005). Simmons' book features the most comprehensive data collection and systematic empirical analysis seen in the area of human rights. Given the typically weak enforcement mechanisms in the issue area of human rights (unlike in trade agreements, retaliation – in the form of violating the human rights of one's own citizens – is impractical and likely to be ineffective), these findings make a strong case for the relevance of international law in shaping state behavior. A novel argument, connecting design features to agreement performance, is made by Alter (2010), who argues that international courts can act as "tipping point actors," enabling domestic compliance constituencies.

In the field of international humanitarian law, and specifically the laws of war, Morrow (2007) finds that enforcement mechanisms have more bite. Here, deterrence by reciprocity induces compliance by those states that ratified a treaty; moreover, Morrow argues that the ratification of treaties generates dynamics of its own by generating domestic political costs for violating the treaty terms. Another important part of Morrow's argument is the role of non-state actors and individuals in causing noncompliance – if the central government lacks control over individual subjects, it becomes difficult for other states to evaluate and respond to noncompliance. Arguably, Morrow's test is a particularly difficult one for theories of compliance, given that international humanitarian law operates in an environment in which any higher enforcement mechanism is lacking – being already at war, states have no recourse to more severe enforcement measures.

The work just reviewed is exemplary of the recent wave of research on enforcement and compliance. Theoretically, these writings pay careful attention to the specific mechanisms through which international law enhances compliance and thereby changes state behavior. Rather than operating at the abstract level of early institutionalist theories, these works elaborate on these effects and trace them to domestic institutions and domestic politics, showing how these generate their own dynamics that may induce treaty compliance. Similar arguments highlighting the importance of domestic institutions and politics appear in writings by international legal scholars as well (Koh 1996, 1998; Trachtman 2013). Such arguments push forward the extant literature in an important respect: rather than assuming a "propensity to comply" that is identical for all countries, they show how this propensity can vary across governments and specify the factors and mechanisms that influence it.

Empirically, the recent literature collected an impressive amount of original data to test the various arguments quantitatively, rather than relying on anecdotal evidence, as was the case in much of the earlier literature. This, again, contributes to the extant literature in important ways, but it also underscores a central limitation of the literature on enforcement and compliance: because data collection on compliance is such a time-consuming endeavor (not only do agreements need to be coded, but so do specific agreement outcomes over time for potentially dozens of countries), these studies remain focused on specific agreements within a specific issue area. On the one hand, this allows for a holistic and detailed perspective; on the other hand, it renders comparisons across agreements – let alone issue areas – difficult.

IV. FRONTIER ISSUES: INFORMALITY AND CHANGE

A. *What's Left Out?*

Although the focus on formal law, including its details, is a tremendously important step in deepening our understanding of why and how international cooperation occurs, this very focus thus far has precluded what could be a very significant issue: cooperation that fails to be formalized.

Some scholars (e.g., Lipson 1991; Downs and Rocke 1997) have noted that some cooperation is optimally left informal. These earlier insights, to my knowledge, have not been systematically tested or refined in the past decades, perhaps because of the obstacles to quantifying what is informal.

Recently, however, Randall Stone (2010) has tackled the issue of informal governance within three very formal institutions: the IMF, the WTO, and the EU. In his theoretically rigorous analyses, Stone argues that the balance of informal and formal is an equilibrium outcome, deriving from the member states' power and interests. He states:

> Formal and informal governance represent alternative social choice mechanisms – the former based on voting and formal rules, the latter based on power and informal influence – and these two mechanisms coexist in international organizations. The choice of procedures that incentivize or delegitimate the use of informal power is a critical step in institutional design, and in equilibrium the mixture of these modes of governance in international organizations balances the power and interests of strong and weak states.

Stone's contributions are important because, although there have been wonderfully rich case studies of particular institutions, especially the EU (Kleine 2010; Reh *et al.* 2010), theorists in the institutionalist tradition have been slow to add to the earlier works of Downs and Rocke, as well as Lipson, in a way that might transcend particular cases. Stone concludes:

> Formal rules are also important in each organization, but in each case, the functioning of the organization cannot adequately be understood without taking into account the many ways in which informal governance mechanisms modify or overrule the formal procedures. Scholars who study the EU and the WTO have devoted considerable attention to this phenomenon, but they have generally failed to connect the dots, because they have not appreciated that informal governance

mechanisms exist primarily to serve the interests of powerful states, while formal rules are generally designed to protect the weak.[9]

What is needed next is even more theoretical elaboration to generate comparative static predictions and truly systematic empirical work to test these predictions. Of course, this is easier said than done. Research design obstacles are tremendous. How does one quantify informal rules reliably across more than the small number of EU-type cases already studied?

Koremenos (2012) argues that, under certain circumstances, states leave out certain design provisions not because they are unnecessary to solve the problem at hand but because they want the flexibility that comes from not formalizing these provisions. Take, for instance, the Nuclear Nonproliferation Treaty. There are no formal punishments articulated in the treaty, yet states are punished for defecting; moreover, it is hard to argue that these defections and ensuing punishments were not anticipated. What made states leave out punishment provisions in the Nuclear Nonproliferation Treaty but articulate them in great detail in the series of International Coffee Agreements that began in the early 1960s? Also, when we see no punishment provisions, how can we distinguish between situations for which punishments are part of the informal design and those for which they are not intended at all, like certain multilateral human rights agreements? The paper articulates conditions under which we might expect punishment provisions (as one example) to be informal (power asymmetries, great heterogeneity among state participants, and non-renegotiation proof punishment [i.e., punishment that is costly to the punisher(s)]) and features a research design that exploits Koremenos' random sample of formal international agreements across the issue areas. By looking more closely at the agreements not correctly predicted by theories of institutional design – that is, times when, given the cooperation problems at hand, the expected institutional solutions were left out – we can see if those agreements are characterized by the underlying features articulated by the theory (i.e., they feature great heterogeneity among the membership, costly punishment, etc.). Additionally, case study work can identify if these agreements did feature punishment over time as states were found to be non-compliant.

B. *Institutional Change*

Institutional change is another topic ripe for consideration now that we have some robust results regarding initial institutional design (Koremenos and Snidal 2012). In international politics, change is of great consequence, and contemporary IR theory has a wide range of substantive views on change. At one end of the spectrum lies

---

[9] One could argue that IL scholars have long understood precisely this point, which is why they insist on the importance and the relative autonomy of the law. I thank the editors for this insight.

realism, which argues that, at some level, not a lot changes because IR begins and ends with the enduring nature of anarchy (structure) and states as the enduring actors with fairly fixed concerns (preferences) for security. At the other end lies constructivism, which often implicitly assumes that the world is fluid and change is relatively easy. Consider Wendt's famous motto: "Anarchy is what states make of it." Similar arguments have been made for actors and preferences.

Between these two extremes is institutionalism. It sometimes presents itself as a theory of change within the existing systemic constraints or structure ("cooperation under anarchy").[10] But sometimes the structure changes, as in the evolution from anarchy to institutionalized cooperation – seemingly the case in Europe. Usually, actors and preferences are fixed, but in other versions, institutionalism sometimes entertains shifts in the interests of the actor (from "warring" states to "trading" states) and inclusion of new actors in international politics (domestic interests, non-governmental organizations [NGOs], international organizations [IOs]). I would argue that institutionalism is best suited to study change because of its combination of disciplined theoretical development and its flexibility in its attitude toward change.[11]

REFERENCES

Abbott, Kenneth W., and Duncan Snidal (2000). "Hard and Soft Law in International Governance," *International Organization*, Vol. 54, No. 3, pp. 421–56.

Allee, Todd, and Paul Huth (2006). "The Pursuit of Legal Settlements to Territorial Disputes," *Conflict Management and Peace Science*, Vol. 23, No. 4, pp. 285–307.

Alter, Karen J. (2010). "Tipping the Balance: International Courts and the Construction of International and Domestic Politics," Working Paper (Evanston, IL: Northwestern University, The Roberta Buffett Center for International and Comparative Studies).

———— (2013). "The Multiple Roles of International Courts and Tribunals: Enforcement, Dispute Settlement, Constitutional and Administrative Review," in Jeffrey L. Dunoff and Mark A. Pollack (eds.), *Interdisciplinary Perspectives on International Law and International Relations: The State of the Art* (New York: Cambridge University Press), pp. 345–70.

Alter, Karen J., and Sophie Meunier (2009). "The Politics of International Regime Complexity," *Perspectives on Politics*, Vol. 7, No. 1, pp. 13–24.

Axelrod, Robert (1984). *The Evolution of Cooperation* (New York: Basic Books).

Axelrod, Robert, and Robert O. Keohane (1985). "Achieving Cooperation under Anarchy: Strategies and Institutions," *World Politics*, Vol. 38, No. 1, pp. 226–54.

Baccini, Leonardo (2010). "Explaining Formation and Design of EU Trade Agreements: The Role of Transparency and Flexibility," *European Union Politics*, Vol. 11, No. 2, pp. 195–217.

Blum, Gabriella (2008). "Bilateralism, Multilateralism, and the Architecture of International Law," *Harvard International Law Journal*, Vol. 49, No. 2, pp. 323–78.

---

[10] Historical institutionalism is a branch within the institutionalist literature that puts institutional change at the core of its research program (Fioretos 2010). (Rational choice) institutionalism, as it was discussed in this chapter, may have a great deal to learn from this branch of the literature.

[11] See, too, Helfer (2002) on the possibility of detrimental change in the human rights issue area.

Bradley, Curtis A., and Judith G. Kelley (2008). "The Concept of International Delegation," *Law and Contemporary Problems*, Vol. 71, No. 1, pp. 1–36.

Brewster, Rachel (2013). "Reputation in International Relations and International Law Theory," in Jeffrey L. Dunoff and Mark A. Pollack (eds.), *Interdisciplinary Perspectives on International Law and International Relations: The State of the Art* (New York: Cambridge University Press), pp. 524–43.

Brunnée, Jutta, and Stephen Toope (2013). "Constructivism and International Law," in Jeffrey L. Dunoff and Mark A. Pollack (eds.), *Interdisciplinary Perspectives on International Law and International Relations: The State of the Art* (New York: Cambridge University Press), pp. 119–45.

Busch, Marc L., and Eric Reinhardt (2003). "Developing Countries and General Agreement on Tariffs and Trade/World Trade Organization Dispute Settlement," *Journal of World Trade*, Vol. 37, No. 4, pp. 719–35.

Busch, Marc L., and Eric Reinhardt (2007). "Three's a Crowd: Third Parties and WTO Dispute Settlement," *World Politics*, Vol. 58, No. 3, pp. 446–77.

Carneiro, Cristiane (2007). "From the United Nations Arms Register to an Arms Trade Treaty – What Role for Delegation and Flexibility," *ILSA Journal of International & Comparative Law*, Vol. 14, pp. 477–98.

Chayes, Abram, and Antonia Handler Chayes (1993). "On Compliance," *International Organization*, Vol. 47, No. 2, pp. 175–205.

Davis, Christina L., and Sarah Blodgett Bermeo (2009). "Who Files? Developing Country Participation in GATT/WTO Adjudication," *Journal of Politics*, Vol. 71, No. 3, pp. 1033–49.

Downs, George W., David M. Rocke, and Peter N. Barsoom (1996). "Is the Good News about Compliance Good News about Cooperation?" *International Organization*, Vol. 50, No. 3, pp. 379–406.

Downs, George W., and David M. Rocke (1997). *Optimal Imperfection? Domestic Uncertainty and Institutions in International Relations*, (Princeton, NJ: Princeton University Press).

Duffield, John S. (2003). "The Limits of 'Rational Design'," *International Organization*, Vol. 57, No. 2, pp. 411–30.

Fearon, James D. (1998). "Bargaining, Enforcement, and International Cooperation," *International Organization*, Vol. 52, No. 2, pp. 269–305.

Finnemore, Martha, and Kathryn Sikkink (1998). "International Norm Dynamics and Political Change," *International Organization*, Vol. 52, No. 4, pp. 887–917.

Fioretos, Orfeo (2012). "Historical Institutionalism in International Relations," *International Organization*, Vol. 65, No. 2, pp. 367–99.

Ghosh, Arunabha (2010). "Developing Countries in the WTO Trade Policy Review Mechanism," *World Trade Review*, Vol. 9, No. 3, pp. 419–55.

Goldstein, Judith O., Miles Kahler, Robert O. Keohane, and Anne-Marie Slaughter (2000). "Introduction: Legalization and World Politics," *International Organization*, Vol. 54, No. 3, pp. 385–99.

Grieco, Joseph M. (1988). "Anarchy and the Limits of Cooperation: A Realist Critique of the Newest Liberal Institutionalism," *International Organization*, Vol. 42, No. 3, pp. 485–507.

Guzman, Andrew T. (2008). *How International Law Works: A Rational Choice Theory*. (Oxford: Oxford University Press).

Guzman, Andrew T., and Beth A. Simmons (2002). "To Settle or Empanel? An Empirical Analysis of Litigation and Settlement at the World Trade Organization," *Journal of Legal Studies*, Vol. 31, No. 1, pp. S205–S235.

Hafner-Burton, Emilie M., and Kiyoteru Tsutsui (2005). "Human Rights in a Globalizing World: The Paradox of Empty Promises," *American Journal of Sociology*, Vol. 110, No. 5, pp. 1373–1411.

Haftel, Yoram Z., and Alexander Thompson (2006). "The Independence of International Organizations: Concept and Applications," *Journal of Conflict Resolution*, Vol. 50, No. 2, pp. 253–75.

Helfer, Laurence R. (2002). "Overlegalizing Human Rights: International Relations Theory and the Commonwealth Caribbean Backlash against Human Rights Regimes," *Columbia Law Review*, Vol. 102, No. 7, pp. 1832–1911.

———— (2006). "Not Fully Committed? Reservations, Risk, and Treaty Design," *Yale Journal of International Law*, Vol. 31, No. 2, pp. 367–82.

Kay, Adrian, and Robert Ackrill (2009). "Institutional Change in the International Governance of Agriculture: A Revised Account," *Governance*, Vol. 22, No. 3, pp. 483–506.

Keohane, Robert O. (1984). *After Hegemony: Cooperation and Discord in the World Political Economy* (Princeton, NJ: Princeton University Press).

Kleine, Mareike (2010). "Making Cooperation Work: Informal Governance in the EU and Beyond," Paper Presented at the 2010 Annual Meeting of the American Political Science Association.

Koh, Harold (1996). "Transnational Legal Process," *Nebraska Law Review*, Vol. 75, pp. 181–207.

———— (1998). "How Is International Human Rights Law Enforced?" *Indiana Law Review*, Vol. 74, pp. 1397–1417.

Koremenos, Barbara (2001). "Loosening the Ties That Bind: A Learning Model of Agreement Flexibility," *International Organization* Vol. 55, No. 2, pp. 289–325.

———— (2002). "Can Cooperation Survive Changes in Bargaining Power? The Case of Coffee," *Journal of Legal Studies*, Vol. 31, No. 1, pp. S259–S283.

———— (2005). "Contracting around International Uncertainty," *American Political Science Review*, Vol. 99, No. 4, pp. 549–65.

———— (2007). "If Only Half of International Agreements Have Dispute Resolution Provisions, Which Half Needs Explaining?," *Journal of Legal Studies*, Vol. 36, No. 1, pp. 189–212.

———— (2011). "An Economic Analysis of International Rulemaking," Working Paper (Ann Arbor, MI: University of Michigan, Department of Political Science).

———— (2012). "What's Left Out and Why? Informal Provisions in Formal International Law." Manuscript, Presented at the Political Economy of International Organizations Conference, January 2012.

———— (forthcoming). "The Continent of International Law," *Journal of Conflict Resolution*.

Koremenos, Barbara, Charles Lipson, and Duncan Snidal (2001). "The Rational Design of International Institutions," *International Organization*, Vol. 55, No. 4, pp. 761–99.

Koremenos, Barbara, and Allison Nau (2010). "Exit, No Exit," *Duke Journal of Comparative and International Law*, Vol. 21, No. 1, pp. 81–119.

Koremenos, Barbara, and Mihwa Hong (2011). "The Rational Design of Human Rights Agreements," Working Paper (Ann Arbor: University of Michigan, Department of Political Science).

Koremenos, Barbara, and Timm Betz (2013). "The Design of Dispute Settlement Procedures in International Agreements," in Jeffrey L. Dunoff and Mark A. Pollack (eds.), *Interdisciplinary Perspectives on International Law and International Relations: The State of the Art* (New York: Cambridge University Press), pp. 371–93.

Koremenos, Barbara, and Duncan Snidal (2012). "Fixing What's Fixed: A Preliminary Agenda for Thinking about International Change." Manuscript.

Krasner, Stephen D. (1982). "Structural Causes and Regime Consequences: Regimes as Intervening Variables," *International Organization*, Vol. 36, No. 2, pp. 185–205.

———— (1991). "Global Communications and National Power: Life on the Pareto Frontier," *World Politics*, Vol. 43, No. 3, pp. 336–66.

Leeds, Brett, Jeffrey Ritter, Sara McLaughlin Mitchell, and Andrew Long (2002). "Alliance Treaty Obligations and Provisions, 1815–1944," *International Interactions*, Vol. 28, No. 3, pp. 237–60.

Levit, Janet (2004). "The Dynamics of International Trade Finance Regulation: The Arrangement on Officially Supported Export Credits," *Harvard International Law Journal*, Vol. 45, No. 1, pp. 65–182.

Lipson, Charles (1991). "Why Are Some International Agreements Informal?" *International Organization*, Vol. 45, No. 4, pp. 495–538.

McLaughlin Mitchell, Sara, and Paul R. Hensel (2007). "International Institutions and Compliance with Agreements," *American Journal of Political Science*, Vol. 51, No. 4, pp. 721–37.

Mearsheimer, John J. (1994). "The False Promise of International Institutions," *International Security*, Vol. 19, No. 3, pp. 5–49.

Mitchell, Ronald B. (2002–12). *International Environmental Agreements Database Project (Version 2010.3)*, available at: http://iea.uoregon.edu/.

Moravcsik, Andrew (2000). "The Origins of Human Rights Regimes: Democratic Delegation in Postwar Europe," *International Organization*, Vol. 54, No. 2, pp. 217–52.

———— (2008). "The New Liberalism," in Christian Reus-Smit and Duncan Snidal (eds.), *The Oxford Handbook of International Relations* (Oxford: Oxford University Press), pp. 234–54.

———— (2010). "Liberal Theories of International Relations: A Primer," Manuscript (Princeton, NJ: Princeton University Press).

Morrow, James D. (2007). "When Do States Follow the Laws of War?" *American Political Science Review*, Vol. 101, No. 3, pp. 559–72.

Odell, John (2010). "Three Islands of Knowledge about Negotiation in International Organizations," *Journal of European Public Policy*, Vol. 17, No. 5, pp. 619–32.

Oye, Kenneth A. (1986). "Explaining Cooperation under Anarchy: Hypotheses and Strategies," in Kenneth A. Oye (ed.), *Cooperation under Anarchy* (Princeton, NJ: Princeton University Press), pp. 1–24.

Pauwelyn, Joost, and Manfred Elsig (2013). "The Politics of Treaty Interpretation: Variations and Explanations Across International Tribunals," in Jeffrey L. Dunoff and Mark A. Pollack (eds.), *Interdisciplinary Perspectives on International Law and International Relations: The State of the Art* (New York: Cambridge University Press), pp. 445–73.

Putnam, Robert D. (1988). "Diplomacy and Domestic Politics: The Logic of Two-Level Games," *International Organization*, Vol. 42, No. 3, pp. 427–60.

Raustiala, Kal (2005). "Form and Substance in International Agreements," *American Journal of International Law*, Vol. 99, No. 3, pp. 581–614.

———— (2013). "Density and Fragmentation in International Institutions," in Jeffrey L. Dunoff and Mark A. Pollack (eds.), *Interdisciplinary Perspectives on International Law and International Relations: The State of the Art* (New York: Cambridge University Press), pp. 293–320.

Raustiala, Kal, and David G. Victor (2004). "The Regime Complex for Plant Genetic Resources," *International Organization*, Vol. 58, No. 2, pp. 277–309.

Reh, Christine, Adrienne Héritier, Edoardo Bressanelli, and Christel Koop (2010). "The Informal Politics of Legislation: Explaining secluded Decision-Making in the European

Union," Paper Prepared for the 2010 Annual Meeting of the American Political Science Association.

Risse, Thomas, and Mareike Kleine (2010). "Deliberation in Negotiations," *Journal of European Public Policy*, Vol. 17, No. 5, pp. 708–26.

Rixen, Thomas (2010). "Bilateralism or Multilateralism? The Political Economy of Avoiding International Double Taxation," *European Journal of International Relations*, Vol. 16, No. 4, pp. 589–614.

Rosendorff, B. Peter (2005). "Stability and Rigidity: Politics and Design of the WTO's Dispute Settlement Procedure," *American Political Science Review*, Vol. 99, No. 3, pp. 389–400.

Rosendorff, B. Peter, and Helen V. Milner (2001). "The Optimal Design of International Trade Institutions: Uncertainty and Escape," *International Organization*, Vol. 55, No. 4, pp. 829–57.

Sattler, Thomas, and Thomas Bernauer (2010). "Gravitation or Discrimination? Determinants of Litigation in the World Trade Organisation," *European Journal of Political Research*, Vol. 50, No. 2, pp. 143–67.

Shaffer, Gregory C., and Mark A. Pollack (2013). "Hard Law and Soft Law," in Jeffrey L. Dunoff and Mark A. Pollack (eds.), *Interdisciplinary Perspectives on International Law and International Relations: The State of the Art* (New York: Cambridge University Press), pp. 197–222.

Simmons, Beth A. (2000). "International Law and State Behavior: Commitment and Compliance in International Monetary Affairs," *American Political Science Review*, Vol. 94, No. 4, pp. 819–35.

———— (2002). "Capacity, Commitment, and Compliance: International Institutions and Territorial Disputes," *Journal of Conflict Resolution*, Vol. 46, No. 6, pp. 829–56.

———— (2009). *Mobilizing for Human Rights: International Law and Domestic Politics* (Cambridge: Cambridge University Press).

———— (2010). "Treaty Compliance and Violation," *Annual Review of Political Science*, Vol. 13, No. 1, pp. 273–96.

Simmons, Beth A., and Daniel J. Hopkins (2005). "The Constraining Power of International Treaties: Theory and Methods," *American Political Science Review*, Vol. 99, No. 4, pp. 623–31.

Smith, James (2004). "Inequality in International Trade? Developing Countries and Institutional Change in WTO Dispute Settlement," *Review of International Political Economy*, Vol. 11, No. 3, pp. 542–73.

Stone, Randall W. (2010). "Controlling Institutions: International Organizations and the Political Economy," Paper Presented at the 2010 Annual Meeting of the American Political Science Association.

Swaine, Edward T. (2006). "Reserving," *Yale Journal of International Law*, Vol. 31, No. 2, pp. 307–66.

Thompson, Alexander (2009). "The Rational Enforcement of International Law: Solving the Sanctioners' Dilemma," *International Theory*, Vol. 1, No. 2, pp. 307–21.

———— (2010). "Rational Design in Motion: Uncertainty and Flexibility in the Global Climate Regime," *European Journal of International Relations*, Vol. 16, No. 2, pp. 269–96.

———— (2013). "Coercive Enforcement in International Law," in Jeffrey L. Dunoff and Mark A. Pollack (eds.), *Interdisciplinary Perspectives on International Law and International Relations: The State of the Art* (New York: Cambridge University Press), pp. 502–23.

Trachtman, Joel P. (2013). "Open Economy Law," in Jeffrey L. Dunoff and Mark A. Pollack (eds.), *Interdisciplinary Perspectives on International Law and International Relations: The State of the Art* (New York: Cambridge University Press), pp. 544–67.

Verdier, Daniel (2008). "Multilateralism, Bilateralism, and Exclusion in the Nuclear Proliferation Regime," *International Organization*, Vol. 62, No. 3, pp. 439–76.

von Stein, Jana (2005). "Do Treaties Constrain or Screen? Selection Bias and Treaty Compliance," *American Political Science Review*, Vol. 99, No. 4, pp. 611–22.

———— (2013). "The Engines of Compliance," in Jeffrey L. Dunoff and Mark A. Pollack (eds.), *Interdisciplinary Perspectives on International Law and International Relations: The State of the Art* (New York: Cambridge University Press), pp. 477–501.

4

Liberal Theories of International Law

Andrew Moravcsik

Liberal theories of international relations (IR) focus on the demands of individuals and social groups, and their relative power in society, as fundamental forces driving state policy. For liberals, every state is embedded in an interdependent domestic and transnational society that decisively shapes the basic purposes or interests that underlie its policies, its interaction with other states, and, ultimately, international conflict and order. This "bottom-up" focus of liberal theories on state–society relations, interdependence, and preference formation has distinctive implications for understanding international law (IL). In recent years liberal theory has been among the most rapidly expanding areas of positive and normative analysis of international law. As the world grows more and more interdependent and countries struggle to maintain cooperation amid diverse economic interests, domestic political institutions, and ideals of legitimate public order, international law will increasingly come to depend on the answers to questions that liberal theories pose.

The first section of this chapter ("Liberal Theories of International Relations") elaborates the assumptions and conclusions of liberal international relations theory. Section II ("What Can Liberal Theories Tell Us about International Law-Making?") develops liberal insights into the substantive scope and depth of international law, its institutional form, compliance, and long-term dynamic processes of evolution and change. Section III ("International Tribunals: Liberal Analysis and Its Critics") examines the specific case of international tribunals, which has been a particular focus of liberal theorizing, and treats both conservative and constructivist criticisms of liberal theory. Section IV ("Liberalism as Normative Theory") considers the

I am grateful to Chris Kendall and Justin Simeone for excellent research assistance and for stylistic and substantive input, and to William Burke-White, Jeffrey Dunoff, Laurence Helfer, Mark Pollack, Anne-Marie Slaughter, and participants at a conference at Temple University Beasley School of Law for detailed comments.

contribution of liberal theory to policy, as well as to conceptual and normative analyses of international law.

I. LIBERAL THEORIES OF INTERNATIONAL RELATIONS

The central liberal question about international law and politics is: who governs? Liberals assume that states are embedded in a transnational society comprising individuals, social groups, and substate officials with varying assets, ideals, and influence on state policy. The first stage in a liberal explanation of politics is to identify and explain the preferences of relevant social and substate actors as a function of a structure of underlying social identities and interests. Among these social and substate actors, a universal condition is *globalization*, understood as variable transnational interdependence, material or ideational, among social actors. It creates varying incentives for cross-border political regulation and interaction. State policy can facilitate, block, or channel globalization, thereby benefitting or harming the interests or ideals of particular social actors. The state is a representative institution that aggregates and channels those interests and ideals according to their relative weight in society, ability to organize, and influence in political processes. In each state, political organization and institutions represent a different subset of social and substate actors, whose desired forms of social, cultural, and economic interdependence define the underlying concerns (preferences across "states of the world") that the state has at stake in international issues. Representative functions of international organizations may have a similar effect.

The existence of social demands concerning globalization, translated into state preferences, is a necessary condition to motivate any purposeful foreign policy action. States may seek to shape and regulate interdependence. To the extent this creates externalities, positive or negative, for policy-makers in other states seeking to realize the preferences of their individuals and social groups, such preferences provides the underlying motivation for patterns of interstate conflict and cooperation. Colloquially, what states want shapes what they do.

Liberal theory highlights three specific sources of variation in state preferences and, therefore, state behavior. Each isolates a distinctive source of variation in the societal demands that drive state preferences regarding the regulation of globalization. To avoid simply ascribing policy changes to ad hoc or unexplained preference changes, liberal theory seeks to isolate the causal mechanisms and antecedent conditions under which each functions. In each case, as the relevant domestic and transnational social actors and contexts vary across space, time, and issues, so does the distribution of state preferences and policies.

Ideational liberal theories attribute state behavior to interdependence among social demands to realize particular forms of public goods provision. These demands are, in turn, based on conceptions of desirable cultural, political, and socioeconomic identity and order, which generally derive from both domestic and transnational socialization processes. Common examples in modern world politics include conceptions of national (or civic) identity and self-determination, fundamental political ideology (such as democratic capitalism, communism, or Islamic fundamentalism), basic views of how to regulate the economy (social welfare, public risk, environmental quality), and the balance of individual rights against collective duties. The starting point for an ideational liberal analysis of world politics is the question: How does variation in ideals of desirable public goods provision shape individual and group demands for political regulation of globalization?

Commercial liberal theories link state behavior to material interdependence among societal actors with particular assets or ideals. In international political economy, conventional "endogenous policy" theories of trade, finance, and environment posit actors with economic assets or objectives, the value of which depends on the actors' position in domestic and global markets (i.e., patterns of globalization). The starting point for a commercial liberal analysis of world politics is the question: How does variation in the assets and market position of economic actors shape their demands for political regulation of globalization?

Republican liberal theories stress the role of variation in political representation. Liberals view all states (and, indirectly, international organizations) as mechanisms of political representation that privilege the interests of some societal actors over others in making state policy. Instruments of representation include formal representation, constitutional structure, informal institutional dynamics, appointment to government, and the organizational capacity of social actors. By changing the "selectorate" – the individuals and groups who influence a policy – the policy changes as well. The starting point for a republican liberal analysis of world politics is the question: How does variation in the nature of domestic representation alter the selectorate, thus channeling specific social demands for the political regulation of globalization?

Although for analytical clarity we distinguish the three categories of liberal theory, they are generally more powerful when deployed in tandem. Interdependence can have significant implications for both collective goods provision (ideational liberalism) and the realization of material interests (commercial liberalism). Moreover, whether underlying preferences are ideational or material, they are generally represented by some institutionalized political process that skews representation (republican liberalism). Even the simplest conventional theories of the political economy of international trade, for example, assume that all three strands are important: private economic interest is balanced against collective welfare concerns, whether in the form of a budget constraint or countervailing public policy goals, and these social pressures are transmitted to the state through representative institutions that privilege some voices over others (Grossman and Helpman 1994).

It is important to be clear what liberal theory is *not*. Theoretical paradigms in international relations are defined by distinctive causal mechanisms that link fundamental causes, such as economic, technological, cultural, social, political, and behavioral changes among states in world politics, to state behavior. Hence the term *liberal* is not used here to designate theories that stress the importance of international institutions; the importance of universal, altruistic, or utopian values, such as human rights or democracy; or the advancement of left-wing or free market political parties or policies. In particular, institutionalist regime theory, pioneered by Robert Keohane and others, often termed "neo-liberal," is distinctly different. Kenneth Abbott has written that:

> Institutionalism . . . analyzes the benefits that international rules, organizations, procedures, and other institutions provide for states in particular situations, viewing these benefits as incentives for institutionalized cooperation. . . . [R]elatively modest actions – such as producing unbiased information, reducing the transactions costs of interactions, pooling resources, monitoring state behavior, and helping to mediate disputes – can help states achieve their goals by overcoming structural barriers to cooperation (2008: 6).

This institutionalist focus on the reduction of informational transaction costs differs from the focus of liberalism, as defined here, on variation in social preferences – even if the two can coexist, with the former being a means of achieving the latter.

The distinctiveness of liberal theories also does not stem from a unique focus on "domestic politics." True, liberal theories often accommodate and explain domestic distributional and political conflict better than most alternatives. Yet, it is unclear what a *purely* "domestic" theory of rational state behavior would be, liberal or otherwise. Liberal theories are international in at least three senses. First, in the liberal view, social and state preferences are driven by transnational material and ideational globalization, without which liberals believe foreign policy has no consistent purpose. Second, liberal theories stress the ways in which individuals and groups may influence policy, not just in domestic but also in transnational politics. Social actors may engage (or be engaged by) international legal institutions via domestic institutions, or they may engage them directly. They may organize transnationally to pursue political ends. The liberal assumption that political institutions are conduits for political representation is primarily directed at nation-states simply because they are the preeminent political units in the world today; it may also apply to subnational, transnational, or supranational institutions. Third, liberal theories (like realist, institutionalist, systemic constructivist theories, and any other intentionalist account of state behavior) are strategic and thus "systemic" in the sense that Kenneth Waltz (1979) employs the term: they explain collective international outcomes on the basis of the interstate distribution of the characteristics or attributes of states, in this case their preferences. The preferences of a single state alone tell us little about its probable strategic behavior with regard to interstate interaction, absent knowledge of the preferences of other relevant states, since liberals agree that state preferences and policies are interdependent and that the strategic games states play matter for policy – assumptions shared by all rationalist theories.

The critical quality of liberal theories is rather that they are "bottom-up" explanations of state behavior that focus on the effect of variations in state–society relations on state preferences in a context of globalization and transnational interdependence. In other words, liberalism emphasizes the distribution of one particular attribute (socially determined state preferences about the regulation of social interdependence), rather than attributes favored by other major theories (e.g., coercive power resources, information, or nonrational standards of appropriate strategic behavior). Other theories have traditionally defined themselves in contrast to this liberal emphasis on social preferences.

II. WHAT CAN LIBERAL THEORIES TELL US ABOUT INTERNATIONAL LAW-MAKING?

Liberal theories can serve as the "front-end" for multicausal syntheses with other theories of institutions, explaining the substance of legal regimes; can generate their own autonomous insights into the strategic and institutional aspects of legal regimes; and can provide explanations for the longer-term dynamic evolution of international law. Let us consider each function in turn.

A. *Liberal Explanations for the Substantive Scope and Depth of International Law*

One way to employ liberal theory is as the first and indispensable step in any analysis of international law, focusing primarily on explaining the substantive content of international interaction. Explaining the substantive focus of law, a task at which few IR theories excel, is a particular comparative advantage of liberal theory. Realism and institutionalism seek to explain the outcome of strategic interaction or bargaining over substantive matters, but they take as given the basic preferences, and hence the substance, of any given interaction. Constructivists do seek to explain the substantive content of international cooperation, but do so not as the result of efforts to realize material interests and normative ideals transmitted through representative institutions, but rather as the result of conceptions of appropriate behavior in international affairs or regulatory policy divorced from the instrumental calculations of societal actors empowered by the state.

For liberals, the starting point for explaining why an instrumental government would contract into binding international legal norms, and comply with them thereafter, is that it possesses a substantive purpose for doing so. From a liberal perspective, this means that a domestic coalition of social interests that "benefits" (ideally or materially) directly and indirectly from particular regulation of social interdependence is more powerfully represented in decision-making than the countervailing coalition of losers from cooperation – compared to the best unilateral or coalitional alternatives. This is sometimes mislabeled a realist ("interest-based") claim, yet most such formulations follow more from patterns of convergent state preferences than from specific patterns of state power (e.g., Abbott 2008). Thus, liberals have no reason to disagree with Jack Goldsmith and Eric Posner's claim that much important state behavior consistent with customary international law arises from pure coincidence (independent calculations of interest or ideals), the use of international law as a coordination mechanism (in situations where symmetrical behavior increases payoffs), or the use of international law to facilitate cooperation where coordinated self-restraint from short-term temptation increases long-term issue-specific payoffs (as in repeated bilateral prisoners' dilemma, where payoffs to defection and discount rates are low) (Goldsmith and Posner 1999: 1127). Contrary to Goldsmith and Posner, however, liberals argue that such cases do not exhaust the potential for analyzing or fostering legalized cooperation. The decisive point is that if social support for and opposition to such regulation varies predictably across time, issues, countries, and constituencies, then a liberal analysis of the societal and substate origins of such support for and against various forms of regulation is a logical foundation for any explanation of when, where, and how regulation takes place (Keohane 1982; Legro 1997; Milner 1997; Moravcsik 1997; Lake and Powell 1999; Wendt 1999).

The pattern of preferences and bargaining outcomes helps define the underlying "payoffs" or "problem structure" of the "games" states play – and, therefore, help define the basic potential for cooperation and conflict. This generates a number of basic predictions, of which a few examples must suffice here. For liberals, levels of transnational interdependence are correlated with the magnitude of interstate action, whether essentially cooperative or conflictual. Without demands from transnationally interdependent social and substate actors, a rational state would have no reason to engage in world politics at all; it would simply devote its resources to an autarkic and isolated existence. Moreover, voluntary (noncoercive) cooperation, including a sustainable international legal order that generates compliance and evolves dynamically, must be based on common or compatible social purposes. The notion that some shared social purposes may be essential to establish a viable world order, as John Ruggie observes (1982), does not follow from realist theory – even if some so-called realists, such as Henry Kissinger, assumed it (1993: 79). The greater the potential joint gains and the lower the domestic and transnational distributional concerns, the greater the potential for cooperation. Within states, every coalition generally comprises (or opposes) individuals and groups with both "direct" and "indirect" interests in a particular policy: direct beneficiaries benefit from domestic policy implementation, whereas indirect beneficiaries benefit from reciprocal policy changes in other states (Trachtman 2010). Preferences help explain not only the range of national policies in a legal issue, but also the outcome of interstate bargaining, since bargaining is often decisively shaped by *asymmetrical interdependence* – the relative intensity of state preferences for inside and outside options (Keohane and Nye 1977). States that desire an outcome more will pay more – either in the form of concessions or coercion – to achieve it.

Trade illustrates these tendencies. Shifts in comparative advantage and intra-industry trade over the past half-century have generated striking cross-issue variations in social and state preferences. Trade creates coalitions of direct and indirect interests: importers and consumers, for example, generally benefit from trade liberalization at home, whereas exporters generally benefit from trade liberalization abroad. Patterns of trade matter as well. In industrial trade, intra-industry trade and investment means liberalization is favored by powerful economic interests in developed countries, and cooperation has led to a massive reduction of trade barriers. A long period of exogenous change in trade, investment, and technology created a shift away from North–South trade and a post–World War II trade boom among advanced industrial democracies. Large multinational export and investment interests mobilized behind it, creating ever-greater support for reciprocal liberalization, thereby facilitating efforts to deepen and widen Generalized Agreement on Tariffs and Trade/World Trade Organization (GATT/WTO) norms (Milner 1988; Gilligan 1997*a*). In agriculture, by contrast, inter-industry trade patterns and lack of developed-country competitiveness has meant that powerful interests oppose liberalization, and agricultural trade has seen a corresponding increase in protection. Both policies have massive consequences for welfare and human life. In trade negotiations, as liberal theory predicts, asymmetrical interdependence is also a source of bargaining power, with governments dependent on particular markets being forced into concessions or costly responses to defend their interests.

More recently, as developed economies have focused more on environmental and other public interest regulation, liberalization has become more complex and conflict ridden, forcing the GATT/WTO and European Union (EU) systems to develop new policies and legal norms to address the legal complexities of "trade and" issues. In environmental policy, cross-issue variation in legal regulation (the far greater success of regulation of ozone depletion than an area such as climate change, for example) reflects, most fundamentally, variation in the convergence of underlying economic interests and public policy goals (Keohane and Victor 2011). The willingness of EU member states to move further than the more diverse and less interdependent WTO is similarly predictable. The "fragmentation" of the international legal system due to multiple, overlapping legal commitments reflects, from a liberal perspectives, underlying functional connections among issues due to interdependence, rather than autonomous tactical or institutional linkage (Alter and Meunier 2009).

In global financial regulation, regulatory heterogeneity under conditions of globalization (especially, in this case, capital mobility) undermines the authority and control of national regulators and raises the risk of "races to the bottom" at the expense of individual investors and national or global financial systems (Simmons

2001; Drezner 2007; Singer 2007; Helleiner, Pagliari, and Zimmermann 2010; Brummer 2011). Major concerns of international legal action include banking regulation, the effectiveness of which is threatened when banks, investors, and firms can engage in offshore arbitrage, seeking the lowest level of regulation; regulatory competition, where pressures for lower standards are created by professional, political, and interest group competition to attract capital; and exacerbation of systemic risk by cross-border transmission of domestic financial risks arising from bad loans or investments, uninformed decisions, or assumed risk without adequate capital or collateral. Coordination of international rules and cooperation among regulators can address some of these concerns, but in a world of regulatory heterogeneity, it poses the problem of how to coordinate policy and overcome political opposition from those who are disadvantaged by any standard. High levels of heterogeneity in this issue area, and the broad impact of finance in domestic economies, suggest that legal norms will be difficult to develop and decentralized in enforcement.

Similar variation can be observed in human rights. The most important factors influencing the willingness of states to accept and enforce international human rights norms involve domestic state–society relations: the preexisting level and legacy of domestic democracy, civil conflict, and such. Even the most optimistic assessments of legalized human rights enforcement concede that international legal commitments generally explain a relatively small shift in aggregate adherence to human rights (Simmons 2009). By contrast, liberal factors account for much more geographical, temporal, and substantive variation in the strength of international human rights norms. The fact that democracies and postauthoritarian states are both more likely to adhere to human rights regimes explains in part why Europe is so far advanced – and the constitutional norms and conservative legacy in the United States is an exception that proves the rule. Recent movement toward juridification of the European Convention on Human Rights (ECHR) system, with mandatory individual petition and compulsory jurisdiction, as well as the establishment of a court, occurred in part in response to exogenous shocks – the global spread of concern about human rights and the "second" and "third" waves of democratization in the 1980s and 1990s – and in part in order to impose them on new members. Political rights are firmly grounded in binding international law, but socioeconomic and labor rights are far less so – a reflection not of the intrinsic philosophical implausibility of the latter, but of large international disparities in wealth and social pressures on governments to defend existing domestic social compromises (Moravcsik 2002, 2004). Even existing political rights are constrained in the face of economic interests, as when member states ignore indigenous rights in managing large developmental projects.

Liberal theories apply also to security areas, such as nuclear nonproliferation. Constructivists maintain that the behavior of emerging nuclear powers – such as India, Pakistan, Israel, North Korea, and Iran – is governed by principled normative concerns about fairness and hypocrisy: if existing nuclear states were more willing to accept controls, new nuclear states would be. Realists argue that the application and enforcement of the nonproliferation regime is simply a function of the cost-effective application of coercive sanctions by existing nuclear states; were they not threatened with military retaliation, states would necessarily be engaged in nuclear arms races. Both reasons may be important causes of state behavior under some circumstances. The liberal view, by contrast, hypothesizes that acceptance of nonproliferation obligations will reflect the underlying pattern of material and ideational interests of member states and their societies. Insofar as they are concerned about security matters, it reflects particular underlying ideational or material conflicts. Recent research findings on compliance with international nonproliferation norms confirm the importance of such factors. The great majority of signatories in compliance lack any evident underlying desire to produce nuclear weapons. Those that fail to sign face particular exogenous preference conflicts with neighbors or great powers (Hymans 2006; Grotto 2008; Sagan 2011).

B. *Liberal Explanations for the Institutional Form and Compliance*

So far, we have considered the implications of liberal IR theory for explaining the substance of cooperation, not its form: when states cooperate legally, but not how they go about it. This may seem appropriate. One might suppose that such a liberal theory is all one needs, for international law is no more than a simple coordination mechanism that ratifies what states would do anyway. (This sort of explanation is often mislabeled "realist," but it is more often a crude version of liberal theory, since, in most accounts, it is a convergence of social preferences, not interstate centralization of coercive power, that explains most of the variation in underlying state interests.) This may sometimes be enough.

Yet in some cases international law surely plays a more independent role. For such cases, liberal theories almost always must still be properly employed as a "first stage," explaining the distribution of underlying preferences. After that, analysts may handoff to other (realist or institutionalist) theories to explain choice of specific legal forms, compliance pull, and long-term endogenous evolution. These "later-stage" theories may contribute to defining the ultimate problem structure by considering factors such as information and transaction costs, coercive power resources, various types of beliefs, and various process variables. As long as one assumes purposive state behavior, as all these theories do, however, liberal theory's focus on variation in social interdependence, the substantive calculations of powerful domestic and transnational groups, and state preferences must properly be considered first. One cannot theorize the efficient matching of means to ends without first explaining the choice of ends. Indeed, liberal theory may constrain (or even supplant) the theories that are appropriate to employ in later stages of the multicausal synthesis, because the nature of underlying preferences is a decisive factor shaping the nature of strategic interaction (Moravcsik 1997, 1998; Lake and Powell 1999). Realist theories, for example, assume an underlying expected conflict of interest sufficient to

motivate costly coercive strategies, whereas institutionalist theories assume underlying positive-sum collective action problems. (The role of nonrational theories is
more complex.) In this view – to extend Stephen Krasner's celebrated metaphor –
once liberalism defines the shape of the Pareto frontier, realism explains distributional outcomes, and institutionalism explains efforts to maximize efficiency and
compliance (1991).

This role of liberal theory as the primary stage of multicausal explanation is an
important and increasingly widely recognized one. Yet, to limit the scope of liberal international theories solely to a "first-stage" explanation for initial preference
formation and the substance of legal norms would be to ignore many of the fundamental contributions that liberal theory has made, or can potentially make, to the
study of the institutionalization, enforcement, and evolution of international law.
There are three specific ways in which involvement of social actors can have a direct
influence on institutional form and compliance pull. First, the future preferences
of individuals and groups have influence decisions about institutionalization and
compliance; second, many international legal rules directly regulate the behavior of
non-state actors; and third, many international enforcement systems are "vertical,"
functioning primarily by embedding international norms in domestic institutions
and politics. Let us consider each in turn.

1. Social Preferences Influence Institutional Delegation and Compliance

On a conventional functional understanding, international law influences behavior
by precommitting governments with short time horizons or uncertainty about future
social circumstances and preferences. States maintain international legal regimes to
enhance their capacity for elaborating and enforcing regime norms by enhancing
reciprocity, reputation, and retaliation. Yet, from a liberal perspective, cooperation
is also what Keohane and Nye (1977) term "complex interdependence" and Robert
Putnam (1988) calls a "two-level game," in which national leaders bargain not just
with foreign counterparts, but also with domestic social actors at home and abroad.
Legal institutions are, in essence, efforts to establish current arrangements that will
appropriately shape not just future interstate interaction, but also future domestic and
transnational state–society relations. Future state-society relations are to some degree
inherently uncertain, due to exogenous trends and shocks or endogenous feedback
induced by commitment to international law. Were this not the case, governments
would not need to establish international regimes or overarching norms, such as
"legality," but could simply enter into specific narrow substantive agreements on
whatever subject is of importance to them. It is uncertainty that generates much of the
demand for transaction cost–reducing international regimes. *To analyze or evaluate
such processes precisely, we must depart from the horizontal state-to-state politics
and incorporate information about the current and future demands of social groups
and the nature of representative institutions.* Variation in present and future social

preferences – the direction, intensity, risk and uncertainty, and time horizon of social demands – can have a direct impact on institutional design and compliance. Smart policy-makers will design institutions so as to shift and channel social preferences in the future in a direction consistent with their favored view of elaboration of and compliance with the legal regime.

Variation in the flexibility of compliance mechanisms is just one example of the way in which the institutional design of international legal agreements takes into account expected shifts in preferences. When entering into a legal commitment, a rational state must weigh the advantages and disadvantages of being bound in the future. The design problem is delicate: excessive rigidity might encourage defection, yet excessive flexibility might encourage abuse. Recent work has sought to locate the "optimal" level and form of *ex ante* commitment (Goldstein and Martin 2000: 604). The critical factor is not primarily whether the domestic sector in question is "sensitive" or "sovereign": it is often in the most sensitive areas, such as diplomatic immunity, arms control, or agricultural policy, where we see the most rigid rules. The critical point is rather the level of current uncertainty and intensity of concern about future exogenous shocks, which might tempt states to defect.

There are a number of institutional solutions to this problem. Rosendorff and Milner argue for establishing proper *ex ante* penalties (2001). Sykes (1991), Downs and Rocke (1995) and Pelc (2009) likewise argue for the utility of escape clauses in international agreements. Koremenos (2002) argues that sunset clauses would permit risk-averse states to renegotiate agreements. Chayes and Chayes (1995) argue for capacity building for governments in trouble. Kleine (2011) observes that the EU employs *ex post* negotiation over exceptions, which may be more efficient than the more rigid solutions above, because it permits governments to elicit new information about the true nature of social demands for exceptions and amendments *ex post*, while insulating governments against pressures from domestic special interests. For example, it would hardly have been useful for European governments to have set "optimal" penalties for ignoring European Court of Justice (ECJ) judgments in 1957, when the entire legal evolution of the system was unforeseen, and it is suboptimal to do so in any given case solely on the basis of prior knowledge (Burley and Mattli 1993; Slaughter-Burley 1993; Weiler 1996).

The pattern of social preferences, present and future, often defines whether inter-state interaction approximates a game of coordination or a game of collaboration, with implications for institutional form. Some international agreements govern coordination games, in which bargaining to agreement may be difficult, but a coalition of social actors has little incentive to press for unilateral defection from an agreement (Keohane 1982, 1984). Coordination games require mechanisms to overcome bargaining problems, the intensity of which depends on informational challenges and the extent of distributional conflict. Other agreements govern collaboration games, in which social actors have a strong incentive to press for defection, creating a prisoners' dilemma structure (Martin 1992). Collaboration games require multi-issue linkages, stronger oversight, and enforcement mechanisms to secure compliance. Even the extent to which a regime is based on reciprocity at all is a function of the distribution of social interests.

Consider, for example, postwar international trade cooperation. Industrial tariff reductions among developed country members of the European Economic Community (EEC) and the GATT in the 1950s and 1960s appear to have generated a coordination game. Negotiation among many detailed issues was sometimes technically complex, but once a handful of "sensitive sectors" had been excluded, cross-cutting ties of intra-industry trade and investment created reciprocal interest in membership and a low incentive to defect unilaterally. There is some reason to believe that institutionalization of implementation and binding interstate dispute resolution added little (Gilligan 1997*b*). Contrast this with contemporaneous efforts to liberalize declining industrial sectors and agriculture, where strong veto groups existed, and patterns of factor abundance and sectoral advantage were cross-cutting, and with the rise of "trade and" issues, in which trade liberalization comes in conflict with increasingly varied public regulatory concerns. These issues created sectoral conflicts of interest requiring oversight, dispute resolution, and enforcement to clarify obligations and secure compliance. Within Europe, cooperation was impossible in areas like agriculture without a complex regional subsidy regime, a set of exceptions and safeguards in the GATT, and far more centralized oversight.

Another example of how *ex ante* social preferences influence institutional design, which feeds back on *ex post* social preferences, arises when leaders exploit international norms to impose favored domestic policies at home. The conventional view of international cooperation focuses on "indirect" benefits, treating domestic commitments solely as a necessary *quid pro quo* to secure foreign adherence to international norms. Yet, domestic coalitions generally also include those who gain "direct" benefits, sometimes led by politicians who seek to impose domestic competitiveness, democracy, environmental quality, or other longer-term reform goals. Mexican entry into the North American FreeTrade Agreement, Chinese entry into the WTO, Republican support for free trade in the United States, and East European entry into the EU have all been interpreted in this way. The tendency of new democracies to favor international human rights commitments and to respond with greater compliance has been seen as a self-interested effort to entrench human rights in domestic institutions and practices (Moravcsik 2000; Hathaway 2007). Traditionally, more advanced democracies have also joined human rights regimes to gain foreign policy externalities in situations of underlying ideological conflict (Moravcsik 2000; Landman 2005).

One methodological implication of the liberal approach is that any study of institutional impact must be rigorously controlled for variation in exogenous preferences: this discussion of compliance and impact is closely connected with the previous discussion of delegation and substantive content. The analyst needs to understand the basic elements that lead a state to commit to international legal mechanisms initially, because states often sign agreements with which they intend to comply. High rates of compliance may not suggest anything about the power of international law, but could simply signal prior convergent preferences. In order to distinguish the independent effect of legal institutions from background preferences, an analysis of international law must take place in two stages. Scholars have attempted to cope with this issue with "two-stage" selection models, in which one explains which states sign which treaties, and then model how treaties then affect compliance decisions with a new specification of preferences that seeks to isolate circumstances in which compliance is costly (e.g., Simmons 2009).

2. International Law Directly Regulates Social Actors

A second way in which variation in social preferences helps explain institutional choice and compliance is that *international law and organizations may regulate or involve social ("non-state") actors directly*. Many international legal rules and procedures are not primarily designed to shape state policy and compliance, as in the classic model of public international law or conventional WTO dispute resolution, but to assist states in regulating domestic and transnational social actors (Alter 2008). When states cooperate to manage matters such as transnational contract arbitration, money laundering, private aircraft, multinational firms, emissions trading, or the behavior of international officials, for example, or when they assist refugees; establish institutions within failed states; or combat terrorism, criminality, or piracy; recognize nationalist movements; or grant rights of participation or representation to private actors in international deliberations, they directly influence domestic and transnational non-state actors such as corporations, nongovernmental organizations (NGOs), private individuals, political movements, international organizations, and criminal and terrorist organizations. The legal enforcement of many such regulatory regimes functions by empowering individuals and groups to trigger international legal proceedings vis-à-vis states. As we shall see, the greater the range of private access to an international regime, all other things being equal, the more likely it is to be effective and dynamic. Often, such access is a function of the issue area itself. It is customary within nations for individuals to trigger litigation about rights, independent prosecutors to trigger criminal prosecutions, and interested parties to sue to assert economic rights and enforce contracts, and the international system is no different.

Many, perhaps most, international legal instruments are not "self-binding" for states at all, but are instead "other-binding" (Alter 2008). They do not force the signatory states to delegate direct sovereignty over government decisions, but are designed primarily to constrain non-state actors. Some regulate international organizations, establishing international procedures or regulating the actions of international officials. Many other international legal rules oversee the behavior of private actors. Much private international law governs corporate activity, individual transactions, investment, communications, and other transnational activities, mostly economic, by non-state actors (Alter 2008). Which non-state actors are regulated and how they are regulated by international law is itself determined by the interests and political strength of those and other social groups (e.g., Keohane and Victor 2011). Other rules govern different aspects of individuals and NGOs. It is conceivable that a government may find such rules onerous, just as it may find an entrenched domestic law onerous, but there is no particular reason to assume that this is more likely in international than domestic life – or that there are "sovereignty costs" associated with international legal obligations of this kind (Goldsmith and Posner 2005). We cannot understand the attitude of states without the subtle understanding of state–society relations provided by liberal theory.

3. Vertical Enforcement of International Law on the Domestic Plane

A third way in which social preferences help explain institutional choice and compliance issues relating to international law is that *compliance with many international legal norms does not rely on "horizontal" interstate reciprocity and retaliation, but instead on "vertical" enforcement embedded in domestic politics ("internalization").*

Many, perhaps most, international legal regimes are enforced vertically rather than horizontally. A traditional "horizontal" perspective treats international legal obligations as external institutional constraints on state sovereignty, enforced by interstate retaliation, mediated by via reciprocity, reputation, or linkage (Posner and Yoo 2005*a*). The horizontal path envisages a role for institutions to render efforts to manipulate interdependence more transaction cost efficient. Institutions may establish norms for granting or revoking reciprocal policy concessions, including or excluding countries in a club, or responding in a linked issue area. The "vertical" path to compliance foresees compliance and enforcement without retaliation. Instead, it seeks to alter the preferences and relative influence of social (non-state) actors who favor and oppose compliance, locking in international norms domestically or transnationally by establishing new legal institutions, shifting coalitions, and creating new ideas of public legitimacy (Burley and Mattli 1993; Chayes and Chayes 1993; Moravcsik 1998; Dai 2005; Alter 2008; Simmons 2009).

Many analyses assume that, in issues such as trade, where reciprocal concessions are exchanged at the bargaining stage, enforcement also rests on such mechanisms. Thus, horizontal enforcement is often seen as the core of international relations, whereas vertical enforcement is often seen (particularly by political scientists) as a secondary mechanism that functions almost exclusively in exceptional areas such as human rights, where reciprocity is rarely a credible enforcement tool and opportunities for linkages are scarce. In fact, however, vertical mechanisms may be the primary enforcement mechanisms in most international legal regimes, while reciprocity and retaliation remain secondary. Consider, for example, the EU, the world's most ambitious and effective international economic regime and, in the eyes of leading liberal international lawyers Anne-Marie Slaughter and William Burke-White, the world's most advanced liberal international order (2006). The EU's founding Treaty of Rome not only does not facilitate retaliation, it bans it. Hence, it is impossible to analyze compliance with EU law without theorizing vertical enforcement through domestic social coalitions, political institutions, ideational frameworks, transnational networks, and judicial mechanisms. Similarly, in the GATT/WTO, it is possible to view compliance mechanisms as largely constructed at the domestic level, for example, through insulating and adopting internationally compliant trade law and bureaucratic structures, mobilizing interest group support, or spreading free-trade norms. The GATT possessed notably ineffective enforcement mechanisms, and, although those of the WTO are somewhat stronger, it is unclear whether retaliation, legalized or not, actually explains levels of compliance (Goldstein and Martin 2000; Abbott 2008; Davis and Bermeo 2009).

Vertical enforcement may take three forms, each consistent with a different variant of liberal theory. Law may alter state–society relations and state preferences via interests, institutions, or ideas.

The first and simplest mechanism of vertical enforcement, in accordance with republican liberal theory, is a change to domestic and transnational representative institutions. Many international obligations are incorporated as constitutional amendments, domestic legislation, treaty law, or through bureaucratic bodies, rules, and procedures. Such changes are important, on the liberal understanding, insofar as they tilt the domestic representative bias among decision-makers on various issues (Moravcsik 1995, 2000; Simmons 2009). Legal or bureaucratic incorporation can place international norms onto the national legislative and executive agenda, increase their salience, and give sympathetic public officials and private individuals a bureaucratic edge. In rule-of-law systems, national officials and courts have some obligation to implement and enforce these norms. Individual litigants, lawyers, and especially NGOs and corporations, may be able to cite international norms in domestic courts and international tribunals, as occurs in the human rights realm (Risse and Sikkink 1999; Sikkink 2011). Christina Davis and Sarah Bermeo have analyzed WTO dispute settlement as a mechanism used by leaders to "manage domestic politics" by signaling resolve at home and abroad (2009: 1037). Participation in ongoing international negotiation and enforcement procedures may strengthen the autonomy of executives, foreign ministries, trade ministries, and others whose "public interest" view can reliably be expected to prevail in favor of cooperation over special interest opposition, as is often the case in trade (Moravcsik 1994; Davis 2004). Finally, involvement in legal institutions may link issues domestically, empowering counter-coalitions at home against those who would violate international norms, as occurs within trade policy.

Another republican liberal mechanism of vertical institutional enforcement works through the adoption and implementation of soft-law norms by national regulators – often working in networks, a characteristic Slaughter associates with "the new world order" (2004). Much EU governance can be understood as coordination run through the Council of Ministers and its committees, in which national officials play a permanent, but in many ways informal, role in legislation, regulation, and enforcement. At the global level, we see a similar process in international finance. Of the Basel financial system, Brummer observes:

> In this decentralized regulatory space, the national–international dichotomies associated with public international law do not apply. National regulators are responsible for devising rules and participating in international standard-setting bodies. International standard-setting bodies serve as inter-agency forums; they are run by consensus and their members (national regulators) are responsible for implementing legislative products. (2011: 273)

Public–private partnerships perform a similar function for policy implementation. Shared international legal norms and ideological interdependence can create situations for domestic courts with domestic legal autonomy to enter into transnational judicial dialogues with international tribunals and domestic judges in other countries (Alter 1998; Raustiala 2002; Slaughter 2004). Slaughter argues that "[n]ational courts are the vehicles through which international treaties and customary law that have not been independently incorporated into domestic statutes enter domestic legal systems" (2000: 1103). This is particularly true in human rights areas, where common law courts have become the agents of incorporating international norms – a process Melissa Waters calls "creeping monism" (2007). Domestic courts have become mediators of transnational norms on issues such as the death penalty, human rights, and a range of free speech issues, including hate speech, defamation, and Internet activity (Waters 2005).

A second mechanism of vertical enforcement, this time in accordance with commercial liberalism, is to transform the interests of domestic and transnational social groups. From a liberal perspective, the purpose of international cooperation is rarely simply to fix a particular static interstate bargain, but to engineer beneficial and enduring transformation of the domestic and transnational economy, society, and politics. (Recall that international legal regimes are, by their very nature, established in circumstances of repeat play under uncertainty, with a time horizon into the future; otherwise, spot agreements would do.) If new policies were not "locked in" in this way by fundamental social, institutional, and cultural feedback, governments would still be fighting and refighting the same battles over international cooperation with the same supporters and opponents, decade in and decade out. Issues would never be resolved, except by exogenous social, economic, or cultural change. Inducing endogenous shifts in preferences – "internalization" of norms – is thus not simply a side effect of cooperation essential to enforcement and compliance; it is often, although not always, the objective (Abbott 2008). To the extent that domestic economic groups reorient their behavior around these norms, making investments in economic activity predicated on their continued validity, the norms are internalized. When a state implements a trade liberalization agreement, for example, the resulting import competition eliminates some domestic firms that opposed liberalization, causes others to adjust in ways that reduce their demand for protection, and expands or creates exporting firms that benefit from free trade. The result is greater support for enforcement of trade liberalization (Bailey, Goldstein, and Weingast 1997; Hathaway 1998). Even Chayes and Chayes' "managerial approach" contemplates the possibility that states might generate the desired and required social and economic changes in the legally specified time (1993). To be sure, if domestic groups are strong enough to block adaptation and secure subsidies, as is the case in agriculture and some other declining sectors, this process will not take place (Gilligan 1997b; Hiscox 2002; Desbordes and Vauday 2007).

Another example is the issue of nonproliferation. Governments that promote uniform enforcement of nonproliferation norms tend to have minimal exogenous preference conflicts with neighbors or great powers, whereas those that oppose them tend to have important conflicts. Although they are unlikely to eschew nuclear weapons, studies show that democracies are less likely to cheat on nonproliferation treaty (NPT) commitments; we do not know whether this is because they are more constrained in what they select, more cautious about hypocrisy, or more vulnerable to whistleblowers (Sagan 2011: 239–40). Much research suggests, however, that genuine compliance requires deeper "NPT-plus" obligations. Understanding whether governments are likely to comply with such norms requires an analysis of economic interests, local security conflicts, global market connections of the civilian nuclear power industry, and leadership structure of states, which can inhibit them from accepting the onerous obligations of committing to goals such as the prevention of smuggling, restrictions on domestic fuel cycle activities, the proper management of spent-fuel resources, the implementation of container shipping protocols, and such (Grotto 2008: 17–18, 23–24).

A third mechanism of vertical enforcement, this time in keeping with ideational liberalism, is to encourage enforcement by embedding new collective objectives in the minds of domestic and transnational actors. International organizations can render ideas more salient in the minds of groups able to transmit and publicize favorable international norms. Commonly cited examples include the impact of national human rights commissions, human rights units in foreign ministries, independent financial institutions, and scientific establishments on the substantive preferences of domestic and transnational actors (P. Haas 1989; Risse and Sikkink 1999; Dai 2005). Liberals believe this is most likely to occur when such domestic groups are inclined, or can be socialized, to sympathize with the values and interests underlying international norms or can benefit professionally or in other ways from such values. International legal regimes may also affect opportunities and incentives for social actors to organize, mobilize, and represent their views domestically and transnationally. International law can accord NGOs, corporations, or individuals formal rights of representation, participation, or observation in transnational deliberations or international activities (Keck and Sikkink 1998). This differs from the constructivist view of preference change, whereby groups engage in a process of "acculturation" in which they seek conformity with the rules of an international reference group for its own sake. Here the emphasis is on self-interest or persuasion to adhere to substantive ideals in tune with preexisting concerns (e.g., Goodman and Jinks 2004: 670–73). Liberals argue that domestic groups must have an interest or ideal at stake, even if that interest may simply be professional advancement – any of which may also lead them to avoid exclusion and social stigmatization – as in Slaughter's analysis of European integration. One example from public international law is United Nations (UN) Security Council decisions on intervention. Nonliberals might view such decisions as epiphenomenal to power politics, or as means to coordinate the expectations and actions of governments. Liberals view them as a means of shaping the preferences of individuals and groups. Subsequent social support for intervention, both elite and popular, is in part a function of the process and outcome of Security Council decision-making – not least in third countries uninvolved in the decision itself (Voeten 2005).

C. *Exogenous and Endogenous Evolution of International Law*

A particular advantage of the liberal accounts of the substance, form, and enforcement of international law is that they can be extended to particularly detailed and plausible accounts of the long-term evolution of international legal norms. International law can evolve through liberal mechanisms of either exogenous or endogenous change.

Exogenous change takes place when autonomous changes in underlying ideational, commercial, and republican factors drive the elaboration, expansion, and deepening of international legal norms over time. Since exogenous trends in core liberal factors such as industrialization, competitiveness, democratization, globalization, and public ideologies often continue for decades and centuries, and vary widely geographically and functionally, such theories can support explanations for "big-picture" regularities in the scope and evolution of international law over the long term, among countries and across issues (Milner and Keohane 1996; Kahler 1999). This offers a particularly powerful means of explaining trends in substantive content. For example, nineteenth- and twentieth-century waves of democracy and industrialization have driven a steady shift away from treaties governing military, territorial, and diplomatic practice to treaties governing economic affairs, which now dominate international law-making and the activity of international tribunals, and in recent years toward human rights and human security, although the latter still remain only 15 percent of the total (Ku 2001). Also consistent with factors such as democratization, industrialization, and education is the fact that the development of international law has been geographically focused in developed countries, notably Europe, and has emanated outward from there.

Endogenous evolution occurs when initial international legal commitments trigger feedback, in the form of a shift in domestic and transnational state–society relations that alters support for the legal norms. In liberal theory, such feedback can influence material interests (commercial liberalism), prevailing conceptions of the public good (ideational liberalism), or the composition of the "selectorate" (republican liberalism), thereby changing state preferences about the management of interdependence. Each of these three liberal feedback loops creates opportunities for "increasing returns" and internalization, but they do not assure that it will take place. It does take place, on the liberal account, only if the net preferences of groups mobilized by cooperation are positively inclined toward its continuation, and if those groups are powerful enough to have a net impact in domestic political systems. Isolating examples and conditions under which this takes place is an ongoing liberal research program.

Exogenous and endogenous effects are often found together. There is, for example, broad agreement that exogenous shifts in technology, underlying market position, and a desire to expand permanently the size, wealth, and efficiency of the tradable sector of the economy explains the general direction of postwar changes in trade policies. Bailey, Goldstein, and Weingast (1997) argue that postwar, multilateral trade liberalization generated domestic economic liberalization, thereby increasing the underlying social support for further rounds of trade liberalization in a continuing virtuous circle of deepening international obligations. A strategy like EU enlargement is expressly designed to use this sort of incentive not just to induce a shift in trade policy, but also to engineer broader economic and political reform, as well as more cooperative international policies in the future (Berman 1995; Hitchcock 2004).

In the EU and elsewhere, vertical and horizontal judicial networking can encourage deeper forms of tacit cooperation, such as "judicial comity," in which judges mutually recognize that "courts in different nations are entitled to their fair share of disputes . . . as co-equals in the global task of judging" (Slaughter 2000: 1113). As a result, domestic courts no longer act as mere recipients of international law, but instead shape its evolution (Benvenisti and Downs 2009; Conant 2013). Moreover, as we saw in the area of multilateral trade, legal cooperation may have broader effects on political and economic systems, both intended and unintended. Even French President Charles de Gaulle, in many ways an archetypical defender of traditional sovereignty, committed France to firm legal developments with the deliberate goal of fundamentally reforming and modernizing the French economy – adaptations that altered French attitudes over the long term and facilitated more cooperation. More recently, EU enlargement has been employed as a means to encourage broad reforms in domestic politics, economics, and societies. Even the distant prospect of enlargement, as was the case in Turkey, encouraged movements toward Islamist democracy that are now irreversible (Tocci 2005; Robins 2007).

What is the relative impact of exogenous and endogenous effects on international law? Here, research still progresses and, obviously, the answer depends on the specific case. Nonetheless, the available evidence suggests that, in general, exogenous factors seem to have a more significant effect than endogenous ones on substantive state policies. The broad constraints on compliance and elaboration tend to be set by patterns of interdependence among countries with underlying national preferences – even if endogenous effects can dominate on the margin and in particular cases. Consider two examples. One is European integration. "Neo-functionalists," such as Ernst Haas, long stressed the essential importance of endogenous processes ("spillovers") in explaining integration. Recently, Alec Stone Sweet and Wayne Sandholtz (1997) have sought to revive the argument for endogenous effects, presenting legal integration as the primary cause of economic integration. Yet, it is now widely accepted that Europe has responded primarily to exogenous economic and security shocks. Nearly all basic economic analyses, which leave little doubt that exogenous liberal processes (factors such as size, proximity, level of development, common borders, common language) explain the bulk (around 80 percent) of postwar economic integration in Europe, leaving about 20 percent for all other factors, such as endogenous legal development (Frankel 1997: 80–88). Similarly, in the area of human rights, the consensus in the literature is that the effect of international human rights norms on state behavior is marginal (Hathaway 2007; Hafner-Burton, forthcoming). Even those scholars who claim the most for legal norms concede that their impact is uneven and secondary to underlying exogenous factors (Simmons 2009).

Yet, the focus on substantive outcomes may underestimate some endogenous effects. In the same case of the EEC, Weiler, Slaughter, Alter, and others have persuasively demonstrated that initial legal delegation and intervening feedback processes (sometimes unforeseen and even, in part, unwanted by national governments) can decisively influence the form of legal cooperation – even if they are not the primary cause of substantive cooperation. European Court of Justice jurisprudence embedded itself in domestic legal systems and helped establish "supremacy," "direct effect," and other doctrines. Explaining this process requires close attention to the liberal micro-incentives of litigants, domestic judges, and international courts under supranational tribunals – to which we now turn (Alter 1998; Burley and Mattli 1993; Weiler 1991; Alter, Guerzovich and Helfer 2009).

III. INTERNATIONAL TRIBUNALS: LIBERAL ANALYSIS AND ITS CRITICS

Institutional conditions for successful enforcement and endogenous feedback have been most intensively analyzed in studies of international tribunals. As we have just seen, Slaughter helped pioneer the analysis of "supranational adjudication" in the EU, arguing that the key is not simply international enforcement but the internationalization of norms in domestic legal systems: litigants bring cases to domestic courts, which interact with international tribunals, and international norms feed back into domestic legal systems (Burley and Mattli 1993). The European experience, according to Slaughter and Helfer,

> challenges us to transcend the traditional framework of "state versus tribunal," summoning an image of a confrontation between two discrete entities in which the outcome depends upon whether the state defines its (unitary) national interest to include compliance with international law. The ECJ and the ECHR have succeeded in becoming effective supranational tribunals by looking not to states per se but to their component institutions, using the link to private parties granted them as supranational tribunals to penetrate the surface of the state [with decisions being made by] courts, ministries, and legislative committees competing and cooperating with one another as part of the normal domestic political process. (1997: 337)

Helfer and Slaughter, and many other scholars since, have generalized this approach to other international tribunals, seeking to specify conditions under which they are effective. The process of externalizing and internalizing norms can be analyzed in three stages of a transnational legal process: access, adjudication, and implementation (Keohane, Moravcsik, and Slaughter 2000).

A. Access

The most critical dynamic in vertical enforcement is not one state bringing pressure to bear on another, but private parties bringing pressure to bear on national governments. This requires institutional mechanisms whereby individuals and social groups can influence the agenda of international tribunals. These include individual petition, referral of cases by domestic courts, and, in criminal cases, independent prosecution. The key is that they be independent of the policy-makers against whom pressure is brought to bear.

If this is correct, we should expect to observe the following: *The lower the cost of access for individuals and social groups with an incentive to use an international tribunal, the more dynamic potential the system has.* This is confirmed by the striking empirical correlation between breadth of individual access and the use, effectiveness, and dynamism of international legal arrangements (Table 4.1).

The basic factors motivating access, and thus internalization, may vary. In the EU, they have been largely economic. Slaughter and Mattli, followed by Weiler, Alter, and others, argue that mobilization of interest groups with an interest in liberalization within a legal system that both grants them standing in domestic courts and offers domestic courts an incentive to recognize European law was a precondition for European legal integration. Systems of economic law enforcement with individual or administrative petition can be robust, even under conditions that may seem unpropitious, as in the case of the Andean Pact (Alter and Helfer 2009). In the human rights area, similarly, underlying trends, such as democratization and the growth of civil society, are the most important determinants of human rights

TABLE 4.1. *Access rules and dockets of international courts and tribunals*

Level of access	International court or tribunal	Average annual number of cases since founding
Low	PCA	0.3
Medium	ICJ	1.7
	GATT	4.4
	WTO	30.5
	Old ECtHR	23.5
High	EC	100.1

EC, European Court; ECtHR; European Court on Human Rights; GATT, Generalized Agreement on Tariffs and Trade; ICJ, International Court of Justice; PCA, Permanent Court of Arbitration; WTO, World Trade Organization
Source: Keohane, Moravcsik, and Slaughter (2000: 475).

performance, but international legal institutions can have a secondary impact. This impact is dependent on access in the form of individual petition (and, in criminal systems, private prosecution). Human rights arrangements without these institutional forms are far less dynamic.

B. *Adjudication*

For legalization, access is necessary but insufficient. International and domestic tribunals must also have incentives to adjudicate cases in a way consistent with the enforcement, internalization, and deepening of international norms. Without "autonomous domestic institutions committed to the rule of law and responsive to citizen interests," international norms are unlikely to be internalized. Although the receptivity of domestic courts to international jurisprudence may depend in part on a common cultural commitment to legal process per se, it depends more on the institutional independence of domestic actors and common substantive values, such as "individual rights and liberties in systems where the individuals themselves are ultimately sovereign" (Helfer and Slaughter 1997: 334). In systems where judges are not independent, or where the divergence between the domestic and international normative systems at stake in individual rulings is too high, domestic judges will not have incentives to make common cause with a supranational tribunal against the government. This requires that courts be relatively autonomous. If this is correct, we should observe that *where the domestic polity has elements of a rule-of-law system, granting autonomy to judges and legal adjudicators, and where judges possess sympathetic values, international legal systems will tend to function better.* It also helps if international or domestic adjudicators are competent, autonomous, and neutral, and they possess a manageable caseload, fact-finding capacity, high quality of legal reasoning, and an ability to engage in judicial networking (Helfer and Slaughter 1997).

Liberals hypothesize that the density of "vertical" international legal commitments and overall legal cooperation tends to be highest among advanced industrial democracies. Yet, this is not to say that democracies are, in all cases, more likely to promote or adhere to international law. Instead, the relationship is subtle and contingent – and therefore the subject of ongoing research. To be sure, democratic and interdependent Europe has emerged predictably as the major promoter of transnational legal norms in the world today, with a regional density of law higher than anywhere else. Yet, although the United States is a democratic, individualist, and rule-of-law country at home, it takes an "exceptionalist" attitude toward international law. One liberal explanation would be that U.S. constitutional culture, deeply embedded over two centuries, embodies distinctive U.S. values (e.g., unique conception of human rights, regulatory style, constitutional norms) that diverge significantly from the norms of advanced industrial democracies. These are bolstered by libertarian and social conservatives, an institutionalized judiciary insufficiently powerful to overcome it, and a constitution uniquely resistant to amendment and subject to veto group obstruction (Moravcsik 2001, 2005). Nondemocratic countries may be more likely to defend traditional state-to-state horizontal conceptions of international law, particularly those that privilege expansive notions of sovereignty. In a substantial tier of industrializing nondemocratic countries, moreover, economic law enjoys some autonomy, and this may permit a vertical dynamic by which a substantial body of international economic law is "internalized" – even if such dynamics are limited by the ever-present possibility of discretionary state action.

C. Implementation

Helfer and Slaughter argue that "the overall boundaries for [courts] are set by the political institutions of [regimes], above all the member states." If courts become too "teleological," that is, if they adopt a mode of interpretation biased toward achieving further legal integration "too far too fast," the member states may not comply, or might even act "to curtail its jurisdiction or urge their national courts to disregard its judgments," or to "shift the composition of the Court" (Helfer and Slaughter 1997: 314–18). This principle can be formulated as follows: *national governments must have interests that incentivize them to implement the judgments of domestic courts, or at least not to defy them outright.* The more effective courts are "those charged with policing modest deviations from a generally settled norm or modifying a particular rule or set of rules incrementally" (Helfer and Slaughter 1997: 330) – a quality that is linked both to interest-based politics and to preexisting rule-of-law norms.Helfer and Slaughter continue, "the link between liberal democracy and effective supranational adjudication" is "complex and contingent, particularly at the margins" (1997: 334).

Recent studies confirm this close relationship between evolution of legal norms and national institutions and interests concerning compliance. In environmental cooperation, for example, liberal states are more likely than illiberal states to create and maintain structures for regularized monitoring and implementation review that often enhance compliance (Raustiala and Victor 1998). One study of compliance with European social and legal norms concludes that "the structure of domestic institutions seems to be key in explaining variance in the mechanisms through which compliance occurs" (Checkel 2000: 34). The domestic political, administrative, and financial cost of compliance is a further constraint on the willingness of states to follow international legal norms. Raustiala and Slaughter (2002: 545) stress that "[c]ompliance with the International Whaling Convention, for example, which requires little action by most states, should be higher than compliance with many narcotics agreements, which require pervasive and costly domestic regulation." In the European Court of Human Rights (ECtHR), states almost uniformly implement legal judgments in a strictly formal sense, but the way in which they choose to do so substantively – quickly or slowly, broadly or narrowly, by financial settlement or by implementing policy change – depends on the size of the stakes and the government interest. Where a judgment threatens a core state interest, implementation will tend to be very narrow – limited, for example, to granting compensation to a single plaintiff, rather than changing a policy (Von Staden 2009).

D. *Critics of the Liberal Analysis of Tribunals*

Liberal theorists such as Helfer and Slaughter contend that international legal regimes more deeply internalized in society often generate more effective compliance and more dynamism over time than do conventional state-to-state legal arrangements. This argument is sometimes stated as a liberal ideal type and, perhaps as a result, the Helfer–Slaughter view of international tribunals has often been criticized for positing an unrealistically linear relationship between "democracy" and the effectiveness and dynamism of international law. The resulting debates have received much scholarly attention, but the underlying critique seems misplaced. As we have seen, liberal theory in fact predicts considerable variation in the effectiveness and dynamism of international law, both among democracies and among autocracies, based on variation in domestic and transnational ideas, interests, and institutions – a finding that may coexist with the observation that democracies are, as a whole, more law abiding. This liberal claim (properly understood) has been accepted by its critics, and today their queries are best viewed as friendly amendments or extensions to liberal theory.

Neo-conservative critics, such as Eric Posner and John Yoo, allege that liberal theory overestimates the extent of vertical internalization (2005*a*, *b*; also Alvarez 2001). Yet, in fact, Posner and Yoo accept most of the liberal empirical argument. They concede that interest group pressures shape state interests in the promulgation and enforcement of international law. They acknowledge that vertical enforcement and evolutionary dynamics sometimes occur – notably in the significant areas of

WTO enforcement and in promoting democratic peace (2005a). They also accept that the EU and the ECHR exhibit more dynamism than other legal systems, though they seek to exclude Europe from consideration as an exceptional "political union." Yet, excluding Europe paints an arbitrary and misleading picture of international law, not simply because it eliminates over a quarter of the global economy and a much greater proportion of global trade, investment, and law-making, but also because EU scholars do not view the institutions as an exceptional "federation," but rather, as do Helfer and Slaughter, as the most interdependent and uniformly democratic of continents (Posner and Yoo 2005a: 55).

Posner insists, further following liberal theory, that dominant interest group coalitions lack "a commitment to international law" per se and thus may oppose the promulgation and enforcement of international norms if they are inconsistent with social interests (Posner 2005). He and liberals also agree that liberal analysis of international law requires underlying theories to explain variation in social and state preferences across issues, countries, and time. Mills and Stephens make a similar point, from an "English school" perspective (2005: 18), when they argue that

> it is difficult to disagree with Slaughter's argument that vertical(through domestic courts) rather than horizontal (through international bodies) enforcement of rules of international law offers the greatest potential at present for an international rule of law. However, Slaughter must confront the reality of domestic politics when it comes to the actual use of domestic courts or highly integrated international courts. Nowhere is this more apparent than from an analysis of the failings of the United States and many other liberal states to accept or internalize international human rights standards by allowing their enforcement in domestic courts . . . [A]t least part of the explanation for the failure of vertical enforcement in this context must derive from the actions of individuals and groups as political actors within democratic states.

Perhaps early formulations of liberal theory were too dichotomous, but the theory, properly understood, is based on precisely the need to theorize the state–society foundations of the variation in the response of liberal states to international law. The fact that compliance requires such an analysis seems an argument for, not against, the centrality of liberal theory.

Harold Koh similarly criticizes liberals for exaggerating the link between democracy and the dynamic success of international law. He presents himself as a "constructivist" and seeks to argue the contrary of the conservative case, namely, that Helfer and Slaughter underestimate the extent to which internalization may occur in non-European and especially nondemocratic settings (Koh 1998; Alvarez 2001). Yet, Koh's most important conclusions, too, dovetail with those of liberal theory.

First, his claim that some vertical enforcement can take place in nondemocracies is consistent with liberal theory. To present this fact as a critique creates disagreement where none exists. Helfer and Slaughter do maintain that democratic states are

more likely to establish dynamic and successful vertical "supranational" adjudication systems, yet, as we have seen, they do not view this relationship as dichotomous:
"Non-democracies may have democratic impulses, embodied in specific institutions; illiberal states may have strong liberal leanings" (1997: 335). For example,
international economic law can be developed with a nondemocratic China, while
even the most advanced democracies, such as the United States in human rights,
have incentives to resist compliance with international norms, which is why courts
always need be jurisprudentially incremental and politically cautious (Helfer and
Slaughter 1997: 314–17).

Second, although Koh superficially rejects the importance of regime type for
domestic internalization, his view that internalization is promoted by stable, repeated
interactions, the "legal" quality of norms, open transnational legal interaction, and
a rich field of NGOs puts him on a slippery slope to recognizing its importance.
As Joel Trachtman observes, Koh's simple claim that "repeated participation in
the international legal process" leads to norm acceptance "is hardly theoretically
satisfying" on its own because "repeated interaction with duplicity or hostility would
not necessarily change anyone's ideas, or their incentives to comply" or "necessarily
overcome strong incentives to defect" (Trachtman 2010: 13). In fact, this mechanism
is likely to function in the way constructivists imagine only under certain (liberal)
preconditions, as Koh himself concedes: "the structural attributes of liberal systems
undeniably make them more open to some kinds of internalization" (1998: 676).
Indeed, the qualities Koh stresses – stable interaction, legality, open interaction,
and civil society – all depend on democratic institutions. Without transparency,
accountability, issue-advocacy networks, and professional status, legal processes are
unlikely to have a consistently positive effect. As Keohane observes, "[i]nstead of
downplaying the point, it would seem wiser to elaborate it" – something Slaughter
and other liberals have done in work on transnational networks and democratic
institutions (1998: 710).

Third, while Koh's approving references to Thomas Franck, suggestive use of the
term "internalization," and self-identification as a "constructivist" seem to suggest
that he holds a nonrationalist or "nonliberal" theory of international law, he does
not in fact commit to the distinctive causal mechanisms of these theories, but rather
to liberal ones. Unlike Franck, Goodman, or others, he does not portray states as
governed by "logics of appropriateness" drawn from habit, cognitive framing, psychology, deontological morality, or standard operating procedures – and he avoids
Frank's view that law-abiding states will necessarily be more law-abiding abroad simply because they transfer legalistic habits of mind. Instead, like Helfer and Slaughter, Koh believes that dynamic legal cooperation is possible with semidemocratic or
nondemocratic states in selected areas primarily because states pragmatically seek
to realize interests and ideals. Legal agreements are possible between China and
the United States, for example, because a measure of largely self-interested institutional autonomy has been granted to economic law, even when fundamental

disagreement remains in other areas. These are quintessentially liberal processes of instrumental pursuit of specific material interests and ideals channeled through representative institutions. Overall, Koh's specific use of theoretical language from IR theory seems misplaced – a case of paradigms hindering understanding.

IV. LIBERALISM AS NORMATIVE THEORY: SOVEREIGNTY AND DEMOCRACY

Liberal theories of international law also have implications for the conceptual analysis and normative evaluation of international law. Liberalism can help shape our understanding of core international legal concepts, even those that govern traditional interstate relations. An example is the concept of national sovereignty – and related notions of "intervention," "domestic jurisdiction," and "legitimacy." For liberals, sovereignty, like the state itself, is socially embedded and constructed. Its meaning is thus fluid. Without rejecting entirely the institutionalist view that sovereignty is a transaction cost–reducing means to simplify interstate interaction, the realist view that prevailing conceptions of sovereignty may result from coercion, or the constructivist insight that the sovereignty norm may gain strength from its legal form or habitual acceptance over time, liberals insist that the substantive meaning of the sovereignty norm varies greatly as a function of the domestic and transnational social context.

From a liberal perspective, nearly all unilateral or multilateral engagement with foreign governments involves some de facto "intervention" in domestic politics, since any international legal norm helps or hurts some individuals and social groups (Slaughter and Burke-White 2006). Such intervention may benefit or disadvantage the existing domestic government and ruling coalition, particularly in nondemocratic states. Even formally domestic activities not formally subject to international law or generally viewed as foreign policy matters may have a substantial impact on foreigners. Thus, for liberals, what remains "essentially within the domestic jurisdiction of any state," as Article 2.7 of the UN Charter[1] states, not only varies with the social context but also is inherently ambiguous.

As a result of this ambiguity, the state actions recognized as sovereign prerogatives, or, conversely, subject to international legal restraints, are subject to constant negotiation and renegotiation by states in the international community. Norms about sovereignty vary over time, and not always simply as a function of consent or power. In different eras, powerful states in the international community have recognized as consistent or inconsistent with sovereignty a changing set of activities on the high seas, domestic religious practices, conceptions of dynastic and national legitimacy, regime types and political practices, and economic activities. Under the Concert of Europe, Wilson's conception of self-determination, or modern human rights law and

---

[1] Charter of the United Nations, 1 U.N.T.S. XVI (1945).

the doctrine of "responsibility to protect," governments have – for varying reasons – collectively decided to recognize private individuals, groups, and political movements against ruling governments (Krasner 1999; Philpott 2001; Evans and Sahnoun 2002; Haas 2008). Even in areas of human rights and economic law, where intervention into domestic practices are common today, international tribunals must commonly decide how much respect ("margin of appreciation") to accord domestic practices – a decision made not simply (or even primarily) on the basis of black-letter law, but on the basis of the underlying legitimacy enjoyed by different forms of domestic practices. These are accepted or rejected, in the liberal view, based on their consistency with the prevailing consensus about acceptable interests and ideals.

Liberal theory also has implications for a normative evaluation of international law. One obvious pragmatic sense in which this is so has to do with practical policy implementation. Insofar as liberal theory is empirically valid, it would be both prudent and normatively advisable (from a consequentialist perspective) to tailor international law to an accurate assessment of which laws are likely to be viable, effective, and dynamic, given underlying social constraints. One important question, for example, is under what conditions to insist on strict adherence to ambitious goals, employing direct state-to-state mechanisms to achieve them (such as international legal direction, reciprocity, coercive sanctions, and regime-changing intervention), and under what conditions to work via state–society relations to encourage favorable endogenous long-term social, economic, and political change and the slower establishment of vertical enforcement mechanisms. In areas such as human rights, there can be a divergence between two uses of the term "liberal": what "liberal" political actors (e.g., NGOs) recommend, which is often the former, and what "liberal" IR theory views as more fundamental and enduring, which is generally the latter. Without a theory of the social foundations of law-making and compliance, neither governments nor their critics are likely to generate sound and humane policy recommendations.

Yet, the normative implications of liberal theory go beyond recognition of existing pragmatic policy constraints. This would be to render it conservative and status quo oriented, as some critics charge (Mills and Stephens 2005). In fact, liberal theory supports normative evaluation and critique of existing international law. One such area is in problematizing the democratic legitimacy of international law – on which there is now a burgeoning scholarly interest.

Liberal theory is centrally concerned with the question of social representation; that is, with whose interests and ideals international law represents. Liberal theory, with its focus on the ways in which international engagement alters domestic processes, suggests that the proper way to pose this question is not to ask whether international institutions themselves are democratic, but whether domestic democratic processes are enhanced or degraded by participation in transnational legal processes (Keohane, Macedo, and Moravcsik 2009). To be sure, judging whether a system of social representation is fair and equitable requires a sophisticated set of normative standards from democratic theory to judge them – about which different analysts may disagree (Buchanan 2004: 18; Dahl 1999; Held 2003; Keohane *et al.* 2009). It also requires a valid understanding of the empirical functioning of domestic and international systems of representation provided by liberal theory. For example, pluralist, libertarian, deliberative, and social democratic critics may differ in assessing the same pattern of facts (Moravcsik 2004).

Still, most democratic theorists would accept certain conclusions that follow from liberal theory. In general, recent liberal research challenges the notion, widespread among both conservative and radical critics, that multilateral institutions are presumptively democracy degrading because they are more distant and insulated from individuals and groups in civil society than are domestic institutions. This threat is generally less significant than many fear it to be.

One reason to be less concerned about a global "democratic deficit" is that, from a liberal perspective, the center of gravity of legal commitment remains largely domestic. International legal norms change the legal and policy processes, but they remain essentially domestic. In the final analysis, decisions to enact, enforce, and extend legal norms remain subject to whatever domestic constitutional provisions states see fit to impose. As a practical matter, enforcement of nearly all international norms remains at home.

Another reason to be relatively sanguine about the effect of international law on domestic democracy is that the proper "applied" standard – if we use prevailing domestic practices to judge international commitments – would not be the pure majoritarian norm adopted by many critics, but a "constitutional democratic" standard. All modern democratic systems are based on complex systems of domestic constitutional delegation; most acts of international legal delegation are no different in kind – and not necessarily any less subject to public control – than these (Goldsmith and Levinson 2009; Keohane *et al.* 2009). Both types of institutional commitment are designed to permit peoples and their leaders to achieve political goals they would not otherwise be able to achieve by managing the impact of interdependence. From this perspective, international law might be viewed by national publics as sovereignty enhancing. People ought to maintain the right to enter into such arrangements, just as they retain the right to enter into constitutional arrangements (Chayes and Chayes 1993, 1998).

From a liberal perspective, moreover, such interstate exchanges of democratic authority are essential policy-making instruments in an interdependent world, where citizens of one nation, in exchange for committing to limit domestic discretion in areas that affect other nations, secures the precommitment of foreign counterparts to adopt particular policies in areas that affect them – policies over which they otherwise would have no control. In essence, this bargain does not necessarily differ from the bargain struck among citizens in a domestic constitutional polity, who precommit to particular policies to secure the commitment of others within an interdependent society (Beitz 1979; Goldsmith and Levinson 2009).

Yet another reason to be suspicious of conservative critics of multilateralism is that there is no reason to assume, as many do, that preexisting domestic democratic institutions are themselves ideal. All national political and social systems are unfair in one or more ways, and domestic institutions as modified by international law may better realize democratic ideals than would autonomous domestic ones (Keohane *et al.* 2009). This is most obvious when international legal regimes are explicitly designed to promote democracy, but this may also occur in other ways (Mansfield and Pevehouse 2006). Even where international legal commitments do undermine everyday domestic majoritarian control over policy, perhaps by virtue of the more diffuse, distant, insulated, or technocratic nature of multilateral processes or the absence of domestic deliberation over foreign policy issues, this need not mean that they debase domestic democracy. Rather, we should judge involvement in international legal institutions by the same standards that are used in everyday domestic constitutional practice.

In modern democracies, well-functioning constitutional institutions are not simply designed to maximize popular control over individual issues – nor is it normatively advisable that they do so (Moravcsik 2004; Keohane *et al.* 2009). Instead, majoritarian control is balanced against other essential democratic virtues, including the defense of individual and minority rights, the suppression of powerful special-interest factions, and the improvement in the epistemic quality of domestic deliberation via new information and ideas. In areas such as foreign trade, central banking, human rights protection, and pharmaceutical regulation, democracies normally delegate to insulated experts. International cooperation seems to consist disproportionately of such issues, whereas issues that inspire the most broad and active popular engagement – such as fiscal policy, social welfare provision, medical care, pension reform, education, local infrastructure, third-country immigration, and such – tend to remain largely national. Still, there may well be areas – European monetary integration is possibly one – where international bodies enjoy an autonomy that exceeds the norm in most domestic democratic systems, without any clear technocratic or normative justification. In such cases, liberal theory treats current international legal institutions as presumptively lacking in democratic legitimacy (Moravcsik 2004).

Even if one concludes that certain international legal practices are democratically legitimate initially upon delegation, it might be objected that legal systems can develop a life of their own that can eventually escape democratic control. Although this may occur in some cases, we have seen – based on trade and human rights – that endogenous legal processes of this kind generally seem to have a much less significant effect on the evolution of substantive policy-making than do exogenous factors. One reason is, as we have seen in liberal analyses of tribunals, is that access, adjudication, and implementation remain closely bound up with domestic politics. This makes it difficult to argue that autonomous evolution of legal systems generally traps national publics into entirely unexpected and unwelcome substantive outcomes – even if individual cases may sometimes diverge from the norm. To the extent that exceptions occur, it is not clear from a normative standpoint why this is any more troubling than analogous legal developments within domestic politics, where a certain degree of isolation from political concerns is instead seen as a favorable indicator of the rule of law. This is good news for those who believe that international law rests on a firm basis of consent. The fate of the Euro is putting this proposition to the test.

There is much more work to be done in assessing the democratic legitimacy of specific international legal arrangements, and debates must be conducted between those with different normative starting points. It is clear, however, that estimating the impact of specific international legal institutions on domestic democratic practice – assessed in terms of popular control, the quality of deliberation, individual and minority rights, and suppression of special interests – requires the type of detailed empirical analysis of the real-world behavior of domestic social interests and representative institutions that liberal theory offers.

REFERENCES

Abbott, Kenneth W. (2008). "Enriching Rational Choice Institutionalism for the Study of International Law," *University of Illinois Law Review*, No. 1, pp. 5–46.

Alter, Karen J. (1998). "Explaining National Court Acceptance of European Court Jurisprudence: A Critical Evaluation of Theories of Legal Integration," in Anne-Marie Slaughter, Alec Stone Sweet, and Joseph H. H. Weiler (eds.), *The European Court & National Courts: Doctrine and Jurisprudence* (Evanston, IL: Northwestern University Press), pp. 227–52.

———— (2008). "Delegating to International Courts: Self-Binding vs. Other-Binding Delegation," *Law and Contemporary Problems*, Vol. 71, No. 1, pp. 37–76.

Alter, Karen J., M. Florencia Guerzovich, and Laurence R. Helfer (2009). "Islands of Effective International Adjudication: Constructing an Intellectual Property Rule of Law in the Andean Community," *American Journal of International Law*, Vol. 103, No. 1, pp. 1–46.

Alter, Karen J., and Laurence R. Helfer (2009). "The Andean Tribunal of Justice and Its Interlocutors: Understanding Preliminary Reference Patterns in the Andean Community," *New York University Journal of International Law & Politics*, Vol. 41, No. 4, pp. 871–930.

Alter, Karen J., and Sophie Meunier (2009). "The Politics of Regime Complexity," *Perspectives on Politics*, Vol. 7, No. 1, pp. 13–24.

Alvarez, José E. (2001). "Do Liberal States Behave Better? A Critique of Slaughter's Liberal Theory," *European Journal of International Law*, Vol. 12, No. 2, pp. 183–246.

Bailey, Michael A., Judith Goldstein, and Barry R. Weingast (1997). "The Institutional Roots of American Trade Policy: Politics, Coalitions, and International Trade," *World Politics*, Vol. 49, No. 3, pp. 309–38.

Beitz, Charles R. (1979). *Political Theory and International Relations* (Princeton, NJ: Princeton University Press).

Benvenisti, Eyal, and George W. Downs (2009). "National Courts, Domestic Democracy, and the Evolution of International Law," *European Journal of International Law*, Vol. 20, No. 1, pp. 59–72.

Berman, Harold J. (1995). "World Law," *Fordham International Law Journal*, Vol. 18, No. 5, pp. 1617–22.

Brummer, Chris (2011). "How International Financial Law Works (and How It Doesn't)," *Georgetown Law Journal*, Vol. 99, No. 2, pp. 257–327.

Buchanan, Allen (2004). *Justice, Legitimacy, and Self-Determination: Moral Foundations for International Law* (New York: Oxford University Press).

Burley, Anne-Marie, and Walter Mattli (1993). "Europe before the Court: A Political Theory of Legal Integration," *International Organization*, Vol. 47, No. 1, pp. 41–76.

Chayes, Abram, and Antonia Handler Chayes (1993). "On Compliance," *International Organization*, Vol. 47, No. 2, pp. 175–205.

———— 1995. *The New Sovereignty: Compliance with International Regulatory Agreements* (Cambridge, MA: Harvard University Press).

Checkel, Jeffrey T. (2000). "Compliance and Domestic Institutions," Paper presented at Annual Meeting (Washington, DC: American Political Science Association).

Conant, Lisa (2013). "Whose Agents? The Interpretation of International Law in National Courts," in Jeffrey L. Dunoff and Mark A. Pollack (eds.), *Interdisciplinary Perspectives on International Law and International Relations: The State of the Art*(New York: Cambridge University Press), pp. 394–420.

Dahl, Robert A. (1999). "Can International Organizations Be Democratic? A Skeptic's View," in Ian Shapiro and Casiano Hacker-Cordón (eds.), *Democracy's Edges* (New York: Cambridge University Press), pp. 19–36.

Dai, Xinyuan (2005). "Why Comply? The Domestic Constituency Mechanism," *International Organization*, Vol. 59, No. 2, pp. 363–98.

Davis, Christina L. (2004). "International Institutions and Issue Linkage: Building Support for Agricultural Trade Liberalization," *American Political Science Review*, Vol. 98, No. 1, pp. 153–69.

Davis, Christina L., and Sarah Blodgett Bermeo (2009). "Who Files? Developing Country Participation in GATT/WTO Adjudication," *The Journal of Politics*, Vol. 71, No. 3, pp. 1033–49.

Desbordes, Rodolphe, and Julien Vauday (2007). "The Political Influence of Foreign Firms in Developing Countries," *Economics & Politics*, Vol. 19, No. 3, pp. 421–51.

Downs, George W., and David M. Rocke (1995). *Optimal Imperfection? Domestic Uncertainty and Institutions in International Relations* (Princeton, NJ: Princeton University Press).

Drezner, Daniel W. (2007). *All Politics Is Global: Explaining International Regulatory Regimes* (Princeton, NJ: Princeton University Press).

Evans, Gareth, and Mohamed Sahnoun (2002). "The Responsibility to Protect," *Foreign Affairs*, Vol. 81, No. 6, pp. 99–110.

Frankel, Jeffrey A. (1997). *Regional Trading Blocs in the World Economic System* (Washington, DC: Institute for International Economics).

Gilligan, Michael J. (1997a). *Empowering Exporters: Reciprocity, Delegation, and Collective Action in American Trade Policy* (Ann Arbor: University of Michigan Press).

———— (1997b). "Lobbying as a Private Good with Intra-industry Trade," *International Studies Quarterly*, Vol. 41, No. 3, pp. 455–74.

Goldsmith, Jack, and Daryl Levinson (2009). "Law for States: International Law, Constitutional Law, Public Law," *Harvard Law Review*, Vol. 122, No. 7, pp. 1791–868.

Goldsmith, Jack L., and Eric A. Posner (1999). "A Theory of Customary International Law," *The University of Chicago Law Review*, Vol. 66, No. 4, pp. 1113–77.

———— (2005). *The Limits of International Law* (New York: Oxford University Press).

Goldstein, Judith, and Lisa L. Martin (2000). "Legalization, Trade Liberalization, and Domestic Politics: A Cautionary Note," *International Organization*, Vol. 54, No. 3, pp. 603–32.

Goodman, Ryan, and Derek Jinks (2004). "How to Influence States: Socialization and International Human Rights Law," *Duke Law Journal*, Vol. 54, No. 3, pp. 621–703.

Grossman, Gene M., and Elhanan Helpman (1994). "Protection for Sale," *American Economic Review*, Vol. 84 No. 4, pp. 833–50.

Grotto, Andrew J. (2008). "What Drives States to Support New Nonproliferation Obligations? An Empirical and Theoretical Exploration," Discussion paper for: International Implications for and Levers on U.S. Nuclear Weapons Policy, U.S. Nuclear Policy Review Project, The Stanley Foundation (Washington, DC: Henry L. Stimson Center).

Haas, Michael (2008). *International Human Rights: A Comprehensive Introduction*, 1st ed. (New York: Routledge).

Haas, Peter M. (1989). "Do Regimes Matter? Epistemic Communities and Mediterranean Pollution Control," *International Organization*, Vol. 43, No. 3, pp. 377–403.

Hafner-Burton, Emilie (forthcoming). "International Human Rights Regimes," *Annual Review of Political Science*, Vol. 15, pp. 3.1–3.22.

Hathaway, Oona A. (1998). "Positive Feedback: The Impact of Trade Liberalization on Industry Demands for Protection," *International Organization*, Vol. 52, No. 3, pp. 575–612.

———— (2007). "Why Do Countries Commit to Human Rights Treaties?" *The Journal of Conflict Resolution*, Vol. 51, No. 4, pp. 588–621.

Held, David. (2003). "Cosmopolitanism: Globalization Tamed?," *Review of International Studies*, Vol. 29, No. 4, pp. 465–80.

Helfer, Laurence R., and Anne-Marie Slaughter (1997). "Toward a Theory of Effective Supranational Adjudication," *Yale Law Journal*, Vol. 107, No. 2, pp. 273–82.

Helleiner, Eric, Stefano Pagliari, and Hubert Zimmermann (2010) (eds.). *Global Finance in Crisis: The Politics of International Regulatory Change*, 1st ed. (New York: Routledge).

Hiscox, Michael J. (2002). "Commerce, Coalitions, and Factor Mobility: Evidence from Congressional Votes on Trade Legislation," *American Political Science Review*, Vol. 96, No. 3, pp. 593–608.

Hitchcock, William I. (2004). *The Struggle for Europe: The Turbulent History of a Divided Continent, 1945–Present* (New York: Anchor Books).

Hymans, Jacques E. C. (2006). "Theories of Nuclear Proliferation: The State of the Field," *The Nonproliferation Review*, Vol. 13, No. 3, pp. 455–65.

Kahler, Miles (1999). "Evolution, Choice, and International Change," in David A. Lake and Robert Powell (eds.), *Strategic Choice and International Relations* (Princeton, N.J: Princeton University Press), pp. 165–96.

Keck, Margaret, and Kathryn Sikkink (1998). *Activists beyond Borders: Advocacy Networks in International Politics* (Ithaca, NY: Cornell University Press).

Keohane, Robert O. (1982). "The Demand for International Regimes," *International Organization*, Vol. 36, No. 2, pp. 325–55.

———— (1984). *After Hegemony: Cooperation and Discord in the World Political Economy* (Princeton, NJ: Princeton University Press).

———— (1998). "When Does International Law Come Home?," *Houston Law Review*, Vol. 35, No. 3, pp. 699–713.

Keohane, Robert O., Stephen Macedo, and Andrew Moravcsik (2009). "Democracy-Enhancing Multilateralism," *International Organization*, Vol. 63, No. 1, pp. 1–31.

Keohane, Robert O., Andrew Moravcsik, and Anne-Marie Slaughter (2000). "Legalized Dispute Resolution: Interstate and Transnational," *International Organization*, Vol. 54, No. 3, pp. 457–88.

Keohane, Robert O., and Joseph S. Nye (1977). *Power and Interdependence: World Politics in Transition* (Boston, MA: Little, Brown and Company).

Keohane, Robert O., and David G. Victor (2011). "The Regime Complex for Climate Change," *Perspectives on Politics*, Vol. 9, No. 1, pp. 7–23.

Kissinger, Henry (1995). *Diplomacy* (New York: Simon & Schuster).

Kleine, Mareike (2011). "Making Cooperation Work: Informal Rules and Flexibility in the European Union," Paper for presentation at the Workshop "Institutional Dynamics in World Politics" (Berlin: Wissenschaftszentrum Berlin).

Koh, Harold Hongju (1998). "Bringing International Law Home," *Houston Law Review*, Vol. 35, No. 3, pp. 623–81.

Koremenos, Barbara (2002). "Can Cooperation Survive Changes in Bargaining Power? The Case of Coffee," *Journal of Legal Studies*, Vol. 31, No. S1, pp. S259–83.

Krasner, Stephen D. (1991). "Global Communications and National Power: Life on the Pareto Frontier," *World Politics*, Vol. 43, No. 3, pp. 336–66.

———— (1999). *Sovereignty: Organized Hypocrisy* (Princeton, NJ: Princeton University Press).

Ku, Charlotte (2001). *Global Governance and the Changing Face of International Law*. ACUNS Reports and Papers No. 2 (Puebla: Academic Council on the United Nations System).

Lake, David A., and Robert Powell (1999) (eds.). *Strategic Choice and International Relations* (Princeton, NJ: Princeton University Press).

Landman, Todd (2005). *Protecting Human Rights: A Comparative Study* (Washington, DC: Georgetown University Press).

Legro, Jeffrey W. (1997). "Which Norms Matter? Revisiting the 'Failure' of Internationalism," *International Organization*, Vol. 51, No. 1, pp. 31–63.

Mansfield, Edward D., and Jon C. Pevehouse (2006) "Democratization and International Organizations," *International Organization*, Vol. 60, No. 1, pp. 137–67.

Martin, Lisa. "Interests, Power, and Multilateralism," *International Organization*, Vol. 46, No. 4 (Autumn 1992), pp. 765–92.

Mills, Alex, and Tim Stephens (2005). "Challenging the Role of Judges in Slaughter's Liberal Theory of International Law," *Leiden Journal of International Law*, Vol. 18, No. 1, pp. 1–30.

Milner, Helen V. (1997). *Interests, Institutions, and Information: Domestic Politics and International Relations* (Princeton, NJ: Princeton University Press).

Milner, Helen V., and Robert O. Keohane (1996). "Internationalization and Domestic Politics: An Introduction," in Robert O. Keohane and Helen V. Milner (eds.), *Internationalization and Domestic Politics* (New York: Cambridge University Press), pp. 3–24.

Moravcsik, Andrew (1994). "Why the European Union Strengthens the State: Domestic Politics and International Institutions," Working Paper No. 52 (Cambridge, MA: Harvard University, Center for European Studies).

———— (1995). "Explaining International Human Rights Regimes: Liberal Theory and Western Europe," *European Journal of International Relations*, Vol. 1, No. 2, pp. 157–89.

———— (1997). "Taking Preferences Seriously: A Liberal Theory of International Politics," *International Organization*, Vol. 51, No. 4, pp. 513–53.

———— (1998). *The Choice for Europe: Social Purpose and State Power from Messina to Maastricht* (Ithaca, NY: Cornell University Press).

———— (2000). "The Origins of Human Rights Regimes: Democratic Delegation in Postwar Europe," *International Organization*, Vol. 54, No. 2, pp. 217–52.

———— (2001). "The New Abolitionism: Why Does the U.S. Practice the Death Penalty While Europe Does Not?," *European Studies Newsletter*, Vol. 4, No. 1.

———— (2002). "In Defense of the 'Democratic Deficit': Reassessing Legitimacy in the European Union," *Journal of Common Market Studies*, Vol. 40, No. 4, pp. 603–24.

———— (2004). "Is There a 'Democratic Deficit' in World Politics? A Framework for Analysis," *Government and Opposition*, Vol. 39, No. 2, pp. 336–63.

———— (2005). "The Paradox of U.S. Human Rights Policy," in Michael Ignatieff (ed.), *American Exceptionalism and Human Rights* (Princeton, NJ: Princeton University Press), pp. 147–97.

Pelc, Krzysztof J. (2009). "Seeking Escape: The Use of Escape Clauses in International Trade Agreements," *International Studies Quarterly*, Vol. 53, No. 2, pp. 349–68.

Philpott, Daniel (2001). *Revolutions in Sovereignty: How Ideas Shaped Modern International Relations* (Princeton, NJ: Princeton University Press).

Posner, Eric A. (2005). "International Law and the Disaggregated State," *Florida State University Law Review*, Vol. 32, No. 3, pp. 797–842.

Posner, Eric A., and John C. Yoo (2005a). "Judicial Independence in International Tribunals," *California Law Review*, Vol. 93, No. 1, pp. 1–74.

———— (2005b). "Reply to Helfer and Slaughter," *California Law Review*, Vol. 93, No. 3, pp. 957–73.

Putnam, Robert D. (1988). "Diplomacy and Domestic Politics," *International Organization*, Vol. 42, No. 3, pp. 427–60.

Raustiala, Kal (2002). "The Architecture of International Cooperation: Transgovernmental Networks and the Future of International Law," *Virginia Journal of International Law*, Vol. 43, No. 1, pp. 1–92.

Raustiala, Kal, and Anne-Marie Slaughter (2002). "International Law, International Relations and Compliance," in Walter Carlsnaes, Thomas Risse, and Beth A. Simmons (eds.), *Handbook of International Relations* (London: Sage Publications, Ltd.), pp. 538–57.

Raustiala, Kal, and David G. Victor (1998). "Conclusions," in David G. Victor, Kal Raustiala, and Eugene B. Skolnikoff (eds.), *The Implementation and Effectiveness of International Environmental Commitments: Theory and Practice* (Cambridge, MA: International Institute for Applied Systems Analysis), pp. 659–708.

Risse, Thomas, and Kathryn Sikkink (1999). "The Socialization of International Human Rights Norms into Domestic Practice: Introduction," in Thomas Risse, Steve C. Ropp, and Kathryn Sikkink (eds.), *The Power of Human Rights: International Norms and Domestic Change* (Cambridge: Cambridge University Press), pp. 1–38.

Robins, Philip (2007). "Turkish Foreign Policy since 2002: Between a 'Post-Islamist' Government and a Kemalist State," *International Affairs*, Vol. 83, No. 2, pp. 289–304.

Rosendorff, B. Peter, and Helen V. Milner (2001). "The Optimal Design of International Trade Institutions: Uncertainty and Escape," *International Organization*, Vol. 55, No. 4, pp. 829–57.

Ruggie, John Gerard (1982). "International Regimes, Transactions, and Change: Embedded Liberalism in the Postwar Economic Order," *International Organization*, Vol. 36, No. 2, pp. 379–415.

Sagan, Scott D. (2011). "The Causes of Nuclear Weapons Proliferation," *Annual Review of Political Science*, Vol. 14, pp. 225–44.

Sikkink, Kathryn (2011). *The Justice Cascade: How Human Rights Prosecutions Are Changing World Politics* (New York: W. W. Norton & Company).

Simmons, Beth A. (2001). "The International Politics of Harmonization: The Case of Capital Market Regulation," *International Organization*, Vol. 55, No. 3, pp. 589–620.

_____ (2009). *Mobilizing for Human Rights: International Law in Domestic Politics* (New York: Cambridge University Press).

Singer, David Andrew (2007). *Regulating Capital: Setting Standards for the International Financial System* (Ithaca, NY: Cornell University Press).

Slaughter, Anne-Marie (2000). "Judicial Globalization," *Virginia Journal of International Law*, Vol. 40, No. 4, pp. 1103–24.

_____ (2004). *A New World Order* (Princeton, NJ: Princeton University Press).

Slaughter, Anne-Marie, and William Burke-White (2006). "The Future of International Law Is Domestic (or, The European Way of Law)," *Harvard International Law Journal*, Vol. 47, No. 2, pp. 327–52.

Slaughter-Burley, Anne-Marie (1993). "New Directions in Legal Research on the European Community," *Journal of Common Market Studies*, Vol. 31, No. 3, pp. 391–400.

Stone Sweet, Alec, and Wayne Sandholtz (1997). "European Integration and Supranational Governance," *Journal of European Public Policy*, Vol. 4, No. 3, pp. 297–317.

Sykes, Alan O. (1991). "Protectionism as a 'Safeguard': A Positive Analysis of the GATT 'Escape Clause' with Normative Speculations," *The University of Chicago Law Review*, Vol. 58, No. 1, pp. 255–305.

Tocci, Nathalie (2005). "Europeanization in Turkey: Trigger or Anchor for Reform?," *South European Society and Politics*, Vol. 10, No. 1, pp. 73–83.

Trachtman, Joel P. (2010). "International Law and Domestic Political Coalitions: The Grand Theory of Compliance with International Law," *Chicago Journal of International Law*, Vol. 11, No. 1, pp. 127–58.

Voeten, Erik (2005). "The Political Origins of the UN Security Council's Ability to Legitimize the Use of Force," *International Organization*, Vol. 59, No. 3, pp. 527–57.

Von Staden, Andreas (2009). *Shaping Human Rights Policy in Liberal Democracies: Assessing and Explaining Compliance with the Judgements of the European Court of Human Rights*, Princeton University, Ph.D. dissertation.

Waltz, Kenneth N. (1979). *Theory of International Politics* (New York: McGraw-Hill).

Waters, Melissa A. (2005). "Mediating Norms and Identity: The Role of Transnational Judicial Dialogue in Creating and Enforcing International Law," *Georgetown Law Journal*, Vol. 93, No. 2, pp. 487–574.

_____ (2007). "Creeping Monism: The Judicial Trend toward Interpretive Incorporation of Human Rights Treaties," *Columbia Law Review*, Vol. 107, No. 3, pp. 628–705.

Weiler, J. H. H. (1991). "The Transformation of Europe," *The Yale Law Journal*, Vol. 100, No. 8, pp. 2403–83.

_____ (1994). "A Quiet Revolution: The European Court of Justice and Its Interlocutors," *Comparative Political Studies*, Vol. 26, No. 4, pp. 510–34.

_____ (1996). "European Neo-constitutionalism: In Search of Foundations for the European Constitutional Order," *Political Studies*, Vol. 44, No. 3, pp. 517–33.

Wendt, Alexander (1999). *Social Theory of International Politics* (New York: Cambridge University Press).

5

Constructivism and International Law

Jutta Brunnée and Stephen J. Toope

Over the last decade or so, a new dialogue has emerged between international relations (IR) theorists interested in the social creation of identity and who focus attention on the role of norms in international politics, and international law (IL) scholars for whom normative evolution is a stock-in-trade. These norm-interested IR thinkers have been labeled "constructivists." Constructivists are interested in many questions, of which the social creation of norms is only one. However, because international law is, of its very nature, norm focused, it is a fascination with norm creation, evolution, and destruction that has proven to be the strongest bridging point between some IL theorists and the constructivists. This bridge will form the core of our analysis in this chapter.

Because we focus considerable attention on how international lawyers and constructivists understand and deal with norms, it is useful to specify at the outset that, in the most general terms, "norms" are standards of behavior created through mutual expectation in a social setting. Many social norms are never transformed into legal norms. Moreover, the category of "legal norm" is not fixed. What norms will be included in the category depends on one's concept of law. For legal theorists called "pluralists," there may be no significant distinction, for example, between "law" produced by state authorities and norms created by voluntary associations: each may or may not be effective in shaping behavior. For other international lawyers, often called "positivists," legal norms can only exist when they are produced through fixed hierarchies, usually state hierarchies. It is their formal pedigree that creates legal norms, according to positivists; therefore law exists regardless of its link to "social norms." As we will see, other theoretical perspectives fall between these two points, or draw upon elements of each, to produce competing explanations of how international law works.

The authors thank Hélène Mayrand, Andrew McLean, and Sean Tyler for their excellent research assistance, and Chris Tenove for his thoughtful background work. We appreciate the incisive commentary by Richard Price and Chris Tenove on draft versions of this chapter.

Our point for present purposes is that the connection between international law and IR theory should not be viewed as a one-way street, with the various IR approaches canvassed in this volume simply being mapped onto a static, and often caricatured, version of "law." Unfortunately, that technique seems to have dominated the interdisciplinary literature, a point to which we will return. What interests us in the particular connections between constructivism and international legal theory is the possibility of genuine interplay. This interplay may be productive for legal theorists, who have often attempted to apply to international law the categories, concepts, and methods developed through the study of domestic legal systems. Insights from IR may help us correct, or at least identify, the shortcomings of this approach. For IR theorists, insights from IL can help to tease out how this specific kind of normative structure can shape actor identity and interests, and how legal norms are created, maintained, and destroyed.

Some leading international lawyers express great concern about interdisciplinary dialogue with IR. These lawyers articulate the need for legal autonomy. For them, law's goal is to shape and judge behavior, and not primarily to explain or predict behavior, which they take to be the purpose of IR theorizing. It is feared that to draw the two fields together will inevitably result in a watering down of law's ability to provide an external critique of social interaction. What is more, some international lawyers suggest that IR is so U.S. centric and bound up with projections of American power that the diversity of international society will be further undermined if international law, a bastion of "sovereign equality," is diluted by IR approaches.

We are not unsympathetic to these concerns, considering the broad sweep of IR theories. As we will see from other contributions to this volume, some IR approaches do tend to undermine what we call the "relative autonomy" of international law. Realist approaches tend to devalue the role of norms in international society, leaving little space for the operation of law. Although "classical" realists such as Hans Morgenthau saw law as a means of addressing uncertainty in international relations, all realists believe law will inevitably be trumped by power and interest calculations. Neo-liberal institutionalists, who claim great interest in the role of norms, tend to treat international law instrumentally as a signaling device or a product of effective interest projection through explicit negotiation and formal adjudication. Classical or ideological liberal theories are open to norms, but tend to project a homogenous normativity that undermines the value diversity of international society.

Constructivists are different. Although we argue that they have yet to fully exploit the mutual learning that is possible in the interaction of constructivist IR thinking and international legal theorizing, there is a promising openness to dialogue. Constructivism helps explain how international law can exist and influence behavior, and international law can help inform a richer understanding of the particular roles of different categories of norms in international society. Constructivist work has so far focused on the building of social norms through interaction and on the pathways through which they come to influence actors. Overall, too little effort has been expended in tracing out the distinctions between social and legal norms, but nothing in constructivism denigrates the distinction or resists such analysis, as some recent work has shown.

In this chapter, we will canvass the reasons underlying the emergence of constructivist thought in IR and will trace out its major preoccupations (in Section I). We will then highlight key themes in constructivist engagement with international law (in Section II), before detailing how international lawyers have deployed constructivist insights (in Section III). Next, we will canvass central themes in the interdisciplinary dialogue between constructivism and international law (in Section IV). Finally, in the Conclusion, we will evaluate the most salient insights and contributions of the literature to date and will identify gaps and productive directions for future work.

I. THE EMERGENCE OF CONSTRUCTIVIST THOUGHT IN INTERNATIONAL RELATIONS THEORY

Constructivist scholars reject the dominant assumption of contemporary IR theory that the interests of states and other actors are formed prior to social interaction. Instead, constructivists claim that identity formation is relational and occurs before, or at least concurrently with, interest formation (Hurd 2008). Interests are therefore defined both in material and nonmaterial terms. While acknowledging the importance of power and material interests, constructivists focus attention upon the role that culture, ideas, institutions, discourse, and social norms play in shaping identity and influencing behavior. For this reason, constructivist thought is especially compelling when seeking to explain the constitution of actors, institutions, and social structures, and their change over considerable periods of time (Ruggie 1986).

Constructivism emerged in IR scholarship as a reaction, as a means of incorporating learning from cognate disciplines, and as an expression of hope. It was a reaction to the powerful strains of neo-realism and neo-liberalism in American IR theory. According to John Ruggie, these two dominant strains share a commitment to neo-utilitarian explanations of behavior. For neo-utilitarians, "ideational factors, when they are examined at all, are rendered in strictly instrumental terms, useful or not to self-regarding individuals (units) in the pursuit of typically material interests, including efficiency concerns" (1998: 855). For constructivists, ideas and norms seemed to have more salience – and a different pattern of influence – than the neo-utilitarians would allow.

Contemporaneously, critical and postmodern scholars in international relations began to draw upon philosophical approaches and social theories that were influential in other social science disciplines. These included the language turn in philosophy (especially Foucault, Derrida, Rorty, and Searle) and structuration in sociology (especially Giddens). In an influential 1988 publication, Keohane grouped all adherents to critical and postmodern approaches together as "reflectivists" and contrasted them to "rationalists" (1988). However, at roughly the same time, Kratochwil and

Ruggie showed that neo-utilitarians themselves were incorporating idea-focused explanatory elements into their approaches. In particular, regime theory claimed that regimes were composed of principles, norms, rules, and decision-making procedures. Principles, norms, and rules are all ideas that must be shared, Kratochwil and Ruggie argued, and for IR to address them it had to incorporate, at least to some degree, a theory of how ideas exist and a methodology focused on interpretation (1986). Constructivists attempted to bridge the divide between neo-utilitarians and their critics and show in methodologically robust ways how ideas and identities matter in international politics.

Even in early theoretical forays, leading constructivist scholars argued that no social theory could explain everything (Wendt 1999; Fearon and Wendt 2002). Jeffrey Checkel has produced some of the most influential explorations of the relationship between rationalism and constructivism. He contrasted constructivist mechanisms, such as persuasion and learning that lead to changes in identities and interests, with rationalist factors, such as the mobilization of domestic and international pressure. Checkel then identified *conditions* that could lead to persuasion and learning rather than the strategic adoption of norms (2001). He has also suggested that there are three generic mechanisms for socialization, which include strategic calculation, as well as role-playing and moral suasion (2005).

The hope associated with constructivism derives from its emergence just as the Cold War was ending and the future of East–West relationships was being reconsidered. Neither neo-realism nor institutionalism had been able to predict or explain the relatively peaceful dissolution of the Soviet bloc. Substantial systemic change occurred without a correspondingly significant change in the distribution of capabilities. As Price and Reus-Smit argue, "[t]hough critical theorists had been making their case well before, international change proved a more effective catalyst of theoretical change than the dialectical interplay of competing theoretical perspectives" (1998: 265). These events may have assisted constructivism's rise, but we argue that constructivism is not uncritically hopeful, and that it has survived the pessimistic turn in world affairs linked to the events of September 11, 2001.

The term *constructivism* was coined by Nicholas Greenwood Onuf (1989), but some of the key tenets of the constructivist worldview were present as early as the 1950s, in the "security communities" work undertaken by Karl Deutsch and his students (1957). Constructivism also finds deep roots in broader social theory, especially in the work of Max Weber. From Weber, constructivists draw the insight that the social world is constructed by intersubjective understandings. These understandings are neither external to individuals (i.e., purely material) nor are they simply inside the heads of individuals (i.e., purely subjective). The work of John Searle, building on Weber, has also been influential. Searle argues that "facts" are not all material, instead distinguishing among brute facts, social facts, and institutional facts. For Searle "institutional facts exist only within systems of constitutive rules" (1995: 28). In a constitutive rule, a new status is assigned to something (e.g., paper becomes money). Because the material features are insufficient to guarantee success in function – paper does not declare itself to be money – "there must be *continued* collective acceptance or recognition of the validity of the assigned function; otherwise the function cannot be successfully performed" (1995: 45). In society, Searle describes a "Background" that shapes all decision making. Constructivists sometimes call this Background "shared understandings" (Ruggie 1998), "habitus" (Kratochwil 1989), or "habits" (Hopf 2010).

The work of sociologist Anthony Giddens (1984) and other "structurationists" has been extremely influential (Bhaskar 1979). For structurationists, neither agents (meaning actors within a given setting) nor social structures are logically preexistent or determining; each is constituted through interaction with the other. Both structure and agency are created in large measure by ideas, not only by material facts. As argued by Alexander Wendt, all social structures "are inseparable from the reasons and self-understandings that agents bring to their actions" (1987: 359).

One of the major theoretical controversies within constructivism today relates to the power of shared understandings to shape the perceptions and decisions of social actors. How does one understand the balance between the explanatory power of structure, including structures of ideas and discourse, and of agency? Do people retain significant agency over their own behavior, or do they tend to replicate intersubjective habits, discursive patterns, or preexisting practices? Commonly in the literature, disagreements over these questions are phrased in terms of competing "logics." At first, the contrast was made, borrowing from the work of March and Olsen (1998: 952), between logics of consequences (instrumentalism) and appropriateness (morality and ethics). More recently, scholars have described logics of arguing (rational oppositional discourse) (Risse 2000), of practicality (practice) (Pouliot 2008), of purposive role-playing (Checkel 2005), of habit (unreflective action) (Hopf 2010), and of emotion (Mercer 2010). The logic of arguing is one example of constructivist work that draws on the thinking of Jürgen Habermas. Constructivists have used Habermas' concepts of "communicative action" and "discourse ethics" to test the existence of genuine persuasion and moral decision-making in international politics (see Deitelhoff and Müller 2005; Price 2008).

Although early contributions to constructivist thought focused primarily on the evolution of intersubjective understandings shaped by ideas, recent work has begun to emphasize more strongly the role of practice, what actors actually do. Early constructivist thinkers suggested that social structures cannot exist without instantiation in practices, but they did not explain what counts as practice or how we should study such practices (Wendt 1994). They suggested only that practice should encompass both material acts and rhetorical commitments (Onuf 1982; Kratochwil 1989). The focus on practice was influenced by American philosophical pragmatism (Dewey 1988; Rorty 1989) and by the work of social theorist Pierre Bourdieu, who argued against rational choice theory, suggesting instead that social agents act through implicit practical logic – a practical sense (1977). Bourdieu's insights have been pursued most systematically by Emanuel Adler, who focuses attention on "communities of practice" (2005: 15–27), furthering the work of social learning theorists Jean Lave and Etienne Wenger (Wenger 1998). For Adler, people's understandings of the world and of themselves are produced and reproduced through continuous interactions and negotiation of meanings (2005: 52–53; Adler and Pouliot 2011). Inherent in this account is the proposition that it is through their participation in social practice that actors generate and maintain collective understandings (Adler 2005: 55–56).

Constructivists do not argue that culture, ideas, shared knowledge, and social norms operate as direct causes of action. Rather, social structures constrain, enable, and constitute actors in their choices, and thus help to shape world politics (Ruggie 1998: 875). The resistance to a direct "causal" explanation of behavior is one of the reasons that constructivists and other IR theorists sometimes engage in dialogues of the deaf. For realists and rational institutionalists, "cause" and hence prediction are the very points of theorizing. But constructivists are more inclined to describe social interactions that shape, mold, or constrain choice, rather than cause action. How does this shaping take place? The clearest attempts to address the "how" questions are found, not in the theory of constructivism, but in empirical work grounded in constructivist predispositions. Martha Finnemore and Kathryn Sikkink provide a thorough catalogue of first-generation constructivist explanations of normative influence, derived from a wide variety of empirical studies (1998: 892–912). More recent work by Autesserre (2009), Deitelhoff (2009), and Orchard (2010) furthers the attempt to show how norms evolve and gain traction. Some constructivist empiricists have focused on what they call the "norm cascade," when norm entrepreneurs succeed in promoting normative evolution, and adoption reaches a "tipping point" at which norms become widely accepted and fully socialized (Finnemore and Sikkink 1998). Others focus on how norms can "entrap" actors (Keck and Sikkink 1998). Most recently, a new generation of empiricists has explored the constructivist political economy, examining cases that reveal how ideas and identities shape the global economy (Hall 2008; Weaver 2008; Abdelal, Blyth, and Parsons 2010).

An interesting substrain of "critical constructivism" has emerged in recent years. Some constructivists have argued that constructivism is inherently "critical" because it shares with critical social theory a rejection of positivist epistemology and value-neutral theorizing (Price and Reus-Smit 1998). Critical constructivists like Adriana Sinclair remain interested in the role of ideas and culture in shaping identity and behavior, but they suggest that mainstream constructivism is too focused on a narrative of liberal progress and too committed to agency, ignoring the structures of power that inhibit challenges to the status quo (Sinclair 2010). Kurki and Sinclair further argue that much constructivist research ignores these structures of power because of its focus on discourse, and its de-emphasis of material resources and unspoken assumptions (2010). A perceived constructivist failure to attend to structures of power has also prompted work by Amitav Acharya on norm localization. Acharya argues that the conventional approach to norm diffusion treats Western norms as cosmopolitan and universal, and fails to recognize how local actors actively reconstruct foreign ideas, creating greater congruence with local beliefs and practices (2004; 2011). Antje Wiener, too, draws on critical constructivism to show that norms are not stable in their interpretation and use, but rather evolve through "interaction in context." Hence, she argues, international norms are inevitably contested and may acquire different meanings in different national settings (2008).

In sum, there is vibrant debate within constructivism, with competing understandings of agency, structure, logics of interaction, areas of explanatory advantage, and normative implications. Constructivist research has therefore shifted its focus from skirmishes with rationalist approaches to explaining social phenomena and addressing its internal diversity.[1]

II. CONSTRUCTIVIST SCHOLARSHIP AND INTERNATIONAL LAW

Constructivism, and its sophisticated understanding of norms, makes possible a sociologically rich and historically grounded understanding of international law. But such insights have been hampered to some extent by narrow understandings of law itself. In the 1990s, two of the most influential contributors to the emergent constructivist approach to IR focused attention on international law. Nicholas Onuf and Friedrich Kratochwil each posited an important role for international law in helping to construct the identities of sovereign states and in shaping their behavior. Yet, even such sympathetic readers of international law as Kratochwil and Onuf failed to allow full scope for the influence of law because they were constrained by their implicit adoption of the framework of analytical positivism.

In brief, Onuf argued that discourse and the social world are mutually constituted. Onuf defined "rules" as general, prescriptive statements. Speech acts become rules through repetition and social acceptance over time; in other words, through "practice." Practices are not merely the application of preexisting rules; they are language and acts that take place in awareness of and reflecting on rules (Onuf 1989). Practices can therefore change rules, and individuals have significant capacity to shape the rules that make up their world, at least within national societies. For Onuf, the operation of law in international society was not straightforward. When Onuf applied his three criteria of "lawness" – formalization of rules, the institutionalization of external supports for rules, and the presence of enforcement officers – international law was found wanting.

Kratochwil was primarily interested in examining how norms and rules function to shape the decisions of actors in international society. He argued that action is

---

[1] Note that a recent survey by the Teaching, Research, and International Policy (TRIP) project found that nearly half (48 percent) of U.S. IR scholars reported that they use either a "constructivist" or "both rationalist and constructivist" approaches. Rates were higher still among IR scholars in Australia, Canada, and the United Kingdom.

generally rule governed. Rules and norms help to constitute individual autonomy by serving to solve problems. They "simplify choice-situations by drawing attention to factors which an actor has to take into account" (1989: 72). But rules and norms are not merely "guidance devices." They are tools to pursue goals, to communicate, and to construct claims. Hence, Kratochwil's focus on deliberative processes and interpretation (1989).

For Kratochwil, law is defined by its particular process of reasoning, which is highly dependent on the use of analogy. He criticized most IR accounts of law for undervaluing, or even ignoring, the process of argumentation that produces legal decisions. International law, in Kratochwil's schema, is quite different from domestic law. Law in international society exists "simply by virtue of its role in defining the game of international relations. It informs the respective decision makers about the nature of their interaction and determines who is an actor; it sets the steps necessary to insure the validity of their official acts and assigns weight and priority to different claims" (1989: 251). Crucially, Kratochwil argued that international legal process is inextricably linked to politics. Therefore, the particular style of legal reasoning that pertains in domestic systems, marked in his view by impartiality, cannot exist in international society.

It may be surprising to suggest that Onuf and Kratochwil's contributions to constructivism and law were shaped by an unconscious positivism, as both explicitly defined their positions in opposition to certain strands of the positivist tradition. Onuf rejected the state positivism of Hans Kelsen and the command paradigm of John Austin, preferring a view of law that treats rules as affected by principled norm use and rhetorical acceptance (1985: 395). Similarly, Kratochwil disputed any conception of law derived simply from the "imposition of superior will" (1989: 142). Further, he denied the identity between law and sanction, and between law and a hierarchical rule system (1989: 186). He also accepted that "formality" is not an appropriate test of the existence or nonexistence of law (1989: 200–01).

In different ways, both Onuf and Kratochwil revert to the assumption that law can only be understood in hierarchical forms associated with domestic legal systems. Kratochwil's is the simpler case. Despite his commitment to a practice-focused, discursive understanding of rules, for Kratochwil, the ideal of rhetorical persuasion was the adversarial process of court adjudication, an ideal that will rarely be realized in the international milieu, where compulsory adjudicative jurisdiction is highly limited (1989: 209, 230).

Onuf's positivist bias in reading international law is more pervasive than is Kratochwil's. Onuf attempted to root the distinctiveness of legal rules in aspects of the rules themselves, but more important in the system that generates the rules. Relying expressly on H. L. A. Hart, Onuf suggested that law is a hierarchical ordering system. Primary rules rely on the existence of secondary rules, which in turn rely on the "validating rule," which in the case of international law is simply "custom" (1982: 10–11). With this hierarchical understanding, Onuf came close to recognizing a command paradigm of law (despite his purported rejection of Austin), because he thought legal rules were defined by their "performative sufficiency" (Onuf 1985: 407–08). Law, then, is inherently "declaratory," the voice of authority speaking to the subject, whose role is to obey.

Ultimately, for both Kratochwil and Onuf, law is a unidirectional imposition of authority (implicit judge or implicit rule of recognition). They are not alone. Indeed, more than two decades after they offered their defining contributions, Kratochwil and Onuf present two of the most nuanced, instructive, and fully developed understandings of international law that one will find in the contemporary IR literature. More often, even IR scholars who stress the normative influences in international politics will articulate the potential interest of international law in ways that adopt an almost caricatured version of the positivist view of legal normativity (Bull 1977; Arend 1999). Most constructivist scholars have been preoccupied with norms and institutions but have not tried to investigate whether there is anything distinctive about *legal* norms and institutions (Barnett 1997). Although Martha Finnemore threw down the gauntlet directly in "Are Legal Norms Distinctive?" (2000), she merely traced out various possible responses, suggesting that useful research questions were buried under the umbrella question.

Christian Reus-Smit is one of the few constructivists who took up the challenge (2004). Starting from the proposition that international politics and international law are mutually constitutive, he nonetheless argues that international political actors behave as if there is a distinctly legal realm (p. 37). This realm is characterized by an institutionally autonomous, distinctive discourse that draws on a preexisting set of norms and practices of justification and that delegitimizes the raw pursuit of power and self-interest (p. 38). Reus-Smit rightly argues that, to understand the distinctiveness of law, it is crucial to understand its obligatory character. The obligatory effect of legal norms is rooted in the legal system's legitimacy as a social institution (p. 42). In turn, the legitimacy of the international legal system is grounded in the deep constitutional structure of modern international society, which is bound up in "the prevailing liberal conception of legitimate statehood and attendant norms of procedural justice" (p. 43).

While describing a "legal realm" with some institutional autonomy, Reus-Smit, and the contributors to his edited volume (2004), nevertheless perceive a fluidity between this legal realm and international politics. Not only do international politics and international law constitute and interpenetrate one another, actors move back and forth between legal and nonlegal action and justification to advance their projects. Reus-Smit's framework is promising, but it remains underspecified. As he admits, it is not a theory of international law but a suggestion of a "set of relationships between dimensions of international social life" (pp. 14–15).

With a few exceptions, then, constructivists have assumed a concept of law that is largely hierarchical and "authority" based. For this reason, many constructivists still tend to see law as a set of posited requirements, created through state institutions or with the consent of states. For example, Thomas Risse and Kathryn Sikkink have explored in detail how international human rights norms evolve and socialize actors, particularly through "internalization" into the domestic sphere. Law is part of this dynamic, but Risse and Sikkink seem to assume that "law" comes into play when governments ratify relevant treaties and enshrine them in domestic law (1999: 29). What is more, in much constructivist scholarship, law is merely acknowledged as one type of social norm, and the focus is on how it "works" in society. For example, Ian Hurd has suggested that legal norms, like other types of norms, are constraining for states, but only through "socialization"; they are also "enabling" in that states are "strategic calculators that manipulate" norms (2007: 209). However, he does not appear to challenge the basic proposition that international law consists in rules that flow from formal sources of law, such as custom and United Nations Charter rules (2011). Overall, although some constructivists betray a sense that law has a special quality and that it may have a particular ability to convince, little extended analysis has yet been pursued as to how that ability is created or derived. In a response to a rationalist and materialist account of the "legalization of world affairs" (Abbott *et al.* 2000), Finnemore and Toope presented a brief description of how one might conceptualize legal obligation from a constructivist perspective, but this contribution was little more than a starting point (2001).

Although most constructivists have presented law as benign and as the endpoint in normative development, some critical constructivists have challenged this portrayal. For example, Adriana Sinclair emphasizes the need to develop a critical understanding of law and not merely to treat law as the end of a continuum from social norms to soft law to hard law. Sinclair suggests that scholars who assume that law is the positive endpoint of normative development have adopted a false "common sense idea of law" in which legal norms are imagined to be determinate, coherent, and – once enacted – separate from politics and power relations (2010; 2011). Sinclair argues specifically that Onuf and Kratochwil share three flaws in their approach to law. First, they claim that the success or failure of proposed norms depends on their fit with the existing context (i.e., with society). They therefore legitimize the status quo, even if unjust. Second, they emphasize discursive expressions and understanding of norms and rules, and thereby sideline deep-seated assumptions or practices that support existing power relations. Third, they assume that participation in the social determination of norms resembles a conversation among equals. In doing so, they overestimate *agency*, the possibility for individuals to contest and change shared understandings. Sinclair concludes that Onuf and Kratochwil offer "a picture of the world as viewed by its elite" (2010).

Sinclair's criticisms of the "common sense" approach to law are drawn from well-developed critical traditions in legal theory. However, Sinclair does not engage deeply with scholars of *international* legal theory who have considered the tension between normativity and realism – or "utopia and apology," in the powerful phrasing of Martti Koskenniemi (2005). Although Sinclair's work challenges constructivist scholars to reassess their approach to international law, she has not yet developed her own account of what international law is or how legal obligation works.

III. INTERNATIONAL LAW SCHOLARSHIP AND CONSTRUCTIVISM

Many international lawyers appear to have both rationalist and constructivist intuitions. That is, they seem to take for granted that interests and power predominate in shaping state conduct and that international law will often yield when states pursue the logic of consequences. At the same time, perhaps by professional disposition, international lawyers tend to assume that international law "matters" and that, following a logic of appropriateness, states and other international actors are guided by legal norms as well as interests. Thus, although international lawyers do not delve into theoretical debates that question the relative importance of norms and interests, they appear to be predisposed toward the integration of rationalist and normative processes that Abbott and Snidal insist is needed for a "more sophisticated generation of IR-IL scholarship" (2013).

Constructivism has made important contributions to understanding the operation of international law by showing how norms may constitute or even trump interests. Indeed, constructivism highlights that legal norms can actually help create specific categories of actors, such as refugees, or entities like international financial institutions (Barnett and Finnemore 2004).[2] However, its most important contributions arguably rest in revealing the centrality of social interaction and of international legal practices in making and giving effect to international law. Relatively few international lawyers have taken advantage of this contribution, perhaps because constructivism is a poor fit for those who see the legal status of a norm as exclusively connected to its provenance from a formal source. After all, constructivism can speak to international lawyers only to the extent that they are prepared to understand legal norms as social norms, and so as constituted and powered primarily by social practices.

Explicit engagement by international lawyers with constructivist insights is a relatively recent phenomenon. But international lawyers have long undertaken work that resonates with constructivist intuitions, even if this work was not self-consciously "constructivist" but rather drew on compatible social science insights, running parallel to constructivism's antecedents in sociology, social psychology, or pragmatist philosophy.

A. *Early Points of Convergence of International Law Scholarship and Constructivism*

An early stream of international law theory whose social science underpinnings connect to constructivism was the "New Haven School," pioneered by Harold Lasswell

---

[2] We thank Chris Tenove for reminding us of this point.

and Myres McDougal (1966). The New Haven School had roots in American legal realism of the early twentieth century, which represented the first sustained effort to integrate social science insights and methodology into law (Tipson 1973–74: 542; Karber 1990: 192). McDougal and Lasswell were also influenced by John Dewey and George Mead, both of whom were prominent figures in the pragmatist school that emerged at the University of Chicago during Lasswell's tenure as a student there (Tipson 1973–74: 539). In developing their "world public order" framework, McDougal and Lasswell built on the proposition that norms typically grow from the interaction of various actors and increasingly fixed patterns of expectations about appropriate behavior. McDougal and Michael Reisman later developed a model that envisaged international law-making as a continuous communicative process (1980). This model aimed to show how normative expectations are maintained and changed through "communication about the authority and credible control intentions of those whose support is needed for the norms' efficacy" (Reisman 1981: 113). The New Haven School's description of legal expectations as emerging from continuing processes of authoritative decision making provided a groundbreaking account of the foundations of international law. However, the New Haven School has not been especially focused on distinguishing among material capabilities, interests, and normativity. It has also been frankly instrumentalist, understanding international law as serving certain policy purposes, notably the promotion of "human dignity" (Toope 1990).

The American legal process school, which also has roots in legal realism, rose to prominence in the 1950s and 1960s (Hart and Sacks 1994). It spawned an international legal process school that examined how international law, through formal and informal processes of decision-making and justification, enables, constrains, and influences international actors (O'Connell 1999). One of the most prominent outgrowths of this perspective on international law was Abram Chayes and Antonia Handler Chayes' "managerial" account of compliance with international law (1995). The parallels between this account and contemporary constructivist explanations of state conduct are evident in managerialism's emphasis on continuous processes of argument and persuasion – "justificatory discourse" that ultimately "jawbones" states into compliance (1995: 25–26). International law is said to frame that discourse because states' explanations for their conduct tend to be more compelling when in conformity with a legal rule and because "good legal argument can generally be distinguished from bad" (1995: 119). The Chayesean explanation of compliance, then, also resonates with the constructivist notion of the logic of appropriateness (Raustiala and Slaughter 2002: 548). But the managerial account only goes so far in teasing out the distinctive influence of legal norms. It neither details *how* good legal argument is distinguished from bad, nor does it explain how treaty parties' "general sense of obligation to comply with a legally binding prescription" (Chayes and Chayes 1995: 110), upon which the Chayesean framework rests, is generated. Indeed, managerialism ultimately rests on a rationalist logic of consequences. States are amenable to managerial strategies due to their growing interdependence and enmeshment in a "complex web of international arrangements" (p. 27). Simply put, it is in their interest to maintain orderly international relations and to remain respected and influential players.

Thomas Franck, in his work on legitimacy, attempted to explain how international law influences international actors. Although Franck's account of the "compliance pull" exerted by legitimate rules did not rely on IR theory (1990: 26), it certainly resonates with constructivism. Franck's theory sets itself apart by identifying specific qualities in law itself (rather than factors external to law) that account for compliance, thereby also highlighting features that distinguish law's influence from that of other social norms. According to Franck, legitimate legal rules have four distinctive traits: determinacy (or clarity), symbolic validation (the communication of authority through ritual or stable practice), coherence (or consistency with other rules), and adherence (vertical nexus of a rule to a pyramid of secondary rules) (1995: 30–46). Legitimacy, then, is something that can be cultivated internally, within legal rules. Franck's theory remains explicitly positivist, emphasizing state consent and relying upon a rule of recognition to explain the source of international legal obligation. His account of international law and legal legitimacy nonetheless contains an important intersubjective anchor point. In his later work, Franck was most explicit that the rule of recognition was the general belief in the binding effect of law and, hence, was a "social construct" (2006: 91).

Harold Koh's transnational legal process theory also focuses on the dynamics that promote compliance with international law. For Koh, the key to explaining why states obey international law lies in the internalization of international norms into the domestic sphere (1997: 2603). Koh identifies several stages in the internalization process. First, states, international organizations, nongovernmental organizations (NGOs), business entities, and other norm entrepreneurs provoke interactions with one another in an international arena (1996: 184). These interactions "force an interpretation or enunciation of the global norm applicable to the situation" (1997: 2646) and eventually produce a legal rule that guides future interactions. According to Koh, "repeated participation in the process will help to reconstitute the interests and even the identities of the participants in the process" (1997: 2646). Koh distinguishes social (the legitimacy of a norm results in widespread obedience), political (elites adopt an international norm as government policy), and legal (incorporation of the norm into the domestic legal system) internalization processes (1997: 2656–57).

Koh's framework reinforces some of the central constructivist claims about international norms, both in its focus on repeated interactions and its explicit sensitivity to "identity" (1997: 2646). His account of norm internalization also overlaps with the work on norm entrepreneurship and norm cycles undertaken by constructivist IR scholars such as Finnemore and Sikkink. Koh's central contribution to the literature has been his effort to look beyond a monolithic understanding of the state and to identify the processes that "bring international law home" (1998*a*). At the same time, his *transnational* legal process framework highlights the involvement of both states and non-state actors in promoting norms and compliance.

Koh justifiably critiques constructivist approaches to international law that neglect the specific pathways through which international norms shape the identity of states (2005: 977). However, although Koh has advanced a detailed account of the salient dynamics, it is not clear that his empirical examples fully support his sweeping claims regarding the purchase of transnational legal process. Although his case studies have been drawn primarily from the human rights field, Koh asserts that transnational legal process can promote compliance with international legal rules "of any kind" (1998*b*: 1399, 1401). He does not specify the circumstances under which certain types of norms may be internalized or whether international norms are more or less likely to persuade actors in different types of states (Hathaway 2002: 1962).

In any case, we suggest that it is not enough to examine, as legal process scholars tend to do, "the social mechanisms that help *make* international law matter" (Koh 2005: 977). Some of the potential of a constructivist approach to international law is lost unless we pay attention to both legal process *and* norm properties.

B. *Explicitly Constructivist Accounts of International Law*

Over the last decade, some international law scholars have engaged in explicitly interdisciplinary work, drawing on constructivist theory to illuminate issues in international law. Some of this work is informed by sociological theory; other work is grounded in IR theory.

Ian Johnstone's examination of the role of legal argumentation in international affairs draws on Habermas' theory of communicative action and on Stanley Fish's concept of interpretive community (2011: 4, 35). According to Johnstone, the logic of communicative action is related to the constructivist logic of appropriateness, but assumes that what is appropriate is not fixed but determined through deliberation. Legal discourse, suggests Johnstone, is a "distinctly powerful form of argumentation" that has a manifest impact on state conduct (2011: 3). He ascribes this influence to the nature of legal argumentation and the existence of interpretive communities that distinguish good arguments from unpersuasive claims (2011: 33). Johnstone also sees "justificatory discourse" as an important aspect of legal discourse (p. 6). He augments the Chaysean account by showing that the reasons why states feel compelled to provide legal justifications for their actions are both interest and identity related. States do value the longer term cooperation and predictability that is promoted by appearing to be law-abiding. But their participation in international regimes also leads them to develop a sense of obligation: law becomes internalized or habit. At the very least, posits Johnstone, the persuasive burden rests on those actors who seek to deviate from collective understandings of the law (2011: 33–34). Furthermore, since legal discourse is an intersubjective practice that operates on the basis of common understandings about the meaning of relevant rules, interpretive communities play an important role in maintaining and shifting legal rules (p. 40).

Johnstone's most important contribution to constructivist engagement with international law is his finely grained explanation of how legal discourse comes to be influential. However, like Koh and the Chayeses, he focuses on the *process* of legal justification and neglects the distinctiveness of law itself, which flows in important part from the *properties* of legal norms. These properties, arguably, account for the specificity of legal argumentation and legal practice. Johnstone hints at this dimension when he suggests that "international legal discourse is a highly specialized form of argumentation, the standard techniques of which are widely recognized" (p. 21). But he asserts rather than explains law's distinctiveness.

Ryan Goodman and Derek Jinks have articulated a "state socialization" framework that resonates with constructivism but is anchored primarily in sociology rather than IR theory. Goodman and Jinks argue that states' identities, interests, or organizational structures are all shaped in part by global regimes (2003: 1752). Although Goodman and Jinks note that debates about regime design "inadequately attend to the ways in which law influences state behavior," their focus is on "the social mechanisms of law's influence" (2005: 983). They do not inquire into the distinctive nature and effects of law itself.

Goodman and Jinks argue that neither persuasion nor coercion fully explain the influence of international norms and regimes. They posit that "acculturation" is an important third mechanism for bringing about state conformity with international norms (2004). This approach seems to run parallel to the work of constructivists on socialization and norm internalization (Finnemore and Sikkink 1998; Checkel 2005). Goodman and Jinks distinguish acculturation from coercion by arguing that the latter involves social sanctions, which entail material costs, whereas the former only entails social costs (2004: 645). The social pressure that drives acculturation also serves to distinguish it from persuasion, which involves social learning, and hence acculturation produces "outward conformity . . . without private acceptance" (2004: 643).

Because acculturation is driven by social pressure rather than persuasion, it does not seem central to Goodman and Jinks' account whether the "culture" into which actors are socialized involves legal norms. They note that "[a]cculturation depends less on the properties of the rule than on the properties of the relationship of the actor to the community" (2004: 643). Goodman and Jinks' approach, then, appears to assume that actors are motivated by social costs and benefits rather than a sense of legal obligation.

Moshe Hirsch also examines international law from a sociological standpoint (2005). His "symbolic-interactionist" account resonates with many core assumptions in constructivism. Its emphasis is firmly on the role of individuals in society; social structures and, indeed, society itself are constituted and shaped by interactions among individuals. Over time, patterns of interaction emerge, as do rules that govern social interaction (2005: 902). However, although the stability of social interactions rests on shared understandings of certain background norms, the meanings assigned to social patterns and rules will also remain contested and negotiated (2005: 903). Hence, for Hirsch, international law is not composed of fully autonomous, external rules to which actors may or may not adhere. Rather, international law is generated through international social interaction, and actors' conduct is influenced by the meanings they attribute to the resultant patterns within international institutions or individual states (2005: 921–23). Hirsch is not concerned with distinguishing the influence of legal norms from that of other social norms. But he does stress that the standard, formal conception of international law is insufficient to understand normative change in international society (2005: 938).

A complementary, interactional account has been articulated by Jutta Brunnée and Stephen Toope. Their work is explicitly interdisciplinary, and it aims to tackle head-on the challenge of identifying the distinctive features of international legal norms. By drawing together insights from constructivism and the legal theory of Lon Fuller, Brunnée and Toope have developed a comprehensive theory of international legal obligation (2000; 2010; 2011a, c). First, building on constructivist insights, their theory assumes that legal norms can only arise in the context of social norms based on shared understandings. Second, what distinguishes law from other types of social ordering is not form, but adherence to specific criteria of legality posited by Fuller: generality, promulgation, nonretroactivity, clarity, noncontradiction, not asking the impossible, constancy, and congruence between rules and official action (Fuller 1969: 39, 46–90). When norm creation meets these criteria, and when there exists what Brunnée and Toope call a "practice of legality" (norm application that also satisfies the legality requirements), actors can pursue their purposes and organize their interactions through law. These features and practices of legality are crucial to generating a distinctive legal legitimacy and a sense of commitment – "fidelity" in Fuller's terms – among those to whom law is addressed. Together, they create legal obligation (Brunnée and Toope 2010: 20–33).

Fuller's work was focused on domestic law, and he may even have been skeptical that international society was sufficiently developed to enable a rule of law (Knop 2010: 61). Nonetheless, by directing our attention to markers of legality that are internal to law, Fuller's theory provides an illuminating perspective on international law. It reveals that the formal and hierarchical manifestations that are generally associated with domestic law, such as tests of "validity" or centralized enforcement, do not suffice to characterize "law," whether domestic or international, and may not actually be required (Fuller 1969). Fuller's work shows that law does not depend on hierarchy between law-makers and subjects of law, but on reciprocity between the participants in a legal system. For Brunnée and Toope, "reciprocity" is central to understanding the nature of legal obligation and hence to the interactional account of international law. It encapsulates the proposition that law is not a one-way street, but requires that actors collaborate to build shared understandings and uphold a practice of legality (Brunnée and Toope 2010: 33–42).

The interactional framework instructs, then, that the distinctiveness of law rests not in form or in enforcement but in the creation and effects of legal obligation. But Brunnée and Toope do not dismiss state consent, "sources" of international law, the creation of courts and tribunals, or better enforcement mechanisms as unimportant. Rather, they argue that these elements must be understood in the broader context of the international legal enterprise, so as to better appreciate the roles they play, their potential, and their limitations. The interactional framework also reveals that building and maintaining the reciprocity that grounds legal obligation requires sustained effort. Their work is closely tied to the logic of practice articulated by Adler and other constructivists. Whether a treaty is adopted or brought into force, when a case is decided by an international court, or when the Security Council enforces a resolution through military force – in Brunnée and Toope's constructivist framework, each of these examples represents but a step in the continuing interactions that make, remake, or unmake international law.

IV. KEY THEMES IN THE ENGAGEMENT BETWEEN CONSTRUCTIVISM AND INTERNATIONAL LAW (AND VICE VERSA)

A striking feature of the growing body of constructivist scholarship on international law – or international law scholarship that resonates with constructivism – is the lack of attention to how legal norms (as opposed to norms more broadly speaking) are generated and the absence of an articulated theory of law itself. Instead, most of this scholarship focuses on processes and practices of actors' engagement with international law. For example, among the international law scholars surveyed in the preceding section, adherents to the New Haven School, Chayes and Chayes, Koh, Johnstone, and Goodman and Jinks focus almost exclusively on processes of legal interaction. What is surprising is that, like many of their constructivist colleagues in IR, all of the above-mentioned international lawyers, except the members of the New Haven School, rely on an unarticulated, purely formal, and generally hierarchical concept of international law. Notwithstanding their interest in argumentative, interpretative, or justificatory practices, for these authors, law itself is not primarily a "practice" nor is it generated by practices. Rather, law is the "product" of formal sources, such as custom and treaty, a product that is then implemented through legal practice.[3] This separation of practice from the underlying concept of law is found even in the work of IR scholars or legal scholars who explicitly draw on

---

[3] We draw here on the helpful distinction between "law as practice" and "law as product" that has been articulated by the legal philosopher Wibren van der Burgh in "Two Models of Law and Morality," *Associations*, Vol. 3 (1999), p. 61; and "Essentially Ambiguous Concepts and the Fuller-Hart-Dworkin Debate," *Archives for Philosophy of Law and Social Philosophy*, Vol. 95 (2009), p. 305.

constructivism (Risse and Sikkink 1999; Goodman and Jinks 2004; Hurd 2011; John-stone 2011). Conceptually, it seems difficult to reconcile constructivism's premise of the *interplay* between actors and norms or institutions with the proposition that the validity of law can be separated from social practice.[4] And yet, in much of this scholarship, legal norms are assumed to operate like social norms, while it appears that "law" itself is assumed to be a formal category rather than a social construct.

The common assumption that "law" is identified through formal validity criteria likely accounts for the fact that very few scholars explore the properties that might distinguish legal norms from other norms. Franck's concept of legitimacy does focus on norm properties, without, however, engaging in any detail with legal processes. Furthermore, Franck did not view his legitimacy factors as constitutive of law but as something that could be promoted in otherwise valid rules to enhance their compliance pull. Brunnée and Toope's international law framework is the only one that emphasizes both norm properties and legal practices and sees them, in keeping with their constructivist premises, as inextricably linked to one another. By tracing out distinctive features of legality, they can conceive of international law as a social practice while also positing its relative autonomy from politics (2011*b*: 354).

When considered against the backdrop of this pattern, it also becomes easier to appreciate why the bulk of the scholarship explored in this chapter is preoccupied with compliance issues. After all, if the category of law itself is taken for granted, there is little reason for engagement with underlying questions of what law is and how it may be distinctive from other forms of social normativity. Hence, relatively little direct attention is paid to how actors turn social norms into law. Of course, as our survey of the salient literature has illustrated, constructivists are interested in the emergence of international norms in general. And yet, when it comes to international law, even the emergence of customary law has received relatively little close attention (Price 2004) – which is odd, given its strong connection to practice. To be fair, even fewer international lawyers have mined constructivism to shed light on customary law. Instead, much of the literature focuses on why existing legal rules do or do not have compliance pull, or on the social processes (argumentation, interpretation, justification, social pressure) through which law comes to matter or can be promoted by various actors. Some of the frameworks considered in this chapter appear to imply a continuous interplay between law-making, implementation, and compliance. But few are explicit that, seen through a constructivist lens, compliance promotion and, indeed, compliance itself, cannot be separated from the processes that create, maintain, reshape, or even destroy international law.

In terms of subject matter, most of the work seeking to draw together the insights of constructivism and international legal theory has focused on examples drawn from

---

4 Wiener (2008: 65, 124) seeks to address this issue by distinguishing formal validity, social recognition, and cultural validation. And see Reus-Smit (2004), explaining how the mutual constitution of law and politics can be reconciled with international law's institutional autonomy.

international environmental law (Nagtzaam 2009; Akhtarkhavari 2010; Brunnée and Toope 2010; Methmann 2010; Stevenson 2011), human rights (Risse and Sikkink 1999; Lutz and Sikkink 2001*a*, *b*; Krebs and Jackson 2007; Walldorf 2010), international criminal law (Deitelhoff 2009; Sagan 2010), and discussions of the role of international institutions, especially courts (Johnston 2001; Barnett and Finnemore 2004; Deitelhoff 2009; Avant, Finnemore, and Sell 2010). This has led some critics to suggest that constructivist-legal interdisciplinary work is overly optimistic, even idealist. We disagree.

The scholarly focus on the above-mentioned fields should not be surprising, for they happen to be areas that, during the last part of the twentieth century and the beginning of the twenty-first, saw extraordinary normative evolution. For people interested in the social construction of norms, including legal norms, it would be foolish not to examine the dramatic changes in human rights after World War II or the explosion of international environmental law after the Brundtland Report. In any event, a number of interdisciplinary studies have focused on international security, the use of force, and arms control (Price 1995; Gheciu 2005; Adler 2008; Heinze 2011), which are hardly fields that engender naïve optimism. It is true that scholars of constructivism and international law should do more work in economic law and trade law, to show how their approaches do or do not yield helpful perspectives in areas that seem so clearly interest and not norm driven. However, recent empirical work on the role of international institutions in the context of international political economy and international finance has begun to fill this gap (Blyth 2002; Abdelal 2007; Hall 2008; Abdelal, Blyth, and Parsons 2010).

What is more, a constructivist analysis can show how power relations and even violence can be hidden or justified by new norms, including new legal norms. As we have suggested, a growing group of "critical" constructivists argues that constructivism should further develop such an analysis, even though constructivist research has not focused deeply on this issue so far. Our own work has revealed that constructivist analysis can lead to conclusions that are far from optimistic, even in areas where we, as international lawyers, would very much want to show normative progress. For example, we show how continual discursive challenges and state noncompliance has undermined the *jus cogens* norm prohibiting torture (Brunnée and Toope 2010).

V. CONCLUSION: CONTRIBUTIONS, GAPS, AND FUTURE DIRECTIONS

The most important contributions of constructivist scholarship, in both IR and IL, are related to the insights it offers into the social processes that drive the creation and operation of international law. At the most general level, constructivist scholarship has provided alternative and richer explanations of behavior than neo-utilitarian models. More specifically, because of its focus on discursive and other practices, constructivism is able to speak about legal reasoning and legal justification, and their relationship to legitimacy, in a way that other IR approaches cannot. Hence, constructivist scholarship has added greatly to our understanding of compliance with international law. Some strands in the growing body of constructivist work have laid the foundations for deeper engagement with the distinctiveness of law itself. Beyond opening up avenues for exploring the social dynamics that might produce and maintain a sense of legal obligation, some scholars have begun to tease out the markers of legal legitimacy and legality. Finally, through its emphasis on the intersubjective nature of shared understandings, norms, and practices, constructivism provides new explanations for the expanding category of "participants" that international law has seen over the last fifty years or so.

We have already alluded to some of the main gaps in the current literature. Most notably, much of the existing constructivist scholarship on international law continues to employ, by default, an uncritical positivist account of international law. As we suggested in the preceding section, although some scholars have sought to fill this particular gap, the vast majority of the literature does not connect the constructivist emphasis on social processes to the concept of international law itself. As a result, constructivist insight into distinctions between legal and nonlegal international norms remains undeveloped. Further, although constructivism has the potential to illuminate how various non-state actors can help shape international law and promote compliance with it, much more work is needed to tease out the varying roles played by states and other actors. This latter observation points to a broader gap in constructivist scholarship on international law. As we outlined in the preceding section, constructivist scholarship has moved beyond meta-theory to explorations of specific issue areas and application of theoretical insights to concrete case studies. However, more systematic empirical work remains to be done to bolster constructivist claims concerning the emergence of shared understandings, the emergence and functioning of legal regimes, and the impact of factors such as legitimacy and legality.

Our observations about gaps in the existing scholarship lead directly to a number of suggestions for a future research agenda. First, at the most basic level, even after some fifteen years of engagement between the two disciplines, more work is required to inform international lawyers about normative or ideas-centered approaches in IR that might shed light on the unique role of international law. Relatively few IL scholars have yet taken up the insights offered by constructivism, and it is unknown whether constructivist theory has influenced the practice of international law. Realist and utilitarian accounts of international society seem to be assumed by many international lawyers, even though they are deeply uncongenial to law. At the same time, IR scholars need to delve more deeply into theories of international law that challenge the dominant positivist account. This dominant account tends to reinforce rationalist assumptions about the role and potential of law in international society, and to undercut constructivist claims concerning the emergence and influence of international norms.

Second, constructivist IR scholars and legal scholars alike must recognize and grapple with the apparent disconnect between constructivist social theory and an implicit positivist legal theory, which assumes a strictly formal, generally hierarchical concept of legal validity. To begin to address this issue, legal scholars and IR scholars need to be more explicit about the concept of law that underpins their work. We believe that many fundamental insights into international law can be gained if interdisciplinary scholarship pursues this path. For example, constructivism can help provide a more coherent account of customary international law, especially the concepts of *opinio juris* and *jus cogens*, than other IR theories and even than international law itself.

A third item for a future research agenda concerns the need to focus more attention on empirical studies that illustrate the distinctiveness of law (according to whatever concept of law a given author adopts) and that explore how that distinctiveness plays out in specific contexts and issue areas. We highlighted some of the issue areas and conceptual questions that warrant increased empirical inquiry.

Fourth, constructivism can contribute to a more integrated exploration of compliance with international law. In particular, it can help to build a richer understanding of the interplay between material power and interests on the one hand, and identity, culture, and norms on the other. Steven Ratner's recent work on "law promotion" and "law talk" by the Red Cross is one example of such work (Ratner 2011, 2013). Ratner's approach is eclectic and illustrates the value of constructivist and rationalist insights in exploring the role of international law, legal argumentation, and various efforts to promote compliance with international law.

Finally, because one strand of constructivism examines how norms and background understandings vary between cultures and over long periods of time (Ruggie 1992; Reus-Smit 2004), constructivism could shed light on possible changes in the nature and practices of the international legal system that purely interest-driven accounts may miss. Interests tend to be more short term than identities. At the same time, through a more in-depth and critical exploration of shared understandings in a deeply diverse international society, future scholarship could help address more systematically the critique that constructivist approaches – and the international legal theory now connected to those approaches – is inherently liberal and Western in bias. It is also important for constructivists to tackle head-on the internal critique of critical theorists and the external critique of realists that constructivism may privilege agency and neglect the constraints of power relationships.

Constructivism and IL have begun a useful conversation, and some insights have been gained. However, a fair evaluation would suggest that the full potential of interdisciplinary scholarship has yet to be seized. For that to happen, IR scholars will have to question their received understanding of law and challenge conceptions that are hierarchical and rooted in formal validity. International lawyers will have to open their minds to conceptions of international politics that do not assume the exclusive explanatory weight of power and material interests. Strangely, only a few scholars on either side of the "divide" have managed to apply insights from within their own discipline that make reaching out to the other both congenial and fruitful. We hope that this review might reveal productive ways in which constructivists and international law scholars can learn from and actually reinforce each other's work.

REFERENCES

Abbott, Kenneth, Robert O. Keohane, Andrew Moravcsik, Anne-Marie Slaughter, and Duncan Snidal (2000). "The Concept of Legalization," *International Organization*, Vol. 54, No. 3, pp. 401–19.

Abbott, Kenneth W., and Duncan Snidal (2013). "Law, Legalization and Politics: An Agenda for the Next Generation of IL/IR Scholars," in Jeffrey L. Dunoff and Mark A. Pollack (eds.), *Interdisciplinary Perspectives on International Law and International Relations: The State of the Art* (New York: Cambridge University Press), pp. 33–56.

Abdelal, Rawi (2007). *Capital Rules: The Construction of Global Finance* (Cambridge, MA: Harvard University Press).

Abdelal, Rawi, Mark Blyth, and Craig Parsons (2010) (eds.). *Constructing the International Economy* (Ithaca, NY: Cornell University Press).

Acharya, Amitav (2004). "How Ideas Spread: Whose Norms Matter? Norm Localization and Institutional Change in Asian Regionalism," *International Organization*, Vol. 58, No. 2, pp. 239–75.

———— (2011). "Dialogue and Discovery: In Search of International Relations Theories Beyond the West," *Millennium – Journal of International Studies*, Vol. 39, No. 3, pp. 619–37.

Adler, Emanuel (2005). *Communitarian International Relations: The Epistemic Foundations of International Relations* (New York: Routledge).

———— (2008). "The Spread of Security Communities: Communities of Practice, Self-Restraint, and NATO's Post–Cold War Transformation," *European Journal of International Relations*, Vol. 14, No. 2, pp. 195–230.

Adler, Emanuel, and Vincent Pouliot (2011) (eds.). *International Practices* (Cambridge: Cambridge University Press).

Akhtarkhavari, Afshin (2010). *Global Governance of the Environment: Environmental Principles and Change in International Law and Politics* (Cheltenham, UK: Edward Elgar).

Arend, Anthony Clark (1999). *Legal Rules and International Society* (New York: Oxford University Press).

Autesserre, Séverine (2009). "Hobbes and the Congo: Frames, Local Violence, and International Intervention," *International Organization*, Vol. 63, No. 2, pp. 249–80.

Avant, Deborah D., Martha Finnemore, and Susan K. Sell (2010) (eds.). *Who Governs the Globe* (Cambridge: Cambridge University Press).

Barnett, Michael (1997). "Bringing in the New World Order: Liberalism, Legitimacy, and the United Nations," *World Politics*, Vol. 49, No. 4, pp. 526–51.

Barnett, Michael, and Martha Finnemore (2004). *Rules for the World: International Organizations in Global Politics* (Ithaca, NY: Cornell University Press).

Bhaskar, Roy (1979). *The Possibility of Naturalism: A Philosophical Critique of the Contemporary Human Sciences* (Brighton: Harvester Press).

Blyth, Mark (2002). *Great Transformations: Economic Ideas and Institutional Change in the Twentieth Century* (New York: Cambridge University Press).

Bourdieu, Pierre (1977). *Outline of a Theory of Practice* (Cambridge: Cambridge University Press).

Brunnée, Jutta, and Stephen J. Toope (2000). "International Law and Constructivism: Elements of an Interactional Theory of International Law," *Columbia Journal of Transnational Law*, Vol. 39, pp. 19–74.

––––––– (2010). *Legitimacy and Legality in International Law: An Interactional Account* (Cambridge: Cambridge University Press, 2010).

––––––– (2011a). "Interactional International Law: An Introduction," *International Theory*, Vol. 3, No. 2, pp. 307–18.

––––––– (2011b). "History, Mystery and Mastery," *International Theory*, Vol. 3, No. 2, pp. 348–54.

––––––– (2011c). "Interactional International Law and the Practice of Legality," in Emanuel Adler and Vincent Pouliot (eds.), *International Practices* (Cambridge: Cambridge University Press), pp. 108–35.

Bull, Hedley (1977). *The Anarchical Society: A Study of Order in World Politics* (London: Macmillan).

Chayes, Abram, and Antonia Handler Chayes (1995). *The New Sovereignty: Compliance with International Regulatory Agreements* (Cambridge, MA: Harvard University Press).

Checkel, Jeffrey T. (2001). "Why Comply? Social Learning and European Identity Change," *International Organization*, Vol. 55, No. 3, pp. 553–88.

––––––– (2005). "International Institutions and Socialization in Europe: Introduction and Framework," *International Organization*, Vol. 59, No. 4, pp. 801–26.

Deitelhoff, Nicole (2009). "The Discursive Process of Legalization: Charting Islands of Persuasion in the ICC Case," *International Organization*, Vol. 63, No. 1, pp. 33–65.

Deitelhoff, Nicole, and Harald Müller (2005). "Theoretical Paradise – Empirically Lost? Arguing with Habermas," *Review of International Studies*, Vol. 31, No. 1, pp. 167–79.

Deutsch, Karl W., Sidney A. Burrell, Robert A. Kann, Maurice Lee, Jr., Martin Lichterman, Raymond E. Lindgren, Francis L. Loewenheim, and Richard W. van Wagenen (1957). *Political Community and the North Atlantic Area: International Organisation in the Light of Historical Experience* (Princeton, NJ: Princeton University Press).

Dewey, John (1988). "The Nature of Aims," in John Dewey (ed.), *The Middle Works of John Dewey, Volume 14, 1899–1924* (Carbondale: Southern Illinois University Press), pp. 154–63.

Fearon, James, and Alexander Wendt (2002). "Rationalism vs. Constructivism: A Skeptical View," in Walter Carlsnaes, Thomas Risse, and Beth Simmons (eds.), *Handbook of International Relations* (London: Sage Publications), pp. 52–72.

Finnemore, Martha (2000). "Are Legal Norms Distinctive?," *New York University Journal International Law & Politics*, Vol. 32, No. 3, pp. 699–706.

Finnemore, Martha, and Kathryn Sikkink (1998). "International Norm Dynamics and Political Change," *International Organization*, Vol. 52, No. 4, pp. 887–917.

Finnemore, Martha, and Stephen J. Toope (2001). "Alternatives to 'Legalization': Richer Views of Law and Politics," *International Organization*, Vol. 55, No. 3, pp. 743–58.

Franck, Thomas M. (1990). *The Power of Legitimacy among Nations* (New York: Oxford University Press).

––––––– (1995). *Fairness in International Law and Institutions* (Oxford: Clarendon Press, 1995).

––––––– (2006). "The Power of Legitimacy and the Legitimacy of Power: International Law in an Age of Power Disequilibrium," *American Journal of International Law*, Vol. 100, No. 1, pp. 88–106.

Fuller, Lon L. (1969). *The Morality of Law*, rev. ed. (New Haven, CT: Yale University Press).

Gheciu, Alexandra (2005). "Security Institutions as Agents of Socialisation? NATO and the 'New Europe,'" *International Organization*, Vol. 59, No. 4, pp. 973–1012.

Giddens, Anthony (1984). *The Constitution of Society: Outline of the Theory of Structuration* (Cambridge: Polity Press).

Goodman, Ryan, and Derek Jinks (2003). "Toward an Institutional Theory of Sovereignty," *Stanford Law Review*, Vol. 55, No. 5, pp. 1749–88.

———— (2004). "How to Influence States: Socialization and International Human Rights Law," *Duke Law Journal*, Vol. 54, No. 3, pp. 621–703.

———— (2005). "International Law and State Socialization: Conceptual, Empirical, and Normative Challenges," *Duke Law Journal*, Vol. 54, No. 4, pp. 983–98.

Habermas, Jürgen (1990). *Moral Consciousness and Communicative Action*, Christian Lenhardt and Shierry Weber Nicholsen, trans. (Cambridge: MIT Press).

Hall, Rodney Bruce (2008). *Central Banking as Global Governance: Constructing Financial Credibility* (Cambridge: Cambridge University Press).

Hart, Henry M., Jr., and Albert M. Sacks (1994). *The Legal Process: Basic Problems in the Making and Application of Law* (Westbury, NY: Foundation Press).

Hathaway, Oona A. (2002). "Do Human Rights Treaties Make a Difference?," *Yale Law Journal*, Vol. 111, No. 8, pp. 1935–2042.

Heinze, Eric A. (2011). "The Evolution of International Law in Light of the 'Global War on Terror,'" *Review of International Studies*, Vol. 37, No. 3, pp. 1045–67.

Hirsch, Moshe (2005). "The Sociology of International Law: Invitation to Study International Rules in Their Social Context," *University of Toronto Law Journal*, Vol. 55, No. 4, pp. 891–939.

Hopf, Ted (2010). "The Logic of Habit in International Relations," *European Journal of International Law*, Vol. 16, No. 4, pp. 539–62.

Hurd, Ian (2007). "Breaking and Making Norms: American Revisionism and Crises of Legitimacy," *International Politics*, Vol. 44, pp. 194–213.

———— (2008). "Constructivism," in Christian Reus-Smit (ed.), *The Oxford Handbook of International Relations* (Oxford: Oxford University Press), pp. 298–316.

———— (2011). "Is Humanitarian Intervention Legal? The Rule of Law in an Incoherent World," *Ethics & International Affairs*, Vol. 25, No. 3, pp. 293–313.

Johnston, Alastair Iain (2001). "Treating International Institutions as Social Environments," *International Studies Quarterly*, Vol. 45, No. 4, pp. 487–515.

Johnstone, Ian (2011). *The Power of Deliberation: International Law, Politics and Organizations* (Oxford: Oxford University Press).

Jordan, Richard, Daniel Maliniak, Amy Oakes, Susan Peterson, and Michael J. Tierney (2009). "One Discipline or Many? TRIP Survey of International Relations Faculty in Ten Countries." Institute for the Theory and Practice of International Relations, College of William and Mary, available at http://irtheoryandpractice.wm.edu/projects/trip/Final_Trip_Report_2009.pdf.

Karber, Phillip A. (1990). "'Constructivism' as a Method in International Law" *Proceedings of the Annual Meeting (American Society of International Law)*, Vol. 94, pp. 189–92.

Keck, Margaret, and Kathryn Sikkink (1998) *Activists beyond Borders: Advocacy Networks in International Politics* (Ithaca, NY: Cornell University Press).

Keohane, Robert O. (1988). "International Institutions: Two Approaches," *International Studies Quarterly*, Vol. 32, No. 4, pp. 379–96.

Knop, Karen (2010). "The Hart-Fuller Debate's Silence on Human Rights," in Peter Cane (ed.), *The Hart-Fuller Debate in the Twenty-First Century* (Oxford: Hart Publishing), pp. 61–78.

Koh, Harold Hongju (1996). "'Transnational Legal Process': The 1994 Roscoe Pound Lecture," *Nebraska Law Review*, Vol. 75, No. 1, pp. 181–207.

——— (1997). "Why Do Nations Obey International Law?" *Yale Law Journal*, Vol. 106, No. 8, pp. 2599–659.

——— (1998a). "The 1998 Frankel Lecture: Bringing International Law Home," *Houston Law Review*, Vol. 35, No. 3, pp. 623–81.

——— (1998b). "How Is International Human Rights Law Enforced?" *Indiana Law Journal*, Vol. 74, No. 4, pp. 1397–417.

——— (2005). "Internalization through Socialization," *Duke Law Journal*, Vol. 54, No. 4, pp. 975–82.

Koskenniemi, Martti (2005). *From Apology to Utopia: The Structure of International Legal Argument* (Cambridge: Cambridge University Press).

Kratochwil, Friedrich (1989). *Rules, Norms, and Decisions: On the Conditions of Practical and Legal Reasoning in International Relations and Domestic Affairs* (Cambridge: Cambridge University Press).

Kratochwil, Friedrich, and John G. Ruggie (1986). "International Organization: A State of the Art on an Art of the State," *International Organization*, Vol. 40, No. 4, pp. 753–75.

Krebs, Ronald R., and Patrick Thaddeus Jackson (2007). "Twisting Tongues and Twisting Arms: The Power of Political Rhetoric," *European Journal of International Relations*, Vol. 13, No. 1, pp. 35–66.

Kurki, Milja, and Adriana Sinclair (2010). "Hidden in Plain Sight: Constructivist Treatment of Social Context and Its Limitations," *International Politics*, Vol. 47, No. 1, pp. 1–25.

Lutz, Ellen, and Kathryn Sikkink (2001a). "The Justice Cascade: The Evolution and Impact of Foreign Human Rights Trials in Latin America," *Chicago Journal of International Law*, Vol. 2, No. 1, pp. 1–34.

——— (2001b). "International Human Rights Law and Practice in Latin America," in Judith L. Goldstein, Miles Kahler, Robert O. Keohane and Anne-Marie Slaughter (eds.), *Legalization and World Politics* (Cambridge: MIT Press), pp. 249–75.

McDougal, Myres, and Harold Lasswell (1966). "The Identification and Appraisal of Diverse Systems of Public Order," in Richard Falk and Saul Mendlovitz (eds.), *The Strategy of World Order: International Law* (New York: World Law Fund), pp. 55–113.

McDougal, Myres, and W. Michael Reisman (1980). "The Prescribing Function in World Constitutive Process: How International Law Is Made," *Yale Studies in World Public Order*, Vol. 6, No. 2, pp. 249–84.

March, James G., and Johan P. Olsen (1998). "The Institutional Dynamics of International Political Orders," *International Organization*, Vol. 52, No. 4, pp. 943–69.

Mercer, Jonathan (2010). "Emotional Beliefs," *International Organization*, Vol. 64, No. 1, pp. 1–31.

Methmann, Chris Paul (2010). "'Climate Protection' as Empty Signifier: A Discourse Theoretical Perspective on Climate Mainstreaming in World Politics," *Millennium – Journal of International Studies*, Vol. 39, No. 2, pp. 345–72.

Nagtzaam, Gerry (2009). *The Making of International Environmental Treaties: Neoliberal and Constructivist Analyses of Normative Evolution* (Cheltenham, UK: Edward Elgar).

O'Connell, Mary-Ellen (1999). "Symposium on Method in International Law: New International Legal Process," *American Journal of International Law*, Vol. 93, No. 2, pp. 334–51.

Onuf, Nicholas G. (1982). "Global Law-Making and Legal Thought," in Nicholas G. Onuf (ed.), *Law-Making in the Global Community* (Durham, NC: Carolina Academic Press), pp. 1–81.

————— (1985). "Do Rules Say What They Do? From Ordinary Language to International Law," *Harvard International Law Journal*, Vol. 26, No. 2, pp. 385–402.

————— (1989). *World of Our Making: Rules and Rule in Social Theory and International Relations* (Columbia: University of South Carolina Press).

Orchard, Phil (2010). "Protection of Internally Displaced Persons: Soft Law as a Norm-Generating Mechanism," *Review of International Studies*, Vol. 36, No. 2, pp. 281–303.

Pouliot, Vincent (2008). "The Logic of Practicality: A Theory of Practice of Security Communities," *International Organization*, Vol. 62, No. 2, pp. 257–88.

Price, Richard (1997). *The Chemical Weapons Taboo* (Ithaca, NY: Cornell University Press).

————— (2004). "Emerging Customary Norms and Anti-personnel Landmines," in Christian Reus-Smit (ed.), *The Politics of International Law* (Cambridge: Cambridge University Press), pp. 106–30.

————— (2008). "Moral Limit and Possibility in World Politics," *International Organization*, Vol. 62, No. 2, pp. 191–220.

Price, Richard, and Christian Reus-Smit (1998). "Dangerous Liaisons? Critical International Theory and Constructivism," *European Journal of International Relations*, Vol. 4, No. 3, pp. 259–94.

Ratner, Steven R. (2011). "Law Promotion beyond Law Talk: The Red Cross, Persuasion, and the Laws of War," *European Journal of International Law*, Vol. 22, No. 2, pp. 459–506.

————— (2013). "Persuading to Comply: On the Deployment and Avoidance of Legal Argumentation," in Jeffrey L. Dunoff and Mark A. Pollack (eds.), *Interdisciplinary Perspectives on International Law and International Relations: The State of the Art* (New York: Cambridge University Press), pp. 568–90.

Raustiala, Kal, and Anne-Marie Slaughter (2002). "International Law, International Relations and Compliance," in Walter Carlsnaes, Thomas Risse and Beth Simmons (eds.), *Handbook of International Relations* (London: Sage Publications Ltd.), pp. 538–58.

Reisman, W. Michael (1981). "International Law-Making: A Process of Communication: The Harold D. Lasswell Memorial Lecture," *Proceedings of the Annual Meeting (American Society of International Law)*, Vol. 75, pp. 101–10.

Reus-Smit, Christian (2004). "The Politics of International Law," in Christian Reus-Smit (ed.), *The Politics of International Law* (Cambridge: Cambridge University Press), pp. 14–44.

Risse, Thomas (2000). "Let's Argue!: Communicative Action in World Politics," *International Organization*, Vol. 54, No. 1, pp. 1–40.

Risse, Thomas, and Kathryn Sikkink (1999). "The Socialization of International Human Rights Norms into Domestic Practices: Introduction," in Thomas Risse, Steve C. Ropp, and Kathryn Sikkink (eds.), *The Power of Human Rights: International Norms and Domestic Change* (Cambridge: Cambridge University Press), pp. 1–38.

Rorty, Richard (1989). *Contingency, Irony, and Solidarity* (Cambridge: Cambridge University Press).

Ruggie, John G. (1986). "Continuity and Transformation in the World Polity: Toward a Neorealist Synthesis," in Robert O. Keohane (ed.), *Neorealism and Its Critics* (New York: Columbia University Press), pp. 131–57.

————— (1992). "Multilateralism: The Anatomy of an Institution." *International Organization*, Vol. 46, No. 3, pp. 561–98.

————— (1998). "What Makes the World Hang Together? Neo-utilitarianism and the Social Constructivist Challenge," *International Organization*, Vol. 52, No. 4, pp. 855–85.

Sagan, Ann (2010). "African Criminals/African Victims: The Institutionalised Production of Cultural Narratives in International Criminal Law," *Millennium-Journal of International Studies*, Vol. 39, No. 1, pp. 3–21.

Searle, John R. (1995). *The Construction of Social Reality* (New York: The Free Press).

Sinclair, Adriana (2010). *International Relations Theory and International Law: A Critical Approach* (Cambridge: Cambridge University Press).

————— (2011). "Law, Caution: Towards a Better Understanding of Law for IR Theorists," *Review of International Studies*, Vol. 37, No. 3, pp. 1095–112.

Stevenson, Hayley (2011). "India and International Norms of Climate Governance: A Constructivist Analysis of Normative Congruence Building," *Review of International Studies*, Vol. 37, No. 3, pp. 997–1019.

Tipson, Frederick Samson (1973–1974). "The Lasswell-McDougal Enterprise: Toward a World Public Order of Human Dignity," *Virginia Journal of International Law*, Vol. 14, No. 3, pp. 535–85.

Toope, Stephen J. (1990). "Confronting Indeterminacy: Challenges to International Legal Theory," *Proceedings of the Canadian Council on International Law*, pp. 209–12.

van der Burgh, Wibren (1999). "Two Models of Law and Morality," *Associations*, Vol. 3, No. 1, pp. 61–82.

————— (2009). "Essentially Ambiguous Concepts and the Fuller-Hart-Dworkin Debate," *Archives for Philosophy of Law and Social Philosophy*, Vol. 95, No. 3, pp. 305–26.

Walldorf, C. William (2010). "Argument, Institutional Process, and Human Rights Sanctions in Democratic Foreign Policy," *European Journal of International Relations*, Vol. 16, No. 4, pp. 639–62.

Weaver, Catherine (2008). *Hypocrisy Trap: The World Bank and the Poverty of Reform* (Princeton, NJ: Princeton University Press).

Wendt, Alexander (1987). "The Agent-Structure Problem in International Relations Theory," *International Organization*, Vol. 41, No. 3, pp. 335–70.

————— (1994). "Collective Identity Formation and the International State," *American Political Science Review*, Vol. 88, No. 2, pp. 384–96.

————— (1999). *Social Theory of International Politics* (Cambridge: Cambridge University Press).

Wenger, Etienne (1998). *Communities of Practice: Learning, Meaning, and Identity* (Cambridge: Cambridge University Press).

Wiener, Antje (2008). *The Invisible Constitution of Politics: Contested Norms and International Encounters* (Cambridge: Cambridge University Press).

6

Wanted – Dead or Alive:

Realism in International Law

Richard H. Steinberg

"Realism" is the theory international lawyers love to hate. Dozens of commentators have attacked realism or written its epitaph. Some commentators have even asked: is anybody still a realist? (Legro and Moravcsik 1999).

Many international law (IL) scholars challenge "realism" because most think it means that international law is epiphenomenal and so devoid of meaning – which could make their jobs irrelevant, wasteful, and quixotic. But they also seem to love realism – or a version of it – because the misunderstood and mischaracterized structural realist straw-man claim that "international law does not matter" serves for them as the perfect foil for arguments that international law is important. It is the null hypothesis that enables international lawyers to show that their argument and life's work does have meaning. So, in a sense, even those who hate "realism" actually love it – in the same way that prohibitionists hated alcohol, Joe McCarthy hated Communism, and family values conservatives hate pornography. What would they do without it?

And there's another reason IL scholars may dislike realism: it is seen as an amoral theory, at best. Realism is almost exclusively positivist (in Comte's scientific sense of the term, not the Austinian jurisprudential sense). It offers a basis for attacking the feasibility of much of the normative work that espouses changing the status quo in international law. In IL, a field that remains driven largely by normative agendas, realists constantly raise annoying facts and analyses that spoil the party.

Moreover, most realists are skeptical of the extent of shared international norms, the existence or longevity of an international "society" or "community," and the evolution of soft law into hard law (Krasner 1999). Realists are skeptical of many assertions

The author thanks Jeffrey Dunoff, Judith Goldstein, Oona Hathaway, Barbara Koremenos, Robert Keohane, Andrew Moravcsik, Athanassios Platias, Mark Pollack, and Kal Raustiala for their useful comments on earlier drafts.

of customary international law: they want unambiguous state-by-state expressions of *opinio juris* that would evidence consent. Hence, realists don't see nearly as much customary law in the world as most international lawyers who aspire to build a more legalized world order.

What's not to hate?

This essay argues that realism remains very much alive, not only because international lawyers have kept it alive by attacking a straw man misinterpretation of the structural realist variant, but also because it is a useful tool for positive analysis of international law: even its structural realist variant (correctly understood) has heuristic power, and realist concepts may be combined with insights of other approaches – for example, cooperation theory in economics, liberalism, social construction theory, or empiricism – to constitute a valuable research program in international law, with substantial explanatory and predictive power. Finally, realism is critical for the advancement of normative agendas in international law. Realism's epitaph is premature. Realism in international law remains alive and vibrant.

The first section of this chapter, "Realism's Core Elements and Causal Narratives in International Law," distills the core elements of the realist tradition in international law over the millennia: the state, state power, state interests. It then briefly posits realism's main causal narratives.

The next section, "Varieties of Realism in International Law," presents a revisionist intellectual history of realism, showing how different versions of realism have put these elements together in different ways. Thucydides, Machiavelli, and Morgenthau all thought that powerful states (or their rulers) conclude treaties to advance state interests. Interests were sometimes divergent and sometimes convergent. Hence, powerful states could sometimes impose international law on weaker states, and sometimes states could agree among themselves on issues of common interest. Classical (Thucydides), early modern (Machiavelli), and traditional (Morgenthau) realist approaches to international law included some additional elements, however – such as norms, religion, and type of government – that affect the making of or complying with treaty obligations. A more contemporary version of realism, the structural realism distilled by Kenneth Waltz and applied to international regimes by Stephen Krasner, presented a highly stylized theory devoid of these additional elements and argued, *inter alia*, that international law can't contradict the structure of the international system. A version of that structural argument was misinterpreted by scores of commentators as a broader claim that international law has no effect on any international outcomes or state behavior – a claim that would never have been made by realist predecessors and that does not follow logically from structural premises. And it is that straw man that has been confounded by many as "realism" over the past thirty years.

The third section, "You Can't Live with It; You Can't Live without It: The Endurance of Realism in Hybrid Theories," shows how realist elements have been used in hybridized accounts of international law. Realism has been regularly combined with elements of other major international relations (IR) theories (rationalism, domestic politics theories, constructivism) and empiricism to yield useful hybrid models that are theoretically progressive and do not subvert realist concepts. These hybrid models add complexity to (and diminish the parsimony of) the structural realist approach, but they expand the explanatory power of realist-oriented argumentation and carve out more broadly effective roles for international law.

The fourth section, "Realist Understanding of International Law-Making, Interpretation, Compliance, and Global Legal Structure," discusses what we have learned about international law from realist and hybrid approaches that employ realist elements. Realism is powerful for explaining international law-making, interpretation, and compliance with international law, which are the microfoundations of realism's insights about the structure of international law.

The final section concludes the chapter, distilling the limits and strengths of realism, and suggesting the importance of the realist tradition for advancing the science and art of international law.

I. REALISM'S CORE ELEMENTS AND CAUSAL NARRATIVES IN INTERNATIONAL LAW: THE STATE, STATE POWER, AND STATE INTERESTS

Realism has a long pedigree that runs back at least two-and-a-half millennia through some of history's most important political thinkers. Although many historians, philosophers, lawyers, political scientists, and commentators could be considered realists, four stand out for their paradigmatic realist approach to international law[1] in the particular epoch in which they wrote. Thucydides (classical realism), Machiavelli (early modern realism), Morgenthau (traditional realism), and Waltz as applied by Krasner (structural realism) have their differences (which are examined in the section "Varieties of Realism in International Law"), but all share three core elements and three causal narratives in their approach to international law. Nonrealists emphasize other factors and narratives to explain international law and its effects.[2]

First, realists see the state as the central actor in international law.[3] The *state* is, of course, an analytic abstraction. The form of the state varies across history –

---

[1] "International law" is a fairly new term that emerged with the rise of the nation-state. In previous epochs, references were made to treaties, customary law, the law of peoples, and the like. For convenience, I will refer here to all of it as "international law," regardless of epoch.

[2] For example, rational institutionalists emphasize international institutions and information. Liberals emphasize the key role that the interests of subnational and transnational groups have in driving the development of international law. See Moravcsik (2013). Constructivists emphasize norms, ideas, and identities. See Brunnée and Toope (2013). None of these other schools of thought places state power at the center of its analysis and must address power only as an afterthought.

[3] Many nonrealist theorists also see the state as the central actor in international law. Aquinas' elaborate taxonomy includes *lex humana* (human law), consisting of *jus civile* (akin to municipal law) and *jus gentium* (the law of peoples), which extends across societies; the latter is a medieval conceptualization

from city-states in ancient Greece, to the absolutist state in early eighteenth-century France, to the contemporary nation-state. Type of government, which partly defines the role of the state, varies as well – whether a democracy, autocracy, theocracy, or something else. Hence, sometimes the state is embodied in a prince or a ruler (Machiavelli 1908). Sometimes it is a bureaucracy (Weber 1947). Or, it may be a set of domestic institutions that interact with each other or with substate actors to generate state behavior (Goldstein and Steinberg 2008). In a weak version, it could be liberal processes that generate state behavior, with the state as intermediator between political parties or domestic interests. But, if the "state" is merely a conveyer belt, then it does not have autonomy in the way most realists conceptualize it (Moravcsik 1997). Notwithstanding the counterclaims of Vernon's *Sovereignty at Bay* (1971), Kindlebebrger's claim that the state is through as an analytic entity (1969), or other approaches that diminish the centrality of the state – for example, transnationalism (Keohane and Nye 1972; Koh 2004), transgovernmentalism (Slaughter 2004), global norms cascades (Sunstein 1996; Finnemore and Sikkink 1998), cosmopolitanism (Charnovitz 2002), and global administrative law (Kingsbury, Krisch, and Stewart 2005) – for realists, the state remains the central actor in international law (Steinberg 2004*a*), as it is for legal positivists.

Second, each state is endowed with interests. Interests are usually determined exogenously or posited. Material interests are often assumed, but not implausibly: survival is posited as a goal of every state, and states are often assumed to be welfare-enhancing, seeking economic gain (measured now by such things as gross domestic product [GDP] growth, job creation, establishment or maintenance of strategic sectors, etc.). Normative or ideational interests are also sometimes posited, assumed, generated from other theories, or otherwise injected, such as the protection of culture, the spread of democracy or human rights, or acceptance of the Washington Consensus. Interests among states are sometimes divergent and at other times convergent; in Waltz's structural realism, which was focused on explaining the structure of the international system and its effects, interests are depicted as divergent (zero-sum, focused on relative gains for survival and accretion of power) (Waltz 1979). Other than the assumption that states seek survival, realism does not require a commitment to any particular assumption about the content of state interests, but state interests are placed at the heart of the analysis.

Third, each state is endowed with material power capabilities that are brought to bear in the international battle to shape the substance and structure of international law. The definition of "power" is contested, but it is defined here conventionally as the ability to get another to do what it would not otherwise do (Dahl 1957). Measuring power is notoriously difficult. In some contexts, state power is measured and employed by issue area – for example, in terms of GDP when measuring

of international law (Aquinas 1947). For John Austin (1832) and Hans Kelson (1942), state consent is the touchstone of international law.

trade or bargaining power (Steinberg 2002); in other contexts, it may be measured in the aggregate, as in efforts to evaluate the structure of the international system (Waltz 1979; Gilpin 1981). But state power – particularly when used by powerful states to coerce weaker states to accept international laws they would not otherwise accept (Krasner 1999) – is central to realist theory and is its most distinctive feature. Indeed, whereas liberal and constructivist theories import sociological concepts and processes to explain international law, and rationalist institutionalism is built on the back of economics, realism is – by virtue of the centrality of power – the most distinctly political of contemporary approaches to international law.

Building on these three core assumptions, realists tend to make three types of causal claims about the role of international law in international politics. First, state capabilities are brought to bear to advance interests that become embodied in international law, so international law reflects the interests of powerful states. Second, international law may make states better off than otherwise. Third, if an international law contradicts the long-term interests of a powerful state, then it will not comply with it. These narratives will be described more expansively below.

In summary, all realists employ three core factors and three causal narratives to understand international law. But realism in international law is not monolithic: it has many variants. Its core elements and causal narratives are put together in various ways.

II. VARIETIES OF REALISM IN INTERNATIONAL LAW

These three realist factors and narratives have been used in theories about international law for millennia, but classical, early modern, and traditional realism each employed additional factors to explain international law and its meaning. In the early 1980s, structural realism exposed some shortcomings of those past efforts to blend realist elements with additional factors: the additional factors led to indeterminacy. Structural realism then offered its own account, the main deduction from which was misunderstood in much of the law and political science literature, thus enabling it to become the whipping boy for IL and IR scholars for the next thirty years. Properly understood, the use of core realist concepts and causal narratives in international law has great heuristic strength.

A. *Realist and "Nonrealist" Factors in Classical, Early Modern,*
and Traditional Realism

In addition to the three core factors identified above, classical, early modern, and traditional realists each used additional factors to help explain treaty commitment and compliance. When those approaches are distilled into a theory of international law, the additional factors, and their interaction with the core elements, add post hoc explanatory power to realist analysis of international law, but at the cost of predictive indeterminacy.

Thucydides' *History of the Peloponnesian War* (1954) is the paradigmatic classical realist account. City-states are the fundamental unit of analysis, and Thucydides explains their motivation for each strategic move. Treaties of alliance and peace are concluded to advance city-state interests. Treaties of alliance, such as the founding of the Delian League, and the various arrangements between Sparta and Persia starting in 407 BC, are depicted as arrangements in the strategic interest of the parties, making them more secure than otherwise (Platias and Koliopoulos 2010). Similarly, the major treaties of peace, such as the Thirty Years' Peace between Athens and Sparta (445 BC), as well as the Peace of Nicias (421–415 BC) following the Archidamian War, were also concluded in the strategic interest of the parties (Kagan 1974). Hence, the classical realist paradigm used the three core realist elements identified above to explain international law and its consequences.

At the same time, Thucydides' account includes other factors affecting treaty commitment and compliance. Religion permeated ancient Greek city-states, motivating some decisions about treaty commitments that ran counter to a city-state's strategic interest: for example, Thucydides wrote that Corinth delayed alliance with Athens because it had "sworn upon the faith of the gods" not to give up Thrace. Similarly, Thucydides believed that a state's form of government could impact its international behavior. For example, he argued that leaders of democracies were often corrupt, greedy, and ambitious, pursuing their own honor and profit at the expense of the city-state's interests, and, at other times, the democracies of Athens and Argos allied with each other less out of strategic interest than out of a kinship with a "sister democracy."[4]

Niccolo Machiavelli famously revived realism during the Italian Renaissance. Normatively, Machiavelli's early modern realist princes are corrupt and cynical, usually lacking any religious inclinations – unlike some leaders in Thucydides' Greece and the Roman Catholic international law philosophers who dominated Western European legal thought in the Dark Ages. Hence, Machiavelli was a constant target for criticism by naturalist and Christian international law philosophers (and their moral philosophical progeny) for centuries, including Grotius[5] (who, although he had elements that would coalesce into positivism, was fundamentally naturalist) (Lauterpacht 1946).

For Machiavelli, treaty commitment and compliance depended fundamentally on the strategic interests and relative power of Italian city-states. He wrote that alliances are broken by consideration of interests; kings will break treaties if it suits them, and treaties concluded by force will hold until the threat of force disappears. Like Thucydides, however, Machiavelli introduced additional factors affecting treaty

---

4 Thucydides (1954), Book 5.21, 11th Year Summer.
5 Grotius (1901), Prolegomena.

commitment and compliance, such as form of government and sense of moral obligation. Machiavelli wrote that democracies are more likely to comply with their treaty commitments than are kings, and he wrote that Athens had once rejected using a treaty in a way that was in Athens' interest, but was dishonest.[6]

Contemporary IL scholarship owes a huge debt to Hans Morgenthau, who brought behavioralism to the field in the United States in the mid-twentieth century (Morgenthau 1940). Before Morgenthau, American IL scholarship was idealistic and doctrinal: states did what international law said they [should] do; international law was international relations. Morgenthau demanded an ontological shift in understanding international law – from considering only treaty texts and treatises, to also considering state behavior, a shift analogous to that which had started taking place in American law scholarship more than a half-century earlier, starting with Holmes' skepticism of the science of law (Holmes 1881) and becoming explicit with Roscoe Pound's American legal realism (Pound 1921).

Morgenthau's theory was that international law exists only if it is in the common interest of all parties to adhere to it or if a power configuration enforces it – a formulation employing the three core concepts identified in the preceding section. He argued that international law could be divided into two types: "non-political international law" includes treaties and customary rules that benefit all states regardless of international power constellations (e.g., the law of treaties, diplomatic immunity, international commercial law, and admiralty) and "political international law," which could also be beneficial for all states, but depends on a particular power constellation (e.g., treaties of alliance and peace) (Morgenthau 1940).

For Morgenthau, state interests could be determined materially or normatively. He argued that shared norms are a powerful basis for international law, rules backed by both interests and norms are more likely to enjoy compliance than are those backed by interest alone, and that compliance with international law is the norm (Morgenthau 1940, 1978). However, as the Cold War became deeply institutionalized, realist commentators (eventually including Morgenthau) made it increasingly clear that where international norms (and international law backed by norms) run contrary to state security interests, security interests will prevail and norms-based international law will not constrain behavior (Hoffmann 1971; Morgenthau 1978).

B. *Structural Realism*

As politics scholars increasingly came to view themselves as hard scientists, studying, explaining, and predicting state behavior, they more rigorously applied philosophy of science criteria to work on IR and IL. In the late 1970s, Kenneth Waltz applied those criteria to critique the existing IR literature, including traditional realism and its earlier forms. In doing so, he identified a core problem: in theoretical terms,

---

[6] Machiavelli (1970), Bk. I, Ch. LIX.

all three of the realist approaches described above are predictively indeterminate. If the material or strategic interests of the state are in conflict with the additional nonrealist factors, then which prevails? If religious oaths, or norms, or democratic sisterhood conflict with the strategic interests of a state, how can we predict whether that state will join a treaty that is in its strategic interest or whether it will comply with such a treaty? And, why would international law backed by norms and interests be more likely to enjoy compliance than law backed by material interests alone? In short, material interests, norms, religion, and different forms of government could all coexist in a model of international law, but the model will be indeterminate unless those elements are theorized, weighted, prioritized, or otherwise reconciled – a move that traditional realist scholars never successfully made. Moreover, Waltz argued, a model in which nonrealist domestic factors could prevail over material geostrategic interests was not a realist theory at all: it was a "reductionist" theory in which religion, form of government, normative movements, or other domestic political factors drive state behavior (Waltz 1979).

Waltz solved these problems, purifying realism and eliminating the indeterminacy of earlier versions, by ridding them of the nonrealist factors – norms, domestic institutions, and religion. States are unitary actors. State interests are exogenous to the model, except for an overriding state interest in survival, which is inherent in a statist model. Relative power among states varies, so the structure of the international system varies over time from hegemonic (one state dominates), to bipolar, to multipolar. Maximizing the probability of national survival drives the model, so states care primarily about relative gains – maintaining or acquiring power. Hence, interests among states are divergent, and focus is on the structure or the international system.

Waltz made no express deductions about international law, but Stephen Krasner used Waltz's structural realism to generate the most controversial and important claim about international law in the twentieth century: he posited that Waltz's structural realism implies that international regimes are not autonomous and have no independent effect on "related behavior and outcomes." In this view, Krasner argued, the self-interest and relative power of states shapes the content of international regimes, which in turn drives "related behavior and outcomes." Hence, international law is merely ephiphenomenal of underlying state power and interests (1983*a*: 6–7). In this sense, international law does not matter.

That deduction, however, was not framed as clearly as it could have been, and it was interpreted more broadly than the logic of structural realism implies. Framed sharply and narrowly, structural realist assumptions imply that international regimes depend on the structure of the system and that regimes can have no independent effect on structure. In that limited sense, international law may be epiphenomenal, lack autonomy, and lack effect. With a focus on structure and relative power in the system, realism was unconcerned with positive-sum possibilities (Krasner 1991): for structural realists, "outcomes" meant system structure, or preservation of or domination by a particular state, and the "related behavior" was that associated with a change in the distribution of power. Hence, properly framed, the structural realist deduction is useful for understanding effects of regimes on the structure of the international system, but it is agnostic on the effects of international law on many matters other than structure.[7]

C. *Confusion over International Law as Epiphenomena*

Nonetheless – and here I offer an expressly revisionist intellectual history of the IL and IR debate – most IL commentators misinterpreted and misstated the argument in two ways. First, most oversimplified and confounded "structural realism" (the highly stylized realist theory that emerged in the late twentieth century) with "realism" (an approach to international law and international relations that was thousands of years old).[8] As a result, many international lawyers largely ignored the insights and conceptualizations offered by classical, early modern, and traditional realists.

Second, they broadened and oversimplified the structural claim into a straw man: "realists" believe that international law is epiphenomenal of underlying power and has no effect on state behavior or welfare.[9] Of course, that was never a realist claim, nor was it a proper deduction from structural realism. As demonstrated above, the idea that international law can benefit all states is consistent with the stance of all major realists: as shown above, Thucydides, Machiavelli, and Morgenthau believed that treaties can make state parties better off than otherwise – as did other twentieth-century realists like E. H. Carr, Winston Churchill, and Henry Kissinger (Carr 1946; Kissinger 1973; Hughes 1974).[10] Moreover, the logic of structural realism is entirely consistent with the conclusion that international law could make all states better off in absolute terms – a positive-sum effect of law. This simply was not something that hardcore structural realists cared about when they referred to "outcomes."

Hence, what should have been Krasner's narrow deduction about international regimes from structural realism morphed into a straw man that was perpetuated by the academy but that no one (not even structural realists) actually supported: "realism argues that international law does not matter." This became a call to arms

---

[7] This brief history of realism is not intended to suggest that realism ends with Waltz. In addition to subsequent applications described below, important variations have been offered, including offensive realism (Mearsheimer 2001), defensive realism (Grieco 1996; Wohlforth 2008), and neo-classical realism (Rose 1998), each of which offers a distinctive take on international law (Pollack 2011).These intellectual movements have not, however, been seen as benchmarks of realism that are as important as those offered by Thucydides, Machiavelli, Morgenthau, and Waltz – the core variants analyzed in greater depth in this chapter.

[8] See, for example, Slaughter (1993), Bederman (2002), Dickinson (2002), and Guzman (2008).

[9] See, for example, Slaughter (1993) and Abbott (1999).

[10] There are hundreds of contemporary treaties that realists would argue make all states better off: the Vienna Convention on the Law of Treaties (and the customary law it represents), the Agreement Establishing the World Trade Organization, and the Articles of Agreement of the International Monetary Fund, just to name a few (Morgenthau 1978; Gruber 2000; Steinberg 2002).

for international lawyers and law scholars. It became the null hypothesis that scores of scholars could use as a vehicle to motivate their argument that law does, in fact, affect behavior and outcomes.[11]

III. YOU CAN'T LIVE WITH IT; YOU CAN'T LIVE WITHOUT IT: THE ENDURANCE OF REALISM IN HYBRID THEORIES

Although many international law and international relations scholars condemned realism, few could live without it. Whether reading the *New York Times* or rationalist-institutionalist, liberal, or constructivist accounts of international law, the concept of the state and its fundamental place in international relations – which owes its lineage to classical realism – remains central to the way most people think about international relations, and the way they explain commitment to and compliance with international law. Yet, realism permeates approaches to international law in more complex ways.

As shown above, history's main realist figures – Thucydides, Machiavelli, and Morgenthau – sometimes blended nonrealist elements with the core elements of realism, in those cases offering hybrid accounts of international phenomena. Despite Waltz's critique of that approach, hybrid theories that use core realist elements endure. The effort to build pure, parsimonious, meta-theories of IL and IR that explain all levels of analysis – an effort associated with the debate over "isms" – has been unsuccessful (Katzenstein, Keohane, and Krasner 1998). As suggested in Dunoff and Pollack's introduction to this volume, Sil and Katzenstein's "analytic eclecticism," and Fearon and Wendt's "toolbox approach" to understanding international relations, particular questions – often mid-level inquiries – demand a broad set of tools, techniques, concepts, and factors drawn from multiple theoretical traditions (Fearon and Wendt 2002; Sil and Katzenstein 2010; Dunoff and Pollack 2013).

Hence, many analysts carefully blend realist concepts and causal narratives, particularly the role of state power in shaping international law, with elements of other traditions to create hybridized frameworks or theories that are progressive, expanding explanatory scope, and not subversive of realism. These hybrid approaches have increased the complexity of theories of international law (i.e., diminishing structural realism's parsimony), but they have also expanded the heuristic power of realism in international law.

A. *State Power, Interests, and Rationalism*

The ink hadn't dried on that part of the *International Regimes* volume in which Krasner posited a structural realist claim that international law might have no effect on "outcomes and related behavior" before Krasner distilled (in the same chapter)

---

[11] See, for example, Slaughter (1993), Abbott (1999), Bederman (2002), and Dickinson (2002).

a "modified structural" argument explaining how international law can affect outcomes and behavior in a manner consistent with the premises of structural realism
(1983a). Pioneered by Robert Keohane and Arthur Stein, this line of argument used
economic analysis to show how international law could facilitate cooperation that
could not otherwise occur (Keohane 1983, 1984; Stein 1983). International regimes,
which are constituted in large part by international law, reduce transactions and
communications costs of negotiating; credible commitments in treaties could solve
the prisoners' dilemma (Abbott 1993), which became the paradigmatic game for
showing that international law has effects; and international law could constitute
focal points that solved simple coordination problems (Garrett and Weingast 1993).[12]

Even though it is entirely consistent with structural realism and is built on the same
assumptions and concepts on which structural realism is premised, this approach
became known as "rationalist institutionalism," and arguments that employed the
approach often began by purporting to distinguish themselves from "realism." In fact,
the approach is better understood as an economic explanation as to how international
law can improve the welfare of states, consistent with the claims of realists throughout
history.

The use of economic analysis and the assumptions of structural realism have
allowed a clearer understanding of how law can move states along the Pareto frontier or toward it, symmetrically or asymmetrically. Early regime theorists, often
preferring to be called "rationalist" or "institutionalist," emphasized international
law that facilitates cooperation and is Pareto improving, and focused on examples
that replicated the prisoners' dilemma, implying that all cooperation was Pareto
improving and implicitly assuming away distributive conflict. Realists responded
with examples of pure distributive conflict along the Pareto frontier (Krasner 1983a).
Morrow (1994) and Fearon (1998) later noted that there are many ways to cooperate,
that the terms of cooperation influence who gains more, and that power is likely
to be used in negotiations over international law to set the terms of cooperation
and determine who wins more and who wins less. Subsequent realist scholarship
has shown how relative state power has shaped the content of international law,
yielding international law bargaining outcomes that may be Pareto improving but
are still skewed distributively in favor of powerful states (Krasner 1999; Gruber
2000; Steinberg 2002). Work on the rational design of international institutions,
which uses similar premises and economic argumentation to systematically explain
when international law employs particular types of legal mechanisms, has recapit-
ulated this line of argument to explain both symmetric Pareto-improving outcomes
and some asymmetric outcomes (Koremenos, Lipson, and Snidal 2001). Barbara
Koremenos's chapter on institutionalism in this volume (2013) expands on this
approach. Taken together, this body of work, using realist elements and premises in

---

[12] Subsequent work suggested employing many of these concepts and the economic method to better
understand international law (Dunoff and Trachtman 1999).

conjunction with economic analysis and other factors, has shown how rational unitary states, with varying power and all pursuing self-interest, can drive international law so as to facilitate movement along the Pareto plane in any direction – thus providing a way to explain the negotiated content of essentially all treaties.[13]

B. *State Power, Interests, Liberalism – and Feedback from International Law*

Analysis of the formulation of state interests may be combined with assessments of relative power among states to explain the formation of international law. As argued above, interests (other than survival) are exogenous to realism. Liberalism can fill that hole, offering a way to understand the formation of state interests based on competition among substate actors with varying interests (Moravcsik 1997). Andrew Moravcsik's chapter in this volume expands on this approach. Interest groups, political parties, branches of government, bureaucratic agencies – or all of the above – may compete with one another to define the national interest. International law may then be seen as a product of power-based negotiations among states, each of which has sorted out its own interests through liberal, bottom-up processes.[14]

In these kinds of hybrid arguments, state agency varies in scale and form. Robert Putnam, for example, conceptualized international treaty negotiations as a two-level game – simultaneous negotiations between competing interests at the domestic level and negotiations between states over treaty content at the international level, with each state's negotiator intermediating at both levels (Putnam 1998). Combined with realism, this analysis could be used to suggest that powerful countries' chief negotiators represent state interests in ways consistent with realism and that they have agency to choose from among two-level solutions, enabling them to simultaneously shape international law, as well as domestic political structure and outcomes at home and abroad.[15]

More broadly, disaggregating the state in conjunction with realist analysis allows us to see how international law may feed back onto domestic politics, shaping state institutions (Gourevitch 1978). Powerful states may use international law as a vehicle for shaping the form and capacity of the state in weaker countries (Steinberg forthcoming). In powerful countries, the state may make international law that transforms the authority of the various branches of its own government (Goldstein and Steinberg 2006).

---

[13] This is the tack taken in Goldsmith and Posner (2005) and Guzman (2008), although they deny that their approach is realist.

[14] Waltz (1954) captures this model in his "second image." For an account of international trade negotiations using this approach, see Bauer, de Sola Pool, and Dexter (1963).

[15] Of course, Putnam's negotiating strategies, focused on manipulation of one's own and other states' domestic interests, are distinctive from the state centrism of the realist tradition, and Putnam's conception of bargaining power was fundamentally different from the material capabilities approach of most realists.

C. *State Power, Interests, and Social Theory*

Realist elements have also been blended with social theory to offer hybrid explanations of international law. Social theory is described in Jutta Brunée and Stephen Toope's (2013) chapter on constructivism in this volume, and in it one can see elements of realist argumentation.

State interests may be defined by social processes and then mediated in negotiations among states, becoming embodied in international law to the extent that powerful states advance them. For example, Peter Haas conceptualized transnational epistemic communities as framing certain types of international problems and solutions, which could be embodied in treaties, but Haas frames his theory as an add-on to realism: the views of the epistemic community are mediated through states of varying power, some of which may not always defer to the views of the epistemic community (Haas 1992).

Several scholars have argued that social norms may become part of international law when advanced by a powerful state. For example, Krasner combined realism with Louis Hartz's argument that liberalism has driven U.S. foreign policy, explaining the conclusion of treaties advancing U.S. objectives in Vietnam and liberal objectives elsewhere (Hartz 1955; Krasner 1978). Edward Said and others have argued that the Western (Grotian) law of war has spread across the globe in a process led by the United States and Europe, but has encountered resistance from Asian states (Said 1978; Engle 2000). Beth Simmons explains treaties combating human trafficking as resulting partly from Western norms and political pressure on weaker, non-Western states (Simmons 2011). More broadly, Judith Goldstein and Robert Keohane argued that ideas have shaped U.S. foreign policy, which in some cases has been transferred into treaties (Goldstein and Keohane 1993). In all of these accounts, normative impulses become causally important through the application of state power, not through the power of ideas alone.

The social concept of "organized hypocrisy" has also been joined with realism to explain the persistence of declared legal norms that are routinely ignored by powerful states. For example, Krasner argued that powerful states routinely intervene in the internal structures of weaker states, but the fiction of Westphalian sovereignty persists, partly because it legitimizes the domestic sovereignty of rulers in all states (Brunsson 1989; Krasner 1999). Similarly, this author has argued that international decision-making rules derived from the principle of the sovereign equality of states are based on a fiction, as sources of power extrinsic to those rules are used to drive outcomes favored by powerful states; the rules persist because of their normative appeal to weak states and because they enable powerful states to discover the preferences of weaker states, which is useful for shaping politically feasible international legal outcomes (Steinberg 2002).

Most broadly, some critical social constructivists have argued that the structure and content of international legal rules replicate power relations within and across states

(Kratochwil 1989; Charlesworth, Chinkin, and Wright 1991; Meyer *et al.* 1997), a line of argument that resonates with realists. David Kennedy argues that sovereignty is an organizing principle that is sure to perpetuate war and replicate processes between states that lead to war (Kennedy 1988). And Alexander Wendt has argued that realism is itself a social construction that defines a world in which states, if they subscribe to the theory, will behave as prescribed by it (Wendt 1992).

D. *State Power, Interests, and Empiricism*

Empiricism, particularly the use of models and regressions, is all the rage in political science. Econometric models that employ and test the significance of state power for explaining international law are the ultimate hybrid, with investigators willing to combine realism's distinctive causal factors with a myriad of other factors from multiple traditions to answer a carefully framed question about international law – without the straightjacket of a particular or limited set of theoretical traditions. Careful empiricists must often test whether power matters in explaining the phenomenon central to their inquiry: failure to do so may yield omitted variable bias or nonconsideration of the obvious hypothesis that power matters. And doing so often reveals that state power (in terms of per capita GDP, alliance power, total military spending, or some other measure) is a significant explanatory factor,[16] as realism predicts.

E. *Evaluating Hybrids*

Three criteria may be useful in evaluating the heuristic power of combining realist elements with other traditions. These criteria reveal some potential limits of realist hybrid theories.

First, one goal of hybridizing realism with other traditions could be to generally expand explanatory and predictive capacity: optimally, the injection of realist elements should be theoretically progressive (Popper 1959; Kuhn 1962; Lakatos 1970). The realist factors should not only add post hoc explanatory power to the case or cases being considered, but should also add explanatory or predictive power to other cases. Otherwise, realism is just supplementing an inadequate theory to save it in a particular case and not enhancing that theory's utility more generally.

Second, in evaluating purported or apparent hybrid approaches, attention must be paid to see whether realism is being subverted by nonrealist factors or dynamics. "Subversion" refers to an instance in which the main factors used in a framework

---

[16] Examples of good empirical work that confirms the significance of power as an explanatory factor include Goldstein, Rivers, and Tomz (2007), in showing effects of GATT/WTO rules, they controlled for GNP per capita; Gowa and Kim (2005), GNP per capita and alliance power; Busch and Reinhardt (2003), weak countries use WTO dispute settlement less than do powerful countries because of cost; and Sattler and Bernauer (2011), dyads of powerful and weak countries settle in WTO dispute settlement to the disadvantage of weak.

are supplemented by other factors, and in the application of the framework the supplementary factors do all the work – subverting the significance of the main factors.[17] When does a hybrid realist story remain realist? The key is that the state must remain the central actor in the international system, and either state power or convergent state interests must play a role in the explanation of international law. For example, consider what might appear to be a realist–liberal hybrid: if interests become transnational and no longer nationally distinct, and states uniformly act as conveyer belts of substate interests, then the story is not realist even though the state may appear to be an actor in it. Consider a purported realist–social theory hybrid: if a norms cascade spills across all states to explain a new international consensus, or if state delegates in international negotiations become "transgovernmental actors" that together define new universal interests that are not reflective of their state's preferences, then any elements that might have appeared realist do not matter. And if a regression result fails to confirm that state power is significantly related to commitment or compliance, then the explanation has no realist element to it.

Third, realist factors in a hybrid theory must be weighted relative to other factors. Without weighting, merely a framework for analysis has been offered: if state power is one of many factors explaining the negotiation of an international law, then it must be weighted against the other factors in order to constitute a clear explanation. Weighting can be achieved through statistical methods (as in a regression) or by establishing contingencies in which a variable is effective or determinative, or by other means.

IV. REALIST UNDERSTANDING OF INTERNATIONAL LAW-MAKING, INTERPRETATION, COMPLIANCE, AND GLOBAL LEGAL STRUCTURE

Given the expansive realist literature on international relations and law, a complete review of all that has been learned from realism is beyond the scope of this chapter. Instead, some basic lessons are recounted.

A. *Making International Law*

From the perspective of Austinian positivism and most other contemporary theories of international law, state consent remains the touchstone of international law-making. As suggested by the realist–rationalist hybrid recounted in the section "You Can't Live with It; You Can't Live without It," *nonpolitical* international law may solve coordination or cooperation problems, yielding outcomes that are beneficial to all states, so consent to that international law could be voluntary. At the other

---

[17] Robert Keohane (forthcoming) has used this concept to critique Stephen Krasner, accusing him of subverting realism in his argument.

extreme, realism teaches that some *political* international law is made by powerful states coercing the "consent" of weaker states (Krasner 1999; Steinberg 2002). Other political international law, such as treaties of alliance, may be catalyzed by system structure and so may be in the mutual self-interest of the state parties, with no coercion required.

Most international law is made in the contemporary epoch through treaties or international organizations. Whenever treaty law yields asymmetric distributive consequences favoring powerful states, it is likely that some element of coercion was at play. Asymmetry may or may not be accompanied by Pareto improvement of the parties: often, international law produces an asymmetric coordination outcome or focal point that favors powerful states (Garrett and Weingast 1993). Coercion may be overtly military, as in Japan's Treaty of Surrender to the United States, in which treaty "consent" was derived through duress, or it may be achieved less overtly through economic pressure, as when the International Monetary Fund (IMF) imposes conditionality agreements on countries in the midst of a financial crisis.

Hard law made by international organizations results from decision-making procedures that usually reflect underlying power. United Nations Security Council actions, for example, are made through weighted voting: the five permanent members, each powerful states, each have a veto over Security Council actions. Similarly, IMF voting is weighted by special drawing right (SDR) contributions, giving the United States more votes than any other country. Voting in the European Union (EU) Council, its most important legislative body, is cast by country, with each country's vote weighted by population.

Realists have long argued that – empirically – powerful countries permit majoritarianism only in organizations that are legally competent to produce only soft law, which poses little risk that powerful states would be bound by legal undertakings they might disfavor (Riches 1940, 297, 894; Morgenthau 1978, 327; Zamora 1980; Krasner 1983*b*). There have been efforts to redefine the distinction between "hard" and "soft" law and to argue that soft law may be effective or might transform into hard law,[18] but conventionally the distinction has turned on whether the public international law in question is mandatory or hortatory. Conventionally, most public international lawyers, realists, and positivists consider soft law to be inconsequential.[19]

But even when decision-making in an international organization is not formally weighted, such as actions taken according to the sovereign equality principle of consensus, decisions reflect underlying power because powerful states use sources of power extrinsic to the decision-making rules to pressure weaker states into joining the consensus. For realists, state "consent" in international law-making is often a fiction (Steinberg 2002; Steinberg 2004*a*).

---

[18] See, for example, Raustiala and Victor (1998) and Abbott and Snidal (2000).
[19] See, for example, Hart (1961: 77–96), Simma and Paulus (1999: 304), and Shaffer and Pollack (2013).

In nonpolitical areas of international law, custom is easily accepted from a realist perspective. For example, the law of treaties is easily accepted because it is in every state's self-interest to have a system that enables Pareto-improving contracts. Similarly, the customary law of diplomatic immunity is easily accepted because it is in every state's interest to support unfettered communication between states.

In contrast, declarations of customary law that contradict powerful countries' interests are usually contested. Contestation typically focuses on *opinio juris*, whether an action was carried out because of legal obligation – the required "psychological" prong of the two-part test for custom. Those aspiring to have customary law used to complete the international legal order and fetter power have an expansive view of what evidences *opinio juris*.[20] Realists (and some other theoretical traditions) demand a clear expression of consent in order to demonstrate *opinio juris*. Some now take the position that it is possible to withdraw from customary law (Bradley and Gulati 2010): if consent is the touchstone of international law, and states may withdraw their consent to treaties, then why can't they withdraw from customary law that no longer serves their interest? Powerful states bristle at efforts to impose custom upon them through an expansive stance on *opinio juris*, and they do not abide by purported custom resulting from that stance.

Thus, whether we focus on treaties, customary international law, or soft law, international law is made through processes, rules, and assertions of power that ensure it will reflect the interests of powerful states.

B. *Interpreting International Law*

Realists do not believe that judicial interpretation of international law can fundamentally shift the balance of rights and responsibilities established through the law-making process because judicial interpretation of international legal commitments is constrained and determined by international politics. Legal interpretation by an international tribunal involves a discursive process of legal reasoning that takes place within a constitutional system of checks and balances established in the treaty that created the international tribunal.[21] But both the discursive process and constitutional structure are constrained by an international power structure that can change constitutional rules or otherwise influence the process of interpretation. As long as interpretations by international tribunals do not fundamentally shift the balance of rights and responsibilities established in a treaty, then powerful states will generally support and comply with tribunal decisions: after all, realism tells us that the rules were made in accordance with the interests of powerful states.

---

[20] See, for example, Simma and Paulus (1999).
[21] For a variant of this claim, see Pauwelyn and Elsig (2013).

However, if interpretations do change the balance of rights and responsibilities to the detriment of powerful states, those states may refuse to comply with the tribunal's decision, operate through the constitutional structure of the regime to reverse or check the tribunal, or rewrite constitutional structure to change judicial decisions, processes, or authority (Steinberg 2004*b*). Hence, interpretation replicates power.[22]

C. Compliance with and Enforcement of International Law

Realists believe that compliance with public international law is generally quite good (Morgenthau 1978). Moreover, compliance usually does not require an overt act of enforcement. States often formulate treaties that require them to do little more than they would do in the absence of a treaty (Downs, Rocke, and Barsoom 1998). Nonpolitical international law is in the self-interest of all states, so they generally comply with it. Similarly, political international law necessitated by system structure often enjoys compliance because it is in the interest of the affected states to comply.

Compliance with treaties made through coercion is more complicated: it often requires a threat by powerful states to coerce compliance. Compliance with coerced treaty law may require boots on the ground or constant coercive diplomacy (George 1991), particularly when security issues are at stake. Usually, however, compliance is secured in the shadow of coercive action.

Since laws made by international organizations reflect the interests of powerful states (by processes described above), powerful states support compliance with those rules by all parties (themselves included). Hence, powerful states are generally happy to support enforcement procedures in international organizations, even if those procedures are not biased in their favor. For example, compliance with multilateral trade law is generally achieved by using the World Trade Organization's (WTO) dispute settlement process, which was designed to allow all states to threaten retaliation against products from a country that persists in contravening its WTO obligations. That threat catalyzes targeted industries in the contravening country to lobby their government to lift the illegal measure, a process that has resulted in a greater than 90 percent rate of compliance with WTO dispute settlement decisions, even among powerful countries (Steinberg 2004*b*). Contrary to a common misperception, therefore, realist theory does not posit that powerful states will never accept or comply with judicial decisions against them in any particular case.

[22] There is increasing evidence that international dispute settlement systems, such as the WTO's, may operate to the advantage of powerful countries. Weak countries may tend to use international adjudication less than more powerful ones because doing so is costly (Busch and Reinhardt 2003). And dyads of powerful and weak countries tend to settle cases in at least some fora to the disadvantage of the weak (Sattler and Bernauer 2011).

D. *Realism and the Structure of International Law*

The preceding realist account of international law-making, interpretation, compliance, and enforcement provides the microfoundations for realism's explanation of the structure of international law.

Morgenthau's view that international law must be in the interest of states subscribing to it, and his distinction between political and nonpolitical international law, were mirrored by Soviet theorists, who argued that international law is a superstructure reflecting the Cold War's capitalist–communist split and distinguishing between international law among "capitalist states" and international law among all states (Hazard 1950; Lissitzyn 1952).

The structure of political international law reflects the structure of the international system. During the Cold War, the United States built a Western international legal system (Gruber 2000; Ikenberry 2000) and the Soviet Union built its own. The General Agreement on Tariffs and Trade (GATT) defined the Western trade regime, with the European Economic Community embedded in it (partly so that economics would harden the bulwark of containment on the Soviet western flank); the Council for Mutual Economic Assistance (COMECON) defined the Eastern bloc's trade regime. The North Atlantic Treaty (NATO), with the Coordinating Committee for Multilateral Export Controls (COCOM) export control list bolstering the West's military-technological advantage, defined the Western security regime; the Warsaw Pact defined the East's. In human rights, the Covenant on Civil and Political Rights enjoyed broad Western support, whereas the Covenant on Economic, Social, and Cultural Rights enjoyed more support from the East.

The structure of political international law changed in the immediate post–Cold War era. In the early post–Cold War years, COMECON and the Warsaw Pact collapsed. NATO, EU, and GATT/WTO membership all surged, in large part to solidify in law the West's Cold War gains. The COCOM regime also collapsed, as its raison d'être had disappeared. The Euro was created, in large part to embrace and contain a reunified Germany that would thereafter be at the heart of the EU.

More subtle, slower changes in international legal structure have accompanied the gradual decline of U.S. economic hegemony and the attendant dispersion of economic power. The 2008 financial crisis and the 2011–12 Euro crisis exposed the weakness of the once almighty IMF. During the Cold War, the GATT was the world's predominant trade regime, and only a handful of customs unions and free-trade areas were embedded within it. Since the end of the Cold War, as U.S. and European shares of GATT/WTO GDP have declined, and those of China, Brazil, India (and now Russia) have increased, it has become impossible to conclude new, substantial multilateral trade agreements in the WTO. Instead, trade agreements are being struck bilaterally, plurilaterally, and regionally: the number of operational, preferential trade agreements in the world grew from less than 50 in 1991 to more than 500 by 2010. Consistent with the prediction of realist hegemonic stability theory (Krasner 1976; Gilpin 1981), the international trade treaty system appears to be fracturing and fragmenting,[23] with the liberalization dynamic shifting from multilateralism to regionalism.

Nonpolitical international law, by contrast, transcends changes in the political structure of the international system. The law of treaties, admiralty, and international commercial law, for example, enjoy the same universal support and are interpreted the same way now as during the Cold War. The law of treaties is constitutive of an international legal system that enables contracting based on state consent. Admiralty law solves simple coordination problems, without bias favoring any one country or countries. And international commercial law solves information problems facing private traders, facilitating transactions when they are mutually beneficial. These laws do not depend on any particular political structure, and it is in the self-interest of all states to commit and comply with them.

Constructivists have argued that thousands of years of realist thinking and teaching has taught rulers to act like realists. Another possibility is that material factors, geography, and historical paths have conspired to make the state the central unit of governance, and the dynamics of interaction between states competing to advance their interests have yielded behavior well-described and explained by realism. Either way, realism appears to have broad explanatory power.

V. CONCLUSIONS: LIMITS, STRENGTHS, AND NORMATIVE AGENDAS IN INTERNATIONAL LAW

Like any other tradition in or theory of international law, realism has strengths and limits. It is but one of several lenses that brings into focus some parts of the mosaic that is international law, but leaves other parts blurred or unobservable.

A. Some Limits

To be sure, realism has limited explanatory power. Without elaboration from other disciplines and approaches, it is hard to identify what "work" law is doing – how and why it affects behavior and outcomes, and the contexts in which it does so. Realism is also better at explaining the development of international law that affects material interests (such as economic welfare and security) than areas of international law that are aimed at advancing normative agendas (such as human rights). Structural realism also has some difficulty explaining the end of the Cold War and the associated end of bipolarity: this crucial change in the structure of the system and international law cannot be understood without reference to what took place within the Soviet Union – a reductionist analysis. Realism does not account for feedback from the international

---

[23] On fragmentation, see Raustiala (2013).

institutions that have been created by state parties: those institutions can reinforce or modify the interests of member states and nonmember states. Moreover, it has often been observed that there are lags between a shift in the distribution of power and changes in the substance or structure of international law; this suggests that not all international law can be deduced from knowing only which states are powerful and what their interests are.

Perhaps most problematic for realism: where do interests come from? When the substance of international law changes because the interests of powerful states have shifted, then explanation derives at least as much from the nonrealist story about the source of interests as from the realist framework that helps us understand how the normative shift translates into new international law.

B. *Some Strengths*

Properly understood, realism has many strengths. The preceding section showed that the core elements of realism can explain much about international law. Many of our most basic behavioralist generalizations about international law are derived from realism: states consent to treaties that advance their interests, noncompliance with a treaty often takes place because the treaty is no longer in the interest of one or more parties to it, powerful states have more influence over the content of a treaty than weaker states, and the like.

Moreover, realism offers this explanatory and predictive power with parsimony. Particularly in its structural form, devoid of complicating reductionist elements, realism offers explanations and predictions about international law – law-making, interpretation, compliance, and structure – using relatively few variables. It is elegantly simple.

By privileging the state as the main unit of analysis, realism reaches across the international law and international relations divide. For almost all international jurists, lawyers, and scholars, international law is premised on the consent of sovereign states – the entities that create public international law. Hence, with the state as the central actor, realism resonates louder with public international law scholars and practitioners than other behavioralist theories that privilege substate, transnational, or transgovernmental actors.

C. *Science and Art in the Cloudlike World of International Law*

The limits of realism (and every other ism) may suggest that it is better employed as a tradition than as a theory. As noted above, efforts to explain and predict all aspects of international law and international relations through the lens of any particular meta-theory have proven fruitless. New ideas about the world keep norms and epistemologies in a constant state of change, so social reality is constantly transforming. The social world may be better understood as cloudlike, with indeterminate edges and in constant flux, than clocklike, with precise, easily predictable mechanical movement (Popper 1959).

In that world, using a single set of heuristic tools to explain and predict international law and associated behavior across long spans of time and broad geographic space will be of limited utility. Hybrid theories are necessary to understand at least some phenomena. And empiricism's effort to explain mid-level phenomena, using concepts and causal narratives from multiple traditions, offers the promise of making precise explanatory and predictive claims about phenomena within narrowly specified time periods and geographic contexts. But, given the broad explanatory power of realist concepts, causal narratives, insights, and intuitions, the realist tradition must be part of the tool kit.

The realist tradition must also be central to the art of international law and international relations. Realism does have a modest normative component. Machiavelli's conceptualization of and preference for the economy of violence[24] should not be underestimated: realism has saved (and could have saved) countless lives by challenging the foolishness of various proposed policies. But this prescriptive element, premised on a widely held norm about the sanctity of human life, hardly counts as a moral compass in the way offered by naturalism and moral philosophy. For the most part, normative agendas will be derived from traditions other than realism.

Yet, it would be hard to assess a strategy for advancing any particular normative agenda in international law without considering which states are powerful and what their interests may be. A lawyer within the foreign ministry of a powerful state, charged with advancing a particular objective in international law, would err by not considering the interests of other states and the sources of power all states could bring to a negotiation. Whether the objective is advancing international law favoring liberalization, civil and political rights, humanitarian law, or national security, considerations of state power and state interests must be central.

No one trying to understand or practice international law can ignore the state, state power, or state interests. The realist tradition remains important to positive theory about international law and to normative agendas. In that sense, everybody is still a realist.

REFERENCES

Abbott, Kenneth W. (1993). "'Trust But Verify': The Production of Information in Arms Control Treaties and Other International Agreements," *Cornell International Law Journal*, Vol. 26, pp. 1–58.

——— (1999). "International Relations Theory, International Law, and the Regime Governing Atrocities in Internal Conflicts," *American Journal of International Law*, Vol. 93, No. 2, pp. 361–79.

---

[24] Machiavelli (1908), Ch. XVII; Bull (1966).

Abbott, Kenneth W., and Duncan Snidal (2000). "Hard Law and Soft Law in International Governance," *International Organization*, Vol. 54, No. 3, pp. 421–56.

Aquinas, Thomas (1947). *Summa Theologica*, translated by the Fathers of the English Dominican Province (New York: Benziger Brothers).

Austin, John (1832). *The Province of Justice Determined* (London: John Murray, Albemarle Street).

Bauer, Raymond, Ithiel de Sola Pool, and Lewis Anthony Dexter (1963). *American Business and Public Policy: The Politics of Foreign Trade* (New York: Atherton Press).

Bederman, David J. (2002). *The Spirit of International Law* (Athens: University of Georgia Press).

Bradley, Curtis A., and G. Mitu Gulati (2010). "Withdrawing from International Custom," *Yale Law Journal*, Vol. 120, No. 2, pp. 202–75.

Brunnée, Jutta, and Stephen Toope (2013). "Constructivism and International Law," in Jeffrey L. Dunoff and Mark A. Pollack (eds.), *Interdisciplinary Perspectives on International Law and International Relations: The State of the Art* (New York: Cambridge University Press), pp. 119–45.

Brunsson, Nils (1989). *The Organization of Hypocrisy: Talk, Decisions and Actions in Organizations* (New York: John Wiley & Sons).

Bull, Hedley (1966). "International Theory: The Case for a Classical Approach," *World Politics*, Vol. 18, No. 3, pp. 361–77.

Busch, Marc L., and Eric Reinhardt (2003). "Developing Countries and GATT/WTO Dispute Settlement," *Journal of World Trade*, Vol. 37, No. 4, pp. 719–35.

Carr, E. H. (1946). *The Twenty Years' Crisis, 1919–1939*, 2nd ed. (London: Macmillan).

Charlesworth, Hillary, Christine Chinkin, and Shelley Wright (1991). "Feminist Approaches to International Law," *American Journal of International Law*, Vol. 85, No. 4, pp. 613–45.

Charnovitz, Steve (2002). "WTO Cosmopolitics," *New York University Journal of International Law and Politics*, Vol. 34, No. 2, pp. 299–354.

Dahl, Robert A. (1957). "The Concept of Power," *Behavioral Science*, Vol. 3, No. 2, pp. 201–15.

Dickinson, Laura A. (2002). "Using Legal Process to Fight Terrorism: Detentions, Military Commissions, International Tribunals and the Rule of Law," *Southern California Law Review*, Vol. 75, No. 6, pp. 1407–92.

Downs, George W., David M. Rocke, and Petern N. Barsoom (1998). "Managing the Evolution of Multilateralism," *International Organization*, Vol. 52, No. 2, pp. 397–420.

Dunoff, Jeffrey L., and Mark A. Pollack (2013). "International Law and International Relations:Introducing an Interdisciplinary Dialogue," in Jeffrey L. Dunoff and Mark A. Pollack (eds.), *Interdisciplinary Perspectives on International Law and International Relations: The State of the Art* (New York: Cambridge University Press), pp. 3–32.

Dunoff, Jeffrey L., and Joel P. Trachtman (1999). "Economic Analysis of International Law," *Yale Journal of International Law*, Vol. 24, No. 1, pp. 1–59.

Engle, Karen (2000). "Culture and Human Rights: The Asian Values Debate in Context," *New York University Journal of International Law and Politics*, Vol. 32, No. 2, pp. 291–333.

Fearon, James D. (1998). "Bargaining, Enforcement, and International Cooperation," *International Organization*, Vol. 52, No. 2, pp. 269–305.

Fearon, James, and Alexander Wendt (2002). "Rationalism v. Constructivism: A Skeptical View," in Walter Carlsnaes, Thomas Risse, and Beth Simmons (eds.), *Handbook of International Relations Theory* (London: Sage Publications), pp. 52–72.

Finnemore, Martha, and Kathryn Sikkink (1998). "International Norm Dynamics and Political Change," *International Organization*, Vol. 52, No. 4, pp. 887–917.

Garrett, Geoffrey, and Barry R. Weingast (1993). "Ideas, Interests, and Institutions: Constructing the European Community's Internal Market," in Judith Goldstein and Robert O. Keohane (eds.), *Ideas and Foreign Policy: Beliefs, Institutions, and Political Change* (Ithaca, NY: Cornell University Press), pp. 173–206.

George, Alexander (1991). *Forceful Persuasion: Coercive Diplomacy as an Alternative to War* (Washington, DC: United States Institute of Peace Press).

Gilpin, Robert (1981). *War and Change in International Politics* (Cambridge: Cambridge University Press).

Goldsmith, Jack L., and Eric A. Posner (2005). *The Limits of International Law* (New York: Oxford University Press).

Goldstein, Judith L., and Robert O. Keohane (eds.) (1993). *Ideas & Foreign Policy: Beliefs, Institutions and Political Change* (Ithaca, NY: Cornell University Press).

Goldstein, Judith L., Douglas Rivers, and Michael Tomz (2007). "Institutions in International Relations: Understanding the Effects of the GATT and the WTO on World Trade," *International Organization*, Vol. 61, No. 1, pp. 37–67.

Goldstein, Judith L., and Richard H. Steinberg (2008). "Negotiate or Litigate? The Effects of WTO Judicial Delegation on U.S. Trade Politics," *Law & Contemporary Problems*, Vol. 71, No. 1, pp. 257–82.

Gourevitch, Peter (1978). "The Second Image Reversed: The International Sources of Domestic Politics," *International Organization*, Vol. 32, No. 4, pp. 881–912.

Gowa, Joanne, and Soo Yeon Kim (2005). "An Exclusive Country Club: The Effects of the GATT on Trade, 1950–1994," *World Politics*, Vol. 57, No. 4, pp. 453–78.

Grieco, J. (1996). "State Interests and International Rule Trajectories: A Neorealist Interpretation of the Maastricht Treaty and European Economic and Monetary Union," *Security Studies*, Vol. 5, pp. 176–222

Grotius, Hugo (1901). *The Rights of War and Peace, Including the Law of Nature and of Nations*, translated by A. M. Campbell (New York: M. Walter Dunne).

Gruber, Lloyd (2000). *Ruling the World: Power Politics and the Rise of Supranational Institutions* (Princeton, NJ: Princeton University Press).

Guzman, Andrew T. (2008). *How International Law Works: A Rational Choice Theory* (New York: Oxford University Press).

Haas, Peter M. (1992). "Banning Chlorofluorocarbons: Epistemic Community Efforts to Protect Stratospheric Ozone," *International Organization*, Vol. 46, No. 1, pp. 187–224.

Hart, H. L. A. (1961). *The Concept of Law* (Oxford: Oxford University Press).

Hartz, Louis (1955). *The Liberal Tradition in America: An Interpretation of American Political Thought since the Revolution* (New York: Harcourt, Brace & World).

Hazard, J. N. (1950). "The Soviet Union and International Law," *Soviet Studies*, Vol. 1, pp. 189–99.

Hoffmann, Stanley (1971). "Weighing the Balance of Power," *Foreign Affairs*, Vol. 50, No. 4, pp. 618–43.

Holmes, Oliver Wendell (1881). *The Common Law* (Boston: Little, Brown, and Co.).

Hughes, E. J. (1974). "Winston Churchill and the Formation of the United Nations Organization," *Journal of Contemporary History*, Vol. 9, No. 4, 177–94.

Ikenberry, G. John (2000). *After Victory: Institutions, Strategic Restraint, and the Rebuilding of Order after Major Wars* (Princeton, NJ: Princeton University Press).

Kagan, Donald (1974). *The Archidamian War* (Ithaca, NY: Cornell University Press).

Katzenstein, Peter J., Robert O. Keohane, and Stephen D. Krasner (1998). "International Organization and the Study of World Politics," *International Organization*, Vol. 52, No. 4, pp. 645–85.

Kelson, Hans (1942). *Law and Peace in International Relations* (Cambridge, MA: Harvard University Press).

Kennedy, David (1988). "International Law and the Nineteenth Century: History of an Illusion," *Quinnipiac Law Review*, Vol. 19, pp. 99–136.

Keohane, Robert O. (1983). "The Demand for International Regimes," in Stephen D. Krasner (ed.), *International Regimes* (Ithaca, NY: Cornell University Press), pp. 325–55.

——— (1984). *After Hegemony: Cooperation and Discord in the World Political Economy* (Princeton, NJ: Princeton University Press).

——— (forthcoming). "Stephen Krasner: Subversive Realist" in Martha Finnemore and Judith Goldstein (eds.), *Power in the Contemporary Era* (Cambridge: Cambridge University Press).

Keohane, Robert O., and Joseph Nye (1972). "Transnational Relations and World Politics: An Introduction," *International Organization*, Vol. 25, No. 3, pp. 329–49.

Kindleberger, Charles P. (1969). *American Business Abroad* (New Haven, CT: Yale University Press).

Kingsbury, Benedict, Nico Krisch, and Richard B. Stewart (2005). "The Emergence of Global Administrative Law," *Law & Contemporary Problems*, Vol. 68, No. 1, pp. 15–61.

Kissinger, Henry (1973). *A World Restored: Metternich, Castlereagh, and the Problems of Peace, 1812–1822* (New York: Houghton Mifflin).

Koh, Harold H. (2004). "International Law as Part of Our Law," *American Journal of International Law*, Vol. 98, No. 1, pp. 43–57.

Koremenos, Barbara (2013). "Institutionalism and International Law," in Jeffrey L. Dunoff and Mark A. Pollack (eds.), *Interdisciplinary Perspectives on International Law and International Relations: The State of the Art* (New York: Cambridge University Press), pp. 59–82.

Koremenos, Barbara, Charles Lipson, and Duncan Snidal (2001). "The Rational Design of International Institutions," *International Organization*, Vol. 55, No. 4, pp. 761–99.

Krasner, Stephen D. (1976). "State Power and the Structure of International Trade," *World Politics*, Vol. 28, No. 3, pp. 317–47.

——— (1978). *Defending the National Interest: Raw Materials, Investments, and U.S. Foreign Policy* (Princeton, NJ: Princeton University Press).

——— (1983a). "Structural Causes and Regime Consequences: Regimes as Intervening Variables," in Stephen D. Krasner (ed.), *International Regimes* (Ithaca, NY: Cornell University Press), pp. 1–21.

——— (1983b). "Regimes and the Limits of Realism: Regimes as Autonomous Variables," in Stephen D. Krasner (ed.), *International Regimes* (Ithaca, NY: Cornell University Press), pp. 355–68.

——— (1991). "Global Communications and National Power: Life on the Pareto Frontier," *World Politics*, Vol. 43, No. 3, pp. 336–66.

——— (1999). *Sovereignty: Organized Hypocrisy* (Princeton, NJ: Princeton University Press).

Kratochwil, Friedrich (1989). *Rules, Norms and Decisions: On the Conditions of Practical and Legal Reasoning in International Relations and Domestic Society* (Cambridge: Cambridge University Press).

Kuhn, Thomas S. (1962). *The Structure of Scientific Revolutions* (Chicago: University of Chicago Press).

Lakatos, Imre (1970). Falsification and the Methodology of Scientific Research Programmes, in Imre Lakatos and Alan Musgrave (eds.), *Criticism and the Growth of Knowledge* (Cambridge: Cambridge University Press), pp. 91–196.

Lauterpacht, Hersch (1946). "The Grotian Tradition in International Law," *The British Year Book of International Law*, Vol. 23, pp. 1–53.

Legro, Jeffrey W., and Andrew Moravcsik (1999). "Is Anybody Still a Realist?," *International Security*, Vol. 24, No. 2, pp. 5–55.

Lissitzyn, O. J. (1952). "Recent Soviet Literature on International Law," *The American Slavic and East European Review*, Vol. 11, No. 4, pp. 257–73.

Machiavelli, Niccolò (1908). *The Prince*, translated by W. K. Marriott (London: J. M. Dent).

Mearsheimer, John J. (2001). *The Tragedy of Great Power Politics* (New York: Norton).

Meyer, John W., John Boli, George M. Thomas, and Francisco O. Ramirez (1997). "World Society and the Nation State," *American Journal of Sociology*, Vol. 103, No. 1, pp. 144–81.

Moravcsik, Andrew (1997). "Taking Preferences Seriously: A Liberal Theory of International Politics," *International Organization*, Vol. 51, No. 4, pp. 513–53.

——— (2013). "Liberal Theories of International Law," in Jeffrey L. Dunoff and Mark A. Pollack (eds.), *Interdisciplinary Perspectives on International Law and International Relations: The State of the Art* (New York: Cambridge University Press), pp. 83–118.

Morgenthau, Hans J. (1940). "Positivism, Functionalism and International Law," *American Journal of International Law*, Vol. 34, No. 2, pp. 260–84.

——— (1978). *Politics among Nations: The Struggle for Power and Peace*, 5th ed. (New York: Alfred Knopf).

Morrow, James D. (1994). "Modeling the Forms of International Cooperation: Distribution Versus Information," *International Organization*, Vol. 48, No. 3, pp. 387–423.

Pauwelyn, Joost, and Manfred Elsig (2013). "The Politics of Treaty Interpretation: Variations and Explanations across International Tribunals," in Jeffrey L. Dunoff and Mark A. Pollack (eds.), *Interdisciplinary Perspectives on International Law and International Relations: The State of the Art* (New York: Cambridge University Press), pp. 445–73.

Platias, Athanasios, and Constantinos Koliopoulos (2010). *Thucydides on Strategy: Grand Strategies in the Peloponnesian War and Their Relevance Today* (New York: Columbia University Press).

Pollack, Mark A. (forthcoming). "Theorizing the European Union: Realist, Intergovernmentalist and Institutionalist Approaches," in Erik Jones, Anand Menon, and Stephen Weatherill (eds.), *The Oxford Handbook of the European Union* (New York: Oxford University Press).

Popper, Karl (1959). *The Logic of Scientific Discovery* (New York: Basic Books).

Pound, Roscoe (1921). *The Spirit of the Common Law* (Francestown, NH: Marshall Jones Company).

Putnam, Robert (1988). "Diplomacy and Domestic Politics: The Logic of Two-Level Games," *International Organization*, Vol. 42, No. 3, pp. 427–61.

Raustiala, Kal (2013). "Institutional Proliferation and the International Legal Order," in Jeffrey L. Dunoff and Mark A. Pollack (eds.), *Interdisciplinary Perspectives on International Law and International Relations: The State of the Art* (New York: Cambridge University Press), pp. 293–320.

Raustiala, Kal, and David Victor (1998). "Conclusions," in Kal Raustiala, David G. Victor, and Eugene V. Skolkinoff (eds.), *The Implementation and Effectiveness of International Environmental Commitments: Theory and Practice* (Cambridge, MA: MIT Press), pp. 659–707.

Riches, Cromwell A. (1940). *Majority Rule in International Organization* (Baltimore: Johns Hopkins Press).

Rose, Gideon (1998). "Neoclassical Realism and Theories of Foreign Policy," *World Politics*, Vol. 51, No. 1, pp. 144–72.

Said, Edward W. (1978). *Orientalism* (New York: Pantheon).

Sattler, Thomas, and Thomas Bernauer (2011). "Gravitation or Discrimination? Determinants of Litigation in the World Trade Organization," *European Journal of Political Research*, Vol. 50, No. 2, pp. 143–67.

Shaffer, Gregory C. and Mark A. Pollack (2013). "Hard Law and Soft Law," in Jeffrey L. Dunoff and Mark A. Pollack (eds.), *Interdisciplinary Perspectives on International Law and International Relations: The State of the Art* (New York: Cambridge University Press), pp. 197–222.

Sil, Rudra, and Peter J. Katzenstein (2010). *Beyond Paradigms: Analytic Eclecticism in the Study of World Politics* (New York: Palgrave Macmillan).

Simma, Bruno, and Andreas L. Paulus (1999). "The Responsibility of Individuals for Himan Rights Abuses in Internal Conflicts: A Positivist View," *American Journal of International Law*, Vol. 93, No. 2, pp. 302–16.

Simmons, Beth (2011). "The Global Diffusion of Law: Transnational Crime and the Case of Human Trafficking," in American Political Science Association (APSA), 2011 Annual Meeting (Washington, DC: APSA), available at SSRN: http://ssrn.com/abstract=1910623.

Slaughter Burley, Ann-Marie (1993). "International Law and International Relations Theory: A Dual Agenda," *American Journal of International Law*, Vol. 87, No. 2, pp. 205–39.

———— (2004). *A New World Order: Government Networks and the Disaggregated State* (Princeton, NJ: Princeton University Press).

Stein, Arthur (1983). "Coordination and Collaboration: Regimes in an Anarchic World," in Stephen D. Krasner (ed.), *International Regimes* (Ithaca, NY: Cornell University Press), pp. 115–40.

Steinberg, Richard H. (2002). "In the Shadow of Law or Power? Consensus-Based Bargaining and Outcomes in the GATT/WTO," *International Organization*, Vol. 56, No. 2, pp. 339–74.

———— (2004a). "Who Is Sovereign?," *Stanford Journal of International Law*, Vol. 40, No. 2, pp. 329–45.

———— (2004b). "Judicial Law-Making at the WTO: Discursive, Constitutional, and Political Constraints," *American Journal of International Law*, Vol. 85, No. 4, pp. 613–45.

———— (forthcoming). "International Trade Law as a Mechanism for State Transformation," in Martha Finnemore and Judith Goldstein (eds.), *Power in the Contemporary Era* (Cambridge: Cambridge University Press).

Sunstein, Cass S. (1996). *Legal Reasoning and Political Conflict* (New York: Oxford University Press).

Thucydides (1954). *History of the Peloponnesian War*, translated by Rex Warner (New York: Penguin Classics).

Vernon, Raymond (1971). *Sovereignty at Bay: The Multinational Spread of U.S. Enterprises* (New York: Basic Books).

Waltz, Kenneth N. (1979). *Theory of International Politics* (New York: McGraw-Hill).

Weber, Max (1947). *The Theory of Social and Economic Organization*, translated by A. M. Henderson and Talcott Parsons (New York: Oxford University Press).

Wendt, Alexander (1992). "Anarchy Is What States Make of It: The Social Construction of Power Politics," *International Organization*, Vol. 46, No. 2, pp. 391–425.

Wohlforth, William C. (2008). "Realism," in Christian Reus-Smit and Duncan Snidal (eds.), *The Oxford Handbook of International Relations* (New York: Oxford University Press), pp. 131–49.

Zamora, Stephen (1980). "Voting in International Economic Organizations," *American Journal of International Law*, Vol. 74, No. 3, pp. 566–78.

PART III

Making International Law

7

Flexibility in International Agreements

Laurence R. Helfer

The form and substance of international agreements are intimately linked. This insight, recently articulated by scholars working at the intersection of international law (IL) and international relations (IR) (Guzman 2005; Hathaway 2005; Raustiala 2005), has important implications for the study of legalized interstate cooperation. The relationship between form and substance affects issues central to the international legal system, including treaty design, the choice between hard and soft law, delegation of authority to international organizations and tribunals, and treaty compliance. The form and substance equation is, in turn, shaped by the many uncertainties that pervade international affairs, including insufficient information about future events, the preferences of other states, and shifts in domestic politics (Koremenos, Lipson, and Snidal 2001).

The linkage between form and substance also illuminates the choices and constraints that governments face, both when they negotiate international agreements and when they decide whether to comply with those agreements over time. Consider as a preliminary example a country that favors the adoption of a "deep" multilateral agreement that requires extensive changes to existing behavior. The state can pursue a range of different strategies to achieve its goal. It may limit participation to a smaller number of countries with similar preferences that will accept the treaty's onerous requirements. Or, it may broaden participation by offering incentives or concessions to nations reluctant to ratify the agreement. These inducements can take many forms, such as side payments, technical assistance, and other treaty membership benefits. But they can also include flexibility mechanisms that make the treaty more attractive by authorizing the parties to manage the risks of joining the agreement. These provisions function as insurance policies. They provide a hedge against uncertainty that allows a state to revise, readjust, or even renounce its commitments if the anticipated benefits of treaty-based cooperation turn out to be overblown (Bilder 1981; Sykes 1991; Helfer 2005).

Flexibility mechanisms also affect a state's calculus regarding treaty compliance. Continuing the previous example, deep international agreements may, notwithstanding their drafters' best efforts, turn out to be too deep, in that they require overly ambitious or unrealistic modifications of state behavior (Raustiala 2005: 613–14). Or, international tribunals or domestic courts may expansively interpret the agreements, resulting in treaties that become "overlegalized" (Helfer 2002). In either instance, when the costs of compliance outweigh the benefits, widespread violations are more likely to result. If, however, these deep agreements contain flexibility mechanisms, states may adjust their commitments instead of violating them.

On the other hand, overly capacious flexibility provisions may engender opportunistic behavior whenever economic, political, or other pressures make compliance inconvenient. Such opportunism also has wider pernicious consequences. Fearing that other treaty members may later invoke a treaty's flexibility mechanisms to shirk compliance, states that prefer to cooperate have a reduced incentive to invest the resources needed to implement and comply with the agreement (Swaine 2003).

As these introductory illustrations suggest, a principal challenge facing treaty negotiators is to select a suite of appropriately constrained flexibility mechanisms that facilitate agreement among states *ex ante* while deterring opportunistic uses of those mechanisms *ex post* after the treaty enters into force. Flexibility tools that are too easy to invoke will encourage self-serving behavior and lead to a breakdown in cooperation. Tools that are too onerous will discourage such behavior, but may prevent the parties from reaching agreement in the first instance, or, if agreement is reached, may lead to widespread violations if the costs of compliance increase unexpectedly (Ress 1994; Helfer 2005).

This chapter provides an overview of flexibility mechanisms in treaties and the role of such mechanisms in promoting or inhibiting international cooperation. The next section reviews the many flexibility devices available to treaty makers. It divides these tools into two broad categories – formal mechanisms (such as reservations, escape clauses, and withdrawal provisions) and informal practices (such as auto-interpretation, nonparticipation, and noncompliance). Section II, "The Study of Flexibility Mechanisms," reviews the IL/IR scholarship on the design and use of treaty flexibility mechanisms, focusing on studies of exit and escape clauses. The last section, "Stock Taking on the Study of Treaty Flexibility Mechanisms," highlights several conclusions that emerge from the burgeoning literature on treaty flexibility and suggests avenues for future research.

I. FLEXIBILITY MECHANISMS IN INTERNATIONAL AGREEMENTS: A BRIEF PRIMER

Government officials, international lawyers, and diplomats have long been interested in shaping the form and content of treaties to manage the risks of international cooperation. These risks include a tendency to gravitate toward "lowest common denominator" provisions that reflect the preferences of "the most intransigent or risk-averse nations," uncertainty over which nations will join an agreement, difficulty in predicting the future behavior of treaty parties, uncertainty over what the "eventual outcomes from participating in the agreement are likely to be," and the possibility that international courts or review bodies will interpret the agreement in a manner contrary to the interests of one or more treaty parties (Bilder 1981: 64–65).

State representatives have responded to these risks by devising an array of formal flexibility mechanisms and incorporating them into the multilateral and bilateral agreements they negotiate. These mechanisms are the subject of several handbooks and model treaty clauses published by the United Nations and other international organizations (United Nations Legal Department 1951, 1957, 2003). In addition, prominent international lawyers and diplomats have authored detailed guides to treaty making that contain numerous examples of flexibility provisions (Blix and Emerson 1973; Boockmann and Thurner 2006; Aust 2007, 2010; United Nations Environment Programme 2007).

A review of these materials reveals the breadth and diversity of formal flexibility tools. Those tools include unilateral reservation and declaration clauses; entry-into-force requirements; limitations on territorial application; duration provisions; amendment and revision procedures; and rules governing suspension, withdrawal, and termination. There is considerable variation within each of these categories. For example, some multilateral agreements prohibit reservations, others allow reservations only to particular clauses, and still others impose substantive conditions on reserving (Helfer 2006a; Swaine 2006). Whatever their precise combination and content, flexibility provisions usually appear at the end of the agreement and are referred to collectively as the treaty's "final clauses."

Formal flexibility mechanisms do not, however, exhaust the flexibility tools available to states. The decentralized and partly anarchic nature of the international legal system means that compliance with treaty commitments cannot be taken for granted, nor can the existence of decision-makers authorized to settle disputes or interpret treaty texts. In this environment, "it is not unusual to discover . . . that the authority formally provided in a written [agreement] may be ignored, or totally redefined by unwritten practice" (McDougal, Lasswell, and Reisman 1967: 260). Informal or unwritten practices that enhance the flexibility of treaties include ad hoc supplementary accords (Aust 1986), "understandings, practices and usages, traditions, conventions, and gentleman's agreements" (Cogan 2009: 215; see also Reisman 2002), de facto modification of treaty obligations through conduct (Aceves 1996), auto-interpretation of ambiguous terms, withholding of financial support, and nonparticipation in treaty activities (van Aaken 2009). Some commentators have even argued that noncompliance itself is a type of flexibility mechanism, one that can sometimes function "as a sort of necessary safety valve . . . rather than an inherent flaw in the system" (Alter 2005: 141; see also Cogan 2006; Pauwelyn 2008).

Table 7.1 provides a simplified typology of common treaty flexibility mechanisms, both formal and informal. It groups these mechanisms into three broad categories: (a) those concerning entry into force, (b) those that operate after the agreement enters into force, and (c) those concerning the cessation of treaty obligations. Table 7.1 also organizes these mechanisms according to whether they are invoked by a single state unilaterally or require a collective decision by all negotiating nations or treaty parties.

Table 7.1 illustrates a number of key points about the universe of treaty flexibility mechanisms. First, such mechanisms exist throughout a treaty's lifecycle, from gestation and birth (negotiation and entry into force) to death (termination). In addition, multiple unilateral and collective options are available at each stage of that cycle.

Second, different flexibility tools serve very different functions. To take one obvious example, unilateral mechanisms typically reduce uncertainty only for the states that invoke them. Collective mechanisms, in contrast, generally mitigate risk for all treaty parties.

A third point follows from the previous two: treaty negotiators can attempt to design "an effective risk management system [by making] a careful choice of those techniques best suited to meet the parties' concerns" (Bilder 1981: 20). The tradeoff among formal flexibility tools is illustrative. "[W]here an agreement includes strong general risk management provisions limiting the subject matter or duration of the agreement or providing for easy withdrawal, there will be less need for other more specific risk management provisions" (Bilder 1981: 20).

A fourth point concerns the relationship between formal and informal flexibility tools – for example, whether they substitute for or complement each other. To understand this relationship, scholars must consider not only the design of flexibility clauses on paper but also the behavior of treaty parties in practice.[1] As the next section explains, scholars have made considerable progress in addressing the first issue but have given shorter shrift to the second.

II. THE STUDY OF FLEXIBILITY MECHANISMS: EXAMPLES FROM TREATY EXIT AND ESCAPE CLAUSES

Over the last decade, IL and IR scholars alike have devoted growing attention to formal flexibility mechanisms. In the legal literature, studies have analyzed reservations (Goodman 2002; Swaine 2006), membership and voting rules (Goodman and Jinks 2004; Helfer 2008a), framework conventions and protocols (Setear 1999), soft law (Guzman and Meyer 2010; Shaffer and Pollack 2010), delegation to international organizations (Alvarez 2005; Helfer 2006b; Guzman and Landsidle 2008) and to

---

[1] Gathii (2011), for example, provides an insightful recent analysis of the design and operation of flexibility mechanisms in African regional trade agreements.

TABLE 7. 1. *Flexibility mechanisms*

Treaty action or process	Formal flexibility mechanisms	Informal flexibility mechanisms
Entry into Force	Unilateral: • Reservations • Declarations • Interpretive statements • Territorial application Collective: • Provisional application • Breaking into multiple treaties or parts • Phasing in treaty obligations • Ratifications requirements • Minimum number of states • Membership by specific states	Unilateral: • Statements of future intent Collective: • Modus vivendi • Practices based on unperfected legal acts (e.g., unratified treaties)
Treaty in Force	Unilateral: • Subsequent notifications • Escape • Escalator clauses • Self-judging exclusions Collective: • Exceptions and limitations • Special and differential treatment (e.g., for developing countries) • Delegation to international courts or international organizations • Amendment and revision	Unilateral: • Autointerpretation • Withholding funds for treaty activities • Noncompliance Collective: • Interpretation through conduct • De facto delegation • Informal processes and practices (e.g., regarding consultations, appointments to treaty offices) • Unwritten supplementary accords
Cessation of Treaty Obligations	Unilateral: • Denunciation and withdrawal Collective: • Limited duration • Formal suspension • Termination	Unilateral: • Nonparticipation in treaty activities Collective: • De facto suspension (e.g., during armed conflict) • Desuetude (e.g., treaty in force but moribund in practice)

international tribunals (Guzman 2002, 2008; Helfer and Slaughter 2005; Posner and Yoo 2005), escape clauses (Gross and Ní Aoláin 2006; see also Sykes 1991; Oraá 1992), exit provisions (Helfer 2005; Meyer 2010), and the relationship between treaty form and substance more generally (Guzman 2005; Hathaway 2005; Raustiala 2005).

Among political scientists, flexibility has figured prominently in the rational design literature, most notably in the 2001 special issue of *International Organization* (Koremenos *et al.* 2001). According to the authors of the special issue, flexibility determines how an institution's member states respond to different forms of uncertainty, such as "unanticipated circumstances or shocks," or "new demands from domestic coalitions or clusters of states wanting to change important rules or procedures" (Koremenos *et al.* 2001: 773). The authors posit three conjectures about flexibility: flexibility increases with uncertainty about the state of the world, flexibility increases with the severity of the distribution problem, and flexibility increases with number. Each of these conjectures takes account of the benefits and costs of flexibility. On the one hand, "the possibility of adjusting [an] agreement when adverse shocks occur allows states to gain from cooperation without tying themselves to an arrangement that may become undesirable as conditions change" (Koremenos *et al.* 2001: 793). But flexibility also has a downside: "Renegotiation of treaty terms, as well as dealing with unilateral invocations of flexibility such as escape clauses, is costly. Moreover, individual states have incentives to free ride on an agreement by developing self-serving interpretations" of flexibility clauses (Koremenos *et al.* 2001: 794).

In the decade following publication of the rational design volume, social science studies of treaty flexibility have proliferated. One set of studies focuses on the design of individual flexibility clauses, including those relating to duration and renegotiation (Koremenos 2005), reservations (Parisi and Ševčenko 2003; Neumayer 2007; Miles and Posner 2008; Kearney and Powers 2011), dispute settlement (Koremenos 2007), escape (Rosendorff and Milner 2001; Neumayer 2011), and withdrawal (Koremenos and Nau 2010). A second, smaller body of scholarship considers how these clauses operate in different issue areas, with an emphasis on trade (Koremenos 2002; Kucik and Reinhardt 2008; Pelc 2009*a*, 2009*b*) and human rights agreements (Neumayer 2007, 2011; Cole 2009; Hafner-Burton, Helfer, and Fariss 2011; Koremenos 2013).

A comprehensive review of the burgeoning legal and social science scholarship on treaty flexibility is beyond the scope of this chapter. Favoring depth over breadth, the sections that follow analyze the design and operation of two formal flexibility tools – exit and escape. These mechanisms provide interesting case studies for exploring advances in the study of treaty flexibility. Exit and escape were long ignored by scholars, dismissed as mere boilerplate, or disparaged by those anxious to prove that nations habitually obey international law. Recent empirical work, however, has revealed wide variation in the design of these clauses and in the situations in which states invoke the clauses to suspend or terminate their treaty obligations. This variation suggests that preserving an exit or escape option is often a rational response to a world plagued by uncertainty, an option that enhances the prospects for interstate cooperation *ex ante*, but that also engenders troubling possibilities for opportunistic behavior *ex post*. In addition, empirical analyses of exit and escape provide fresh evidence to evaluate the claims and conjectures about treaty flexibility advanced in the legal and social science literatures.

A. *The Design and Use of Treaty Exit Clauses*

The term "exit" describes a state's unilateral withdrawal from or denunciation of an international agreement that a state has previously ratified, an act that terminates the state's legal obligations under the agreement and ends the state's status as a treaty party. In the case of multilateral agreements, denunciation or withdrawal generally does not affect the treaty's continuation in force for the remaining states parties. For bilateral agreements, in contrast, denunciation or withdrawal by either party results in the termination of the treaty.

A state that seeks to disengage from a treaty in these ways usually invokes a denunciation or withdrawal clause set forth in the treaty itself. A treaty that does not contain such an express clause "is not subject to denunciation or withdrawal unless: (a) it is established that the parties intended to admit the possibility of denunciation or withdrawal; or (b) a right of denunciation or withdrawal may be implied by the nature of the treaty."[2]

Denunciation and withdrawal provisions reduce the uncertainty of international agreements. They do so by providing what is in effect an insurance policy – a low-cost option for states to end treaty-based cooperation if an agreement turns out badly. All other things being equal, such provisions encourage the ratification by a larger number of states than would join the treaty in the absence of such a clause. Exit clauses also enable the negotiation of deeper or broader commitments than could otherwise be attained (Tobin 1933: 202; Helfer 2005: 1599). Viewed in isolation, these benefits counsel government officials to include broad and permissive withdrawal and denunciation provisions in the treaties they negotiate.

Although the *ex ante* benefits of exit are considerable, treaties that permit easy withdrawal also create disincentives to future cooperation. One such disincentive is that states will invoke exit clauses opportunistically (or credibly threaten to do so) whenever economic, political, or other pressures make compliance costly or inconvenient. In addition, states that would prefer to cooperate but fear that their treaty partners may quit the agreement have less incentive to invest in treaty compliance. These deterrents to cooperation suggest that governments should make treaties more

---

[2] Vienna Convention on the Law of Treaties, 1153 U.N.T.S. 331 (1969), Article 56. Helfer (forthcoming) provides an overview of the history of the Vienna Convention on the Law of Treaties (1969), Article 56 and its application to situations in which a state attempts to exit from a treaty that lacks a denunciation or withdrawal clause.

durable by eliminating or restricting exit opportunities – a position directly contrary
to the *ex ante* perspective that favors broad withdrawal rights.

These competing perspectives on the costs and benefits of exit suggest that a key
challenge treaty negotiators face is to set optimal conditions on exit *ex ante*, so as to
deter opportunistic exit *ex post*. Exit clauses that are too easy to satisfy will encourage
self-serving denunciations and lead to a breakdown in cooperation. Exit provisions
that are too onerous will discourage such behavior, but may either prevent the parties
from reaching agreement in the first instance or trigger widespread treaty violations
if the costs of compliance rise unexpectedly.

1. Variation in the Design of Exit Clauses

Treaty provisions that authorize unilateral exit are common, but they are not ubiquitous. The clauses are found in a wide array of multilateral and bilateral agreements
in issue areas including human rights, arms control, trade, investment, and environmental protection. A recent study of a random sample of 142 treaties published in the
United Nations Treaty Series finds that 60 percent of treaties surveyed contain an
exit clause. The incidence of these clauses "varies by issue area, with human rights
agreements almost always incorporating them but more than half of the security
agreements in the sample failing to do so" (Koremenos and Nau 2010: 106).[3]

More intriguingly, denunciation clauses impose different types and degrees of
restrictions on a state's ability to withdraw. Treaty handbooks and model rules illustrate the wide variation in exit provisions.

> A review of these [drafting] guides... reveals that denunciation and withdrawal
> clauses cluster around [five] ideal types: (1) treaties that may be denounced at any
> time; (2) treaties that preclude denunciation for a fixed number of years, calculated
> either from the date the agreement enters into force or from the date of ratification
> by the state; (3) treaties that permit denunciation only at fixed time intervals; (4)
> treaties that may be denounced only on a [particular] occasion, identified either by
> time period or upon the occurrence of a particular event; [and] (5) treaties whose
> denunciation occurs automatically upon the state's ratification of a [subsequent]
> agreement. (Helfer 2005: 1597)

Divergences also exist as to the procedures for providing notice of a denunciation,
including the period of time that must elapse before a denunciation takes effect,
to whom notice must be given, and whether the denouncing state's obligations
continue after the withdrawal takes effect. For some categories of treaties, such as
humanitarian law conventions, the effective date of withdrawal is contingent upon

---

3 These findings may be influenced by the fact that most treaties in the random sample are bilateral.
   Anecdotal evidence suggests that exit clauses are more pervasive in multilateral treaties (Helfer 2005:
   1596–98).

external events, such as the cessation of an existing armed conflict.[4] Others, most notably bilateral investment agreements, "contain a continuing effects clause that provides that investments made, acquired, or approved prior to the date of the termination of the treaty will be protected by the treaty's provisions for a further period of ten, fifteen, or twenty years" (Salacuse 2010: 472).

The most common unilateral exit clauses require advance notice (most often of twelve or six months) of a decision to withdraw, sometimes with the additional condition that the treaty has been in force for a specified number of years (Koremenos and Nau 2010: 106–07). The large majority of exit provisions do not, however, require a state to justify its decision to withdraw. To the contrary, notices of denunciation are generally short, stylized letters of two or three paragraphs that inform the treaty depository that a state is quitting a particular agreement on a specified future date. A few treaties – most notably arms-control agreements – require states to explain a decision to withdraw, although they generally allow the denouncing nation to decide whether the factual predicate for withdrawal has been satisfied (Chayes 1972; Perez 1994). In addition, states often provide explanations when denouncing international labor conventions, although the treaties do not require them to do so (Widdows 1982).

Koremenos and Nau (2010) offer a theory of exit clause design to explain the variation in the length of notice periods and waiting periods prior to withdrawal. They find empirical support for two propositions. First, treaties that address an underlying "enforcement problem" are more likely to include longer notice periods than other types of agreements; and second, treaties that address an underlying "commitment problem" are more likely to have longer waiting periods than treaties that do not have such a goal (Koremenos and Nau 2010: 108–10). These findings provide intriguing evidence that government negotiators tailor the details of exit provisions to the type of cooperation challenge they seek to overcome.

2. Variation in the Use of Exit Clauses

As compared to the design of denunciation and withdrawal clauses, scholars have devoted less attention to how often or in which circumstances states actually exit from treaties. To the limited extent that the topic is mentioned in the legal literature, the conventional wisdom holds that exit is a highly unusual act or one that merits international condemnation – assertions based on anecdotes of a few high-profile denunciations and withdrawals from international organizations (Jenks 1969: 180; Rudzinski 1977: 806; Schlesinger 2003: 26–27). Recent empirical studies, however, belie these claims.

Helfer (2005) analyzes data on exit collected from several international organizations. He identifies 1,546 instances of denunciation and withdrawal from 5,416

---

[4] Common Article 63 of four Geneva Conventions of 1949.

multilateral agreements registered with the United Nations between 1945 and 2004.[5] His study finds that, although older treaties are denounced more frequently than recently adopted ones, the rate of exit "has held relatively constant or declined only slightly over the last fifty years, even after controlling for the large increase in . . . ratifications and the emergence of new nations in the 1960s and 1970s" (Helfer 2005: 1604–05). Based on these findings, the study concludes that "denunciations and withdrawals are a regularized component of modern treaty practice – acts that are infrequent but hardly the isolated or aberrant events that the conventional wisdom suggests" (Helfer 2005: 1602).

Data from Helfer (2005), supplemented with the additional examples discussed below, suggest that the situations in which states denounce or withdraw from treaties can be grouped into four broad categories. These categories are not mutually exclusive. There may be more than one explanation for a state's decision to exit in a particular instance, and multiple states that exit the same treaty may have different reasons for doing so. Nevertheless, the four categories provide a basic framework for reviewing the empirical landscape of treaty denunciations and withdrawals.

The most high profile – and often the most controversial – of the four situations involves states that quit a treaty to challenge disfavored international legal rules or rebuke international institutions. In the late 1990s, for example, three Caribbean nations denounced human rights treaties and withdrew from the jurisdiction of international human rights bodies in response to treaty interpretations that resulted in the de facto abolition of the death penalty in those countries (Helfer 2002).[6] More recently, several Latin American nations denounced bilateral investment agreements (BITs) and their associated dispute settlement mechanisms, charging that the international investment regime "is not transparent, . . . does not account for the disparity in economic situation of regime members," is staffed by arbitrators who "have an investor bias[, and whose] decisions infringe on the legitimate exercise of sovereignty by host countries . . . " (Salacuse 2010: 469). These and other examples illustrate how states use unilateral exit to disengage from or radically reconfigure existing forms of international cooperation (Helfer 2002; Swaine 2003; Tzanakopoulos 2011).

Second, withdrawing from an agreement (or threatening to withdraw) can increase a denouncing nation's negotiating leverage with other states parties and its influence in international organizations. The United States' denunciation in the 1970s and 1980s of the agreements establishing the International Labor Organization (ILO) and the United Nations Educational, Social and Cultural Organization (UNESCO) follow this pattern. In each instance, the United States used exit and threats of

---

[5] Of the 5,416 multilateral treaties in the study, 191, or 3.5 percent, have been denounced at least once. This small percentage suggests that a few treaties have resulted in withdrawals by multiple countries (Helfer 2005: 1606).

[6] Another example of exit precipitated by dissatisfaction with international human rights institutions involved North Korea's attempt to denounce the ICCPR, which does not contain an express provision for denunciation or withdrawal (Evatt 1999; Bates 2008).

exit – and the loss of organizational support and funding these entailed – to pressure the organizations' members to change their behavior, after which it rejoined the treaties. The Soviet Union and its allies pursued a similar approach in the 1950s, temporarily withdrawing from but later rejoining the World Health Organization, UNESCO, and the ILO. In the mid-1990s, the United States and the European Communities used an exit strategy to close the Uruguay Round of trade talks that created the World Trade Organization (WTO). They withdrew from the old General Agreement on Tariffs and Trade (GATT) – a treaty that contained special provisions for developing countries – and then ratified the WTO Agreements as a "single undertaking," forcing developing nations to accept a broad package of obligations favorable to U.S. and European interests. These examples reveal how states use exit and threats of exit to increase their voice within treaty-based negotiating forums and to reshape treaty commitments to more accurately reflect their interests (Hirschman 1970).

A third circumstance concerns what might be termed "forced exit," which occurs when one state or group of states requires another nation to withdrawal from a treaty as a condition of joining or retaining membership in an international organization. The most striking example of forced exit occurred in the mid-2000s, when the European Union (EU) demanded that countries seeking EU membership denounce BITs with the United States that had been in force since the early 1990s. The EU "announced that the treaties, which broadly prohibited. . .discrimination against foreign investment, violated European (protectionist) laws that had governed the region's economic policies for nearly fifty years" (Brummer 2007: 1372).[7] Commentators have noted the possibilities of similar forced exits from bilateral trade and investment agreements between the United States and the members of Mercosur, South America's largest regional trading block (Brummer 2007: 1389). These examples illustrate that forced exits lie at the intersection of law and power in international relations.

A fourth and very different type of exit occurs when the denunciation of one treaty is linked to joining a subsequent agreement that relates to the same subject matter. In the ILO and the International Maritime Organization, for example, the ratification of certain revising conventions or protocols triggers the automatic or compulsory denunciation of earlier agreements (Helfer 2006b). Similarly, a few Council of Europe treaties that supersede earlier agreements on the same topic require ratifying nations to denounce the earlier agreements as a condition of membership (Polakiewicz 1999: 37). Such paired treaty actions update a state's international obligations without diminishing its overall level of commitment. Unlike the previous three circumstances, denunciations and withdrawals of this type are fundamentally cooperative in nature. They often occur in groups or waves, a pattern that suggests

---

[7] The EU later modified this position somewhat, declaring that all EU-incompatible BIT provisions would have to be removed from the treaties. The countries seeking accession to the EU complied with this demand.

a collective effort to shift to a new equilibrium point that benefits all or most states parties (Helfer 2005).

The four situations in which states invoke the option to exit from treaties also highlight the limitations of analyzing the design of denunciation and withdrawal clauses in isolation. For example, the hedge against uncertainty that exit clauses provide may be greater in some issue areas than in others, depending on such factors as the type of cooperation problem that states are seeking to resolve and power differentials among member nations. In addition, the incidence of exit may vary with the types of international institutions that a treaty establishes and the independent authority that those institutions exercise.

B. *The Design and Use of Escape Clauses*

The term "escape" describes a unilateral act by which a treaty party temporarily suspends or derogates from some or all of its obligations without, however, withdrawing from membership or violating the treaty. The authority to put treaty commitments on hold is provided by a suspension or derogation clause set forth in the agreement itself.[8] Such clauses authorize a state to deviate – generally for a limited period of time, under particular conditions, and in response to extraordinary circumstances – from otherwise applicable treaty commitments (Pelc 2009*b*).

According to recent studies, escape clauses provide a mechanism for responding to conditions of domestic political or economic uncertainty. "States may agree to particular terms of cooperation but then suffer domestic shocks that make these terms politically difficult. What they require is a temporary relief from their obligations" (Koremenos 2005: 561). Anticipating that shocks, emergencies, and other exceptional circumstances will generate domestic opposition to treaty compliance, states will be hesitant to commit to a treaty that may be subject to these events unless it includes an *opt out* clause (Sykes 1991: 279). Such a provision facilitates international agreement *ex ante* by authorizing a temporary deviation from compliance if the anticipated exigent circumstances later arise. *Ceteris paribus*, an escape option also encourages more states to ratify a treaty, and it enables the negotiation of deeper international obligations than would be possible without such a provision (Hafner-Burton *et al.* 2011: 674).

After a treaty enters into force, however, escape clauses may have deleterious consequences for international cooperation. The most basic concern is that escape mechanisms authorize deviant behavior precisely when treaty compliance is needed most. The risks of noncompliance are especially acute for capacious opt-out provisions, which are "prone to abuse by ... members, to the point where [the treaty] loses its credibility and becomes irrelevant" (Pelc 2009*a*: 350). To obviate this possibility, many escape clauses impose costs on the states that invoke them, for

---

[8] Treaties may also be suspended due to the outbreak of armed conflict, although the circumstances in which such suspensions are lawful are disputed (Aust 2007: 308–11).

example, by requiring compensation to adversely affected actors, or by triggering disclosure to and scrutiny by international monitoring bodies. If properly calibrated, some scholars argue, these costs create a stable equilibrium in which treaties bend rather than break in response to domestic shocks that might otherwise cause international cooperation to unravel altogether (Rosendorff and Milner 2001: 831–32).

1. Variation in the Design of Escape Clauses

The incidence of escape clauses across issue areas is not well explored. Although there is some evidence that these mechanisms are less prevalent than other formal flexibility tools, escape clauses in trade and human rights agreements are quite common and have attracted considerable scholarly interest (Hoekman and Kostecki 1995: 303; Koremenos 2005: 561).

In the trade context, attention has focused on the safeguards clause in GATT Article XIX, which, during nearly half a century between 1947 and 1994, permitted a GATT contracting party temporarily to suspend its obligation to not raise trade barriers when, "as a result of unforeseen developments," domestic producers suffer a "serious injury" from foreign imports.[9] This safeguards provision was subject to a compensation and retaliation clause, which allowed adversely affected GATT members to suspend "substantially equivalent concessions" if the escaping country did not voluntarily provide compensation. Infant industry and balance-of-payments provisions in GATT were similarly designed.[10]

The conventional wisdom among legal scholars and social scientists is that escape clauses in trade agreements are self-enforcing. "Escaping members themselves have the strongest incentive to offer compensation, since they are looking to make their future return to compliance credible" (Pelc 2009a: 352). As a result, states can avoid delegating broad enforcement authority to international institutions. Instead, such institutions need "only record and publicize instances of escape and compensation" to maintain an efficient equilibrium (Pelc 2009a: 352).

In the human rights context, the drafters of several key international conventions anticipated that states would come under enormous pressure to restrict civil and political liberties during national emergencies. Yet, the drafters also recognized that such crises provide a convenient justification to enhance executive power, dismantle democratic institutions, and repress political opponents. To balance these competing concerns, the treaties included derogations clauses that authorize states to suspend certain rights during emergencies but subject those temporary restrictions to a detailed international regime of limitations, notifications, and review procedures (Fitzpatrick 1994; Gross and Ní Aoláin 2006).

Notwithstanding these restrictions, most legal scholars are highly suspicious of derogations. They fear that states will invoke these opt-out clauses to justify

---

[9] General Agreement on Tariffs and Trade, 55 U.N.T.S. 194, Article XIX.
[10] Ibid., Articles XII and XVIII.

widespread human rights violations and impose so-called permanent emergencies (Gross and Ní Aoláin 2006). In response to these concerns, commentators have emphasized the "utmost importance" that derogations be "strictly monitored and do not operate as a shield for the destruction of rights" (Joseph, Schultz, and Castan 2005: 824). And they have argued for expansive interpretations of legal doctrines that restrict a state's power to opt out, such as the principle of exceptional threat, nonderogability of fundamental rights, proportionality, nondiscrimination, and consistency with other international rules (El Zeidy 2003; Lorz 2003).

2. Variation in the Use of Escape Clauses

As with studies of treaty exit clauses, recent empirical work that analyzes when states actually exercise the option to suspend or derogate from their treaty commitments challenges the conventional wisdom about escape clause design.

In the trade regime, commentators often highlight the popularity of GATT Article XIX, which member states invoked on 150 occasions between 1950 and 1994. But this escape clause did not function as the rational design literature predicts. "While the total number of Article XIX measures increased with time, the use of compensation and retaliation" – the linchpin for the self-enforcing equilibrium that rational design scholars find so appealing – declined precipitously until it "came to play a trivial role" in the operation of the safeguards regime (Pelc 2009a: 357). In its place, GATT/WTO members adopted "appeals to exception" – criteria that describe the specific domestic circumstances that a state must prove to justify a temporary deviation from normal free-trade rules. Self-serving claims of having met these criteria are deterred not by requiring the payment of compensation, but rather by the ability of other nations to challenge the escaping state's assertions before the WTO dispute settlement body – as occurred, for example, when the United States imposed emergency tariffs on steel imports in 2002 (Patterson 2002). The more general insight for treaty design scholarship is that compensation schemes and appeals to exception may function as "alternative institutional means of providing flexibility without leading to its abuse" (Pelc 2009a: 350).

A disconnect between the design and use of escape clauses also exists for human rights agreements. The legal literature emphasizes the danger that states will invoke derogations as an excuse to repress civil and political liberties. To avoid this highly problematic outcome, international courts and treaty bodies have imposed progressively more stringent restrictions and limitations over time on the use of derogations.[11]

Two recent studies reveal that the empirical picture is more complex. The first study, drawing on two new datasets of derogations and states of emergency around

---

[11] U.N. Human Rights Committee, General Comment 29, States of Emergency (article 4), U.N. Doc. CCPR/C/21/Rev.1/Add.11 (2001); *A. and Others v. United Kingdom*, App. No. 3455/05, 2009–__ Eur. Ct. H.R. (Grand Chamber) (2009).

the world from 1976 to 2007, finds that countries most likely to derogate are a subset of stable democracies in which domestic courts can exercise strong oversight of the executive, and voters can hold governments politically accountable for repressing rights. These countries also generally provide information about a derogation's duration and the rights being suspended. The study theorizes that these derogations are carried out with a specific goal in mind: to enable governments facing serious threats to buy time and legal breathing space from voters, courts, and interest groups to confront crises while signaling to these audiences that rights deviations are necessary, temporary, and lawful. Conversely, in countries where the judiciary is weak or voters cannot easily remove leaders from office, governments have little need to escape because they are unlikely to be held accountable for rights violations. When these insincere derogating countries do opt out, however, they generally do not provide information about the rights suspended, and they maintain derogations for multiple consecutive years (Hafner-Burton *et al.* 2011: 698–704).

The second study, based on similar empirical evidence, also concludes that the use of derogation clauses varies by regime type. In particular, the study finds that autocratic governments step up their violations of civil and political liberties during declared states of emergency, including some rights that the treaties designate as nonderogable. In contrast, the study finds no evidence of increased rights violations in either category when democracies derogate (Neumayer 2011).

The findings of these two studies are in tension with the expectations of the drafters of human rights treaties and of scholars of escape clause design. The drafters sought to limit repression during emergencies by creating international notification and monitoring procedures to review the legality of derogations and their associated rights restrictions. The studies suggest, however, that these flexibility mechanisms are influential not because they require states to disclose and justify derogations internationally, but rather because they enable democratic governments to signal to domestic audiences that rights suspensions are necessary, temporary, and lawful. In addition, whereas the literature on human rights escape clauses emphasizes the danger of abuse by all treaty parties, these studies suggest that these concerns are valid for autocracies but not for stable democracies – the countries that are the most likely to escape.[12] Stated more pointedly, derogation clauses appear to matter least where they are needed most.

III. STOCK TAKING ON THE STUDY OF TREATY FLEXIBILITY MECHANISMS AND AVENUES FOR FUTURE RESEARCH

The previous sections of this chapter have analyzed the variation in the design and use of exit and escape clauses in international agreements. Scholars have recently

---

[12] Neumayer (2007) and Bradley and Goldsmith (2000) reach a similar conclusion – that democracies are more likely than other types of states to file reservations to human rights treaties.

identified similar variation in other formal flexibility tools listed in Table 7.1, including devices that relate to a treaty's entry into force, its operation, and its termination. Taken together, these studies suggest a number of general conclusions about how flexibility tools promote or inhibit cooperation among nations, as well as avenues for future research.

A. *Stock Taking on the Study of Treaty Flexibility Mechanisms*

The studies reviewed in this chapter provide increasing evidence that formal flexibility mechanisms are not superfluous, boilerplate, or symbolic provisions that appear in the final clauses of treaties out of habit or happenstance. To the contrary, the studies support the central claim of rational design scholars – that governments manage the risks of international cooperation not only by adjusting a treaty's substantive standards and its membership rules, but also by selecting from among an array of flexibility devices. The studies also suggest a more specific finding – that states make tradeoffs among potentially available flexibility tools in an attempt to calculate an overall level of treaty risk.[13] To be clear, these conclusions do not rule out the possibility that certain categories of treaties or types of flexibility mechanisms are not in fact designed, or are not designed rationally. But they do suggest that rational design should be a baseline assumption for those who study treaty flexibility.

A second general conclusion that emerges from the literature reviewed in this chapter is that the use of flexibility mechanisms sometimes diverges from the expectations of a treaty's drafters and the conjectures of rational design scholars. In some instances, the unanticipated behavior relates to how frequently states invoke the flexibility tools available to them. In others, states with certain domestic characteristics – such as those with democratic or autocratic governments – are, contrary to predictions, the predominant users of particular flexibility tools. And, in still other cases, there are unanticipated interaction or substitution effects among formal and informal flexibility mechanisms, some of which may impose fewer costs or offer greater benefits.[14]

---

[13] The nearly 200 conventions negotiated under the auspices of the ILO provide an example. None of these treaties permit reservations, which would be inconsistent with the organization's tripartite membership structure of governments, workers, and employers (McMahon 1965–66). However, the conventions include other flexibility tools that enable states to customize their legal obligations in much the same way as reservations. Some conventions contain standards that apply only to designated countries. Others set forth general principles and relegate more detailed rules to nonbinding recommendations on the same topic. And still others allow ratification in parts or exclude designated industries or types of workers (Servais 1986).

[14] One example of a substitution effect is the finding, discussed above, that states have used the escape clause in Article XIX and appeals to exception as alternative flexibility tools in the GATT. An illustration of how Article XIX did not function as expected concerns so-called gray area measures in which one GATT member convinces another to "voluntarily" restrain exports or agree to other forms of managed trade. These gray area measures have often been more pervasive than invocations of Article XIX's formal escape clause (Dunoff 2010).

B. *Avenues for Future Research*

The importance of flexibility tools to treaty negotiators, as well as the divergences between flexibility tools as they appear on paper and as they are applied in practice, suggests several lines of inquiry that scholars might pursue in future studies.

First, although much can be learned from analyzing individual flexibility mechanisms in isolation, a deeper understanding of how nations cooperate requires considering the relationship among different flexibility tools. A study of treaty duration by Koremenos (2005) is a pioneer in this regard. It considers whether exit and escape clauses and delegation to international institutions are substitutes for finite duration provisions. Koremenos finds that exit and escape clauses "seem to resolve different problems than finite duration," but that the delegation of decision-making authority may be a viable alternative to limiting a treaty's life span (Koremenos 2005: 561). Other studies might consider whether certain flexibility tools are complements or substitutes. This research would be especially welcome for issue areas – such as environment and national security – for which treaty flexibility tools have thus far received less attention.

A second promising avenue for research involves going beyond the analysis of treaty texts and institutional design features to consider when and how states actually exercise the formal and informal flexibility mechanisms available to them. Failure to address how flexibility tools actually function in practice risks two types of errors. On the one hand, treaties with few flexibility mechanisms (i.e., agreements that are highly sovereignty-restrictive on paper) may turn out to be far less constraining in fact, for example, due to informal flexibility practices not reflected in treaty texts (Helfer 2008b). Conversely, factors such as reputational concerns, asymmetric distributions of power, or entrenched behavioral norms may deter states from invoking flexibility clauses, with the result that those clauses exist only in principle (Guzman and Landsidle 2008). Examining the use of flexibility provisions also helps to guard against the *post hoc ergo propter hoc* errors to which rational design conjectures are sometimes prone.

Third, future research could investigate how flexibility tools interact with the form and substance of international agreements more generally (Raustiala 2005). For example, scholars might consider how the number, type, scope, and combination of flexibility devices are influenced by four overarching constraints that treaty negotiators face: (a) a "participation constraint" that results from a desire to induce all states affected by a particular cooperation problem to join an agreement (Downs, Rocke, and Barsoom 1998; Barrett 2003; Helfer 2008a); (b) a "sovereignty constraint," characterized by an aversion to delegating authority to international institutions, even where doing so provides an effective way to resolve transborder collaboration problems (Bradley and Kelley 2008); (c) an "information constraint" caused by pervasive uncertainties relating to future events and the preferences of other states (Koremenos *et al.* 2001); and (d) a "problem structure constraint" that is a function of the externally determined features of a substantive issue area, such as its public goods or club goods character (Sandler 2004; Mitchell 2006).

A fourth line of inquiry might probe whether flexibility mechanisms are especially appealing to – and most likely to be used by – particular types of domestic regimes. As noted previously, several recent studies of human rights treaties find that democracies reserve and derogate more frequently than do other states. Scholars might consider whether the design and use of flexibility tools in other issue areas exhibit similar patterns and, if they do, develop and test hypotheses to explain these findings. These hypotheses should take into account the four constraints on treaty negotiators listed in the previous paragraph, each of which relates to factors external to states. But they should also consider whether domestic politics and domestic institutions explain the observed correlations between regime type and the design and use of particular flexibility tools.

REFERENCES

Aceves, William J. (1996). "The Economic Analysis of International Law: Transaction Cost Economics and the Concept of State Practice," *University of Pennsylvania Journal of International Economic Law*, Vol. 17, No. 4, pp. 995–1068.

Alter, Karen J. (2005). "International Courts Are Not Agents! The Perils of the Principal-Agent Approach to Thinking about the Independence of International Courts," *American Society of International Law Proceedings*, Vol. 99, pp. 138–41.

Alvarez, José E. (2005). *International Organizations as Law-Makers* (Oxford: Oxford University Press).

Aust, Anthony (1986). "The Theory and Practice of Informal International Instruments," *International and Comparative Law Quarterly*, Vol. 35, No. 4, pp. 787–812.

——— (2007). *Modern Treaty Law and Practice*, 2nd ed. (Cambridge: Cambridge University Press).

——— (2010). *Handbook of International Law*, 2nd ed. (Cambridge: Cambridge University Press).

Barrett, Scott (2003). *Environment and Statecraft: The Strategy of Environmental Treaty-Making* (Oxford: Oxford University Press).

Bates, Ed (2008). "Avoiding Legal Obligations Created by Human Rights Treaties," *International and Comparative Law Quarterly*, Vol. 57, No. 4, pp. 751–88.

Bilder, Richard B. (1981). *Managing the Risks of International Agreement* (Madison: University of Wisconsin Press).

Blix, Hans, and Jirina H. Emerson (1973) (eds.). *The Treaty Maker's Handbook* (New York: Oceana Publications).

Boockmann, Bernhard, and Paul W. Thurner (2006). "Flexibility Provisions in Multilateral Environmental Treaties," *International Environmental Agreements: Politics, Law and Economics*, Vol. 6, No. 2, pp. 113–35.

Bradley, Curtis A., and Jack Landman Goldsmith III (2000). "Treaties, Human Rights, and Conditional Consent," *Pennsylvania Law Review*, Vol. 149, No. 2, pp. 399–468.

Bradley, Curtis A., and Judith G. Kelley (2008). "The Concept of International Delegation," *Law & Contemporary Problems*, Vol. 71, No. 1, pp. 1–36.

Brummer, Chris (2007). "The Ties That Bind? Regionalism, Commercial Treaties, and the Future of Global Economic Integration," *Vanderbilt Law Review*, Vol. 60, No. 5, pp. 1349–1408.

Chayes, Abram (1972). "An Inquiry into the Workings of Arms Control Agreements," *Harvard Law Review*, Vol. 85, No. 5, pp. 905–69.

Cogan, Jacob Katz (2006). "Noncompliance and the International Rule of Law," *Yale Journal of International Law*, Vol. 31, No. 1, pp. 189–210.

———— (2009). "Representation and Power in International Organization: The Operational Constitution and Its Critics," *American Journal of International Law*, Vol. 103, No. 2, pp. 209–63.

Cole, Wade M. (2009). "Hard and Soft Commitments to Human Rights Treaties, 1966–2000," *Sociological Forum*, Vol. 24, No. 3, pp. 563–88.

Downs, George W., David M. Rocke, and Peter N. Barsoom (1998). "Managing the Evolution of Multilateralism," *International Organization*, Vol. 52, No. 2, pp. 397–419.

Dunoff, Jeffrey L. (2010). "How *Not* to Think about Safeguards," in Kyle W. Bagwell, George A. Bermann, and Petros C. Mavroidis (eds.), *Law and Economics of Contingent Protection in International Trade* (Cambridge: Cambridge University Press), pp. 401–12.

El Zeidy, Mohamed M. (2003). "The ECHR and States of Emergency: Article 15 – a Domestic Power of Derogation from Human Rights Obligations," *San Diego International Law Journal*, Vol. 4, pp. 277–318.

Evatt, Elizabeth (1999). "Democratic People's Republic of Korea and the ICCPR: Denunciation as an Exercise of the Right of Self-Defence," *Australian Journal of Human Rights*, Vol. 5, No. 1, pp. 215–24.

Fitzpatrick, Joan (1994). *Human Rights in Crisis: The International System for Protecting Human Rights during States of Emergency* (Philadelphia: University of Pennsylvania Press).

Gathii, James, T. (2011). *African Regional Trade Agreements as Legal Regimes* (Cambridge: Cambridge University Press).

Goodman, Ryan (2002). "Human Rights Treaties, Invalid Reservations, and State Consent," *American Journal of International Law*, Vol. 96, No. 3, pp. 531–60.

Goodman, Ryan, and Derek Jinks (2004). "How to Influence States: Socialization and International Human Rights Law," *Duke Law Journal*, Vol. 54, No. 3, pp. 621–704.

Gross, Oren, and Fionnuala Ní Aoláin (2006). *Law in Times of Crisis: Emergency Powers in Theory and Practice* (Cambridge: Cambridge University Press).

Guzman, Andrew T. (2002). "The Cost of Credibility: Explaining Resistance to Interstate Dispute Resolution Mechanisms," *Journal of Legal Studies*, Vol. 31, No. 1, pp. 303–26.

———— (2005). "The Design of International Agreements," *European Journal of International Law*, Vol. 16, No. 4, pp. 579–612.

———— (2008). "International Tribunals: A Rational Choice Analysis," *The University of Pennsylvania Law Review*, Vol. 157, No. 1, pp. 171–236.

Guzman, Andrew T., and Jennifer Landsidle (2008). "The Myth of International Delegation," *California Law Review*, Vol. 96, No. 6, pp. 1693–1724.

Guzman, Andrew T., and Timothy L. Meyer (2010). "International Soft Law," *Journal of Legal Analysis*, Vol. 2, No. 1, pp. 171–225.

Hafner-Burton, Emilie M., Laurence R. Helfer, and Christopher J. Fariss (2011). "Emergency and Escape: Explaining Derogation from Human Rights Treaties," *International Organization*, Vol. 65, No. 4, pp. 673–707.

Hathaway, Oona A. (2005). "Between Power and Principle: An Integrated Theory of International Law," *University of Chicago Law Review*, Vol. 72, No. 2, pp. 469–536.

Helfer, Laurence R. (2002). "Overlegalizing Human Rights: International Relations Theory and the Commonwealth Caribbean Backlash against Human Rights Regimes," *Columbia Law Review*, Vol. 102, No. 7, pp. 1832–1911.

———— (2005). "Exiting Treaties," *Virginia Law Review*, Vol. 91, No. 7, pp. 1579–1648.

_____ (2006a). "Not Fully Committed? Reservations, Risk, and Treaty Design," *Yale Journal of International Law*, Vol. 31, No. 2, pp. 367–82.

_____ (2006b). "Understanding Change in International Organizations: Globalization and Innovation in the ILO," *Vanderbilt Law Review*, Vol. 59, No. 3, pp. 649–726.

_____ (2008a). "Nonconsensual International Lawmaking," *University of Illinois Law Review*, No. 1, pp. 71–126.

_____ (2008b). "Monitoring Compliance with Unratified Treaties: The ILO Experience," *Law and Contemporary Problems*, Vol. 71, No. 1, pp. 193–218.

_____ (forthcoming). "Terminating Treaties," in Duncan Hollis (ed.), *The Oxford Guide to Treaties* (Oxford: Oxford University Press).

Helfer, Laurence R., and Anne-Marie Slaughter (2005). "Why States Create International Tribunals: A Response to Professors Posner and Yoo," *California Law Review*, Vol. 93, No. 3, pp. 899–956.

Hirschman, Albert O. (1970). *Exit, Voice, and Loyalty: Responses to Decline in Firms, Organizations, and States* (Cambridge, MA: Harvard University Press).

Hoekman, Bernard M., and Michel M. Kostecki (1995). *The Political Economy of the World Trading System from GATT to WTO* (Oxford: Oxford University Press).

Jenks, C. Wilfred (1969). *A New World of Law? A Study of the Creative Imagination in International Law* (London: Longmans).

Joseph, Sarah, Jenny Schultz, and Melissa Castan (2005). *The International Covenant on Civil and Political Rights: Cases, Materials, and Commentary*, 2nd ed. (Oxford: Oxford University Press).

Kearney, Patrick Michael, and Ryan M. Powers (2011). "Veto Players and Conditional Commitment to U.N. Human Rights Agreements," *APSA 2011 Annual Meeting Paper*, pp. 1–27.

Koremenos, Barbara (2002). "Can Cooperation Survive Changes in Bargaining Power? The Case of Coffee," *Journal of Legal Studies*, Vol. 31, No. 1, S259–S284.

_____ (2005). "Contracting around International Uncertainty," *American Political Science Review*, Vol. 99, No. 4, pp. 549–65.

_____ (2007). "If Only Half of International Agreements Have Dispute Resolution Provisions, Which Half Needs Explaining?" *Journal of Legal Studies*, Vol. 36, No. 1, pp. 189–212.

_____ (2013). "Institutionalism and International Law," in Jeffrey L. Dunoff and Mark A. Pollack (eds.), *Interdisciplinary Perspectives on International Law and International Relations: The State of the Art* (New York: Cambridge University Press), pp. 59–82.

Koremenos, Barbara, and Allison Nau (2010). "Exit, No Exit," *Duke Journal of Comparative and International Law*, Vol. 21, No. 1, pp. 81–120.

Koremenos, Barbara, Charles Lipson, and Duncan Snidal (2001). "The Rational Design of International Institutions," *International Organization*, Vol. 55, No. 4, pp. 761–99.

Kucik, Jeffrey, and Eric Reinhardt (2008). "Does Flexibility Promote Cooperation? An Application to the Global Trade Regime," *International Organization*, Vol. 62, No. 3, pp. 477–505.

Lorz, Ralph Alexander (2003). "Possible Derogations from Civil and Political Rights under Article 4 of the ICCPR," *Israel Yearbook on Human Rights*, Vol. 33, pp. 85–103.

McDougal, Myres S., Harold D. Lasswell, and W. Michael Reisman (1967). "The World Constitutive Process of Authoritative Decision," *Journal of Legal Education*, Vol. 19, No. 3, pp. 253–300.

McMahon, J. F. (1965–66). "The Legislative Techniques of the International Labour Organization," *British Yearbook of International Law*, Vol. 41, pp. 1–102.

Meyer, Timothy (2010). "Power, Exit Costs, and Renegotiation in International Law," *Harvard International Law Journal*, Vol. 51, No. 2, pp. 379–425.

Miles, Thomas J., and Eric A. Posner (2008). "Which States Enter into Treaties, and Why?" *University of Chicago Law & Economics, Olin Working Paper No. 420; University of Chicago, Public Law Working Paper No. 225*, pp. 1–36.

Mitchell, Ronald B. (2006). "Problem Structure, Institutional Design, and the Relative Effectiveness of International Environmental Agreements," *Global Environmental Politics*, Vol. 6, No. 3, pp. 72–89.

Neumayer, Eric (2007). "Qualified Ratification: Explaining Reservations to International Human Rights Treaties," *Journal of Legal Studies*, Vol. 36, No. 2, pp. 397–430.

———— (2011). "Do Governments Mean Business When They Derogate? Human Rights Violations during Notified States of Emergency," Working Paper, pp. 1–42.

Oraá, Jaime (1992). *Human Rights in States of Emergency in International Law* (Oxford: Clarendon Press).

Parisi, Francesco, and Catherine Ševčenko (2003). "Treaty Reservations and the Economics of Article 21(1) of the Vienna Convention," *Berkeley Journal of International Law*, Vol. 21, No. 1, pp. 1–26.

Patterson, Eliza (2002). "The US Provides Section 201 Relief for the American Steel Industry," *ASIL Insights*, available at http://www.asil.org/insights/insigh84.htm.

Pauwelyn, Joost (2008). *Optimal Protection of International Law: Navigating between European Absolutism and American Voluntarism* (Cambridge: Cambridge University Press).

Pelc, Krzysztof J. (2009a). "Seeking Escape: The Use of Escape Clauses in International Trade Agreements," *International Studies Quarterly*, Vol. 53, No. 2, pp. 349–68.

———— (2009b). *The Cost of Wiggle-Room: On the Use of Flexibility in International Trade Agreements*, Georgetown University, PhD thesis.

Perez, Antonio F. (1994). "Survival of Rights under the Nuclear Non-proliferation Treaty: Withdrawal and the Continuing Right of International Atomic Energy Agency Safeguards," *Virginia Journal of International Law*, Vol. 34, No. 4, pp. 749–830.

Polakiewicz, Jörg (1999). *Treaty-Making in the Council of Europe* (Strasbourg: Council of Europe Publishers).

Posner, Eric A., and John C. Yoo (2005). "Judicial Independence in International Tribunals," *California Law Review*, Vol. 93, No. 1, pp. 1–74.

Raustiala, Kal (2005). "Form and Substance in International Agreements," *American Journal of International Law*, Vol. 99, No. 3, pp. 581–614.

Reisman, W. Michael (2002). "Unratified Treaties and Other Unperfected Acts in International Law: Constitutional Functions," *Vanderbilt Journal of Transnational Law*, Vol. 35, No. 3, pp. 729–47.

Ress, Georg (1994). "Ex Ante Safeguards Against Ex Post Opportunism in International Treaties: Theory and Practice of International Public Law," *Journal of Institutional and Theoretical Economics*, Vol. 150, No. 1, pp. 279–303.

Rosendorff, B. Peter, and Helen V. Milner (2001). "The Optimal Design of International Trade Institutions: Uncertainty and Escape," *International Organization*, Vol. 55, No. 4, pp. 829–57.

Rudzinski, Aleksander Witold (1977). "Denunciation of International Treaties," *Book Review, American Journal of International Law*, Vol. 71, No. 4, pp. 805–07.

Salacuse, Jeswald W. (2010). "The Emerging Global Regime for Investment," *Harvard International Law Journal*, Vol. 51, No. 2, pp. 427–74.

Sandler, Todd (2004). *Global Collective Action* (Cambridge: Cambridge University Press).

Schlesinger, Stephen C. (2003). *Act of Creation: The Founding of the United Nations: A Story of Superpowers, Secret Agents, Wartime Allies and Enemies and Their Quest for a Peaceful World* (Boulder, CO: Westview Press).

Servais, J. M. (1986). "Flexibility and Rigidity in International Labour Standards," *International Labour Review*, Vol. 125, No. 2, pp. 193–208.

Setear, John K. (1999). "Ozone, Iteration, and International Law," *Virginia Journal of International Law*, Vol. 40, No. 1, pp. 193–310.

Shaffer, Gregory C., and Mark A. Pollack (2010). "Hard vs. Soft Law: Alternatives, Complements, and Antagonists in International Governance," *Minnesota Law Review*, Vol. 94, No. 3, pp. 706–99.

Swaine, Edward T. (2003). "Unsigning," *Stanford Law Review*, Vol. 55, No. 5, pp. 2061–89.

———— (2006). "Reserving," *Yale Journal of International Law*, Vol. 31, No. 2, pp. 307–66.

Sykes, Alan O. (1991). "Protectionism as a 'Safeguard': A Positive Analysis of the GATT 'Escape Clause' with Normative Speculations," *University of Chicago Law Review*, Vol. 58, No. 1, pp. 255–305.

Tobin, Harold J. (1933). *The Termination of Multipartite Treaties* (New York: Columbia University Press).

Tzanakopoulos, Antonios (2011). "Denunciation of the ICSID Convention under the General International Law of Treaties," in Rainer Hofman and Christian Tams (eds.), *International Investment Law and General International Law: From Clinical Isolation to Systemic Integration* (Baden-Baden: Nomos Verlagsgesellschaft Mbh & Co), pp. 75–93.

United Nations Environment Programme (2007). *Multilateral Environmental Agreement Negotiator's Handbook*, 2nd ed. (Joensuu: University of Joensuu, Department of Law).

United Nations Legal Department (1951). *Handbook of Final Clauses* (New York: Treaty Section of the United Nations Office of Legal Affairs).

———— (1957). *Handbook of Final Clauses* (New York: Treaty Section of the United Nations Office of Legal Affairs).

———— (2003). *Handbook of Final Clauses* (New York: Treaty Section of the United Nations Office of Legal Affairs).

van Aaken, Anne (2009). "International Investment Law between Commitment and Flexibility: A Contract Theory Analysis," *Journal of International Economic Law*, Vol. 12, No. 2, pp. 507–38.

Widdows, Kelvin (1982). "The Unilateral Denunciation of Treaties Containing No Denunciation Clause," *British Yearbook of International Law*, Vol. 53, pp. 83–114.

8

Hard and Soft Law

Gregory Shaffer and Mark A. Pollack

Political scientists and legal scholars have increasingly explored the concepts of hard and soft law in international governance.[1] Although the concept of soft law remains to some extent controversial in the legal academy, the burgeoning literature of the past decade has generated valuable insights regarding the adoption of hard and soft law as a design choice, the advantages and disadvantages of each form under different conditions, the ways in which hard and soft legal instruments interact over time, and the impact and effectiveness of hard and soft legal provisions in various issue areas.

In this chapter, we review and assess this literature, with a focus on the insights generated by interdisciplinary international law/international relations (IL/IR) scholarship. The first four parts cover the four core areas of IL/IR theorizing about hard and soft law: definition, design, interaction, and impact. That is, we first address a key *definitional* question, noting the substantial disagreements among positivist, rational institutionalist, and constructivist scholars about the definitions and the key features of hard and soft law, respectively. Next, we examine the question of hard and soft law as a *design* choice, asking under what conditions states (or other actors) might opt for hard- or soft-law commitments in international relations. Here, we distinguish between a nearly ubiquitous functionalist approach and a nascent but promising distributive approach distinctive to contemporary IL/IR scholarship. Third, we examine the question of how hard and soft law *interact* in an increasingly complex and fragmented international legal landscape, arguing that hard and soft

We wish to thank Mary Rumsey and Nate Nesbitt for their research assistance and Claire Kelly, Jeffrey Dunoff, and the other participants at the IL/IR conference for their extremely helpful comments. All errors remain our own. This chapter borrows from and builds upon our earlier work. See, for example, Pollack and Shaffer (2009, 2012) and Shaffer and Pollack (2010, 2011).

[1] See, for example, Chinkin (1989), Lipson (1991), Boyle (1999), Abbott and Snidal (2000, 2004), Shelton (2000a), Guzman and Meyer (2009, 2010), Shaffer and Pollack (2009, 2010), and the sources cited in the pages that follow.

law can interact not only as alternatives or complements, but also, under certain conditions, as antagonists. Fourth, we examine the sparse but suggestive scholarship on the *impact* of hard and soft law beyond the law-making stage (i.e., in terms of legal interpretation, as well as compliance and effectiveness). A brief final section concludes with a discussion of the value-added contributions, as well as the lacunae and blind spots, of the IL/IR literature in this area.

I. DEFINITIONS: THEORIZING HARD AND SOFT LAW

One fundamental challenge of studying hard and soft law is that definitions of these terms vary dramatically across different schools of thought in legal and political science scholarship. Simplifying slightly, we identify three basic positions in the literature: a legal positivist view that associates the hard/soft distinction with a binary binding/nonbinding dichotomy, a constructivist view that considers the purported hardness or softness of law as secondary to its social effects, and a rational institutionalist position that takes a multidimensional and continuous view of hard and soft law. Let us consider each view, very briefly, in turn.

A. *Positivism*

Positivist legal scholars generally adopt a simple binary binding/nonbinding divide to distinguish hard law from soft law. In this view, what makes law distinctive with respect to other norms is its claim to bind actors, to impose legal obligation, and the fundamental distinction between hard and soft law is the distinction between legally binding and nonbinding commitments. Indeed, taking the legal positivist argument to its logical conclusion, some scholars go further and reject the very concept of soft law. They do so because, from the *internal* perspective of a judge or legal advocate, law is by definition "binding" (Weil 1983; Klabbers 1996, 1998; Raustiala 2005). Other legal scholars remain open to the idea that nonbinding agreements may retain some characteristics and effects of law, but generally agree that the fundamental distinction between hard and soft law is determined by its binding or nonbinding nature (Shelton 2000*b*: 4; Reinicke and Witte 2000; Guzman and Meyer 2010). Distilling this view, we might conceive of soft law in positivist terms as a codified instrument that is publicized, issued through an institutionalized process, with the aim of exercising a form of authority or persuasion, even though the instrument is not formally legally binding.[2]

---

[2] Although most of the literature limits the concept of soft law to agreements among states and non-state actors, including international organizations and civil society, Guzman and Meyer (2009, 2010) compellingly extend the concept to what they call "international common law," namely, the decisions of international courts that are either advisory or else not binding on states that are not party to the litigation but that nevertheless issue interpretations of law that are widely accepted and shape actors' subsequent expectations.

B. *Constructivism*

Constructivist scholars, by contrast, focus less on the formal terms of law as understood at a single point of time, such as the enactment stage, and more on law as part of a process of social interaction that can shape shared social understandings of appropriate behavior. Many constructivist scholars have thus questioned the characterization of law as either "hard" or "soft" because such characterizations focus too narrowly in the interpretation and enforcement of law by courts and fail to capture how law operates normatively as part of an interactional process over time (Finnemore and Toope 2001; Trubek, Cottrell, and Nance 2006). Their counterparts in interdisciplinary debates in international relations and international law tend to discount the efficacy of soft law because it does not create binding obligations on states, which can thus more easily ignore it in light of their interests.[3] Constructivists, in contrast, explicitly address how international law can lead states to change their perceptions of their interests through transnational processes of interaction, deliberation, persuasion, or acculturation over time (Ruggie 1998; Boyle and Meyer 1998; Goodman and Jinks 2004; Brunnée and Toope 2013). Scholars working in an experimentalist "new governance" tradition sometimes go further, arguing that soft law approaches should generally be privileged to promote responsive governance (e.g., Sabel and Simon 2006). Indeed, for constructivists, the creation of soft law might not reflect a "choice" at all, but the accumulation and gradual transformative effect of shared understandings and state practices over time.

C. *Rational Institutionalism*

Rationalist international relations scholars, by contrast, frequently express skepticism about the binding nature of international law, noting that "the term 'binding agreement' in international affairs is a misleading hyperbole" (Lipson 1991: 508) and that "most international law is 'soft' in distinctive ways" as compared to most domestic law (Abbott and Snidal 2000: 421). Institutionalist scholars in IR nonetheless note that the language of "binding commitments" often matters because, through it, states signal the seriousness of their commitments, so that noncompliance can entail greater reputational costs and justify reprisals (Lipson 1991; Guzman 2005, 2008; Raustiala 2005).

In the most influential statement of the institutionalist approach, Kenneth Abbott and Duncan Snidal sought to integrate the preexisting concept of soft law into the interdisciplinary effort to theorize about the "legalization" of world politics. Following the editors of the project, Abbott and Snidal define *legalization* in international

---

[3] For example, Richard Steinberg (2002: 340) contends, from a realist perspective, that "most public international lawyers, realists and positivists, consider soft law to be inconsequential." Similarly, Andrew Guzman maintains, from a rational institutionalist perspective, that "soft law represents a choice by the parties to enter into a weaker form of commitment" (Guzman, 2005: 611).

relations as varying across three dimensions, (i) precision of rules, (ii) obligation, and (iii) delegation to a third-party decision-maker such as an international secretariat or a dispute settlement body. In this context, hard and soft law can be defined along a continuum depending on the qualities of a given instrument along these three dimensions (cf. Boyle 1999). Hence, hard law "refers to legally binding obligations that are precise (or can be made precise through adjudication or the issuance of detailed regulations) and that delegate authority for interpreting and implementing the law" (Abbott and Snidal 2000: 421).

In contrast with this ideal type of hard law, Abbott and Snidal (2000: 38) define soft law as a residual category: "The realm of 'soft law' begins once legal arrangements are weakened along one or more of the dimensions of obligation, precision, and delegation." Thus, if an agreement is not formally binding, it is soft along one dimension. Similarly, if an agreement is formally binding but its content is vague, so that the agreement leaves almost complete discretion to the parties as to its implementation, then the agreement is soft along a second dimension. Finally, if an agreement does not delegate any authority to a third party to monitor its implementation or to interpret and enforce it, then the agreement again can be soft (along a third dimension) because there is no third party providing a focal point around which parties can reassess their positions; thus the parties can discursively justify their acts more easily in legalistic terms with less consequence, whether in terms of reputational costs or other sanctions.

Over the past decade, the rational institutionalist definition has been adopted by a growing number of IL/IR scholars, including us – yet, the positivist critique suggests four important notes of caution about its use. First, although Abbott and Snidal recognize the importance of legal obligation in their definition, their conception of hard and soft law assigns no weighting or priority to these three dimensions: obligation is considered, but is assigned no greater weight than precision or delegation in determining the hardness or softness of a legal provision. From an internal perspective adopted by legal actors who must make and weigh arguments at court, obligation matters most. From an external perspective adopted by scholars assessing the impact of these dimensions on outcomes, however, there is greater debate regarding these dimensions' relative weights.

Second, the authors of the legalization volume model the "obligation" dimension of hardness and softness along a continuum ranging from an explicit negation of an intent to be legally bound to an unconditional obligation to be legally bound, with multiple intermediate points. Yet, as noted above, legal positivists contest whether legal obligation indeed varies along a continuum or is rather a binary, on–off question (Raustiala 2005). Whether obligation varies dichotomously or continuously is a question that again divides those taking an internal legal perspective (dichotomous view) and those taking an external perspective focusing on parties' intentions in designing an agreement (continuous view). Those taking an external view contend that intentions behind the extent of obligation vary, as exemplified by unconditional obligations, reservations, escape clauses, hortatory obligations, political treaties with implicit conditions on obligations, and norms adopted without law-making authority (Hollis and Newcomer 2009).

Third, the primary virtue of the Abbott and Snidal definition, in our view, is precisely its multidimensionality, yet much of the work that has applied Abbott and Snidal's definition loses this multidimensionality, effectively flattening the definition into a single dimension and theorizing about the effects of "hard and soft law" without examining the impact of possible combinations of obligation, precision, and delegation in any given case. Indeed, just as various flexibility mechanisms may represent alternative means of addressing uncertainty, each with its own strengths and weaknesses, variations in obligation, precision, and delegation in legal agreements may represent *alternative responses to similar challenges,* with states choosing particular combinations of the three dimensions to address particular challenges. To take full advantage of the multidimensional character of Abbott and Snidal's definition, scholars would need to disaggregate hardness and softness into their component parts, and seek to understand the choice of – and effects of – each of these parts individually and in combination. We attempt to do this briefly in this chapter, but our effort is at best a preliminary one that currently finds no echo in the existing literature.

A fourth and final critique is that institutionalist scholars in the legalization project implicitly assumed that the three dimensions of legalization combine in an additive fashion, namely:

Obligation + Precision + Delegation = High Legalization [or Hard Law]

However, it seems likely that these three dimensions interact in complex but systematic ways that are not considered in the legalization project. Consider, for example, the relationship between precision and delegation. If we imagine an international agreement that is high in both obligation (e.g., a legally binding treaty) and delegation (e.g., featuring a binding dispute settlement mechanism), then, by definition, such a treaty would become "harder" as it increased along the third dimension of precision. Such a claim, however, ignores the potential interaction of precision and delegation. An agreement that scores high on obligation, precision, and delegation would empower a neutral third party to settle disputes about the interpretation of the agreement – yet, the high precision of the agreement might reduce the need to resort to dispute settlement in the first place, and, in any case, it would constrain the discretion of the arbitrators or adjudicators were cases brought. By contrast, an agreement that scored high on obligation and delegation but low on precision (i.e., an agreement with vague provisions) would score *lower* in terms of hardness, according to Abbott and Snidal. Yet, such an agreement would clearly provide potential litigants (either states or private actors) with the ability to file cases, and judges or adjudicators hearing these cases would have greater freedom to interpret, elaborate, and apply its vague positions. These features, in turn, would increase the likelihood that the resulting legal order would be dynamic and evolve over time in ways that might not have been anticipated by its founders (Stone Sweet and Brunell 1998; Keohane, Moravcsik, and Slaughter 2000; Moravcsik 2013). Hence, although the Abbott and Snidal conceptualization of hard and soft law offers a promising enrichment of the simple binary binding/nonbinding distinction, understanding how these three dimensions interact in combination remains undertheorized and largely unexplored, both in terms of design and effect.

II. DESIGN: THE CHOICE OF HARD AND SOFT LAW

Regardless of one's preferred classification of hard and soft law, it is clear that states (and other actors) seeking to regulate their interactions have a large menu of choices when it comes to designing agreements that may be harder or softer along several dimensions. Over the past two decades, both legal and political science scholars have sought to explain why and under what conditions states might opt to conclude agreements of a hard or soft nature, and what advantages and disadvantages hard and soft law present to states from an *ex ante* negotiating perspective. The dominant approach to this question has been *functionalist*, theorizing about the respective advantages and disadvantages of hard and soft law in responding to problems of collective action, incomplete contracting, and uncertainty, and making predictions about the conditions under which states might choose hard or soft law and law-making processes. This functionalist literature has generated considerable insight into the reasons that states might choose hard and soft law, but it runs into difficulties in explaining why different states might have different preferences over hard and soft law, and why states might establish multiple, overlapping, and inconsistent hard- and soft-law norms to govern a single issue in international politics. In this context, we identify a second, *distributive*, approach that emphasizes the distributive consequences of international law-making, and notes how distributional concerns can explain varying state preferences for hard and soft law, as well as the existence of multiple, overlapping regimes. This distributive approach will also, we argue in the next section, help explain why and under what conditions hard and soft law can interact as antagonists as well as complements. We begin, in the rest of this section, by examining the functionalist and distributive approaches to the choice and design of hard and soft law, respectively.

A. *A Functionalist Approach*

Within international relations theory, there is a strong tradition, dating back to Robert Keohane's (1984) groundbreaking work, which takes a functional approach, explaining the nature and the specific features of international institutions and international law in terms of the functions that these institutions perform and the types of problems they are designed to solve. Culminating in the rational design research program, the functionalist approach seeks to explain a wide variety of design features of international law and institutions, including the choice of formal versus informal agreements, and, more recently, of hard and soft law-making processes, identifying the advantages and disadvantages of each in different contexts (Lipson 1991; Abbott and Snidal 2000; Koremenos, Lipson, and Snidal 2001).

As an institutional form, hard law features many advantages. In particular, functionalist scholars argue that:

- Hard-law instruments allow states to commit themselves more credibly to international agreements. They make state commitments more credible because they increase the cost of reneging, whether because of legal sanctions or because of the costs to a state's reputation when it is found to have violated its legal commitments.[4]
- Hard-law instruments are more credible because they can have direct legal effects in national jurisdictions or require domestic legal enactment, thereby creating new tools that mobilize domestic actors, increase the audience costs of a violation, and thus make state commitments more credible.
- Hard-law instruments solve problems of incomplete contracting by creating mechanisms for the interpretation and elaboration of legal commitments over time.
- Hard-law instruments better permit states to monitor and enforce their commitments, including through the use of dispute settlement bodies.

Note that this functionalist scholarship generally articulates the functional advantages of hard law as a simple, one-dimensional phenomenon. However, if we take seriously the notion of hard and soft law as a multidimensional distinction, we can, in principle, make finer distinctions, formulating more specific hypotheses about the effects of obligation, precision, and delegation separately. Obligation, for example, seems particularly important with respect to certain functions of hard law, such as engaging states' reputations and entrenching international commitments in state law. Precision similarly is implicated in engaging states' reputations and should also facilitate monitoring and enforcement, on the logic that it is easier to measure, identify, and punish noncompliance with more precise rules. Delegation, finally, confers distinct functional advantages, including not only monitoring and enforcement of contracts (and, once again, implicating states' reputations), but also, and distinctively, the elaboration of incomplete contracts over time.

In any event, functionalists point out, hard law also entails significant costs. Binding law creates formal commitments that restrict the behavior of states, infringing on national sovereignty in potentially sensitive areas. Precise rules are more likely to

---

[4] The increased reputational engagement of hard law is a core theme in the literature. See, for example, Guzman (2005, 2008), Abbott and Snidal (2000), and Lipson (1991: 508). For a critique of this view, see Brewster (2013).

constrain states than are vague obligations, all else being equal. And delegation of dispute settlement to a third-party decision-maker further constrains state discretion and unleashes the possibility of an agreement's terms being interpreted in ways contrary to a state's initial understanding. As a result, hard law can encourage states to bargain fiercely and at length, increasing transaction costs and diverting resources from other endeavors. In addition, hard-law agreements can be rigid and more difficult to adapt to changing circumstances (Lipson 1991; Abbott and Snidal 2000: 433). Hard law is particularly problematic, sociolegal scholars contend, where it requires uniformity when a tolerance of national diversity is needed, where it presupposes a fixed condition when situations of uncertainty demand constant experimentation and adjustment, and where it is rigid and difficult to amend when frequent change may be essential (Raustiala and Victor 1998; Trubek *et al.* 2006).

Defending soft law, functionalist scholars argue that soft-law instruments offer significant offsetting advantages over hard law. They find, in particular, that:

- Soft-law instruments provide greater flexibility for states to cope with uncertainty and learn over time through information sharing and deliberation.
- Soft-law instruments allow states to be more ambitious and engage in deeper cooperation than they would if they had to worry about enforcement.
- Soft-law instruments impose lower sovereignty costs on states in sensitive areas.
- Soft-law instruments are easier and less costly to negotiate.
- Soft-law instruments are more efficient in simple coordination games in which the creation of a focal point is sufficient to induce compliance.
- Soft-law instruments can be propagated by non-state actors, including international secretariats, state administrative agencies, substate public officials, and business associations and nongovernmental organizations, and they may be used to complement or displace state authority in transnational governance.[5]

In short, the functionalist view holds that hard- and soft-law instruments offer particular advantages for different contexts, and these scholars generally advocate a pragmatic approach, contending that hard- or soft-law instruments should be selected depending on the characteristics of the issue and the negotiating and institutional context in question. As Abbott and Snidal write, although "soft law sometimes [is] designed as a way station to harder legalization, . . . often it is preferable on its own terms" (Abbott and Snidal 2000: 421, 423; Abbott and Snidal 2004). In this sense, the literature on the choice of hard and soft law finds echoes in the related literature on the choice and design of flexibility provisions, in which rational states are assumed to fine-tune a variety of flexibility provisions in response to the functional demands of specific cooperation problems (Koremenos 2013; Helfer 2013).

---

[5] For good discussions on the purported functional advantages of soft law, see, for example, Lipson (1991: 500–01, 514–27), Abbott and Snidal (2000: 38–39), Kirton and Trebilcock (2004: 9), Sindico (2006: 832), Trubek *et al.* (2006), and Guzman and Meyer (2009, 2010).

B. A *Distributive Approach*

The functionalist approach reviewed above has generated significant insights into the design of international institutions and international law, yet functionalist approaches have been criticized for relying too heavily on the metaphor of the prisoners' dilemma (PD) game in assessing the role of international law (McAdams 2009). The distributive challenge to regime theory calls into question the appropriateness of the PD game as the proper model for most instances of international cooperation because it fails to capture the potential for distributive conflicts among the participants.[6] The classic PD model assumes that states share a common interest in reaching a cooperative outcome, and the primary impediment to successful cooperation is the fear that other states will cheat on their agreements. In PD models of international relations, these problems are typically addressed by creating mechanisms for monitoring state behavior and sanctioning states that violate the terms of the agreement – that is, international law.

However, the PD game ignores another important obstacle to successful cooperation: namely, conflicts among states with *different interests* over the *distribution* of the costs and benefits of cooperation. That is to say, when states cooperate in international politics, they do not simply choose between cooperation and defection, the binary choices available in PD games, but rather they choose specific *terms* of cooperation, such as the specific level of various tariffs in a trade regime, or the precise levels of greenhouse gas emissions in an environmental regime, and so on. In game-theoretic terms, there may be multiple equilibria – multiple possible agreements that both sides prefer to the status quo – and states face the challenge of choosing among these many possible agreements. In an international trade agreement, for example, one side may prefer to drastically reduce tariffs on industrial goods, whereas another may place a stronger emphasis on reducing agricultural tariffs or agricultural subsidies. As a result, states face not only the challenge of monitoring and enforcing compliance with a trade agreement, but also of deciding on the *terms* of that agreement (e.g., the mix of industrial and agricultural tariffs). Yet, PD models, with their binary choice of cooperation or defection, fail to capture these elements of international cooperation.

In international politics, as Stephen Krasner (1991: 339) argues, efforts at cooperation often take the form of a battle of the sexes (or battle) game, in which different states have clear preferences for different international norms or standards. Even if all states benefit from a common standard, raising the prospect of joint gains, the distribution of those gains depends on the specific standard chosen, and the primary question is whether and how states can secure cooperation on their preferred terms. The canonical example, from which the battle game takes its name, is one in which

---

[6] Among important works on the problem of distribution in world politics are Krasner (1991), Fearon (1998), Drezner (2007), and Büthe and Mattli (2011).

two players (say, a husband and wife) agree that they want to take a vacation together, but disagree on the destination (he prefers the mountains; she, the beach). In such a game, the primary challenge is not the threat of cheating (since both players prefer *some* joint vacation to being alone), but rather of deciding which of two possible equilibrium outcomes (the mountains or the beach) will be selected. Any agreement in battle is likely to be self-enforcing once adopted, with little need for monitoring or enforcement mechanisms, since both players prefer either cooperative outcome to uncoordinated behavior. By contrast with the PD game, however, the battle game is characterized by a strong distributive conflict over the terms of cooperation. Put differently, the most important question is not whether to move toward the Pareto frontier of mutually beneficial cooperation, but rather *which point* on the Pareto frontier will be chosen. Under such circumstances, Krasner (1991: 340) suggests, outcomes are determined primarily by the use of state power, with more powerful states securing cooperation on terms closest to their own preferences.

Looking beyond the specific features of the battle game, James Fearon has argued that it is misleading to attempt to characterize international cooperation over any given issue as *either* a prisoner's dilemma *or* a battle game. Rather, Fearon maintains, all areas of international cooperation involve both a bargaining stage, in which the actors bargain to resolve distributive conflicts, and an enforcement stage, in which actors design institutions to monitor and enforce compliance with agreed-upon rules (Fearon 1998; see also Mattli and Büthe 2003).

The story does not end here, however, for it is also clear that different international law-making procedures and forums are likely to influence the terms of cooperation, and hence the distribution of joint gains, in more or less predictable ways. This phenomenon is the subject of a growing literature in IR that examines the politics of "regime complexity" and the phenomenon of "forum shopping." As theorized by Kal Raustiala and David Victor, a regime complex is "an array of partially overlapping and nonhierarchical institutions governing a particular issue-area" (Raustiala and Victor 2004; see also Helfer 2004; Alter and Meunier 2009). One characteristic feature of such regime complexes is that they provide states, and other actors, with an incentive to forum shop, selecting particular regimes that are most likely to support their preferred outcomes. More specifically, states will select regimes based on characteristics such as their membership (e.g., bilateral, restricted, or universal), voting rules (e.g., one-state-one-vote vs. weighted voting, and consensus vs. majority voting), institutional characteristics (e.g., presence or absence of dispute settlement procedures), substantive focus (e.g., trade, finance, environment, or food safety), and predominant functional representation (e.g., by trade, finance, environment, or agricultural ministries), each of which might be expected to influence substantive outcomes in more or less predictable ways (Helfer 2004; Jupille and Snidal 2006).

If this analysis is correct, then the choice of hard and soft law and law-making procedures is likely to be a function, not simply of the nature of the cooperation problem, but also of the varying preferences of individual states (and other actors) about the specific terms of cooperation. For our purposes here, the core claim of the distributive approach is that individual states, and other actors, are likely to have conflicting preferences for hard or soft law-making procedures in any given issue area, as a function of their substantive preferences in that issue area, and therefore champion multiple, competing procedures and forums in practice.[7] For example, the countries of the European Union (EU), concerned about the problem of climate change and already undertaking considerable efforts to reduce their own greenhouse gas emissions, evinced an early and strong preference for formal law-making procedures within the United Nations (UN) Framework Convention on Climate Change, whereas the United States, faced with the same collective action problem and the same degree of uncertainty about the state of the world, sought to avoid the imposition of costly limits on its ever-growing greenhouse gas emissions and therefore strongly favored informal law-making forums and agreements to deal with the issue. Problem structure, in other words, may dictate the general level of distributive conflict, but a single problem structure can spur states with different substantive preferences to champion different institutional designs.[8] The result, in the climate change arena as in other areas, has been a proliferation of hard- and soft-law forums, each championed by a diverse coalition of states and non-state actors, and each competing to formulate international rules and norms. This last observation, in turn, directs our attention to the third question motivating this chapter: how do these various, overlapping hard and soft law-making procedures interact in practice?

III. INTERACTION: HARD AND SOFT LAW AS COMPLEMENTS OR ANTAGONISTS

A. Hard and Soft Law as Complements

Although the respective costs and benefits of hard and soft law as alternatives remain a subject of contention, legal and political science scholars have moved increasingly toward a view that hard and soft international laws can *interact* and build on each other as complementary tools for international problem solving. These scholars contend that hard- and soft-law mechanisms can build on each other in two primary

---

[7] This point, to be clear, is where our distributive approach differs from the rational design approach. The rational design project, unlike most of the functionalist literature, explicitly theorizes about the existence of distributive conflict, and it hypothesizes that distributive problems will lead states *collectively* to design international institutions with larger memberships, wider scope, and greater flexibility; see Koremenos, Lipson, and Snidal (2001: 783–97). Our argument, by contrast, is that *individual* states, and other actors, will have distinct and often conflicting institutional design preferences, as a function of their substantive preferences, resulting different choices over hard- and soft-law instruments.

[8] In a compelling paper, Meyer (2012) similarly employs a distributive model to understand the subject of customary law codification, arguing that states seek to codify existing customary law not to clarify that law or enforce compliance, but to "capture" the law and move it toward their own preferred outcomes.

ways: nonbinding soft law can lead the way to binding hard law, and binding hard law can subsequently be elaborated through soft-law instruments. For example, a leading U.S. international law casebook introduces the concept of soft law by noting both that "soft law instruments are consciously used to generate support for the promulgation of treaties or to help generate customary international law norms [i.e., binding hard law]," and that "treaties and state practice give rise to soft law that supplements and advances treaty and customary norms" (Dunoff, Ratner, and Wippman 2010: 95). In both cases, hard- and soft-law instruments serve as complements to each other in the progressive development of international law, leading to greater international cooperation and coordination over time (Chinkin 1989, 2000: 30–31; Shelton 2000*b*).

In their examination of hard and soft law acting as complements, scholars of hard and soft law can be divided into the same three camps we discussed above: positivist legal scholars, who find that soft law is inferior to hard law but recognize that nonbinding instruments can potentially lead to hard law; rationalist scholars, who view soft law as a complement to hard law that serves state interests in many contexts; and constructivist scholars, who view soft law as a complement to hard law that can facilitate dialogic and experimentalist transnational and domestic processes that transform norms, understandings, and perceptions of interests.

Positivist legal scholars generally view soft law as a second-best alternative to hard law, either as a way-station on the way to hard law, or as a fall-back when hard law approaches fail (Weil 1983; Klabbers 1998). Sindico (2006: 846) summarizes this view when he writes, "[s]oft law, and voluntary standards in particular, are a stage in the creation of international legal norms. It is as a pioneer of hard law that soft law finds its raison d'être in the normative challenge for sustainable global governance."

These scholars tend to view soft law solely in terms of its *relationship* to a hard law ideal. Reinicke and Witte (2000: 76), for example, stress how soft-law agreements "can and often do represent the first important element in an evolutionary process that shapes legal relationships among and between multiple actors, facilitating and ultimately enhancing the effectiveness and efficiency of transnational policy-making." Similarly, Kirton and Trebilcock (2004: 27) conclude that soft law is not a replacement for hard international law. "At best, it is a complement."

By contrast with positivist scholars, institutionalist scholars are generally agnostic as to whether hard or soft law is preferable. In their work on "pathways to cooperation," Abbott and Snidal (2004) nonetheless define three pathways, two of which explicitly involve the progressive hardening of soft law. The three pathways are (a) the use of a framework convention, which subsequently deepens in the precision of its coverage; (b) the use of a plurilateral agreement, which subsequently broadens in its membership; and (c) the use of a soft-law instrument, which subsequently leads to binding legal commitments. They note how these three pathways can be blended and sequenced, once more resulting in a mutually reinforcing, evolutionary interaction between hard- and soft-law mechanisms (Abbott and Snidal 2004: 80).

Constructivist-oriented scholars also focus on hard and soft law as complements. Trubek *et al.* (2006: 32), for example, contend that soft-law instruments can help to generate knowledge (as through the use of benchmarking, peer review, and exchange of good practices), develop shared ideas, build trust, and, if desirable, establish "non-binding standards that can eventually harden into binding rules once uncertainties are reduced and a higher degree of consensus ensues." Janet Levit (2004), working in a legal pluralist framework, finds that international hard- and soft-law regimes engage in ongoing interactions in which each is reconstitutive of the other (Levit 2004: 107, 162).

B. *Hard and Soft Law as Antagonists*

Although the bulk of legal scholarship assumes a complementary interaction, or progressive development, of hard and soft law, a few legal scholars have recognized the possibility of tension, or conflict, between existing and emerging norms in the process of international law's development. For example, in an early article on soft law, Christine Chinkin acknowledges that soft law "has both a legitimising and deligitimising direct effect. . . . While there is no doctrine of desuetude in international law, the legitimacy of a previously existing norm of international law may be undermined by emerging principles of soft law" (Chinkin 1989: 866). Similarly, Michael Reisman (1992: 144) noted the challenge of the rise of soft law in terms of generating an "inconsistent normativity to the point where, in critical matters, international law has become like a camera whose every shot is a double exposure."

In our own recent work, we have articulated a distributive model of hard- and soft-law interaction, specifying two scope conditions – the degree of distributive conflict and the unity or fragmentation of the legal order – under which hard and soft law might interact either as complements or as antagonists. Put simply, we argue that distributive conflict provides states (and other actors) with the incentive to use both soft and hard legal provisions strategically and often antagonistically to shape and reorient international law in line with their substantive preferences, whereas the existence of legal fragmentation and regime complexes offers them the opportunity to do so at a relatively low cost. Our argument is summarized in Table 8.1, which illustrates our expectations about the interaction of hard and soft law under different combinations of distributive conflict and regime complexity.

Three core claims arise from this model. First, where distributive conflict among states is low, hard and soft law do indeed tend to work as complements in an evolutionary or progressive manner. This scenario particularly arises when powerful states have convergent interests. In the field of international political economy, for example, Daniel Drezner (2007) argues that, as a general rule, agreement between the United States and the European Union is both a necessary and sufficient condition for successful international regulation. The existing literature on international regulation provides numerous examples of such complementary interaction, including

TABLE 8.1. *Distributive conflict, regime complexes, and the interaction of hard and soft law*

	Distributive conflict low	Distributive conflict high
Single, Isolated Regime	Complementary interaction of hard and soft law, as per existing literature.	Possible antagonistic interaction of hard and soft law within the regime, although opportunities limited by invariant memberships, rules, and substantive content of regime.
Regime Complex	Possible complementary interaction of hard and soft law, although differing memberships, rules, and substantive foci may render coordination difficult even in the absence of major distributive conflicts.	Likely antagonistic interaction of hard and soft law between regimes with different decision-making rules, memberships, and substantive foci.

in areas such as the conclusion of the international agreements to protect the ozone layer, the anti-bribery convention, and anti-money laundering regulation: in each area, U.S. and EU preferences converged over time, yielding soft-law agreements in a first stage that later hardened into binding international agreements (Pollack and Shaffer 2012). Our argument, therefore, is not that hard and soft legal provisions cannot interact in a complementary fashion, but that much of the existing literature exhibits selection bias by drawing disproportionately from cases in which the most powerful states agree on the aims and terms of regulation.

Second, where distributive conflict among states is high, hard and soft law can interact as antagonists, in two senses. From a legal perspective, hard and soft legal norms can be antagonistic in a conflict-of-laws sense; that is, a proliferation of legal norms can and often does lead to inconsistencies and conflicts among norms, creating confusion rather than clarity in a fragmented international legal order. From a political perspective, states and non-state actors can strategically create and deploy hard and soft legal norms and processes in an attempt to undermine, change, and reorient substantive legal provisions with which they disagree, and can advocate for legal norms that most closely fit their substantive preferences. In this second, political sense, inconsistency among hard and soft law is not an unintended consequence of unplanned proliferation of regimes, but rather a strategic choice. In practice, we argue, the most common pattern has been for states to contribute to the creation of new soft-law norms, which can be negotiated or even asserted at a relatively low cost, in an effort to challenge existing hard-law norms.

Third, the antagonistic interaction of hard and soft law will often have the effect of undermining the purported advantages of each type of law, leading to the *hardening of soft-law processes*, resulting in more strategic bargaining and reducing their purported advantages of consensus building through information sharing and persuasion, and the *softening of hard-law regimes*, resulting in reduced legal certainty and predictability as a result of multiple, conflicting legal provisions. That is, where states deploy hard and soft law in opposition to each other, the soft-law regimes and fora can lose some of their technocratic, flexible, and deliberative features, and the hard-law regimes and fora can become less clear and determinate in their requirements. Where distributive conflict is ongoing, international legal instruments will not simply converge into a new synthesis, but may remain in conflict for a prolonged period. Such a stalemated outcome is particularly likely when powerful states line up on multiple sides of the issue (Drezner 2007), but even in so-called North–South disputes, countries of the global South may deploy extended soft-law challenges to existing hard law favored by the global North (Helfer 2004).

Examples of such antagonistic interactions between hard and soft law are readily found, and our simple model provides an overarching theoretical framework for explaining the findings of case study analyses that cut across issue areas in economic regulation, human rights, and international security. A number of distributive conflicts pit coalitions of great powers against each other and demonstrate the strategic use of hard and soft law as antagonists. The United States and the European Union have, for example, taken dramatically different approaches to the regulation of genetically modified organisms (GMOs), with each side seeking to advance its views in competing forums, with the U.S. favoring the free trade–oriented World Trade Organization (WTO) and the EU fostering the negotiation of the Cartagena Biodiversity Protocol; meanwhile, both sides have sought to "upload" their regulatory frameworks for food safety through the soft-law Codex Alimentarius Commission, a classic soft-law body traditionally dominated by technically oriented experts. Under the terms of WTO's Sanitary and Phytosanitary (SPS) Agreement, implementation of a Codex standard creates a presumption of compliance with harder WTO law provisions, subject to binding dispute settlement. As a result, the traditionally softer and more deliberative Codex has also become a forum for hard strategic bargaining among states that recognize that the content of Codex standards on GMOs could significantly influence the outcome of formal litigation about the marketing of genetically modified foods and crops (Veggeland and Borgen 2005; Pollack and Shaffer 2009).

Other prominent examples of great-power stalemates and antagonistic interaction of hard and soft law include:

- the protection of cultural diversity, where the EU took a leadership role in negotiating a series of soft-law provisions that ultimately evolved into a hard-law

UNESCO convention (to which the United States is not a party), with the aim of enshrining a cultural exception to free-trade rules that the EU had failed to secure in WTO law (Graber 2006; Voon 2006; Pollack and Shaffer 2012).

- the issue of climate change, where the United States has fostered the creation of a growing number of soft-law negotiating forums, such as the Major Economies Forum and the Asia-Pacific Partnership for Clean Development and Climate, as alternatives to the EU-sponsored, hard-law Kyoto Protocol (van Asselt, Sindico, and Mehling 2008; Andonova, Betsill, and Bulkeley 2009; Vihma 2009; Andonova and Elsig 2012; Pollack and Shaffer 2012).
- the issue of humanitarian intervention, where a coalition of Western states and non-state actors have championed a soft-law "responsibility to protect" (R2P), which would challenge an "absolute sovereignty" reading of the hard-law Article 2(4) of the United Nations Charter, supported by Russia, China, and a large bloc of authoritarian regimes (Shaffer and Pollack 2011).

In other areas, we find a great-power consensus enshrined in existing hard law, but challenged by coalitions of weaker states attempting to undermine existing hard law through the use of soft-law proclamations, particularly in sovereign-equality negotiating forums such as the UN General Assembly. The most well known example here is intellectual property rights, where Helfer has explored how developing countries can "engage in regime shifting," adopting "the tools of soft lawmaking" (Helfer 2004: 32; see also Raustiala and Victor 2004). In doing so, they often work with nongovernmental groups who serve as allies to help generate development-oriented "counter norms" (Helfer 2004: 53–54). Specifically, Helfer demonstrates how developing countries have attempted to counter the creation of formal intellectual property rights rules under the WTO Trade-Related Intellectual Property Rights (TRIPS) Agreement and bilateral TRIPS-plus agreements through forum shifting tactics involving the Convention on Biodiversity, World Intellectual Property Organization (WIPO), and the World Health Organization (WHO), within which they constitute a majority voting bloc. Shaffer and Pollack (2011) find a similar process at work in the security realm, where a large bloc of non–nuclear-weapons countries have sought to challenge the threat or use of nuclear weapons by nuclear-weapons countries through a series of soft-law resolutions in the UN General Assembly, as well as by requesting an advisory opinion from the International Court of Justice in the famous 1996 *Nuclear Weapons* case. In both cases, coalitions of weaker states sought with some success to use their numerical advantages in universal membership bodies to create "counter-norms," although, in both cases, a competing coalition of powerful states has prevented any fundamental change to existing hard law.

In each of these cases, IL/IR scholars have demonstrated that hard and soft law do not automatically interact in a complementary fashion, but are often deployed strategically and antagonistically – the result being not the progressive development of law, but an indefinite stalemate and, in many cases, a muddying of the international legal waters.

IV. IMPACT: THE INTERPRETATION AND EFFECTIVENESS OF HARD AND SOFT LAW

By and large, the literature on hard and soft law has focused on the choice and design of legal instruments, thus justifying its placement in the "making" section of this volume. By contrast, there have been few studies comparing compliance with and effectiveness of hard and soft legal commitments, respectively, and virtually no systematic analysis regarding the interpretation of hard and soft legal instruments. These issues are nevertheless significant, and, indeed, the purported advantages of hard and soft law at the design stage are often predicated on thinly theorized or unspoken assumptions about these later stages. We therefore offer a few observations on each of these questions.

A. *Interpretation*

At first blush, it would seem as if soft law agreements are likely to be deeply problematic when it comes to the interpretation stage of the international legal process. Here again, however, it is useful (and indeed vital) to distinguish among the three dimensions – obligation, precision, and delegation – identified by Abbott and Snidal, each of which has distinct implications for the interpretation stage.

Reversing the traditional order of Abbott and Snidal's typology, we can begin with delegation, and in particular delegation to third-party arbitrators and adjudicators as authoritative interpreters of international agreements. Here, it is clear that such delegation shifts the primary locus of interpretation from states to arbitrators and courts. Legal agreements that are soft along the delegation dimension leave broad scope for auto-interpretation of treaties by states parties, minimizing sovereignty costs but also increasing the risk of opportunistic interpretation. By contrast, agreements that are hard on the delegation dimension ensure that interpretation will take place among third parties, which in turn raises important questions about the independence or dependence, and the neutrality or bias, of third-party judges or arbitrators (Voeten 2013). In between these extremes, nonjudicial "management" regimes (Chayes and Chayes 1995) or "systems of implementation review" (Raustiala and Victor 1998) can provide some degree of centralization of legal interpretation within a given regime, thus limiting the scope for auto-interpretation even in the absence of legal sanctions for noncompliance.

The effects of variation along the second dimension, precision, are more complex, and are likely to interact, as noted above, with the delegation dimension. That is to say, low precision combined with a low degree of delegation provides a wide range of state and non-state actors with the ability to interpret opportunistically a vague set of legal provisions, and is therefore likely to impose few, if any, real constraints on states parties. By contrast, low precision combined with high delegation to third-party dispute settlement systems grants international judges or arbitrators wide latitude to issue authoritative interpretations of vague treaty provisions and can result in growing constraints on states over time.

The effects of variation in the obligation dimension would seem to be the most straightforward, since nonbinding legal agreements would seem by definition to be nonjusticiable before an international dispute settlement body. This purely formal distinction, however, can be questioned on two counts. First, although international courts may not explicitly enforce nonbinding norms of international law, in practice, it is possible that nonbinding norms, such as the precautionary principle, may inform judges' interpretations of specific treaty provisions (Shaffer and Pollack 2010: 753). Second, international legal interpretation is not limited to international courts, but takes place as well among national governments and/or international implementation review systems, as well as in the court of international public opinion, which may not distinguish clearly between binding and nonbinding commitments. Political scientist Daniel Thomas (2001), for example, has demonstrated how the human rights provisions of the Cold War–era Conference on Security and Cooperation Agreement, despite being explicitly nonbinding, were seized on by Western governments, human rights nongovernmental organizations (NGOs), and Soviet-bloc dissidents to criticize and delegitimate communist governments in the 1970s and 1980s.

Our point here is not that there are no important differences in interpretation between hard and soft law, but rather that the differences are likely to be more fine-grained than a simple hard/soft distinction might imply, and additional research will clearly be needed to understand how varying degrees of obligation, precision, and delegation – and the interactions among them – influence the interpretation of international legal provisions by judicial and nonjudicial actors alike.

B. *Compliance and Effectiveness*

In assessing the impact of hard and soft law, we must distinguish between the concepts of compliance and effectiveness (Raustiala and Victor 1998; Raustiala 2000). As Kal Raustiala (2000: 398) writes, "compliance as a concept draws no causal linkage between a rule and behavior, but simply identifies a conformity between the rule and behavior. To speak of effectiveness is to speak directly of causality: to claim that a rule is 'effective' is to claim that it led to certain behavior or outcomes, which may or may not meet the legal standard of compliance."

Strictly speaking, soft-law provisions – which are either nonbinding, vague, or nonjusticiable before international courts – are problematic in terms of assessing compliance. For this reason, some of the few studies of the impact of soft-law agreements focus instead on effectiveness (as Martin [2013] advocates in Chapter 24 of this volume), asking whether soft law is more or less effective than hard law in changing the behavior of states and thereby addressing the problems that international agreements are designed to manage. Intriguingly, these studies challenge the popular view that soft-law agreements are necessarily less effective in changing behavior and solving international problems than their hard-law counterparts. In one multi-issue study of the effectiveness of international environmental agreements, Raustiala and Victor (1998: 685–89) conclude that soft-law agreements can, under certain circumstances, be more effective than hard-law agreements in the same area. The reason is that, in the face of significant uncertainty about the nature of environmental problems and the costs of addressing them, states are more willing to engage in ambitious or deep cooperation through nonbinding instruments. In many cases, such nonbinding agreements set in train a process of "learning-by-doing," through which the nature of the problem and the means of addressing it are clarified. Finally, they claim, both compliance and effectiveness of nonbinding agreements are increased where these agreements are paired with systems of implementation review, which increase transparency, build capacity, and shame noncomplying countries. Other studies of international environmental cooperation have produced similar findings (Brown Weiss 1997).

There has, to date, been only one major, cross-issue study that examined the impact of soft-law agreements. In a study funded by the American Society of International Law, a group of legal scholars examined compliance with soft-law provisions across four issue areas – human rights, the environment, arms control, and trade and finance – asking whether the formal status of a norm (binding or nonbinding) makes a difference when it comes to compliance by state and non-state actors (Shelton 2000a). Compliance with nonbinding norms, they hypothesized, may be affected by four factors: (a) the context of norm creation, and in particular whether a soft-law norm is freestanding or adopted pursuant to a hard-law agreement; (b) the content, or precision, of a norm, with precise norms more likely to elicit compliance; (c) the institutional setting, and, in particular, the existence of compliance review mechanisms; and (d) the targets of the norm, where compliance is more likely when states alone can comply, as opposed to when the behavior of private actors is implicated (Shelton 2000b: 13–17). Drawing on the findings of many rich case studies of multiple soft-law agreements, the project concludes with mixed findings:

> [I]n some cases the binding instrument evokes much greater compliance, in others there may be little difference, and in still others a non-binding legal instrument may evoke better compliance than would a binding one. In general the same factors are at play and the pathways through which compliance takes place are the same. But domestic institutions for enforcing law, such as the judiciary, are not available, in the absence of domestic legislation or a customary international law rule, and the various international and national incentives to comply may often be less. Moreover, it is less likely that the institutions often associated with agreements will be created for soft law instruments. (Brown Weiss 2000: 536)

Elaborating on these findings, the study found support for several key hypotheses, including the claim that context (i.e., the link between a soft-law norm and a related hard-law agreement) made compliance with soft-law agreements more likely, as did the existence of a compliance review system. These findings, and those of the individual case studies in the volume, are significant, yet the research design of the project limits our ability to draw clear lessons from it. As a matter of research design, the authors seek to determine whether soft law produces greater or lesser compliance than hard law, yet no systematic effort is made to compare hard- and soft-law agreements in each issue area. Furthermore, one could argue that the project's focus on compliance – rather than effectiveness – is misplaced. As Raustiala and Victor (1998: 686) note, soft-law agreements may, as a result of their greater depth, produce greater effectiveness despite imperfect compliance, a possibility that is missed by focusing primarily on compliance as the object of study. In addition, the authors may repeat the long-standing danger of overstating the causal significance of a legal norm, which may in some circumstances reflect a shallow, lowest-common-denominator agreement. Indeed, several of the key findings of the project – that compliance with soft-law norms is higher where a broad international consensus exists (Brown Weiss 2000: 537) and where the costs of compliance are low (Brown Weiss 2000: 538) – point precisely to depth or shallowness, rather than the binding or nonbinding nature of the agreement, as the most significant predictor of compliance.

Despite the difficulties in studying the effectiveness of, and compliance with, soft and hard international agreements, cutting-edge empirical work continues to identify potential causal mechanisms and scope conditions for the effectiveness of different types of international agreements. In the realm of international financial standards, for example, Daniel Ho (2002) finds some support for the claim that market forces (i.e., a desire for a positive reputation in global financial markets) partially explain state decisions to implement the soft-law Basle accord on capital adequacy standards, particularly among democratic systems, whereas divided government and corruption are both negatively associated with such compliance. In a study of compliance with voluntary financial standards in East Asia, however, Andrew Walter (2007) finds that both official and market incentives for compliance often fail, resulting in weak or "mock" compliance with standards by countries following the 1997 Asian financial crisis. In the field of EU studies, a lively debate has emerged around the soft-law "Open Method of Coordination," which was designed and celebrated as a soft-law, deliberative exercise in collective learning and benchmarking and an alternative to hard-law regulation (Trubek *et al.* 2006), but which has been shown in subsequent studies to be largely ineffective in changing either the views or the behavior of EU member states (Rhodes and Citi 2009).

Our point here is not that soft law does not produce high levels of compliance or effectiveness, but rather that the empirical study of the impact of hard and soft law presents extraordinarily difficult research design challenges, which existing scholarship has addressed imperfectly at best. Future research should therefore identify clearly the nature of the dependent variable in question, whether compliance or effectiveness; engage in explicit comparisons between hard- and soft-law agreements in a given issue area; and engage in explicit comparisons across issue areas as well.

V. CONCLUSION

Sustained scholarly consideration of soft as well as hard law is barely two decades old, and IL/IR scholars have been in the forefront of this scholarship, seeking to theorize, explain, and empirically analyze the increasing use and effects of soft law in international affairs. This scholarship, in our view, has made considerable strides forward in the four areas of definition, design, interaction, and impact. With respect to definition, scholars from various theoretical traditions have explored the meaning and content of the terms hard and soft law, offering competing and overlapping accounts of how harder or softer legal provisions are chosen and operate in practice. The design or choice of hard and soft law has received perhaps the greatest scholarly attention, and, collectively, the literature has identified clear advantages and disadvantages of agreements that are harder and softer along various dimensions. Both functionalist and distributive theoretical approaches have begun to identify the conditions under which states (and non-state actors) might choose one or the other. The study of the interaction of hard and soft law is in its early stages, but here the addition of a distributive approach has shed light on the ways in which hard and soft law can be used not only in a complementary but also, under certain conditions, in an antagonistic fashion. We know less about the impact of both soft and hard law, in terms of both interpretation and effectiveness, but the existing literature can be mined for systematic hypotheses about the interpretation of soft law and for preliminary findings about its effectiveness. Clearly, more research is called for in these areas.

Although we, therefore, see great promise in the scholarly study of both soft and hard law, we have also found evidence of two major weaknesses in the literature, one theoretical and the other empirical. On the theoretical side, we have seen how scholarship on this subject is characterized by some confusion about the basic definitions or characteristics of hard and soft law, with legal scholars tending to focus on the question of bindingness, while political science and IL/IR scholars have largely adopted the multidimensional institutionalist definition. As a result, scholars, in many instances, speak past each other, using the same terms but defining them in fundamentally different ways. Furthermore, scholars who adopt the Abbott and Snidal approach have generally failed to operationalize and study individually the three dimensions – obligation, precision, and delegation – of their chosen definition. In the IL/IR study of institutional design and flexibility provisions, scholars like Koremenos (2013) and Helfer (2013) have distinguished multiple flexibility mechanisms, each with its own characteristics, advantages, and disadvantages, and they have begun to examine the tradeoffs and interactions among different flexibility mechanisms. The literature on hard and soft law can, in principle, make a similar theoretical move, understanding the choice of and interaction among the dimensions of obligation, precision, and delegation, but the extant literature has only begun to do so. Finally, the existing literature on hard and soft law has drawn almost exclusively on the functionalist approach, although recent work suggests that a distributive approach (emphasizing distributive conflict, strategic choice, and power) and a constructivist approach (emphasizing the communicative and constitutive impact of soft-law norms) have much to offer as accounts of how soft and hard law are designed and work in practice.

Empirically, one could argue that the literature on hard and soft law again lags behind that on flexibility mechanisms. Existing studies of soft-law design, interaction, and impact have thus far focused disproportionately on a few issue areas (most notably the environment), with far more preliminary and equivocal results in other issue areas. With a few exceptions, moreover, this literature has been more case study driven, with far less comparative or large-*n* research. To some extent, this choice is an artifact of the subject matter: in the study of flexibility mechanisms, scholars have focused exclusively on hard-law treaties, which they have drawn from existing databases like the UN Treaty Series and coded for the existence of specific flexibility provisions. By contrast, soft-law agreements, and particularly nonbinding agreements, have not been systematically collected in the same way, and these resist easy quantification. Despite these limitations, a handful of studies have attempted to study comparatively the design, interaction, and impact of hard and soft law across multiple issue areas (e.g., Shelton 2000a; Pollack and Shaffer 2012), and there is a clear need for more such comparative work, including work that incorporates the activities of non-state actors (e.g., Abbott and Snidal 2009; Pauwelyn, Wessel, and Wouters 2012). In addition, the hard- and soft-law literature suffers from the same problem identified by Helfer in his review of the flexibility literature; namely, a nearly exclusive focus on the initial choice and design of agreements, with far less discussion of their use or impact in practice.

Taken together, these criticisms allow us to identify an agenda for future research that would be more self-aware in its definition of terms, more attuned to distributive as well as functional considerations, and more geared to systematic, comparative empirical study of the interaction and impact, as well as the design, of hard- and soft-law agreements.

REFERENCES

Abbott, Kenneth W., and Duncan Snidal (2000). "Hard and Soft Law in International Governance," *International Organization*, Vol. 54, No. 3, pp. 421–56.
Abbott, Kenneth W., and Duncan Snidal (2004). "Pathways to Cooperation," in Eyal Benvenisti and Moshe Hirsch (eds.), *The Impact of International Law on International Cooperation: Theoretical Perspectives* (New York: Cambridge University Press), pp. 50–84.

Abbott, Kenneth W., and Duncan Snidal (2009). "The Governance Triangle: Regulatory Standards Institutions and the Shadow of the State," in Walter Mattli and Ngaire Woods (eds.), *The Politics of Global Regulation* (Princeton, NJ: Princeton University Press), pp. 44–88.

Alter, Karen J., and Sophie Meunier (2009). "The Politics of International Regime Complexity," *Perspectives on Politics*, Vol. 7, No. 1, pp. 13–24.

Andonova, Liliana B., Michele M. Betsill, and Harriet Bulkeley (2009). "Transnational Climate Governance," *Global Environmental* Politics, Vol. 9, No. 2, pp. 52–73.

Andonova, Liliana, and Manfred Elsig (2012). "Informal International Lawmaking – a Conceptual View from International Relations," in Joost Pauwelyn, Ramses Wessel, and Jan Wouters (eds.), *Informal International Lawmaking* (Oxford: Oxford University Press).

Boyle, Alan E. (1999). "Some Reflections on the Relationship of Treaties and Soft Law," *International Law Quarterly*, Vol. 48, No. 4, pp. 901–13.

Boyle, Elizabeth Heger, and John W. Meyer (1998). "Modern Law as a Secularized and Global Model," *Sociale Welt*, Vol. 49, No. 3, pp. 213–32.

Brewster, Rachel (2013). "Reputation in International Relations and International Law Theory," in Jeffrey L. Dunoff and Mark A. Pollack (eds.), *Interdisciplinary Perspectives on International Law and International Relations: The State of the Art* (New York: Cambridge University Press), pp. 524–43.

Brown Weiss, Edith (1997). *International Compliance with Nonbinding Accords* (Washington, DC: The American Society of International Law).

——— (2000). "Conclusions: Understanding Compliance with Soft Law," in Dinah Shelton (ed.), *Commitment and Compliance: The Role of Non-binding Norms in the International Legal System* (New York: Oxford University Press), pp. 535–53.

Brunnée, Jutta, and Stephen J. Toope (2013). "Constructivism and International Law," in Jeffrey L. Dunoff and Mark A. Pollack (eds.), *Interdisciplinary Perspectives on International Law and International Relations: The State of the Art* (New York: Cambridge University Press), pp. 119–45.

Büthe, Tim, and Walter Mattli (2011). *New Global Rulers: The Privatization of Regulation in the World Economy* (Princeton, NJ: Princeton University Press).

Chayes, Abram, and Antonia Handler Chayes (1995). *The New Sovereignty: Compliance with International Regulatory Agreements* (Cambridge, MA:Harvard University Press).

Chinkin, Christine (1989). "The Challenge of Soft Law: Development and Change in International Law," *International and Comparative Law Quarterly*, Vol. 38, No. 4, pp. 850–66.

——— (2000). "Normative Development in the International Legal System," in Dinah Shelton (ed.), *Commitment and Compliance: The Role of Non-binding Norms in the International Legal System* (New York: Oxford University Press), pp. 21–42.

Drezner, Daniel W. (2007). *All Politics Is Global: Explaining International Regulatory Regimes* (Princeton, NJ: Princeton University Press).

Dunoff, Jeffrey, Steven Ratner, and David Wippman (2010). *International Law: Norms, Actors, Process: A Problem-Oriented Approach*, 3rd ed. (New York: Aspen Law and Business Publishers).

Fearon, James (1998). "Bargaining, Enforcement, and International Cooperation," *International Organization*, Vol. 52, No. 2, pp. 269–305.

Finnemore, Martha, and Stephen J. Toope (2001). "Alternatives to 'Legalization': Richer Views of Law and Politics," *International Organization*, Vol. 55, No. 3, pp. 743–58.

Goodman, Ryan, and Derek Jinks (2004). "How to Influence States: Socialization and International Human Rights Law," *Duke Law Journal*, Vol. 54, No. 3, pp. 621–703.

Graber, Cristoph Beat (2006). "The New UNESCO Convention on Cultural Diversity: A Counterbalance to the WTO?," *Journal of International Economic Law*, Vol. 9, No. 3, pp. 553–74.

Guzman, Andrew T. (2005). "The Design of International Agreements," *The European Journal of International Law*, Vol. 16, No. 4, pp. 579–612.

_____ (2008). *How International Law Works: A Rational Choice Theory* (New York: Oxford University Press).

Guzman, Andrew T., and Timothy L. Meyer (2009). "International Common Law: The Soft Law of International Tribunals," *Chicago Journal of International Law*, Vol. 9, No. 2, pp. 515–35.

_____ (2010). "International Soft Law," *Journal of Legal Analysis*, Vol. 2. No. 1, pp. 171–225.

Helfer, Lawrence R. (2004). "Regime Shifting: The TRIPS Agreement and New Dynamics of Intellectual Property Lawmaking," *Yale Journal of International Law*, Vol. 29, pp. 1–83.

_____ (2013). "Flexibility in International Agreements," in Jeffrey L. Dunoff and Mark A. Pollack (eds.), *Interdisciplinary Perspectives on International Law and International Relations: The State of the Art* (New York: Cambridge University Press), pp. 175–96.

Ho, Daniel E. (2002). "Compliance and International Soft Law: Why Do Countries Implement the Basle Accord?," *Journal of International Economic Law*, Vol. 5, No. 3, pp. 647–88.

Hollis, Duncan B., and Joshua J. Newcomer (2009). "'Political" Commitments and the Constitution," *Virginia Journal of International Law*, Vol. 49, No. 3, pp. 507–84.

Jupille, Joseph, and Duncan Snidal (2006). "The Choice of International Institutions: Cooperation, Alternatives and Strategies," available at http://papers.ssrn.com/sol3/papers.cfm?abstract_id=1008945, accessed March 25, 2012.

Keohane, Robert O. (1984). *After Hegemony: Cooperation and Discord in the World Political Economy* (Princeton, NJ: Princeton University Press).

Keohane, Robert O., Andrew Moravcsik, and Anne-Marie Slaughter (2000). "Legalized Dispute Resolution: Interstate and Transnational," *International Organization*, Vol. 54, No. 3, pp. 457–88.

Kirton, John J., and Michael J. Trebilcock (2004). "Introduction: Hard Choices and Soft Law in Sustainable Global Governance," in John J. Kirton and Michael J. Trebilcock (eds.), *Hard Choices, Soft Law: Voluntary Standards in Global Trade, Environment, and Social Governance* (London: Ashgate), pp. 3–32.

Klabbers, Jan (1996). "The Redundancy of Soft Law," *Nordic Journal of International Law*, Vol. 65, No. 2, pp. 167–82.

_____ (1998). "The Undesirability of Soft Law," *Nordic Journal of International Law*, Vol. 67, No. 4, pp. 381–91.

Koremenos, Barbara (2013). "Institutionalism and International Law," in Jeffrey L. Dunoff and Mark A. Pollack (eds.), *Interdisciplinary Perspectives on International Law and International Relations: The State of the Art* (New York: Cambridge University Press), pp. 59–82.

Koremenos, Barbara, Charles Lipson, and Duncan Snidal (2001). "The Rational Design of International Institutions." *International Organization* Vol. 55, No. 4, pp. 761–800.

Krasner, Stephen D. (1991). "Global Communications and National Power: Life on the Pareto Frontier," *World Politics*, Vol. 43, No. 3, pp. 336–56.

Levit, Janet Koven (2004). "The Dynamics of International Trade Finance Regulation: The Arrangement on Officially Supported Export Credits," *Harvard International Law Journal*, Vol. 45, No. 1, pp. 65–182.

Lipson, Charles (1991). "Why Are Some Agreements Informal?" *International Organization*, Vol. 45, No. 4, pp. 495–538.

Martin, Lisa L. (2013). "Against Compliance," in Jeffrey L. Dunoff and Mark A. Pollack (eds.), *Interdisciplinary Perspectives on International Law and International Relations: The State of the Art* (New York: Cambridge University Press), pp. 591–610.

Mattli, Walter, and Tim Büthe (2003). "Setting International Standards," *World Politics*, Vol. 56, No. 1, pp. 1–42.

McAdams, Richard (2009). "Beyond the Prisoners' Dilemma: Game Theory, Coordination, and Law," *Southern California Law Review*, Vol. 82, No. 2, pp. 209–58.

Meyer, Timothy L. (2012). "Codifying Custom," *University of Pennsylvania Law Review*, Vol. 160, No. 4, pp. 995–1069.

Moravcsik, Andrew (2013). "Liberal Theories of International Law," in Jeffrey L. Dunoff and Mark A. Pollack (eds.), *Interdisciplinary Perspectives on International Law and International Relations: The State of the Art* (New York: Cambridge University Press), pp. 83–118.

Pauwelyn, Joost, Ramses Wessel, and Jan Wouters (2012) (eds.). *Informal International Lawmaking* (Oxford: Oxford University Press, forthcoming).

Pollack, Mark A., and Gregory C. Shaffer (2009). *The International Law and Politics of Genetically Modified Foods* (Oxford: Oxford University Press).

——— (2012). "The Interaction of Formal and Informal Lawmaking," in Joost Pauwelyn, Ramses Wessel and Jan Wouters (eds.), *Informal International Lawmaking* (Oxford: Oxford University Press, forthcoming).

Raustiala, Kal (2000). "Compliance and Effectiveness in International Regulatory Cooperation," *Case Western Reserve Journal of International Law*, Vol. 32, No. 3, pp. 387–440.

——— (2005). "Form and Substance in International Agreements," *American Journal of International Law*, Vol. 99, No. 3, pp. 581–610.

Raustiala, Kal, and David G. Victor (1998). "Conclusions," in David G. Victor, Kal Raustiala, and Eugene B. Skolnikoff (eds.), *The Implementation and Effectiveness of International Environmental Commitments: Theory and Practice* (Cambridge, MA: MIT Press), pp. 659–707.

——— (2004). "The Regime Complex for Plant Genetic Resources," *International Organization*, Vol. 58, No. 2, pp. 277–309.

Reinicke, Wolfgang, and Jan Martin Witte (2000). "Interdependence, Globalization and Sovereignty: The Role of Non-binding International Legal Accords," in Dinah Shelton (ed.), *Commitment and Compliance: The Role of Non-binding Norms in the International Legal System* (New York: Oxford University Press), pp. 75–100.

Reisman, W. Michael (1992). "The Concept and Functions of Soft Law in International Politics," in Emmanuel G. Bello and Bola A. Ajibola (eds.), *Essays in Honour of Judge Taslim Olawale Elias, Volume I: Contemporary International Law and Human Rights* (Heidelberg: Springer), pp. 135–45.

Rhodes, Martin, and Manuele Citi (2007). "New Modes of Governance in the European Union: A Critical Survey and Analysis," in Knud Erik Jørgensen, Mark A. Pollack, and Ben Rosamond (eds.), *The Handbook of European Union Politics* (New York: Sage Publications), pp. 463–82.

Ruggie, John Gerard (1998). "What Makes the World Hang Together? Neo-utilitarianism and the Social Constructivist Challenge," *International Organization*, Vol. 52, No. 4, pp. 855–885.

Sabel, Charles F., and William H. Simon (2006). "Epilogue: Accountability without Sovereignty," in Gráinne de Búrca and Joanne Scott (eds.), *Law and New Governance in the EU and the US* (Oxford: Hart Publishing), pp. 395–412.

Shaffer, Gregory C., and Mark A. Pollack (2010). "Hard Law vs. Soft Law: Alternatives, Complements and Antagonists in International Governance," *Minnesota Law Review*, Vol. 94, No. 3, pp. 706–99.

———— (2011). "Hard Law, Soft Law, and International Security: The Cases of Nuclear Weapons and the Responsibility to Protect," *Boston College Law Review*, Vol. 52, No. 4, pp. 1147–1241.

Shelton, Dinah (ed.) (2000a). *Commitment and Compliance: The Role of Non-binding Norms in the International Legal System* (New York: Oxford University Press).

———— (2000b). "Law, Non-law, and the Problem of 'Soft Law,'" in Dinah Shelton (ed.), *Commitment and Compliance: The Role of Non-Binding Norms in the International Legal System* (New York: Oxford University Press), pp. 1–18.

Sindico, Francesco (2006). "Soft Law and the Elusive Quest for Sustainable Global Governance," *Leiden Journal of International Law*, Vol. 19, No. 3, pp. 829–46.

Steinberg, Richard (2002). "In the Shadow of Law or Power? Consensus-Based Bargaining and Outcomes in the GATT/WTO," *International Organization*, Vol. 56, No. 2, pp. 339–74.

Stone Sweet, Alec, and Thomas L. Brunell (1998). "Constructing a Supranational Constitution: Dispute Resolution and Governance in the European Community," *American Political Science Review*, Vol. 92, No. 1, pp. 63–81.

Thomas, Daniel (2001). *The Helsinki Effect: International Norms, Human Rights, and the Demise of Communism* (Princeton, NJ: Princeton University Press).

Trubek, David, Patrick Cottrell, and Mark Nance (2006). "'Soft Law,' 'Hard Law,' and European Integration: Toward a Theory of Hybridity," in Gráinne de Búrca and Joanne Scott (eds.), *Law and New Governance in the EU and the US* (Oxford: Hart), pp. 65–94.

van Asselt, Harro, Francesco Sindico, and Michael A. Mehling (2008). "Global Climate Change and the Fragmentation of International Law," *Law and Policy*, Vol. 30, No. 4, pp. 423–49.

Veggeland, Frode, and Svein Ole Borgen (2005). "Negotiating International Food Standards: The World Trade Organization's Impact on the Codex Alimentarius Commission," *Governance*, Vol. 18, No. 4, pp. 675–708.

Vihma, Antto (2009). "Friendly Neighbor or Trojan Horse? Assessing the Interaction of Soft Law Initiatives and the UN Climate Regime," *International Environmental Agreements*, Vol. 9, No. 3, pp. 239–62.

Voeten, Erik (2013). "International Judicial Independence," in Jeffrey L. Dunoff and Mark A. Pollack (eds.), *Interdisciplinary Perspectives on International Law and International Relations: The State of the Art* (New York: Cambridge University Press), pp. 421–44.

Voon, Tania (2006). "UNESCO and WTO: A Clash of Cultures?" *International and Comparative Law Quarterly*, Vol. 55, No. 3, pp. 635–52.

Walter, Andrew (2007). "Do Voluntary Standards Work among Governments? The Experience of International Financial Standards in East Asia," in Ngaire Woods and Dana Brown (eds.), *Making Global Self-Regulation Effective in Developing Countries* (Oxford: Oxford University Press), pp. 32–61.

Weil, Prosper (1983). "Towards Relative Normativity in International Law?," *American Journal of International Law*, Vol. 77, No. 3, pp. 413–42.

9

Nongovernmental Organizations in International Relations (Theory)

Peter J. Spiro

Non-state power is now a fact of international life. Nonetheless, the role of non-governmental organizations (NGOs) in international relations remains undertheorized. A burgeoning social science literature relating to NGOs has emerged in recent years. However, this work tends to be narrow in scope, confronting discrete elements of NGO activity. This is unsurprising, given the novelty of much of the activity and the need for descriptive accounts in a range of contexts. International relations (IR) theorists have been late to the party. To the extent that IR theorists have attempted to situate NGOs in international process, for the most part, it has been relative to the state. This approach fails to recognize the consequentiality of NGO activity not directly implicating state action.

This chapter sketches a systematization of NGO activity relating to international relations. It describes four primary pathways for the exercise of NGO power: through and against states, international organizations (IOs), firms, and each other. Only by situating NGO power relative to state and non-state entities does the breadth and novelty of the NGO role in today's global decision-making come into full relief.

International relations theory is helpful in mapping NGOs relative to states. The more holistic posture of recent IR theory may also be helpful in processing activity that bypasses the state altogether. It is unclear how that contribution would be distinctive, however. In the first decade of the interdisciplinary collaboration, IR theory offered international law (IL) scholars a range of useful optics. International relations theory brought empirical systematization to a discipline that had long suffered the flabbiness of positivist wishful thinking. Going forward, IR may have less to offer IL. The inability of legacy IR models to capture the rise of non-state actors may limit interdisciplinary utility.

International legal scholarship is itself only now beginning to pick up the analytical ball. As a matter of traditional international law, non-state actors lacked international legal personality; these actors were processed only as the creatures of states. This translated into a lack of legal doctrine respecting NGOs. Even as the state centrism of international law breaks down, it is difficult to speak of meaningful international law doctrine relating to NGOs. However, IL scholarship is moving to catalogue institutional and extrainstitutional practices relating to NGOs, which should contribute to a theoretical understanding of the place of NGOs in international law and decision-making as both IR and IL move to account for the non-state actors. A move to eclecticism on both sides of the disciplinary divide should facilitate this trajectory.

I. FRAMING NONGOVERNMENTAL ORGANIZATIONS

Much of the literature on NGOs disaggregates NGO participation in terms of their roles and functions at various stages in the decision-making process. This approach is linear, considering the sequence of decision-making phases and how NGOs are participating in each. Although this approach facilitates a descriptive account of NGO participation, it may fail to address foundational questions. A more useful typology can be constructed from agency relationships and causal chains. Mapping out the features of NGO activity across the decision-making cycle isolates the ways in which NGO participation is (or is not) novel in the realm of world politics.

The term "nongovernmental organization" is a negative definition and, as such, cuts a wide swath. It is generally understood to exclude for-profit entities. That still leaves a range of entities. This chapter considers groups that are politically activist as a matter of institutional identity, a subset cannot be exactly drawn. It includes groups that focus on law development and enforcement, with Amnesty International and Greenpeace as archetypes. But it also includes service-oriented NGOs, most of whom pursue parallel political activities. The category aims beyond expert groups and epistemic communities. These groups often have political agendas, however. Many thus are also subject to the analysis offered here.

All NGOs are political. Generalist organizations such as Amnesty and Greenpeace purport to represent universal values and the interests of humanity in general. They nonetheless represent sympathetic constituencies. That is, even generalist NGOs work to advance the preferences of supporters. This is more obviously the case for NGOs representing particular identity groups (e.g., organizations advancing the rights of gays, women, indigenous peoples, the disabled, and scores of other bounded communities). Likewise for environmental groups that reference particular issues, often defined in terms of protecting such nonhuman resources as whales or rain forests. NGOs must pick and choose among possible agenda items. In this respect, all NGOs are interest groups. As Wapner observes (2007), "[m]uch like other political actors, [NGOs] are self-interested entities engaged in advancing their own agendas."

Some analyses distinguish transnational and national NGOs. This distinction may be artificial. Constructivist accounts of NGO participation in international relations show how even the most local NGOs can work transnational channels (Keck and Sikkink 1998). The United Nations (UN) no longer makes a hard distinction for accreditation purposes.[1] National NGOs may have more limited institutional entry points than transnational NGOs, especially in IOs, but this may be just another way of saying that national NGOs will be on average less powerful than transnational ones. There does not appear to be an intrinsic difference between national and transnational NGOs. The categorization merely reifies the former importance of boundaries in a way that NGO activity is otherwise transcending. In either case, NGOs will seek to advance discrete interests, whether on behalf of national or transnational constituencies.

A distinction might be made between activist and service NGOs. Service NGOs have constituency relationships (donors on the one hand, aid recipients on the other). Service NGOs are primarily in the business of transferring goods and services. They do not aim to establish or enforce rights, or they do so only incidentally to their primary mission of delivery. Service NGOs supply public and other goods otherwise provided by governments. They are often funded by governments as contractors. The distinction is imperfect, however, as these NGOs increasingly press a parallel political agenda. Among them are such humanitarian NGOs as Oxfam, CARE, and Médecins sans Frontières (Kamminga 2005: 93; Barnett 2009), as well as such environmental groups as the World Wildlife Fund (WWF) and the Nature Conservancy. To the extent that service NGOs are oriented to the international law-making and enforcement process, the models sketched here apply.

Finally, epistemic communities may be oriented to law-changing activities. Experts aspire to policy-making salience. The notion, however, that expert groups are neutral or objective has been challenged (Guilhot 2005: 166–85; Mutua 2001: 155–57). Expert groups are in the business of advancing agendas, even if under cover of objective (or even transcendent) principles. They are amenable to description as interest groups, albeit ones empowered with something more than represented constituencies. Expert groups can thus be included in the category of activist NGOs for the purposes of this analysis.

At this point, a more elaborated actor typology is unhelpful in addressing the channels of their influence. These channels do not appear correlated to organizational form, which may reflect the fact that such channels are only crudely institutionalized. Unlike in more mature political systems, new global decision-making processes have yet to sort organizational identities. In the meantime, any group with power will be able to use it. Nonetheless, there are patterns in how this power is deployed.

The existing literature of NGO activity typically breaks down the decision-making sequence into three or more phases, in effect amounting to a before, during, and after. The "before" phase consists of agenda setting and events that bring a particular issue into the policy-making orbit; the "during" phase pertains to the

---

[1] ECOSOC Resolution 1996/31, which governs NGO accreditation, provides for the recognition of national-level NGOs on the same basis as international NGOs so long as they can demonstrate that "their programme of work is of direct relevance to the aims and purposes of the United Nations."

negotiations themselves; and the "after" phase comprises implementation and enforcement. Raustiala disaggregates NGO participation in the negotiations phase to include the monitoring of national delegations for domestic publics, reporting on negotiations, and facilitating domestic political compromises both during negotiations and for purposes of domestic ratification (Raustiala 1997, 2012). Keck and Sikkink evaluate the success of non-state networks by isolating "stages" in issue politics to include "defining an issue area, convinc[ing] policymakers and publics that the problems thus defined are soluble, prescrib[ing] solutions, and monitor[ing] their implementation" (Keck and Sikkink 1998: 201). A number of case studies of NGO participation in international relations implicitly take the same sort of approach by organizing analysis on a chronological basis, considering NGO inputs along the road to establishing an international law regime. Abbott and Snidal's important recent work on NGO participation in standard setting addresses arrangements that have already been institutionalized (Abbott and Snidal 2009).

This approach has utility in establishing the fact of NGO influence. Decisions (especially in the context of treaty development) are undertaken on a linear basis. Even if actor influence is difficult to measure precisely, describing the totality of NGO participation in the context of any particular process is likely at least to demonstrate the proposition that NGOs are consequential. The effect is both to demonstrate cumulative influence (established by the possibility of influence at any number of points in the policy process), as well as to highlight particular junctures at which such influence is probable. To the extent that this has been the baseline for assessing the place of NGOs in international relations, it may explain the tendency to highlight decision-making phases as a controlling variable.

This silo approach fails to isolate essential and causal qualities of NGO participation, however. One could undertake a similar analysis of state influence without necessarily shedding any more light on the nature of state power, other than that it exists. Accounts that break out decision-making phases are prone to describe different mechanisms of influence under cover of different kinds of decisions. Unless common elements are extracted, this may result in something less than a full understanding of NGO participation. Such analysis fails to isolate sources of NGO power and essential qualities of NGO participation.

International legal scholarship relating to NGOs falls short in a similar fashion. Traditional positivist approaches to international law capture activity only to the extent that it is reflected in textual instruments and in formal procedures. Under that approach, international law scholars catalogue the participation of NGOs in international institutions along three vectors. First, as NGOs have become more prominent in the contemporary landscape, legal scholars and historians have undertaken historical surveys of NGO participation in international law-making (e.g., Korey 1998; Charnovitz 2006). This work describes activity that had gone largely ignored in state-centered histories and establishes continuities to contemporary developments.

Second, as in IR, there has been sector-specific work considering the role of NGOs in particular areas of international law (e.g., Chinkin 1998). This work has been characterized by narrative description, the equivalent of recent history. This work is important to the extent that it documents episodes or processes in which NGOs have participated in international law-making. It may also allow for more granular treatments of informal NGO participation. However, its utility may be limited by atypical features of particular issue areas.

Third, there has been some cross-sectoral cataloguing by law scholars of NGO activity. As this participation becomes denser, the cataloguing exercise should contribute to understanding the role of NGOs in new global institutional arrangements. However, this approach may fail to capture NGO influence exercised outside of formal channels. As with IR scholarship, it has also typically focused on particular entry points. Examples include studies of NGO participation in international conferences, standing IOs, before treaty committees, and in regional dispute resolution bodies (e.g., Shelton 1994; Lindblom 2005; Ripinsky and van den Bossche 2007). In this respect, international legal scholarship has also tended to focus on slices of the decision-making sequence. For instance, studies relating to the procedural participation of NGOs in treaty negotiation may isolate NGO influence in agenda setting, but this activity may not be generalizable to other decision-making phases. Perhaps the most important contribution of IL scholarship to understanding the changing role of NGOs flows from its normative orientation. Applying accountability and transparency metrics, for example, helps to explain the rise of NGOs and to critically confront the appropriateness of various modes of NGO participation.

To the extent that the existing literature in both IR and IL focuses on conventional decision-making, it suffers a selection error. Conventional decision-making involves state actors. Analysis of the before, during, and after phases of treaty negotiations will tend to focus on how NGOs influence states. To the extent that the literature has taken the form of case studies, it has tended to be sector specific. This may retard systematization in a similar way. Case studies focused on human rights norms, for instance, may privilege states as consequential actors to the extent that human rights norms are defined to comprehend state action only.

Models that maintain relational variables are less vulnerable to this critique. Liberal theory, for instance, situates NGO activity as it bears on state decision-making. The virtue of this approach is also its limitation: by situating all NGO activity relative to one other type of actor, it misses the rest of the spectrum. Although constructivism is more plastic, it has also tended to situate NGOs relative to the state (Wendt 1999: 193). Similarly, legal scholarship has focused on formal institutional arrangements, which will also tend to privilege analysis situating NGOs relative to the state. By surveying the range of relational possibilities across sectors, this chapter assesses the strengths of the dominant IR models and traditional IL approaches.

II. RELATING NGO POWER

Multiactor relational dynamics are tiered. In advancing agendas, NGOs have levers and targets of influence. That is, in some contexts they aim to influence an actor to influence other actors in turn (levers). In other contexts, they may seek to influence actors with respect to their own conduct (targets). NGOs interact with states, IOs, firms, and other NGOs in both respects. These dynamics apply throughout the decision-making sequence, including the making, interpretation, and enforcement of international law.

A. NGOs → States

The state remains the most powerful international actor. As a result, NGOs focus their efforts on influencing state conduct, either as levers or targets. Enlisting state allies as levers against other actors will typically pose the most effective channel for advancing NGO interests. To the extent that states are end players, they are also most often the ultimate target of NGO activity. Variants of IR theory comfortably account for this activity. International relations theory has mostly worked from state-centric premises (Spiro 2000; Ochoa 2011). To the extent that it accepts the consequentiality of non-state actors, it is through state channels. International law scholarship is also comfortable on this terrain. Narrative descriptions of treaty negotiations by law scholars, for example, have accounted for NGO participation as it influences state action.

As levers, states are brought to bear as agents against other states and other actors. This process plays out familiarly in the sphere of domestic politics. A domestic NGO lobbies its own government to press an agenda with other states and in IOs through the channels of interstate relations. The domestic NGO works with the standard tools of domestic politics, including money and votes, as well as offering expertise in the way of conventional lobbyists. In effect, NGOs enlist their governments as agents against other states and other actors. The strategy allows NGOs to enlist traditional state power.

Once states are enlisted, the remaining sequence looks much like international relations in its conventional mode: states pressing their interests on other states through the exercise of diplomatic and economic power backed (at least in extreme cases) by military force. This account fits within theoretical accounts of international relations, the logic of two-level games, and liberal IR theory: domestic politics helps explain international outcomes (Moravcsik 1997). Chayes and Chayes conclude, for instance, that NGOs "exert their major influence through the domestic polit-ical process" (Chayes and Chayes 1998: 252). Under these approaches, NGOs are consequential insofar as they partially constitute home state interests.

Nongovernmental organizations also act outside the confines of domestic politics: NGOs from one state will work to influence other states with respect to the conduct of a third state, or even of their home state. For instance, the U.S.-based Human Rights Watch lobbies the government of the United Kingdom with respect to its position regarding Myanmar or with respect to post-9/11 antiterror policies in the United States itself. The U.S.-based NRDC does the same with respect to climate change negotiations, pressuring foreign governments with respect to ongoing negotiations.

In some cases, NGO and state agendas will coincide, in which case NGOs serve state interests as much as the other way around. One legal scholar explains the Landmines Treaty as a case in which some states put NGOs to work against the "political hegemony of the United States." The undertaking presented a context in which "small and medium-sized states [could], in partnership with global civil society, overcome great power opposition; the US does not always have to lead the new post-Cold War environment" (Anderson 2000: 107–08).

Where state and NGO interests are not aligned, constructivism identifies NGO power based not on the ordinary currency of politics (votes and money) but rather on the power of shared knowledge and learning. Nongovernmental organizations advance ideas that become important to states' identities as such (e.g., Finnemore and Sikkink 1998), and NGOs facilitate the internalization of the ideas they help to shape. Advocates facing "blockages" in their domestic political contexts develop transnational networks, who then teach other states and international institutions, which will in turn pressure the home state in which the blockage is suffered. This "boomerang effect" supplies a model for transnational advocacy efforts. The basic innovation here is to recognize transnational NGO activism both below and beyond the state.

This constructivist model is informed by and mirrored on the law side in Transnational Legal Process (Koh 1997). This school highlights the iterative role of courts in incorporating international law into domestic legal regimes. It departs from a traditional international law optic insofar as it recognizes the international agency of judicial actors. In Transnational Legal Process, NGOs play the part of law entrepreneurs, applying persuasive powers through their institutionalized role as litigants. Changed state behavior is the end result.

Although it is not typically deployed to describe transnational advocacy, liberal theory also supplies a useful heuristic, one that remains rooted in power rather than shared knowledge.[2] Nongovernmental organizations are able to exert influence on states because they are in a position to mobilize powerful agents against them, even outside ordinary politics. In securing action from the United Kingdom against a third state, for instance, the British government is aware that Human Rights Watch can mobilize sympathetic constituencies in the United Kingdom with respect to the third-country policy at issue or with respect to unrelated policies of the UK. With respect to the latter, Human Rights Watch can also mobilize other agents (including other states) to act against the United Kingdom.

[2] For an elaboration of what I call liberal transnationalism, see Spiro (2004).

States thus can be both levers and targets. In either case, states have reason to accommodate NGO demands because NGOs can deploy powerful agents against them, including other states, and corporate and other nongovernmental entities. In other words, NGOs can make states pay for nonconforming practices. This is the price of "shaming" strategies on the part of NGOs.

B. NGOs → *International Organizations*

International organizations have become an important site for international law making (Johnstone 2013). NGOs with law-related agendas have an incentive to influence IOs. NGOs work various channels to use IOs as levers against target actors. In some contexts, IOs are themselves the target of NGO activity. International law scholarship facilitates our understanding of this activity through its historical, narrative, and cross-sectoral cataloguing exercises; IR theorists have also undertaken case studies of this activity. Both disciplines continue to center the state in the IO context, however, even as the institutional role of NGOs is elevating.

The category of IOs represents a broad institutional range of intergovernmental entities, including the United Nations and its component parts (including treaty bodies), regional organizations, international financial institutions, ad hoc world conferences, and international tribunals. These institutions (and/or components thereof) are variably engaged in standard setting; applying standards in particular cases; and, more broadly, managing international responses to global issues. Nongovernmental organizations engage with the full spectrum of IOs. Activity can be undertaken on a direct basis or indirectly through state agents. In many IO contexts, states remain the ultimate decision makers, and, to that extent, NGO influence will be indirect.

Nongovernmental organizations impact IO decision-making indirectly through state actors. States can be influenced, as described above, through domestic or transnational political interaction. This was an important element of the land mines negotiations; the success of an NGO network (working as the International Campaign to Ban Landmines) in persuading Canada to support their efforts was a watershed on the way to securing the convention (Mekata 2000). Nongovernmental organizations will secure the support of states to advance agendas in intergovernmental fora. Particular to the IO context is the now-common practice of including NGO representatives on state delegations; NGO representatives routinely participate on state delegations at international environmental negotiations. NGOs were included in state delegations in negotiations leading to the Land Mines convention (Price 1998: 624–25). They have also participated in IO proceedings involving women's and other group rights, as well as in the Rome conference negotiations leading to the establishment of the International Criminal Court (Kamminga 2005: 94; Schiff 2008: 146–52).

This activity fits within liberal parameters. It also computes from an institutional-ist perspective. Raustiala explains this NGO activity as facilitating the effectiveness of international environmental institutions and the place of states within them. Given that NGOs are politically powerful and sometimes possess superior informa-tion, states have various incentives to integrate NGOs into the structure of inter-national decision-making. On the information side, the resulting benefits of NGO participation include supplying "off budget" policy research and development to states; providing states with information about the compliance of other parties with multilateral regimes; policing national delegations in the context of international negotiations, thus tipping off home governments as necessary to the possibilities of bureaucratic misbehavior; and undertaking on-site reporting for delegates of often complex negotiations as they unfold. On the political side, because NGOs are powerful domestic political players, their inclusion on negotiating delegations can smooth domestic acceptance of international regimes and enhance the probability of co-opting political actors that might otherwise oppose government preferences, both during negotiations and in the postnegotiations context of domestic ratification efforts; and they also undertake capacity-building programs in national settings to advance treaty compliance. In the end, however, states retain control of the decision-making process.

Where liberal theory seeks to explain how transnational NGO activity impacts policy-making at the national level, institutionalism considers the NGO role in cementing intergovernmental regimes. In both cases, the state remains the rela-tional constant. As Raustiala asserts, "in order to work, international environmental cooperation must rely on the legitimate coercion over private actors which only state, and their organizations, wield" (Raustiala 1997).

Institutionalist logic has more difficulty processing the phenomenon of delegation capture. For example, Greenpeace and other groups have paid membership dues for smaller states that would not otherwise have joined the International Whaling Commission, in order to stack state votes in favor of a whaling moratorium. Green-peace was reported to have prepared required member submissions, and then to have assigned Greenpeace members to sit as delegates for these "states of convenience" (Chayes and Chayes 1998: 265). The London-based Foundation for International Environmental Law and Development was instrumental in establishing the Associ-ation of Small Island States (AOSIS) in 1989. The CIEL, together with Greenpeace, coordinated the positions of thirty-seven state members of AOSIS for purposes of climate change policy. The AOSIS has been, in turn, a prominent force in the climate change negotiations.[3]

---

[3] A similar phenomenon was observed with the request for an advisory opinion from the International Court of Justice on nuclear weapons, which some criticized as a front job for anti-nuclear NGOs – in effect, a case of IO capture (Charnovitz 2006: 364).

Insofar as these NGOs were nominally representing state parties, the practice does not directly challenge traditional paradigms of state primacy, and it would be accurate to say that the power of the states involved (as an institutionalist would argue) was greatly enhanced by the NGO effort. But the groups involved, especially the member-based Greenpeace, are also representing the interests of constituencies beyond the states behind whose nameplates they sit. Given the disparity in resources – in this case weighing heavily in favor of the NGOs, in contrast to the examples of environmentalist NGOs sitting in large, developed-state delegations – there are cases in which the NGOs have been formulating the policy (both goals and specifics) in a sort of tail-wagging-the-dog dynamic.

Nongovernmental organizations also act directly on IOs to advance their discrete agendas. Some of this activity follows a constructivist script. Keck and Sikkink use Brazilian rain forest deforestation as a case study. Facing a blockage in Brazil, local activists turned to U.S. and European NGOs, who in turn pressured the multilateral banks (both directly and through their own governments), who in turn pressured Brazil to attend to deforestation. In the mid-1980s, prominent U.S. NGOs, including the Environmental Defense Fund and Natural Resources Defense Council, worked with Brazilians to enact U.S. legislation calling on the World Bank to pay closer heed to environmental aspects of its financing activities. The Bank, in turn, forced subnational (not central government) authorities to accept the institutional participation of local NGOs in forest-related policy-making. When that deal soured, Brazilian NGOs together with the Friends of the Earth and Oxfam filed a complaint with the World Bank Inspection Panel, established in 1993 as a channel for direct NGO input into Bank oversight. Although that complaint was rejected, in the wake of the episode the World Bank was sensitized to the environmental implications of Bank projects. The case study presents an example of activists "'shop[ping]' the entire global scene for the best venues to present their issues [to] seek points of leverage at which to apply pressure" (Keck and Sikkink 1998: 200).

Nongovernmental organizations have had formal standing and limited rights of participation in the United Nations since its founding, in the form of consultative status before the Economic and Social Council (Otto 1996). The major world conferences of the 1990s extended formal participation rights to NGOs (Clark et al. 1998). The World Bank has established an advisory committee composed of NGO representatives, with an aim to bring human rights and environmental values into Bank decision-making. NGOs were able to initiate so-called 1503 procedures before the United Nations Commission on Human Rights. NGOs are given a formal role in the Universal Periodic Review of all member state human rights practices in the new UN Human Rights Council. Secondary participation rights have been extended to NGOs in such IOs as UNAIDS, the World Health Organization (WHO), the Global Environment Facility (GEF), and the UN Environment Program (UNEP). As described by Gartner, NGO participation in the Global Alliance for Vaccines and Immunization and the Global Fund to Fight Aids has been on the basis of full membership. Law scholars working in the school of global administrative law have usefully imported domestic administrative law values, including procedural regularity, accountability, transparency, and regulatory efficacy, in assessing the role of NGOs in these institutions (Kingsbury, Kirsch, and Stewart 2005; Gartner 2011).

Some treaty regimes extend formal roles to NGOs in their implementation and enforcement. Nongovernmental organizations have been centrally involved in the enforcement of the Convention on International Trade in Endangered Species. In the human rights context, NGOs are playing an increasingly important role in the elaboration of treaty regimes through treaty committee practice and procedure (Lindblom 2005: 395–406). NGOs assist UN working groups and special rapporteurs on an informal basis, and their participation, in a variety of ways, both direct and indirect, in working groups, with special rapporteurs, and in the treaty committees present opportunities to press the evolution of conventional norms. Nongovernmental organizations interact with secretariats and other entities acting in their IO capacity. NGO participation has also advanced in regional institutions; NGOs are routine amicus participants in proceedings before the African Commission on Human and Peoples' Rights, the European Court of Human Rights, and the Inter-American Court of Human Rights. This work has been catalogued by international law scholars (Shelton 1994; Charnovitz 2006: 354).

Expertise is particularly valuable in the IO context. As monitors, NGOs supply IOs with information that would otherwise be hard for them to come by, given limited resources and the inherent conflicts of interest that may incline states to underresource IO fact-finding. International organization secretariats are often staffed with former NGO officials, and thus receptive to NGO teaching. IOs find themselves in a competitive institutional environment, and NGOs can offer legitimacy by delivering the approval of powerful constituencies. To the extent that IO action is driven by states, moreover, NGOs are in a position to influence IO decision-making through political power.

Nongovernmental organizations also contribute to the development of norms of customary international law, often coupled with treaty regimes to the end of instant custom (where treaty obligations are asserted to bind nonparty states). NGOs cannot independently erect international norms on a clean slate. However, they can graft on to existing norms and treaty regimes to establish rights coverage. This occurs in the context of interpretation and application, in something like a common law process. NGOs are positioned to press novel but not discontinuous conceptions of human rights norms. Those conceptions will be accepted by states and other actors in some cases.[4] In other words, NGOs can use states and other actors, including IOs, as levers in the formation of customary international law, itself a kind of nonformal international institution.

---

[4] On the NGO role in norm emergence, see Clark (2001).

In all of these settings, standard setting supplies an efficient mechanism for advancing international agendas in the same way that affecting legislation will be efficient for advancing domestic agendas (however much the mechanisms of influence will differ). Nongovernmental organizations undertake to influence standard setting through all of the many vehicles by which international law is made. Treaty and other legal regimes help NGOs advance their agendas by giving target state actors a focal point for conforming their practices to a standard. Once a convention is in place, NGOs and their allies can work to secure accession by states.

The establishment and expansion of legal regimes enable NGOs to engage in monitoring and other follow-up activities. NGOs measure state conduct against legal metrics, which they have had a hand in making, and then seek to mobilize agents against target states to secure compliant behavior. This is a core NGO strategy. NGO positions are legitimated with agents insofar as they reflect legal norms. In this sense, international law is a use of IOs as a lever, fitting into Barnett and Duvall's taxonomy as an example of institutional power (Barnett and Duvall 2005: 51–52), at least insofar as IOs make international law. For target states, the use of legal norms is shorthand for establishing the bona fides of NGO positions (Ratner 2013).

Nongovernmental organizations primarily seek to influence IOs as levers, that is, as a means to the end of conforming behavior on the part of target actors. There are also contexts in which IO conduct itself implicates international norms, as with respect to peacekeeping operations. NGOs are also bringing human rights law to bear on the policy-making apparatus of international economic organizations, such as the World Trade Organization, the International Monetary Fund, and the World Bank. At the World Bank, for instance, NGOs are allowed to bring complaints on behalf of affected communities before an Inspection Panel (Bradlow 2005). Where IOs are targets, they can be influenced indirectly and directly, as when they are pursued as levers. The calculus of legitimacy is particularly powerful in this context to the extent that IO operations are fledgling and institutionally fragile. In the absence of salient empirical studies, the normative frames of legal scholarship are helpful to understanding how NGO participation impacts perceptions of legitimacy and how legitimacy may in turn impact efficacy (Gartner 2011).

C. NGOs → Firms

As firms become more powerful (and states less so), NGOs have moved to influence corporate behavior directly. In the past, NGO–firm interaction was largely filtered through state intermediaries, with states acting as levers to secure corporate conformities. Nongovernmental organizations interact directly with firms as both levers and targets, in many cases without state or IO intermediation. Although there has been some recent IR work addressing this activity, the phenomenon has gone understudied. It is unclear how the dominant schools of IR theory help us to understand NGO–firm interaction at the global level, other than to steer analysis away from formalistic conceptions of international legal personality and to demand systematization of institutional incentives and performance. International law scholars (along with IR theorists working outside the confines of received models) are working to describe this diverse activity.

As levers, firms are an important resource for advancing NGO interests. Firms are politically powerful. In the realm of domestic politics, they are a source of campaign money. In transnational politics, corporations also have the power of siting decisions. That is, corporate decisions to invest or not to invest in one jurisdiction or another can present a make-or-break difference to local economic prosperity. This power has increased with the enhanced mobility of capital. To the extent that corporate decision-making takes international norms into account, NGOs can leverage their power against states (Barnett and Duvall 2005).

Firms are also the target of NGO activity. Although states have traditionally been the sole object of international human rights regimes, transnational firms are being held accountable to international human rights with respect to core human rights relating to physical injury and liberty from restraint (Ratner 2001). Some doctrine has emerged in this context, with the application of the Alien Tort Statute (ATS) in the United States as one focal point. The ATS has, in turn, been centered by Transnational Legal Process as a key vehicle for the internalization of international law (Koh 1997). With respect to labor rights, constraining corporate conduct is the ultimate aim of rights initiatives, in which context firms are the natural target of rights proponents. Constraining firm (not state) behavior is the ultimate objective in most environmental protection contexts.

In some cases, firms will find themselves in the crosshairs as both levers and targets. When a firm has operations within a state engaged in serious human rights violations, NGOs will seek to constrain the conduct of both the state and the firm itself, using the firm as a channel for achieving both ends. Recent examples include NGO targeting of firms doing business in Myanmar and the Sudan.

Nongovernmental organizations are able to influence firm behavior as both levers and targets to the extent that they command consumer constituencies. In highly competitive and brand-sensitive business contexts, NGO activity can have a nontrivial impact on corporate bottom lines. Firms understand the potential of NGO "naming and shaming" campaigns. This gives NGOs leverage over firm behavior, whether NGOs are seeking to have firms press their influence with states or to have corporations conform their own conduct to NGO objectives. As firms recognize the potential of NGO power, it is unnecessary for NGOs to deploy it in all, or even many, cases. Nongovernmental organizations may exercise power over firms well short of a boycott call.[5]

---

[5] This may qualify in Barnett and Duvall's taxonomy as a kind of structural power, in which the consumer–corporate relationship is becoming constitutive of firm capacities and in which firms are coming to accept social responsibilities (Barnett and Duvall 2005: 52–54).

The result has been an elaborated superstructure arising from the interaction of repeat players. Interaction between NGOs and firms in recent years has become more cooperative, not unlike interaction between regulators and regulated entities in the conventional public sphere. In work not easily characterized as either IR or IL, Abbott and Snidal conclude that these arrangements have "arguably been the most vibrant area of [regulatory standard setting] in recent years" (Abbott and Snidal 2009: 518; see also Murphy 2005).

As firms seek certainty, they have been amenable to negotiating "voluntary" regimes with NGO counterparts. These undertakings (often executed as contracts) serve corporate interests because they provide guidance on what sort of conduct will be insulated from punitive NGO responses. They serve NGO interests because they directly advance NGO agendas where national regulation may be failing (in the face of mobile capital) and supranational regulation remains institutionally immature.

Most of the codes are not backed by governmental or intergovernmental enforcement, but they can be (at least in theory) effectively monitored by nongovernmental agents. To the extent that monitoring is effective, NGOs can punish violations through shaming. Although these regimes do not constitute formal legal regimes, they have the capacity to secure corporate conformity with international norms.

At a more general level, as agents of sympathetic constituencies, NGOs have played an important role in the movement toward corporate social responsibility. Leaving specified codes of conduct aside, transnational corporations have been sensitized to taking account of human rights and other social values. Corporate social responsibility (CSR) creates an environment in which such values (again, at least in theory) condition all corporate decision-making. It becomes unnecessary to apply outside pressure in every case (from either governments or NGOs) as the values become internalized to corporate and shareholder culture. Corporate social responsibility is no longer optional for large multinationals (Kocher 2004: 411–12; Ochoa 2011).

These arrangements and values remain unstable. Corporate social responsibility runs the risk of veering toward whitewash (or "greenwash," in the context of environmental protection), with corporations using image enhancement as a cloak for business as usual on the ground. Similarly, NGOs may not have the resources to effectively monitor codes of conduct and "principles" regimes, in which case corporate interests get the benefit of looking virtuous without having to pay the price in terms of constrained decision-making (Barenberg 2007). Abbott and Snidal highlight significant regulatory gaps that have arisen across products and industries (Abbott and Snidal 2009: 547).

Such regimes could migrate to more broadly institutionalized settings at the supranational level, in either IOs or in private standard-setting venues such as the International Organization for Standardization (ISO) or umbrella accounting rule-making bodies such as Financial Accounting Standards Board. There is also the possibility of innovating hybrid regimes, which include governmental and nongovernmental actors in nonpyramidal structures. Abbott and Snidal call this (and call for more) state "orchestration." The Kimberley Process supplies an example of a recently established standard-setting entity in which states are key players; the International Labor Organization (ILO) of an older one. In some cases, IOs may play the role of the orchestrator autonomously from states, reflecting the fact that IOs now comprise something more than simply intergovernmental institutions. The UN Global Compact is an example that appears to be gaining institutional momentum (Barnett and Duvall 2005: 60–61). In both instances, NGOs push for and accede to the enlistment of state and IO actors, as described above, to discipline corporate conduct.

International relations theory has been late to address the phenomenon of NGO–firm interaction (Ochoa 2011). To the extent that IR theorists have processed NGO power, they seem to be drawing from non-IR approaches. For example, Abbott and Snidal's work applies new governance theory to transnational arrangements involving firms and NGOs. Brunnée and Toope (2010) more clearly situate their work as IR theory, but draw heavily from Fuller's (legal) theory of communities of practice. As NGO–firm relationships become more consequential, IR as a discipline will have more incentive to address the dynamic. Any theory of international relations that does not process this interaction will be incomplete. International legal scholarship, meanwhile, is contributing important descriptive analysis (e.g., Murphy 2005; Meidinger 2006).

D NGOs → NGOs

Nongovernmental organizations also act on each other in a range of contexts. Much of this interaction is cooperatively undertaken in the establishment of networks, in which NGO interests coincide and coordinated action serves mutual interests. This activity has been described as part of IR case studies (e.g., Khagram, Riker, and Sikkink 2002). Less studied are potentially adversarial relationships, in which NGOs seek to advance their agendas by influencing and constraining other NGOs, both as levers and as targets.

To the extent that NGOs have power that can be applied against other actors (as in the iterations described above), NGOs may find it useful to enlist other NGOs to secure objectives against target actors. The mandates and priorities of individual NGOs will be bounded. To shift or broaden a powerful NGO's brief may advance the interests of another NGO or network of NGOs.

As a powerful human rights NGO, Amnesty International is the object of such activity. Amnesty was founded with the strictly bounded mission to work for the release of political prisoners (Korey 1998: 166). It took many years for it to broaden this mandate to, for instance, condemn the apartheid regime in South Africa. More recently, it was pressed to take up persecution on account of sexual orientation as a matter of official organization policy. There is now an effort to have it work on behalf of abortion rights (Mutua 2001: 156; Hopgood 2006: 158–59). Amnesty's support for such particular causes can leverage the efforts of relevant identity-oriented NGOs and the constituencies they represent. Amnesty frames its work in terms of norms, and it is in a position to facilitate their recognition. Enlisting the group marks a greater advance for entrenching any given right than does the support of all but the most powerful states.[6]

For the same reason, southern NGOs have pressed Amnesty and other prominent northern human rights NGOs to broaden their missions to press economic and social rights in addition to political ones. These efforts have enjoyed only mixed success and have provoked sometime bitter exchanges on an NGO–NGO basis.[7] The tension demonstrates the power dynamics of NGO–NGO interaction. Southern NGOs have few material resources to mobilize against their northern counterparts. NGOs pressing sexual orientation and abortion rights have various tools for enlisting the support of other NGOs, including access to money and powerful media. Nongovernmental organizations from the north have not been blind to southern concerns; some have become vigorous advocates for economic and social rights,[8] and the acknowledgment of distinctive developing world interests is now an important point of legitimation. But violations of civil and political rights present more manageable metrics (Steiner 1991: 19).[9] Southern NGO perceptions that their perspectives are given shorter shrift in the mix of global human rights advocacy further demonstrate the fact that all NGOs are political in one way or another (Chinkin 2000: 144; Mutua 2001; Rajagopal 2003: 261).

Nongovernmental organizations may also work to influence other NGOs as targets. This activity is along the lines of NGO efforts to influence firm conduct; corporations share with NGOs the central characteristic of being nongovernmental. NGOs may become targets when they act beyond the ultimately representative functions of political activism. Religions supply an example among non-state actors. Gender rights NGOs have pressed the Catholic Church on issues relating to reproductive freedom. Relief NGOs may also be monitored for adherence to best practices for humanitarian operations, as, for instance, in the wake of the 2004 Asian tsunami. Relief and human rights groups have clashed over strategies in crisis areas, creating conflicts with respect to competing lobbying efforts with government and IO officials, as well as attempts to influence each other's agendas (Rieff 2007). A group of NGOs, including Amnesty, Save the Children, Oxfam, and World Vision, have signed on to an "Accountability Charter" to guide management, fund-raising, and advocacy practices. On much the same model as interaction with other actors, NGOs can impact other NGOs by steering the support of interested publics (Bob 2005).

---

[6] For a case study in a national NGO seeking – and failing to secure – Amnesty's support, see Bob (2005: 72–76), describing efforts by Ken Saro-Wiwa on behalf of Nigeria's Ogoni in the early 1990s.

[7] For an example, see the exchange between Human Rights Watch director Kenneth Roth and University of Delhi professor Neera Chandhoke (Bell and Coicaud 2007: 169–203).

[8] Oxfam International is an example of such an NGO (Green 2008).

[9] On Amnesty's difficulties in assimilating Southern concerns into its organizational culture (see Hopgood 2006: 161–75).

NGO–NGO interaction illustrates the strategic nature of NGO activity. In order to succeed in advancing agendas, NGOs will often find themselves using each other to advance particularistic ends, and they may find themselves in conflict where interests diverge. A variant of the non-state/non-state relationship of NGOs to firms, the NGO–NGO coupling has been studied by constructivist scholars as networks. Although this work acknowledges asymmetries in power among NGOs, the emphasis is on alliances. The network itself is the actor (Keck and Sikkink 1998: 207). Network formation depends in part on the transmission of information, in the boomerang model from southern NGOs to northern ones. This approach does not appear to have predictive capacities in the sense that it does not predict when the transmission of information will result in network formation. It may also underestimate conflicting interests among NGOs. Institutionalists understand the role of epistemic communities, which also frames non-state actors as providers of information. But NGOs have resources other than information in efforts to secure the support of other NGOs.

To the extent that NGOs act strategically and marshal material resources, rationalist approaches may be useful. Empirical IR work is beginning to address inter-network dynamics and causal explanations for issue adoption by NGOs.[10] Otherwise, rationalist approaches have not centered NGO relationships among themselves. This could owe in part to a persistent state focus: admitting NGO power would require a departure from the isomorphism of state-centered approaches. It would also expand the number of players in international games.[11]

Nor has IL scholarship contributed much to the development of generalizable approaches to NGO–NGO interaction. This may in part be explained by a tendency to lump NGOs together as a progressive force in a less systematic version of the way that IR has worked with the network as a unit (e.g., Willetts 1996). Doctrine relating to the development of customary international law may have also hindered the recognition of NGO–NGO activity. To the extent that states are still held out as necessary players in the development of customary norms, NGO–NGO activity may seem too attenuated from law development. Other disciplines, especially anthropology (e.g., Rajagopal 2003), may help both IR and IL in understanding NGO interaction with other NGOs in an international law frame.

III. CONCLUSION

International legal scholarship and IR theory have been slow to recognize the consequentiality of NGOs in the making and enforcement of international law. Both

---

[10] Carpenter (2011, 2007). Carpenter describes the causal importance of "agenda vetting" by "gatekeeper" or "hub" NGOs in issue adoption among networks.

[11] Cf. Ochoa (2011), describing how IR theory must adopt to actor sets whose number and instability is greater than among states.

disciplines inherited state-oriented conventions. In international law, doctrine defined international legal personality to the exclusion of non-state actors. In IR theory, realism and second-generation models considered non-state actors epiphenomenal. This reflected the reality that non-state actors played only a marginal role on the ground in the Westphalian order.

As non-state actors, including NGOs, have assumed a higher level of global activity, both disciplines are beginning to process the shift. Liberalism sees a place for NGOs in the formation of state preferences. Institutionalism puts NGOs in the service of international organizations. Constructivism has allocated a place for NGOs in norm development models. But all continue largely to tether NGO activity to the state. More recent work, outside of the major IR schools and sometimes denominated as eclecticism, appears to be filtering NGO activity in autonomous terms. This work will be useful to IL scholars to the extent that it illuminates causal chains (involving either power or ideas) in which NGOs represent a link.

For their part, IL scholars have assembled important descriptive accounts of NGO activity, especially in the context of international organizations. As the activity grows denser, institutional patterns will be more easily identifiable, in both public and private institutions. New IL scholarship is sufficiently plastic to generalize these patterns short of doctrine, in the form of best practices, soft law, and international norms. In contrast to IR theory, IL scholarship is more attuned to normative assessments of institutional arrangements. Although not wholly foreign to the IR project, applying accountability, legitimacy, democracy, and transparency norms sits more comfortably in IL scholarship. On these fronts, IR theorists should find growing utility in IL scholarship relating to NGOs.

REFERENCES

Abbott, Kenneth W., and Duncan Snidal (2009). "Strengthening International Regulation through Transnational Governance: Overcoming the Orchestration Deficit," *Vanderbilt Journal of Transnational Law*, Vol. 42, pp. 501–78.

Anderson, Kenneth (2000). "The Ottawa Convention Banning Landmines, the Role of International Non-governmental Organizations, and the Idea of International Civil Society," *European Journal of International Law*, Vol. 11, No. 1, pp. 91–120.

Barenberg, Mark (2007). "Corporate Social Responsibility and Labor Rights in U.S.-Based Corporations," in Michel Feher (ed.), *Nongovernmental Politics* (Cambridge: Zone Books), pp. 223–35.

Barnett, Michael (2009). "Evolution without Progress? Humanitarianism in a World of Hurt," *International Organization*, Vol. 63, No. 4, pp. 621–64.

Barnett, Michael, and Raymond Duvall (2005). "Power in International Politics," *International Organization*, Vol. 59, No. 3, pp. 39–75.

Bell, Daniel A., and Jean-Marc Coicaud (2007) (eds.). *Ethics in Action: The Ethical Challenges of International Human Rights Nongovernmental Organizations* (Cambridge: Cambridge University Press).

Bob, Clifford (2005). *The Marketing of Rebellion* (Cambridge: Cambridge University Press).

Bradlow, Daniel D. (2005). "Private Complainants and International Organizations: A Comparative Study of the Independent Inspection Mechanisms In International Financial Institutions," *Georgetown Journal of International Law*, Vol. 36, No. 2, pp. 403–94.

Brunnée, Jutta, and Stephen J. Toope (2010). *Legitimacy and Legality in International Law* (Cambridge: Cambridge University Press).

Carpenter, R. Charli (2007). "Studying Issue (Non)-Adoption in Transnational Advocacy Networks," *International Organization*, Vol. 61, No. 3, pp. 643–67.

———— (2011). "Vetting the Advocacy Agenda: Network Centrality and the Paradox of Weapons Norms," *International Organization*, Vol. 65, No. 1, pp. 69–102.

Charnovitz, Steve (2006). "Nongovernmental Organizations and International Law," *American Journal of International Law*, Vol. 100, No. 2, pp. 348–72.

Chinkin, Christine (1998). "The Role of Non-governmental Organisations in Standard Setting, Monitoring and Implementation of Human Rights," in Joseph J. Norton et al. (eds.), *The Changing World of International Law in the Twenty-First Century* (The Hague: Kluwer Law International), pp. 45–66.

———— (2000). "Human Rights and the Politics of Representation," in Michael Byers (ed.), *The Role of Law in International Politics* (Oxford: Oxford University Press), pp. 131–47.

Chayes, Abram, and Antonia Chayes (1998). *The New Sovereignty: Compliance with International Regulatory Agreements* (Cambridge, MA: Harvard University Press).

Clark, Anne Marie, Elisabeth J. Friedman, and Kathryn Hochstetler (1998). "The Sovereign Limits of Global Civil Society: A Comparison of NGO Participation in UN World Conferences on the Environment, Human Rights and Women," *World Politics*, Vol. 51, No. 1, pp. 1–35.

Clark, Anne Marie (2001). *Diplomacy of Conscience: Amnesty International and Changing Human Rights Norms* (Princeton, NJ: Princeton University Press).

Finnemore, Martha, and Kathryn Sikkink (1998). "International Norm Dynamics and Political Change," *International Organization*, Vol. 52, No. 4, pp. 887–917.

Gartner, David (2011). "Beyond the Monopoly of States," *University of Pennsylvania Journal of International Law*, Vol. 32, No. 2, pp. 595–641.

Green, Duncan (2008). *From Poverty to Power* (Oxford: Oxfam Publishing).

Guilhot, Nicholas (2005). *The Democracy Makers: Human Rights and International Order* (New York: Columbia University Press).

Hopgood, Stephen (2006). *Keepers of the Flame: Understanding Amnesty International* (Ithaca, NY: Cornell University Press).

Johnstone, Ian (2013). "Law-Making by International Organizations: Perspectives from IL/IR Theory," in Jeffrey L. Dunoff and Mark A. Pollack (eds.), *Interdisciplinary Perspectives on International Law and International Relations: The State of the Art* (New York: Cambridge University Press), pp. 266–92.

Kamminga, Menno T. (2005). "The Evolving Status of NGOs in International Law: A Threat to the Inter-state System?," in Philip Alston (ed.), *Non-state Actors and Human Rights* (Oxford: Oxford University Press), pp. 93–112.

Keck, Margaret E., and Kathryn Sikkink (1998). *Activists beyond Borders: Advocacy Networks in International Politics* (Ithaca, NY: Cornell University Press).

Khagram, Sanjeev, James V. Riker, and Kathryn Sikkink (2002). *Restructuring World Politics: Transnational Social Movements, Networks, and Norms* (Minneapolis: University of Minnesota Press).

Kingsbury, Benedict, Nico Kirsch, and Richard B. Stewart (2005). "The Emergence of Global Administrative Law," *Law and Contemporary Problems*, Vol. 68, Nos. 3 & 4, pp. 15–61.

Kocher, Eva (2004). "Private Standards in the North – Effective Norms for the South?," in Anne Peters *et al.* (eds.), *Non-State Actors as Standard Setters* (Cambridge: Cambridge University Press).

Koh, Harold Hongju (1997). "Why Do Nations Obey International Law?," *Yale Law Journal*, Vol. 106, No. 8, pp. 2599–659.

Korey, William (1998). *NGOs and the Universal Declaration of Human Rights: "A Curious Grapevine"* (New York: Palgrave).

Lindblom, Anna-Karin (2005). *Non-governmental Organisations in International Law* (Cambridge: Cambridge University Press).

Meidinger, Errol (2006). "The Administrative Law of Global Private-Public Regulation: The Case of Forestry," *European Journal of International Law*, Vol. 17, No. 1, pp. 47–87.

Mekata, Motoko (2000). "Building Partnerships toward a Common Goal: Experiences of the International Campaign to Ban Landmines," in Ann M. Florini (ed.), *The Third Force: The Rise of Transnational Civil Society* (Washington, DC: Carnegie Endowment for International Peace).

Moravcsik, Andrew (1997). "Taking Preferences Seriously: A Liberal Theory of International Politics," *International Organization*, Vol. 51, No. 4, pp. 513–53.

Murphy, Sean D. (2005). "Taking Multinational Codes of Conduct to the Next Level," *Columbia Journal of Transnational Law*, Vol. 43, No. 2, pp. 389–433.

Mutua, Makau (2001). "Human Rights International NGOs: A Critical Evaluation," in Claude E. Welch, Jr. (ed.), *NGOs and Human Rights: Promise and Performance* (Philadelphia: University of Pennsylvania Press), pp. 151–66.

Ochoa, Christiana (2011). "Corporate Social Responsibility and Firm Compliance: Lessons from the International Law – International Relations Discourse," *Santa Clara Journal of International Law*, Vol. 9, No. 1, pp. 169–78.

Otto, Dianne (1996). "Nongovernmental Organizations in the United Nations System: The Emerging Role of International Civil Society," *Human Rights Quarterly*, Vol. 18, No. 1, pp. 107–41.

Price, Richard (1998). "Reversing the Gun Sights: Transnational Civil Society Targets Land Mines," *International Organization*, Vol. 52, No. 3, pp. 613–44.

Princen, Thomas, and Matthias Finger (1994). *Enviromental NGOs in World Politics: Linking the Local and the Global* (London: Routledge).

Rajagopal, B. (2003). *International Law from Below: Development, Social Movements, and Third World Resistance* (Cambridge: Cambridge University Press).

Ratner, Steven (2001). "Corporations and Human Rights: A Theory of Legal Responsibility," *Yale Law Journal*, Vol. 111, No. 3, pp. 443–546.

_____ (2013). "Persuading to Comply: On the Deployment and Avoidance of Legal Argumentation," in Jeffrey L. Dunoff and Mark A. Pollack (eds.), *Interdisciplinary Perspectives on International Law and International Relations: The State of the Art* (New York: Cambridge University Press), pp. 568–90.

Raustiala, Kal (1997). "State, NGOs and International Environmental Institutions," *International Studies Quarterly*, Vol. 41, No. 4, pp. 719–40.

_____ (2012). "NGOs in International Treatymaking," in Duncan Hollis (ed.), *Oxford Guide to Treaties* (Oxford: Oxford University Press).

Rieff, David (2007). Good vs. Good, *Los Angeles Times*, 24 June.

Ripinsky, Sergey, and Peter van den Bossche (2007). *NGO Involvement in International Organizations* (London: British Institute of International and Comparative Law).

Schiff, Benjamin N. (2008). *Building the International Criminal Court* (Cambridge: Cambridge University Press).

Shelton, Dinah (1994). "The Participation of Nongovernmental Organizations in International Judicial Proceedings," *American Journal of International Law*, Vol. 88, No. 4, pp. 611–42.

Spiro, Peter J. (2000). "Globalization, International Law, and the Academy," *New York University Journal of International Law and Policy*, Vol. 32, No. 2, pp. 567–90.

—— (2004). "Disaggregating U.S. Interests in International Law," *Law and Contemporary Problems*, Vol. 67, No. 4, pp 195–219.

Steiner, Henry J. (1991). *Diverse Partners: Non-governmental Organizations in the Human Rights Movement* (Cambridge, MA: Harvard Law School).

Wapner, Paul (2007). "The State or Else! Statism's Resilience in NGO Studies," *International Studies Review*, Vol. 9, No. 1, pp. 85–89.

Wendt, Alexander (1999). *Social Theory of International Politics* (Cambridge: Cambridge University Press).

Willetts, Peter (ed.) (1996). *"The Conscience of the World": The Influence of Non-governmental Organisations in the UN System* (Washington, DC: The Brookings Institution).

10

Regulatory Networks:

Power, Legitimacy, and Compliance

Abraham L. Newman and David Zaring

Cross-border collaboration among domestic regulatory agencies has become a defining feature of contemporary global governance. Substate actors meet with their peers from other jurisdictions to exchange information, coordinate enforcement, and even to harmonize the regulatory rules applied at home (Keohane and Nye 1977; Raustiala 2002; Slaughter 2004). Both the international relations (IR) and international law (IL) literatures have taken note of this form of transgovernmental cooperation, and a term in both literatures has been minted and widely adopted. "Regulatory networks" appear in myriad areas where globalization has affected a regulatory project shared across borders by agencies, industries, and interest groups. In many instances, economic interdependence forges interactions among jurisdictions with distinct domestic rules. The resulting governance frictions produce the impetus for regulatory interactions among domestic authorities delegated with responsibilities for market oversight. There are regulatory networks in antitrust (Whytock 2005; Damro 2006), aviation (Bermann 1993), data privacy (Bignami 2005; Newman 2008a), human rights (Cardenas 2003), national security (Krahmann 2003; Lipson 2005), and telecommunications (Bermann 1995) regulation, just to name a few.

In the world of financial regulation alone, which has been a particularly welcoming one for such networks, American regulators have joined the International Organization of Securities Commissions (IOSCO), the Basel Committee on Banking Supervision, the Participants Group of major export credit agencies, the Financial Action Task Force (which deals with money laundering), the International Association of Insurance Supervisors (IAIS) the semi-private International Accounting Standards Board, and the mostly private World Federation of Exchanges. In addition, the new Financial Stability Board (FSB) is meant to serve as a network of networks, coordinating the harmonization of financial regulation done by other financial regulatory networks and staffed, like them, by domestic agency officials (Singer 2004; Zaring 2005; Baker 2009; Posner 2009; Helleiner 2010; Bach and Newman 2010a; Brummer 2012).

We begin by describing these regulatory networks, although we do not claim that regulatory networks stand in for *every* kind of network – the term, after all, applies not just to international regulation, but to the Internet, to ways that ideas are propagated, and to social organization. Our concern here is with the international and regulatory variant of the network.

We then review some of the insights offered by international relations scholars and international law scholars interested in such regulatory networks. Although generalizations are necessarily imprecise, we suggest that the IR oeuvre has proved particularly attentive to the way that power is wielded within these networks. International law scholars have focused more on the description of networks and considerations of their legitimacy. Of course, legal scholars have not completely ignored the way that power is wielded within and by regulatory networks, just as political scientists have not turned a blind eye to questions of legitimacy posed by the phenomenon. In our view, the disciplinary focuses are more trends than iron laws, but they do reflect different foci of attention. We suggest that, although the literatures have diverged, future work may be ripe for reintegration, as both IL and IR scholars increasingly turn their attention to the same issue: compliance with network mandates. Thus, we present a collaborative research agenda on regulatory networks highlighting issues of participation, authority resources, regime complexity, and interdependent implementation, which we hope will be of interests to scholars from both fields.

I. DEFINING NETWORKS

The term "regulatory network" has been bestowed on a wide array of relatively young international institutions. Although each institution is unique in its own way, networks tend to share a number of common features, including (usually) agency/ministry membership, action through rule-making, a taste for subsidiarity, enforcement through peer review, small secretariats, and informal process. Even as they differ in size, scope, and in the sorts of rules that they promulgate, networks share characteristics of *participation, process, enforcement,* and *institutionalization.* However, in each of these areas, as networks are created without benefit of treaty or staffing by diplomats, they look rather different from international organizations (IOs).

Participation in these networks is frequently limited to various task-specific regulators responsible for market or governance oversight, be they public, private, or even, on occasion, regulatory advocates. In rare cases, entities like the FSB, which has admitted the International Monetary Fund (IMF) and World Bank to its ranks, have invited formal IOs to participate. But the usual arrangements include representatives of domestic, nondiplomatic agencies responsible for the regulatory enterprise in which the network itself is engaged (Verdier 2009), and, on occasion, their counterparts in industry (Levi-Faur 2005).

Networks almost always act through rule-making in lieu of other bureaucratic processes; that is, they promulgate generally applicable, forward-looking regulations meant to guide the conduct of the membership when it returns home. The administrative process that the networks use whenever they promulgate their various types of rules is voluntary and often extremely informal, although it frequently becomes more institutionalized over time (Zaring 2008).

Moreover, these networks rarely have coercive enforcement tools at the international level. Rather, they rely on self-reporting and peer review to police compliance with the network's standards. Far from only being expert-driven coordination mechanisms, however, the networks have also firmly embraced a principle of subsidiarity, especially in enforcement. The idea is that the network will delegate questions of implementation and policing to its members, who enjoy considerable administrative law powers in their home markets, while the international institution will focus on agenda setting and policy deliberations.

In this way, and in others, even though the goal is some form of international administration, the international network does not look like a domestic agency. Networks are lightly institutionalized, with very small secretariats incapable of doing much more than coordinating meetings (and to do that or whatever else the network does, the institutions often rely on the bureaucrats of their membership, either in their domestic capacity or as officials seconded to the network). Networks tend to have broad and flexible mandates, rather than the sorts of specific and carefully constrained authorities that ordinarily characterize the treaties that create IOs or the domestic laws that authorize domestic agency action. The founding documents of networks, if they exist at all, are modest affairs, with broad authorization that, however worded, never appear to be taken very seriously after the network is created. If a network has ever eschewed a course of action because of the limitations of its founding document, there has not yet been a fuss made of it (Zaring 1998, 2008). Thus, participants in the network (and not the network secretariat) and their interactions with each other become the key to understanding what the network does and how it functions.

Network proponents have argued that the informal nature of such cooperation offers a fast and flexible alternative to traditional forms of international law. Sidestepping drawn-out treaty ratification procedures, transgovernmental initiatives can quickly respond to emerging global challenges. Moreover, such networks include those technical experts who are well positioned to navigate the quickly shifting demands of international interdependence conflicts. Slaughter has concluded that such networks provide a "blueprint for the international architecture of the 21st century" (Slaughter 2004).

Skeptics, by contrast, view such networks merely as appendages of states, limiting their ability to independently influence international dynamics or provide effective governance solutions (Drezner 2007; Verdier 2009). Their effectiveness for actionable global problems remains, in many instances, an empirical question that needs to be studied across sectors.

II. OUR APPROACH

Although research into regulatory networks is vibrant and growing, along with the institutions themselves, our own sense about the state of network scholarship in IL and IR is that the integration of insights across disciplines has slowed. Political science scholarship has moved in an empirical, although broad, direction, while the legal scholarship has more narrowly focused on the identification of networks as a source of legal semi-obligation, the search for constraints being one of the animating ones of international law.[1] And so, while the scholars most emblematic in the network field – lawyers such as Anne-Marie Slaughter and political scientists such as Robert Keohane – have been active in both IL and IR, the fields have grown apart. International relations regulatory network scholarship has been active, with a relatively large literature embracing a wide range of methodological and theoretical approaches. In IL, network scholarship has taken on the more limited goal of documenting the way that regulatory networks have evolved into lawlike institutions that create rules in the international system. Or, to put it another way, recent work in IR has focused on neo-realist impulses underscoring the power relationships embedded in network architectures, whereas IL has frequently identified and more simply celebrated the institutions that either mask or generate those sorts of power imbalances.

After reviewing the divergent paths taken across the fields, we identify and develop a research agenda considering the role of regulatory networks as an international governance mechanism. The bulk of the chapter, then, considers how IR and IL could consider variation in the legal structures, power dynamics, and implementation issues that arise, as well as makes an initial attempt to explain such variation. In reintegrating legal and political perspectives, we hope to fertilize both and engage researchers across disciplines to consider this novel and still relatively underexplored research domain. Although many IR scholars have considered the way that powerful interests within and among states have engaged with networks, legal scholars have embraced the possibility of the institutions and either justified or critiqued their legitimacy. From both perspectives, the ability of networks to get states or agencies to comply with their mandates has been critical. And the systematic evaluation

---

[1] The study of networks has antecedents in other traditions of international legal scholarship. For example, legal scholars had long accepted the idea that transnational law – law regulating international relationships between non-state actors – was worthy of study (Jessup 1956). Steiner and Vagts' (1976) *Transnational Legal Problems* casebook delved into the sort of below-the-state-level coordination that characterizes network analysis from the legal perspective.

of compliance and implementation issues is probably the next step for regulatory network research.

III. REGULATORY NETWORKS IN INTERNATIONAL RELATIONS: POLICY NETWORKS, COORDINATION MECHANISMS, AND SOCIAL NETWORK ANALYSIS

Network concepts entered the IR lexicon in the 1970s as scholars confronted the demise of traditional state-centered diplomacy (Keohane and Nye 1977; Risse-Kappan 1995). At its most basic, and divorced from any particular context, a network consists of a node connected to other nodes through a set of ties. This abstract definition, however, offers few a priori expectations about how regulatory networks function, the politics within them, or their likely ability to confront coordination challenges. Researchers have thus developed at least three unique (but often overlapping) images of networks, which have potentially distinct implications for those interested in the role of regulatory networks in mitigating global governance challenges. The following section reviews these three perspectives – policy networks, coordination mechanisms, and social network approaches – before applying their lessons directly to issues of global regulatory networks.

A. Policy Networks

Early work in IR that explored network concepts borrowed the metaphor of the network from public policy research. The fundamental idea was that society and state structures were not discrete units and often permeated one another. Each could be decomposed and disaggregated into a number of distinct actors (with distinct interests), which engage collectively in policy coordination of a particular functional governance domain (Hopkins 1976; Keohane and Nye 1977). In such policy networks, private actors (including firms and nongovernmental organizations) took on a greater role. Particularly in the agenda-setting and implementation phases of policy development, these nontraditional actors made a critical contribution to global regulatory debates (Abbott and Snidal 2009; Büthe and Mattli 2011). At the same time that private actors were brought in, the state itself was disaggregated. Substate actors, such as judges, regulators, or parliamentarians, who had not traditionally been considered part of the foreign policy apparatus of the state, began to engage their counterparts in other states, along with relevant private actors. The channels through which diplomacy operated multiplied along with the actors participating in these debates (Risse-Kappan 1995; Peterson 1995; Börzel 1998; Cerny 2010). Regulatory networks, then, vary in terms of the primary types of actors involved. In some issue areas (e.g., banking regulation and securities markets), public authorities such as central banks and financial services regulators dominate global governance debates. In others (e.g., accounting standards or Internet domain names), by contrast, private actors are primarily responsible for setting the basic standards concerning market participation. In either case, there is considerable interaction between public and private authorities (Farrell 2006).

A second contribution of this research stream highlights the multiple and overlapping sites of authority present in global regulatory efforts. Policy networks comprised of public and private actors enjoy varying levels of power resources across regimes. In many policy domains, jurisdiction is overlapping, creating multilevel governance processes. In such circumstances, network actors can potentially leverage opportunity structures within the multilevel system to shape agenda setting and policy decision-making (Hooghe and Marks 2001; Zito 2001). Authority opportunities at the international level can be activated to shape policy domestically or regionally. In their path-breaking study, Keck and Sikkink described how international activist networks employed global norms in order to press for policy change at the domestic level (Keck and Sikkink 1998). Similarly, Newman demonstrates how networks of domestic regulators use their delegated authority, expertise, and network ties to transform regional policy initiatives (Newman 2008*b*). Building on Keohane and Nye's concept of transgovernmental coalitions, these studies suggest that participants in regulatory networks have unique policy preferences and that the network offers a pathway through which they can assert those interests vis-à-vis other actors, such as heads of state or IOs (Cameron 1995; Cardenas 2003; Newman 2008*a*). Importantly, regulatory network participants enjoy varying types and levels of power resources (Barnett and Duvall 2005). As argued in the epistemic communities literature, some rely primarily on the authority derived from their technical expertise to shape the policy agenda (Haas 1992). Perry and Nolke (2006), for example, have argued that the International Accounting Standards Board's success is largely a product of its considerable expertise in this area. Other network participants may have additional regulatory capacity, including the delegated authority to control market access or mobilize ties to regulatory constituents (Newman 2008*b*). Posner (2009), for example, has argued that changes in internal regulatory delegation within the European Union enhanced the authority of European participants in international financial rule-making. Singer (2007) underscores the importance of relationships between financial regulators to domestic constituencies to account for international regulatory preferences. The policy network research stream, then, opens up the number and types of actors participating in global governance, potential areas of entrepreneurial agency that such actors might enjoy, and sources of inequality or power disparities among the network participants.

B. *Networks – Between Hierarchies and Markets*

A second strand of research in IR has drawn more explicitly from sociology and the new economics of organizations (Williamson 1981; Powell 1990). Here, the central research question concerns various coordination mechanisms, their relative efficiency, and potential limitations. From managing a global production supply chain to an international humanitarian relief effort, IR scholars following this tradition argued that coordination dilemmas centered on the nature of the problem–actor constellation (Abbott and Snidal 2000; Koremenos 2013). In some settings, where, for example, extensive monitoring is necessary, hierarchy guarantees information exchange and proper surveillance. In other domains, however, where pure coordination is required, distributed coordination through market mechanisms might be sufficient. Networks offer a middle ground between hierarchy and markets, offering less centralization and control than hierarchy, but possibly facilitating information flows and providing a focal point for slightly more complicated coordination problems. Kahler and Lake argue that states purposively choose among hierarchy, networks, and markets when they design international regimes depending on the problem that they face and the capacity of the governance design to resolve that specific problem (Kahler and Lake 2009). Similarly, Slaughter has argued that informal regulatory networks offer a fast and flexible alternative to more cumbersome hierarchical international treaties, which often get bogged down in domestic ratification processes. Such networks promote the distribution of best practices and allow for technical standardization and enforcement assistance (Slaughter 2004). Raustiala (2002) highlights the role of such coordinating networks in regulatory areas ranging from the environment to financial market oversight. Regulatory authorities construct links with peers in other jurisdictions to promote information sharing and monitoring capacities. Although less concerned with agency interests or power resources, this second research strain suggests the purposive use of networks by international actors as a strategy to overcome some specific types of coordination dilemmas. It thus offers testable expectations concerning when such regulatory networks might be more or less effective. At the same time, the research suggests the possible limits of intermediate forms of organizational adjustment for solving highly contentious policy problems.

C. Social Network Approaches

The final and most recent literature takes a structural approach developed in sociology – known as *social network analysis* – and applies the basic concepts and finding to international network phenomena (Hafner-Burton, Kahler, and Montgomery 2009). The basic assumption of this research is that social interactions (known as *ties*) create connections between nodes that, when aggregated, form network structures (Wasserman and Faust 1994). Ties comprise a range of types of interaction, including material, social, and normative, and do not necessarily need to be intentional. Social network studies, for example, have looked at marriage relations, citation patterns, and hyperlinks among websites (Padgett and Ansell 1993). As the ties between nodes are aggregated, distinct structural patterns emerge, which can then shape the behavior of network participants. From this perspective, hierarchies, networks, and markets are not distinct structures. Rather, networks may be characterized as more or less centralized. In some cases, a few nodes are highly connected to other nodes in the network, whereas those other nodes share few connections with each other, thus creating a *star network*. Such star networks place hubs in a privileged position as they become brokers of information for other network participants and have access to most of the information that passes through the network. Star networks are both extremely efficient and fragile at the same time. The hub-and-spoke structure allows information to quickly pass across the farthest reaches of the network. If, however, something should happen to the hub, the network could quickly break down.

Other network structures, by contrast, are less centralized, with ties distributed more equally among nodes. In such *mesh networks*, the redundancy of ties increases the robustness of the network but may produce inefficient coordination. Such structural variation has been used across a host of studies in IR to explain diverse research questions such as patterns of diffusion, sources of authority, and agenda setting (Lake and Wong 2009; Carpenter 2011). Bach and Newman (2010*a*) demonstrate, for example, how distinct ties within the regulatory network for securities market governance influence different parts of the regulatory process. The central position of the U.S. Securities and Exchange Commission as a hub has shaped the global regulatory agenda, whereas more diffuse ties among regulators serve to affect policy implementation. Social network approaches highlight structural constraints forged through iterative interactions among the actors involved and underscore the potential inequalities and power dynamics that can arise from regulatory network interactions. As with the policy network literature, the focus is less on the effectiveness of such cooperation and more on the politics, power, and inequalities that might arise.

IV. LEGITIMACY

International lawyers, for their part, tend to wax enthusiastic about the wide array of networks seeking to solve cross-border problems. Networks, which are not traditional creatures of international law, have accomplished a great deal in areas where the usual tools of international law have made little or no impact. As Richard Stewart has observed, they can, and have, set standards, coordinated enforcement, or built regulatory capacity. They have acted through an agreement on principles or committed to a memorandum of understanding, or, after setting some rules of the road, served simply as a coordinative clearinghouse by offering information exchanges or the aforementioned capacity and enforcement assistance (Stewart 2005).

Describing these variations and documenting the effects of regulatory networks in international governance has been a preoccupation of international legal scholars, but their work is not without familiar issues of normative implication and process design.[2] Some of these implications may be derived from the interest among international lawyers in identifying institutions that "work" – that is, that constrain the action of states and that are susceptible to a recognizably legal form of analysis. The predilection for this form of success, although not shared by all international lawyers, makes for a scholarly ethos that endorses effective cooperation. In reviewing the writings of legal network scholars, we will first consider their descriptive work, then the normative implications of the legal corpus.

A. Describing Networks

Descriptively, one challenge for scholars of regulatory networks has been categorization. What counts as a network and what does not? It has not always been easy for international scholars to move beyond identification to broader maintenance, a likely function of the fact that very narrow or specific definitions are unrealistic in practice.

One problem is that, institutionally, some treaties provide for network-like relationships, making it difficult to cleanly identify networks as simple alternatives to treaties for countries interested in international governance (Raustiala 2002). The World Trade Organization (WTO), for example, has, pursuant to its agreement on sanitary and phytosanitary (SPS) measures, delegated authority to quasi-networks designed to encourage the harmonization of national standards on food, animal, and plant health and safety (Lang and Scott 2009). The resulting SPS institution has both network elements of soft law and treaty elements of hard law. Is it a network? It operates like a network, but the work product has certain binding legal effects in WTO dispute settlement proceedings, rather than the soft-law encouragement offered by other networks. Other networks, like the Basel Committee on Banking Supervision, have no treaty component and expressly declaim any legal force whatsoever (Zaring 1998). And the regulatory network overseeing antitrust arguably was created because a formal treaty would have been impossible to conclude (Damtoft and Flanagan 2009).

Conversely, international regulatory cooperation can be discerned in examples of bilateral cooperation or even barely explicitly cooperative structures at all – these are the sorts of institutionalization that some capital markets regulators have particularly preferred (Brummer 2010). Some of the instantiations might better be characterized as clubs, where regulators invite their peers to join them in coordinating regulation not through an increasingly formal informal network, but through a multilateral or bilateral arrangement that amounts to something less, such as a mutual regulation agreement among regulators, or an "I'm okay, you're okay" agreement to enforce matters together (Kapczynski 2009; Brummer 2010, 2011). Are all of these

---

[2] The approach has resulted in a uniquely legal form of empiricism, with qualitative description and particular attention to institutionalization.

organizations networks? It may not entirely make sense to put informal collaboration in the WTO in the same category as friendly meetings among, say, treasury officials interested in limiting tax flight. To be sure, it is a problem, we suspect, that is unlikely to be solved by precisely and exactly specifying what "counts" as a network and what does not – an arid exercise. Definitional obliqueness, however, does raise the possibility that difficulties in defining networks have led legal scholars to invest the institutions with a form of mission creep, as they become capable of anything and organizable by anyone.

The second critical descriptive question, after definition, has been one of means. How do networks do what they do? Once again, the process has not been entirely specified. The noninstitutionalists have proposed an almost mystical process of disaggregated coordination. For example, David Mitrany and Charles Sabel both posit that the mere act of interaction can take on some sort of independent momentum that results in coordinated outcomes, even though the coordination itself is hard to institutionalize, define, or predict (Sabel and Zeitlin 2010). Mitrany described this as a process of *enmeshment*, where some transnational coordination might lead to more (Mitrany 1966). Sabel, writing with Michael Dorf, characterized it, in the domestic sphere, as *democratic experimentalism*, whereby disaggregated groups would try a number of different approaches to regulatory problems, and the best of those approaches would be used as benchmarks offered up to everybody and then replaced by a new effort to exceed the benchmarks (Sabel and Dorf 1998). In their view, the design of the institution of cooperation does not matter very much. Others have been more willing to look to power dynamics to explain what happens within the network, and they suggest that this dynamic is most interesting in the decision-making process (Scott 1995; Posner 2005). Still others point to the growing adoption of good government process by networks as something that has made the content of what they do tractable to outsiders (Zaring 2008). The problem is a striking one for lawyers, who care very much about decision-making processes (at least ordinarily), but find it difficult to observe these in the often secretive network scheme, making this a descriptive enterprise in which further research could be valuable.

B. Normative Implications

Amid the descriptive work, two different types of normative issues have received substantial attention. First, some legal scholars argue explicitly (and many others who study various networks suggest implicitly) that networks promote international cooperation and that this cooperation is a good thing. Anne-Marie Slaughter, the progenitor of much international legal network scholarship, endorses this view; she believes that the continued interaction of substate actors such as regulators will advance international cooperation and reduce international conflict (Slaughter 2004).

This sort of implicit normative commitment also defines some of the work of other network scholars, such as Raustiala, who views networks as a tool that nations can use to meet international challenges, and Zaring, who argues that problems created by globalization require global responses and networks are often efficient at such responses (Zaring 1998; Raustiala 2002).

The second normative strand in international legal scholarship argues that regulatory networks promote the rule of law. Networks do so either by enhancing and improving formal international institutions, or, alternatively, by adopting some of the trappings of legal rule themselves. The capacity-building advantage of networks might be seen in the worldviews of scholars like Lang and Scott, who see the informal, harmonization-oriented aspects of the current WTO order – regulators are trying to agree on minimum food and product safety standards that can cross borders, for example – as something that can deepen the effect of the formal treaty and its purpose (Lang and Scott 2009). Others, like Dunoff, see the growing networks of advocates before these institutions as something that may contribute to the civil society of formal international arrangements (Dunoff 2004).

But another way that networks help promote the rule of law is by increasingly adopting lawlike trappings themselves. Zaring has identified the way that regulatory network processes have incorporated increasingly lawlike features of openness, notice and comment, and administrative good governance (Zaring 2005, see also Giovanoli 2009).

It is not always clear how these normative commitments do their work. Is there some sort of compliance pull? If so, it would be consistent with Franck's account about the way that international law enjoys both legitimacy and respect. To Franck, compliance with international rules depended in part on their quality and justice; the better the rules, the stronger their compliance pull and the more intense the virtuous circle leading to further respect for network (or other forms of international governance) pronouncements (Franck 1988).

Relatedly, the growth of this obedience to international rule of law might come from the enmeshment that networks offer as countries that participate in their processes find it increasingly impossible to exit (or – perhaps more important – to even partially exit from full participation). Joseph Weiler found these points of no return to be critical in explaining the transformation of Europe from a set of warring states into a body in which those states cooperated and exercised the voice that we expect robust political institutions to provide (Weiler 1991). Moreover, enmeshment via network and international issue-specific technocratic cooperation is what David Mitrany thought would be the locus of a realistic version of global governance (Mitrany 1966).

Some political scientists have identified a similar process of enmeshment in the European Union, which features, via the union's comitology and Open Method of Coordination (OMC) processes, efforts to get domestic regulators to coordinate their approaches at the supranational level (Bignami 1999). Enthusiasts view OMC and comitology as opportunities for constant improvement through ever more edifying dialogue, peer review, and compromise among regulators (e.g., Joerges and Neyer

1997; Heidenreich and Zeitlin 2009). Others contend that the dialogue can be opaque, and, ultimately, a rather inefficient mechanism for the promulgation of pan-European policy (e.g., Rhodes 2010).

Finally, there are network skeptics in the international legal literature. Some of these scholars argue that networks do not work (or do not work well) even as they grudgingly concede the necessity of some sort of international structure to respond to globalization (Posner 2005). The critique is reminiscent of that given against informal international cooperation that could be found in John Jackson's work on the international trade regime. Jackson believed that a formal WTO with a highly legalized dispute resolution process was a much better prospect for the development of trade law than were the relatively informal and ad hoc Generalized Agreement on Tariffs and Trade (GATT) decision-making and dispute resolution processes (Jackson, Davies, and Sykes 2008).

Along these lines, in financial regulation today, which is often posited as the epitome of effective network coordination, Hal Scott has concluded that regulatory networks such as the Basel Committee on Banking Supervision have often been ineffective mechanisms for this sort of supervision and that, when they have not been ineffective, they have been counterproductive. Scott particularly indicts the Basel Committee for its treatment of the Japanese banking system (Scott 1995). Verdier has also criticized Basel and its network cognates in finance for ineffectiveness (Verdier 2009).

Other skeptics argue that networks will likely become particularly opaque venues for the exercise of unfair and inequitable power, either by regulated industry, which could capture the networks, or by the powerful states that wield disproportionate influence in the network (Singer 2007). Networks, after all, operate outside of the public eye, by and large, and usually lack strong procedures designed to ensure voice for all. One example of such a critique might be found in Macey's work (2003). He has offered a public choice account of the development of the Basel Committee, arguing that the regulators have joined the committee more as a move toward cartelization and to forestall regulatory competition, lest finance be offshored to more efficiently regulated jurisdictions.

Underlying the public choice skepticism adopted by scholars such as Macey and Singer is a lawyerly suspicion of nontransparent exercises of public power, which make networks, in the view of some, look deficient in both accountability and legitimacy. Eric Pan, for example, has argued that international banking regulation needs a multilateral treaty to regain both its legitimacy and its effectiveness (Pan 2010). And even network proponents such as Slaughter and Zaring have felt compelled to address the legitimacy issues posed by the institutions (Slaughter 2001, Zaring 2008).

Secretive exercise of police power is the epitome of those issues meant to be solved by what lawyers call *administrative law*, which concerns the imposition of procedural and open governance requirements on domestic administrative agencies.

Unsurprisingly then, a concerted research effort into the promise and capabilities of global administrative law has taken the legitimacy of transnational institutions such as networks as its subject and has explored a variety of mechanisms that might be used to import good governance practices to these institutions (Stewart 2005; Kingsbury and Krisch 2006). Indeed, Barr and Miller have argued that the Basel Committee, taken in the context of research about what might be useful inclusions in global administrative law, might exemplify some of the promise of procedurally legitimate international institutions (Barr and Miller 2006).

V. A COLLABORATIVE RESEARCH AGENDA

Although research in regulatory networks has grown across both fields, considerable empirical and theoretical gaps remain. In the next section, we highlight four issues that should appeal to scholars from both IL and IR and move forward our understanding of the role such regulatory networks play in global governance.

A. *Who Participates and Why?*

Much of the literature, regardless of discipline, takes the network metaphor as a given and then asks whether regulatory networks have an effect on global governance. To better understand issues of power and legitimacy, however, one must examine the prior question concerning who participates and why.

In contrast to the network enthusiasts' image of egalitarian universalist organizations, network participation often varies in terms of breadth, depth, and institutional form (Bach 2010). Institutionally, some regulatory networks have a clublike, formal membership structure. The Basel committee, for example, is limited to G20 members, while others, such as IOSCO, have an open membership process (Helleiner 1996; Singer 2007). Even in universal membership networks, however, some jurisdictions choose not to participate. Moreover, institutional rules within many networks privilege some actors over others. The technical committee in IOSCO and the IAIS drive standards debates, and the members of the technical committees frequently represent the regulators from the largest markets (Underhill 1995). More informally, cooperative dynamics place some regulators in more focal positions than others (Raustiala 2002; Bach and Newman 2010a). Regulators frequently sign memoranda of understanding (MoU) with each other as informal mechanisms to promote cooperation on enforcement and standards implementation. As is the case with more institutionalized networks, MoU participation varies considerably. South Africa, for example, is highly connected in the field of financial securities, whereas Brazil is not. Although we know that such inequality exists across and within networks, little research exists as to the factors driving differences in participation. Since research has demonstrated that these networks play a significant role in policy diffusion and global governance, for issues of power and legitimacy, it is critical to understand why some jurisdictions are more represented in regulatory networks than are others.

B. *Sources of Authority*

Skeptics of network governance frequently deny the importance of these forms of regulatory cooperation. International relations scholars argue that networks are epiphenomenal to great-power politics, and their legal counterparts contend that they do not produce measurable outputs. To address more fully the autonomous causal significance of such actors and their potential effectiveness, research from both fields should consider in greater depth the authority resources that network participants can leverage to influence policy and politics.

Initial work by Newman (2008*b*) and Bach and Newman (2010*b*) finds that network actors employ their regulatory capacity to have an independent measurable effect on agenda setting. Regulatory capacity includes the expertise of participants, their delegated legislative authority to control market access, and their ties to constituents and other actors. Expertise offers technical authority over an issue space and allows network actors to define and monitor a set of market rules. Control over market access provides regulators tools to shift the costs of inaction by other market and government actors. Ties to constituents and other regulators create potential allies in lobbying efforts. When engaged in agenda-setting activities with other sub-state actors, IOs, or executive agency representatives, they can use these authority resources to bolster their case and alter the cost–benefit calculus of potential political allies. In short, networks that enjoy considerable regulatory capacity are in a position to become policy entrepreneurs, upending the agendas of powerful states. Importantly, many of these authority resources are grounded in the domestic legal setting. Although agreements reached in a transgovernmental forum may appear informal and nonbinding, participants often have the domestically delegated authority to monitor and sanction those agreements as hard law in the domestic realm (Eberlein and Newman 2008). Additional research could apply this perspective to alternative outcomes of interest and investigate in more detail the conditions under which regulatory capacity might be more or less effective or present. Legal scholarship concerning administrative law and the moral and institutional authority of the law might offer a complementary set of factors that could explain both the independent causal effect of such networks and their variable efficacy.

C. *Regime Complexity and Regulatory Networks*

Network proponents often speak of the networks of networks active in global governance (Slaughter 2004). Moreover, regulatory networks coexist with a variety of alternative international coordination mechanisms, ranging from treaty-based international law to extraterritorial application of domestic rules. Although it is clear that

TABLE 10.1. *Regime complex dynamics with regulatory networks*

		Relative authority of network in the regime complex	
		High	Low
Relative Legitimacy of Network in the Regime Complex	Broad	Competitive	Supplement – Information
	Limited	Supplement – Hub Power	Dependent

these informal alternatives may at times compete with and at times complement traditional treaty-based regimes (Raustiala 2002), research is lacking as to the conditions under which one or the other situation might be the case.

Building on the prior two research domains, we propose a set of exploratory hypotheses concerning the relationship of such networks to other components in a regime complex (Raustiala 2004; Alter and Meunier 2009; Raustiala 2013) that examine the relative legitimacy and authority resources of regulatory networks compared to other global governance mechanisms (Table 10.1). Imagine that such networks can have either broad or limited participation, which connotes more or less legitimacy, and high or low regulatory capacity, which determines their authority resources. In cases in which the network has greater legitimacy and authority than other international institutions in the regime complex, then the likelihood of competition is greatest. The network supplants the traditional IO and serves as an alternative site for regime governance. By contrast, when legitimacy and authority are low, the network depends more heavily on the broader regime complex to accomplish its goals and likely has little independently measurable effect on global governance. The mixed cases, however, are the most interesting and offer more nuanced expectations of how regulatory networks might complement more traditional governance regimes. In cases in which the network has broader participation, following more functional accounts, it may serve as a scanning and monitoring device in the more general regime. Acting as part of peer review systems or information sharing and accountability, the network can fill an important vacuum in many global governance regimes. Similarly, in cases in which the network lacks broad-based participatory legitimacy but enjoys significant authority, it can bring a useful set of enforcement tools to relatively weak international regimes. Here, network hubs from key markets can leverage their domestically delegated authority to enforce informal network or regime standards.

Clearly, other testable expectations exist concerning the interaction between regulatory networks and traditional treaty law. We offer these merely as examples of where research might go so as to better specify the relationship.

D. *Regulatory Networks and Interdependent Implementation*

International relations and IL scholars have become increasingly interested in issues of treaty compliance (Hathaway 2001; Hafner-Burton and Tsutsui 2007; Vreeland 2008). The motivating question across these studies is whether international law and global governance actually alter actor behavior. Complementary scholarship has highlighted the ways in which implementation itself may serve as an important locus of international change (Sandholtz 2007; Mahoney and Thelen 2010). Work on regulatory networks could open up both research agendas by exploring the interdependent nature of policy implementation and enforcement. Examining the international interdependence of policy implementation and enforcement would improve debates about compliance and diffusion, which frequently focus on de jure legislative changes rather than on-the-ground shifts in regulatory behavior. Taking the more general case of policy implementation, research on regulatory networks can examine the ways through which international interaction might alter such on-the-ground behavior.

Initial research suggests at least two pathways. First, and perhaps the more traditional view, is that regulatory cooperation serves as a means to enhance regulatory capacity. Information sharing and training promote expertise and ties among network participants. As a result, individual members are better positioned to implement and enforce their domestic legislation. This begs the question of how the network might have shaped domestic policy agendas in the first place, a point we examined in the section on authority resources. In any case, capacity building has long been seen as a soft-law function of regulatory networks, and research in the field of financial services offers initial evidence that network interactions alter the regulatory behavior of participants (Bach and Newman 2010*a*).

A second and less explored mechanism for interdependent implementation concerns the dual-hatted character of regulatory network participants. Regulatory bodies often serve simultaneously as participants in the international network and as domestic market supervisors (Newman 2010). Standards harmonization has long been seen in the network literature as a soft-law global governance approach. But this view fails to recognize that network participants are endowed with domestic legal authority that frequently transforms international standards into interpretations of domestic rules. In this subtle move, domestic law serves to offer a hard edge to international soft law (Putnam 2009).

Although either capacity building or dual delegation may serve to bolster compliance with international law, they do not rely on the existence of an international treaty. Rather, they ultimately depend on the existence of national legislation that can be triggered by network cooperation (Kaczmarek and Newman 2011). Although international law is one way to promote domestic legal harmonization, it is not the only means to do so. By more fully incorporating regulatory networks into debates on compliance and diffusion, researchers will be able to tap into the more general category of interdependent implementation and, in turn, explore the multiple pathways through which such networks might matter.

VI. CONCLUSION

Since the 1970s, IL and IR scholars have highlighted the role that regulatory networks play in global governance. This research has proven convincingly that such networks are important for many international domains (Bermann 1993; Slaughter 2004). This leaves open, however, many questions as to who participates, the conditions under which they might matter, or how they interact with other forms of international law. Recent work in IR has begun to address these issues, focusing both on power dynamics and social network relations within the networks (e.g., Bach and Newman 2010a).

Building on the issues of power and legitimacy that drive many research efforts across the academic disciplines, this chapter not only maps the state of play in each but attempts to highlight common areas of interest. In examining who participates in regulatory networks, with what authority resources, how they interact with other forms of international cooperation, and the role of such networks in internationally interdependent policy implementation, we hope to spark a new round of research interested in global regulatory networks.

As economic interdependence deepens further and international trade negotiations continue to stall, regulatory cooperation will be at the fore of global economic debates. Regulatory networks offer one mechanism to resolve such conflicts. It is critical to underscore, however, that such cooperation is not merely about fixing problems. Network participants have unique interests and authority resources that they can deploy to shape policy agendas and implementation. Similarly, variation in the makeup of these networks shapes the agendas that make it to the table. We thus conclude with a call to take both power and legitimacy issues more seriously in regulatory network debates. Although regulation or administrative law can induce a sense of technocratic banality, they are often just as political and consequential as treaty-based international law.

REFERENCES

Abbott, Kenneth, and Duncan Snidal (2000). "Hard and Soft Law in International Governance," *International Organization*, Vol. 54, No. 3, pp. 421–56.

―――― (2009). "The Governance Triangle: Regulatory Standards Institutions and the Shadow of the State," in Walter Mattli and Ngaire Woods (eds.), *The Politics of Global Regulation* (Princeton, NJ: Princeton University Press), pp. 44–88.

Alter, Karen J., and Sophie Meunier (2009). "The Politics of International Regime Complexity," *Perspectives on Politics*, Vol. 7, No. 1, pp. 13–24.

Bach, David (2010). "Varieties of Cooperation: Regulating Transnational Markets for Information Goods," *International Studies Review*, Vol. 36, pp. 561–89.

Bach, David, and Abraham Newman (2010a). "Transgovernmental Networks and Domestic Policy Convergence: Evidence from Insider Trading Regulation," *International Organization*, Vol. 64, No. 3, pp. 505–28.

Bach, David, and Abraham Newman (2010b). "Governing Lipitor and Lipstick: Capacity, Sequencing, and Power in International Pharmaceutical and Cosmetics Regulation," *Review of International Political Economy*, Vol. 17, No. 4, pp. 665–95.

Baker, Andrew (2009). "Deliberative Equality and the Transgovernmental Politics of the Global Financial Architecture," *Global Governance*, Vol. 15, No. 2, pp. 195–218.

Barnett, Michael S., and Raymond Duvall (2005). *Power in Global Governance* (Cambridge: Cambridge University Press).

Barr, Michael S., and Geoffrey P. Miller (2006). "Global Administrative Law: The View from Basel," *European Journal of International Law*, Vol. 17, No. 1, pp. 15–46.

Bermann, George A. (1993). "Regulatory Cooperation with Counterpart Agencies Abroad: The FAA's Aircraft Certification Experience," *Law and Policy in International Business*, Vol. 24, No. 3, pp. 669–781.

———— (1995). "Regulatory Cooperation between the European Commission and U.S. Administrative Agencies," *Administrative Law Journal of the American University*, Vol. 9, No. 4, pp. 933–83.

Bignami, Francesca E. (1999). "The Democratic Deficit in European Community Rulemaking: A Call for Notice and Comment in Comitology," *Harvard Journal of International Law*, Vol. 40, No. 2, pp. 451–515.

———— (2005). "Transgovernmental Networks vs. Democracy: The Case of the European Information Privacy Network," *Michigan Journal of International Law*, Vol. 26, No. 3, pp. 807–68.

Börzel, Tanja A. (1998). "Organizing Babylon: On Different Conceptions Of Policy Networks," *Public Administration*, Vol. 76, No. 2, pp. 253–73.

Brummer, Chris (2010). "Post-American Securities Regulation," *California Law Review*, Vol. 98, No. 2, pp. 327–83.

———— (2011). "How International Financial Law Works (and How It Doesn't)" *Georgetown Law Journal*, Vol. 99, No. 2, pp. 257–327.

———— (2012). *Soft Law and the Global Financial System: Rule Making in the 21st Century* (Cambridge: Cambridge University Press).

Buthe, Tim, and Walter Mattli (2011). *The New Global Rulers* (Princeton, NJ: Princeton University Press).

Cameron, David R. (1995). "Transnational Relations and the Development of European Economic and Monetary Union," in Thomas Risse-Kappan (ed.), *Bringing Transnational Relations Back In: Nonstate Actors, Domestic Structures and International Institutions* (Cambridge: Cambridge University Press), pp. 37–78.

Cardenas, Sonia (2003). "Transgovernmental Activism: Canada's Role in Promoting National Human Rights Commissions," *Human Rights Quarterly*, Vol. 25, No. 3, pp. 775–90.

Carpenter, R. C. (2011). "Vetting the Advocacy Agenda: Network Centrality and the Paradox of Weapons Norms," *International Organization*, Vol. 65, No. 1, pp. 69–102.

Cerny, Philip G. (2010). *Rethinking World Politics: A Theory of Transnational Neopluralism* (Oxford: Oxford University Press).

Damro, Chad (2006). "Transatlantic Competition Policy: Domestic and International Sources of EU-US Cooperation," *European Journal of International Relations*, Vol. 12, No. 2, pp. 171–96.

Damtoft, Russell W., and Ronan Flanagan (2009). "The Development of International Networks in Antitrust," *International Lawyer*, Vol. 43, No. 1, pp. 137, pp. 137–50.

Drezner, Daniel W. (2007). *All Politics Is Global: Explaining International Regulatory Regimes* (Princeton, NJ: Princeton University Press).

Dunoff, Jeffrey L. (2004). "Public Participation in the Trade Regime: Of Litigation, Frustration, Agitation and Legitimation," *Rutgers Law Review*, Vol. 56, No. 4, pp. 961–70.

Eberlein, Burkard, and Abraham Newman (2008). "Escaping the International Governance Dilemma? Incorporated Transgovernmental Networks in the European Union," *Governance*, Vol. 21, No. 1, pp. 25–52.

Farrell, Henry (2006). "Governing Information Flows: States, Private Actors, and e-Commerce," *Annual Review of Political Science*, Vol. 9, pp. 353–74.

Franck, Thomas M. (1988). "Legitimacy in the International System," *American Journal of International Law*, Vol. 82, No. 4, pp. 705–59.

Giovanoli, Mario (2009). "The Reform of the International Financial Architecture after the Global Crisis," *N.Y.U. Journal of International Law and Politics*, Vol. 42, No. 1, pp. 81–123.

Haas, Peter (1992). "Epistemic Communities and International Policy Coordination," *International Organization*, Vol. 46, No. 1, pp. 1–35.

Hafner-Burton, Emilie, Miles Kahler, and Alexander Montgomery (2009). "Network Analysis for International Relations," *International Organization* Vol. 63, No. 2, pp. 559–92.

Hafner-Burton, Emilie, and Kiyoteru Tsutsui (2007). "Justice Lost! The Failure of International Human Rights Law to Matter Where Needed Most," *Journal of Peace Research*, Vol. 44, No. 4, pp. 407–25.

Hathaway, Oona A. (2001). "Do Human Rights Treaties Make a Difference," *Yale Law Journal*, Vol. 111, No. 8, pp. 1935– 2204.

Heidenreich, Martin, and Jonathan Zeitlin (2009). *Changing European Employment and Welfare Regimes: The Influence of the Open Method of Coordination on National Reforms* (London and New York: Routledge).

Helleiner, Eric (1996). *States and the Reemergence of Global Finance* (Ithaca, NY: Cornell University Press).

———(2010). "What Role for the New Financial Stability Board? The Politics of International Standards after the Crisis," *Global Policy*, Vol. 1, No. 3, pp. 282–90.

Hooghe, Liesbet, and Gary Marks (2001). *Multi-level Governance and European Integration* (Lanham, MD: Rowan and Littlefield).

Hopkins, Raymond F. (1976). "The International Role of 'Domestic' Bureaucracy," *International Organization*, Vol. 30, No. 3, pp. 405–32.

Jackson, John, William Davies, and Alan O. Sykes, Jr. (2008). *Legal Problems of International Economic Relations*, 4th ed. (St. Paul, MN: West).

Jessup, Philip C. (1956). *Transnational Law* (New Haven, CT: Yale University Press).

Joerges, Christian, and Jurgen Neyer (1997). "Transforming Strategic Interaction into Deliberative Problem-Solving: European Comitology in the Foodstuffs Sector," *Journal of European Public Policy*, Vol. 4, No. 4, pp. 609–25.

Kaczmarek, Sarah, and Abraham Newman (2011). "The Long Arm of the Law: Extraterritoriality and the National Implementation of Foreign Bribery Legislation," *International Organization*, Vol. 65, No. 4, pp. 745–70.

Kahler, Miles, and David Lake (2009). "Economic Integration and Global Governance: Why So Little Supranationalism?," in Walter Mattli and Ngaire Woods (eds.), *The Politics of Global Regulation* (Princeton, NJ: Princeton University Press), pp. 242–76.

Kapczynski, Amy (2009). "Harmonization and Its Discontents: A Case Study of TRIPS Implementation in India's Pharmaceutical Sector," *California Law Review*, Vol. 97, No. 6, pp. 1571–1649.

Keck, Margaret, and Kathryn Sikkink (1998). *Activists beyond Borders: Advocacy Networks in International Politics* (Ithaca, NY: Cornell University Press).

Keohane, Robert, and Joseph Nye (1977). *Power and Interdependence: World Politics in Transition* (Boston: Little, Brown).

Kingsbury, Benedict, and Nico Krisch (2006). "Introduction: Global Governance and Global Administrative Law in the International Legal Order," *European Journal of International Law*, Vol. 17, No. 1, pp. 1–13.

Koremenos, Barbara (2013). "Institutionalism and International Law," in Jeffrey L. Dunoff and Mark A. Pollack (eds.), *Interdisciplinary Perspectives on International Law and International Relations: The State of the Art* (New York: Cambridge University Press), pp. 59–82.

Krahmann, Elke (2003). *Multilevel Networks in European Foreign Policy* (Hampshire, UK: Ashgate).

Lake, David, and Wendy Wong (2009). "The Politics of Networks: Interests, Power, and Human Rights Norms," in Miles Kahler (ed.), *Networked Politics: Agency, Power, and Governance* (Ithaca, NY: Cornell University Press), pp. 127–50.

Levi-Faur, David (2005). "The Global Diffusion of Regulatory Capitalism," *Annals of the American Academy of Political and Social Science*, Vol. 598, pp. 12–32.

Lang, Andrew, and Joanne Scott (2009). "The Hidden World of WTO Governance," *European Journal of International Law*, Vol. 20, No. 3, pp. 575–614.

Lipson, Michael (2005). "Transgovernmental Networks and Nonproliferation," *International Journal*, Vol. 61, No. 1, pp. 179–98.

Macey, Jonathan R. (2003). "Regulatory Globalization as a Response to Regulatory Competition," *Emory Law Journal*, Vol. 53, No. 3, pp. 1353–79.

Mahoney, James, and Kathleen Thelen (2010). *Explaining Institutional Change: Ambiguity, Agency, and Power*, 1st ed. (New York: Cambridge University Press).

Mitrany, David (1966). *A Working Peace System* (London: Quadrangle).

Newman, Abraham (2008a). "Building Transnational Civil Liberties: Transgovernmental Entrepreneurs and the European Data Privacy Directive," *International Organization*, Vol. 62, No. 1, pp. 103–30.

——— (2008b). *Protectors of Privacy: Regulating Personal Data in the Global Economy* (Ithaca, NY: Cornell University Press).

——— (2010). "International Organization Control under Conditions of Dual Delegation: A transgovernmental Politics Approach," in Deborah D. Avant, Martha Finnemore, and Susan K. Sell (eds.), *Who Governs the Globe* (Cambridge: Cambridge University Press), pp. 131–55.

Padgett, John F., and Christopher K. Ansell (1993). "Robust Action and the Rise of the Medici, 1400–1434," *American Journal of Sociology*, Vol. 98, No. 6, pp. 1259–1319.

Pan, Eric (2010). "Challenge of International Cooperation and Institutional Design in Financial Supervision: Beyond Transgovernmental Networks," *Chicago Journal of International Law*, Vol. 11, No. 1, pp. 243–84.

Perry, James, and Andreas Nolke (2006). "The Political Economy of International Accounting Standards," *Review of International Political Economy*, Vol. 13, No. 4, pp. 559–86.

Peterson, John (1995). "Policy Networks and European Union Policy-Making," *West European Politics*, Vol. 18, No. 2, pp. 389–407.

Posner, Elliott (2009). "Making Rules for Global Finance: Transatlantic Regulatory Cooperation at the Turn of the Millennium," *International Organization*, Vol. 63, No. 4, pp. 665–99.

Posner, Eric A. (2005). "International Law and the Disaggregated State," *Florida State University Law Review*, Vol. 32, No. 3, pp. 797–842.

Powell, Walter (1990). "Neither Market Nor Hierarchy: Network Forms of Organization," *Research in Organizational Behavior*, Vol. 12, pp. 295–336.

Putnam, Tonya L. (2009). "Courts without Borders: Domestic Sources of U.S. Extraterritoriality in the Regulatory Sphere," *International Organization*, Vol. 63, No. 3, pp. 459–90.

Raustiala, Kal (2002). "The Architecture of International Cooperation: Transgovernmental Networks and the Future of International Law," *Virginia Journal of International Law*, Vol. 43, No. 1, pp. 1–92.

———— (2004). "The Regime Complex for Plant Genetic Resources," *International Organization*, Vol. 58, No. 2, pp. 277–309.

———— (2013). "Institutional Proliferation and the International Legal Order," in Jeffrey L. Dunoff and Mark A. Pollack (eds.), *Interdisciplinary Perspectives on International Law and International Relations: The State of the Art* (New York: Cambridge University Press), pp. 293–320.

Rhodes, Martin (2010). "Employment Policy: Between Efficacy and Experimentation," in Helen Wallace, Mark A. Pollack, and Alasdair R. Young (eds.), *Policy-Making in the European Union* (Oxford: Oxford University Press), pp. 279–304.

Risse-Kappan, Thomas (1995). *Bringing Transnational Relations Back In: Nonstate Actors, Domestic Structures and International Institutions* (Cambridge: Cambridge University Press).

Sabel, Charles F., and Michael C. Dorf (1998). "A Constitution of Democratic Experimentalism," *Columbia Law Review*, Vol. 98, No. 2, pp. 267–473.

Sabel, Charles F., and Jonathan Zeitlin (2010). *Experimentalist Governance in the European Union: Towards a New Architecture* (Oxford: Oxford University Press).

Sandholtz, Wayne (2007). *Prohibiting Plunder: How Norms Change* (Oxford: Oxford University Press).

Scott, Hal S. (1995). "The Competitive Implications of the Basle Capital Accord," *Saint Louis University Law Journal*, Vol. 39, No. 3, pp. 885–95.

Singer, David (2004). "Capital Rules: The Domestic Politics of International Regulatory Harmonization," *International Organization*, Vol. 58, No. 3, pp. 531–65.

———— (2007). *Regulating Capital: Setting Standards for the International Financial System* (Ithaca, NY: Cornell University Press).

Slaughter, Anne-Marie (2001). "Agencies on the Loose? Holding Government Networks Accountable" in George A. Bermann, Matthias Herdegen, and Peter L. Lindseth (eds.), *Transatlantic Regulatory Co-operation: Legal Problems and Political Prospects* (Oxford: Oxford University Press), pp. 521–46.

———— (2004). *A New World Order* (Princeton, NJ: Princeton University Press).

Steiner, Henry J., and Detlev Vagts (1976). *Transnational Legal Problems* (Mineola, NY: Foundation Press).

Stewart, Richard B. (2005). "The Global Regulatory Challenge to U.S. Administrative Law," *N.Y.U. Journal of International Law and Politics*, Vol. 37, No. 4, pp. 695–762.

Underhill, Geoffrey R. D. (1995). "Keeping Governments out of Politics: Transnational Securities Markets, Regulatory Cooperation, and Political Legitimacy," *Review of International Studies*, Vol. 21, No. 3, pp. 251–78.

Verdier, Pierre (2009). "Transnational Regulatory Networks and Their Limits," *Yale Journal of International Law*, Vol. 34, No. 1, pp. 113–72.

Vreeland, James (2008). "Political Institutions and Human Rights: Why Dictatorships Enter into the United Nations Convention against Torture," *International Organization* Vol. 62, No. 1, pp. 65–101.

Wasserman, Stanley, and Katherine Faust (1994). *Social Network Analysis: Methods and Applications* (Cambridge: Cambridge Press).

Weiler, Joseph H. H. (1991). "The Transformation of Europe," *Yale Law Journal*, Vol. 100, No. 8, pp. 2403–83.

Whytock, Christopher A. (2005). "A Rational Design Theory of Transgovernementalism: The Case of the E.U.-U.S. Merger Review Cooperation," *Boston University International Law Journal*, Vol. 23, No. 1, pp. 1–54.

Williamson, Oliver (1981). "The Economics of Organization: The Transaction Cost Approach," *American Journal of Sociology*, Vol. 87. No. 1, pp. 548–77.

Zaring, David (1998). "International Law by Other Means: The Twilight Existence of International Financial Regulatory Organizations," *Texas International Law Journal*, Vol. 33, No. 2, pp. 281–330.

——— (2005). "Informal Procedure, Hard and Soft, in International Administration," *Chicago Journal of International Law*, Vol. 5, No. 2, pp. 379–784.

——— (2008). "Rulemaking and Adjudication in International Law," *Columbia Journal of Transnational Law*, Vol. 46, No. 3, pp. 563–611.

Zito, Anthony (2001). "Epistemic Communities, Collective Entrepreneurship and European Integration," *Journal of European Public Policy*, Vol. 8, No. 4, pp. 583–603.

11

Law-Making by International Organizations:

Perspectives from IL/IR Theory

Ian Johnstone

This chapter is about law-making by international organizations (IOs), or what I call "delegated law-making" for short. It is a complex phenomenon, not least because the scope of matters covered by both "law-making" and "delegation" is contested. Although some intergovernmental organizations have been empowered to make law explicitly, the relationship between states and the organizations they create is often more complicated than the term *delegation* connotes. Various strands of international law (IL) and international relations (IR) theory shed light on this relationship, and, as such, delegated law-making is a good laboratory for exploring the value of cross-disciplinary theorizing.

The chapter begins with the concept of delegation, arguing that it comes in three forms when applied to IOs: explicit, implied, and attenuated. The second section, "Law in Its Infinite Variety" is devoted to law-making. I present a pluralistic conception of law that includes five distinct types of IO acts or instruments: treaty law, legislation and regulation, executive decisions, soft law, and judge-made law. I provide examples to illustrate the extent to which delegation tends to be implied and attenuated, as well as explicit.

The third section, "International Law/International Relations Theory: Three Cuts," considers the explanatory power of three strands of IL/IR theory that appear in the literature: rational choice, constructivist, and discursive. The approaches are not mutually exclusive, and, indeed, the third is an offshoot of the second, but they do offer alternative ways of studying and thinking about delegated law-making. The first has proven its worth by generating testable hypotheses and empirical research, but tends to reduce both the concepts of delegation and law-making to propositions that do not fully capture the complexity of what is going on. Constructivism better captures that complexity but is harder to test empirically. Discursive theory is furthest from the social science mainstream but central to legal theory, as making arguments is the stock in trade of lawyers. The fact that the IR/IL literature has focused more on rational choice and constructivism than on discursive theory may be a reflection of an observation made elsewhere in this volume, namely, that the literature has largely been an exercise in the application of IR theory to the study of law (Dunoff and Pollack 2013). Focusing on discourse turns that around by showing how important branches of international legal theory can inform the study of international politics. The chapter concludes with a future IL/IR research agenda on law-making by IOs.

I. DELEGATION ON A SPECTRUM

The notion of delegating powers to IOs has more resonance in the IR literature than in IL. It is rooted in studies of the European Union (EU), combining theories of delegation to administrative agencies at the domestic level with rational choice institutionalism at the international level (Pollack 1997, 2003). It is tied to the literature on the rational design of institutions (Koremenos, Lipson, and Snidal 2001) and became the subject of an influential edited volume in 2006 (Hawkins *et al.* 2006). It is also connected to the growing body of IR literature on the democratic deficit, accountability, and legitimacy of decision making in international institutions (for a recent review of the literature, see Keohane, Macedo, and Moravscik 2009).

Delegation is also a familiar concept to domestic lawyers, not least because much of administrative law concerns the proper scope and oversight of delegation to agencies and regulatory bodies. Administrative law thinking has found its way into international legal scholarship (Boisson de Chazournes *et al.* 2009; Kingsbury, Krisch, and Stewart 2005), and lawyers have begun to look at the law-making role of IOs in terms of delegation (Ku 2000; Swaine 2004; Sarooshi 2005). The disciplines converged in two conferences that culminated in a special journal issue on "The Law and Politics of International Delegation" (Bradley and Kelley 2008a).

An oft-cited definition of international delegation is "a grant of authority by two or more states to an international body to make decisions or take action" (Bradley and Kelley 2008b: 2; see also Guzman and Landsidle 2008: 1698). This definition is broader than others that appear in the literature, like "a conditional grant of authority from a principal to an agent" (Hawkins *et al.* 2006: 7) or "the grant of authority to implement, interpret and apply rules" (Abbott et al. 2000: 401). The broad definition has the virtue of capturing the entire range of functions delegates perform, which Bradley and Kelley list as, including legislative, adjudicative, regulatory, monitoring and enforcement, agenda setting, research and advice, policy implementation, and re-delegation (Bradley and Kelley 2008b: 2). Koremenos offers a longer list of twenty-three internationally delegated tasks (Koremenos 2008: 162–63). Not all of those constitute law-making, but if one employs the pluralistic conception that I present in the next section, many affect the development of law by or in IOs.

The simplest kind of delegation is when a state or states explicitly grant authority to an IO. This type of delegation lends itself to rigorous social scientific analysis, for example, through principal–agent theory, because it is usually quite easy to identify the principals, the agent, and the powers conferred on the agent by the principals. It helps to address a number of important questions associated with delegation, such as how much discretion the principals intend to grant, whether the agent has interests separate from the principals, and how to control "agent drift." As such, it provides a useful frame of reference for exploring the relationship between an IO and its member states.

More difficult, yet as common, are acts of implied delegation. Few IOs are given explicit authority to legislate, but in practice many have acted as law-makers. By joining these organizations, member states consent to their missions, but the passage of time and change of circumstances means that it is not always clear exactly to what the states have consented (Alvarez 2005: 262). The practices of the organization may be more extensive than what the founders contemplated or what members who join later would expect simply by reading their constitutive acts. The doctrine of implied powers holds that an IO has explicit powers, as well as those "conferred upon it by necessary implication as being essential to the performance of its duties."[1] The implied powers doctrine is the most widely accepted school of thought on the competence of IOs – including the competence to engage in law-making.

The application of principal–agent theory to acts of implied delegation is not straightforward. Consider the United Nations (UN) Security Council. Can one reasonably assume that in establishing the UN, the founding members intended for the Security Council to engage in intrusive peace building, create international criminal tribunals, or legislate on terrorism? Is this best understood as falling within the "agent's" margin of discretion, or as an example of unauthorized policy drift? Have the principals acquiesced to those exercises of authority by the Security Council? Implied delegation may be inferred from acquiescence, but that begs the question by what standard can acquiescence be measured.

More difficult still is what may be called "attenuated" delegation. International relations theorists speak of the "unintended consequences" of delegation (Pierson 1996). Organizations may acquire their own preferences, separate from those of the member states, leading to policy drift, slippage, or "shirking" (Pollack 1997). In principal–agent terms, this is undesirable from the principal's point of view, something to be controlled. From other IL/IR perspectives, IO autonomy is both necessary and desirable. The executive head and secretariats of some IOs are expected to act independently, not merely as servants of their member states (Sarooshi 2005; Johnstone 2007). Thus, I use the term "attenuated" to convey the sense that the powers being exercised are several steps removed from member state control, although not necessarily unintended. Subdelegation may fit this description, for example, when the Council of the European Union delegates to the Commission, or when the UN Security Council establishes a transitional administration with governing powers, as it did in Kosovo and East Timor. In the latter case, the relevant principal is hard to

---

[1] International Court of Justice (1949), *Reparation for Injuries* case, at 192; European Court of Justice (1987), *Germany v. Commission*, Joined Cases 281, 283–85 and 287/85.

identify – is it the member states of the UN who delegated authority to the Council, is it the Council as a "collective principal" (Tierney 2008), or are the various members of the Security Council multiple principals with different understandings of what they have done?

The growing role of nongovernmental actors in law-making by IOs is also revealing (Charnovitz 2007; Ripinsky and Van den Bossche 2007; Steffek, Kissling, and Nanz 2008). This is built into the design of the International Labor Organization (ILO), where representatives of employee and employer organizations sit alongside government representatives. Elsewhere, the role of nongovernmental actors is more informal (Peters 2009: 225–27). With no vote, they are not delegated law-making powers per se, but through a diffuse normative process, they have an impact on the development of international law. In these cases of attenuated delegation, the principal and agent may be so far removed from each other that it is misleading to suggest that they are in a relationship at all. Moreover, international bureaucracies and nongovernmental organizations (NGOs) may themselves be "agents of socialization" (Finnemore and Sikkink 1998; Keck and Sikkink 1998). This turns principal–agent theory on its head because the agents affect how the principals (states) define their interests and identities. None of this suggests that "delegation" is too murky a concept for it to be useful, but simply that much of what happens in IOs does not fall neatly into the categories of principal and agent.

II. LAW IN ITS "INFINITE VARIETY"

The formalistic notion that international law is simply a set of black letter rules is outdated. Debates among natural law thinkers, positivists, critical scholars, and other legal theorists have paved the way for a more pluralistic conception of law, and of where, how, and by who it is made. Thus, Jan Klabbers laments that it is no longer clear "what exactly constitutes international law and what does not" (Klabbers 2009: 83). José Alvarez argues that the sources set out in Article 38 of the International Court of Justice Statute no longer fully capture the range of acts and instruments that are treated as law (Alvarez 2005). Even two of those traditional sources – customary law and general principles – leave ample room for debate about what qualifies. Thus, for example, customary law may arise out of the practices of IOs, and therefore – if one assumes IOs are somewhat autonomous – is one step removed from the practices of states (Higgins 1963; Johnstone 2008b). Law in its "infinite variety" (Baxter 1980) also includes decisions, regulations, and administrative acts of IOs, as well as various forms of soft law (Shelton 2000; Boyle and Chinkin 2009).

Theorists of IL/IR have joined the debate on what counts as law, most notably with the publication of a special issue of *International Organization* on legalization (Goldstein *et al.* 2001). This group of scholars sees law as falling on a spectrum from non- to soft to hard depending on the degree of obligation, precision, and delegation. That particular characterization has been criticized for presenting too narrow a conception of both IL (heavily positivist) and IR theory (mainly neo-liberal institutionalist) (Finnemore and Toope 2001; Brunnée and Toope 2010), yet the Legalization volume was one of a number of recent interdisciplinary efforts to conceptualize what international law is, who makes it, and how it functions (see also Byers 2000; Reus-Smit 2004; Koh and Hathaway 2005; Simmons and Steinberg 2006; Trachtman 2008).

Although delegation to IOs is common, explicit delegation of law-making power is rare (Koremenos 2008; Bradley and Kelley 2008b; Sarooshi 2005). The EU is the exception, but even there scholars have responded to the democratic deficit critique by arguing that the supranational legislative powers of the EU are less extensive than meets the eye (Majone 1998; Moravscik 2002). From the point of view of "state sovereigntists," this may be comforting, but it misses the point that law and law-making come in many forms. In the following sections, I present five different types of IO "law" and discuss each in terms of the degrees of delegation outlined above: explicit, implicit, and attenuated.

A. Treaty Law

The most common form of international law is treaties. Many IOs have become venues for the negotiation and adoption of treaties. This may not look like delegated law-making at all, since the IO seems to serve as nothing more than a forum (Guzman and Landsidle 2008). All member states of the IO have the opportunity to participate in the negotiating process, and no state is bound unless it signs and ratifies or later accedes to the treaty. Yet, the categorical position that treaty making in IOs is not delegation does not tell the whole story.

To begin with, the constituent instruments of some IOs can be amended by majority vote. For many, like the International Civil Aviation Organization (ICAO), the amendment only takes effect for states that ratify it, hence there is no delegation. But for others, like the International Atomic Energy Agency (IAEA, whose Statute can be amended by a two-thirds vote), all are bound unless they withdraw from the organization. Similarly, the Articles of Agreement of the International Monetary Fund (IMF) can be amended by three-fifths of the members who also have 85 percent of the weighted voting power. For the United States, this does not constitute delegation since it currently has a 17 percent share of the vote, but for other members it does.

Another treaty-making process that, arguably, has an element of delegation, is at work in the ILO. The peer pressure that is built into it suggests that states have committed themselves to a process over which they do not have full control (Kirgis 1997; Alvarez 2005). All ILO members have an obligation to bring labor conventions to the attention of competent domestic authorities for appropriate action, even if they voted against it in the ILO Assembly. If action is not taken domestically, members must report that back to the ILO and explain why not, and then at regular intervals must report to the director-general on "the position of its law and practice in regard to the matters dealt with in the Convention . . . and stating the difficulties which prevent or delay ratification of the Convention."[2] Thus, while each government retains ultimate authority to decide whether it will be bound by the convention, the process dilutes that authority by making it more difficult and politically costly to opt out.

More attenuated still are treaty-making processes that include non-state actors. This is common in IOs, where secretariat officials, expert groups, and NGOs tend to play a significant role. The International Law Commission and UNCITRAL have a major impact on treaty making in the UN system. The UN Environment Program (UNEP) Secretariat has been instrumental in drafting various environmental treaties. Although the World Trade Organization (WTO) is a member-driven organization, the secretariat and its director-general are starting to play a more active role in trade negotiations (Marceau 2011). Although non-state actors have been instrumental in ad hoc conferences (like the Rome Conference on the International Criminal Court), their role tends to be more institutionalized in IOs, through accreditation as observers for example (Ripinsky and Van den Bossche 2007). In all of these examples – and in most regional organizations – each government ultimately decides whether it will be bound, but by accepting the active participation of non-state actors, they have tacitly delegated some law-making power to them. The nature and scope of influence that these actors have in each organization is a topic for IL/IR research and theorizing. The role of transnational actors in EU constitutive treaty making (from Rome to Lisbon), for example, is a source of debate among intergovernmentalists, neo-functionalists, and the various offshoots of these theories (Sandholtz and Stone Sweet 1998; Tsebelis and Garrett 2001; Magnette 2005).

B. *Legislation and Regulation*

From the point of view of delegation theory, secondary legislation made by the EU is more consequential than treaty making (the primary legislation). European Union legislation comes in the form of regulations, directives, and decisions.[3] Regulations are directly binding on member states; decisions are directly binding on states or individuals (depending on to whom they are addressed); and directives require national implementation measures to have binding force within member states. Some decisions are adopted by the European Commission alone (discussed below), but the more "political" and significant legislation is adopted by the Council or by co-decision of the Council and European Parliament. Voting procedures range

---

[2] ILO Constitution, Article 19(5)(e).

[3] The proposed Constitutional Treaty tried to clarify the situation by distinguishing between legislative acts (laws) and implementing acts (regulations and decisions). The Lisbon Treaty maintained this hierarchy but not the terminology, instead distinguishing "political" from "nonpolitical" legislation and dividing the latter into delegated and implementing acts (Nugent 2010: 209–10, 307).

from unanimity to simple majority, with most decisions now subject to qualified majority vote.

These variations in the form, content, and process of EU law make it difficult to generalize about the scope of delegation. One kind of delegation occurs when decisions are adopted by majority or qualified majority vote in the Council: here, all member states have delegated law-making powers to some subset of states. Another occurs when the European Parliament has co-decision authority: here, EU member states have delegated law-making power to a body of representatives that are directly elected by their own citizens, separate from national elections. Another kind of delegation is the power of the Commission to propose legislation. Proposing is not the same as adopting, of course, but it is an important delegated power that is integral to the law-making process.

The EU is not the only IO that has regulatory powers. The World Health Organization, World Meteorological Organization, and International Maritime Organization can all make regulations through a tacit consent/opt out procedure. Adopted by simple majority vote, these regulations are nevertheless binding on all members of the organizations unless they explicitly opt out. Like the ILO system of peer pressure, this modifies without eliminating the positivist principle that states are bound only by rules to which they have consented (Kirgis 1997). Consent is still required, but the mechanism by which that consent is granted – or deemed to be granted – is less demanding than a formal vote.

In some highly technical but important areas, UN specialized agencies have been given full legislative powers. Thus, the ICAO Council can make binding rules regulating aircraft over the high seas. The power was delegated by the parties of the Chicago Convention on Civil Aviation to the ICAO Council, a body of thirty-six states that can make rules by a two-thirds majority vote. Other than in the context of the EU, this is a rare example of regulative authority being delegated to a subset of an IO's membership, seen as necessary in the case of ICAO, given the importance of safety and efficiency in regulating air traffic.

C. Executive Decisions

Some decisions of IOs adopted by executive bodies are binding law. Article 25 of the UN Charter states that all members of the UN agree "to accept and carry out decisions of the Security Council in accordance of the present Charter." What constitutes a decision as opposed to a recommendation or nonbinding appeal for action is a vexed question,[4] but few lawyers dispute that if a Security Council resolution uses the words "decides" or "demands," then the decision is binding and, as such, hard law. The UN member states have thereby delegated law-making authority to an executive body composed of fifteen states, only nine of which

---

[4] International Court of Justice (1966), *Southwest Africa* case.

must vote in favor of a resolution – with no veto by one of the five permanent members.

In the post–Cold War era, Security Council "law-making" has taken on unexpected forms. The Council has made determinations that function as authoritative interpretations of the UN Charter (Ratner 2004). In 1992, for example, the Security Council declared that the proliferation of weapons of mass destruction constitutes a threat to international peace and security. This had no automatic legal consequences at the time, but it set down a marker that acts of proliferation would meet the Article 39 threshold for measures under Chapter VII of the Charter. In that sense, the determination has a law-making character.

The Security Council has also subdelegated law-making power to peacekeeping operations, most notably in 1999, to the transitional administrations in Kosovo and East Timor (Caplan 2006; Chesterman 2004). These unusual peace operations were given full governing powers for transitional periods. The founders of the UN never imagined the Security Council would grant this kind of power to its field missions, nor did most states that joined the UN in the years before 1999. Other peacekeeping missions have had an important impact on the evolution of international law, but none have been explicitly subdelegated this kind of law-making authority.

Another recent Security Council innovation is its "quasi-legislative" resolutions on terrorism and the proliferation of weapons of mass destruction. Resolutions 1373 (2001) and 1540 (2004) are unique in that they impose binding obligations on all states in broad issue areas for an indefinite period. Unlike most Security Council resolutions, they are not tied to a particular incident, nor do they seek to enforce a decision against a particular state. Qualitatively different from the Council's normal crisis management role, the Security Council acted not like an executive branch of government but like a legislature.

Another executive body with the ability to adopt binding decisions is the EU Commission. This is another example of subdelegation, whereby member states of the EU delegate to the Council of Ministers, which in turn delegates to the Commission. Commission regulations, decisions, and directives tend to be administrative measures designed to implement the more significant law adopted by the Council and Parliament. Yet, some Commission acts fill gaps in EU law, suggesting that the line between political legislation and nonpolitical administration is fine indeed. An important feature of Commission rule making is *comitology*, whereby committees composed of governmental representatives oversee the work of the Commission. Prior to the Lisbon Treaty, there were five comitology procedures that gave varying degrees of control to the committees, ranging from the ability to block a decision to merely advising. By dividing Commission acts into "delegated" and "implementing," the Lisbon Treaty changed the comitology arrangements and, more generally, the mechanisms for scrutiny and control that the Council and Parliament have over the Commission (Hix and Hoyland 2011; Georgiev 2011).

D. *Soft Law*

International lawyers use the term "soft law" to describe norms that are formally nonbinding but habitually obeyed (Shelton 2000; Abbott and Snidal 2000; Boyle and Chinkin 2007). As noted above, interdisciplinary work has elaborated on the concept by placing soft law on a spectrum between purely political instruments and hard law, depending not only on the degree of obligation but also the precision of the language used and the extent to which monitoring, dispute resolution, and enforcement are delegated to a third party. Among lawyers, soft law is a contested concept because it implies what a strict legal positivist would deny – that a continuum exists between political and legal commitments, and that the difference between the two is a matter of degree (Weil 1983; Klabbers 2009). Yet, the term is firmly embedded in the law-making lexicon, spawning a body of IL/IR literature on whether and in what ways legal norms are distinctive (Finnemore 2000; Brunnée and Toope 2010).

Soft law comes in various forms, including norms expressed in obligatory language, but contained in a nonbinding instrument (like UN General Assembly resolutions) and norms enshrined in a binding treaty but in vague, imprecise, or hortatory terms (like some provisions of human rights treaties). Most interesting from the point of view of delegated law-making are the many codes of conduct, guidelines, and recommendations adopted by IOs like the ICAO Standards and Recommended Practices, IAEA Safety Standards, World Bank guidelines, and Food and Agricultural Organization (FAO) and UN Educational, Scientific, and Cultural Organization (UNESCO) recommendations (Sands and Klein 2009; Alvarez 2005). Soft law exists outside the UN system as well, for example, in the form of EU recommendations and opinions and in the international trade regime (Kirton and Trebilcock 2004).

Although many of these "recommendations" are truly that, some can acquire binding force. The ILO's Equal Remuneration Convention, for example, demands equal pay for work of equal value but contains no precise obligations on how or even when the principle must be brought into effect. Those more precise standards appear in the companion ILO recommendations. If widely adhered to in practice, the recommendations can come to be seen as authoritative interpretations of the treaty. Indeed, there may even be some obligation on the part of a state ratifying the Convention to also ratify companion recommendations. Article 19(5)(d) of the ILO Constitution stipulates that "states must take action to make the convention effective"; arguably, the only way of making some conventions "effective" is by implementing the companion recommendations (Kirgis 1997).

The World Health Organization (WHO) has the authority to adopt health conventions and make binding regulations, but it has done so less than the ILO. Nevertheless, as a "technical" agency where considerable expertise resides, its nonbinding instruments tend to carry a great deal of weight. The Codex Alimentarius, a joint undertaking of the WHO and FAO, produces a variety of food safety standards that are considered to be nonbinding. A WTO agreement related to food safety does not confer binding status on Codex standards, but does give them enhanced status by making them a benchmark against which WTO members must justify their food safety regulations in dispute-resolution processes. Like ILO recommendations, this is an example of formally nonbinding standards being treated as authoritative in interpretations of harder law (Büthe 2008: 227; Klabbers 2009: 188).

Another unusual (and contested) form of law-making by IOs is the hardening of soft law through operational activities (Johnstone 2008*b*). The term "operational activities" describes the programmatic work of IOs, like humanitarian action or development assistance. These operational activities are often undertaken against the backdrop of widely acknowledged but not well-specified norms. The activities may trigger reactions from affected governments, and the discourse that accompanies the action and reactions can cause soft law to harden. Examples include the hardening of the right to political participation through electoral assistance activities by IOs (Fox 1992); the hardening of some of the Guiding Principles on Internal Displacement through humanitarian action (Bagshaw 2005); the crystallization of minority rights through the work of the Organization for Security and Cooperation in Europe (OSCE) High Commissioner on National Minorities (Ratner 2004); and the revision of the International Health Regulations triggered by actions of the WHO director-general in response to the SARS crisis (Burci and Koskemäki 2009; Kingsbury and Casini 2009). This is a highly attenuated form of delegation in that the member states of the organization give the secretariat a broad mandate to engage in the activity, and then the practices of the organization have the effect of making law. This is law-making through the back door, if not quite by stealth.

E. Judge-Made Law

The extent to which courts and quasi-judicial bodies do and should make law is contested in domestic and international legal theory. Conventional wisdom is that courts apply and interpret the law: they do not make new law. The International Court of Justice (ICJ) itself has stated that "its task is to engage in its normal judicial function of ascertaining the existence or otherwise of legal principles . . . It states the existing law and does not legislate."[5] Empirical studies suggest that, out of respect for state sovereignty or institutional self-protection, international tribunals refrain from judicial activism (Guzman and Landsidle 2008). They interpret their dispute resolution and advisory jurisdiction narrowly, employing a strict constructionist approach to interpretation that does not leave much scope for law-making from the bench.

Yet, Article 38 of the ICJ Statute itself describes judicial decisions as a subsidiary source of law. No less an authority than a past president of the ICJ wrote (before she joined the Court) that, "the very determination of specific disputes, and the provision

---

[5] International Court of Justice (1996), *Legality of the Threat or Use of Nuclear Weapons*, para 18.

of specific advice, does develop international law" (Higgins 1993: 202). Even if decisions are formally binding only on the parties (or not at all if an advisory opinion),
the Court's reasoning is often invoked in subsequent disputes. The European Court
of Justice (ECJ) certainly plays a law-making role – not by design necessarily, but
through judicial practice and acquiescence to that practice (Alter 1998; Pollack 2003;
Stone Sweet 2004; Nugent 2010). The extent to which the WTO Appellate Body
engages in law-making is more contested (Steinberg 2004). Even quasi-judicial bodies like the human rights treaty committees can "make" law through interpretations
of vague provisions in treaties that come to be accepted as authoritative.

This has obvious implications for an analysis of delegated law-making, not only in
terms of whether courts make law but how. In some cases, a court may give content
to general norms, thereby converting soft law in to hard (Boyle and Chinkin 2007).
In others, it may fill gaps in the law, sometimes described as completing "incomplete
contracts" (Trachtman 1999). In others still, judicial decisions can have the effect
of "constitutionalizing" the legal order they purport to regulate (de Burca and Scott
2001; Dunoff 2009; Trachtman 2009; Peters 2009). Which, if any, of these forms of
judicial activism constitute delegated law-making? Are the courts acting as agents of
the states that create them, or autonomously? Or, are the dynamics not well explained
in terms of agency and better illuminated by other theoretical frameworks?

III. INTERNATIONAL LAW/INTERNATIONAL RELATIONS THEORY: THREE CUTS

In this section, I turn to three clusters of IR theory that serve as alternative lenses
for analyzing delegated law-making: rational choice, constructivism, and discursive
theory. The three theoretical approaches correspond to three distinct logics: the
logic of consequences, the logic of appropriateness, and the logic of arguing (March
and Olsen 1989; Risse 2000). Although discursive theory is not typically separated
from constructivism in the IR literature, for the purposes of understanding delegated
law-making, it is usefully discussed separately. Following Habermas, Thomas Risse
explains that the logic of appropriateness drives actors with a given identity to act in
a manner that is consistent with accepted norms; the logic of arguing helps them to
identify what those norms are and how they apply in a given situation (Risse 2000,
2004). Both are captured by constructivism, but the latter is a distinct mode of social
interaction that has a good deal to say about how law is made and implemented.

A. Rational Choice: The Logic of Consequences

Rational choice theory starts from the premise that political actors (primarily states)
are motivated by self-interest and act strategically to advance those interests. Informed
by microeconomics and driven by the logic of consequences, rational choice theory

sees actors acting instrumentally to advance fixed preferences. Neo-realism, neo-liberal institutionalism, and at least two variants of "new institutionalism" – rational choice and historical institutionalism – all share rationalist assumptions (Pollack 2010: 23).

The most common explanation for delegation to IOs in the IR literature, principal–agent theory, is rational choice: "In this framework, a principal, the initial holder of executive power, decides to delegate certain powers to an agent who is responsible for carrying out the task" (Hawkins *et al.* 2006; Hix and Hoyland 2011: 23). The principal does so for instrumental reasons, calculating that its goals can best be achieved by empowering agents to act on its behalf. Principal–agent theorists have identified several reasons why states may delegate to IOs: to benefit from specialized expertise, to lock in policy preferences, to help manage disputes, and to enhance the credibility of commitments (Hawkins *et al.* 2006: 12–20; Bradley and Kelly 2008*b*: 25–27). Moreover, delegation can make it possible for governments to do internationally what may be difficult for them domestically, shifting responsibility to the IO and avoiding blame at home if things turn out badly (Büthe 2008: 235; Hathaway 2008: 126).

Principal–agent theory has been applied fruitfully to the study of the EU (Tallberg 2002; Pollack 2003; Hix and Hoyland 2011). It is increasingly being applied to other organizations and issue areas, like the World Bank (Nielson and Tierney 2003), the IMF (Martin 2006), the WTO (Büthe 2008), the ILO (Helfer 2008), and the UN Security Council (Tierney 2008). Most of these delegations are not about law-making, but rather about monitoring, the dissemination of information, dispute resolution, and other lesser forms of authority (Koremenos 2008). In light of the pluralization of law-making processes described above, however, even these other functions can have a significant impact on development of the law.

Rational choice has found its way into the IL scholarship from several directions. Goldsmith and Posner claim that "international law emerges from states acting rationally to maximize their interests, given their perceptions of the interests of other states and the distribution of power" (Goldsmith and Posner 2005: 3). This line of reasoning has provoked a skirmish in the United States between rational choice lawyers who worry about too much power being delegated to IOs (Ku 2000; Swaine 2004; Yoo 2005) and those who believe the concerns are exaggerated. The former complain that delegation is stripping power from domestic institutions. The latter respond that the delegation of true legislative powers to IOs is rare and, when it does occur, highly constrained. Not only are the "sovereignty costs" low, but these writers also stress the benefits of delegation, pointing to some of the same factors that principal–agent theorists have identified – to overcome collective action problems for example – as well as more normative goals, like the promotion of human rights (Guzman and Landsidle 2008; Hathaway 2008).

Law and economics is another branch of rational choice IL/IR theory – indeed, Joel Trachtman describes economic methods as simply another term for "rational social scientific analysis" (Trachtman 2008). Trachtman and his co-author Jeffrey Dunoff note that the law and economics movement was just starting to find its way into international law in 1999 (Dunoff and Trachtman 1999; Posner 2000; Sykes 2007). They draw an analogy to the business firm and – among other things – use economic analysis to ask what powers are most efficiently delegated by states to IOs, and, once delegated, what powers should be subdelegated by the plenary body to its constituent parts. They also use game theory to illuminate interaction among states that are members of the organization, between the states and the organization, and between IOs (like the WTO and World Intellectual Property Organization on intellectual property issues). That seminal article concludes with a research agenda for law and economics that encompasses everything from transnational legal process (Koh 1997, 1998) and transgovernmentalism (Slaughter 2004) to "fiscal federalism" and the related principle of subsidiarity. What ties these fields together from the point of view of delegated law-making is the allocation of competencies to institutions and the interactions among them, at the substate, national, regional, and global levels.

As applied to delegated law-making, rational choice theory helps to explain why states give up authority to IOs; for example, when the IO has expertise to offer in return (Mayer 2008). It also helps to explain *how* states delegate – namely, by granting no more authority than necessary to achieve the principal's goals while establishing control mechanisms to oversee the agent (Hawkins *et al.* 2006; Hix and Hoyland 2011). From this perspective, EU comitology is a device by which the representatives of national governments keep a check on the Commission. Principal–agent theory can also help to explain the problem that multiple or collective principals have in trying to rein in rogue bureaucracies, and, conversely, the room for maneuver that these bureaucracies may have when the principals are divided (Nielsen and Tierney 2003).

Finally, principal–agent theory has generated a lively debate on the degree of autonomy of international courts and the mechanisms that may constrain that autonomy. Thus Karen Alter, Mark Pollack, and Jonas Tallberg all argue that international courts are quite autonomous and the control mechanisms are weak (Tallberg 2002; Pollack 2003; Alter 2008). National governments (principals) appoint judges (agents) to tribunals, but their ability to remove them is constrained, as is their ability to reverse rulings or rewrite the mandates of the courts. Geoffrey Garrett and Paul Stephan, conversely, see more limited judicial independence and stronger control mechanisms (Garrett 1995; Stephan 2002).

The lens of rational choice has also been turned on the so-called democratic deficit of IOs. A central aspect of that critique is that the chain of delegation between citizens and decision-makers in IOs is so long that it cannot be called democratic (Dahl 1999). This is a challenge to the legitimacy of IOs only if one assumes they have some autonomous power; otherwise, the only legitimacy question would be how democratic its member states are. One line of debate among rational choice theorists is essentially between those who do not see much delegation of significant law-making powers by governments to IOs (Majone 1998; Moravscik 2002) versus those who see a great deal of delegation, especially in the EU (Follesdal and Hix 2006).

However, rational choice and especially principal–agent theory do not explain implied and attenuated delegation well. These tend to get characterized as "slack," "slippage," and "unintended consequences" in the literature, implying they are deviations that need to be prevented or fixed. Yet, from a lawyer's perspective, they are not deviations but rather an expected, even desirable feature of international decision-making. To paraphrase an institutionalist critique of realism: rational choice explains a few big things about delegation well, but it does not explain everything.

B. *Constructivism: The Logic of Appropriateness*

A defining feature of constructivism is its focus on ideas, norms, and culture in world politics, stressing the role of collectively held or shared understandings about social life. Principal–agent theory does not sit well with constructivism, and, indeed, the whole notion of delegation from a principal to an agent is problematic. Constructivists are concerned with agency, but the relationship they focus on is agent–structure. From the perspective of delegated law-making, states are the agents and international law and institutions the structure. The relationship between them is mutually constitutive: whereas states create most IOs, the IOs in turn shape state identity and interests. The process is interactive, involving contestation and cooperation, with states driven as much by the logic of appropriateness as by the logic of consequences – they behave in a way that is appropriate for actors with their identity, and not solely by making instrumental calculations of how to advance fixed interests.

Constructivist theory is more open to the possibility of IO autonomy than is principal–agent theory. The autonomy may lead to beneficial results, for example, when IOs serve as platforms for norm entrepreneurs or as agents of socialization (Florini 1996; Abbot and Snidal 1998; Finnemore and Sikkink 1998). The process tends to be led by states, but networks of individuals, NGOs, and secretariat officials also play independent roles. Alternatively, the IOs may display dysfunctions – even pathologies – that lead to undesirable results (Barnett and Finnemore 2004). Either way, this feature of IOs is better or at least differently explained by social constructivists than rational choice theorists. The questions they ask are not whether, why, and how state-principals delegate to IO-agents, but whether, why, and how the IOs are able to shape the behavior, interests, and even identities of the states.

Lawyers who write in a constructivist mode trace a similar pattern of international socialization. Harold Koh describes a transnational legal process of "interaction," "interpretation," and "internalization" (Koh 1997). New norms emerge and take shape through interaction within and between states, in a process that involves representatives of NGOs, the private sector, and officials of IOs, as well as domestic bureaucrats and courts. Brunnée and Toope present an interactional theory of legal obligation that claims the compliance pull of law depends on its congruence with shared understandings, accepted criteria of legality, and enmeshment in "an interactive practice of legality" (Brunnée and Toope 2010: 100–25). Goodman and Jinks posit an acculturation model, whereby compliance depends not so much on internal acceptance but rather on mimicry of the "beliefs and behavior patterns of the surrounding [global] culture" (Goodman and Jinks 2004: 626). Although these are mainly theories of compliance, they point to the fact that the line between implementation of existing law and interstitial law-making is blurry. Actors are not only affected by rules, but they also change by their practice the normative structures within which they act (Kratochwil 1989: 61). In other words, international law affects practice and that practice in turn affects the law.

Thus, constructivism offers a less positivist, more fluid perspective on international law. The law-making, law-interpreting, and law-applying process is not easily traceable to principals delegating specified powers to agents and reining them in when those powers are exceeded. Rather, it is a complex, dynamic form of social interaction. Constructivism is better able to capture the multiplicity of actors involved in law-making. Not just governments, but NGOs, private sector entities, and enterprising individuals play a role. The heads of IOs can be norm entrepreneurs either by pushing for norms to be concretized as legal obligations or by managing operational activities that have the effect of hardening the law (Johnstone 2011).

Implied and attenuated forms of law-making are better explained by constructivism than by rational choice theory, starting from the observation that a good amount of "norm-generation and norm-acceptance [by IOs] is only shakily related to the will of states" (Boisson de Chazournes et al. 2009; Kingsbury and Casini 2009: 354). State consent is often attenuated – either because the normative process itself is diffuse or because the IO has subdelegated authority to another international institution, like a peace operation or an international court. Judicial behavior may be better explained by theories of legitimacy and accountability that look to evolving practice and normative expectations rather than rules about the appointment and removal of judges or legislative oversight (Alter 2006; Hurd 2008).

Finally, the literature on international constitutionalism sits well with IL/IR constructivism (MacDonald, St. John, and Johnston 2005; Joerges and Petersmann 2006; Loughlin and Walker 2007; Dunoff and Trachtman 2009; Klabbers, Peters, and Ulfstein 2009). It bears on IO law-making in three ways. First, it asks whether the founding instruments of IOs should be viewed as treaties or as constitutions. The EU constitutional convention failed, but the treaties of the EU are often described in constitutional terms, including by the ECJ (Weiler and Wind 2003). Many of the founding acts of UN specialized agencies are officially called constitutions (UNESCO, the ILO, FAO, and WHO). There is a substantial body of literature on the "constitution" of the WTO (Joerges and Petersmann 2006; Dunoff 2009; Trachtman 2009). European and increasingly North American scholars are asking whether the UN Charter is a constitution (Dupuy 1997; Franck, Chesterman, and

Malone 2008; Doyle 2009; Fassbender 2009). An implication of calling founding instruments constitutions is that their provisions are more likely to be interpreted flexibly, as "living trees," in light of changing circumstances – opening the door to judicial law-making.

Second, the constitutionalism literature draws attention to the distinction between constitutive and regulative rules popularized by social constructivists (Wendt and Duvall 1989; Katzenstein 1996; Ruggie 1998). Regulative rules are prescriptions that order and constrain behavior. Constitutive rules define social activities and categories of action. Arguably state sovereignty, noninterference, and *pacta sunt servanda* are constitutive rules of the international system, rules that give it its form and create the conditions for international interaction. Social constructivism provides a better way of thinking about those rules than does rational choice. After all, if state sovereignty is a constitutive norm (states are what they are because of the norm), then principal–agent theory does not take you very far in understanding how that norm came into being or how it functions.

A third body of literature that bridges IL and IR is on the "constitutionalization" of the international system. The questions here concern whether and to what extent an international constitutional order exists, despite the absence of formal government. Is there an emerging "unwritten global constitution" that seeks to create order out of globalization, fragmentation, and overlapping jurisdiction of different bodies of law (Dunoff and Tracthman 2009; Klabbers *et al.* 2009)? Questions at the IR/IL intersection include what constitutionalization means, whether nonhierarchical pluralism is possible in a global constitutional order, and who are the actors that create and recreate it.

C. Discursive Theory: The Logic of Arguing

Discursive theory looks at the power of rhetoric, argumentation, and justifications for action in international affairs. Friedrich Kratochwil, Thomas Risse, Harald Müller, and other IR theorists draw on Habermas' theory of communicative action to posit a logic of arguing, separate from but related to the logics of consequences and appropriateness (Kratochwil 1989; Risse 2000; Crawford 2002; Reus-Smit 2004; Müller 2004; Adler 2005; Bjola and Kornprobst 2009; Johnstone 2011). In rational choice theory, arguments are used strategically in order to win instrumental benefits, such as support of allies for a given policy. In constructivist theory, argumentation is a device for arriving at intersubjective understandings about what constitutes appropriate behavior. The purpose of arguing is not only to win support but to try to persuade others of the merits of a particular course of action. In Habermas' ideal of communicative action, it also means being open to persuasion, to changing one's mind in response to "the force of the better argument" (Habermas 1996: 305).

From the perspective of IL/IR theory, legal discourse is a highly structured type of argumentation, which may or may not be categorically different from other forms (Kratochwil 1989: 211; Reus-Smit 2004: 40). Legal argumentation can be especially powerful because its conventions are widely understood and accepted within the discipline. But, borrowing from deliberative democrats, I claim that the difference between it and political deliberation should not be overstated (Bohman 1999; Gutmann and Thompson 2004; Johnstone 2011). Both entail appeals to impartial (as opposed to purely self-serving) arguments, understood by all affected as relevant to the nature and purpose of the enterprise in which the discourse occurs.

In the IR literature, Habermas' discourse ethics (and the Frankfurt School more generally) informs not only "mainstream" constructivists, but also critical thinkers like Andrew Linklater (1990), Richard Devetak (2005), and Mark Hoffman (1987). Among other things, critical theorists argue that the quality of international decision-making processes depends on the quality of the discourse that surrounds them: if hegemonic, exclusionary, and obfuscating, then it is not legitimate.

Similarly, in the IL literature, a focus on discourse is common to critical, as well as certain mainstream theories. The latter includes Abram Chayes and Antonia Handler Chayes, and Tom Franck, who emphasize "justificatory discourse" and "fairness discourse," respectively, to explain compliance with international law (Chayes and Chayes 1995; Franck 1995). Critical legal studies have long paid attention to the "structure of legal argumentation," seeking to expose the hidden ideologies and inherent contradictions of international law through a close examination of legal arguments made in judicial and nonjudicial settings (Kennedy 1999; Koskenniemi 1999). The difference between the two schools is that the former sees the discourse as a vehicle for managing the tensions inherent in any pluralistic society, whereas the latter sees it as a vehicle for masking those tensions and the value choices inherent in legal decisions, no matter how apolitical the argumentation may seem to be (Johnstone 2011).

What does discursive theory tell us about delegated law making? First, law-making is a process of discursive interaction that begins not when states sit around a table but as part of an ongoing relationship and set of practices. As noted above, treaty making in IOs is not purely a matter of bargaining among states on the basis of power and interests, but also includes deliberation and appeals to principle and evidence in which secretariat officials, experts, and other non-state actors play a role (Katzenstein 1996). The Vienna Convention and Montreal Protocol on Ozone Depletion are a case in point. The Convention, adopted in 1985, set out general principles; more precise obligations followed in the Protocol, adopted in 1987. Even when the Protocol was adopted, there remained considerable scientific uncertainty about ozone loss and economic uncertainty about the costs of mitigation. So, a review mechanism was set up to allow for further adjustments requiring only a two-thirds majority vote among the parties. The UNEP, under the leadership of Mostafa Talba, played a critical role by convening a number of meetings at key moments among diplomats, scientists, and industry leaders to undercut opposition leading to agreements on a complete phase-out of chlorofluorocarbons (CFCs) well ahead of schedule.

Other, more diffuse forms of IO law-making are also illuminated by discursive theory – legislating by the UN Security Council, for example. Security Council resolution 1540, designed to stop weapons of mass destruction from falling into the hands of terrorists, was adopted through a law-making process that was formally restricted to the fifteen Council members but deliberately porous, enabling other UN member states and NGOs to provide organized input to the negotiating process (Datan 2005). Law-making authority in that case was implicitly delegated to the Security Council by UN member states, but the Security Council tacitly sought deliberative input from all UN member states, as well as from non-state actors. The vote in the Security Council came down to its fifteen members, but the process by which they got to that vote was diffuse and discursive.

Second, discursive theory helps to explain incremental law-making. Norms emerge through the practice of states and bouts of argumentation triggered by international incidents (Reisman, 1988). One state acts, it seeks to justify its actions, and others respond. The ensuing back and forth can cause soft norms to harden. This does not happen in one fell swoop, but incrementally, as a result of state and non-state actors (including IO officials) engaging with each other. Over time, good practice comes to be treated as legal obligation. Conversely, discursive theory can illuminate how hard law may soften if persistently violated or ignored.

Third, discursive theory casts a different light on the control mechanisms over IO law-making. The comitology process associated with the European Commission can be viewed as dialogue between the committee and Commission members (Joerges and Neyer 1997; Pollack 2010). Judicial review of IO acts may function in a similar way. Among international courts, only the ECJ clearly has the power of formal judicial review, but the ICJ in the *Lockerbie* and *Bosnia Genocide* cases engaged in what has been called an "expressive" mode of review (Alvarez 1996). The ICJ did not strike down Security Council resolutions, but in effect warned Council members to take care not to overstep the limits of their authority when imposing binding obligations. Moreover, this "dialogic" mode of review is not restricted to the ICJ. In the *Kadi* case, the ECJ declined to pass judgment on the legality of a Security Council sanctions regime, but, by striking down the European regulations that implemented the regime, it sent a strong signal to the Security Council. Many national courts also commented on the propriety of the Security Council's resolution, as did UN officials like the Legal Counsel and High Commissioner for Human Rights (Johnstone 2008a). These examples of what may be called discursive checks on IO law-making tie in to the constitutionalization literature that speaks of "constitutional discourse" among multiple international actors and agents (Dunoff 2009).

Fourth, an impetus behind the "global administrative law" initiative is to identify and develop the checks that exist on law-making by IOs. Although this can be explained partly in principal–agent terms, it can also be understood in terms of discursive theory: accountability achieved through hearings, transparency, reason-giving, and inclusive participation. (Kingsbury and Casisini 2009: 325; Boisson de Chazournes *et al.* 2009). This corresponds with the IR literature on IO account-ability. Buchanan and Keohane speak of the transnational civil society channel of accountability, in which "every feature of the institution becomes a potential object of principled, informed, collective deliberation . . . " (Buchanan and Keohane 2006: 432, 434). Sabel and Cohen draw an analogy to the accountability provided by domes-tic administrative law through systems of reporting, mutual reason-giving, and peer review. They note that even the EU does not have a coherent body of administrative law structuring how broad policy objectives are translated into specific regulations, but decision- making at key steps is "transparent, accessible to relevant parties in civil society as well as affected administrators, and deliberative in the sense of providing reasons for decisions" (Cohen and Sable 2005).

Fifth, discursive theory has something important to say about the legitimacy of IO decision- making. Inclusive deliberation is one way of addressing the democratic deficit in IOs (Bohman 1999; Johnstone 2008a; Steffek *et al.* 2008). Those who see evidence of such deliberation in IOs are less worried about the legitimacy deficit; those who do not see it argue for more inclusive deliberation.

IV. CONCLUSION

In this chapter, I have argued that the concept of delegation has been useful to understand law-making by IOs, but, in some cases, the line between the initial power holder (states) and those to whom law-making power is delegated is diffuse and attenuated. Moreover, the line between making, interpreting, and implementing law is blurry, which creates problems for the standard account of explicit state consent as the basis for all legal obligation.

This more fluid picture of delegated law-making suggests several avenues for fur-ther interdisciplinary research. First, the empirical research on delegation concludes that when states delegate to IOs, it is usually to preform functions other than law-making. Yet, a more expansive picture of law suggests that this conclusion needs to be revisited. In her seminal work on when, what, and why states choose to dele-gate, Barbara Koremenos lists twenty-three tasks (Koremonos 2008: 162–63). Only a handful involve legislating in its pure form, and the cases are few. Yet, many of the other functions (and many IO functions she does not list) have "normative ripples" (Alvarez 2005). The research agenda, therefore, is to devise a comprehensive list of IO tasks that have an impact on international law-making broadly defined, and to examine them in terms of explicit, implicit, and attenuated delegation.

Second, the role of non-state actors in international law-making needs be explored more deeply. The literature on transgovernmental networks and NGO participation in IOs should be merged with more traditional legal scholarship on the sources of law, as well as social science scholarship on who are the actors in world politics.

The role of "experts" in IO law-making also deserves more attention. Do they lend legitimacy to the process by bringing information and evidence-based reasoning to the table? Or, do they reduce legitimacy by masking value and political choices behind seemingly technocratic decisions?

Third, better methodologies need to be found for testing constructivist and discursive theories. "Follow the paper trail" (i.e., the official justifications and explanations) is a useful starting point for understanding the power of norms in international politics (Finnemore and Sikkink 1998), and there is a body of IR literature on discourse analysis (Milliken 1999). This must be expanded to include methodologies for determining when, whether, and why norms crystallize as law. If the making, interpretation, and implementation of international law is a discursive, intersubjective process, what techniques can IR scholars deploy to test that proposition?

Fourth, the literature on global constitutionalism and global administrative law has been produced almost entirely by lawyers. This is a fruitful area for IL/IR inquiry, just as these topics have been the subject of interdisciplinary research at the domestic level. What does it mean to talk about global constitutional and administrative law in the absence of world government?

Finally, IO law-making in "its infinite variety" raises more questions about legitimacy and the democratic deficit than are currently being asked in the literature. Does deliberation really add legitimacy to IO decision-making? Are IOs dominated by hegemons, impervious to voices of global civil society and those on the margins? Or, are they nascent public spheres, venues for transnational, inclusive deliberation? In seeking to answer these questions, the value of cross-disciplinary IL/IR theorizing is greater than the sum of its parts.

REFERENCES

Abbott, Kenneth W., Robert O. Keohane, Andrew Moravcsik, Anne-Marie Slaughter, and Duncan Snidal (2000). "The Concept of Legalization," *International Organization*, Vol. 54, No. 3, pp. 401–19.

Abbott, Kenneth W., and Duncan Snidal (1998). "Why States Act through International Organizations," *Journal of Conflict Resolution*, Vol. 42, No. 1, pp. 3–32.

Abbott, Kenneth W., and Duncan Snidal (2000). "Hard and Soft Law in International Governance," *International Organization*, Vol. 54, No. 3, pp. 421–56.

Adler, Emanuel (2005). *Communitarian International Relations: The Epistemic Foundations of International Relations* (London and New York: Routledge).

Alter, Karen J. (1998). "Who Are the Masters of the Treaty? European Governments and the European Court of Justice," *International Organization*, Vol. 52, No. 1, pp. 125–52.

———— (2006). "Delegation to International Courts and the Limits of Re-contracting Political Power," in David Hawkins *et al.* (eds.), *Delegation and Agency in International Organizations* (New York: Cambridge University Press).

———— (2008). "Agents or Trustees? International Courts in Their Political Context," *European Journal of International Relations*, Vol. 14, No. 1, pp. 33–63.

Alvarez, José (1996). "Judging the Security Council," *American Journal of International Law*, Vol. 90, No. 1, pp. 1–38.

―――― (2005). *International Organizations as Lawmakers* (Oxford: Oxford University Press).

Bagshaw, Simon (2005). *Developing a Normative Framework for the Protection of Internally Displaced Persons* (Ardsley, NY: Transnational Publishers).

Barnett, Michael, and Martha Finnemore (2004). *Rules for the World: International Organizations in Global Politics* (Ithaca, NY: Cornell University Press).

Baxter, Richard (1980). "International Law in Her 'Infinite Variety,'" *International and Comparative Law Quarterly*, Vol. 29, No. 4, pp. 549–66.

Bjola, Corneliu, and Markus Kornprobst, eds. (2010). *Arguing Global Governance: Agency, Lifeworld, and Shared Reasoning* (New York: Routledge).

Bohman, James (1999). "International Regimes and Democratic Governance," *International Affairs*, Vol. 75, No. 3, pp. 499–513.

Boisson de Chazournes, Laurence, Lorenzo Casisni, and Benedict Kingsbury (2009) (eds.). "Symposium on Global Administrative Law in the Operations of International Organizations," *International Organizations Law Review*, Vol. 6, No. 2., pp. 315–666.

Boyle, Alan, and Christine Chinkin (2007). *The Making of International Law* (Oxford and New York: Oxford University Press).

Bradley, Curtis, and Judith Kelley (2008a). "The Law and Politics of International Delegation," Special Issue of *Law and Contemporary Problems*, Vol. 71, No. 1, pp. 1–312.

―――― (2008b). "The Concept of International Delegation," *Law and Contemporary Problems*, Vol. 71, No. 1, pp. 1–36.

Brunnée, Jutta, and Stephen J. Toope (2010). *Legitimacy and Legality in International Law: An Interactional Account* (Cambridge: Cambridge University Press).

Buchanan, Allen, and Robert Keohane (2006). "The Legitimacy of Global Governance Institutions," *Ethics and International Affairs*, Vol. 20, No. 4, pp. 405–37.

Burci, Gian Luca, and R. Koskemäki (2009). "Human Rights Implications of Governance Responses to Public Health Emergencies," in Andrew Clapham and Mary Robinson (eds.), *Realizing the Right to Health* (Zurich: Ruffer & Rub).

Büthe, Tim (2008). "The Globalization of Health and Safety Standards," *Law and Contemporary Problems*, Vol. 71, No. 1, pp. 219–56.

Byers, Michael (2000) (ed.). *The Role of Law in International Politics* (New York: Oxford University Press).

Caplan, Richard (2006). *International Governance of War-Torn Territories: Rule and Reconstruction* (New York: Oxford University Press).

Charnovitz, Steve (2007). "Non-governmental Organizations and International Law," *American Journal of International Law*, Vol. 100, No. 2, pp. 348–72.

Chayes, Abram, and Antonia Handler Chayes (1995). *The New Sovereignty: Compliance with International Regulatory Agreements* (Cambridge, MA: Harvard University Press).

Chesterman, Simon (2004). *You the People: The United Nations, Transitional Administration and State-Building* (Oxford: Oxford University Press).

Cohen, Joshua, and Charles Sable (2005). "Global Democracy?," *New York University Journal of International Law and Politics*, Vol. 37, No. 4, pp. 763–97.

Crawford, Neta (2002). *Argument and Change in World Politics* (Cambridge: Cambridge University Press).

Datan, Metav (April/May 2005). "Security Council Resolution 1540: Weapons of Mass Destruction and Non-state Trafficking," *Disarmament Diplomacy*, available at http://www.acronym.org.uk/dd/dd79/79md.htm.

Dahl, Robert A. (1999). "Can International Organizations Be Democratic? A Skeptic's View," in Ian Shapiro and Casiano Hacker-Cordon (eds.), *Democracy's Edges* (Cambridge: Cambridge University Press), pp. 19–36.

De Burca, Grainne, and Joanne Scott (2001) (eds.). *The EU and the WTO: Legal and Constitutional Issues* (Oxford: Hart Publishing).

Devetak, Richard (2005). "Critical Theory," in Scott Burchill et al. (eds.), *Theories of International Relations*, 3rd ed. (New York: Palgrave Macmillan), pp. 137–60.

Doyle, Michael (2009). "The UN Charter – a Global Constitution?," in Jeffrey L. Dunoff and Joel P. Trachtman (eds.), *Ruling the World? Constitutionalism, International Law, and Global Governance* (New York: Cambridge University Press), pp. 113–32.

Dunoff, Jeffrey L. (2009). "The Politics of International Constitutions: The Curious Case of the World Trade Organization," in Jeffrey L. Dunoff and Joel P. Trachtman (eds.), *Ruling the World? Constitutionalism, International Law and Global Governance* (New York: Cambridge University Press), pp. 178–205.

Dunoff, Jeffrey L., and Mark A. Pollack (2013). "International Law and International Relations: Introducing an Interdisciplinary Dialogue," in Jeffrey L. Dunoff and Mark A. Pollack (eds.), *Interdisciplinary Perspectives on International Law and International Relations: The State of the Art* (New York: Cambridge University Press), pp. 3–32.

Dunoff, Jeffrey L., and Joel P. Trachtman (1999). "Economic Analysis of International Law," *Yale Journal of International Law*, Vol. 24, No. 1, pp. 1–59.

———— (2009) (eds.). *Ruling the World? Constitutionalism, International Law and Global Governance* (New York: Cambridge University Press).

Dupuy, Pierre Marie (1997). "The Constitutional Dimension of the Charter of the United Nations Revisited," *Max Planck Yearbook of United Nations Law*, Vol. 1, No. 1, pp. 1–33.

Fassbender, Bardo (2009). "The United Nations Charter as the Constitution of the International Community," in Jeffrey L. Dunoff and Joel P. Trachtman (eds.), *Ruling the World? Constitutionalism, International Law, and Global Governance* (New York: Cambridge University Press), pp. 133–48.

Finnemore, Martha (2000). "Are Legal Norms Distinctive?," *N.Y.U. Journal of International Law and Politics*, Vol. 32, No. 3, pp. 699–705.

Finnemore, Martha, and Katherine Sikkink (1998). "International Norm Dynamics and Political Change," *International Organization*, Vol. 52, No. 4, pp. 887–917.

Finnemore, Martha, and Stephen Toope (2001). "Alternatives to 'Legalization': Richer Views of Law and Politics," *International Organization*, Vol. 55, No. 3, pp. 743–58.

Florini, Ann (1996). "The Evolution of Norms," *International Studies Quarterly*, Vol. 40, No. 3, pp. 363–89.

Follesdad, Andreas, and Simon Hix (2006). "Why There Is a Democratic Deficit in the EU: A Response to Majone and Moravscik," *Journal of Common Market Studies*, Vol. 44, No. 3, pp. 533–62.

Fox, Gregory (1992). "The Right to Political Participation in International Law," *Yale Journal of International Law*, Vol. 17, No. 2, pp. 539–608.

Franck, Thomas (1995). *Fairness in International Law and Institutions* (New York: Oxford University Press).

Franck, Thomas, Simon Chesterman, and David Malone (2007). *Law and Practice of the United Nations* (New York: Oxford University Press).

Garrett, Geoffrey (1995). "The Politics of Legal Integration in the European Union," *International Organization*, Vol. 49, No. 1, pp. 71–81.

Georgiev, Vihar (2011). "Commission on the Loose? Delegated Law Making and Comitology after Lisbon," unpublished working paper.

Goldsmith, Jack L., and Eric A. Posner (2005). *The Limits of International Law* (New York: Oxford University Press).

Goldstein, Judith L., and Miles Kahler, Robert Keohane, and Ann-Marie Slaughter (eds.) (2001). *Legalization and World Politics* (Cambridge: MIT Press).

Goodman, Ryan, and Derek Jinks (2004). "How to Influence States: Socialization and International Human Rights Law," *Duke Law Journal*, Vol. 54, No. 3, pp. 621–703.

Gutmann, Amy, and Dennis Thompson (2004). *Why Deliberative Democracy?* (Princeton, NJ: Princeton University Press).

Guzman, Andrew T. (2007). *How International Law Works: A Rational Choice Theory* (New York: Oxford University Press).

Guzman, Andrew T., and Jennifer Landsidle (2008). "The Myth of International Delegation," *California Law Review*, Vol. 96, No. 6, pp. 1693–1724.

Habermas, Jurgen (2005). *Between Facts and Norms: Contributions to a Theory of Democracy* (Cambridge, MA: MIT Press).

Hathaway, Oona (2008). "International Delegation and State Sovereignty," *Law and Contemporary Problems*, Vol. 71, No. 1, pp. 115–52.

Hawkins, Darren, David Lake, Daniel Nielson, and Michael Tierney (2006) (eds.). *Delegation and Agency in International Organizations* (New York: Cambridge University Press).

Helfer, Lawrence (2008). "Monitoring Compliance with Unratified Treaties," *Law and Contemporary Problems*, Vol. 71, No. 1, pp. 193–218.

Higgins, Rosalyn (1963). *The Development of International Law through the Political Organs of the United Nations* (London: Oxford University Press).

Higgins, Rosalyn (1993). *Problems and Process: International Law and How We Use It* (Oxford: Oxford University Press).

Hix, Simon, and Bjorn Hoyland (2011). *The Political System of the European Union*, 3rd ed. (Basingstoke, Hampshire: Palgrave Macmillan).

Hoffman, Mark (1987). "Critical Theory and the Inter-paradigm Debate," *Millennium*, Vol. 16, No. 2, pp. 231–49.

Hurd, Ian (2008). *After Anarchy: Legitimacy and Power in the United Nations Security Council* (Princeton, NJ: Princeton University Press).

Joerges, Christian, and Jurgen Neyer (1997). "From Intergovernmental Bargaining to Deliberative Political Process: The Constitutionalization of Comitology," *European Law Journal*, Vol. 3, No. 3, pp. 273–99.

Joerges, Christian, and Ernst-Ulrich Petersmann (2006) (eds.). *Constitutionalism, Multi-level Trade Governance and Social Regulation* (Oxford: Harbt).

Johnstone, Ian (2007). "The Secretary-General as Norm Entrepreneur, in Simon Chesterman (ed.), *Secretary or General? The UN Secretary-General in World Politics* (New York: Cambridge University Press), pp. 123–38.

———— (2008a). "Legislation and Adjudication in the UN Security Council: Bringing Down the Deliberative Deficit," *American Journal of International Law*, Vol. 102, No. 2, pp. 275–308.

———— (2008b). "Law-Making through the Operational Activities of International Organizations," *George Washington International Law Review*, Vol. 40, No. 1, pp. 87–122.

———— (2011). *The Power of Deliberation: International Law, Politics, and Organization* (New York: Oxford University Press).

Katzenstein, Peter (1996) (ed.). *The Culture of National Security: Norms and Identity in World Politics* (New York: Columbia University Press).

Keck, Margaret, and Katherine Sikkink (1998). *Activists beyond Borders: Advocacy Networks in International Politics* (Ithaca, NY: Cornell University Press).

Kennedy, David W. (1999). "'The Disciplines of International Law and Policy," *Leiden Journal of International Law*, Vol. 12, No. 1, pp. 9–134.

Keohane, Robert, Stephen Macedo, and Andrew Moravcsik (2009). "Democracy-Enhancing Multilateralism," *International Organization*, Vol. 63, No. 1, pp. 1–31.

Kingsbury, Benedict, Nico Krisch, and Richard Stewart (2005). "The Emergence of Global Administrative Law," *Law and Contemporary Problems*, Vol. 68, No. 1, pp. 15–61.

Kingsbury, Benedict, and Lorenzo Casini (2009). "Global Administrative Law Dimensions of International Organizations Law," *International Organizations Law Review*, Vol. 6, No. 2, pp. 319–58.

Kirgis, Frederic (1997). "Specialized Law-Making Processes" in Christopher Joyner (ed.), *The United Nations and International Law* (Cambridge: Cambridge University Press), pp. 65–96.

Kirton, John, and Michael Trebilcock (2004) (eds.). *Hard Choices, Soft Law: Voluntary Standards in Global Trade, Environment and Social Governance* (Aldershot, UK: Ashgate Publishing).

Klabbers, Jan (2009). *An Introduction to International Institutional Law*, 2nd ed. (Cambridge: Cambridge University Press).

Klabbers, Jan, Anne Peters, and Geir Ulfstein (2009). *The Constitutionalization of International Law* (Oxford: Oxford University Press).

Koh, Harold H. (1997). "Why Do Nations Obey International Law?" *Yale Law Journal*, Vol. 106, No. 8, pp. 2599–2659.

———— (1998). "Bringing International Law Home," *Houston Law Review*, Vol. 35, No. 3, pp. 623–81.

Koh, Harold, and Oona Hathaway (2005) (eds.). *Foundations of International Law and Politics* (New York: Foundation Press).

Koremenos, Barbara (2008). "When, What, and Why States Choose to Delegate," *Law and Contemporary Problems*, Vol. 71, No. 1, 151–92.

Koremenos, Barbara, Charles Lipson, and Duncan Snidal (2001). "The Rational Design of International Institutions," *International Organization*, Vol. 55, No. 4, pp. 761–99.

Koskenniemi, Martti (1989). *From Apology to Utopia* (Cambridge: Cambridge University Press).

Kratochwil, Friedrich (1989). *Rules, Norms, and Decisions: On the Conditions of Practical and Legal Reasoning in International Relations and Domestic Affairs* (Cambridge: Cambridge University Press).

Ku, Julian (2000). "The Delegation of Federal Power to International Organizations: New Problems with Old Solutions," *Minnesota Law Review*, Vol. 85, No. 1, pp. 71–113.

Linklater, Andrew (1990). *Beyond Realism and Marxism: Critical Theory and International Relations* (London: Macmillan Press).

Loughlin, Martin, and Neil Walker (2007) (eds.). *The Paradox of Constitutionalism: Constituent Power and Constitutional Form* (Oxford: Oxford University Press).

Magnette, Paul (2005). *What Is the European Union? Nature and Prospects* (Basingstoke, UK: Palgrave Macmillan).

Majone, Giandomenico (1998). "Europe's Democratic Deficit: The Question of Standards," *European Law Journal*, Vol. 4, No. 1, pp. 5–28.

Marceau, Gabrielle (2011). "IGOs in Crisis? Or New Opportunities to Demonstrate Responsibility?" *International Organizations Law Review*, Vol. 8, No. 1, pp. 1–4.

March, James G., and Johan P. Olsen (1989). *Rediscovering Institutions: The Organizational Basis of Politics* (New York: Free Press/Macmillan).

Martin, Lisa (2006). "Distribution, Information and Delegation to International Organizations: The Case of IMF Conditionality," in David Hawkins *et al.* (eds.), *Delegation and
Agency in International Organizations* (New York: Cambridge University Press), pp. 140–64.

Mayer, Peter (2008). "Civil Society Participation in International Security Organizations," in
Jens Steffek *et al.* (eds.), *Civil Society Participation in European and Global Governance*
(Hampshire, UK: Palgrave Macmillan), pp. 116–39.

McDonald, Ronald St. John, and Douglas M. Johnston (2005) (eds.). *Towards World Constitutionalism: Issues in the Legal Ordering of the World Community* (Leiden: Martinus
Nijhoff).

Milliken, Jennifer (1999). "The Study of Discourse in International Relations: A Critique
of Research and Methods," *European Journal of International Relations*, Vol. 5, No. 2,
pp. 225–54

Moravcsik, Andrew (2002). "In Defense of the Democratic Deficit: Reassessing Legitimacy in the European Union," *Journal of Common Market Studies*, Vol. 40, No. 4,
pp. 603–24.

Müller, Harald (2004). "Arguing, Bargaining and All That," *European Journal of International
Relations*, Vol. 10, No. 3, pp. 395–435.

Nielson, Daniel, and Michael Tierney (2003). "Delegation to International Organizations:
Agency Theory and World Bank Environmental Reform," *International Organization*,
Vol. 57, No. 2, pp. 241–76.

Nugent, Neill (2010). *The Government and Politics of the European Union*, 7th ed. (Basingstoke, Hampshire: Palgrave).

Peters, Ann (2009). "Membership in the Global Constitutional Community," in Jan Klabbers
et al. (eds.), *The Constitutionalization of International Law* (Oxford: Oxford University
Press), pp. 153–262.

Pierson, Paul (1996). "The Path to European Integration: A Historical Institutionalist Analysis," *Comparative Political Studies*, Vol. 29, No. 2, pp. 123–63.

Pollack, Mark A. (1997). "Delegation, Agency and Agenda-Setting in the European Union,"
International Organization, Vol. 51, No. 1, pp. 99–134.

———— (2003). *The Engines of European Integration* (New York: Oxford University Press).

———— (2010). "Theorizing EU Policy-Making" in Helen Wallace, Mark Pollack, and Alasdair
Young (eds.), *Policy-Making in the European Union* (Oxford: Oxford University Press), pp.
15–43.

Posner, Eric A. (2000). *Law and Social Norms* (Cambridge, MA: Harvard University Press).

Ratner, Steven (2004). "The Security Council and International Law," in David Malone (ed.),
The U.N. Security Council: From the Cold War to the 21st Century (Boulder, CO: Lynne
Rienner Publishers) pp. 591–605.

Reisman, W. Michael (1988). "International Incidents: Introduction to a New Genre in
the Study of International Law," in W. Michael Reisman and Andrew R. Willard (eds.),
International Incidents: The Law That Counts in World Politics (Princeton, NJ: Princeton
University Press).

Reus-Smit, Christian (2004) (ed.). *The Politics of International Law* (Cambridge: Cambridge
University Press).

Ripinsky, Sergey, and Peter Van den Bossche (2007). *NGO Involvement in International
Organizations* (London: British Institute of International Law).

Risse, Thomas (2000). " ' Let's Argue!': Communicative Action in World Politics," *International Organization*, Vol. 54, No. 1, pp. 1–39.

———— (2004). "Social Constructivism and European Integration," in Antje Wiener and Thomas Diez (eds.), *European Integration Theory* (New York: Oxford University Press), pp. 159–76.

Ruggie, John G. (1998). "What Makes the World Hang Together?" *International Organization*, Vol. 52, No. 3, pp. 855–86.

Sands, Philippe, and Pierre Klein (2009) (eds.). *Bowett's Law of International Institutions*, 6th ed. (London: Sweet & Maxwell).

Sandholtz, Wayne, and Alec Stone Sweet (1998). *European Integration and Supranational Governance* (New York: Oxford University Press).

Sarooshi, Dan (2005). *International Organizations and Their Exercise of Sovereign Powers* (Oxford: Oxford University Press).

Shelton, Dinah (2000) (ed.). *Commitment and Compliance: The Role of Non-binding Norms in the International Legal System* (New York: Oxford University Press).

Simmons, Beth, and Richard Steinberg (2006) (eds.). *International Law and International Relations* (New York: Cambridge University Press).

Slaughter, Anne-Marie (2004). *A New World Order* (Princeton, NJ: Princeton University Press).

Steffek, Jens, Claudia Kissling, and Patricia Nanz (2008) (eds.). *Civil Society Participation in European and Global Governance* (Hampshire, UK: Palgrave Macmillan).

Steinberg, Richard H. (2004). "Judicial Law-Making at the WTO: Discursive, Constitutional and Political Constraints," *American Journal of International Law*, Vol. 99, No. 2, pp. 247–75.

Stephan, Paul (2002). "Courts, Tribunals, and Legal Unification: The Agency Problem," *Chicago Journal of International Law*, Vol. 3, No. 2, pp. 333–52.

Stone Sweet, Alec (2004). *The Judicial Construction of Europe* (New York: Oxford University Press).

Swaine, Edward (2004). "The Constitutionality of International Delegations," *Columbia Law Review*, Vol. 104, No. 6, pp. 1492–1614.

Sykes, Alan (2007). "The Economics of Public International Law," in A. Mitchell Polinsky and Steven Shavell (eds.), *Handbook of Law and Economics* (Amsterdam: Elsevier), pp. 757–822.

Tallberg, Jonas (2002). "Delegation to Supranational Institutions: Why, How and With What Consequences?" *West European Politics*, Vol. 25, No. 1, pp. 23–46.

Tierney, Michael (2008). "Delegation Success and Policy Failure: Collective Delegation and the Search for Iraqi Weapons of Mass Destruction," *Law and Contemporary Problems*, Vol. 71, No. 1, pp. 283–312.

Trachtman, Joel (2009). "Constitutional Economics of the World Trade Organization," in Jeffrey L. Dunoff and Joel P. Trachtman (eds.), *Ruling the World? Constitutionalism, International Law, and Global Governance* (Cambridge: Cambridge University Press), pp. 206–29.

———— (1999). "The Domain of WTO Dispute Resolution," *Harvard International Law Journal*, Vol. 40, No. 2, pp. 333–77.

———— (2008) (ed.). *International Law and International Politics* (Burlington: Ashgate).

Tsebelis, George, and Geoffrey Garrett (2001). "The Institutional Foundations of Intergovernmentalism and Supranationalism in the European Union," *International Organization*, Vol. 55, No. 2, pp. 357–90.

Weil, Prosper (1983). "Towards Relative Normativity in International Law," *American Journal of International Law*, Vol. 77, No. 3, pp. 13–42.

Weiler J. H. H., and Marlene Wind (2003) (eds.). *European Constitutionalism beyond the State* (Cambridge: Cambridge University Press).

Wendt, Alexander, and Raymond Duvall (1989). "Institutions and International Order," in Ernst-Otto Czempiel and James Rosenau (eds.), *Global Changes and Theoretical Challenges: Approaches to World Politics for the 1990s* (Lexington, MA: Lexington Books), pp. 51–73.

Yoo, John (2005). *The Powers of War and Peace: The Constitution and Foreign Affairs after 9/11* (Chicago: University of Chicago Press).

12

Institutional Proliferation and the International Legal Order

Kal Raustiala

Since the cataclysm of World War II, the international order has grown increasingly institutionalized. Hundreds of international organizations (IOs) and tens of thousands of treaties now exist, many with widespread – and in some cases nearly universal – membership. International institutions existed before 1945, of course, and even before the outbreak of World War I. But compared to these earlier eras, the international system today is far more densely populated by rules and institutions.

At one level, this is a sign of the robustness of international cooperation. Great wars yield great reorderings, and the reordering that took place after 1945 was unusual in its focus on the construction of a rule-based and multilateral system (Ikenberry 2000; Patrick 2009). Yet, the significance of the postwar growth of rules and institutions is contested. For some, it is a sign of healthy maturation toward a more cooperative world, increasingly "lapt in universal law" (Tennyson 1881: 54). For others, international institutions are simply big government writ global: irrelevant at best and, at worst, a menace to national sovereignty (e.g., Rabkin 2004). Even those inclined toward a positive view of international institutions, however, sometimes see a dark side to the robust growth that has taken place in recent decades. Too many rules, and too many institutions to administer and adjudicate them, can fragment and complicate the international order.

This concern can be seen in fields as varied as trade, environment, human rights, and investment. International institutions have multiplied in recent decades and, increasingly, they overlap and even clash. Rising institutional density is particularly apparent with regard to courts (Shany 2004). In the realm of criminal law sits the International Criminal Court, the tribunals for the former Yugoslavia and Rwanda, and the many special and hybrid courts of Sierra Leone, Cambodia, and elsewhere.

I thank Nell Moley for research assistance and Karen Alter, Larry Helfer, Cesare Romano, Richard Steinberg, and David Victor for helpful comments on earlier drafts of this chapter, and thank the editors of this volume for feedback and forbearance.

In the realm of human rights law are regional courts for the Americas, Europe, and Africa. There is a special tribunal for the Law of the Sea, and others for Central America and Eastern and Southern Africa. The World Trade Organization's (WTO) Appellate Body has a healthy docket of cases. And the International Court of Justice (ICJ) continues to hear disputes, as it and its predecessor, the Permanent Court of International Justice, have done since the 1920s.

No one international court sits above another, however, and judgments on related topics can exhibit considerable tension in reasoning as well as results. As the president of the ICJ – not coincidentally, the institution with most to lose from this judicial flourishing – declared in a speech before the United Nations (UN) General Assembly, tribunals have proliferated "in an anarchic manner." "Unfortunate consequences" have ensued, he suggested, chief among them forum shopping, conflicting decisions, and ultimately, a fragmented system of international law (Guillaume 2000). Rising fragmentation, a contemporaneous UN report declared, poses a serious threat to the "credibility, reliability, and consequently, authority of international law" (Hafner 2000). In short, some fear this "kaleidoscopic reality" may be a recipe for a disjointed and dysfunctional legal order (Koskenniemi and Leino 2002: 559). Not all observers share this sense of foreboding, however. Some offer qualified praise – and even encomiums – for institutional proliferation and fragmentation (e.g., Charney 1998).

Institutional proliferation is not limited to courts, nor has it only been noticed by lawyers. Political scientists, who have long studied institutionalization (Krasner 1983; Keohane 1984), have also begun to consider density's implications. Early scholarship on international institutions focused primarily on their impact. Did institutions (or "regimes") alter outcomes in meaningful ways? Or did they simply ratify existing policies and preferences – and, as such, serve largely as an irrelevant sideshow to the real game of power politics? More recently, research has turned to the microdesign of institutional features. But alongside this focus is new attention to proliferation. Does a densely institutionalized order yield distinctive politics? What happens when institutions overlap and even contradict one another? Is rising density the result of a deliberate strategy by powerful states, or simply an unintended outcome of a more cooperative world politics? Either way, how do states use such a complicated international order to advance their interests?[1]

This chapter explores institutional density, and the conflict and competition such density inevitably creates in an anarchical system of states. This topic is explored somewhat differently in law and political science. For legal scholars, who look predominantly at international courts, the primary focus is normative: is fragmentation – the key animating concept for lawyers – a threat, or simply a welcome indicator of a maturing legal system? For political scientists, the primary focus is positive, and

---

[1] On these and other questions, see, for example, Aggarwal (1998), Raustiala and Victor (2004), Young (2008), Alter and Meunier (2009), Keohane and Victor (2011).

concepts such as "regime complexity" and "institutional overlap" are deployed to analyze strategic behavior within a crowded and intersecting institutional matrix. These divergent analytic modes are not surprising. But they should not be over-drawn, as there is increasingly sophisticated interaction between the two fields on these (and many other) issues.[2] Still, there remains substantial room for fruitful debate, as these literatures have not fully engaged the many possible connections. Perhaps the best example of an emergent common agenda is the question of who benefits from rising density.

In short, rising density has interesting implications for world politics. (I will gen-erally use *density* as shorthand for the related but sometimes distinct issues of prolif-eration, overlap, and fragmentation.) Once we think in terms of interaction among a multiplicity of institutions, we can see that institutionalization is not per se con-straining. States can more readily pick and choose which rules to follow – and, most interestingly, which rule to interpret. They can create competing institutions as well as compete within institutions. Politics becomes less a 2 × 2 matrix than a three-dimensional game of chess.

Existing research provides some preliminary insights into these issues, but, to date, these insights are less empirical than conceptual. The main contribution has been to recognize the phenomenon of institutional density and to begin to theorize about its nature. That issues in world politics overlap and connect, and that linkages may alter outcomes, is of course no mystery to policy-makers. Nixon and Kissinger famously pursued linkage diplomacy in the 1970s, and no doubt Kissinger's hero Metternich did so far earlier. But linkage politics is different from institutional density, even if there is substantial overlap in practice. Nixonian linkage was an almost purely political strategy pursued outside of (and with contempt for) the role of international institutions. It was about substantive connections. A dense institutional order, by contrast, certainly makes some policy linkages easier – and yields new forms of leverage – but it also creates linked and fragmented procedures and structures. These, in turn, may produce distinct and even novel behaviors, such as forum shopping and "strategic inconsistency" (Raustiala and Victor 2004). These phenomena are newer, since they fundamentally rest on the dramatic increase in institutionalization that has taken place in recent decades.

Is a dense international order a significant problem, a welcome development, or a largely superficial phenomenon? Is density an inadvertent outgrowth of inten-sifying interdependence, or a deliberate strategy? How does density vary – by issue area, over time, and across regions? These questions represent important lines of thinking that are either under way or incipient in the growing literature on institutional density. The first part of this chapter ("The Rise of Institutional Density") looks at the empirics of institutional density. Part II ("Density: Two

---

[2] For an overview of recent interdisciplinary research, with some reference to cognate issues of density, delegation, and institutional design, see Hafner-Burton, Victor, and Lupu (2012).

Optics") surveys the emerging scholarship in law and political science. Part III ("The Debate over Density") explores some fundamental questions. Part IV concludes the chapter

I. THE RISE OF INSTITUTIONAL DENSITY

For most of its history, the states system was lightly institutionalized, if at all. Proto-institutions, such as the Concert of Europe, allowed the great powers of the day to manage their interactions, but these arrangements had no real organizational basis and only barely resembled contemporary international institutions.[3] Treaties of the nineteenth century were likewise limited in number and, because only a small number of entities were considered members of international society, were largely bilateral or plurilateral. Some specialized, functional IOs were created late in the nineteenth century, such as the International Telecommunications Union. But the number remained quite small. The creation of the League of Nations in 1919 ushered in the modern age of international organizations (Claude 1988), and the early twentieth century also saw many more multilateral treaties and a general proliferation of rule-making, led in part by the move to codify what had long been the core of international law: custom.

But the real break point came with the creation of the UN and the explosion of institution building that followed – or, in some cases, such as the Bretton Woods institutions, accompanied – the San Francisco conference of 1945. Institutions with sweeping scope and meaningful capacity multiplied in the wake of World War II, as did a wide range of agreements, some in areas that had hitherto simply not existed as subjects of international law. Arms control, human rights, foreign investment, environmental protection – these and many other topics were the focus of extensive rule-making in the postwar order. The number of treaties deposited with the UN grew from fewer than 4,500 in 1959 to more than 45,000 fifty years later. By one estimate, there were 37 IOs in the system in 1909; a century later, 1,839.[4]

Slowly – or not so slowly – the "space" of the international system began filling up. Many areas of state behavior were now governed by some regime or another, and increasingly, by more than one. Trade is illustrative. From 1947 onward, the General Agreement on Tariffs and Trade (GATT) – the surviving pillar of the stillborn International Trade Organization – governed a wide swath

---

[3] Interactions between great powers and many weaker entities were often structured via overseas empires, a fundamentally coercive mode of organization that has few direct parallels today. David Lake (2009) explores less overt modes of dominance.

[4] Union of International Associations (2012). Compare with Shanks, Jacobson, and Kaplan (1996) (stating that, in 1981, there were 1,063; by 1992, 1,147). Shanks *et al.* compare the same UIA dataset with one of their own and argue that IOs die more frequently than many imagine, leading the birthrate of IOs to be even higher than it appears – in particular for "emanations," which are IOs formed by existing IOs. For an earlier study, see Wallace and Singer (1970).

of world trade. But, in later decades, free-trade accords multiplied dramatically. This new institutional density had repercussions for compliance and dispute settlement. Since now the parties to a dispute could be members of more than one such accord, there were multiple ways to seek reconciliation (or delay). To be sure, in the 1950s and 1960s, when the mode of settlement was more firmly diplomatic, there was not much in the way of difference among differing regimes – and fewer differing regimes to begin with. But as trade regimes increasingly legalized and developed more refined settlement procedures, the differences became more pointed.

The negotiation of the North American Free Trade Agreement (NAFTA), for instance, took note of the contemporaneous negotiations of the WTO, the effective successor of the GATT system. NAFTA declares that "disputes regarding any matter arising under both this Agreement and [GATT], any agreement negotiated thereunder, or any successor agreement, may be settled in either forum at the discretion of the complaining Party."[5] Nonetheless, respondents can require that certain disputes be settled under NAFTA and not the WTO, including challenges to measures adopted pursuant to certain environmental agreements, as well as disputes arising under "the NAFTA Chapters 7 (sanitary and phytosanitary measures) and 9 (standards related measures) relating to human, animal, or plant life, or health, or protection of the environment, or raising factual issues concerning the environment, health, safety, or conservation, including directly related scientific matters" (Gantz 1999: 1044).[6] In 2009, the United States invoked this provision in requesting NAFTA dispute settlement over Mexico's failure to move the long-running tuna–dolphin dispute from the WTO to NAFTA.[7]

This complicated relationship between overlapping treaty regimes plainly creates much scope for strategic behavior. Consider the softwood lumber dispute between the United States and Canada. Begun prior to NAFTA's entry in force, it was heard by eleven NAFTA Chapter 19 panels, four NAFTA Chapter 11 panels, and was featured in six WTO disputes, as well as in several U.S. Court of International Trade and federal court decisions (Dunoff 2007). The multiplicity of rulings was no accident. The players, all sophisticated and well-lawyered, jockeyed for advantage by employing (and reemploying) varied forums.

Today, there are more than 500 plurilateral trade agreements, in addition to the many WTO accords (and nearly 3,000 bilateral investment treaties). A prevailing

---

[5] North American Free Trade Agreement, U.S.-Can.-Mex., Dec 17, 1992, 32 I.L.M. 289 (1993), art. 2005(1).

[6] Nevertheless, NAFTA members settle most of their trade disputes in the WTO (Davis 2009).

[7] United States Trade Representative (November 2009). United States Initiates NAFTA Dispute with Mexico over Mexico's Failure to Move Its Tuna-Dolphin Dispute from the WTO to the NAFTA [press release], available at http://www.ustr.gov/about-us/press-office/press-releases/2009/november/united-states-initiates-nafta-dispute-mexico-over.

metaphor among trade analysts is "the spaghetti bowl," a reference to the arresting image that results from drawing lines around the various trade zones.[8]

None of this is unique to trade, even if it may be most pronounced in trade. NAFTA and the WTO were both treaties of the 1990s, an era that witnessed an explosion of international conferences (or circuses, depending on your viewpoint) and produced many new treaties, resolutions, and "outcome documents." These texts contained rules and norms that often touched on or overlapped with rules and norms already in existence. As early as 1992, legal scholars warned of the growing problem of "treaty congestion" (cf. Palmer 1992; Weiss 1993: 675).

And it was not a coincidence that concern with treaty congestion was first raised in the context of the global environment. Environmental cooperation was a major growth area in this period, and the focus was largely on negotiating new agreements rather than implementing existing ones. Many environmental issues are also intrinsically linked in ways (perhaps no different than in other arenas of international cooperation, but seemingly more apparent to scholars and practitioners) that led to concern over the ramifications of treaty overlap. If a treaty on transboundary air pollution, for example, also had implications for climate change – and the two issues are plainly connected as economic and ecological matters – ought they not be connected as well in terms of negotiation and implementation? At least that is how many scholars and participants began to think.

There were, as a result, increasing calls for a common institutional home that would rationalize environmental cooperation and reduce "congestion," and soon after a debate over creating a World Environment Organization to provide coherence to the multiplying and sometimes fractious array of institutions (Charnovitz 2002). Negotiators began to include clauses purporting to govern the relationships among the growing number of accords. Consider the 1998 Rotterdam Convention on the Prior Informed Consent Procedure for Certain Hazardous Chemicals and Pesticides in International Trade.[9] The convention's preamble amply illustrates both the rising density of agreements and the difficulty inherent in addressing this density frontally:

The Parties to this Convention

Aware of the harmful impact on human health and the environment from certain hazardous chemicals and pesticides in international trade,

Recalling the pertinent provisions of the *Rio Declaration on Environment and Development* and Chapter 19 of *Agenda 21* on 'Environmentally sound management

---

[8] There are many versions of this image, some reflecting regions, some the globe. See, e.g., Baier et al (2007). But the impression given is always the same: a mess. (Or, for lawyers, an opportunity for larger bills as client's advice needs rise).

[9] United Nations Rotterdam Convention on the Prior Informed Consent Procedure for Certain Hazardous Chemicals and Pesticides in International Trade, February 24, 2004, 2244 UNTS 337.

of toxic chemicals, including prevention of illegal international traffic in toxic and dangerous products',

Mindful of the work undertaken by the United Nations Environment Programme (UNEP) and the Food and Agriculture Organization of the United Nations (FAO) in the operation of the voluntary Prior Informed Consent procedure, as set out in the *UNEP Amended London Guidelines for the Exchange of Information on Chemicals in International Trade* (hereinafter referred to as the 'Amended London Guidelines') and the *FAO International Code of Conduct on the Distribution and Use of Pesticides* (hereinafter referred to as the 'International Code of Conduct'),

. . .

Recognizing that good management practices for chemicals should be promoted in all countries, taking into account, inter alia, the voluntary standards laid down in the *International Code of Conduct* and the *UNEP Code of Ethics on the International Trade in Chemicals*,

Desiring to ensure that hazardous chemicals that are exported from their territory are packaged and labelled in a manner that is adequately protective of human health and the environment, consistent with the principles of the *Amended London Guidelines and the International Code of Conduct*,

Recognizing that trade and environmental policies should be mutually supportive with a view to achieving sustainable development,

Emphasizing that nothing in this Convention shall be interpreted as implying in any way a change in the rights and obligations of a Party under any existing international agreement applying to chemicals in international trade or to environmental protection,

Understanding that the above recital is not intended to create a hierarchy between this Convention and other international agreements . . .

Italicized (my emphasis) in this short preamble are five other international agreements explicitly mentioned; implicitly recognized in the final two clauses are scores more related to environment, trade, and hazardous chemicals.

Indeed, the final two clauses constitute what diplomats refer to as a "savings clause": language meant to ensure that one accord does not alter commitments undertaken in another. Savings clauses are not specific to the environment, although the myriad trade and environment linkages provide ample cause for their negotiation. Savings clauses both reflect and accentuate the fundamental problem of rising density in the international system. Since there is generally no hierarchy among international institutions, and since by their terms agreements such as the Rotterdam Convention do not alter other agreements, conflicts are left to be sorted out – or to fester – in some political fashion. This is the basic intuition behind the concept of a "regime complex": rather than a single, coherent regime, there is, in practice, often an array of partially overlapping institutions governing a particular issue area (Raustiala and Victor 2004).

Just as agreements increasingly began to (metaphorically) bump into one another, so too did IOs and other bodies. Consider international courts. For most of the twentieth century, international courts were almost nonexistent: aside from the usually sleepy ICJ there were few examples, and those dispute settlement procedures that did exist, such as the GATT panels, were avowedly uncourt-like (Hudec 1987). As recently as 1986, for example, a leading British international lawyer could write (correctly) that, "it is a rarity in the international field for there to be any possibility of more than one forum" for a given dispute (Fitzmaurice 1986: 437).

Several momentous changes altered this story. One was the rise and rise of international criminal law, which spawned several new tribunals and an array of complex judgments that sometimes addressed common doctrinal issues, even if the underlying facts and crimes differed. Another was the creation of the WTO Appellate Body, which increasingly took the trade order away from the diplomatic-consultative approach of the past toward a world of careful legal briefs and rulings in the hundreds of pages. Other courts also popped up, such as the International Tribunal for the Law of the Sea (Romano 1999). A third change was the revival of regional integration efforts, many of which featured courts as dispute settlers. (What deeper factors drove some of these changes is a topic I turn to below.)

Courts, by nature, issue rulings, follow precedent, and interpret texts.[10] But the lack of hierarchy among international courts creates scope for inconsistent decisions and divergent reasoning. In turn, this encourages forum shopping as litigants use these differences to seek advantage. For some international lawyers, the phenomenon (or problem) of fragmentation in the international system begins and ends here: the proliferation of courts, and therefore of rulings, they believe, fundamentally challenges the coherence and integrity of the international legal system.

But institutional density is by no means limited to overlapping treaty rules or contradictory legal decisions. Negotiating forums can also overlap. The existence of multiple institutions with plausible jurisdiction over a shared set of issues, often exercised in different ways, among different parties, and with different procedures, provides ample opportunity for maneuvering – or "regime-shifting" (Helfer 2004) – by actors interested in a particular bargaining outcome (or no outcome). Should questions of essential medicines and patents be negotiated at the World Health Organization (WHO), the WTO, the World Intellectual Property Organization (WIPO), or the many bilateral "TRIPs-plus" accords? Should agreements on food grow out of the Food and Agricultural Organization (FAO), the WTO, the CGIAR system, or the UN General Assembly? And which agreement, norm, or process prevails in the event of a conflict?

---

[10] Strictly speaking, there is no doctrine of *stare decisis* in international law, but, as a practical matter, international courts do follow precedents, however construed, in many cases.

The problem is not limited to existing institutions. States can create new institutions (and exit existing ones) if they prefer new rules and structures. The UN replaced the League; the WTO, the GATT. Because different institutions often have different procedures and different members, there may be strong incentives to pursue one or another venue for rule-making. Nothing stops parallel rule-making efforts, nor prevents the resulting rules from conflicting. In short, *a denser international order yields more institutional choice*. Relatedly, *the desire for more (or better) choices may yield more density*. This, as I will discuss later in this chapter, has potentially significant implications for how we understand the constraining role of international institutions.

To be sure, not all institutions that overlap – or coexist in the same juridical space – do so in an uncoordinated or nonhierarchical fashion. Some are explicitly "nested" in others. Work dating from the 1980s, for example, described how various textile agreements, as well as regional institutions such as Asia-Pacific Economic Cooperation (APEC), were nested within the larger GATT system (Aggarwal 1985). Others have looked at nestedness in other contexts (Alter and Meunier 2009). Nested regimes remain an important part of the institutional fabric of the global order. But what is more striking is the plethora of institutions that are decidedly not nested, yet by inadvertence – or intent – address many of the same subjects.

Some of these non-nested institutions are multilateral and even universal in ambition; others are regional in nature. There is, as a result, a sort of geography of density. Some regions are clearly more densely institutionalized than others; one need only to compare Europe to East Asia. Why this is so is an outstanding question in both senses of the word. Geography may matter in another way. Although the simple accretion of treaties, institutions, and tribunals is likely to correlate at least roughly with more fragmentation, overlap (and conflict) is most likely when more relevant institutions operate in the same geographic zone. If, conversely, much of the growth in institutions is via regional regimes, the resulting fragmentation may have a different character: segmented by area and more parallel than overlapping. One might even describe it as more akin to a federal system of rule, whereas an array of partially overlapping regimes with broadly global ambits is more reminiscent of the complexity of rule and authority in feudal Europe (Ruggie 1993). This distinction should not be overdrawn, however, since even parallel regimes with different regional focuses may still engage common legal or policy questions – and do so differently.

II. DENSITY: TWO OPTICS[11]

Institutional density is growing, but it is not new. International lawyers, who are typically closer to the practice of institution building than their counterparts in the social sciences, have been contemplating the specter of a denser and more

---

[11] The term comes from Keohane (1997).

fragmented system for decades.[12] In 1958, for example, Baxter (1958: 178–79) examined the law governing armed forces stationed abroad, in particular the North
Atlantic Treaty Organization (NATO) Status of Forces Agreement, and asked "is the
law progressing in the direction of greater uniformity or, on the contrary, has there
been a disintegration and fragmentation of the law since the period of the Second
World War?" A few years earlier, Jenks (1953: 405) observed that "the conflict of law-
making treaties . . . must be accepted as being in certain circumstances an inevitable
incident of growth" of international law. Likewise, Szasz wrote in 1966 that

> what is lacking is a generally accepted codification of international law, or even a
> definitive and complete encyclopedia wherein the established international legal
> norms can conveniently be found. As a matter of fact, it is unduly difficult to
> determine, without extensive and often involved research, the various rules of
> international law that may bear upon a given point. (Szasz 1966: 852)

Szasz did not invoke fragmentation per se in this passage – or at least did not use
that exact term – but he did have his finger on a basic attribute of it, as did many
other prominent international lawyers of the time. Even in 1966, there were lots of
legal rules, too many for even an able lawyer in the UN legal counsel's office (such
as Szasz) to keep track of. As a result, there was no easy way to make sense of what
was and what was not required in a given situation. Again, there is no necessary
connection between a multiplicity of rules and overlapping or contradictory rules.
But practice – and common sense, if not the basic laws of entropy – suggests that two
phenomena are related: a rising tide of disconnected rules, of which no one person
or office can keep track, will surely yield conflict if not contradiction.[13]

And lawyers were perhaps primed to see this. Litigation provides ample incentive
to seek out conflicting rules and differing forums. Domestic law had long addressed
the problem (or issue) of conflicts, which arise even in well-functioning national
systems. This is a point worth underscoring: while the international system may be
particularly prone to conflict because it lacks a clear and accepted legal hierarchy,
conflict is inherent in many legal systems – particularly federal ones like that of the
United States or Germany. The study of "conflicts of laws" has been a mainstay of
Anglo-American legal study for centuries and dates back, in one form or another, to
Roman law. The typical conflicts problem involves multiple legal rules grounded in
multiple sovereigns, such as a contract signed in one state but breached in another.
But the basic concept – how to choose when seemingly parallel rules or systems
diverge in result – is neither novel nor inapplicable to the international legal plane.

---

[12] A Google Ngram search of "legal fragmentation" shows essentially no mention of the phrase until the
mid-1950s, and then a dramatic rise peaking around 2000.
[13] As discussed further later in the chapter, however, these conflicts may not always be as great as some
fear or imagine; Charney's (1998) extensive survey of how basic questions of international law have
been treated in international courts, while now dated, suggests that most rulings are broadly aligned.

Indeed, international law has long contained doctrines, simple to be sure, that are meant to alleviate such conflicts. The doctrine of *lex specialis*, for example, declares that particular rules prevail over general rules. Similarly, later treaties generally trump earlier ones.[14] These sorts of basic rules of the road can be helpful, but are plainly limited in a world of tens of thousands of treaties, many highly specialized and often updated (leading to confusion about which is prior, let alone more specialized). The Vienna Convention on the Law of Treaties codifies some of these rules, but hardly solves the fundamental problem. A direct consequence of this weak arsenal of conflict-dampening tools has been the angst demonstrated by some over the rising number – or specter, depending on one's view – of legal conflicts.

This angst – although concentrated in The Hague – stems from real events. Remarkably, international courts have issued more than 25,000 decisions (Alter 2013). Nearly all are innocuous with regard to conflicts, but a few high-profile judgments illustrate the consequences of a nonhierarchical system. In 1995, for example, the International Criminal Tribunal for the former Yugoslavia (ICTY) rejected a prior interpretation of the law of state responsibility announced by the ICJ. In justifying this move, the ICTY wrote that international law "lacks a centralized structure [and] does not provide for an orderly division of labor" among tribunals. As a result, "every tribunal is a self-contained system."[15]

This decision sparked attention. Judges such as ICJ President Guillaume spoke out on the need for an organizing structure, and some scholars bemoaned the implications of this new juridical landscape. Others pushed back, however, arguing that these concerns were overwrought and "the more [courts] the merrier" (Charney *et al.* 2002: 369). New courts, they urged, "strengthen the system of international law, notwithstanding some loss of uniformity." Moreover, in the end, "multiple courts are better than no courts at all" (Charney 1998; Pauwelyn and Salles 2009: 80). In 2006, however, the International Law Commission (ILC) produced a nearly 500-page report, revealingly subtitled "difficulties arising from the diversification and expansion of international law" (International Law Commission 2006: Chapter XII). This report, unsurprisingly, took a less positive view of judicial proliferation. Among the many points made, the ILC noted that there is "astonishingly little" judicial practice on conflicts; that is to say, international courts have tended to avoid resolving such conflicts. Instead, they are far more often resolved, in the ILC's phrasing, by negotiation – otherwise known as politics.

Across campus in political science departments, however, there was little worry over the specter of inconsistent legal decisions, nor much consideration of whether (in Judge Guillaume's words) the "privileged position" and "special authority" of the

---

[14] At least those on the same topic, an often-crucial caveat. See also Gourgourinis (2011).
[15] *Prosecutor v. Tadic*, Case No. IT-94-1-I, Decision on Defence Motion for Interlocutory Appeal on Jurisdiction, ¶ 70 (Int'l Crim. Trib. for the Former Yugoslavia Oct. 2, 1995). See also Application of the Convention on the Prevention and Punishment of the Crime of Genocide (*Bosnia and Herzegovina v. Serbia and Montenegro*), 2007 I.C.J. Case 91 (February 26).

ICJ made it *primus inter pares*, and therefore the appropriate apex of a restructured international legal order. But political scientists did have a long-standing interest in one aspect of international law – treaties – and the cooperation they represented. Regimes in world politics had been a central concern since the early 1980s. Regimes were generally thought of, if only implicitly, as self-contained institutions that operated in a specified issue area. At the core was usually a legal document (although, as the late Abram Chayes liked to say, political scientists rarely used the "L Word").[16]

The regimes literature that emerged from this era was rich and varied. But, until recently, it rarely acknowledged a growing reality: regimes were not self-contained, but instead frequently overlapped and even competed with one another.[17] That regimes were multiplying was well understood. The larger implications of institutional density, however, were not given much attention. Yet, as Drezner has recently argued, density has begun to transform the fundamental challenge of cooperation in ways that have major implications for theories of international relations. "In a world thick with institutions, the central problem for institutionalists is no longer surmounting the transaction costs of policy coordination, but selecting among a welter of possible governance arrangements" (Drezner 2009: 66).

By the turn of the new millennium, international relations (IR) scholars were more actively exploring the issue of rising density. Although the particular spin and nomenclature varied – some spoke of "overlap" or "interplay," while others analyzed regime "complexes" and "complexity" – the basic orientation was the same (Young 2002; 1996; Raustiala and Victor 2004; Stokke 2004; Alter and Meunier 2009). International institutions were not free-standing, nor did state choices in one institution fail to affect those in others. Rising density moves more of the action of cooperation to implementation, and leads to a more complex "chessboard politics" in which different pieces move in different ways (Alter and Meunier 2009: 16). As noted above, earlier scholarship had introduced the idea of nested regimes. Although this provided an analytic point of entry, it had a different orientation than most of the work on institutional density that followed. And, conceptually, nested regimes were distinct if not diametrically opposed to the concerns about fragmentation raised by some lawyers: indeed, it was precisely a nested and organized relationship that Cassandras like Judge Guillaume sought.[18]

Adding to this new wave of scholarship was the remarkable growth of trade law, which spurred a burst of attention to the overlap inherent in what were dubbed "trade and" problems. "The 'trade and . . .' industry is booming," noted one knowledgeable observer in 2002 (Leebron 2002: 15). Trade's connection to human rights,

---

[16]   That is much less true today. See Hafner-Burton *et al.* (2012).

[17]   This reflected reality; for much of the postwar period, regimes were indeed "'decomposable' from the rest of the system, in the sense that they operated without close links to other regimes in other issue-areas" (Keohane and Nye 2001).

[18]   Even so, Aggarwal (1998: 213) noted the problems with nested institutions, writing that "the temptation to create new institutions as a solution to new problems may be a perilous illusion."

environment, labor, intellectual property, cultural practices – these and other combinations led to a more focused examination of how regimes interacted, clustered, or undermined one another. (Moreover, it was nearly always the "and" part of the "trade and" equation that was being undermined by the trade part – leading partisans of various "ands" to dig deeper into the underlying structural features that favored trade institutions.)

Indeed, the concept of a "regime complex" was introduced in the pages of the leading journal of international relations with regard to an obscure issue – plant genetic resources – that nonetheless bridged the very heated arenas of trade, environment, intellectual property, and agriculture (Raustiala and Victor 2004). The role of regime complexes in a wide array of areas of international cooperation, from human rights, security in Europe, election monitoring, trade, intellectual property, refugees, to climate change, have all been explored since (Helfer 2004; Busch 2007; Alter and Meunier 2009; Gehring and Oberthur 2009; Keohane and Victor 2011).

Meanwhile, international lawyers continue to debate the merits, or peril, of a fragmented legal order, in a torrent that far outmatches, in size at least, the work done by political scientists. A search of "fragmentation w/5 'international law'" on the Westlaw database in early 2012 produced nearly 600 articles, many published in the last few months alone (although, to be sure, not all fully focused on fragmentation). To paraphrase an earlier scribe on the subject, for lawyers, the fragmentation industry is booming.

III. THE DEBATE OVER DENSITY

Why are international institutions proliferating and, increasingly, overlapping and conflicting? How does this phenomenon affect the behavior of states and other actors? Is institutional density good or bad – and for whom? These questions are central, but their answers are still emerging. The sheer fact of rising density appears almost undisputed.[19] But, beyond this, there is substantial room for debate and only a small (but growing) body of scholarship. Perhaps the most basic question raised by institutional density is why it is increasing. The limited research that directly engages this issue tends to focus on the dynamics of specific examples of density, rather than on why density *across the system* appears to be increasing.

Existing explanations for rising density also vary depending on what facet is emphasized. An early study by Romano of international courts argued that their rapid proliferation could be attributed "largely to the expansion of international law into domains that were either solely within states' domestic jurisdiction (e.g., criminal justice) or not the object of multilateral discipline ... when conceived in this manner, the multiplication of [courts] becomes the precipitate of the accrued normative density of the international legal system" (Romano 1999: 728–29). Although it

[19] Although surely someone will seize this opening soon.

is uncontroverted that international law increasingly addresses subjects traditionally thought of as domestic, this is somewhat question-begging: why has this happened? (I will return to this in a moment.) And, in any event, as Romano (1999: 728–29) points out, this argument "fails to explain why the 1990s have given birth to more international judicial bodies than any other decade." Nor does it explain why this expansion comes replete with new courts. Romano instead looks to the end of the Cold War as a key trigger. By revitalizing the Security Council and weakening Russia, the Cold War's demise directly aided the establishment of several international criminal tribunals and may have indirectly assisted the development of others, such as the Law of the Sea Tribunal.

Other legal scholars have suggested, not necessarily inconsistently, that the dramatic proliferation of courts is a consequence of new politics and preferences on a grand scale – a shift from a state-centered conception of international law to a more universalistic, human-centered, and individually accessible system. This shift is perhaps best exemplified by the tremendous postwar expansion of the human rights regime (Koskenniemi and Leino 2002: 574–79; see also Teitel 2011). Whereas ordinary state disputes can be dealt with diplomatically, or in fora that add a veneer of legal process to diplomatic negotiation, individual rights issues require, or are thought to require, institutions of adjudication that more closely resemble Western-style domestic courts. Still, determining what is driving the move toward a more person-centered conception of international law is no easier a question to answer than what is driving the move to internationalize once-domestic policy concerns. But both seem to reflect a kind of meta-ideational change in how international law is conceived and in the broad understandings of the acceptable purposes of international cooperation. In other words, this is likely a topic that transcends the narrow and rationalist analysis that tends to dominate contemporary scholarship on institutions in political science.

Rising density is, of course, not limited to international courts; there are many more treaties and IOs as well. But the rate of recent change in agreements and organizations is somewhat less dramatic and, moreover, does not appear keyed to the demise of Cold War politics. One prominent study argues that, for IOs, "the birthrate peaked in the mid 1970s, remained high in the early 1980s, and has steadily declined since."[20] Other data suggest that intergovernmental organizations grew from fewer than 100 at the end of World War II to close to 350 fifty years later, in a fairly steady rise – and the number has generally plateaued since (Pevehouse 2010). These numbers are sensitive to conceptual choices about what counts as an organization, but the basic picture appears reasonably clear and consistent: the growth of IOs has continued since the end of the Cold War, but is slowing down from its early postwar peak.

---

[20] Shanks, Jacobson, and Kaplan (1996: 598). Their study ends in 1992, however.

International agreements are similar. The number of treaties registered with the UN exhibits the following pattern:

UN Treaty Registrations by Decade

1950–59: 4,318
1960–69: 5,106
1970–79: 8,098
1980–89: 8,146
1990–99: 9,461
2000–09: 9,809

Total as of May 2011: 48,566

As this shows, treaty proliferation was most marked in the 1970s, when the rate of increase jumped substantially. As with IOs, the end of the Cold War did not seem to bring about a major disjuncture; in fact, the rate of change in the 1990s was slower than in some earlier decades. It may well be that the type of agreement we see in recent decades is different – and certainly that is the perception held by many observers – but the data do not speak to that issue. Still, when one takes the long view, there is no denying the great rise in the number of treaties: more than a tenfold increase since 1945. In sum, the different forms of institutionalization have exhibited different patterns of growth. Yet, overall, international institutions are clearly far more numerous today than a half century ago.

A very basic claim about this growth, alluded to earlier in this chapter, is that overall rising levels of density and fragmentation may simply be a product of time: perhaps higher levels of density reflect a natural and organic process, unfolding over time as the wheels of diplomacy grind along and produce new agreements and organizations.[21] This process may have been further bolstered by an even more basic change: the increasing numbers of states in the international system. As postwar decolonization took root, the number of states in the system doubled, and then doubled again. As a result there are many more dyads in the system now than in 1945.

These basic changes may explain a substantial part of the rise in density. Yet increased density appears to be more than the mere accumulation of decades of negotiations and summitry among a rapidly growing cast of sovereigns. Even if it were, one would still need to explain why there are so many negotiations and so many summits producing so many rules and so many institutions. Perhaps rising institutional density reflects not just the proliferation of sovereigns but also a greater dispersal of power in the international order. As new or newly resurgent players – such as China, Brazil, India, Turkey – grow more powerful, and older powers, such as the United States and Europe, diminish in at least relative terms, these new, or at least more powerful, actors may seek to create new institutions that better serve

[21] I thank Karen Alter for emphasizing this point.

their interests (Steinberg 2013). But much of the growth of international institutions is connected to traditional great powers, and so this factor, although of an as-yet unknown quantum, is probably not sufficient to account for much of the expansion in density we observe.

The early regimes literature offered some ideas about institutionalization that may be helpful in pondering these questions. Keohane invoked the concept of density when he asked, three decades ago, the very basic question of why we observe regimes rather than simply ad hoc arrangements among states. He argued that "the denser the policy space, the more highly interdependent are different issues." And where issue density is high,

> one substantive object may well impinge on another and regimes will achieve economies of scale, for instance in establishing negotiating procedures that are applicable to a variety of potential agreements within similar substantive areas of activity. Furthermore, in dense policy spaces, complex linkages will develop among substantive issues. . . . As linkages such as these develop, the organizational costs involved in reconciling distinct objectives will rise and demands for overall frameworks of rules, norms, principles, and procedures to cover certain clusters of issues – that is, for international regimes – will increase. (Keohane 1982: 339–40)

More succinctly, he wrote, there is "a link between interdependence and international regimes: increases in the former can be expected to lead to increases in demand for the latter" (Keohane 1982: 341).

Two things stand out. First, Keohane hypothesized that, as issues overlapped and the costs of reconciliation increased, states would rationalize their cooperation via the creation of regimes. Pushed further, that logic suggests that as regimes themselves overlap and conflict, meta-regimes of some kind should arise to rationalize the (now larger and more complicated) issue area. Although this may sometimes occur – and perhaps that is the story of the WTO's "single undertaking" – clearly many issue areas follow a different and messier path toward not regimes, but regime complexes. Second, at a deeper level it does seem intuitive that rising interdependence may be a sort of master variable that yields more demand for agreements, which in turn spur the creation of more institutions to organize cooperation, adjudicate disputes, and interpret provisions. Coupled to a far larger number of putative bargaining parties, growing interdependence may drive a substantial portion of rising institutional density.

The qualitative changes in the nature of international institutions discussed above – more "behind the border" issues, more focus on individual rights and access – are less easily connected to changes in interdependence – and not obviously connected to the numerical growth of sovereigns – but they too can be seen as its product. As states grow more interdependent economically, for example, they have a greater interest in the seemingly neutral domestic regulations that may alter conditions of international competition, such as food safety inspections. That requires a new set of rules to govern what was formerly a purely domestic matter (such as the Sanitary and Phytosanitary [SPS] and Technical Barriers to Trade [TBT] Agreements in the WTO). And, as liberal values spread via commerce, and knowledge of other political and cultural systems grows, we might expect to see a spread of rights-consciousness and of individualistic approaches to the law as well. Add in an increasing number of states, eager to demonstrate their sovereignty via participation in the full fabric of international life, and you may have a recipe for substantial institutional proliferation.

These speculations are consistent with a world in which international institutions are plentiful and increasingly intersect with domestic law and life. But do they explain the rise not just in the number of institutions, but in overlap and conflict among these institutions? In a simple sense, perhaps: more regimes likely yield a higher probability of overlap and conflict. Yet, an increase in rules and institutions does not *necessarily* lead to substantial fragmentation or conflict; the fact that national legal systems also accumulate many new rules over time as well (just consider the *Federal Register*) suggests that the problem of density – to the degree that there is a problem – transcends mere numerical growth. National rules emerge, even in federal systems, within a constitutional structure that provides for a process of rule-reconciliation over time. Conflicts may well occur, but there is an established method for resolving them. In the international arena, there is no such constitutional structure, and thus the impact of sheer numerical growth may be far more meaningful.

So, at one level, rising density may simply be the wages of success in a more cooperative, peaceful, and truly global world. But the existing patterns of institutional overlap and conflict suggest that overlap and fragmentation in this process is not randomly distributed. In recent work, Keohane and Victor theorize about the conditions under which some issues become more complexly institutionalized than others. They describe a continuum, with integrated regimes at one end, "highly fragmented collections of institutions" at the other, and regime complexes somewhere in the middle (Keohane and Victor 2011). They theorize that three forces explain where a given issue, and its associated agreements, is situated on this spectrum. First, when the interests of key powers vary, regime complexes are more likely. Second, when states face high uncertainty about cooperative risks and rewards, they will favor smaller club-like structures that often will overlap. Third, the harder it is to link relevant issues, the more fragmentation is likely to increase.

Some studies even suggest that rising levels of complexity and overlap may reflect a deliberate strategy to create new institutional options and rules and undermine existing ones (Leebron 2002; Helfer 2004; Raustiala and Victor 2004; Benvenisti and Downs 2009). If true, this raises very interesting puzzles. The guiding assumption in the pioneering work on regimes was that states created regimes to reduce the transaction costs of cooperation and to create focal points that promote agreement. Institutionalization, as a result, channels decisions and over time restricts freedom of action, thus promoting stable cooperation.

By contrast, a multiplicity of institutions in a given issue area can enlarge choice and latitude, allowing states to pursue multiple and even contradictory tracks. This is likely to be especially true for those states with the resources and bureaucratic capacity to operate effectively across multiple forums. Consequently, the existence of overlap and inconsistency may be broadly beneficial for the most powerful states, and may even reflect an intention to *raise* transaction costs, not lower them. As transaction costs grow in a given area, cooperation may shift to regimes more favorable to powerful actors (Helfer 2004).[22] And, in general, the greater difficulty of maneuvering in a more complex, high-transaction-costs world can be much more readily borne by powerful states. This, in turn, gives them a relative advantage over other actors. (It also bears at least a family resemblance to the argument that dominant firms in an industry may counterintuitively favor complex regulation, because they are relatively better able to navigate such a system and therefore are advantaged vis-à-vis smaller rivals or newcomers.)

In short, rising levels of density may undermine some of the power-restraining effects of institutionalization. In a denser system, states and other actors can more readily chose among rules and procedures. Which then become dominant – if any – is ultimately more a matter of politics and power than of law and rules. This logic suggests that institutionalization relates to power in a sort of U-curve. Powerful states are advantaged by either low levels of institutionalization – which more closely approximate a state of nature – or by very high levels, in which a dense and overlapping thicket of institutions both saps the resources of smaller states and provides greater scope for choice and strategy for major players. How these varied motivations and strategies interact, and whether and when states seek to increase transaction costs so as to slow down cooperation or divert it into other forums, is a central area in need of more study.

As this suggests, while the causes of rising density remain murky, so too are the consequences. In addition to advantaging some states over others, possible consequences adverted to in the emerging scholarship on density include a greater role for implementation in determining outcomes, a greater reliance on bounded rationality in actor decision-making, more social interaction among key actors, more forum shopping, more institutional competition, and more feedback among institutions (Alter and Meunier 2009). The normative attractiveness of this more complex cooperative climate is also unclear. Lawyers in particular have debated whether legal fragmentation is broadly beneficial or a peril to be avoided. The aforementioned Tadic ruling, in which the upstart ICTY appeared to reject the authority of the World Court, became "a flashpoint for the anxiety of fragmentation" (Teitel and Howse 2009: 963). If different courts could announce different rules for similar problems,

---

[22] Helfer notes, however, that in some cases "weaker states and networks of states and NGOs can engage also engage in regime shifting, although the specific rationales and the strategies they employ may differ from those of well-resourced nations" (Helfer 2004: 17).

then international law – often derided as weak at best, meaningless at worst – now also seemed more malleable and even arbitrary than many had feared.

Nonetheless, whether fragmentation bears greater virtue than vice is often viewed differently depending on the context. Regional fragmentation rarely raises concerns, perhaps because it corresponds to a basic geographic presumption about law: legal rules (appropriately) vary depending on location. Location, in turn, is often thought to be a powerful proxy for preferences. This Tieboutian view appears to have widespread adherence, even if it is rarely expressed directly (Tiebout 1956). Yet, it is not obvious why regional fragmentation should be more acceptable. All treaty regimes are consent-based, and hence each reflects the considered deliberation of a set of a parties that have chosen to join together to form, for at least a given set of issues, a community of commitment. Whether that community of commitment rests on a geographic basis or some other ground seems normatively immaterial. Indeed, a fair case can be made that regional groupings, which rest on accidents of geography, should be accorded less deference than other forms.

Still, the primary concern of many legal scholars is that fragmentation will yield divergence in similarly oriented legal rules. In other words, it is not fragmentation per se that is the concern, but that, as in *Tadic*, doctrines or reasoning on common issues will vary across juridical domains. This variation, in turn, may yield two sorts of problems, one direct and one indirect. First, it creates direct uncertainty and perhaps even conflict over rules and their meanings. Whether a given human rights treaty applies extraterritorially, for instance, is not always plain from the treaty text, and different adjudicators may opine differently on it. Some agreements may even contain "counterregime norms," norms that directly undermine rules in other, perhaps older, forums (Helfer 2009). Such rule uncertainty may mean that foreign ministries and other actors will lack clear guidance, or will selectively choose which guidance to adhere to, and hence law will not serve to channel behavior effectively. This may, in turn, lead to higher levels of noncompliance as states violate one rule while complying with another. Second, and more indirectly, divergence creates incentives to forum shop. Lawyers have long looked askance at forum shopping, which seems to undermine fundamental principles of evenhandedness by making outcomes turn on the vagaries of the forum chosen.

How grave are these problems? For the first, rule uncertainty, there is good reason to be skeptical that it is a serious concern. International law is sufficiently malleable already that there is often substantial wiggle room for good lawyers to make a range of reasonable claims about the meaning of an international legal rule. It is hard to see how divergent results or doctrines from different treaties or international forums will substantially alter this preexisting latitude. To be sure, rising levels of rule uncertainty will make it easier for states, as well as other actors, to make self-serving legal claims. But they seem perfectly capable of doing so already.

Moreover, actors seem able to work within a rule-uncertain environment in domestic legal systems. Within the United States, for example, appellate circuits often split on major issues, and while, in theory, the Supreme Court stands ready to resolve splits, in practice, many persist for decades. Because the circuits are geographically defined, actors know that legal rules vary based on what region of the nation the relevant behavior occurs in. For international courts, jurisdiction is not always geographic in nature, and so it may be more likely that a given dispute will fall within the purview of multiple rule interpretations or interpreters. But international courts have their jurisdiction delimited in other ways. The ICTY, for instance, has limited time and place jurisdiction – over acts committed in the former Yugoslavia from 1991 onward. Likewise, the ICC's jurisdiction is limited to certain crimes and inapplicable to events that occurred before July 1, 2002. There is no obvious reason why such differentiated jurisdiction cannot be sustained in the international plane in much the same way it is (sometimes) sustained in domestic law. In short, higher institutional density may well lead to more rule uncertainty. Yet, uncertainty is already pervasive for many areas of international law, and hence any added uncertainty from divergence is likely to be small. And experience in the domestic realm suggests that legal systems can survive a fair bit of divergence with little ill effect.

What about the risks of forum shopping? The answer depends in part on whether the likely result is a race to the bottom or to the top – however defined – or simply a distribution of options that allows actors more latitude to pick their own rules and rule-makers. Some analyses of the proliferation of international tribunals implicitly assume a race to the bottom—that is, a dynamic in which forum shopping leads to weaker or worse rules. (Worse, of course, being very much in the eye of the beholder.) But others see a race to the top. A more densely populated international system can lead to fruitful competition among international institutions, including courts. This "competitive multilateralism," may "ultimately be as beneficial for the international regulatory regime as the competition among political interests is for democracy" (Wedgewood 2005; Benvenisti and Downs 2009: 596–97). The existence of multiple forums is certainly good news for complainants, who have more options as a result. Proponents of this view go further, however, and argue that competition "may also improve the quality of rulings and the expediency of proceedings" (Pauwelyn and Salles 2009: 80). "Competitive adjudication" may serve to keep the power and reach of often-insufficiently unaccountable international courts in check (Cogan 2008).

Even if these views are seen as a bit Panglossian, concerns raised by forum shopping in the domestic context do not necessarily transpose to the international plane. Pauwelyn and Salles, for example, argue that some of these concerns, such as the cost to the parties of multiple proceedings, have little bite in the international context where litigation costs are very small relative to the stakes at play and the resources of the players. In a context in which the primary actors are very sophisticated and – most important – may have the ability to create or change rules and institutions, forum shopping seems far less of a concern than it would be in a domestic context. The most significant issue, they argue, is likely to be inconsistent rulings, which may both "leave the dispute unresolved" and threaten the legal system's stability and legitimacy (Pauwelyn and Salles 2009: 82–83). In any event, a persuasive accounting of the costs and benefits has yet to be done, and further study of international forum shopping is essential.

In short, the legal literature raises concerns about proliferation but also highlights advantages. Some political scientists agree. Although a well-designed single regime is usually preferable in terms of regulatory effectiveness, "regime complexes have some distinctive advantages over integrated, comprehensive regimes" (Keohane and Victor 2011: 19).[23] In particular, regime complexes are often more flexible and adaptable; the variegated architecture of agreement within a regime complex may allow for multiple paths forward in an uncertain cooperative climate. This argument is not so different from the notion of "competitive multilateralism." Like Justice Brandeis' famous depiction of the states in a federal system as laboratories for policy experimentation,[24] a less uniform approach to cooperation permits both experimentalism and competition. As multilateral cooperation embraces ever more complicated and technical issues, these features may prove attractive.

Whatever the merits and demerits of rising institutional density, density is unlikely to decrease. For the near term, at least, it seems to be a durable feature of the international system. And so perhaps the most interesting question is: who benefits? The most common answer is that powerful states benefit.[25] Fragmentation, write Benvenisti and Downs, favors the great powers, for it "operates to sabotage the evolution of a more democratic and egalitarian international regulatory system and to undermine the normative integrity of international law" (Benvenisti and Downs 2009: 597). Just as corporations use the threat of exit to extract favorable tax or regulatory concessions from local governments, so too can powerful states more credibly threaten to exit a given international institution in a world in which there are other, similar institutions with plausible jurisdiction over issues they care about.

Perhaps the most dramatic example of this phenomenon is the WTO. The major trading states strategically exited one regime (the old GATT) and entered a new one more to their liking (the WTO). A dense and fragmented international order increases the opportunity for great powers to choose particular forums that favor them or use the threat of exit to enact rules more consistent with their preferences. This ability to choose and to exit and to generally seek advantage in the briar patch of institutions that characterizes many complex issues today is not uniquely the province of the powerful, but it appears far more easily deployed by them. In a related fashion, the powerful can more easily deploy "strategic inconsistency" – the deliberate creation of inconsistent rules and norms in other forums – simply because

---

[23] These advantages are not guaranteed, however; as they note, "dispersed institutions can also be associated with chaos, a proliferation of veto points and gridlock . . ." (Keohane and Victor 2011: 16).

[24] *New State Ice Co. v. Liebmann.* 285 U.S. 262 (1932); c.f. Dorf and Sabel (1998).

[25] But see Alter and Meunier (2009: 14): "sometimes complexity empowers powerful state actors, while at other times NGOs and weaker actors gain for the overlap of institutions and rules."

they have a greater bureaucratic capacity to participate in and strategize about a wide range of negotiations and institutions (Raustiala and Victor 2004). It is no surprise that many scholars point to the most powerful state in the system – the United States – as the most "adroit" at shifting between (and creating new) regimes (Helfer 2004: 17).

There are at least two additional reasons to believe that rising levels of density and fragmentation will favor the powerful. First, the proliferation of institutions can dilute the power of the constructed focal points that institutions so often create and contain, making institutions less effective as organizers of cooperation. That freedom of movement is likely to be more beneficial to the powerful. Paradoxically, a very dense and overlapping institutional order may provide as much freedom of movement to a great power as a thinly institutionalized "state of nature." As hypothesized above, institutional density and freedom of action may exhibit a U-shaped relationship, especially for the strong. Second, and equally important, the transaction costs of cooperation will likely rise as density rises. This again is likely to favor the powerful, who can more readily bear these costs. Together, these factors "create dynamics that favor the great powers more than would be expected under the institutionalist paradigm" (Drezner 2009: 66).

In a similar fashion, by undermining the coherence and therefore the normative force of the international legal order fragmentation is likely to further disadvantage the weak. In other words, fragmentation may limit the fundamental ability of the international order to remain – or become – a rule-based system that constrains the strong as well as the weak. As Teitel and Howse (2009: 966) perceptively put it, "the more so called international law there is, and the more lawyers and judges there are, the less clear and certain this purported law becomes." A more ambiguous or variegated international legal framework is one that cannot be as effectively deployed in lawfare-like efforts to tie down Gulliver with so many regulatory threads. More, in short, may be less.

Courts, of course, are traditionally thought to be relatively neutral venues for dispute settlement, focused on law rather than power; right over might. There may even be some truth to this aspiration, and, to the degree there is, it suggests that the rapid judicialization of international relations ought to influence the assessment of who benefits from rising density and fragmentation. Perhaps whatever advantages the strong gain from, say, the proliferation of negotiating forums may be partially counterbalanced by advantages that accrue to the weak in dispute settlement. But there is some reason for skepticism. In the WTO context, for instance, many have pondered how the move to a more legalized process of dispute resolution has altered the balance between the weak and the strong. In recent work, Busch, Reinhardt, and Shaffer conclude that while there are some benefits for weak states, legal capacity is a serious constraint on their ability to prevail in disputes. In their words, the "greater legalization of the multilateral trade regime poses asymmetric challenges for developing countries, perhaps allaying some concerns over the distribution of economic power, but raising new ones over the distribution of legal capacity" (Busch, Reinhardt, and Shaffer 2009: 576–77).

A final consideration is this: whether rising complexity is welcome or not, is it intentional or accidental? The idea that it is largely unintentional – perhaps, as described above, simply a sort of natural corollary of the growth of cooperation – has a strong intuitive appeal in a vast and complex international system. But there are reasons to think otherwise. The strong case for intentionality is laid out by Benvenisti and Downs (2009: 597–98):

> A fragmented system's piecemeal character suggests an absence of design and obscures the role of intentionality. As a result, it is often considered to be solely the accidental byproduct of historical events and broad social forces. This has helped obscure the fact that fragmentation is in part the result of a calculated strategy by powerful states to create a legal order that both closely reflects their interests and that only they have the power to alter.

If they are correct that intentionality has a strong role to play, their argument opens up a fascinating coda to the literature on postwar order-building by the United States – the most obvious protagonist in Benvenisti and Downs's "calculated strategy." As Ikenberry (2000, 2011) has most famously argued, the United States used its overwhelming power in the wake of World War II to build a variegated and multilateral system that would, by restraining its freedom of action, ultimately husband its strength and extend its dominance over time. The core of that approach was the creation of a set of significant rule-governed institutions that knit together the economic and security interests of the West.

Is the United States pursuing a different strategy today? Turning institutionalism on its head, perhaps it (and perhaps others) may be slowly – and surreptitiously – untying these fetters by proliferating treaties and IOs. This denser system allows the United States, through a diversity of forums, to have much greater latitude to pursue the policies it desires. To what degree this assessment is accurate, and what it means in a world increasingly focused on the rise of powers like China, is a question that ought to be explored in much greater detail (Hachigian and Sutphen 2008; Zakaria 2008).[26]

IV. CONCLUSION

The "move to institutions" that characterized the twentieth century continues (Kennedy 1987). Institutional proliferation may be less dramatic than it was in

---

[26] This strategy may also reflect declining American power, in that a weaker United States may prefer to pursue bilateral and plurilateral cooperation, where it can wield greater influence over outcomes. I thank Richard Steinberg for this suggestion.

the crucial years of the 1940s, but it is undeniable that the international system is more densely populated and fragmented than ever before. Certainly, more rules and, perhaps most important, many more authoritative rule interpreters, exist, and the cumulative output of this strikingly complex system is bewildering.

What these developments mean for international order is a question that has only begun to be asked. Yet, as the international system continues to grow in complexity, this question will become even more significant. The prospect of another great war, and concomitant great reordering, is too terrible to imagine – and, in the view of many, increasingly remote as a practical matter (Goldstein 2011). If that belief is accurate, the international system we have today will not be swept clean as new powers, such as China and India, rise to the fore and cast a new world order on the ashes of the old. The existing system will instead be augmented, layer-cake-like, by new institutions expressly created to address new (or even old) problems and, increasingly, to serve the differing interests of these rising powers. These new institutions will inevitably rub up against or even clash with existing institutions, leading to more overlap, more conflict, and more forum shopping. In short, the most interesting question for the future is probably not whether international institutions matter – they do – nor why they are designed the way they are. It will be how to manage and navigate an international order that is growing ever more complex.

REFERENCES

Aggarwal, Vinod K. (1985). *Liberal Protectionism: The International Politics of Organized Textile Trade* (Berkeley: University of California Press).
———— (1998) (ed.). *Institutional Designs for a Complex World: Bargaining, Linkages, & Nesting* (Ithaca, NY: Cornell University Press).
Alter, Karen J. (2013). "The Multiple Roles of International Courts and Tribunals: Enforcement, Dispute Settlement, Constitutional and Administrative Review," in Jeffrey L. Dunoff and Mark A. Pollack (eds.), *Interdisciplinary Perspectives on International Law and International Relations: The State of the Art* (New York: Cambridge University Press), pp. 345–70.
Alter, Karen J., and Sophie Meunier (2009). "The Politics of International Regime Complexity," *Perspectives on Politics*, Vol. 7, No. 1, pp. 13–24.
Baier, Scott L., Jeffrey H. Bergstrand, and Peter Egger (2007). "The New Regionalism: Causes and Consequences," *Économie Internationale*, Vol. 1, No. 109, pp. 9–29.
Baxter, R. R. (1958). "Jurisdiction over Visiting Forces and the Development of International Law," *Proceedings of the American Society of International Law at Its Annual Meeting*, Vol. 52, No. 4, pp. 174–80.
Benvenisti, Eyal, and George W. Downs (2009). "Toward Global Checks and Balances," *Constitutional Political Economy*, Vol. 20, No. 3–4, pp. 366–87.
Biermann, Frank, Philipp Pattberg, Harro van Asselt, and Fariborz Zelli (2009). "The Fragmentation of Global Governance Architectures: A Framework for Analysis," *Global Environmental Politics*, Vol. 9, No. 4, pp. 14–40.

Busch, Marc L. (2007). "Overlapping Institutions, Forum Shopping, and Dispute Settlement in International Trade," *International Organization*, Vol. 61, No. 4, pp. 735–61.

Busch, Marc L., Eric Reinhardt, and Gregory C. Shaffer (2009). "Does Legal Capacity Matter? A Survey of WTO Members," *World Trade Review*, Vol. 8, No. 4, pp. 559–77.

Charney, Jonathan I. (1998). "Is International Law Threatened by Multiple International Tribunals?," *Recueil des Cours*, Vol. 271, pp. 101–382.

Charney, Jonathan I., Richard B. Bilder, Bernard H. Oxman, and Patricia M. Wald (2002). "The 'Horizontal' Growth of International Courts and Tribunals: Challenges or Opportunities?, " *Proceedings of the American Society of International Law at Its Annual Meeting*, Vol. 96, pp. 369–80.

Charnovitz, Steve (2002). "A World Environment Organization," *Columbia Journal of Environmental Law*, Vol. 27, No. 2, pp. 323–62.

Claude, Inis L., Jr. (1988). *Swords into Plowshares: The Problems and Progress of International Organization*, 4th ed. (New York: Random House).

Cogan, Jacob Katz (2008). "Competition and Control in International Adjudication," *Virginia Journal of International Law*, Vol. 48, No. 2, pp. 411–49.

Davis, Christina L. (2009). "Overlapping Institutions in Trade Policy," *Perspectives on Politics*, Vol. 7, No. 1, pp. 25–31.

Dorf, Michael C., and Charles F. Sabel (1998). "A Constitution of Democratic Experimentalism," *Columbia Law Review*, Vol. 98, No. 2, pp. 267–473.

Drezner, Daniel W. (2009). "The Power and Peril of International Regime Complexity," *Perspectives on Politics*, Vol. 7, No. 1, pp. 65–70.

Dunoff, Jeffrey L. (2007). "The Many Dimensions of Softwood Lumber," *Alberta Law Review*, Vol. 45, No. 2, pp. 319–56.

Fitzmaurice, Sir Gerald (1986). *The Law and Procedure of the International Court of Justice*, Vols. 1–2 (Cambridge: Grotius).

Gantz, David A. (1999). "Dispute Settlement under the NAFTA and the WTO: Choice of Forum Opportunities and Risks for the NAFTA Parties," *American University International Law Review*, Vol. 14, No. 4, pp. 1025–106.

Gehring, Thomas, and Sebastian Oberthür (2009). "The Casual Mechanisms of Interaction between International Institutions," *European Journal of International Relations*, Vol. 15, No. 1, pp. 125–56.

Goldstein, Joshua S. (2011). *Winning the War on War: The Decline of Armed Conflict Worldwide* (New York: Dutton).

Gourgourinis, Anastasios (2011). "General/Particular International Law and Primary/Secondary Rules: Unitary Terminology of a Fragmented System," *European Journal of International Law*, Vol. 22, No. 4, pp. 993–1026.

Guillaume, Gilbert (2000). "The Proliferation of International Judicial Bodies: The Outlook for the International Legal Order," Speech by His Excellency Judge Gilbert Guillaume, President of the International Court of Justice (New York: Sixth Committee of the General Assembly United Nations).

Hachigian, Nina, and Mona Sutphen (2008). *The Next American Century: How the U.S. Can Thrive as Other Powers Rise* (New York: Simon & Schuster).

Hafner, G. (2000). *Risks Ensuing from Fragmentation of International Law*, United Nations International Law Commission, Report on the Work of Its Fifty-Second Session, Fifty-Fifth-session, Supplement No.10.

Hafner-Burton, Emilie M., David G. Victor, and Yonatan Lupu (2012). "Political Science Research on International Law: The State of the Field," *American Journal of International Law*, Vol. 106, No. 1, pp. 47–97.

Helfer, Laurence R. (2004). "Regime Shifting: The TRIPs Agreement and New Dynamics of International Intellectual Property Lawmaking," *Yale Journal of International Law*, Vol. 29, No. 1, pp. 1–83.

_____ (2009). "Regime Shifting in the International Intellectual Property System," *Perspectives on Politics*, Vol. 7, No. 1, pp. 39–44.

Hudec, Robert E. (1987). "'Transcending the Ostensible': Some Reflections on the Nature of Litigation between Governments," *Minnesota Law Review*, Vol. 72, No. 2, pp. 211–26.

Ikenberry, G. John (2000). *After Victory: Institutions, Strategic Restraint, and the Rebuilding of Order after Major Wars* (Princeton, NJ: Princeton University Press).

_____ (2011). *Liberal Leviathan: The Origins, Crisis, and Transformation of the American World Order* (Princeton, NJ: Princeton University Press).

International Law Commission (2006). *Conclusions of the Work of the Study Group on the Fragmentation of International Law: Difficulties Arising from the Diversification and Expansion of International Law*, Study Group on the Fragmentation of International Law, Report (New York: United Nations).

Jenks, C. Wilfred (1953). The Conflict of Law-Making Treaties, *British Yearbook of International Law*, Vol. 30, pp. 401–53.

Kennedy, David (1987). "The Move to Institutions," *Cardozo Law Review*, Vol. 8, No. 5, pp. 841–988.

Keohane, Robert O. (1982). "The Demand for International Regimes," *International Organization*, Vol. 36, No. 2, pp. 325–55.

_____ (1984). *After Hegemony: Cooperation and Discord in the World Political Economy* (Princeton, NJ: Princeton University Press).

_____ (1997). "International Relations and International Law: Two Optics," *Harvard International Law Journal*, Vol. 38, No. 2, pp. 487–502.

Keohane, Robert O., and Joseph S. Nye, Jr. (2001). "The Club Model of Multilateral Cooperation and Problems of Democratic Legitimacy," in Roger B. Porter et al. (eds.), *Efficiency, Equity, Legitimacy: The Multilateral Trading System at the Millennium* (Washington, DC: Brookings Center for Business and Government), pp. 264–307.

Keohane, Robert O., and David G. Victor (2011). "The Regime Complex for Climate Change," *Perspectives on Politics*, Vol. 9, No. 1, pp. 7–23.

Koskenniemi, Martti, and Päivi Leino (2002). "Fragmentation of International Law? Postmodern Anxieties," *Leiden Journal of International Law*, Vol. 15, No. 3, pp. 553–79.

Krasner, Stephen D. (1983) (ed.). *International Regimes* (Ithaca, NY: Cornell University Press).

Lake, David A. (2009). *Hierarchy in International Relations* (Ithaca, NY: Cornell University Press).

Leebron, David W. (2002). "Linkages," *American Journal of International Law*, Vol. 96, No. 1, pp. 5–27.

Palmer, Geoffrey (1992). "New Ways to Make International Environmental Law," *American Journal of International Law*, Vol. 86, No. 2, pp. 259–83.

Patrick, Stewart. (2009). *The Best Laid Plans: The Origins of American Multilateralism and the Dawn of the Cold War* (Lanham, MD: Rowman & Littlefield).

Pauwelyn, Joost, and Luiz Eduardo Salles (2009). "Forum Shopping before International Tribunals: (Real) Concerns, (Im)possible Solutions," *Cornell International Law Journal*, Vol. 42, No. 1, pp. 77–118.

Pevehouse, Jon (2010). "Global Governance Snapshot," *Current History*, Vol. 109, No. 730, inside cover.

Rabkin, J. A. (2004). *The Case for Sovereignty: Why the World Should Welcome American Independence*, 2nd ed. (Washington, DC: American Enterprise Institute for Public Policy Research).

Raustiala, Kal, and David G. Victor (2004). "The Regime Complex for Plant Genetic Resources," *International Organization*, Vol. 58, No. 2, pp. 277–309.

Romano, Cesare P. R. (1999). "The Proliferation of International Judicial Bodies: The Pieces of the Puzzle," *New York University Journal of International Law and Politics*, Vol. 31, No. 4, pp. 709–51.

Ruggie, John Gerard (1993). "Territoriality and Beyond: Problematizing Modernity in International Relations," *International Organization*, Vol. 47, No. 1, pp. 139–74.

Shanks, Cheryl, Harold K. Jacobson, and Jeffrey H. Kaplan (1996). "Inertia and Change in the Constellation of International Governmental Organizations, 1981–1992," *International Organization*, Vol. 50, No. 4, pp. 593–627.

Shany, Yuval (2004). *The Competing Jurisdictions of International Courts and Tribunals* (Oxford: Oxford University Press).

Steinberg, Richard H. (2013). "Wanted–Dead or Alive: Realist Approaches to International Law," in Jeffrey L. Dunoff and Mark A. Pollack (eds.), *Interdisciplinary Perspectives on International Law and International Relations: The State of the Art* (New York: Cambridge University Press), pp. 146–72.

Stokke, Olav Schram (2004). "Trade Measures and Climate Compliance: Institutional Interplay between WTO and the Marrakesh Accords," *International Environmental Agreements: Politics, Law and Economics*, Vol. 4, No. 4, pp. 339–57.

Szasz, Paul C. (1966). "How to Develop World Peace through Law," *American Bar Association Journal*, Vol. 52, September, pp. 851–57.

Teitel, Ruti G. (2011). *Humanity's Law* (Oxford: Oxford University Press).

Teitel, Ruti, and Robert Howse (2009). "Cross-Judging: Tribunalization in a Fragmented but Interconnected Global Order, *New York University Journal of International Law and Politics*, Vol. 41, No. 4, pp. 959–90.

Tennyson, Baron Alfred Tennyson (1881). *The Works of Alfred Tennyson: Locksley Hall, and Other Poems* (Philadelphia, PA: Gebbie & Co).

Tiebout, Charles M. (1956). "A Pure Theory of Local Expenditures," *Journal of Political Economy*, Vol. 64, No. 5, pp. 416–24.

Union of International Associations (2012). "Statistics: International Organizations by Year and Type 1909–1999" (Table 2) Yearbook of International Organizations (Brussels: Union of International Associations), available at http://www.uia.be/statistics-international-organizations-year-and-type-1909-1999.

United States Trade Representative (2009). "United States Initiates NAFTA Dispute with Mexico over Mexico's Failure to Move Its Tuna-Dolphin Dispute from the WTO to the NAFTA," USTR Press Office, November.

Wallace, Michael, and J. David Singer (1970). "Intergovernmental Organization in the Global System, 1815–1964: A Quantitative Description," *International Organization*, Vol. 24, No. 2, pp. 239–87.

Wedgwood, Ruth (2005). "Give the United Nations a Little Competition," *New York Times*, 5 December.

Weiss, Edith Brown (1993). "International Environmental Law: Contemporary Issues and the Emergence of a New World Order," *Georgetown Law Journal*, Vol. 81, No. 3, pp. 675–710.

Young, Oran R. (1996). "Institutional Linkages in International Society: Polar Perspectives," *Global Governance*, Vol. 2, No. 1, pp. 1–23.

_____ (2002). *The Institutional Dimensions of Environmental Change: Fit, Interplay, and Scale* (Boston: Massachusetts Institute of Technology).

Young, Oran R., W. Bradnee Chambers, Joy A. Kim, and Claudia ten Have (2008) (eds.). *Institutional Interplay: Biosafety and Trade* (Hong Kong: United Nations University Press).

Zakaria, Fareed (2008). *The Post-American World* (New York: W. W. Norton & Company, Inc.).

13

Legitimacy in International Law and International Relations

Daniel Bodansky

Over the past couple of decades, there has been an explosion of interest, both among international lawyers and international relations scholars, in the legitimacy of international institutions (IOs) – what Ian Clark (2005: 12) has described as a "veritable renaissance of international legitimacy talk." Studies have:

- historically traced the changing conceptions of legitimacy in "international society" and "world society" (Clark 2005, 2007);
- theorized about the concept of legitimacy (Simmons 1999; Applbaum 2010; Buchanan 2010; Tasioulas 2010);
- advanced general normative conceptions of legitimacy (Buchanan 2003; Buchanan and Keohane 2006; Caney 2009);
- surveyed the legitimacy of different types of international institutions, including global governance organizations (Koppell 2010), international financial institutions (Porter 2001; Woods 2003, 2006); private governance systems (Cashore 2002; Bernstein and Cashore 2007; Schaller 2007); and public–private partnerships (Bäckstrand 2006); and
- examined the legitimacy of particular international institutions, including, among others, the World Trade Organization (WTO) (Howse 2000, 2001; Weiler 2000; Howse and Nicolaidis 2001; Esty 2002; Cass 2005; Picciotto 2005; Conti 2010), the International Criminal Court (Danner 2003), the Security Council (Caron 1993; Sato 2001; Jodoin 2005; Voeten 2005; Hurd 2008), the treaty bodies of multilateral environmental agreements (Brunnée 2002), investor–state arbitral tribunals (Brower 2003; Franck 2005), the Global Reporting Initiative (Beisheim and Dingwerth 2008), the World Commission on Dams (Dingwerth 2005), and the International Organization for Standardization (ISO) (Clapp 1998; Raines 2003).

This recent burgeoning of interest in legitimacy represents a significant shift. Historically, neither international law (IL) nor international relations (IR) had paid much attention to the issue.[1] International lawyers tended to focus on legality rather than legitimacy. And political scientists tended to focus on power and interests, rather than on normative factors such as legitimacy. The newfound concern about legitimacy reflects the growing interest by international lawyers in interdisciplinary studies and the greater openness of political scientists to constructivist perspectives.

Several substantive changes in international relations have contributed to the focus on legitimacy.[2] First, international governance is increasing both in depth and breadth. Second, international governance increasingly affects not only states, but also individuals and other non-state actors. Finally, international governance is increasingly being exercised by private and public–private institutions, as well as by intergovernmental institutions. The focus on legitimacy is one of several responses to these trends toward greater international governance; others include the streams of work on good governance (Woods 1999; Esty 2006), constitutionalism (Kumm 2004; Dunoff and Trachtman 2009; Klabbers, Peters, and Ulfstein, 2009), accountability (Grant and Keohane 2005; Koppell 2010), and global administrative law (Kingsbury, Krisch, and Stewart 2005).

The issue of international legitimacy raises many important questions:

- Conceptually, what do we mean by "legitimacy," and what is its relation to other concepts such as legality, authority, obedience, power, self-interest, morality, and justice?
- Normatively, what standards should we use to assess the legitimacy of IOs? Are these legitimacy standards uniform, or do they vary depending on an institution's issue area and on the type and extent of authority it exercises?
- Descriptively, what standards do different actors (government officials, international bureaucrats, civil society groups, and business) actually use in assessing the legitimacy of international institutions? Are these factors complementary, or do they sometimes work at cross-purposes?
- Causally, what explains why institutions are accepted as legitimate, and what are the effects of these beliefs? How much practical difference does legitimacy make – for example, for the effectiveness and stability of an institution?

This chapter reviews the IL and IR literatures on legitimacy over the last two decades. To a significant degree, these literatures do not divide up neatly. Books on the legitimacy of international governance contain contributions by both international lawyers and political scientists (for example, Coicaud and Heiskanen 2001; Wolfrum and Röben 2008; Meyer 2009). Some important contributions come from other disciplines, such as philosophy (Buchanan 2003; Caney 2009; Tasioulas 2010)

---

[1] An exception is Claude (1966).
[2] For a general analysis of the causal factors responsible for the increasing attention to legitimacy, see Zürn (2004).

or psychology (Tyler 2006), and others involve collaborations among different disciplines (Buchanan and Keohane 2006). In many cases, the work of international lawyers and political scientists on legitimacy is virtually indistinguishable. And, within each field, there is an enormous variety of approaches. Within political science, for example, Ian Clark's historical books on the legitimacy of world society (2005) and world community (2007) bear little resemblance to the more analytical work of Robert Keohane (Grant and Keohane 2005; Buchanan and Keohane 2006). Similarly, within IL, Joseph Weiler's "geological" approach (2004) is strikingly different from the Fullerian approach of Jutta Brunnée and Stephen Toope (2010). So it is possible to describe only broad tendencies, which gloss over the diversity within both fields.

To date, much of the work on international legitimacy has been of a theoretical nature, clarifying the general concept of legitimacy (Steffek 2003; Meyer 2009; Applbaum 2010; Buchanan 2010; Tasioulas 2010) and elaborating conceptions of legitimacy that are appropriate for international institutions, given their differences from domestic governments (see, e.g., Bodansky 1999; Buchanan 2003; Bernstein 2005; Buchanan and Keohane 2006; Esty 2006). These have generally sought to find a middle ground between state consent on the one hand and democratic decision-making on the other, and have focused largely on procedural factors such as transparency, participation, and neutrality.

By comparison, there has been surprisingly little empirical work by either international lawyers or political scientists to determine what standards of legitimacy actors actually apply and how much difference these beliefs make in practice. Instead, most studies assume that normative standards of legitimacy, such as transparency, participation, and representativeness, are, in fact, widely shared; that actors use these standards to assess the legitimacy of international institutions; and that enhancing these factors will help legitimize international institutions and make them more effective.[3] Going forward, more empirical work is needed both on attitudes about legitimacy and on their causes and effects.

Despite many areas of convergence between the IL and IR literatures on legitimacy, important differences also exist. International relations scholars focus on the legitimacy of international institutions rather than of international law. Although many international lawyers share this institutional orientation, some have attempted to develop a more specific theory of legal legitimacy, based on internal qualities of the legal system (for example, whether rules are clear, prospective, and public, and whether they were adopted in conformity with the legal system's secondary rules about norm creation), rather than on the political process by which the rules were

---

[3] Koppell's study (2010) of twenty-five global governance organizations is one of the few works that explores the divergence between what people believe about legitimacy and what standards are actually justified as a matter of normative theory. Other empirically oriented studies include Beishem and Dingwerth (2008), Breitmeier (2008), and Raines (2003).

produced or their substantive outcomes. This concern with what Lon Fuller (1964) called "the internal morality of the law," characteristic of international lawyers such as Thomas Franck (1990) and Jutta Brunnée and Stephen Toope (2010), has no counterpart among political scientists, who have shown little interest in the legitimacy of international law as such.

The study of legitimacy thus stands in contrast to many topics considered in this volume, where IL has been the consumer of theoretical approaches produced by IR scholars. In the case of legitimacy, political science is itself a consumer of theories produced by other disciplines, such as sociology and psychology, and has yet to develop its own theory of legitimacy. Instead, IL has been the more theoretically active of the two disciplines, developing theories of legitimacy based on the concept of "interactional law" (Brunnée and Toope 2010), constitutionalism (Kumm 2004; Klabbers *et al.* 2009), and global administrative law (Kingsbury *et al.* 2005; Esty 2006).

I. THE CONCEPT OF LEGITIMACY

In thinking about the problem of legitimacy, it is useful initially to distinguish (following Rawls) the general concept of legitimacy from more particular conceptions of legitimacy. Often, "legitimate" and "illegitimate" are used simply as terms of approbation and disapproval. For example, people might characterize nuclear power as "illegitimate," meaning not within the bounds of acceptability, or an argument as "legitimate," meaning logically valid. In both political science and IL, however, the concept of legitimacy is usually understood in a narrower way, as relating to the justification and acceptance of political authority (Beetham 1991). A legitimate institution or leader has a right to exercise authority – it has a right to rule (or to use the more common expression, govern) – whereas an illegitimate one does not.[4]

A wide variety of factors might give an actor the right to govern: democratic accountability, legality, religion, tradition, expertise, preservation of order, success in solving collective problems, respect for human rights, and so forth. These different *conceptions* of legitimacy are all consistent with the general *concept* of legitimacy as the right to rule.

If the concept of legitimacy is understood as the right to govern, this raises two questions: first, what does it means to "govern"? And second, what does it mean to have a "right" to govern? The answer to the first question defines the domain to

---

[4] Although most of the IL and IR literatures on legitimacy consider the legitimacy of particular international institutions, such as the Security Council (Caron 1993; Hurd 2008) or the WTO (Howse 2001), some apply the term more broadly to general political orders, such as the Westphalian state system or the Congress of Vienna's balance of power system (Clark 2005), or more narrowly to particular international rules. An example of the latter is Franck (1990), who focuses on the legitimacy of rules rather than institutions.

which the concept of legitimacy is applicable. The answer to the second addresses the nature of the claim being made in calling governance "legitimate."

Obviously, the concept of legitimacy applies to institutions such as the WTO or the United Nations (UN) Security Council. But does it apply to private governance arrangements such as the Marine Stewardship Council? To the exercise of "soft" power? To market-based institutions such as international emissions trading?

International relations scholars have devoted more attention than international lawyers to the problem of defining the concept of *governance* (Bernstein 2010). Although definitions vary, the essence of governance involves making decisions for a collective – decisions that not merely affect others indirectly, but are directed at them and are intended, in some way, to constrain their behavior. The decisions may be general rules intended to guide behavior or very specific decisions related to a specific case. But, in either case, they have a social (other-directed) quality, aiming to substitute the ruler's judgment for that of its subjects. Components of governance include applying and enforcing decisions as well as making them.

Governance can vary widely in its coerciveness. At one end of the spectrum, an institution may use "hard" power to enforce its rule. Although power and legitimacy represent different types of reasons for compliance, the exercise of power is itself legitimate if the actor involved has a right to do so. Power and legitimacy can thus complement one another as bases of governance.[5] At the other end of the spectrum, people may voluntarily accept and be guided by an institution as a result of its soft power. Although nonbinding regimes lack coercive power, they still could be said to "rule" to the extent that they intend their decisions to guide others. Indeed, beliefs about legitimacy are arguably more crucial for institutions exercising soft rather than hard power, since an institution's lack of coercive power means that it must rely more on perceived legitimacy as a basis of influence. That said, the weaker an institution's rule – the less it is able to compel obedience to its decisions – the less legitimacy concerns it raises (Esty 2006). The imposition of sanctions by the Security Council, for example, raises a greater issue of normative legitimacy than the Marine Stewardship Council's environmental standard for sustainable fishing.

A wide variety of actors exercise authority and hence raise an issue of legitimacy, including governments, IOs, expert groups, market actors, and civil society groups. Increasingly, IR scholarship has focused on private or public–private governance regimes (Cashore 2002; Raines 2003; Dingwerth 2005; Bäckstrand 2006; Bernstein and Cashore 2007; Schaller 2007; Hlavac 2008; Koppell 2010). Indeed, it appears that political scientists have focused more attention in recent years on the legitimacy of private governance arrangements (such as the World Commission on Dams, the Forest Stewardship Council, or the supply-chain authority of Wal-Mart) than on public (binding) regimes (such as the WTO, the Security Council, or the

---

[5] Indeed, Reus-Smit (2007: 19) argues that, as a descriptive matter, power and legitimacy are mutually supportive: power helps create legitimacy and legitimacy reinforces power.

International Criminal Court), which have been of greater interest to international lawyers (Caron 1993; Howse 2001; Weiler 2001; Esty 2002; Danner 2003).

The concept of legitimacy can be understood by comparing it with two other bases of influence: rational persuasion and power. *Rational persuasion* depends on convincing another based on the content of a decision. To the extent that an institution exercises influence through rational persuasion, then this does not raise any issue of legitimacy. In contrast, when an institution governs, it substitutes its judgment for that of those subject to its authority. A decision influences behavior not because it persuades its addressees that it is correct, but because it has an authoritative source.

Consider, for example, two very different reasons why the U.S. Supreme Court might follow a decision of the International Court of Justice (ICJ): first, it might be persuaded by the ICJ's reasoning; second, it might view the ICJ as an authoritative source. The second would raise a question about the ICJ's legitimacy – does it have the right to govern vis-à-vis the Supreme Court? – while the first would not. In general, judges attempt to persuade others that their decisions are correct by writing legal opinions; but their decisions are authoritative even if they fail to convince. In saying that a decision or norm is legitimate, one isn't asserting that the decision is correct as a matter of substance – for example, because it is just or efficient. Instead, one is saying that the author of the decision has a right to rule. It is a legitimate authority, whose decisions are entitled to respect.

Legitimacy also differs as a basis for compliance from *compulsion*. Like legitimacy, compulsion engenders compliance independent of whether those subject to an institution's authority agree with its decisions. But, in contrast to compulsion, legitimacy has a normative quality. A legitimate institution has a right to rule; it is "morally justified in attempting to govern" (Buchanan 2010: 85), and this moral justification has normative consequences for those subject to the institution's authority, and also possibly for third parties as well (for example, by creating a duty not to intervene).[6]

II. DISTINGUISHING AND CONFLATING NORMATIVE AND DESCRIPTIVE LEGITIMACY

Why do we care about the legitimacy of international institutions? There are two possible reasons. First, we might want to know whether an institution is worthy of our support. Do we think that the ICJ, or the International Criminal Court, or the World Bank, or the Security Council has a right to rule in its given domain? Does its exercise of authority have some moral or other normative justification? Second,

---

[6] Philosophers disagree about the nature of those normative consequences. What Buchanan (2010: 82) calls the "dominant political view" holds that the legitimacy of an institution – its right to rule – entails a corresponding moral duty to obey on the part of those subject to the institution's authority (Raz 1986; Simmons 1999; Tasioulas 2010). But others conceptualize the right to rule as a power to create legal as opposed to moral duties (Applbaum 2010: 221).

we might care about legitimacy for instrumental reasons – because we think that a legitimate institution is more likely to be effective or stable. The first issue has to do with an institution's normative legitimacy – with whether it has a right to rule as a matter of moral theory. The second issue has to do with an institution's descriptive or sociological legitimacy – with whether its authority is accepted by relevant audiences, such as states and civil society groups; whether it enjoys a reservoir of support that makes people willing to defer even to unpopular decisions and helps sustain the institution through difficult times.

The relationship between normative and descriptive legitimacy is complex. On the one hand, to some degree, descriptive legitimacy seems conceptually parasitic on normative legitimacy since beliefs about legitimacy are usually beliefs about whether an institution, as a normative matter, has a right to rule.[7] People justify, criticize, and persuade on the basis that an institution is actually legitimate (or illegitimate).[8] On the other hand, some argue the other way around, that normative legitimacy depends on descriptive legitimacy. It has an intrinsically social quality and depends on people's beliefs. An institution could not be normatively legitimate if no one thought it so. As Andrew Hurrell (2005: 29) argues, legitimacy is "quite literally meaningless outside of a particular historical context and outside of a particular set of linguistic conventions and justificatory structures. To paraphrase Ronald Dworkin, legitimacy has no DNA."

But the normative and descriptive/sociological perspectives on legitimacy clearly differ.[9] If we ask what makes an institution *normatively* legitimate, the answer will depend on arguments about moral, political, and legal theory. In contrast, if we ask what makes an institution *descriptively* legitimate, the answer will depend on empirical and explanatory arguments about what people believe and why. Normative legitimacy depends on whether an institution *objectively* has a right to rule – whether its claim is in some sense true. It focuses on qualities of the ruler that morally justify its authority – for example, its democratic pedigree, transparency, or expertise. In contrast, descriptive legitimacy concerns whether actors *subjectively* believe that an institution has a right to rule. It focuses on the attitudes of the ruled, rather than on the qualities of the ruler, and thus reflects "not the truth of the philosopher but the belief of the people" (Clark 2005: 18, quoting T. Schabert). An institution is descriptively legitimate when it is socially sanctioned (Reus-Smit 2007: 158) and

---

[7] According to Steffek (2003: 263), both Weber and Habermas viewed legitimacy as "the conceptual place where facts and norms merge, where the de facto validity (Geltung) of a social order springs from a shared conviction about the normative validity of values (Gültigkeit)."

[8] Some writers sever this conceptual link between normative and descriptive legitimacy by including within the concept of descriptive legitimacy acceptance of an institution's authority for affectual reasons or because people simply take the institution for granted (Suchman 1995).

[9] "Legitimacy" is one of the few words that refer both to beliefs and to the thing about which beliefs are held, and a considerable amount of confusion might be avoided if different terms were used to refer to normative and descriptive legitimacy.

when people tend to follow its decisions not because of self-interest or compulsion, but because they accept the institution's right to rule (Hurd 1999).

Which perspective on legitimacy do international lawyers and political scientists take? Although the answer is not always clear, it appears that, for most international lawyers and political scientists, legitimacy is of interest primarily as a basis of compliance and effectiveness. Both disciplines see legitimacy as particularly important at the international level because of the lack of institutions that can compel compliance with international norms. For example, Thomas Franck (1990) begins his seminal book, *The Power of Legitimacy among Nations*, by framing the issue in terms of compliance:

> In the international system, rules usually are not enforced yet they are mostly obeyed. Lacking support from a coercive power comparable to that which provides backing for the laws of a nation, the rules of the international community nevertheless elicit much compliance on the part of sovereign states. Why do powerful nations obey powerless rules? That is the subject of this excursion into power: more precisely, the power which rules exert on states, both the weak and, more remarkably, the strong. (Thomas Franck 1990: 3)

Similarly, Ian Hurd's article, "Legitimacy and Authority in International Politics" (1999: 379–80) – one of the first international relations pieces on legitimacy – begins:

> What motivates states to follow international norms, rules, and commitments? All social systems must confront what we might call the problem of social control – that is, how to get actors to comply with society's rules – but the problem is particularly acute for international relations, because the international social system does not possess an overarching center of political power to enforce rules . . . [T]he idea that states' compliance with international rules is a function of the legitimacy of the rules or of their source gets less attention. . . . In this article, I address those who would ignore . . . the workings of legitimacy in international relations. . . .

The common interest of both international lawyers and IR scholars in legitimacy as a basis of compliance suggests that both disciplines are concerned primarily with descriptive/sociological legitimacy[10] – with whether people think an institution or rule is legitimate – since that is what influences people's behavior. The same is true of other perceived benefits of legitimacy, such as effectiveness and compliance: they are a function of an institution's descriptive rather than normative legitimacy. They depend on whether an institution is perceived as legitimate, rather than on whether it is legitimate as a matter of normative theory.

Some writers make their focus on descriptive legitimacy explicit. Ian Hurd (1999: 381), for example, states: "I am interested strictly in the subjective feeling by a particular actor or set of actors that some rule is legitimate," not the rule's "moral worth"

---

[10] Exceptions include Buchanan and Keohane (2006) and Kumm (2004), who have an explicitly normative orientation.

or "its justice in the eyes of an outside observer." Many writers, however, never state explicitly that they are interested in descriptive legitimacy, so one must infer it from their work. This is true, for example, of Thomas Franck (1990), who does not distinguish in his book between normative and descriptive legitimacy. Similarly, Andrew Hurrell (2005) develops a very useful typology identifying five dimensions of legitimacy – process, substantive values, expertise, effectiveness, and deliberation – but he does not state explicitly whether these are dimensions of normative or descriptive legitimacy.

The failure to specify whether they are addressing normative or descriptive legitimacy reflects the fact that both international lawyers and IR scholars tend to think that the two go together in practice. Although few say so explicitly, most seem to assume that the normative legitimacy of an institution is a good indicator of its sociological legitimacy; that if an institution is normatively legitimate, it will be accepted as legitimate (see, e.g., Zürn 2004; Buchanan and Keohane 2006: 436). For this reason, neither discipline has distinguished much between the two perspectives on legitimacy or has made a serious effort to study legitimacy empirically – for example, through public opinion surveys about what people think would make an international institution legitimate or illegitimate. Instead, both use a methodology that essentially conflates normative and descriptive legitimacy. Initially, they make some simple assumptions about what makes an institution normatively legitimate – transparency, for example, or public participation or democratic decision making. Then, they assume that these are the criteria that people in fact use in assessing the legitimacy of an institution – that is, these normative criteria are the test of descriptive legitimacy. Finally, they examine whether some international institution – say, the Security Council or the WTO or the Forest Stewardship Council – meets these standards and, on that basis, decide whether the institution is legitimate.

Consider, for example, Alison Danner's article (2003) on the legitimacy of the International Criminal Court prosecutor. Danner states that "good process . . . will enhance the legitimacy of the Prosecutor's exercise of discretion" (552) and that, "by contributing to the impartiality and consistency of [the Prosecutor's] decision-making, [guidelines for prosecutorial decisions] will enhance its legitimacy" (541). But, like most writers about legitimacy, she does not provide empirical support for these propositions. Instead, she simply "assumes that, over time, external perceptions of [the Prosecutor's] legitimacy will mirror the Prosecutor's actual practices" (536). On this approach, descriptive legitimacy tracks normative legitimacy and need not be studied separately.

III. CONCEPTIONS OF NORMATIVE LEGITIMACY

When the issue of international legitimacy emerged in the 1990s, the initial instinct of most political scientists was to apply the same standard of legitimacy – that is, democracy – to international institutions as to domestic governments. This led to frequent criticisms of the "democratic deficit" in international governance (Dahl 1999).

Over the past decade, considerable work has been done by both international lawyers and political scientists to articulate less demanding normative standards that might be appropriate for international governance. Part of the motivation for this intellectual move was pragmatic. If international legitimacy requires international democracy, then it is unachievable according to many writers, given the lack of a global *demos* – a community that is the precondition for democracy.[11] In the sphere of nonideal moral theory, we must take this institutional constraint into account. But the move away from democracy also has a normative justification – namely, that international institutions lack the comprehensive authority of domestic governments and therefore do not require as demanding a normative justification (Steffek 2003). Their functions are more akin to those of an administrative agency – hence the recent focus, particularly by international lawyers, on standards drawn from administrative law (Esty 2006) and on the development of a theory of global administrative law (Kingsbury *et al.* 2005).

Although democratic legitimacy seems too utopian to serve as a useful standard, state consent seems too apologetic. State consent was, of course, the traditional basis of international legitimacy: institutions could trace their legitimacy back to the treaties that created them. But most international lawyers and IR scholars now reject state consent as a sufficient basis of normative legitimacy (see, e.g., Bodansky 1999; Weiler 2004; Zürn 2004; Buchanan and Keohane 2006: 412–14). Problems with state consent as a basis of legitimacy include the fact that many states are undemocratic and therefore lack legitimacy themselves, and that state consent is usually given by the executive branch, which lacks legitimate authority to create rules that bind private actors.

In the middle space between global democracy on the one hand and the state system on the other, authors have advanced a wide array of procedural and substantive factors that arguably contribute to normative legitimacy. Political scientists typically classify these factors in terms of whether they contribute to *input-* or *output-based legitimacy*, to use the terminology originated by Fritz Scharpf (1997, 1999). Input-based legitimacy derives from the process by which decisions are made, including factors such as transparency, participation, and representation. Does a decision result from a democratic process, for example? Was there sufficient participation by civil society? Did it involve adequate deliberation? In contrast, output-based legitimacy derives from the results of governance. Does a regime solve problems effectively? Does it reach equitable outcomes? Is it stable? Does it respect human rights?

Perhaps because they are ostensibly concerned with descriptive rather than normative legitimacy, few international lawyers or political scientists delve deeply into

---

[11] But see Moravcsik (2004: 27), who argues that IOs are not significantly undemocratic when assessed against the "real world practices of existing governments."

moral or legal theory in discussing the issue of legitimacy. Habermas' theory of discursive legitimation is perhaps the most prominent input-based normative theory (Steffek 2003), whereas Raz's "service conception of authority" (1986) sets forth the basic logical structure of instrumental, output-based accounts of normative legitimacy.[12]

Instead of focusing on these general theories, political scientists and international lawyers tend to take a more ad hoc approach to normative legitimacy. For example, Allen Buchanan and Robert Keohane (2006) put forward what they call a "complex standard of legitimacy," which combines a wide variety of factors, including substantive (output-based) elements such as minimal moral acceptability and comparative benefit, procedural (input-based) elements such as transparency and institutional integrity (i.e., conformity with an institution's own procedures), as well as a variety of factors that are more difficult to classify, such as channels of accountability to civil society, ongoing consent by democratic states, and various "epistemic virtues."

A more general organizing principle for discussions of normative legitimacy is accountability (Grant and Keohane 2005). Accountability is a broad concept that captures much of what makes democracy normatively attractive, but appears more achievable internationally (Risse 2006). Democratic elections provide one type of accountability, but so can transparency, liability mechanisms, procedural rules, third-party review, and so forth.

Many international lawyers approach normative legitimacy in much the same way as do political scientists, considering a variety of procedural and substantive factors (e.g., Bodansky 1999, 2007). But some have drawn on specifically legal constructs, such as administrative or constitutional law, in developing a more general theory of international legitimacy. Administrative law combines both input- and output-based elements. Input-based legitimacy is provided by procedural requirements such as notice and comment, reason-giving, and review, whereas output-based legitimacy is provided by technical expertise (Esty 2006). International lawyers have similarly argued that constitutionalism can provide a basis for input- and output-based legitimacy: input-based legitimacy by delineating the procedures for how authority may be exercised and output-based legitimacy by imposing substantive limits on what an institution may do (Kumm 2004).

Finally, some international lawyers have sought to develop a theory of what might be called *legal* or *rule legitimacy*, which focuses on features of legal rules and the international legal system more generally. Thomas Franck's seminal work (1990) on "the power of legitimacy in international law" argued that the legitimacy of international law rests on four properties of legal rules: determinacy (clarity of content), symbolic validation (including ritual and pedigree), consistency, and adherence (conformity with the legal system's secondary rules about norm creation).

---

[12] According to the service conception of authority, authority is justified when "we will do better by following an authority than by working out what to do on our own" (Hershovitz 2003: 206).

Although his theory is ostensibly about international law's descriptive legitimacy, his discussion of these factors suggests that most also have a normative character. Similarly, Jutta Brunnée and Stephen Toope's book, *Legitimacy and Legality in International Law* (2010), develops a theory of legal legitimacy that draws on what Lon Fuller (1964) called the "internal morality of the law," including features of legal rules such as generality, public promulgation, prospectivity, intelligibility, consistency, stability, and congruence with official action.

Much of the work thus far on legitimacy seems to assume a single general normative theory of legitimacy. But, as Monica Hlavac (2008: 210) observes, institutions vary in their "capacities and functions, and as they do what legitimacy demands of them may change too." (In a similar vein, see Bodansky 2008.) Going forward, political scientists and international lawyers may therefore need to take a more differentiated, contextual approach in studying normative legitimacy, which focuses on factors such as:

- *The kind of authority an institution is exercising.* For example, legislative institutions would seem to require a different kind of justification – a different basis of normative legitimacy – than judicial institutions. Political scientists have tended to assume a legislative model for international law, and have accordingly seen democracy as the touchstone of legitimacy. In contrast, international lawyers have seen international law more in administrative law terms and have attempted to analyze the legitimacy of international law using an administrative law model (see, e.g., Kingsbury et al. 2005; Esty 2006; Lindseth 2010).
- *The issue area or domain.* For example, in more technical arenas, such as international environmental law or international health, expertise may provide a basis of normative legitimacy. In contrast, in less technical areas, normative legitimacy may depend more on public participation, transparency, and accountability.
- *How much authority an institution is exercising.* As noted earlier, soft power requires less justification than does hard power. Daniel Esty (2006: 1509) develops a two-dimensional model in which legitimacy concerns are a function of the degree to which international governance is autonomous and binding.

IV. THE EMPIRICAL STUDY OF DESCRIPTIVE LEGITIMACY

Unlike the study of normative legitimacy, which involves issues of morality and political theory, descriptive legitimacy raises primarily empirical questions:

- What standards of legitimacy do actors actually use in assessing the legitimacy of international institutions?
- To what degree are international institutions, in fact, accepted as legitimate?
- What are the causal consequences of an institution's perceived legitimacy (or illegitimacy)? Political scientists and international lawyers generally assume that

an organization perceived to be legitimate will have higher levels of compliance and be more stable (see, e.g., Bodansky 1999; Hurd 2008: 202). But is this empirically true? Does a belief in legitimacy cause greater compliance? Greater effectiveness? More stability? Conversely, to what degree do perceptions of illegitimacy undermine a regime's effectiveness and/or stability? How important are beliefs about legitimacy in determining behavior? How do they compare, as a causal factor, with other factors, such as power and self-interest?

• To what extent is "legitimacy talk" sincere and to what extent is it merely a "strategic move in a political game" (Hurrell 2005: 16)?[13] How important is its role in supporting or undermining an institution's authority? Are weak powers able to use legitimacy arguments as a means to "strengthen the legal and moral constraints" on stronger states (Hurrell 2005: 16)?

One potential problem with the concept of descriptive legitimacy is circularity. If descriptive legitimacy is defined in terms of a propensity to comply with rules, then compliance is part of the meaning of legitimacy, rather than something that might be caused by it.[14] In studying descriptive legitimacy, we need to be careful to specify indicators of legitimacy that can be measured in some objective way, independent of compliance. We can then take this measure of legitimacy either as the dependent variable, to explore what factors might cause an institution to be accepted as legitimate (for example, transparency, participation rules, accountability mechanisms, and so forth), or as the independent variable in attempting to explain behavioral compliance or problem-solving effectiveness.

As noted earlier, most writers assume that an institution's descriptive legitimacy is at least to some degree a function of its normative legitimacy, so their theories of descriptive legitimacy are partly parasitic on their assumptions about normative legitimacy. But whether the normative attractiveness of an institution makes it more likely to be accepted as legitimate is an empirical question that cannot be answered a priori. The fact that a policy is normatively justified – say a carbon tax or a single-payer health care system – does not necessarily mean that it will be popularly accepted, and the same is true of institutions.

Some writers posit that various non-normative factors are also important in causing an institution or legal rule to be accepted. Thomas Franck (1990), for example, argues that the legitimacy of international law depends in part on symbolic validation through ritual or pedigree. Similarly, Jutta Brunnée and Stephen Toope (2010) argue that legal legitimacy depends not only on the "internal morality of the law," but also on the degree to which legal rules are congruent with shared social understandings

---

[13] For example, in his study of UN Security Council reform, Ian Hurd (2008: 212–13) concludes that "legitimacy talk" is insincere, "covering up the political interests of states."

[14] For example, Andrew Hurrell (2005: 16) says that "legitimacy...refers to a particular kind of rule-following, or obedience, distinguishable from purely self-interested or instrumental behavior on the one hand, and from straightforward imposed or coercive rule on the other."

and are upheld by official practice. Other non-normative factors that might be relevant to an institution's acceptance as legitimate include the length of time the institution has existed (since trust often takes time to develop), the size of the group over which the institution exercises authority, and the degree to which the group has a shared identity and common values (Steffek 2003: 256; Esty 2006: 1504–05).

All of these, however, are only theories; they have little if any empirical support. How might we go about empirically studying the descriptive legitimacy of an institution and the factors that actually contribute to (or detract from) the institution's perceived legitimacy? Initially, we would need to identify the relevant community of actors. Then, we would need some way of ascertaining their beliefs about whether the institution has a right to rule, why or why not, and what the effects of those beliefs are.

International institutions have multiple audiences and constituencies and affect many different actors. So a wide variety of actors are potentially relevant in determining an institution's descriptive legitimacy. Many studies of legitimacy focus on the attitudes of states. Ian Hurd (2008), for example, focuses on states in examining the importance of membership and deliberation as legitimating factors for the Security Council. The state, however, is an abstraction that doesn't have attitudes or beliefs of its own. So, in assessing the legitimacy of international institutions for states, we must examine the attitudes and beliefs of government officials. In countries with a separation of powers, an international institution may be accepted as legitimate by one branch of government but not another. For example, since foreign relations is largely subject to executive control, the transfer of authority from national governments to international institutions increases the authority of the executive relative to the legislative branch, and this is likely to raise legitimacy concerns primarily among legislators (Zürn 2004: 264).

As international institutions increasingly address what goes on within countries (rather than simply the interactions between states) and are directed ultimately at private conduct, then they raise concerns primarily for individuals (and, by extension, nongovernmental groups) and business – actors that traditionally have had little if any ability to participate or control international institutions, and to whom international institutions have not been accountable. Not surprisingly, many if not most of the critiques of international institutions as illegitimate come from what Michael Zürn (2004: 283) calls the "societal sphere" rather than from government elites, and assessments of descriptive legitimacy focus on the public's beliefs.

Once the relevant actors are determined, how might we go about determining their views about legitimacy? By necessity, any methodology will be imperfect and often it may be impracticable to get the necessary evidence. As Ian Hurd (2008: 213) notes in his study of the legitimacy of the Security Council, "in practice the evidence needed to confirm or falsify [my hypotheses about legitimacy] is unobtainable." Two possible methods of determining beliefs about legitimacy are *opinion surveys* and *discourse analysis*.

Political scientists and psychologists have used opinion surveys and interview data to study the legitimacy of domestic institutions, despite the formidable methodological challenges involved (Weatherford 1992). For example, in a pioneering study, the psychologist Tom Tyler (1990) used interview data to explore why the losing side in litigation often accepted the result. Political scientists have similarly used survey data to study the legitimacy of the South African Constitutional Court (Gibson and Caldeira 2003), the European Court of Justice (Gibson and Caldeira 1995), national high courts (Gibson, Caldeira, and Baird 1998), and the U.S. Supreme Court and Congress (Gibson, Caldeira, and Spence 2005). To avoid the circularity of measuring legitimacy in terms of compliance and then relying on legitimacy as an explanation of compliance, these political science studies devised separate empirical measures of general support for an institution, knowledge about its particular features (e.g., its procedures), and acceptance of the institution's decisions.

Only a few studies have attempted to determine attitudes about the legitimacy of international institutions through surveys (Raines 2003; Koppell 2010). Instead, most studies infer attitudes about legitimacy from the arguments that actors make – for example, the reasons states give for compliance or noncompliance with legal rules (Hurd 1999: 391), the criticisms by civil society groups of international institutions as illegitimate, and the responses by international institutions in trying to legitimate their authority. For example, in response to criticisms relating to participation, accountability, and transparency, the WTO Appellate Body has allowed *amicus* briefs, the World Bank has established the Inspection Panel, and international organizations generally have sought to provide greater information about their activities. Similarly, in an effort to enhance the legitimacy of the Global Environment Facility (GEF), states adopted a new governing instrument in 1994, giving developing countries greater voting shares and making the GEF more independent from the World Bank. Of course, these attempts to enhance the legitimacy of international institutions may rely on mistaken assumptions about what people (or states) want and may therefore be unsuccessful. So we also need to consider the responses to these reform efforts by affected groups, which provide more direct – and presumably more reliable – evidence of their attitudes about legitimacy.

A complicating factor in empirical studies of legitimacy is the possibility that different actors may have different conceptions of legitimacy, leading an institution to be accepted as legitimate by some actors and not by others. Some may see legitimacy as primarily dependent on procedural justice, for example, and others on speed and efficiency. The Security Council may be accepted as legitimate by the "Perm-5" (the United States, Russia, China, the United Kingdom, and France) but not by other states, which have lesser rights of participation and decision-making. Similarly, international financial institutions may be accepted as legitimate by donor countries, but not by the developing world. Or increased participation by civil society groups may increase an institution's legitimacy in the eyes of those groups, but decrease its legitimacy for governments. Standards of legitimacy may also vary depending on individuals' political or cultural views – for example, whether they are hierarchic or egalitarian in orientation, and individualist or communitarian (Kahan and Braman 2006).

In his discussion of the legitimacy of WTO dispute settlement, Joseph Weiler (2001) distinguishes between insiders, who view diplomatic approaches to dispute settlement as legitimate, and outsiders, who want WTO dispute settlement to be more judicial. Similarly, as Jonathan Koppel (2010) argues, factors that enhance an institution's legitimacy – such as neutrality – often make it more difficult for an institution to serve the needs of important states, which may in turn reduce the institution's authority. Along the same lines, Julia Black (2008: 29–30) argues that polycentric regulatory regimes must appeal to different audiences, with different views about legitimacy. Scientists focus on expertise, for example, while the wider society appraises legitimacy in terms of representativeness. International institutions thus construct multiple narratives, according to Black, aimed at different legitimacy communities.

Even the views of a single actor about legitimacy may not necessarily be consistent. The standards that an actor applies in assessing the legitimacy of an international institution may conflict with one another. To take a simple example, procedural constraints that play an important role in establishing an institution's input-based legitimacy may make it harder for the institution to make decisions and thereby undermine its output-based legitimacy.

Ultimately, descriptive legitimacy is important because it is believed to enhance an institution's effectiveness and stability. If actors perceive an institution as legitimate, they are more likely to accept its decisions and comply with them. That, at least, is the theory. But, as with other assumptions about descriptive legitimacy, it needs to be studied empirically. One of the apparently few studies to assess whether legitimating factors such as transparency and participation are associated with greater success for an institution is Beishem and Dingwerth (2008). More empirical works along these lines are needed.

V. CONCLUSION

During the last twenty years, interest in international legitimacy has blossomed. Surveying the period as a whole, three general trends stand out:

- First, an increasing interest in the views of non-state actors, reflecting the growing impact of international institutions on civil society and business.
- Second, an increasing focus on the legitimacy of private and public–private governance, rather than only intergovernmental organizations.
- Third, an intellectual move away from democracy and toward less-demanding standards of legitimacy such as accountability, deliberation, or administrative procedure.

Despite much work by both international lawyers and political scientists, however, our understanding of the subject is still in its infancy. Writers have identified many factors that arguably contribute to an institution's normative legitimacy – transparency, public participation, deliberation, and so forth. But it is unclear whether, even together, these factors provide a sufficient basis of normative legitimacy – whether they would give international institutions a right to rule. Certainly, they leave many key questions about the design of international institutions unanswered, including the composition of decision-making bodies (should they be inclusive or have a more limited membership?) and the appropriate decision-making rules (consensus or some kind of qualified majority voting?).

Similarly, we know very little about what would make international institutions accepted as legitimate. Writers assume that, if international institutions were more transparent, representative, accountable, and so forth, this would engender the diffuse support – the reservoir of goodwill – that is the essence of descriptive legitimacy. But descriptive legitimacy may depend as much, if not more, on affective factors – common traditions and values, symbols, and the trust that can develop only over time. Thus far, most of the writing about descriptive legitimacy is a version of informed speculation. We need more careful empirical work to determine the key factors that contribute to an international institution's perceived legitimacy and those factors' relationship to compliance and effectiveness.

The study of international legitimacy offers an unusual opportunity for collaboration between political scientists and international lawyers. The two fields approach the issue in largely similar ways. And, in contrast to some topics, in which the flow of insights has run mostly in one direction, from political science to international law, each field has something to contribute to the other in studying legitimacy. Political science can assist in the development of more rigorous empirical studies of descriptive legitimacy. And IL can contribute insights about the particular ways that legality itself can be a legitimating force.

REFERENCES

Applbaum, Arthur Isak (2010). "Legitimacy without the Duty to Obey," *Philosophy and Public Affairs*, Vol. 38, No. 3, pp. 215–39.

Bäckstrand, Karin (2006). "Multi-stakeholder Partnerships for Sustainable Development: Rethinking Legitimacy, Accountability and Effectiveness," *European Environment*, Vol. 16, No. 5, pp. 290–306.

Beetham, David (1991). *The Legitimation of Power* (Basingstoke, UK: Macmillan).

Beishem, Marianne, and Klaus Dingwerth (2008). "Procedural Legitimacy and Private Transnational Governance," SFB-Governance Working Paper Series No. 14.

Bernstein, Steven (2005). "Legitimacy in Global Environmental Governance," *Journal of International Law and International Relations*, Vol. 1, No. 1, pp. 139–66.

———— (2010). "When Is Non-state Global Governance Really Governance?," *Utah Law Review*, Vol. 2010, No. 1, pp. 91–114.

Bernstein, Steven, and Benjamin Cashore (2007). "Can Non-state Global Governance Be Legitimate? An Analytical Framework," *Regulation & Governance*, Vol. 1, No. 4, pp. 347–71.

Black, Julia (2008). "Constructing and Contesting Legitimacy and Accountability in Polycentric Regulatory Regimes," *Regulation & Governance*, Vol. 2, No. 2, pp. 137–64.

Bodansky, Daniel (1999). "The Legitimacy of International Governance: A Coming Challenge for International Environmental Law," *American Journal of International Law*, Vol. 93, No. 3, pp. 596–624.

_____ (2007). "Legitimacy," in Daniel Bodansky, Jutta Brunnée, and Ellen Hey (eds.), *The Oxford Handbook of International Environmental Law* (Oxford: Oxford University Press), pp. 704–23.

_____ (2008). "The Concept of Legitimacy in International Law," in Rüdiger Wolfrum and Volker Röben (eds.), *Legitimacy in International Law* (Berlin: Springer).

Breitmeier, Helmut (2008). *The Legitimacy of International Regimes* (Surrey, UK: Ashgate).

Brower, Charles H., II (2003). "Structure, Legitimacy and NAFTA's Investment Chapter," *Vanderbilt Journal of Transnational Law*, Vol. 36, No. 1, pp. 37–94.

Brunnée, Jutta (2002). "COPing with Consent: Lawmaking under Multilateral Environmental Agreements," *Leiden Journal of International Law*, Vol. 15, No. 1, pp. 1–52.

Brunnée, Jutta, and Stephen J. Toope (2010). *Legitimacy and Legality in International Law: An Interactional Account* (Cambridge: Cambridge University Press).

Buchanan, Allen (2003). *Justice, Legitimacy and Self-Determination: Moral Foundations of International Law* (Oxford: Oxford University Press).

_____ (2010). "The Legitimacy of International Law," in John Tasioulas and Samantha Besson (eds.), *The Philosophy of International Law* (Oxford: Oxford University Press), pp. 79–96.

Buchanan, Allen, and Robert O. Keohane (2006). "The Legitimacy of Global Governance Institutions," *Ethics & International Affairs*, Vol. 20, No. 4, pp. 405–38.

Caney, Simon (2009). "The Responsibilities and Legitimacy of Economic International Institutions," in Lukas Meyer (ed.), *Legitimacy, Justice and Public International Law* (Cambridge: Cambridge University Press), pp. 92–122.

Caron, David D. (1993). "The Legitimacy of the Collective Authority of the Security Council," *American Journal of International Law*, Vol. 87, No. 4, pp. 552–88.

Cashore, Benjamin (2002). "Legitimacy and the Privatization of Environmental Governance: How Non-state Market-Driven (NSMD) Governance Systems Gain Rule-Making Authority," *Governance*, Vol. 15, No. 4, pp. 503–29.

Cass, Deborah Z. (2005). *The Constitutionalization of the World Trade Organization: Legitimacy, Democracy and Community in the International Trading System* (Oxford: Oxford University Press).

Clapp, Jennifer (1998). "The Privatization of Global Environmental Governance: ISO 14000 and the Developing World," *Global Governance*, Vol. 4, No. 3, pp. 295–316.

Clark, Ian (2005). *Legitimacy in International Society* (Oxford: Oxford University Press).

_____ (2007). *International Legitimacy and World Society* (Oxford: Oxford University Press).

Claude, Inis (1966). "Collective Legitimization as a Political Function of the United Nations," *International Organization*, Vol. 20, No. 3, pp. 367–79.

Coicaud, Jean-Marc, and Veijo Heiskanen (eds.) (2001). *The Legitimacy of International Organizations* (Tokyo: UN University Press).

Conti, Joseph A. (2010). "Producing Legitimacy at the World Trade Organization: The Role of Expertise and Legal Capacity," *Socio-Economic Review*, Vol. 8, No. 1, pp. 131–55.

Dahl, Robert A. (1999). "Can International Organizations Be Democratic? A Skeptic's View," in Ian Shapiro and Casiano Hacker-Cordón (eds.), *Democracy's Edges* (Cambridge: Cambridge University Press), pp. 19–36.

Danner, Allison Marston (2003). "Enhancing the Legitimacy and Accountability of Prosecutorial Discretion at the International Criminal Court," *American Journal of International Law*, Vol. 97, No. 3, pp. 510–52.

Dingwerth, Klaus (2005). "The Democratic Legitimacy of Public-Private Rule Making: What Can We Learn from the World Commission on Dams?" *Global Governance*, Vol. 11, No. 1, pp. 65–83.

Dunoff, Jeffrey L., and Joel P. Trachtman (2009). *Ruling the World? Constitutionalism, International Law, and Global Governance* (Cambridge: Cambridge University Press).

Esty, Daniel C. (2002). "The World Trade Organization's Legitimacy Crisis," *World Trade Review*, Vol. 1, No. 1, pp. 7–22.

———— (2006). "Good Governance at the Supranational Scale: Globalizing Administrative Law," *Yale Law Journal*, Vol. 115, No. 7, pp. 1490–1562.

Franck, Susan D. (2005). "The Legitimacy Crisis in Investment Treaty Arbitration: Privatizing Public International Law through Inconsistent Decisions," *Fordham Law Review*, Vol. 73, No. 4, pp. 1521–1625.

Franck, Thomas M. (1990). *The Power of Legitimacy among Nations* (Oxford: Oxford University Press).

Fuller, Lon L. (1964). *The Morality of Law* (New Haven, CT: Yale University Press).

Gibson, James L., and Gregory A. Caldeira (1995). "The Legitimacy of Transnational Institutions: Compliance, Support and the European Court of Justice," *American Journal of Political Science*, Vol. 39, No. 2, pp. 459–89.

———— (2003). "Defenders of Democracy? Legitimacy, Popular Acceptance, and the South African Constitutional Court," *Journal of Politics*, Vol. 65, No. 1, pp. 1–30.

Gibson, James L., Gregory A. Caldeira, and Vanessa A. Baird (1998). "On the Legitimacy of National High Courts," *American Political Science Review*, Vol. 92, No. 2, pp. 343–58.

Gibson, James L., Gregory A. Caldeira, and Lester Kenyatta Spence (2005). "Why Do People Accept Public Policies They Oppose? Testing Legitimacy Theory with Survey-Based Experiment," *Political Research Quarterly*, Vol. 58, No. 2, pp. 187–201.

Grant, Ruth W., and Robert O. Keohane (2005). "Accountability and Abuses of Power in World Politics," *American Political Science Review*, Vol. 99, No. 1, pp. 29–43.

Hershovitz, Scott (2003). "Legitimacy, Democracy, and Razian Authority," *Legal Theory*, Vol. 9, No. 3, pp. 201–20.

Hlavac, Monica (2008). "A Developmental Approach to the Legitimacy of Global Governance Institutions," in David A. Reidy and Walter J. Riker (eds.), *Coercion and the State* (New York: Springer), pp. 203–33.

Howse, Robert (2000). "Adjudicative Legitimacy and Treaty Interpretation in International Trade Law: The Early Years of WTO Jurisprudence," in Joseph H. H. Weiler (ed.), *The EU, the WTO, and the NAFTA* (New York: Oxford University Press), pp. 35–70.

———— (2001). "The Legitimacy of the World Trade Organization," in Jean-Marc Coicaud and Veijo Heiskanen (eds.), *The Legitimacy of International Organizations* (New York: UN University Press), pp. 355–407.

Howse, Robert, and Kalypso Nicolaïdis (2001). "Legitimacy and Global Governance: Why Constitutionalizing the WTO Is a Step Too Far," in Roger B. Porter, Pierre Sauve, Arvind Subramanian, and Americo Beviglia Zampetti (eds.), *Efficiency, Equity, and Legitimacy: The Multilateral Trading System at the Millennium* (Washington, DC: Brookings Institution Press), pp. 227–52.

Hurd, Ian (1999). "Legitimacy and Authority in International Politics," *International Organization*, Vol. 53, No. 2, pp. 379–408.

———— (2008). "Myths of Membership: The Politics of Legitimation in UN Security Council Reform," *Global Governance*, Vol. 14, No. 2, pp. 199–217.

Hurrell, Andrew (2005). "Legitimacy and the Use of Force: Can the Circle Be Squared?" *Review of International Studies*, Vol. 31, Supp. S1, pp. 15–32.

Jodoin, Sébastien (2005). "Enhancing the Procedural Legitimacy of the U.N. Security Council: A Normative and Empirical Assessment," *Sri Lanka Journal of International Law*, Vol. 17, No. 1, pp. 1–54.

Kahan, Dan, and Donald Braman (2006). "Cultural Cognition and Public Policy," *Yale Law and Policy Review*, Vol. 24, pp. 147–70.

Kingsbury, Benedict, Nico Krisch, and Richard B. Stewart (2005). "The Emergence of Global Administrative Law," *Law and Contemporary Problems*, Vol. 68, No. 3–4, pp. 15–61.

Klabbers, Jan, Anne Peters, and Geir Ulfstein (2009). *The Constitutionalization of International Law* (Oxford: Oxford University Press).

Koppell, Jonathan G. S. (2010). *World Rule: Accountability, Legitimacy, and the Design of Global Governance* (Chicago: University Chicago Press).

Kumm, Mattias (2004). "The Legitimacy of International Law: A Constitutionalist Framework of Analysis," *European Journal of International Law*, Vol. 15, No. 5, pp. 907–31.

Lindseth, Peter L. (2010). *Power and Legitimacy: Reconciling Europe and the Nation-State* (New York: Oxford University Press).

Meyer, Lukas H. (2009). *Legitimacy, Justice and Public International Law* (Cambridge: Cambridge University Press).

Moravcsik, Andrew (2004). "Is There a 'Democratic Deficit' in World Politics? A Framework for Analysis," *Government and Opposition*, Vol. 39, No. 2, pp. 336–63.

Picciotto, Sol (2005). "The WTO's Appellate Body: Legal Formalism as a Legitimation of Global Governance," *Governance*, Vol. 18, No. 3, pp. 477–503.

Porter, Tony (2001). "The Democratic Deficit in the Institutional Arrangements for Regulating Global Finance," *Global Governance*, Vol. 7, No. 4, pp. 427–39.

Raines, Susan Summers (2003). "Perceptions of Legitimacy and Efficacy in International Environmental Management Standards: The Impact of the Participation Gap," *Global Environmental Politics*, Vol. 3, No. 3, pp. 47–73.

Raz, Joseph (1986). *The Morality of Freedom* (New York: Oxford University Press).

Reus-Smit, Christian (2007). "International Crises of Legitimacy," *International Politics*, Vol. 44, No. 2–3, pp. 157–74.

Risse, Thomas (2006). "Transnational Governance and Legitimacy" in Arthur Benz and Yannis Papadopoulos (eds.), *Governance and Democracy: Comparing National, European and International Experiences* (London: Routledge), pp. 179–99.

Sato, Tetsuo (2001). "The Legitimacy of Security Council Activities under Chapter VII of the UN Charter at the End of the Cold War," in Jean-Marc Coicaud and Veijo Heiskanen (eds.), *The Legitimacy of International Organizations* (Tokyo: UN University Press), pp. 309–54.

Schaller, Susanne (2007). "The Democratic Legitimacy of Private Governance: An Analysis of the Ethical Trading Initiative," INEF Report 91/2007.

Scharpf, Fritz W. (1997). "Economic Integration, Democracy and the Welfare State," *Journal of European Public Policy*, Vol. 4, No. 1, pp. 18–36.

———— (1999). *Governing in Europe: Effective and Democratic?* (Oxford: Oxford University Press).

Simmons, John A. (1999). "Justification and Legitimacy," *Ethics*, Vol. 109, No. 4, pp. 739–71.

Steffek, Jens (2003). "The Legitimization of International Governance: A Discourse Approach," *European Journal of International Relations*, Vol. 9, No. 2, pp. 249–75.

Suchman, Mark C. (1995). "Managing Legitimacy: Strategic and Institutional Approaches," *Academy of Management Review*, Vol. 20, No. 3, pp. 571–610.

Tasioulas, John (2010). "The Legitimacy of International Law," in John Tasioulas and Samantha Besson (eds.), *The Philosophy of International Law* (Oxford: Oxford University Press), pp. 97–118.

Tyler, Tom R. (1990). *Why People Obey the Law* (New Haven, CT: Yale University Press).

———— (2006). "Psychological Perspectives on Legitimacy and Legitimation," *Annual Review of Psychology*, Vol. 57, pp. 375–400.

Voeten, Erik (2005). "The Political Origins of the UN Security Council's Ability to Legitimize the Use of Force," *International Organization*, Vol. 59, No. 3, pp. 527–57.

Weatherford, M. Stephen (1992). "Measuring Political Legitimacy," *American Political Science Review*, Vol. 86, No. 1, pp. 149–66.

Weiler, Joseph H. H. (2001). "The Rule of Lawyers and the Ethos of Diplomats: Reflections on the Internal and External Legitimacy of WTO Dispute Settlement," in Roger Porter, *et al.* (eds.), *Efficiency, Equity, and Legitimacy: The Multilateral Trading System at the Millennium* (Washington, DC: Brookings Institution Press), pp. 334–50.

———— (2004). "The Geology of International Law – Governance, Democracy and Legitimacy," *ZaöRV*, Vol. 64, pp. 547–62.

Wolfrum, Rüdiger, and Volker Röben (2008) (eds.). *Legitimacy in International Law* (Berlin: Springer).

Woods, Ngaire (1999). "Good Governance in International Organizations," *Global Governance*, Vol. 5, No. 1, pp. 39–61.

———— (2003). "Holding Intergovernmental Institutions to Account," *Ethics and International Affairs*, Vol. 17, No. 1, pp. 69–80.

———— (2006). *The Globalizers: The IMF, the World Bank, and Their Borrowers* (Ithaca, NY: Cornell University Press).

Zürn, Michael (2004). "Global Governance and Legitimacy Problems," *Government and Opposition*, Vol. 39, No. 2, pp. 260–87.

PART IV

The Interpretation and Application of International Law

14

The Multiple Roles of International Courts and Tribunals:

Enforcement, Dispute Settlement, Constitutional and Administrative Review

Karen J. Alter

As this volume demonstrates, scholarly interest in international law's intersection with international politics is growing. Much international law (IL) scholarship excludes international courts (ICs) from the conversation, dismissing as irrelevant or dysfunctional the international legal institutions that elaborate and help enforce the law. The proliferation, rising usage, and growing political importance of international courts around the world makes this standard disclaimer increasingly less viable. Many domains of IL – international economic law, human rights law, criminal law, administrative law, and even constitutional law – have become judicialized. The judicialization of international relations (IR) occurs when courts gain authority to define what the law means and where litigation becomes a useful way to reopen political agreements. Negotiations among actors become debates about what is legally permissible, and politics takes place in the shadow of courts, with the lurking possibility of litigation shaping actor demands and political outcomes.

In an effort to broaden the debate about the role of ICs in the international legal system, this chapter draws from a study of the universe of operational ICs, examining ICs as a category of actors. Section I, "The Twenty-First Century International Judicial Order," gives an overview the international judicial system as it exists today. Section II, "The Four Roles of International Courts," describes the four roles that states have delegated to ICs. The *enforcement role* has ICs assessing state compliance with IL. The *administrative review role* involves ICs reviewing the decisions of administrative actors in cases raised by private litigants. The *constitutional review role* has courts assessing the legal validity of legislative and government actions vis-à-vis higher-order legal obligations. The *dispute settlement role* is perhaps the broadest judicial role, in that ICs have the general jurisdiction to issue binding interpretations in any dispute that is brought. After defining the four roles, I map these roles onto the universe of ICs in operation as of 2006, reporting the result of a coding of the statutes where the jurisdictions of the twenty-five ICs are defined.

Section III, "The Theoretical Payoff from Considering International Courts' Multiple Roles," reflects on what the multiple roles of ICs tell us about two debates in the IL and IR scholarship. I use the four roles to argue that courts can be either agents of states or trustees of law, depending on the judicial role. We might perhaps perceive of ICs as agents and states as principals in other-binding judicial roles, although it probably makes more sense to see international judicial oversight as a policy tool used by states to monitor others. But for self-binding judicial roles, such as constitutional review and enforcement, I stick to the argument that ICs are better conceived of as trustees of the law. I build on this distinction between self-binding and other-binding delegation to ICs to argue that, especially where ICs are monitoring the behavior of other actors, compliance concerns recede in importance. I then apply the four-role typology to debates about IC design, arguing that the multiple roles of ICs help us understand why most ICs today have design features that undermine states' ability to control which cases are litigated. Section IV, "International Courts and Democratic Politics," concludes by considering what the four roles of ICs mean for concerns about how delegation to ICs perhaps undermines domestic democracy.

I. THE TWENTY-FIRST CENTURY INTERNATIONAL JUDICIAL ORDER

I am interested in how creating international judicial bodies affects international relations. My study approaches the international judiciary in holistic terms, allowing us to see common political dynamics at play across international legal bodies. I use the Project on International Court and Tribunal's definition of an international court,[1] focusing on permanent ICs because their permanence combines with the public nature of their rulings to potentially create a stronger shadow of the law that can affect international affairs and state decision-making, but I recognize that decisions of quasi-legal and ad hoc bodies can also be authoritative and politically important. This section reports some of the basic descriptive findings from my study of twenty-five operational ICs.[2]

As of 2006, twenty-five permanent international courts were operational, meaning the statutes defining IC's jurisdictions had been ratified, and the courts were ready to receive legal complaints.[3] Figure 14.1 identifies the twenty-five permanent ICs considered in this analysis, organized by the year the court became operational

---

[1] Available at http://www.pict-pcti.org/. Last accessed, September 20, 2011.

[2] For a through explanation of the data sources and coding criteria, see Alter (forthcoming).

[3] Not all of these courts are particularly active, but I want my sample to include all ICs that can receive cases today. The figure does not include at least seven other formally constituted ICs that appear to be dormant, and six hybrid domestic/international criminal tribunals. For the full listing of active and inactive ICs, see: http://www.pict-pcti.org/publications/synoptic_chart.html. This material is updated in Romano (2011).

	Europe	Latin America	Africa	Asia	Pan-Regional
International Economic Courts 17 ICs	European Court of Justice (1952) Benelux court (1974) Economic Court of the Common-Wealth of Independent States (ECCIS) (1993) European Free Trade Area Court (1992)	Andean Tribunal of Justice (ATJ) (1984) Central American Court of Justice (CACJ) (1992) Caribbean Court of Justice (CCJ) (2001) Southern Common Market (MERCUSOR) (2004)	West African Economic and Monetary Union (WAEMU) (1995) Common Court of Justice and Arbitration for the Organization for the Harmonization of Corporate Law in Africa (OHADA) (1997) Court of Justice for the Common Market of Eastern and Southern Africa (COMESA) (1998) Central African Monetary Community (CEMAC)(2000) Court of Justice of the East African Community (EACJ) (2001) Economic Community of West African States Court of Justice (ECOWAS CCJ) (2001) Southern African Development Community (SADC) (2005)	Association of Southeast Asian States (ASEAN) (2004)	World Trade Organization Appellate Body (1994)
International Human Rights Courts 5 ICs	European Court of Human Rights (1958)	Inter-American Court of Human Rights (1979) CCJ[a]	African Court of Peoples and Human Rights (ACtPHR) (2006) ECOWAS CCJ (2005) [SADC can hear national appeals that can involve human right issues; the EACJ envisions adding a human rights jurisdiction]		
International Criminal Tribunals 3 ICs	International Criminal Tribunal for Former Yugoslavia (ICTY) (1993)		International Criminal Tribunal for Rwanda (ICTR) (1994) [Special Court for Sierra Leone is a hybrid international criminal tribunal]		International Criminal Court (2002)
General Jurisdiction 8 ICs	BCJ	CACJ, CCJ	WAEMU, CEMAC, EACJ, SADC		International Court of Justice (ICJ) (1945)
Specialized Jurisdiction 1 IC					International Law of the Sea Tribunal (ITLOS) (1996)
Total courts by region N = 25	6	5	9	1	4 Pan Regional ICs

Date in parentheses is year IC became operational.

[a] CCJ's de facto human rights jurisdiction applies to countries that allow the CCJ to replace the Privy Council as the highest court of appeals.

FIGURE 14.1. Region and Subject Matter Distribution of Active International Courts.

(in parenthesis).[4] Four of these legal bodies are global in reach – the International Court of Justice (ICJ), International Tribunal of the Law of the Sea (ITLOS), the appellate body of the World Trade Organization (WTO), and the International Criminal Court (ICC). The rest are regional bodies located in Africa (nine ICs), Europe (six ICs), Latin America (five ICs), and Asia (one IC). These bodies have jurisdiction to hear cases involving economic disputes (seventeen ICs), human rights issues (five ICs), and war crimes (three ICs), and/or the courts have a general jurisdiction that allows them to adjudicate any case involving any issue where plaintiffs have legal standing to invoke the court (nine ICs). A court can be listed more than once if its subject matter jurisdiction extends beyond a single category. I indicate a second listing by using the acronym only.

The "new" ICs in the sample not only are recent creations but also are qualitatively different entities. I give the name "old style" international courts to those ICs that lack compulsory jurisdiction. When an IC's jurisdiction is not compulsory, states can decide whether to submit to an IC's jurisdiction on a case-by-case basis. "New style" ICs have compulsory jurisdiction and access for non-state actors to initiate litigation, design features that make them far more likely to be activated and to issue judgments in cases in which states are unwilling participants. Of the twenty-five permanent ICs operational as of 2006, twenty-one (84 percent) have at least partial compulsory jurisdiction, thirteen (52 percent) allow international institutional actors to initiate binding litigation, and sixteen (64 percent) have provisions that allow private actors to initiate litigation. These design features explain, in part, why IC usage has also increased. By the end of 2011, ICs had issued more than thirty-seven thousand binding legal rulings. Eighty-eight percent of the total IC output of decisions, opinions, and rulings were issued since the end of the Cold War (1989). Figure 14.2 shows the increased usage of ICs since the end of the Cold War. The data include binding rulings in concrete cases (excluding advisory decisions, interim rulings, appellate decisions, and rulings in staff cases). The figure excludes the European Court of Justice (ECJ) and European Court of Human Rights (ECtHR) so as to better see the growth in litigation by all ICs. Before the end of the Cold War, there were five permanent ICs, in addition to the ECJ and ECtHR – the ICJ (created 1945), the BENELUX court (BCJ, created 1974), the Inter-American Court of Justice (created 1979), and the Andean Tribunal of Justice (ATJ, created 1984). Although it lacked a permanent judicial body the WTO's precursor body (the dispute settlement system of the General Agreement on Tariffs and Trade [GATT]) also existed, and I include

---

4 The founding dates of ICs are actually not easy to pinpoint, as there may be significant time gaps between when states agree to create an IC, when they ratify the necessary treaties, and when the court is actually created. For example, the founding protocol for the Economic Community of West African States (ECOWAS) court was drafted in 1991, ratified in 1995, and became binding in 1996. Yet, only in 2001 were judges appointed and rules of procedure created. For well-known ICs, I rely on the date that most people know as their founding date. For less-known ICs, I use the date when the first set of judges assumed office.

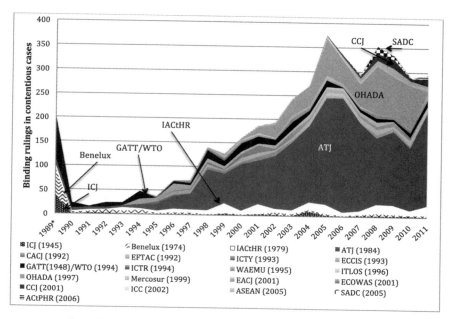

FIGURE 14.2. Growth in International Court Decision Making through 2009 (ECJ and ECtHR excluded). Binding rulings from the IC's founding through 1989. *Source:* Alter, forthcoming.

panel rulings from the GATT era in this count. The first column includes the sum of all international judicial rulings in these five international legal bodies through 1989. The rest of the figure includes litigation for each post–Cold War year from the twenty operational ICs for which I could find data. After the ECJ and ECtHR, the next most active courts are the ATJ (2,197 rulings), the Organization for the Harmonization of Corporate Law in Africa (OHADA) court (569 rulings) and Inter-American Court of Human Rights (IACtHR, 239 rulings), and the WTO legal system (117 GATT-era panel rulings, 176 WTO-era panel rulings) issued by the end of 2011.

If we take litigation as a sign of legal demand, we can see a growing number of litigants seizing ICs in an attempt to influence legal and political outcomes. But we can also see from the narrow bands on the graph that many of the ICs are not very active, often despite having the same design as some of the more active ICs. Sometimes, low levels of activity are easily explained. Some ICs have small memberships, and some oversee a small set of binding rules. Low levels of litigation are also to be expected in the first years of an IC's existence. The level of activity and influence of Europe's Court of Justice and Court of Human Rights today make all other ICs pale in comparison; we forget that, initially, these two ICs were not all that different from today's new ICs. In their first twenty years, the ECJ issued only 558 and the ECtHR only 22 rulings. The lesson: establishing international judicial authority takes time, even in the best of circumstances (Alter 2011*a*).

II. THE FOUR ROLES OF INTERNATIONAL COURTS: ENFORCEMENT, ADMINISTRATIVE REVIEW, CONSTITUTIONAL REVIEW, AND DISPUTE SETTLEMENT

Most of us are familiar with a small handful of international legal bodies and their rulings. These examples loom large in our minds, often defining our understanding of ICs. In keeping with the holistic approach to studying ICs as actors, this section discusses the formal mandates of ICs. International court jurisdictions are defined in treaties, which can be amended over time. There are separate treaty provisions for each jurisdictional role, defining which actors can raise cases, the types of remedies the IC can order, and, in some cases, the scope of legal review allowed.[5] I begin by defining each role, offering examples from international legal systems around the world. Although ICs can end up playing roles that they were never officially delegated, it is nonetheless helpful to understand what states have tasked ICs to do. The jurisdictional grants define the domains of international judges, sending important signals to litigants and thereby shaping the types of legal suits that are raised and the arguments of advocates. Also, the formal grants of jurisdiction represent relative safe zones for ICs, where the assertion of jurisdiction is least credibly contested and where defenders are most likely to rally in support of an IC ruling. Examining IC jurisdictions reveals that these courts have been delegated a broader set of tasks than many people realize.

A. *International Law Enforcement*

Twenty of the twenty-five ICs (80 percent) operational as of 2006 have been formally empowered to oversee state compliance with international rules. The enforcement role involves ICs reviewing the actions of states, public bodies, and, in some cases, individuals, to see whether they cohere with the requirements of IL. International courts primarily name a state practice as legal or illegal, and secondarily authorize remedies designed to compensate victims and create costs associated with illegal behavior. For example, the Court of the Economic Community of West African States found that Niger's government failed to protect Hadijatou Mani from modern-day enslavement, and it awarded her $120,000, which the government immediately paid (Duffy, 2009). The court's contribution to this case was to name the family law practices upheld by national courts as creating the conditions of enslavement, and to specify a remedy.[6] International courts are not unique in primarily flagging noncompliance. Indeed, no court actually enforces its rulings or the remedies judges create. Rather, judges rely on their own authority to encourage compliance, and, if that fails, on the power of others to bring coercive pressure to bear. At the domestic

---

[5] Figure 14.3 reports on the result of coding the treaties where IC's jurisdictional mandates are defined.
[6] *Hadijatou Mani Koraou v. The Republic of Niger*, ECOWAS Case No. ECW/CCJ/JUD/06/08 (Oct. 27, 2008).

level, one can assume that governments will provide support for the enforcement of domestic court rulings because national judges are helping to enforce state law and because coercive power will be employed against individual subjects of the law and not the sovereign itself. With the expectation that states *will* enforce legal rulings, there is perhaps an assumption of coercion behind national legal rulings. Clearly, this assumption does not hold internationally. For most people, this difference – namely, the lack of any international governmental apparatus to enforce IC rulings against states – makes international law unlike domestic law. But, as others have pointed out, the situation of ICs is analogous to the constitutional and public law roles of courts in domestic realm (Goldsmith and Levinson 2009; Hathaway and Shapiro 2011).

As scholars have noted, there are many good reasons for states to commit to international judicial oversight. States might self-bind because they do not trust that future governments will stick to international agreements (Elster 2000). Especially where actors have little faith in national judicial checks, agreeing to international judicial oversight can send a helpful signal to foreign investors, international institutions, foreign governments, and to the broader public that the government is seriously committed to respecting international covenants (Moravcsik 1995; Ikenberry 2001; Cooley and Spruyt 2009). Political leaders may also prefer that disinterested international judges, rather than actors in powerful Western countries or lawyers appointed jointly with private firms, review their compliance with international rules. At least some of these reasons should span time, yet delegating ICs an enforcement role is largely a post–Cold War phenomenon. Indeed, it is more accurate to say that, for many years, states showed an aversion to committing to the compulsory jurisdiction of ICs, preferring instead to require that states first consent before a case proceeded to court (Levi 1976: 70–71). Of the five enforcement systems in existence before the end of the Cold War, only the ECJ had compulsory jurisdiction for its enforcement role. Since the end of the Cold War, however, states have enhanced the enforcement role of many ICs by making their jurisdiction compulsory, allowing non-state actors – supranational commissions, prosecutors, and private litigants – to initiate litigation that reviews state compliance with international law, and expanding the types of laws that are subject to enforcement action (Alter 2011*a*).

Today, one finds ICs with enforcement jurisdiction in all substantive areas where ICs operate. Economic regimes are increasingly likely to include an enforcement role for ICs. Systems modeled on the WTO (including the enforcement system for Mercosur and ASEAN) rely on other states to initiate litigation. Most of the other economic enforcement systems follow the model of the ECJ, often allowing supranational commissions, private litigants, or both to challenge state noncompliance with community rules (Alter 2012). Human rights systems have changed over time. The Inter-American and African Union systems still rely on politically attuned Commissions to vet which cases reach the court. The European Court of Human Rights and Economic Community of West African States Court of Justice (ECOWAS) systems, by contrast, now allow private litigants to initiate litigation directly wherever national actions arguably violate international human rights statutes. International criminal courts rely on independent prosecutors to raise noncompliance cases. Unlike economic and human rights courts that review policies and actions undertaken under the color of state authority, international criminal courts target specific individuals, holding them accountable for committing war crimes and crimes against humanity.

B. *International Administrative Review*

International courts with administrative review jurisdiction hear challenges to the decisions of administrative actors in cases raised by individuals whom the administration's decisions affect.[7] Depending on the standard of review, the judge will be checking to make sure that the administrative decision is faithful to the law, that the administrative decision-maker followed prescribed procedures, and that the administrator had legally defensible reasons for its decision. As of 2006, there were thirteen permanent ICs with administrative review jurisdiction (52 percent of ICs). One finds international administrative review jurisdiction primarily in international economic arenas, where there are supranational regulatory rules and/or supranational administrators charged with implementing international regulatory rules.

The reason to delegate administrative review jurisdiction is to monitor the behavior of administrative actors, who themselves rely on delegated authority. At the international level, administrative review has two forms. International courts can be authorized to hear challenges to the decisions of international organization (IO) administrators, like the European Commission or the International Seabed Authority, or charges that IO administrators failed to act where they were legally required to do so. This type of administrative review usually does not compromise national sovereignty; indeed, it arguably keeps supranational administrators faithful to member state intent.

International courts can also review the decisions of national administrators who are charged with implementing international regulatory rules. For example, the ECJ, BCJ, and Andean courts regularly review national application of common regulatory rules. Where states creatively interpret international rules to promote national policy objectives, international administrative review may serve as a sort of international enforcement system for regulatory decision-making. But, more often than, not international administrative review is not seen as encroaching on national prerogatives. International court review helps to facilitate a uniform interpretation of transnational regulatory rules, providing guidance for domestic administrators and judges regarding new and complex technical legal issues. It provides a legal redress for private actors that fails as often, if not more, than it succeeds, thereby

---

7 Within the specialized world of ICs, the title of "administrative courts" is given to specialized bodies that hear labor disputes involving international employees. Instead, I am interested in international adjudicatory systems that replicate what occurs within domestic administrative review systems.

helping states defend their actions against firm claims of illegalities. For developing countries especially, but even in developed country contexts, it can be helpful to have an IC certify a domestic action as legal or shoulder the blame when a ruling disappoints firms. In the Andean context, the Andean Tribunal's clarification of ambiguous Andean intellectual property rules, its requirement that national administrations give reasons for their rulings, and its willingness to assert the supremacy of Andean rules has ended up improving national administrative decision-making regarding intellectual property issues, and it has helped national intellectual property administrators push back against the political efforts to compromise Andean patent requirements (Helfer, Alter, and Guerzovich 2009: 21–25).

C. *International Constitutional Review*

Constitutional review jurisdiction confers a judicial authority to invalidate laws and government acts on the basis of a conflict with higher-order legal obligations (Stone Sweet 2000: 21). In the international arena, the higher-order laws are usually the founding treaties that "constitute" supranational political systems, and they may also include basic rights protections for member states (Dunoff and Trachtman 2009). There are ten ICs with the formal jurisdiction to review the validity of legislative enactments. Most of these ICs are located within common market systems, where supranational political bodies are empowered to draft and agree to international policies that may be directly binding on member states.

Constitutional review vis-à-vis international acts is a very clear category. But some scholars see IC review of state acts as having a potential constitutional significance. International trade agreements may be elevated to a form of higher-order law, which takes precedence over conflicting national laws and policies. Human rights law is often seen as a higher-order legal obligation, so that the enforcement of international human rights agreements may be seen as largely analogous to constitutional review of state acts. And international criminal law can be seen as creating a higher-order limit on what states are allowed to do as they exercise their monopoly on the legitimate use of force.

Such claims are controversial for a number of reasons. When ICs enforce what are arguably higher-order international laws, they mainly authorize compensation for victims or authorize the punishment of individuals responsible for gross human rights violations. The contested domestic law or policy may even remain legally valid within the national system. Although constitutional law scholars may see analogies between what ICs do and the award of compensation by supreme courts, most people expect constitutional courts to be able to nullify illegal state acts. International courts are, in fact, able to nullify illegal international acts. But IC rulings regarding domestic acts do not invalidate "illegal" national acts. Moreover, many states comply fully with IC rulings by paying compensation while still maintaining the contested practice.

International courts are also considered to be constitutional bodies because of their ability to develop law of constitutional import (Dunoff and Trachtman 2009). The emergence of what might be seen as morphed international constitutional roles with respect to state actions depends, however, on how domestic actors view international legal rulings. If governments or judges see ICs as authoritative, and the laws they apply as supreme, then ICs may be able to foster a culture of constitutional obedience in which state acts condemned by ICs are seen as ipso facto invalid.[8] Like national constitutional courts, the IC will be unable to compel compliance with its rulings, and thus it will rely on evolving public opinion and national mobilization to pressure political actors to respect its rulings (Epp 1998). But where national cultures of international law adherence emerge, national legislators and judges may voluntarily vacate state policies that run afoul of higher-order international laws.[9]

D. *International Dispute Settlement*

International dispute settlement via courts is the archetypical role of ICs. Pretty much all international treaties include provisions for dispute settlement. Usually, the parties can choose nonjudicialized dispute settlement (e.g., arbitration, mediation, good offices), but a specific body is named as a final venue for settling disputes regarding the agreement (often the ICJ or a regional court). Legalized dispute settlement differs from nonlegalized forms in that a predetermined set of judges decides cases based on standing law; the court's ruling will usually be publicly pronounced, binding, and available for nonparties to peruse; and public rulings at least potentially define a legal precedent that can be used going forward. Most often, dispute settlement is triggered by states. But there are some international agreements that allow firms to initiate international dispute settlement to claim rights that exist as part of international treaties.[10]

Most dispute settlement systems are part of an economic and general jurisdiction systems. War crimes bodies and human rights bodies do not include dispute settlement provisions. The ICJ and the ITLOS also have interstate disputes settlement jurisdiction, and, if states consent, the ITLOS system can be invoked by private actors to resolve disputes regarding the seizing of vessels. Figure 14.3 shows that most of the economic systems with dispute adjudication jurisdiction also have enforcement,

---

[8] The term *constitutional obedience* comes from Phelan (2008).

[9] National judges may also serve as filters, pushing back against international law encroachments so as to regulate the effects of global governance on domestic constitutional orders (Alter 2001; Benvenisti 2008; Maduro 2009).

[10] For example, virtually all recent bilateral investment treaties and investment chapters of regional trade agreements, such as the North American Free Trade Agreement, contain provisions authorizing private parties to trigger the establishment of ad hoc arbitral panels that review whether state actions are consistent with their treaty obligations (Goldstein 1996; Franck 2007).

International courts (date created)	Dispute settlement role	Enforcement role	Administrative review role	Constitutional review role
Economic systems				
European Court of Justice (ECJ)/Tribunal of First Instance (TFI) (1952/1988)	X	X	X	X and Morphed role?
Benelux Court (BCJ) (1974)			X	
Andean Tribunal Of Justice (ATJ) (1984)	X	X	X	X
Central American Court of Justice (CACJ) (1992)	X	X	X	X
European Free Trade Area Court (EFTAC) (1992)	X	X	X	
Economic Court of the Common-Wealth of Independent States (ECCIS) (1993)	X			
World Trade Organization Permanent Appellate Body (WTO) (1994)	X	X ——————————————> Morphed role?		
West African Economic and Monetary Union (WAEMU) (1994)	X	X	X	X
Common Court of Justice and Arbitration for the Organization for the Harmonization of Corporate Law in Africa (OHADA) (1997)	X ——————> Morphed role?			
Court of Justice for the Common Market of Eastern and Southern Africa (COMESA) (1998)	X	X	X	X
Central African Monetary Community (CEMAC)(2000)	X	X	X	X
East African Community Court of Justice (EACJ) (2001)	X	X	X	X
Caribbean Court of Justice (CCJ) (2001)[a]	X		X	X
Court of Justice of the Economic Community of West African States (ECOWAS) (2001)[a]	X	X	X	X
Southern Common Market (Mercosur) (2002)	X	X		
Association of Southeast Asian Nations Dispute Settlement Mechanisms (ASEAN) (2004)	X	X		
Southern African Development Community (SADC) (2005)[c]	X	X	X	X
Human rights [a]				
European Court of Human Rights (ECtHR) (1958)		X ——————————————> Morphed role?		
Inter-American Court of Human Rights (IACtHR) (1979)		X ——————————————> Morphed role?		
African Court of Peoples and Human Rights (ACtPHR) (2005)		X		
International Criminal Courts				
International Criminal Tribunal for the Former Yugoslavia (ICTY) (1993)		X		
International Criminal Tribunal for Rwanda (ICTR) (1994)		X		
International Criminal Court (ICC) (2002)		X		
General jurisdiction and Other [b]				
International Court of Justice (ICJ) (1945)	X			
International Tribunal for the Law of the Seas (ITLOS) (1996)	X		Seabed Authority	
Courts with an explicitly delegated role (percentage N = 25)	18 (72 percent)	19 (76 percent)	13 (52 percent)	10 (43 percent)

[a] The ECOWAS court also has a human rights jurisdiction and the CCJ can hear appeals where countries have consented to let the CCJ replace the Privy Council.

[b] General jurisdiction covers any case states choose to bring. The jurisdiction of the International Tribunal for the Law of the Sea, however, will only cover disputes pertaining to the Law of the Sea. See Figure 14.2 for other ICs with general jurisdiction.

[c] Member states revised SADC's jurisdiction in August 2012. Changes were not yet public at the time of publication.

FIGURE 14.3. The Four Judicial Roles Delegated to International Courts (within category by year IC created).

administrative review, and constitutional review jurisdiction. Although the ICs have jurisdiction to hear any case that is validly brought, some international judicial systems clearly expect that most disputes will involve enforcement or challenges to the validity of community acts and thus the other roles of the IC. Dispute settlement in these institutions tends to be reduced to contract disputes with international institutions. Thus, what might be seen as the paradigmatic role of ICs may actually be a secondary or tertiary role for the IC within its legal order. The exception to this argument is the OHADA. This system envisions that private actors will appeal disputes involving the multilateral "Uniform Acts" that govern business transactions within member states.

International dispute settlement can either be noncompulsory – something that both parties must agree to for the case to advance – or compulsory. Where ICs have compulsory jurisdiction, dispute settlement can become a tool used to enforce the agreement, and thus the IC's dispute settlement role can morph into an enforcement role. Eighteen of the twenty-five operational ICs have been delegated dispute settlement jurisdiction (72 percent); of these, thirteen were also delegated the jurisdiction to oversee state compliance with the law (e.g., enforcement jurisdiction). This overlap helps explain why most ICs with dispute settlement jurisdiction have compulsory jurisdiction for this role.

E. *Mapping the Delegation of Judicial Roles across International Courts*

Figure 14.3 reports on the coding of the formally delegated roles of today's operational ICs. The treaties where IC jurisdictions are defined allow more than one role to be delegated to a single court. X indicates that the IC has formally been delegated a given power, meaning that international treaties and protocols explicitly authorize the court to play a given role. I list ICs by their primary subject-matter jurisdiction, but the Caribbean Court of Justice and the Court of Justice of the Economic Community of West African States also have human rights jurisdictions. I also indicate those cases in which scholars see ICs having morphed roles. Judges can engage in judicial law making in all four roles, but it is interesting to note that the places where scholars often suggest that ICs' roles have expanded seem to be more the exception than the rule.

We can see that most of the ICs with dispute settlement jurisdiction (fifteen of nineteen) have also been delegated other roles; most ICs in economic systems have been delegated multiple roles, whereas ICs in human rights and criminal law systems were *only* delegated an enforcement role; ICs with administrative and constitutional review jurisdiction have been delegated more than one role and are mostly located in economic systems with supranational administrators and legislative actors; and nine of the ten ICs that have been delegated a constitutional review role also have an administrative review role.

III. THE THEORETICAL PAYOFF FROM CONSIDERING INTERNATIONAL COURTS' MULTIPLE ROLES

I am interested in the multiple roles ICs play because it allows us to appreciate the many different contributions ICs make to international politics. International courts do oversee state compliance with international agreements, but this is not all they do. Wherever common regulatory rules are to be applied transnationally, policy-makers worry about rules being interpreted and applied differentially across borders. Wherever there are supranational administrators making binding decisions, lawyers and policy-makers worry about how to monitor the international actors to ensure basic competence and as a check against institutional capture. International systems of administrative review are designed to address these concerns. National legislatures and states in federal systems worry that their sovereign rights may be usurped when the executive operates through international institutions. Human rights advocates and national judges worry about unchecked international authority. International constitutional review helps to address these concerns. And dispute settlement does more than resolve legal ambiguities; it transfers private litigant complaints about broken promises to a venue where disinterested actors can investigate the charges and hopefully create some legal finality to the dispute. How do we translate these insights to theoretical debates about ICs and international politics?

This section uses the four IC roles to shine light on two different scholarly debates: whether it makes sense to see ICs as agents of states or trustees of the law, and whether certain legal designs contribute to IC independence, and thereby spur IC activism. Examining the multiple roles of ICs in some respects complicates these debates in that there is no longer a single answer to the question. But it also helps move beyond the disagreeing camps by showing the conditions under which the different arguments gain resonance.

A. *International Courts as Agents or Trustees?*

Scholars disagree as to whether international courts should be seen as agents of states or trustees of the law they oversee. Those who see ICs as state's agents suggest that states are the primary actors shaping IC decision-making, using the threat of relegislation, sanction, or noncompliance to decisively influence judicial decision-making (Garrett and Weingast 1993; Garrett, Kelemen, and Schulz 1998; Stephan 2002; Carrubba, Gabel, and Hankla 2008). Those who see ICs as trustees stress the political autonomy that ICs have, arguing that these courts operate in a realm of rhetorical politics where state sanctioning tools are of little practical relevance (Stone Sweet 2002; Alter 2008a).[11] It is interesting to note that this is primarily an IR debate,

---

[11] *Trustee* comes from the common law practice of *trusts*, where property is held on behalf of a beneficiary and overseen by a designated trustee who has a legal obligation to follow the rules of the trust and act in

reflecting the state-centric perspective that dominates IR scholarship (Hawkins *et al.* 2006). Judicial politics scholars are more likely to consider how a broad range of factors influence judicial outcomes, such as the party in power, the party that appointed the judge, the perspective of powerful interest groups, legal traditions, previous professional experience, and the like (Staton and Moore 2011). American politics and public administration scholars are also less likely to be committed to the idea that states are privileged principals and more willing to conceive of judges as monitors used by governments to watch over the behavior of others (McCubbins, Noll, and Weingast 1989; Kelemen 2011).

The multiple roles of ICs help us to nuance, although perhaps not entirely resolve, the disagreement. Courts can play both self-binding and other-binding roles. In other-binding judicial roles, courts may well be the agents of states. In self-binding roles, however, courts are trustees of the law. I use a stylized narrative from the domestic context to explain how courts can be both other-binding and self-binding institutions.

In earlier times and in smaller societies, there was no delegation to judges; chiefs and kings both made law and served as the interpreters of the law. As territories grew, delegation of interpretive authority became unavoidable. Sovereign actors – those with the authority to make law – primarily delegated dispute settlement authority, the power to make a decision about a controversy or a dispute. While sovereign actors were ceding authority to interpret the law, they were not themselves subject to the interpretations of their judges, mainly because no judge would presume to know better than the sovereign what the law meant. This delegation was other-binding: sovereigns were subjecting others to judicial interpretations of the law. As the state apparatus grew, the role of judges grew. Cases still appeared as controversies that judges were asked to resolve, but when the subject of cases became state actors, judges ended up in a monitoring and enforcing role, reviewing whether the sovereign's other agents (e.g., tax collectors, local rulers, state administrators) were faithfully following the sovereign's laws. Neither type of delegation – dispute settlement or monitoring and enforcing – bound the sovereign, so long as the sovereign himself was never subjected to the jurisdiction of the court.

Thus far, I have only considered delegation in an authoritarian context, where the supreme leader both makes and enforces the law. Constitutional democracy differs from authoritarian rule in that it is premised on the notion of a social contract between leaders and their people. From a social contract perspective, government acts legitimately only when citizens can select their rulers and when governments respect the rule of law. Developments in constitutional democracy led to self-binding delegation, wherein branches of government agreed to limit their powers by binding

---

the best interest of the beneficiary. There are also scholars who give equal weight to law and political factors as they consider how international judges operate within a zone of discretion (Steinberg 2002, 2004; Ginsburg 2005).

themselves to the authority of others, including to the authority of courts.[12] When sovereigns use courts to monitor their agents, as occurs in the administrative review role, delegation to courts remains primarily other-binding. When sovereigns use courts to check their exercise of power, courts help ensure governmental respect of the social compact.

At the domestic level, it is especially easy to see how delegating different judicial roles binds the sovereign in different ways. Courts playing a *dispute settlement* role, hearing private litigant cases, mostly bind others by bringing state law into the resolution of private disputes. In *administrative review*, a judge checks the legal validity of the decisions, actions, and nonactions of public administrative actors, who themselves rely on delegated authority. Administrative actors may find themselves constrained, but that is the point of subjecting administrative authority to judicial oversight. Thus, this role remains primarily other-binding, a tool of the legislatures to police the behavior of administrative actors. Self-binding occurs in the enforcement and constitutional review roles. In the *enforcement* role, a judge monitors police and prosecutors as they use the state's coercive power. Force can only be legitimately used against citizens when it is lawful. *Constitutional review* checks whether the law created by legislatures or interpreted and applied by executive branch actors, or both, cohere with the constitution. These last two roles are pretty much always self-binding and sovereignty compromising, but they also help to reinforce the legitimacy of the sovereign's actions by suggesting that the sovereign is respecting the social compact.

The international level is different from the domestic level in that ICs are often ruling on the actions of sovereign states and their agents. This means that we must amend the above discussion of how judicial roles implicate state autonomy. It is still the case that dispute settlement and administrative review roles primarily bind others, whereas enforcement and constitutional review roles are primarily self-binding for governments. But circumstances can arise in each role that will lead ICs to be issuing interpretations that impinge on national autonomy. Figure 14.4 captures how delegation to ICs has both self-binding and other-binding dimensions. Because all boxes on the table are filled, it may look like ICs are binding states as much as they are binding others. But this would only be true if the number of cases in each box were equal and thus if ICs spent as much time reviewing state compliance with international rules as they did fulfilling the many other-binding tasks they have been delegated.

The larger point is that, even in the international realm, delegation to courts has both self-binding and other-binding dimensions, each of which is animated by a different logic and results in different politics (Alter 2008*a*, 2008*b*). Our preoccupation with national sovereignty often obscures from conversation the useful other-binding roles of ICs, and that self-binding is both intentional and often desirable.

---

[12] Of course, this binding is somewhat fictitious, since the self-binding could be undone through a new constitutional act (see Elster 2000).

	Other-binding situations	Self-binding situations
Dispute Settlement Jurisdiction to hear disputes among specified actors.	Compulsory dispute settlement for transborder disputes between private litigants (e.g., OHADA cases). Compulsory dispute settlement between IOs and private contractors (found in many IOs).	Inter-state dispute settlement. When non-compulsory, states control which cases reach the IC. Compulsory dispute settlement easily morphs into the enforcement role.
Enforcement Jurisdiction to declare state noncompliance with the law.	Ad hoc criminal courts set up by the Security Council and criminal jurisdiction vis-à-vis rebel forces (ICTY and ICTR).	Most international enforcement jurisdiction (trade, human rights, war crimes).
Administrative Review Jurisdiction to review of validity of actions of administrative actors (to ensure procedural regularity and respect for the confines of administrative jurisdiction).	Review of administrative decisions of IO actors (ITLOS, ECJ, ATJ, and others). Review of the national application of international rules (BCJ, ECJ, ATJ, and others) so long as IC review is gap-filling and procedural, leaving fact finding to national actors.	Administrative review that questions administrative fact finding morphs into enforcement.
Constitutional Review Jurisdiction to assess the validity of legislative and executive acts on the basis of a conflict with a higher order legal norm.	Review of the legality of IO actions (ECJ, ATJ, and others).	Review of the legality of state actions (morphed judicial enforcement roles).

FIGURE 14.4. Delegation to International Courts Reflecting Other-Binding and Self-Binding Logics.

The fact that delegation to ICs can be both self- and other-binding has implications for the debate on how compliance concerns shape IC decision-making. In the many places where international legal bodies primarily bind others to follow the law, the interests of ICs and powerful state-principals are likely to align, so that the debate about whether ICs must be concerned about sanctions or compliance with their rulings is largely irrelevant. For example, a coding of every preliminary ruling case sent to the Andean Tribunal of Justice revealed very few cases in which governments intervened to defend a government policy, because most cases involved administrative review of decisions applying Andean intellectual property laws, which governments generally supported (Helfer and Alter 2009; Helfer et al. 2009). Compliance is perhaps more of a concern in constitutional cases and international enforcement cases, although governments may also be happy to let ICs shoulder the blame of angering domestic groups. All of this is to say that compliance is not necessarily the concern that IR scholars expect it to be, which means that threats of noncompliance are not necessarily the political resource that political scientists presume it to be. None of this speaks to whether ICs take into account the legal arguments of governments. But does it really make sense to presume that, without compliance concerns and sanctioning threats, judges would systematically ignore the insight, opinions, and legal arguments of policy-makers?

There is more at stake in this debate than whether ICs are controlled by states. The larger point of contention is whether international judges are able to build and exercise legal and political authority. If ICs are mere agents of states, providing useful information and constructing focal points but nonetheless beholden to the inflexible national interest concerns of governments, there will be very little that international law and ICs can do to influence international politics (Goldsmith and Posner 2005; Posner and Yoo 2005). But if ICs have sufficient autonomy to rule against powerful governments and, by so doing, seriously call into question the legality of government actions, then there is significant room for international law to be a tool to influence international organizations and governments (Goodman and Jinks 2004; Brunnée and Toope 2010) and for litigation to become a way through which legal understandings shift and political change occurs (Alter 2011*b*).

B. *International Judicial Roles and IC Design*

Related to the debate about whether ICs are agents of states is the question of how the design of international legal institutions affects IC independence. Eric Posner and John Yoo argue that those ICs that lack compulsory jurisdiction are more dependent on states wanting to use them. This dependence, they argue, leads ICs to work harder to please governments, especially the governments of powerful states (Posner and Yoo 2005). Although much of Posner and Yoo's analysis is controversial,[13] most agree that ICs with compulsory jurisdiction are in fact more independent, for the reasons Posner and Yoo suggest. At this point, however, most ICs have compulsory jurisdiction and they allow non-state actors to initiate litigation.[14] If Posner and Yoo are right that IC design determines IC dependence on states, and if we presume, as

---

[13] The controversial part of Posner and Yoo's analysis is their claim that dependent ICs will be more effective than independent ICs. It is surely true that where states can block legal proceedings, the only disputes that will be litigated are those in which the state is willing to let the IC determine the legal outcome. For this reason alone, compliance with IC rulings is likely to be higher. Most scholars, however, do not see compliance as a useful measurement of IC effectiveness (Raustiala 2000; von Stein 2013; Martin 2013). Helfer and Slaughter (2005) offer a comprehensive critique of Posner and Yoo's arguments.

[14] Only three ICs out of twenty-five that lack compulsory jurisdiction – the ICJ, ITLOS, and the African Court of People and Human Rights. The Inter-American Court of Human Rights also relies on states opting in to its compulsory jurisdiction, but at this point twenty-two Latin American countries have

most IR scholars do, that states prioritize their control of international actors, then we must wonder why states repeatedly consent to ICs with designs that compromise IC dependence on states?

The four roles help us understand this IC design puzzle. The design of ICs can vary by judicial role. A functional analysis of IC design presumes that states would design ICs to play the roles they delegate to them so that certain judicial roles would bring with them certain IC designs. From a functional design perspective, we should not be surprised when ICs have the design features they need to credibly play their delegated roles. If the IC lacks the design elements needed for a given role, then one must wonder whether states actually intend the IC to play the role. Where IC designs exceed the design features associated with a role, increasing access to the system and the remedies-associated roles, we might want to know more about when and why governments are enhancing the design of an IC. Figure 14.5 identifies design features associated with each role. These features are explained more fully in the study from which this chapter is drawn (Alter, forthcoming). Any IC design that falls into the light gray column corresponds to functional features needed if an IC is to credibly play its designated role. The figure also identifies typical enhancements one finds in busier ICs that arguably help it play its role and the constraints that one often finds in less busy ICs, which usually reflect an effort to maintain control over the legal process. This discussion and coding of IC design is static, obscuring the fact that at least seven ICs, including the most active and politically relevant ones today, have been reformed over time to remove constraints and add enhancements (Alter 2011a). Moreover, one should not equate the existence of enhancements and constraints with the functional effectiveness of such design features. The COMESA legal system has the widest formal access rules of any IC, but litigants never seem to invoke the COMESA system to challenge illegal polices. The ECOWAS system has mechanisms to add sanctions for noncompliance, but they have never been used. And, in practice, the formal requirement that the Dispute Settlement Body endorse WTO panel and appellate body decisions does not serve as a meaningful political check on WTO legal decision-making.

The functional argument expects that ICs with enforcement, administrative, and constitutional review powers will have compulsory jurisdiction, and that ICs with administrative review roles will also have private access. Figure 14.6 identifies the design of ICs within each judicial role, focusing on the features associated with "new style" ICs. Access refers to whether non-state actors have standing to *initiate* a dispute. Gray boxes highlight the functionally required design criteria. If judicial role drives the design of the IC, we should not find it surprising if the gray boxes are marked with an X. White boxes with an X represent a design enhancement feature. The evidence in support of the functional argument comes via correlation. If function were not related to design, we would expect the rules for access and compulsory jurisdiction

---

opted in and withdrawal is extremely unlikely, so that the Inter-American Court increasingly operates under the assumption that its jurisdiction is compulsory (Romano 2007: 820–21).

	Basic Functional Design Elements				
Role	Compulsory jurisdiction	Access to initiate litigation	Remedies	Potential design enhancements	Potential political constraints
Dispute Settlement Jurisdiction to hear disputes among specified actors.	Optional	State access	**Binding rulings**	Compulsory jurisdiction. Private actors authorized to sue governments. Financial remedies.	No compulsory jurisdiction.
Enforcement Jurisdiction to declare state noncompliance with the law.	**Required** Otherwise states would avoid oversight by blocking cases.	State Access	**Findings of noncompliance**	International prosecutorial actor to monitor and pursue noncompliance. Coercive sanctions.	No compulsory jurisdiction. Political controls on prosecutors/ commissions. Requirements of political assent before any remedy can be required.
Administrative Review Jurisdiction to review the validity of administrative actions (to ensure procedural regularity and respect for the confines of administrative jurisdiction).	**Required** Otherwise administrative defendant can avoid oversight by blocking cases.	**Private access to** challenge decisions that affect them.	**Nullification of** illegal administrative decisions; orders for action where administrators have failed to act.	Compensation for injuries incurred by administrative negligence. Preliminary ruling mechanism so that private actors can raise challenges in local courts.	Requiring that governments bring cases on behalf of their citizens in lieu of allowing direct access to the court.
Constitutional Review Jurisdiction to assess the validity of legislative and executive actions on the basis of a conflict with a higher-order legal norm.	**Required** Otherwise legislative defendant can avoid oversight by blocking cases.	**States and Supranational institutions** All constituent units need to be able to challenge *ultra-vires* actions; otherwise, there is no real check against legislative actors doing as they please.	**Nullification of** unconstitutional statutes.	Private access to initiate litigation (e.g., concrete judicial review).	Only states can challenge legality of international acts.

FIGURE 14.5. Design Features for Judicial Roles.

to be more randomly distributed, as opposed to clustered by role. Instead, we can see that ICs with enforcement, administrative, and constitutional review roles are more likely to have the minimum design features of compulsory jurisdiction and access for non-state actors to initiate litigation. It thus seems plausible that the extension of multiple roles to ICs may account at least in part for the trend toward new style ICs.

Of course, nearly all ICs today have compulsory jurisdiction and 85% (21/25) allow non-state actors to initiate litigation. We might thus think that something else

Judicial role and minimum design criteria	ICs with this role	Compulsory jurisdiction	State access	Private litigant access	Supra-national actor access
Dispute settlement Jurisdiction to hear disputes among contracting parties.	ASEAN	X	X	°	
	ATJ	X	X	°	
	CACJ	Partial	X	Limited	Community officials
	CCJ	X	X	Case by case	
	CEMAC	X	X	°	
	COMESA	X	X	°	
	EACJ	X	X	°	
	ECCIS	X	X		
	ECJ	X	X	°	The Commission
	ECOWAS	X	X		
	EFTAC	X	X	Limited	
	ICJ	Optional protocol	X		Advisory opinions only
	ITLOS	Optional protocol	X		
	MERCOSUR	X	X		
	OHADA	X	Advisory opinions only	X	
	SADC	X	X	X	Community officials
	WTO	X	X		
	WAEMU	X	X		
Enforcement Jurisdiction to declare state noncompliance with the law. *Functional design criteria*: Compulsory jurisdiction. Human rights and war crimes system arguably require access for non-state actors. *Enhancements*: Supranational prosecutor or state initiation of litigation. Sometimes private litigant access to initiate litigation.	ASEAN	X	X		
	ACtHPR	Optional protocol	X	Optional protocol	Commission
	ATJ	X	X	X	Secretariat
	CACJ	X	X	X	Any community organ
	CEMAC	X	X	X	Any community organ
	COMESA	X	X	X	Secretary General
	EACJ	X	X	X	Secretary General
	ECtHR	X	X	X	
	ECJ	X	X	Via national courts	Commission
	ECOWAS	X	X	Human rights only	Executive Secretary
	EFTAC	X			Surveillance Authority
	IACtHR	Optional protocol	X		Commission
	ICC	X			Prosecutor
	ICTY	X			Prosecutor
	ICTR	X			Prosecutor
	MERCOSUR	X	X		
	SADC†	X	X	X	
	WAEMU	X	X	Via national courts	Commission
	WTO	X	X		
Administrative Review Jurisdiction to review decisions of administrative actors to ensure procedural regulatory and respect for the confines of administrative jurisdiction. *Functional design criteria*: Compulsory jurisdiction, private access	ATJ	X	X	X	Any community organ
	BCJ	X	X	Via national courts	
	CACJ	Partial	X	X	Any community organ
	CCJ	X	X	X	
	CEMAC	X	X	X	Any community organ
	COMESA	X	X	X	Any community organ
	EACJ	X		X	
	ECJ	X		X	
	ECOWAS	X	X	X	
	EFTAC	X	X	X	
	ITLOS	X	X	X	
	SADC†	X	X	Via national courts	
	WAEMU				

Judicial role and minimum design criteria	ICs with this role	Compulsory jurisdiction	State access	Private litigant access	Supra-national actor access
Constitutional Review Jurisdiction to invalidate acts of legislative and executive bodies on the basis of a conflict with a higher order legal requirement. *Functional design criteria:* Compulsory jurisdiction. Access for participants in the supranational legislative process. *Enhancements:* Private access	ATJ	X	X	X	General Secretariat
	CACJ	X	X	X	Any community organ
	CCJ	Optional Protocol		X	
	CEMAC	X	X	X	Any community organ
	COMESA	X	X	X	
	EACJ	X	X	X	Advisory opinions only
	ECJ	X	X	X	Any community organ
	ECOWAS	X	X		Any community organ
	SADC†	X	X	X	Any community organ
	WAEMU	X	X	X	Any community organ

*Private access pertains only to IO employees and firms that have disputes regarding goods and services supplied to the IO.
†SADC's private access provisions revised in 2012.

FIGURE 14.6. International Court Design and Judicial Roles (organized alphabetically).

explains this trend. But we can also see greater variation in IC designs with respect to design features that are *not* functionally required. The grant of private access for dispute settlement and enforcement roles is far more limited. Although many enforcement and constitutional review systems allow supranational actors to initiate litigation, few administrative review and dispute settlement systems permit these actors to initiate litigation. This suggests that IC design is being varied because of functional requirements, and not because of a greater or lesser desire to create active and independent ICs.

The coding raises many questions, but it does confirm the functional argument. The only exceptions where design does not seem to correlate with function are the Inter-American and African Court of Human Rights, where political constraints still hinder the body's enforcement capacities, and the CCJ's constitutional role, which is quirky because the CCJ's constitutional role is designed to replace the role of the Commonwealth Privy Council. But we also find many enhancements, which suggests that the functional analysis underexplains the design trend.

Why does it matter if function shapes IC design? Many scholars have hypothesized how the design of ICs affects legal outcomes. Posner and Yoo (2005: 6–7) expect compulsory jurisdiction and private access to lead to more judicial activism and less state support for a legal system, whereas Keohane, Moravcsik, and Slaughter (2000) expect international legal systems in which non-state actors can influence the selection, access, and implementation of dispute settlement to generate more litigation, greater compliance with IC rulings, and the deepening and widening of legalization. Stone Sweet (1999) also expects that where interested parties are able to instigate litigation the result will be more judicial law-making, and Helfer and Slaughter (1997) expect that private access will increase the effectiveness of international legal mechanisms. If IC design is an artifact of judicial role, however, then the link between IC design and legal outcome may not be as direct as scholars have hypothesized. For example, one finds compulsory jurisdiction and private access associated with international administrative review systems in all but one international constitutional review system. But my best sense of the data is that one does not find accusations of activist judges in all or even most ICs with administrative and constitutional review jurisdiction.

It could be that the theories are more applicable to IC enforcement roles. Scholars often want to see every review of state action as a form of enforcement. Such a perspective subsumes the notion that governments often choose to use courts to monitor actors within their own states (Kelemen 2011), eliminating entirely the category of other-binding delegation and reinforcing the idea that government and ICs are mostly in an antagonistic relationship. Still, we do not find that IC design shapes judicial law-making in the way that the theories expect. Reviewing the universe of operational ICs reveals that courts with similar designs – like the COMESA, CEMAC, CACJ, ATJ, and SADC courts that share the design of the ECJ and the ECtHR, and the MERCOSUR and ASEAN system that share the design of the WTO – do not share a record for legal activity or judicial law-making. Other factors could be important in shaping judicial law-making (Steinberg 2002; Ginsburg 2005). The larger point is that IC design may be mostly an artifact of judicial role and, for this reason, less shaping of legal and political outcomes than scholars anticipate.

IV. CONCLUSION: INTERNATIONAL COURTS AND DEMOCRATIC POLITICS

Scholars tend to approach the subject of international adjudication with a single example in mind – either a single role, single case, or a single legal regime. This contribution has attempted to broaden our perspective on the role of international courts and international politics by broadly comparing the different roles that ICs have been delegated and, in fact, are playing around the world today. The multiple roles of ICs reveal that these courts do not exist solely to compromise national sovereignty. Delegation to ICs does undermine any individual government's ability to define what international law means, and it creates a rival actor – the IC – that is authorized to define the meaning of international law in concrete cases. But ICs also can be protective of state sovereignty. In their administrative and constitutional review roles, ICs provide checks on the exercise of supranational authority. Administrative review can also help states to defend themselves against private actors that charge them with bias or political interference in the application of law.

The multiple roles of ICs also help nuance conversations about what makes ICs agents of states, and about whether delegation to ICs undermines domestic democracy. If ICs were pure agents of nation-states, then these courts would be unlikely to deviate from what governments want, which might be protective of domestic democracy.[15] But I argued that ICs can also act as trustees of the law in certain circumstances. As trustees of the law, ICs can help to ensure that supranational governance and supranational administrators do not exceed the social contract of the international institution. International court trustees can also, however, interpret the law in ways that the consenting nation-states never intended and that democratic majorities might dislike (Alter 2008a). We need to remember that constitutional review and enforcement roles are intended to create checks on sovereign power. The point of international war crimes and human rights statutes is to prohibit violence against noncombatants, no matter how politically popular such actions may be. But where international legal institutions help transnational legal interests trump domestic interests, international law and IC trustees may be seen as a threat to democracy. In this light, domestic constitutional provisions that demand that IL and IC rulings also respect national constitutional provisions may be the remedy needed to protect national democracy.

I have focused here on the roles states have delegated to ICs, not on whether and under what conditions ICs end up playing their designated roles. The focus on mandate helps us define a baseline from which we can then explore what leads ICs to inhabit a delegated role. We should investigate further how enhancements help and constraints hinder an IC's ability to play its delegated roles. We should also investigate why ICs with similar designs are invoked more or less frequently than we might expect, and thus how context and features woven into the fabric of the law shape IC activation.

REFERENCES

Alter, Karen J. (2001). *Establishing the Supremacy of European Law: The Making of an International Rule of Law in Europe* (Oxford: Oxford University Press).
———— (2008a). "Agents or Trustees? International Courts in Their Political Context," *European Journal of International Relations*, Vol. 14, No. 1, pp. 33–63.
———— (2008b). "Delegating to International Courts: Self-Binding vs. Other-Binding Delegation," *Law and Contemporary Problems*, Vol. 71, No. 1, pp. 37–76.
———— (2009). *The European Court's Political Power: Selected Essays* (Oxford: Oxford University Press).
———— (2011a). "The Evolving International Judiciary," *Annual Review of Law and Social Science*, Vol. 7, pp. 387–415.
———— (2011b). "Tipping the Balance: International Courts and the Construction of International and Domestic Politics," *Cambridge Yearbook of European Legal Studies* Vol. 13, pp. 1–22.

[15] Delegation could still strengthen executive power to the detriment of legislative power, however, and encroach on the prerogatives of states in federal systems.

_____ (2012). "The Global Spread of European Style International Courts," *West European Politics*, Vol. 35, No. 1, pp. 135–54.

_____ (forthcoming). *The New Terrain of International Law: Courts, Politics, Rights* (Princeton, NJ: Princeton University Press).

Benvenisti, Eyal (2008). "Reclaiming Democracy: The Strategic Uses of Foreign and International Law by National Courts," *American Journal of International Law*, Vol. 102, No. 2, pp. 241–76.

Brunnée, Jutta, and Stephen J. Toope (2010). *Legitimacy and Legality in International Law: An Interactional Account* (Cambridge: Cambridge University Press).

Carrubba, Clifford J., Matthew Gabel, and Charles Hankla (2008). "Judicial Behavior under Political Constraints: Evidence from the European Court of Justice," *American Political Science Review*, Vol. 102, No. 4, pp. 435–52.

Cooley, Alexander, and Hendrik Spruyt (2009). *Contracting States: Sovereign Transfers in International Relations* (Princeton, NJ: Princeton University Press).

Duffy, Helen (2009). "*Hadijatou Mani Koroua v. Niger*: Slavery Unveiled by the Ecowas Court," *Human Rights Law Review*, Vol. 9, No. 1, pp. 151–70.

Dunoff, Jeffrey L., and Joel P. Trachtman (2009) (eds.). *Ruling the World? Constitutionalism, International Law, and Global Governance* (Cambridge: Cambridge University Press).

Elster, Jon (2000). *Ulysses Unbound: Studies in Rationality, Precommitment, and Constraints* (Cambridge: Cambridge University Press).

Epp, Charles R. (1998). *The Rights Revolution: Lawyers, Activists, and Supreme Courts in Comparative Perspective* (Chicago: University of Chicago Press).

Franck, Susan D. (2007). "Empirically Evaluating Claims about Investment Treaty Arbitration," *North Carolina Law Review*, Vol. 86, No. 1, pp. 1–87.

Garrett, Geoffrey, R. Daniel Kelemen, and Heiner Schulz (1998). "The European Court of Justice, National Governments, and Legal Integration in the European Union," *International Organization*, Vol. 52, No. 1, pp. 149–76.

Garrett, Geoffrey, and Barry R. Weingast (1993). "Ideas, Interests, and Institutions: Constructing the European Community's Internal Market," in Judith Goldstein and Robert O. Keohane (eds.), *Ideas & Foreign Policy: Beliefs, Institutions, and Political Change* (Ithaca, NY: Cornell University Press), pp. 173–206.

Ginsburg, Tom (2005). "Bounded Discretion in International Judicial Lawmaking," *Virginia Journal of International Law*, Vol. 45, No. 3, pp. 631–73.

Goldsmith, Jack L., and Eric A. Posner (2005). *The Limits of International Law* (Oxford: Oxford University Press).

Goldsmith, Jack, and Daryl Levinson (2009). "Law for States: International Law, Constitutional Law, Public Law," *Harvard Law Review*, Vol. 122, No. 7, pp. 1791–868.

Goldstein, Judith (1996). "International Law and Domestic Institutions: Reconciling North American 'Unfair' Trade Laws," *International Organization*, Vol. 50, No. 4, pp. 541–64.

Goodman, Ryan, and Derek Jinks (2004). "How to Influence States: Socialization and International Human Rights Law," *Duke Law Journal*, Vol. 54, No. 3, pp. 621–703.

Hathaway, Oona, and Scott J. Shapiro (2011). "Outcasting: Enforcement in Domestic and International Law," *Yale Law Journal*, Vol. 111, No. 2, pp. 252–349.

Hawkins, Darren, Daniel Nielson, Michael J. Tierney, and David A. Lake (2006) (eds.). *Delegation and Agency in International Organizations* (Cambridge: Cambridge University Press).

Helfer, Laurence R., and Karen J. Alter (2009). "The Andean Tribunal of Justice and Its Interlocutors: Understanding Preliminary Reference Patterns in the Andean Community," *New York University Journal of International Law and Politics*, Vol. 41, No. 4, pp. 871–930.

Helfer, Laurence R., Karen J. Alter, and M. Florencia Guerzovich (2009). "Islands of Effective International Adjudication: Constructing an Intellectual Property Rule of Law in the Andean Community," *American Journal of International Law*, Vol. 103, No. 1, pp. 1– 47.

Helfer, Laurence R., and Anne-Marie Slaughter (1997). "Toward a Theory of Effective Supranational Adjudication," *Yale Law Journal*, Vol. 107, No. 2, pp. 273–391.

––––– (2005). "Why States Create International Tribunals: A Response to Professors Posner and Yoo," *California Law Review*, Vol. 93, No. 3, pp. 899–956.

Ikenberry, G. John (2001). *After Victory: Institutions, Strategic Restraint, and the Rebuilding of Order after Major Wars* (Princeton, NJ: Princeton University Press).

Kelemen, R. Daniel (2011). *Eurolegalism: The Transformation of Law and Regulation in the European Union.* (Cambridge, MA: Harvard University Press).

Keohane, Robert O., Andrew Moravcsik, and Anne-Marie Slaughter (2000). "Legalized Dispute Resolution: Interstate and Transnational," *International Organization*, Vol. 54, No. 3, pp. 457–88.

Levi, Werner (1976). *Law and Politics in the International Society* (Beverly Hills, CA: Sage Publications).

Maduro, Miguel Poiares (2009). "Courts and Pluralism: Essay on a Theory of Judicial Adjudication in the Context of Legal and Constitutional Pluralism," in Jeffrey L. Dunoff and Joel P. Trachtman (eds.), *Ruling the World: Constitutionalism, International Law and Global Governance* (Cambridge: Cambridge University Press), pp. 356–80.

Martin, Lisa L. (2013). "Against Compliance," in Jeffrey L. Dunoff and Mark A. Pollack (eds.), *Interdisciplinary Perspectives on International Law and International Relations: The State of the Art* (New York: Cambridge University Press), pp. 591–610.

McCubbins, Matthew D., Roger G. Noll, and Barry R. Weingast (1989). "Structure and Process, Politics and Policy: Administrative Arrangements and the Political Control of Agencies," *Virginia Law Review*, Vol. 75, No. 2, pp. 431–82.

Moravcsik, Andrew (1995). "Explaining International Human Rights Regimes: Liberal Theory and Western Europe," *European Journal of International Relations*, Vol. 1, No. 2, pp. 157–89.

Phelan, William (2008). "Why Do EU Member States Offer a 'Constitutional' Obedience to EU Obligations? Encompassing Domestic Institutions and Costly International Obligations," Discussion Paper No. 256 (Dublin: Trinity College Dublin, Institute for International Integration Studies).

Posner, Eric A., and John C. Yoo (2005). "Judicial Independence in International Tribunals," *California Law Review*, Vol. 93, No. 1, pp. 1–74.

Raustiala, Kal (2000). "Compliance & Effectiveness in International Regulatory Cooperation," *Case Western Reserve Journal of International Law*, Vol. 32, No. 3, pp. 387–440.

Romano, Cesare P. R. (2007). "The Shift from the Consensual to the Compulsory Paradigm in International Adjudication: Elements for a Theory of Consent," *New York University Journal of International Law and Politics*, Vol. 39, No. 4, pp. 791–872.

––––– (2011). "A Taxonomy of International Rule of Law Institutions," *Journal of International Dispute Settlement*, Vol. 2, No. 1, pp. 241–77.

Staton, Jeffrey K., and Will H. Moore (2011). "Judicial Power in Domestic and International Politics," *International Organization*, Vol. 65, No. 3, pp. 553–87.

Steinberg, Richard H. (2002). "In the Shadow of Law or Power? Consensus-Based Bargaining and Outcomes in the GATT/WTO," *International Organization*, Vol. 56, No. 2, pp. 339–74.

––––– (2004). "Judicial Lawmaking at the WTO: Discursive, Constitutional, and Political Constraints," *American Journal of International Law*, Vol. 98, No. 2, pp. 247–75.

Stephan, Paul B. (2002). "Courts, Tribunals, and Legal Unification–the Agency Problem," *Chicago Journal of International Law*, Vol. 3, No. 2, pp. 333–52.

Stone Sweet, Alec (1999). "Judicialization and the Construction of Governance," *Comparative Political Studies*, Vol. 32, No. 2, pp. 147–84.

———— (2000). *Governing with Judges: Constitutional Politics in Europe* (Oxford: Oxford University Press).

———— (2002). "Constitutional Courts and Parliamentary Democracy," *West European Politics*, Vol. 25, No. 1, pp. 77–100.

von Stein, Jana (2013). "The Engines of Compliance," in Jeffrey L. Dunoff and Mark A. Pollack (eds.), *Interdisciplinary Perspectives on International Law and International Relations: The State of the Art* (New York: Cambridge University Press), pp. 477–501.

15

The Design of Dispute Settlement Procedures in International Agreements

Barbara Koremenos and Timm Betz

What explains the inclusion of formal dispute settlement procedures in international agreements? Delegating any kind of decision-making comes at a significant sovereignty cost, as Abbott and Snidal (2000: 436) note. From this perspective, instances of delegation are puzzling. Some legal scholars, however, argue that international law becomes more effective the more "lawlike" it is. Helfer and Slaughter (1997: 283), for instance, regard international tribunals as an integral part of "a global community of law." From this perspective, the absence of dispute resolution mechanisms in some agreements is what begs an explanation.

Based on game theory insights, Koremenos (2007) argues that the inclusion of dispute settlement procedures in international agreements is a deliberate choice by governments, made to address specific cooperation problems. The implication is that international law is designed efficiently: dispute settlement procedures are likely to be incorporated into agreements if, but only if, they are needed to solve specific problems. Her data confirm this viewpoint.

Yet, some empirical observations potentially undermine this conclusion. Many formal dispute resolution mechanisms are rarely invoked in practice. This pattern is reinforced by the many agreements that couple formal dispute resolution mechanisms with explicit encouragements to settle informally through, for instance, "friendly" negotiations.[1] Additionally, many formal dispute settlement mechanisms contain options to reject settlements lawfully, thereby rendering the formal mechanisms noncompulsory. Finally, states may attach reservations to their agreements,

The authors are grateful for detailed comments from Jeff Dunoff and Mark Pollack. The material in this chapter is based on research supported by the National Science Foundation under Grant No. 0801581.

[1] In the following, this is what we refer to as "informal dispute resolution" – an explicit provision in the agreement encouraging informal modes of dispute resolution, such as friendly negotiations or diplomacy. Of course, this possibility always exists. However, not all agreements encourage it explicitly. In contrast, we define formal dispute settlement procedures as those engaging a third party in mediation, arbitration, and/or adjudication.

releasing themselves perhaps from the most onerous obligations from their perspective or, more to the point of this chapter, exempting them from compulsory dispute settlement procedures; the United States, in particular, makes active use of such reservations (Henkin 1995). Given these empirical observations, one could argue that dispute settlement mechanisms are, in reality, nothing more than a fig leaf. Although incorporated into agreements, their existence is undermined by reservations and restrictions. The agreements would thus be inefficient, and formal dispute settlement mechanisms ineffective.

This chapter argues that we need to distinguish carefully between the use of dispute settlement mechanisms and their effects. Even if they are rarely invoked, dispute settlement procedures facilitate cooperation. They screen states at the stage of treaty ratification, reducing the likelihood that disputes break out. And, by providing enforcement power, they constrain states once an agreement comes into force, again reducing the likelihood of disputes. Thus, two mechanisms are at work: one regarding the selection of participating states and one regarding the selection of defections. Together, they imply that the infrequent use of dispute settlement mechanisms may be a consequence of properly functioning, carefully designed agreements, not an indication of their failure.

We also counter arguments that informal settlements and reservations are imperiling the functioning of compulsory dispute settlement procedures. First, although we document that informal settlements are explicitly encouraged in the vast majority of agreements with formal procedures, we argue that such informal settlements also take place in the shadow of these more legalized mechanisms. By providing a credible outside option, the presence of formal dispute settlement procedures likely affects the outcome of informal settlements, just as it does in the domestic context (see Muthoo 2002). Second, we show that agreements with formal dispute settlement procedures are less likely to allow for reservations. There is little reason to be concerned that reservations undermine the purpose and functioning of dispute resolution mechanisms on a large scale. Still, how reservations affect the functioning of dispute settlement provisions is an empirical question that deserves more analysis.

The next section reviews some of the recent literature on the design of dispute resolution mechanisms. We then build on rational design (Koremenos, Lipson, and Snidal 2001) to derive conjectures about the design of dispute settlement mechanisms and test these empirically. Speaking to a long-standing debate in the literature, we present new results suggesting that highly legalized dispute settlement mechanisms are used for the solution of punishment problems, and perhaps less so for information provision. By contrast, the explicit encouragement of informal settlements as the least legalized form of dispute resolution is strongly associated with informational problems. We then address the effectiveness of dispute resolution mechanisms, even if they are invoked infrequently, and the role of reservations.

I. WHAT HAS BEEN DONE SO FAR?

Over the last decade, the role of dispute resolution mechanisms has received substantial attention in the literature. In a special issue of *International Organization*, Goldstein *et al.* highlight the delegation of "broad authority to a neutral entity for implementation of the agreed rules" (2000: 387) as one of three key dimensions of legalization in international agreements; notably, the authors argue that delegation often concerns the settlement of disputes about and interpretation of agreed-upon rules.

To date, states have negotiated numerous agreements that either delegate dispute resolution authority to a preexisting body or create their own authority for dispute resolution. Nonetheless, most of these agreements have received little if any scholarly attention. Rather, a few prominent agreements are the subject of extensive literatures, for example, the International Court of Justice (ICJ), the North American Free Trade Agreement, the European Court of Justice, and the dispute settlement mechanism of the General Agreement on Tariffs and Trade, which underwent substantial revisions in the transition to the World Trade Organization (WTO).

The literature on the WTO greatly advanced our understanding of many facets of international dispute settlements but is also emblematic of two shortcomings of the field. First, single agreements, and often only one or two very specific details of an agreement, feature prominently. Although providing a holistic picture of a single institution, the extent to which findings can be generalized is limited. Grando (2006), for instance, examines the allocation of the burden of proof in the WTO's dispute settlement system and derives policy prescriptions from her analysis. Of course, there is much to be gained from paying close attention to such details, especially when done in a theoretically informed manner. An exemplary piece in this regard is Brutger's (2011) analysis of how the participation of private parties affects the selection of complaints in the WTO and how this, in turn, helps explain the perceived dominance of resource-rich countries in the WTO's dispute settlement procedures. Thus, a rather minor design feature – the possibility of private contributions to litigation costs – has far-reaching implications for the pattern of observed disputes.

At the same time, the literature would benefit from more systematic comparative research. Illustrative of the advantages of such an approach is the paper by Helfer and Slaughter (1997) on supranational adjudication. They distill a number of conditions that contribute to effective supranational adjudication and apply this inductively derived theory to explain other cases of adjudication as well. Helfer and Slaughter's work is an impressive improvement with respect to large parts of the literature. It also underscores a substantial difference between the international law (IL) and international relations (IR) literatures. Although the former typically welcomes international adjudication and strives to promote its spread and effectiveness (for a critical discussion, see the introduction in Posner and Yoo [2005]), most political scientists assume a more distanced position, assessing the effects and effectiveness of adjudication (e.g., Huth, Croco, and Appel 2011).

Second, most authors examine the implications of the WTO for its participants (Busch and Reinhardt 2003), make normative prescriptions (Barceló 2009), or remain largely descriptive (Charnovitz 2009). By contrast, few scholars attempt to explain systematically the design choices made by states (for exceptions, see J. Smith 2000; Rosendorff 2005; Betz 2011). This is the more surprising given that a large group of scholars seems dismayed over imbalances in the workings of the WTO dispute settlement system that are thought to disfavor small poor economies (Busch and Reinhardt 2003; Kim 2008) – although there is some evidence that, over time, countries may acquire the necessary expertise and infrastructure to participate effectively in the dispute settlement mechanism (Davis and Bermeo 2009).

This inattention to broader institutional design issues is found not only in the context of the WTO but also in the study of international agreements more generally. In particular, we know little about what affects the choice of the specific form of dispute settlement procedures. In the following, we address these points, examining what accounts for the choice and design of dispute settlement mechanisms in international agreements. In particular, the analysis is concerned not just with a few select, albeit important, cases, but generates general results, based on quantitative comparisons across a random sample of international agreements that features four distinct issue areas.

II. WHY DELEGATE, AND TO WHOM?

A. *Two Ideal-Type Perspectives and a Puzzle*

The extant literature offers two very different takes on the delegation of dispute resolution. At one end of the spectrum, traditional realists argue that states comply with international law only when it is in their "national interest" to do so (Krasner 1978) and that institutions "have minimal influence on state behavior" (Mearsheimer 1994: 7). A variant of this view is that international law does not change behavior because states enter into only those agreements that already align with their interests (Downs, Rocke, and Barsoom 1996). Consequently, it is irrelevant whether international agreements contain dispute resolution mechanisms. If this view is correct, one would expect to see the inclusion of dispute resolution mechanisms either in random patterns across agreements or not at all if the negotiation of dispute resolution mechanisms comes at any cost. Furthermore, since states' interests are presumably so aligned, we would expect that dispute resolution mechanisms would be rarely if ever needed.

By contrast, some legal scholars argue that international law influences state behavior "because it is perceived largely as morally authoritative and legitimate" (Ginsburg and McAdams 2003: 1234). Brunnée and Toope (2011: 308), coming from

TABLE 15.1. *Summary statistics – incidence and form of dispute resolution provisions*

	Any dispute resolution (1)	Forms of dispute resolution				Total (6)
		Informal (2)	Mediation (3)	Adjudication (4)	Arbitration (5)	
Security	18 (38%)	18 (38%)	5 (11%)	1 (2%)	2 (4%)	47 (20%)
Economics	54 (52%)	52 (50%)	17 (17%)	42 (41%)	24 (23%)	103 (44%)
Environment	13 (30%)	10 (23%)	6 (14%)	8 (19%)	9 (21%)	43 (18%)
Human rights	27 (66%)	16 (39%)	8 (20%)	9 (22%)	20 (49%)	41 (18%)
TOTAL	112 (48%)	96 (41%)	36 (15%)	60 (26%)	55 (24%)	234 (100%)

These and all subsequent data are from the Continent of International Law, Koremenos (forthcoming).

a constructivist perspective, emphasize how not only a perception of legitimacy and legality must exist, but "that the obligatory effect of international law must be generated and maintained through practices that sustain legality over time." Based on the premise from the legalization literature that "courts and tribunals represent a key dimension of legalization" (Keohane, Moravcsik, and Slaughter 2000: 457), one may thus conclude that the existence and usage of dispute resolution mechanisms contribute to a more lawlike character of international agreements, thereby enhancing their legitimacy and effectiveness. Thus, we would expect to see the inclusion of dispute resolution mechanisms in most, if not all, international agreements.

How well do these two ideal-type theories perform when put to the data? Table 15.1 shows descriptive statistics from the Continent of International Law (COIL) project, which features a random sample of 234 international agreements drawn from the United Nations Treaties Series (UNTS) database.[2] The agreements are drawn from four issue areas following UNTS definitions: security, environment, economics, and human rights.[3]

Following Koremenos (2007), we identify four different types of dispute resolution mechanisms. *Informal mechanisms* refer to diplomacy, friendly negotiations, or market-based mechanisms, such as side payments. Notably, informal mechanisms do

---

[2] For a more detailed description of COIL, see Koremenos (forthcoming).
[3] This is not to say that other typologies are not important. In fact, the COIL dataset codes for a wealth of other attributes as well – e.g., whether an agreement prescribes, proscribes, or authorizes behavior; whether it is thematic or regional; or whose behavior it principally governs. The randomization, however, was undertaken conditional on these four issue areas. This decision was in part motivated by the extant literature, which typically compares agreements within specific issue areas, as in Mitchell's (2002–11) database of International Environmental Agreements or the Alliance Treaty Obligations and Provisions data set of Leeds *et al.* (2002). In part, the decision was also motivated by COIL's theoretical premise that issue areas are comparable once one looks at the set of underlying cooperation problems that brought states to the negotiating table.

not involve any actors other than the affected parties in the dispute. Moreover, even though states always have the option to settle informally, many agreements explicitly suggest diplomacy and friendly negotiations to be used as a first means for resolving disputes. *Mediation*, the second form of dispute resolution, is more formal. Importantly, mediation involves a neutral third party, but it is nonbinding – the mediator is supposed to assist the disputing parties in finding an agreeable solution, but does not issue a formal ruling. This is different from *arbitration*, the third form of dispute resolution, in which the disputants select a third party for the resolution of the dispute. This arbitrator may issue binding statements or simply recommendations, depending on the provisions in the agreement; however, the arbitrator is supposed to solve the dispute (and not, like a mediator, only help the disputants reconcile their views). The fourth, and final, form of dispute resolution considered is *adjudication*. Here, the agreement either establishes a court or delegates to a preexisting one, and the specified court is authorized to issue a ruling, which may (but need not) be binding.[4]

Table 15.1 presents the incidence of various dispute resolution mechanisms, both for the entire sample and across issue areas. As is evident from the table, neither theory discussed above can adequately explain the data. Given that the negotiation of dispute resolution mechanisms is costly and lengthy (see Alter [2003], on difficult WTO negotiations), realists would predict the absence of dispute resolution mechanisms. Yet, almost half of the agreements in the sample, 48 percent, explicitly mention some form of dispute resolution, and 37 percent include a provision relating to one of the formal mechanisms (mediation, arbitration, or adjudication). On the other hand, not each and every agreement is made more legalized through the inclusion of dispute settlement mechanisms. Finally, it is worth noting that agreements may provide for more than one form of dispute settlement. In particular, 82 percent of the agreements with formal procedures encourage informal settlements as well.

Table 15.1 additionally reveals substantial variation across issue areas, unexplained by these theories. Agreements concerned with economic issues, for example, are almost twice as likely to explicitly encourage the informal settlement of disputes as agreements addressing environmental issues. Another notable result is that human rights agreements rely much more often on adjudication than do agreements in any other issue area. This variation, both across issue areas and across different forms of dispute resolution, begs for an explanation.

B. *The Perspective of Rational Design*

Rational design, as introduced in Koremenos *et al.* (2001) and further developed in the COIL project (Koremenos, forthcoming), provides a theory to explain such

---

4 The standard legal taxonomy of dispute resolution slices the world up slightly differently. See, e.g., United Nations Charter, Article 33 (listing negotiation, enquiry, mediation, conciliation, arbitration, judicial settlement, resort to regional agencies, or other peaceful means of settlement).

variation across agreements. The theoretical premise is that states try to solve recurrent cooperation problems through international institutions, usually manifested in international law. It is these cooperation problems that drive the design of international agreements. With respect to dispute resolution mechanisms, four cooperation problems are especially relevant.[5]

Enforcement problems are present whenever parties to an agreement have an incentive to defect from cooperation. The most prominent example of such an enforcement problem is the prisoners' dilemma. Even if mutual cooperation makes everyone better off compared to mutual noncooperation, some actors may prefer to renege because they can do better individually by cheating. States may try to address underlying enforcement problems through dispute resolution mechanisms. For instance, by explicitly identifying violators (and violations), they incur reputational costs. By authorizing punishments, sometimes collectively, punishments become more credible and thereby more effective. Collective punishments can be especially difficult to achieve, and Thompson (2009) aptly identifies a sanctioners' dilemma that can be alleviated through international institutions.

States are also more likely to include dispute resolution mechanisms into their agreements when one or more of them face a domestic *commitment problem*. Commitment problems arise if an actor's current optimal plan for the future will no longer be optimal once that future arrives and the actor has a chance to reoptimize. Thus, unless the actor has a device to tie its hands to the current plan, the plan is inconsistent over time (therefore, commitment problems are also labeled *time-inconsistency problems*). A variant of such commitment problems often arises in volatile and polarized political systems, where a government's preferences may change dramatically over time. It is important to distinguish commitment problems from enforcement problems, where an actor's *current* optimal plan entails a defection, and no reoptimization or preference change is involved. Moreover, enforcement problems can be alleviated by the existence of future periods, whereas commitment problems exist because of the future. By rendering agreements more legalized, dispute resolution provisions offer a device to solve commitment problems. As Goldstein *et al.* (2000: 393) argue, "Governments and domestic groups may also deliberately employ international legalization as a means to bind themselves or their successors in the future. In other words, international legalization may have the aim of imposing constraints on domestic political behavior." In addition, dispute resolution mechanisms provide recourse for other actors to punish a government for deviations from its announced plans, altering the incentive structure faced by governments.

Third, *uncertainty about the state of the world* refers to uncertainty regarding the consequences of cooperation. States may try to solve a particular problem but be unsure about the future consequences of their own actions, the actions of other states, and/or the actions of international institutions – including the institutions

---

[5] These cooperation problems are elaborated in Koremenos *et al.* (2001).

they create. Such uncertainty may arise because states are unsure about what the world will look like in the future, because they lack the technical expertise to predict the consequences of actions, or because they are unsure about how the agreement will play out. Put differently, uncertainty about the state of the world implies that the future benefits (and costs) of cooperation are not easily predicted, and hence a dispute could easily break out, attributable to an unexpected shift in the distribution of benefits. Although flexibility measures can facilitate cooperation under such circumstances (Koremenos 2005; Kucik and Reinhardt 2008; Helfer 2013), dispute resolution provisions may prove valuable as well.[6]

The fourth relevant cooperation problem is *uncertainty about behavior*. If a party to an agreement is unsure whether another party is following through on its obligations, it may stop cooperating simply because it fears being disadvantaged by maintaining cooperation. Thus, uncertainty about behavior may trigger an unwarranted, and indeed unwanted, breakdown of cooperation – and, in turn, discourage cooperation in the first place. Dispute resolution may address such factual uncertainty in that it provides legalized ways to handle disputes, typically through a formalized procedure that collects and disseminates information. This resonates well with standard institutionalist arguments about the role of international agreements in information provision (Keohane 1984).

It might be helpful to emphasize the difference between the two kinds of uncertainties introduced above. Uncertainty about the state of the world can bring about changes in bargaining power and/or the relative gains from cooperation, making a defection more attractive to one side. Being able to prevent defections is then particularly valuable and not solved by a simple exchange of information. Uncertainty about behavior allows states to take advantage of an information asymmetry and to defect without the other side recognizing (or without the other side recognizing early enough). It is this informational advantage that encourages defections, and it is more easily resolved through a simple exchange of information.

Moreover, uncertainty about behavior as an underlying cooperation problem is different from legal uncertainty, which refers to difficulties in the interpretation and application of rules. Naturally, dispute settlement mechanisms are relevant for legal uncertainty as well. This follows closely the managerial school of compliance (A. Chayes and A. H. Chayes 1993), according to which international institutions play a vital role in the interpretation of ambiguous rules. Similarly, Ginsburg and McAdams (2003) consider how noisy signals and rule ambiguity give rise to violations of international agreements, which then are resolved in legalized dispute settlement procedures. Notably, these authors explicitly consider dispute settlement

---

[6] Indeed, dispute resolution mechanisms can be considered a form of centralization that increases flexibility (Rosendorff 2005; Betz 2011), a view that contrasts with those of many legal and political science scholars that dispute resolution mechanisms reduce flexibility by constraining state actors (Abbott and Snidal 2000; Brewster 2006; Guzman and Meyer 2010).

mechanisms without any punishment power and show how they work effectively in the presence of informational problems. Hence, we expect that ambiguous rules are associated with the presence of dispute settlement mechanisms as well.

To summarize, states try to solve two categories of cooperation problems through dispute resolution mechanisms. First, problems requiring punishment or enforcement power, which arise in the presence of enforcement problems, commitment problems, and uncertainty about the state of the world. By providing enforcement power, material and reputational, dispute resolution mechanisms alleviate these cooperation problems. The second category comprises informational problems, which arise in the presence of uncertainty about behavior, as well as if agreements contain ambiguous rules. By providing information and legalized ways to handle such disputes, dispute resolution mechanisms address this category of cooperation problems.

We can refine these predictions further. If states include dispute settlement mechanisms to solve punishment problems, we would see enforcement problems, commitment problems, and uncertainty about the state of the world to be the driving forces behind the inclusion of dispute resolution provisions in international agreements; this would be so especially for the most legalized mechanisms, given the need to provide the added power of punishment. Hence, arbitration and adjudication in particular should be associated with punishment problems.

If dispute resolution mechanisms solve informational problems, that is, non-compliance due to ambiguous language and noisy signals about the behavior of other states, we would expect uncertainty about behavior and ambiguous rules to affect the inclusion of dispute resolution provisions. Moreover, resolving uncertainty about behavior mainly requires consultations and deliberations, rather than adjudication. Hence, the encouragement of informal settlements and, possibly, mediation is an appropriate design choice. By contrast, in the presence of ambiguous rules, we should see international tribunals for arbitrated or adjudicated rule interpretation.

An empirical analysis of the relationship between rule ambiguity and arbitrated or adjudicated dispute settlement mechanisms, however, is not straightforward. The reason is that both the formulation of ambiguous rules and the inclusion of dispute resolution procedures are simultaneously determined choices made by governments. Standard regression techniques therefore yield invalid inferences about the relationship between these two variables. For this reason, we omit ambiguous rules from the empirical models that follow;[7] we instead refer to Koremenos (2011), who analyzes the simultaneous choice of rule precision and dispute resolution mechanisms in more depth, with evidence in favor of an inverse relationship between these two

---

[7] Instrumental variable techniques provide an alternative way to address such endogeneity concerns. However, the two standard procedures to estimate such endogenous probit models are hugely problematic in a wide range of circumstances (Betz 2010).

Barbara Koremenos and Timm Betz

TABLE 15.2. *Probit analysis – incidence and form of dispute resolution provisions*

	Any	Formal	Arb./Adj.	External
	(1)	(2)	(3)	(4)
Enforcement	0.871** (0.351)	1.011*** (0.073)	1.170*** (0.228)	1.124*** (0.200)
Commitment	1.697*** (0.526)	1.752** (0.806)	1.783** (0.882)	1.577* (0.855)
Uncertainty world	−0.206 (0.580)	0.231 (0.408)	0.248 (0.483)	0.471 (0.361)
Uncertainty behavior	0.430*** (0.115)	0.299 (0.250)	0.062 (0.352)	−0.186 (0.453)
U.S. involvement	−0.394* (0.209)	−0.232 (0.260)	−0.151 (0.254)	−0.085 (0.255)
Ln (number)	0.176** (0.085)	0.382*** (0.050)	0.386*** (0.043)	0.353*** (0.046)
N	234	234	234	234

Note: Issue area dummies omitted. Standard errors in parentheses, heteroscedasticity-robust, clustered on issue areas.
Significance: *** at 1% level; ** at 5% level; * at 10% level.

design elements. Her finding about the role of legal uncertainty is in line with Ginsburg and McAdams's (2003) theory of dispute resolution mechanisms and supports our conjectures above with respect to ambiguous rules.

III. A LOOK AT THE DATA

In this section, we examine the predictions articulated above in a random sample of international agreements. We lean on Koremenos (2007), but use a larger dataset and extend the analysis in several respects. Most important, given the smaller dataset at the time, Koremenos collapsed all four of the above cooperation problems into one variable, labeled *complex cooperation problem*; instead, we evaluate the effects of each cooperation problem *individually*. Parsing out the effects of punishment problems and informational problems allows us to draw some conclusions about the character of dispute resolution mechanisms. Of course, the two explanations need not be exclusive.

Tables 15.2 and 15.3 provide the results from four probit regressions. All data come from the COIL dataset. As in Table 15.1, the forms of dispute resolution become stronger in terms of delegation and legalization when moving from the first to the third column. The first column captures whether there is any kind of dispute resolution provision in the agreement. This category includes informal settlements, which are excluded from the second column, leaving mediation, arbitration, and adjudication. The third column in addition excludes mediation as a form of dispute settlement, counting only adjudication and arbitration, which are the two most legalized mechanisms. The fourth column offers an alternative dimension of variation in dispute settlement design: whether dispute settlements are delegated internally

TABLE 15.3. *Predicted probabilities and average marginal effects*

	Any (1)	Formal (2)	Arb./Adj. (3)	External (4)
Pr(dispute resolution)				
-baseline	26.2%	6.3%	4.4%	3.5%
-enforcement	58.6%	28.4%	26.8%	22.2%
-commitment	84.8%	54.8%	47.0 %	36.5%
-uncertainty world	20.0%	9.6%	7.1%	8.5%
-uncertainty behavior	41.5%	10.7%	5.0%	2.3%
-ln(number)	30.2%	10.1%	7.3%	5.6%
Marginal Effect				
-enforcement	32.4pp	22.1pp	22.4pp	18.7pp
-commitment	58.6pp	48.5pp	42.6pp	33.0pp
-uncertainty world	−6.2pp	3.3pp	2.7pp	5.0pp
-uncertainty behavior	15.3pp	4.4pp	0.6pp	−1.2pp
-ln(number)	4.1pp	3.8pp	2.9pp	2.1pp

Note: Baseline is a bilateral agreement without U.S. involvement and without any of the cooperation problems.

Predicted probabilities and average marginal effects (percentage points) calculated separately for each issue area and then averaged, with weights according to relative frequency of each issue area. For ln(number), marginal effect is for change from an agreement with two participants to an agreement with four participants, which is roughly the sample average.

or externally. With internal delegation, a body composed of or appointed by the member states to an agreement is involved in the dispute settlement. For instance, suppose two states try to resolve a dispute and jointly appoint a judge to serve as arbitrator. In the data, this is coded as internal delegation. By contrast, suppose the dispute is referred to the ICJ. This would be coded as external delegation, in which a third party outside the agreement is involved in the dispute settlement. Aside from international tribunals, this function could be assumed by a third state or a nongovernmental organization. External delegation, especially when it comes with compulsory jurisdiction, does not necessarily imply more legalization, but it implies a relatively larger loss of state autonomy.

A first set of explanatory variables is dictated by the conjectures derived above and includes variables that capture punishment problems (enforcement problem, commitment problem, uncertainty about the state of the world) and informational problems (uncertainty about behavior). The cooperation problems are coded as 1 whenever they are found to be present to a high degree in an international agreement.[8]

The regressions include several control variables. Based on transaction cost arguments, we expect dispute resolution provisions to be more likely as the number of

---

[8] See Koremenos (2005, 2007) for an explanation of the binary coding of cooperation problems.

original participants increases.[9] The number variable is log-transformed in order to capture the effects of percentage increases rather than absolute increases. Second, a superpower dummy is included, coded as 1 whenever the United States is a signatory to an agreement. Partly based on realist accounts, the expectation is that such agreements are less likely to include dispute resolution provisions because the United States, which has the most to lose from international constraints, does not want to be bound by international law in unpredictable ways (Koh 1997: 2615ff.; see also Brewster 2006, with an argument based on domestic politics). Finally, issue area dummies are included (not reported in the table).[10] Table 15.2 presents coefficient estimates and standard errors for the probit regressions. Since probit coefficients are hard to interpret directly, Table 15.3 reports marginal effects. The marginal effects were calculated for each issue separately, then averaged across issue areas to obtain (weighted) average marginal effects.

Two results stand out. First, enforcement and commitment problems always increase the probability that an agreement includes a dispute resolution mechanism. For instance, the probability that an agreement arranges for either adjudication or arbitration increases more than fivefold in the presence of enforcement problems; it increases by a factor of ten in the presence of commitment problems. These effects are still substantial, but less pronounced, when informal mechanisms are considered, as column 1 in Table 15.3 shows. This is much in line with theoretical expectations. Commitment and enforcement problems are particularly severe issues, and hence call for legalized and formal procedures; informal mechanisms and mediation are insufficient to address these problems.

By contrast, for the third variable in the category of punishment problems, uncertainty about the state of the world, the results are much less supportive. The marginal effects are relatively small, even negative for informal mechanisms, and never statistically significantly different from 0 at any conventional level. However, even for this variable, the effects increase in size and significance as more legalized and externally delegated mechanisms are considered.[11] One explanation for this result might be that uncertainty about the state of the world is addressed more effectively by other design elements – escape clauses (Kucik and Reinhardt 2008) or limited duration clauses (Koremenos 2005).

The second main result concerns the variable capturing factual uncertainty, uncertainty about behavior. Problems arising from uncertainty about behavior often can be resolved through the exchange of information and hence do not require

---

9   This follows in part from the rational design conjecture; centralization increases with Number (Koremenos *et al.* 2001).
10 Standard errors are heteroscedasticity-robust and clustered on issue areas.
11 One may suspect that the insignificance of the variables capturing uncertainties is due to collinearity among the variables in the regression. This, however, is not the case – none of the bivariate correlation coefficients exceeds a level of 0.32; similarly, combining variables into dummies or leaving out some of them does not increase the precision of the coefficient estimates.

formalized dispute procedures or court rulings. Thus, it was expected that the effect should be weakest for the more legalized mechanisms. This expectation is consistent with the data – the coefficient is positive and statistically significant at the 1 percent level in the first column of Table 15.5, and the marginal effect is substantively large: an agreement characterized by uncertainty about behavior is about 58 percent more likely to include a dispute resolution provision than is an agreement without such an underlying cooperation problem. The coefficient decreases in size and statistical significance once informal procedures are excluded from the dependent variable. Looking at arbitration and adjudication only, the marginal effect is negligible and statistically insignificant. For external delegation, the coefficient even turns negative and is estimated very imprecisely.

Surprising from the perspective of power politics is that U.S. involvement has a statistically significant effect only when informal procedures are considered as well; the effect weakens substantially in size and significance as dispute resolution procedures become more legalized. By our previous arguments, we would have expected the reverse; additional results below may provide an explanation, in that the United States tends to attach reservations more often than other states, and hence might be exempted from binding settlement mechanisms. The number of signatories has the expected sign and is always statistically significant; the more signatories an agreement has, the more likely is the inclusion of a dispute resolution mechanism. Moreover, the effect is strongest for more formalized (i.e., centralized) procedures, which is not surprising, given the costs of negotiating and implementing them.

On the most general level, our findings suggest that dispute resolution mechanisms assume very different tasks and that these tasks are dictated by the underlying cooperation problems. First, dispute settlement mechanisms help to resolve punishment problems by authorizing and coordinating punishments and by identifying violators explicitly. Punishment problems arise chiefly out of enforcement and commitment problems, which create incentives to cheat in the absence of effective punishments. Effective punishments are best achieved when dispute settlement mechanisms are legalized and centralized and when they are independent of direct state influence. The second purpose served by dispute settlement mechanisms is information provision. Since information provision does not require highly legalized, powerful, or centralized mechanisms, the effect is strongest for informal procedures, a perspective supported by the strong association between uncertainty about behavior and informal dispute settlement procedures, but the absence of such a relationship for arbitration and adjudication.

IV. LOOPHOLES IN AGREEMENTS . . . AND IN THEORIES?

The previous section provided strong support for conjectures based on the rational design framework. Still, two caveats need to be addressed. First, some dispute resolution provisions are nonbinding, and others appear limited, given that states often

TABLE 15.4. *Explicit encouragement to settle disputes informally*

	Mediation	Arbitration	Adjudication	External
	(1)	(2)	(3)	(4)
Yes	32 (89%)	57 (95%)	41 (75%)	61 (82%)
No	4 (11%)	3 (5%)	14 (25%)	13 (18%)
N	36	60	55	74

Note: Percentages in parentheses conditional on Form of Dispute Resolution. For example, 89% of agreements with mediation allow for informal settlements. All differences are statistically significant at p = 0.000.

add reservations to their agreements to the effect that they must give permission before any instance of dispute resolution delegation occurs. Does such allowance for "loopholes" restrict the functioning of dispute settlement mechanisms and, in essence, render them meaningless design elements? This section will start to explore this question and point out the need for further research along these lines. Second, dispute resolution mechanisms may not be used very frequently in practice. Yet, as we argue, this does not mean that dispute settlement mechanisms are useless or ineffective; effective dispute settlement mechanisms generate selection effects and cast a "shadow of the law," both of which have powerful effects on state behavior and, in particular, imply that the dispute settlement mechanisms need not be invoked to be effective.

A. Restrictions and Reservations

Formal dispute settlement mechanisms impose severe restrictions on state sovereignty (Abbott and Snidal 2000: 436). States may try to relax these constraints through two means. Formal dispute settlement mechanisms may be explicitly noncompulsory, allowing for outside settlements; similarly, they may allow for the lawful rejection of settlements and appeals (i.e., the mechanisms are nonbinding).[12] Alternatively, the parties to an agreement may attach reservations at the time of signature, thus gaining an exemption from the treaty provisions pertaining to the settlement of disputes.

Descriptive statistics on design elements encouraging informal dispute resolution are displayed in Table 15.4. The overwhelming majority of agreements with formal settlements explicitly encourage the informal settlement of disputes. Although mechanisms stipulating adjudication and external delegation allow for outside

---

[12] One could argue that no international ruling is ever binding, so the term *nonbinding* is hardly as meaningful in the international law setting as in the domestic setting; but see Alter (2013) for an argument why the distinction between international and national law may not be that important on this dimension.

TABLE 15.5. *Possibility to reject settlements lawfully*

	Arbitration (2)	Adjudication (3)	External (4)
Yes	7 (12%)	13 (24%)	15 (20%)
No	53 (88%)	42 (76%)	59 (80%)
p-value	0.082	0.000	0.000
N	60	55	74

Note: Percentages in parentheses conditional on Form of Dispute Resolution. For example, 12% of agreements with arbitration allow for the lawful rejection of settlements.

settlements less often, the pattern is impressive – very few agreements rule out the informal settlement of disputes in the shadow of formalized procedures. The question, of course, is how often and under what conditions states take advantage of this opportunity, an issue certainly warranting further research.

Table 15.5 provides descriptive statistics on the possibility of rejecting settlements lawfully. Here, the pattern is reversed. The majority of agreements do not provide for this possibility; the percentage increases for adjudication and external delegation, but does not go beyond 25 percent for adjudicated mechanisms. Thus, it might be the binding, and therefore less calculable, character of formal dispute settlements that drives states into using informal procedures – but it may as well be the reduced cost, confidentiality, and expedited procedure that informal settlements provide, compared to the highly legalized and lengthy procedures in adjudicated and externally delegated mechanisms. Detailed case studies would be needed to obtain further insights into these questions.

The use of reservations is documented in Table 15.6. Almost all agreements allow for some kind of reservation – that is, reservations are not explicitly prohibited in the majority of agreements. However, the *form* of the specific dispute resolution provision makes hardly any difference with respect to whether reservations are permissible; the differences are hardly significant. Importantly, however, a difference exists among agreements that include dispute resolution provisions and those that do not: among agreements with any form of dispute resolution, 10 percent explicitly rule out reservations, whereas this figure is at only 3 percent for agreements without any form of dispute resolution; this difference is statistically significant with a p-value of 0.029. That agreements with dispute resolution procedures are *more likely* to rule out the use of reservations than are agreements without dispute resolution procedures suggest that states actively discourage the use of reservations that might exempt them from dispute settlements. This conjecture is supported by the very sparse use that states make of reservations, as the third line of Table 15.6

TABLE 15.6. *Possibility to attach reservations and agreements with at least one reservation attached at time of entry into force*

	Mediation	Arbitration	Adjudication	External
	(1)	(2)	(3)	(4)
Not prohibited	30 (83%)	56 (93%)	49 (89%)	69 (93%)
p-value	0.007	0.438	0.056	0.394
Attached	4 (11%)	5 (8%)	11 (20%)	10 (14%)
p-value	0.331	0.556	0.001	0.039
N	36	60	55	74

Note: Percentages in parentheses conditional on Form of Dispute Resolution. For example, 83% of agreements with mediation allow for reservations to be made; 11% of agreements with mediation have at least one reservation attached.

illustrates.[13] Only one-fifth of agreements with adjudication have any reservations attached (whether concerning substantive provisions or the dispute resolution procedure); thus, there is little reason to be worried that states circumvent formally established dispute settlement procedures by exempting themselves a priori through the use of reservations on a large scale. Likewise, it is an empirical question whether states that attached reservations to their participation in dispute settlement procedures indeed invoke these, or whether they decide to participate despite their reservations, which would further weaken the impact of reservations on the functioning of dispute settlement procedures. Koremenos (book manuscript) will examine these questions regarding reservations in more detail. Notwithstanding, the results showcased here suggest that the design of dispute settlement procedures is not undermined by the use of reservations.

Most significant for this chapter, a closer look at the agreements in the COIL sample reveals that only ten agreements have reservations attached that are concerned with dispute resolution; nine of these agreements fall under the issue area of human rights, and one is concerned with the financing of terrorism.[14]

Moreover, reservations need not be a state's final word. A number of states have withdrawn their respective reservations, mirroring a move toward greater acceptance of legalized dispute settlement mechanisms. The American Convention on Human Rights provides an example, illustrating the power of soft, nonbinding law, especially when viewed in its relationship to hard law, much in line with the argument made by Shaffer and Pollack (2010).[15] The Convention delegates authority to both the Inter-American Commission on Human Rights and the Inter-American Court of Human Rights. The Court is able to issue-binding rulings on contentious cases and

---

[13] We consider only reservations that were attached to an agreement at the time it entered into force.
[14] A table displaying data on reservations in all agreements in the COIL sample is available on the COIL website at http://www.isr.umich.edu/cps/coil/.
[15] The discussion of the American Convention on Human Rights relies heavily on Beck (2011).

also has the authority to submit advisory opinions (i.e., nonbinding statements). In 1982, the Commission urged Guatemala to suspend an extension of the death penalty to certain crimes despite a reservation Guatemala made allowing the practice. The Commission then referred the matter to the Court. Although Guatemala did not recognize the jurisdiction of the Convention's Court in this matter, in response to the request by the Commission, the Court concluded that it was entitled to issue a parallel advisory opinion, which sided with the Commission. As a result of this increased pressure, Guatemala's government eventually ceased the death penalty. In 1986, Guatemala withdrew its reservation, and, in 1987, finally acknowledged the Court's contentious jurisdiction. In essence, the nonbinding advisory opinion exerted pressure on the Guatemalan government that was arguably just as strong as that exerted by a binding ruling. Therefore, even though Guatemala did not fall under the jurisdiction of the Court, a less binding dispute settlement mechanism exerted sufficiently strong pressure on the government to change its behavior.

B. *Effectiveness without Usage*

Although there is little evidence that reservations are frequently used by states to bypass dispute settlement procedures, as Table 15.6 indicates, it could be argued that formal mechanisms are not used with great regularity, outside some presumed exceptional cases like the WTO. Additionally, Table 15.4 suggests that informal procedures might be used frequently instead of the institutionalized mechanisms. This raises the question of whether "practice follows design" – are dispute settlement procedures used in practice and not simply theoretical constructs?

It would be a fallacy to infer from the nonuse of dispute settlement procedures that they are inconsequential, as some realist arguments would imply. Thus, while we and realists make similar predictions about the infrequent use of formal dispute settlement procedures, our explanations contrast starkly.[16] In particular, we contend that making the leap from unused to ineffective settlement procedures overlooks the strategic interaction among and anticipative behavior of states. In fact, infrequent recourse to dispute settlement procedures may just as well indicate the effectiveness of this institutional design choice.

Two mechanisms explain such an inverse relationship between the use of dispute settlement procedures and their effectiveness. The first mechanism relies on the screening power of treaties, the second relies on their constraining power. Notably, each of these mechanisms is linked directly to distinct cooperation problems, enforcement problems, and commitment problems, respectively. Thus, the following discussion directly contributes to the debate whether international treaties constrain or screen (Simmons 2000; von Stein 2005) by identifying conditions under

---

[16] Moreover, even though the prediction with respect to usage is the same, the prediction with respect to design differs, and we provided ample evidence in favor of our argument in the previous sections.

which treaties will exert constraining or screening functions. Finally, we discuss the influence of the shadow of the law on promoting informal settlement, thereby precluding the formal use of dispute settlement procedures.

1. Screening to Solve Underlying Enforcement Problems

First, highly legalized agreement designs may effectively restrict membership through a screening mechanism and thereby limit the potential for enforcement problems to arise. Formalized dispute settlement procedures, especially when coupled with strong enforcement mechanisms, deter dishonest signatories: those that do want to join an agreement, but do not intend to follow through on their obligations (Simmons [2009] provides an excellent discussion of this issue). For instance, in the Chemical Weapons Convention (CWC), intrusive inspections, harsh enforcement mechanisms (such as powerful sanctions and potential referral to the United Nations Security Council), and a highly legalized dispute settlement mechanism allowing for referral to the International Court of Justice, discouraged insincere ratifications. Consequently, compliance with the treaty remained on a very high level, and the few violations were concerned with rather technical details.[17]

The argument made so far, of course, is simply a restatement of Downs, Rocke, and Barsoom's (1996) argument that states self-select into those agreements that they deem to be in their interest anyway – as they put it, "most treaties require states to make only modest departures from what they would have done in the absence of an agreement" (1996: 380). Yet, this does not imply that dispute resolution mechanisms are ineffective. Dispute resolution mechanisms may be effective precisely because they are rarely used, given their screening function. Provided that dispute resolution mechanisms impose some additional cost on violators, they can help reduce the enforcement problem to a tolerable level for a still relatively broad group of states, which then benefit from cooperation. In addition, because disputes are expected to arise less often, cooperation becomes more durable. Cooperation is in danger of breaking down as soon as any party to an agreement reneges on its commitments. By restricting the pool of signatories to signatories who have similar prisoners' dilemma-like payoffs, who expect and who are expected to comply given that mutual cooperation is superior to mutual defection, dispute resolution mechanisms contribute to more stable (and, potentially, deeper) forms of cooperation.[18]

---

[17] In the case of the CWC, a case can be made that insincere ratifiers were screened out primarily by the strong inspection and sanctioning mechanisms rather than by the existence of the dispute settlement mechanism. However, the point remains that the agreement was designed such that only sincere ratifiers were willing to enter it and, as a consequence, there has been little need to invoke the dispute settlement mechanism.

[18] Put differently, states (or their leaders) who have very short shadows of the future, and thus for whom the incentive to defect is higher than that of the average state, are either screened out given the potential punishment or have their payoffs changed by the threat of punishment. In either case, the incidence of cooperation would increase.

2. Constraining to Solve Underlying Commitment Problems (and Some Enforcement Problems)

A second mechanism explaining unused dispute settlement procedures is found in their constraining effects. Even if the parties to an agreement manage to solve enforcement problems through other means, commitment problems may remain. As was argued previously, dispute resolution mechanisms provide an effective means to address them. However, states may still refrain from actually invoking formal settlement procedures.

If states anticipate the rulings of a dispute settlement mechanism and the associated punishment, they may refrain from a violation in the first place. This implies that the mere presence of a dispute settlement mechanism, particularly when fortified with punishment capabilities, will reduce the incidence of rule violations; of course, if there is no rule violation, recourse to the dispute settlement body becomes superfluous as well. Thus, even if the mechanism is not engaged directly and explicitly, it exerts a constraining power on state behavior – it can be a commitment device, helping states tie their hands with respect to domestic constituencies, and it remains unused precisely because of, not despite, its proper functioning. This argument is akin to arguments found in conflict studies: if threats to use force are credible, we will rarely observe the actual use of force (A. Smith 1999).

Koremenos (forthcoming) finds that about a quarter of agreements address commitment problems, and such problems are especially prevalent in the issue areas of human rights and investment. Not coincidentally, these are also the issue areas that are characterized by a high incidence of formal dispute resolution mechanisms. Thus, delegated dispute resolution provisions are one design element helping states to solve commitment problems. For instance, if a new leader comes to power with preferences that favor defection, the ensuing costs imposed by a court could be enough to change the leader's payoffs into favoring cooperation. Thus, if delegated dispute resolution mechanisms function in this way, they are not used on the equilibrium path.

And, of course, this same constraining mechanism works to solve enforcement problems not solved through the screening function. When faced with incentives to defect, even states with stable preferences over time must incorporate into their payoffs for defection the possibility of being punished through a court or other form of formal dispute resolution. As argued above, if the threat is sufficiently high, defection may be deterred.

3. The Influence of the Shadow of the Law

Finally, the rare use of formal dispute resolution may imply that states are resolving their conflicts in the "shadow of the law." As we have shown, the majority of agreements with formal procedures allow for informal settlements as well. Moreover, more than half of the agreements that encourage informal settlements also impose time limits on the dispute resolution process (55 agreements out of 96). Hence, states may try to settle informally; but if they do not manage to resolve their disputes within a specified, finite time period, the formal dispute settlement process kicks in. This implies that the formal procedures cast a rather strong shadow on informal settlements.

What are the implications of power asymmetries for the outcomes of settlements? Sattler and Bernauer (2010) find that WTO disputes involving substantial power asymmetries are more likely to be settled outside the formal dispute settlement mechanism than are disputes among more equal parties; they find this to be a worrisome result, based on the argument that it is "easier to reduce legal capacity differences than to reduce power differences" (Sattler and Bernauer 2010: 162). This, however, overlooks that the shadow of the law works even in the presence of power asymmetries. The potential recourse to the dispute settlement mechanism raises the outside option of the country of lesser power, and sometimes may raise it substantially. Neither party can fall behind its expected payoff under the dispute resolution mechanism – and the fact that, in more than half of the agreements mentioning informal settlements, the formal procedures are invoked if settlement does not succeed within a specified time period further reinforces this effect. This logic works even if both parties have an incentive to strive for a settlement outside the formal mechanisms. If formal dispute settlement procedures are lengthy and costly, it may prove valuable to both sides to circumvent them by settling the issue in question informally in bilateral negotiations; yet, both sides have to acknowledge in their negotiations that the other side cannot be worse off than it would be under the formal procedure minus the costs of participating in the formal process. Again, by its mere presence, the dispute settlement mechanism affects the outcomes under the agreement without being engaged formally.

V. CONCLUSION

In this chapter, we reviewed some of the literature on dispute settlement mechanisms in international agreements and argued that attempts to explain the design and functioning of settlement mechanisms are lacking, in particular, in truly comparative projects. We set out to offer a theory that links the design of dispute settlement provisions to distinct cooperation problems, thereby transcending any particular agreement or even issue area, and showed that specific cooperation problems strongly affect both the existence and the form of dispute settlement procedures: informational problems tend to be addressed by informal mechanisms, whereas punishment problems call for formal mechanisms.

We then countered two concerns: that the use of reservations undermines dispute settlement procedures and that rarely invoked dispute settlement mechanisms are meaningless design elements. We argue that even rarely used dispute settlement mechanisms may have strong effects. First, we addressed the screening mechanism: by providing enforcement power, these mechanisms discourage dishonest signatories from joining an agreement. Second, we addressed the constraining mechanism: the threat of a ruling combined with punishment may be enough to discourage defection by changing the payoffs in favor of cooperation. Finally, even if defection still occurs, the threat of a ruling may still inspire informal settlements outside the formal procedures.

We also point out a number of avenues for further research. Although the analysis hinted at how particular design elements might interact, the relationship among distinct design elements is an important part of any future research agenda because, as negotiators know firsthand, dispute resolution provisions are not designed in a vacuum. Finally, we need to examine more carefully the functioning of international agreements over time once they are in place, including some creative attempts to capture the elusive "shadow of the law" and its implications for both design and practice.[19]

REFERENCES

Abbott, Kenneth W., and Duncan Snidal (2000). "Hard and Soft Law in International Governance," *International Organization*, Vol. 54, No. 3, pp. 421–56.

Alter, Karen J. (2003). "Resolving or Exacerbating Disputes? The WTO's New Dispute Resolution System," *International Affairs*, Vol. 79, No. 4, pp. 783–800.

——— (2013). "The Multiple Roles of International Courts and Tribunals: Enforcement, Dispute Settlement, Constitutional and Administrative Review," in Jeffrey L. Dunoff and Mark A. Pollack (eds.), *Interdisciplinary Perspectives on International Law and International Relations: The State of the Art* (New York: Cambridge University Press), pp. 345–70.

Barceló, John J. III (2009). "Burden of Proof, Prima Facie Case and Presumption in WTO Dispute Settlement," *Cornell International Law Journal*, Vol. 42, No. 23, pp. 23–43.

Beck, Katherine (2011). "The Evolution of Dispute Resolution in the American Convention on Human Rights," Working Paper (Ann Arbor: University of Michigan, Department of Political Science).

Betz, Timm (2010). "Endogenous Variables in Probit Models: Comparing Estimators," Working Paper (Ann Arbor: University of Michigan, Department of Political Science).

——— (2011). "Crime without Punishment: Delegation, Flexibility, and Exploitation in International Agreements," Working Paper (Ann Arbor: University of Michigan, Department of Political Science).

Brewster, Rachel (2006). "Rule-Based Dispute Resolution in International Trade Law," *Virginia Law Review*, Vol. 92, No. 2, pp. 251–88.

Brunnée, Jutta, and Stephen J. Toope (2011). "Interactional International Law: An Introduction," *International Theory*, Vol. 3, No. 2, pp. 307–18.

Brutger, Ryan (2011). "Private Parties: Hidden Actors of WTO Dispute Settlement," Working Paper (Princeton, NJ: Princeton University, Department of Political Science).

---

[19] Koremenos (book manuscript) attempts to overcome some research design obstacles to determining the strength of the shadow of the law through case study research.

Busch, Marc L., and Eric Reinhardt (2003). "Developing Countries and General Agreement
    on Tariffs and Trade/World Trade Organization Dispute Settlement," *Journal of World
    Trade*, Vol. 37, No. 4, pp. 719–35.
Charnovitz, Steve (2009). "The Enforcement of WTO Judgements," *Yale Journal of Interna-
    tional Law*, Vol. 34, No. 2, pp. 558–66.
Chayes, Abram, and Antonia Handler Chayes (1993). "On Compliance," *International Orga-
    nization*, Vol. 47, No. 2, pp. 175–205.
Davis, Christina L., and Sarah Blodgett Bermeo (2009). "Who Files? Developing Country
    Participation in GATT/WTO Adjudication," *Journal of Politics*, Vol. 71, No. 3, pp. 1033–49.
Downs, George. W., David M. Rocke, and Peter N. Barsoom (1996). "Is the Good News
    about Compliance Good News about Cooperation?" *International Organization*, Vol. 50,
    No. 3, pp. 379–406.
Ginsburg, Tom, and Richard H. McAdams (2003). "Adjudicating in Anarchy: An Expressive
    Theory of International Dispute Resolution," *Willam & Mary Law Review*, Vol. 45, No. 4,
    pp. 1229–1339.
Goldstein, Judith O., Miles Kahler, Robert O. Keohane, and Anne-Marie Slaughter (2000).
    "Introduction: Legalization and World Politics," *International Organization*, Vol. 54, No. 3,
    pp. 385–99.
Grando, Michelle T. (2006). "Allocating the Burden of Proof in WTO Disputes. A Critical
    Analysis," *Journal of International Economic Law*, Vol. 9, No. 3, pp. 615–56.
Guzman, Andrew T., and Timothy L. Meyer (2010). "International Soft Law," *Journal of
    Legal Analysis*, Vol. 2, No. 1, pp. 171–225.
Helfer, Laurence R. (2013). "Flexibility in International Agreements," in Jeffrey L. Dunoff and
    Mark A. Pollack (eds.), *Interdisciplinary Perspectives on International Law and International
    Relations: The State of the Art* (New York: Cambridge University Press), pp. 175–96.
Helfer, Laurence R., and Anne-Marie Slaughter (1997). "Toward a Theory of Effective Supra-
    national Adjudication," *Yale Law Journal*, Vol. 107, No. 2, pp. 273–391.
Henkin, Louis (1995). "U.S. Ratification of Human Rights Conventions: The Ghost of Senator
    Bricker," *American Journal of International Law*, Vol. 89, No. 2, pp. 341–50.
Huth, Paul K., Sarah E. Croco, and Benjamin J. Appel (2011). "Does International Law
    Promote the Peaceful Settlement of International Disputes? Evidence from the Study
    of Territorial Conflicts since 1945," *American Political Science Review*, Vol. 105, No. 2,
    pp. 1–22.
Keohane, Robert O. (1984). *After Hegemony. Cooperation and Discord in the World Political
    Economy* (Princeton, NJ: Princeton University Press).
Keohane, Robert O., Andrew Moravcsik, and Anne-Marie Slaughter (2000). "Legalized Dis-
    pute Resolution: Interstate and Transnational," *International Organization*, Vol. 54, No. 3,
    pp. 457–88.
Kim, Moonhawk (2008). "Costly Procedures: Divergent Effects of Legalization in the
    GATT/WTO Dispute Settlement Procedures," *International Studies Quarterly*, Vol. 52,
    No. 3, pp. 657–86.
Koh, Harold Hongju (1997). "Why Do Nations Obey International Law?" *Yale Law Journal*,
    Vol. 106, No. 8, pp. 2599–659.
Koremenos, Barbara (2005). "Contracting around International Uncertainty," *American Polit-
    ical Science Review*, Vol. 99, No. 4, pp. 549–65.
——— (2007). "If Only Half of International Agreements Have Dispute Resolution Provisions,
    Which Half Needs Explaining?," *Journal of Legal Studies*, Vol. 36, No. 1, pp. 189–212.
——— (2011). "An Economic Analysis of *International* Rulemaking," Working Paper (Ann
    Arbor: University of Michigan, Department of Political Science).

―――― (forthcoming). "The Continent of International Law," *Journal of Conflict Resolution*.
―――― (book manuscript). "The Continent of International Law" (Ann Arbor: University of Michigan, Department of Political Science).

Koremenos, Barbara, Charles Lipson, and Duncan Snidal (2001). "The Rational Design of International Institutions," *International Organization*, Vol. 55, No. 4, pp. 761–99.

Krasner, Stephen D. (1978). *Defending the National Interest* (Princeton, NJ: Princeton University Press).

Kucik, Jeffrey, and Eric Reinhardt (2008). "Does Flexibility Promote Cooperation? An Application to the Global Trade Regime," *International Organization*, Vol. 62, No. 3, pp. 477–505.

Leeds, Brett, Jeffrey Ritter, Sara McLaughlin Mitchell, and Andrew Long (2002). "Alliance Treaty Obligations and Provisions," *International Interactions*, Vol. 28, No. 3, pp. 237–60.

Mearsheimer, John J. (1994). "The False Promise of International Institutions," *International Security*, Vol. 19, No. 3, pp. 5–49.

Mitchell, Ronald B. (2002–11). *International Environmental Agreements Database Project* (*Version 2010.3*), available at http://iea.uoregon.edu/.

Muthoo, Abhinay (2002). *Bargaining Theory with Applications* (Cambridge: Cambridge University Press).

Posner, Eric A., and John C. Yoo (2005). "Judicial Independence in International Tribunals," *California Law Review*, Vol. 93, No. 1, pp. 1–74.

Rosendorff, B. Peter (2005). "Stability and Rigidity: Politics and Design of the WTO's Dispute Settlement Procedure," *American Political Science Review*, Vol. 99, No. 3, pp. 389–400.

Sattler, Thomas, and Thomas Bernauer (2010). "Gravitation or Discrimination? Determinants of Litigation in the World Trade Organisation," *European Journal of Political Research*, Vol. 50, No. 2, pp. 143–67.

Shaffer, Gregory C., and Mark A. Pollack (2010). "Hard vs. Soft Law: Alternatives, Complements and Antagonists in International Governance," *Minnesota Law Review*, Vol. 94, No. 3, pp. 706–99.

Simmons, Beth A. (2000). "International Law and State Behavior: Commitment and Compliance in International Monetary Affairs," *American Political Science Review*, Vol. 94, No. 4, pp. 819–35.

―――― (2009). *Mobilizing for Human Rights. International Law and Domestic Politics* (Cambridge: Cambridge University Press).

Smith, Alastair (1999). "Testing Theories of Strategic Choice: The Example of Crisis Escalation," *American Journal of Political Science*, Vol. 43, No. 4, pp. 1254–83.

Smith, James McCall (2000). "The Politics of Dispute Settlement Design: Explaining Legalism in Regional Trade Pacts," *International Organization*, Vol. 54, No. 1, pp. 137–80.

Thompson, Alexander (2009). "The Rational Enforcement of International Law: Solving the Sanctioners' Dilemma," *International Theory*, Vol. 1, No. 2, pp. 307–21.

von Stein, Jana (2005). "Do Treaties Constrain or Screen? Selection Bias and Treaty Compliance," *American Political Science Review*, Vol. 99, No. 4, pp. 611–22.

16

Whose Agents? The Interpretation of International Law in National Courts

Lisa Conant

> It now seems more important to make domestic courts agents of world order than to instruct them to be servants of national policy.
>
> Richard Falk, 1964

National courts' interpretation of international law inspires both high expectations about the potential enforceability and uniformity of international law and doubts about the legitimacy of this activity. Many international lawyers and scholars of international law (IL) and international relations (IR) conceive of national courts as powerful "agents" of enforcement that could promote the development of a more effective system of international law. Enlisting the authority of domestic courts in the service of international law becomes a means to promote adherence to evolving norms. Functionalist approaches highlight the need for dispute resolution in a globalizing world that still lacks adequate international institutional mechanisms. The optional jurisdiction of many international courts and the limited capacity of others to hear the volume of disputes arising within a regional or global jurisdiction creates an institutional vacuum that can only be addressed by national courts (Falk 1964; Martinez 2003; Buxbaum 2005–06; Kirby 2005–06; Whytock 2009–10; Michaels 2011a; Nollkaemper 2011). National courts have responded to this demand, interpreting and applying international legal norms much more often than even the most active international courts (Conant 2002; Geeroms 2004; Sloss 2009; Whytock 2009–10; Sloss, Ramsey, and Dodge 2011a). Chronicles of the globalization of judicial dialogue, in which national judges increasingly refer to each other's interpretations, suggest that domestic courts can contribute toward uniformity and consensus (Slaughter 1999–2000, 2003, 2004). Yet, empirical accounts uncover

I am grateful to Jeffrey Dunoff, Mark Pollack, Ralf Michaels, Rachel Brewster, Steven Ratner, and the participants at the "Interpretation, Application, and Enforcement of International Law Workshop" at Temple University for their helpful suggestions. Any errors or unusual interpretations remain my own.

inconsistent applications of international law that generate legal diversity and uncertainty (Conant 2002; Stephan 2002; Martinez 2003; Hofstötter 2005; Ramos Rameu 2006; Dunoff 2008; Wind 2010). Indeed, many of the international lawyers who see promise in domestic courts are disappointed by inadequate applications of international law in these venues (Franck and Fox 1996; Conforti and Francioni 1997; Hunt 1997; Koh 1997*a*). Finally, conventional accounts identify the United States as an exceptional case of judicial parochialism (Slaughter 1999–2000, 2003; Flaherty 2006; Slaughter and Burke-White 2006), but the pattern of international legal interpretation in U.S. courts defies any isolationist categorization once examined historically and across fields of law (Koh 1991; Martinez 2003; Geeroms 2004; Cleveland 2006; Whytock 2009–10; Sloss *et al.* 2011*a*).

As a result, growing awareness of this judicial activity coincides with disagreements about how national courts should and will engage international law. Much of the legal scholarship articulates normative or descriptive theories about the proper role of national courts, often pitting transnationalists, who urge national courts to be agents of the international system, against a competing nationalist or sovereigntist approach, which conceives of national courts primarily as agents of states that should prioritize domestic laws and constituencies.

By contrast, interdisciplinary and political science scholarship develops positive theories to explain the behavior of national courts. Legalization research on international and transnational dispute resolution posits that much variation in the effectiveness of international law is determined by whether it is embedded in national law, where embeddedness entails the extent to which national courts enforce international rules against governments (Keohane, Moravcsik, and Slaughter 2000). Why and how national courts do this is then the subject of theoretical debate. Socialization processes are prevalent in several of these accounts, whereas domestic institutional features are decisive in others, and relative power in the international system dominates the final theories discussed.

Although transnationalist and socialization approaches identify factors that push toward uniformity, nationalist, liberal, realist, and institutionalist accounts highlight factors that can produce diversity, with the implication that we must necessarily expect at least periodic incoherence and possibly frequent inconsistencies in the application of international law by national courts. Unfortunately, most of the more extensive empirical accounts to date are overwhelmingly doctrinal descriptions that are not organized to inform competing theoretical expectations. Greater interdisciplinary collaboration between those developing theoretical propositions and those with deep knowledge of national case law could inform our understanding of the perils and promise identified in the normative scholarship and test the competing hypotheses advanced in the positivist scholarship.

In the following sections of the chapter, I discuss the central contributions that have emerged from debates among these competing approaches, along with empirical findings that either support or pose puzzles within existing accounts. I begin with transnational approaches and their nationalist critics in the normative scholarship, follow with discussions of discrete positive theories of judicial behavior, and end with realist theories. I conclude by discussing gaps in the literature and avenues for future scholarship.

I. TRANSNATIONALISM AND ITS DISCONTENTS: WHO SHOULD NATIONAL COURTS SERVE?

Richard Falk was an early proponent of using domestic courts as agents to develop a more effective international legal order. Recognizing the unwillingness of states to trust international tribunals to adjudicate many disputes, he anticipated that "we could trust our own courts to apply international law" (1964: 12). He advocated "denationalizing courts in the United States so as to encourage the application of impartial standards of international law formed without reference to the distinctive content of either public policy or foreign policy of the United States" (Falk 1964: 177). He proposed that national courts independently apply international law in areas of international consensus and defer to the executive only in areas where no clear consensus existed. Writing shortly after the postwar proliferation of international human rights treaties and during the height of the Cold War, Falk anticipated that courts could vigorously apply international human rights law but would need to exercise substantial deference in economic disputes (1964: 177). In an era of economic globalization, contemporary transnationalists view national judicial activism across all areas of law as a positive development.

A. *Transnationalist Accounts*

Transnationalists identify a globalization of national judiciaries that they portray as beneficial on functional and normative grounds. A key feature of Anne-Marie Slaughter's transgovernmental "new world order" consists of national courts engaging in a transnational process of dialogue where they invoke both international and foreign sources of law to solve contemporary problems. Most of the dialogue is horizontal, among national judges who influence each other in terms of the persuasive authority of their judgments. Even where relations appear hierarchically vertical, such as in regional legal regimes, including the European Union (EU) and Council of Europe, much of the judicial interaction remains a cooperative dialogue among equals (Slaughter 1997, 1999–2000, 2003, 2004). The fundamental justification for judicial globalization is functional, in promoting problem solving through access to more information, ideas, and arguments. Other transnationalist accounts focus on the nature of the functional demand for an international judicial system to serve the values of predictability, fairness, efficiency, and stability. Given the realities of economic interdependence and universal international human rights commitments, national courts that make "a habitual practice of parochially disregarding the existence of other courts will lead to chaos and dysfunction" (Martinez 2003:

444). To avoid this outcome, "national courts interpreting international law should consider relevant decisions of foreign courts interpreting the same treaty or principle of customary international law and should not depart from those precedents without articulating clear reasons for doing so" (Martinez 2003: 513). Transnationalists identify global problems that concern large parts (or all) of the world simultaneously and must be resolved with comprehensive approaches, for example, global warming, liability for Internet defamation, and worldwide price fixing (Michaels 2011a: 169). The lack of effective world courts to address these problems means that domestic courts are the only possible venues. In doing so, national courts may draw on international law, as Falk proposed, or on domestic law. Thus, Hannah Buxbaum argues that U.S. courts are well positioned to apply *domestic* economic law to resolve global problems, such as price fixing, and thereby provide effective transnational regulation of world markets. The possibility of treble damage awards and utility of several domestic economic regulations uniquely enable U.S. federal courts to deter misconduct that causes global harms (2005–06).

More normatively, transnationalists observe that international agreements and transnational regulatory networks empower the executive, generating an "executive" globalization that is difficult to check (Newman and Zaring 2013). "Judicial" globalization, operating as domestic courts interpret international law, offers one of the few constraints on the expansion of executive power (Flaherty 2006). In the EU context, Andrew Moravcsik (1994) demonstrates the ways in which extensive regional coordination strengthens the executive within states, whereas Karen Alter (1998) shows how national courts in concert with the European Court of Justice (ECJ) can constrain the freedom of the executive to control outcomes. Others observe that contemporary United Nations (UN) Security Council Resolutions operate as global legislation on behalf of the most powerful states without any prescribed system for review (Michaels 2011a; Scheppele, forthcoming). As a result, only domestic courts are available to provide any review of these measures, which can infringe on individual rights. For example, individuals who found their assets frozen, given their alleged support of terrorism, sought recourse in national and then EU courts. In a controversial decision, the ECJ annulled EC regulations that implemented UN Security Council resolutions as violating the right to property and failing to afford due process.[1] Joseph Weiler (2008) and Gráinne de Búrca (2010) chastise the ECJ for deciding the case entirely on the grounds of its internal constitutional order, a practice they associate with the insular approach that the U.S. Supreme Court took in the *Medellin* case.[2] Although both acknowledge that the ECJ provided individual due process protections, in contrast to *Medellin*, de Búrca sharply criticizes the ECJ for taking a "dualist" position that emphasized the autonomy of the EU legal order and prioritized EU fundamental rights over UN instruments that reflect a more

[1] Kadi, 402/05 and 415/05 [2008] ECR 6351.
[2] 552 U.S. 491 2008.

universal international legal order. Castigating the ECJ's approach as one that fragments the international legal order, de Búrca (2010) argues for a more "constitutional" (and "monist") approach that integrates the international legal order.[3] Weiler (2008: 896) likewise chides the ECJ for an approach it would reject if national courts adopted it relative to EU law.

Yet, the ECJ has had to reconcile itself to this approach from national courts for decades, given widespread refusal to accept EU legal supremacy exclusively on the ECJ's terms. Interdisciplinary scholarship has traced national courts' doctrinal responses to the ECJ's declarations of major principles such as direct effect, supremacy, and liability. It took decades for some national courts to accept these rulings, and multiple constitutional courts justify EU legal supremacy in ways that reassert domestic constitutional norms (Alter 1996, 2001; Slaughter, Stone Sweet, and Weiler 1998; Ruggiero 2002). Indeed, even the most enthusiastic participants in transnational judicial activity subordinate international law to clear provisions of the national constitution (Kirby 2005–06). The Federal Constitutional Court of Germany, often praised for its "dialogic" cooperation (de Búrca 2010), nonetheless considers itself able to review EU actions for compatibility with domestic constitutional norms (Boom 1995) and abides by interpretations of the European Convention on Human Rights (the Convention) only to the extent that they increase the level of domestic rights protections (Neuman 2004).

Harold Koh's transnational judicial process approach specifies how national judges reconcile international and national legal systems through a series of interactions instigated by transnational norm entrepreneurs and issue networks and the interpretations of judges who eventually internalize international legal norms within domestic law (1997b, 1998). Here, the transnational judicial process is justified in terms of its promotion of norms that are internationally legitimate. This reflects common assumptions among transnationalists that international law expresses universal values, pursues the highest-order goals of peace and security, and protects human rights. As a result, national judges should accord international law precedence over conflicting national laws. Ultimately, current transnationalist accounts echo Falk in urging judges to see themselves not as representatives of a particular government but as professionals in an endeavor that transcends borders (Slaughter 1999–2000: 1124) and to look beyond narrow national interests to mutual interests in an ordered international system (Koh 2004: 54).

---

[3] Dualist approaches conceptualize the international legal order as separate from the domestic legal order and tend to require the adoption of national measures to bring international law into effect in domestic law. Monist approaches conceptualize the international legal order as part of and supreme to domestic law, such that international laws can take immediate effect in domestic law. Formal distinctions between dualist and monist countries do not necessarily lead to significant differences in the practice of applying international law (Slaughter *et al.* 1998), and it is misleading to portray many countries as strictly dualist or monist since domestic courts may apply international law according to dualist or monist principles depending on the specific circumstances of the case (Sloss *et al.* 2011a).

B. Nationalist Accounts

Transnationalist accounts provoke the ire of nationalists, who fear subordination to international law and the resulting loss of national sovereignty. Much of the criticism focuses on the role of international law in constitutional interpretation, where nationalists see significant problems of democratic accountability. Nationalists specifically reject the notion that conformity to some sort of international consensus should displace domestic laws (Rasmussen 1986; Alford 2004; Young 2005; Weisburd 2005–06; McGinnis 2006). Constitutional interpretation should reflect fundamental commitments within a nation, and differences between conceptions of rights are justifiable in terms of the distinct values societies place on particular liberties. Nationalists in the United States charge that efforts to invoke international law in constitutional cases reflect a strategy of liberals to impose values that they cannot achieve in democratic venues. Ernest Young (2005) and Roger Alford (2004) both assail the invocation of international opinion to shift perceptions of the moral evolution of standards (e.g., the conception of cruel and unusual punishment), where a newly emerging consensus against the death penalty in the United States exists only when foreign countries are added into the calculation. Nationalists also turn transnationalist separation of powers arguments on their head by arguing that the use of international acts enacted by the political branches in constitutional interpretation illegitimately elevates acts of statutory authority, at best, to constitutional status and thereby promotes excessive executive power (Alford 2004: 62). The use of transnational legal materials in constitutional interpretation further undermines self-governance by creating venues for domestic interest groups and foreigners to impose rules on American citizens without the usual institutional checks on the exercise of power (McGinnis 2006: 319).

Moreover, John McGinnis (2006: 303, 313) questions whether trends in international law even reflect democratic consensus anywhere, given that international law reflects the choices of states, not people, through formal processes with deep democratic deficits. The foreign laws most frequently referenced by transnationalists, meanwhile, are European, where "traditions are more favorable to the imposition of elite moral values" (McGinnis 2006: 311). Customary international law suffers the deepest democratic deficit since it is not written anywhere, but is surmised by unelected judges on international courts, who can be unrepresentative of popular opinion and appointed by nations whose leaders are not elected (Bradley 2001: 465, 468; McGinnis 2006: 314). Nationalists contest the inclusion of postwar international human rights law as a source of customary international law because its norms derive predominantly from international resolutions and other agreements and not necessarily from consistent practices that states accept as legally binding. Most problematic are efforts to bind states to human rights norms in conventions that they have not ratified or to provisions from which states have exempted themselves through declarations and reservations. With its frequently stronger protections of individual rights than the federal or state constitutions and statutes in the United States, such customary international human rights law provides one of the clearest potential challenges to U.S. federalism (Goldsmith 1997: 1622, 1641; Bradley and Goldsmith 1997*a,b*).

Notably, many of these nationalist claims react to the specific context of a handful of cases in the U.S. Supreme Court relating to the death penalty and decriminalization of homosexual acts. But the invocation of international opinion and law in these cases has been modest, merely reflecting that Justices have confirmed opinions that they already found compelling; these references are far from that of binding authority and do not even suggest persuasive authority (Neuman 2004; Aleinikoff 2004; O'Brien 2010; Whytock 2010; Goodman and Jinks, forthcoming). As such, the threat of international law to American democracy remains a straw man. Even in Europe, where scholars attribute some of the strongest effects of international law to domestic courts' activity, detailed empirical accounts indicate that the national judges of several countries – Denmark, France, Germany, Spain, Sweden, and the United Kingdom – act as nationalists, insulating domestic law from unwelcome international intrusions (Golub 1996; Chalmers 2000; Alter 2001; Ramos Rameu 2006; Wind 2010).

Nationalists also complain that international sources are selectively used only when they are rights-enhancing and should actually be incorporated when they are rights-constricting as well (Alford 2004; Ramsey 2004). Responding to unwelcome judgments, they echo many internationalist lawyers in complaining that national courts get the "facts wrong" (Ramsey 2004; Ku 2010–11). Yet, historic and contemporary practice indicates that courts have frequently invoked international law to restrict the protection of individual rights by (a) relying on rules of war making, (b) denying the extraterritorial application of constitutional principles while recognizing the extraterritorial right of the government to act, (c) applying the doctrine of "discovery" to appropriate land and govern native populations, (d) invoking "ancient principles of the international law of nation-states" to exempt immigrants from constitutional protections (Cleveland 2006), and (e) applying UN Security Council Resolutions in the post 9/11 "global war on terror" (Scheppele, forthcoming). Whether the restrictions or expansions in rights are justified becomes a normative question divorced from empirical grounding.

Furthermore, nationalists quibble with the partiality of a transnational judicial dialogue dominated by affluent Western countries, common-law courts, and Europeans, not because it is therefore hegemonic, but because European social democracy, secularism, and pacifism render European experience remote from and therefore irrelevant to the United States, going so far as to argue that "it may be that in many nations traditional societal norms impose substantial constraints on the behavior of juveniles. But in our more atomistic, laissez-faire, success-driven society, such norms have much less constraining power. We may therefore need the death penalty for deterrence where most other nations do not" (McGinnis 2006: 312).

Other nationalist analyses explain the historically limited ways that national courts have applied international law in terms of the deference that national courts appropriately show toward the executive branch as it pursues national security interests. In these accounts, courts lack the institutional resources and capacity to assess the implications of their decisions in areas of foreign policy (Goldsmith 1997; Bradley 2001; Nzelibe 2003–04). As a result, the executive should be free to depart from the traditional doctrines that courts have conventionally used to promote international comity, including the interpretation of statutes to conform to international law[4] and reluctance to apply statutes extraterritorially (Posner and Sunstein 2007).

Nationalists are also critical of judicial invocation of international human rights law because of its likelihood to interfere with broader foreign policy goals. In this area, nationalists highlight a dramatic exception to the conventional view that U.S. courts are insular (Posner 2009: 207–25). In litigation on the basis of the Alien Tort Statute (ATS) of 1789, federal courts have enforced the international human rights norms of postwar customary international law and awarded damages to aliens who suffered harm at the hands of public and private actors anywhere in the world (Burley 1989; Aceves 2007; Altschuller, Lehr, and Orsmond 2011). Originally adopted to *prevent* conflict by ensuring that federal courts could provide redress to foreigners injured by Americans (Burley 1989; Bellia and Clark 2011), contemporary ATS cases often target abuses occurring outside the United States and can therefore generate strains in foreign relations. Curtis Bradley argues that ATS litigation "shifts responsibility for official condemnation and sanction of foreign governments away from elected political officials to private plaintiffs and their representatives," who "have neither the expertise nor the constitutional authority to determine U.S. foreign policy" (Bradley 2001: 460). Bradley sees "no reason to expect that . . . the plaintiffs and their lawyers will take into account broader issues relating to the U.S. national interest, . . . and these individuals lack the accountability of elected officials for making bad foreign relations decisions" (Bradley 2001: 460).

Overlap between normative and positive theorizing emerges in the transnational and nationalist accounts, where normative justifications often coexist with the articulation of expectations about behavior. Yet, these debates are primarily motivated by normative concerns, in contrast to the next set of debates that are primarily animated by differing expectations of empirical outcomes.

II. EXPLAINING VARIATIONS IN INTERNATIONAL LEGALIZATION: WHY DO NATIONAL COURTS APPLY INTERNATIONAL LAW?

Scholars from the fields of IL and IR develop positive theories to explain how and why national courts apply international law. Accounts focusing on socialization

---

4 Schooner Charming Betsy 6 U.S. 64, 118 (1804); Von Colson, 14/83 [1984] ECR1891; and Marleasing, 106/89 [1990] ECR I-4135.

processes draw on constructivist IR theory and IR theories of international organization to predict substantial convergence in the application of international law
by national courts. Accounts focusing on domestic institutions draw on liberal IR
theory and comparative institutionalist theory to predict diversity in this case law.
Finally, accounts focusing on power and interests that derive from realist IR theory
also predict variations.

A. Socialization Accounts

Legal scholars have developed explanations based on socialization that engage IR
debates on legalization. The transnational legal process approach developed by Koh
predicts conformity with international law. An evolutionary, transactional process
proceeds through a series of interactions that leads to the interpretations of norms
and ultimately their internalization, where habitual obedience becomes voluntary
(1997b: 2645–46). In areas where international coordination generates mutual benefits, instrumental interests play a key explanatory role (Koh 1998: 636–42; Keohane
1998–99: 703–05). Similarly, interests surface in Koh's discussions of issue linkages,
in which states avoid deviations from their commitments in order to prevent vicious
cycles of retaliation (1998: 653–55). In fields of international law where deviation
does not generate significant costs of noncompliance, constructivist conceptions
become more prominent as "transnational norm entrepreneurs" mobilize to persuade national officials and other political elites of the value of an international
norm. Once persuaded, "governmental norm sponsors" work inside state institutions to promote compliance. National courts specifically contribute to "judicial
internalization" when they incorporate international norms into their interpretation
of domestic law (Koh 1998: 643, 647–55). "Through this repeated cycle of interaction,
interpretation, and internalization – the transnational legal process – international
law acquires its 'stickiness,' and nations come to 'obey' out of a perceived self-interest
that becomes institutional habit" (Koh 1998: 655).

Neofunctionalist scholarship similarly attributes the success of the EU legal system
to strategic socialization of national courts by the ECJ. In this account, the ECJ
appeals to shared professional norms and self-interests to co-opt national judiciaries,
practicing lawyers, and legal scholars. Convincing legal argumentation legitimates
rulings for the legal profession generally, and the creation of a binding system of
EU law serves professional interests as well: the supremacy and direct effect of
EU law empower national courts to exercise judicial review, offer lawyers a new
avenue to pursue client interests, and present academics with new fields of inquiry.
National governments find themselves trapped into accepting EU law because legal
justifications "mask" the implications of rulings and "shield" the ECJ from attack
(Burley and Mattli 1993; Mattli and Slaughter 1995). Once supranational rules govern
transactions, transnational exchange increases and generates new disputes that the
ECJ resolves with its case law, which further encourages both more exchange and

more supranational legislation to address emerging problems. This process sustains an ongoing expansion in legal integration that is difficult to reverse or stop, given the institutional obstacles to treaty revision (Alter 1998; Stone Sweet and Brunell 1998). Ultimately, neofunctionalists expect that compliance with EU law and ECJ rulings will be the most common outcome, and many emphasize the role that national courts play in enforcing the substantial docket of preliminary rulings.

Skeptics have found little empirical support for the convergence predicted in these accounts. Robert Keohane observes more variable outcomes in legal internalization than Koh's theory allows, and argues that international norm cleavages will disrupt the transnational legal process in predictable ways: resistant state elites may align with domestic opponents of international rules that do not link to other issues—for example, the death penalty in the United States (Keohane 1998–99: 712). Scholars have also challenged neofunctionalist assumptions about judicial empowerment by identifying how the EU legal system "demotes" national supreme courts. Serving as the ultimate authority is likely to be more important to courts of last instance than the opportunity to review national law for its compatibility with EU law. In the case of constitutional courts, which already enjoy the power of judicial review, EU judicial review merely opens the door to challenges to their authority by lower courts (Alter 2001). As a result, high courts' cooperation in EU law enforcement is a puzzle worthy of explanation.

Another socialization account theorizes more variations in behavior by specifying an acculturation mechanism that operates independently of the coercive and persuasive mechanisms emphasized in most of the IL and IR literatures. Goodman and Jinks argue that acculturation results from cognitive pressures to assimilate. Unlike persuasion, which requires that actors are consciously convinced of the validity of a norm, acculturation requires only the perception that an important reference group subscribes to the norm or engages in the practice. Processes of acculturation lead states to create structurally similar institutions even when these structures fail to address needs, and to incorporate norms that reflect prevalent ideas (Goodman and Jinks 2004: 635, 638, 640, 642). Variations in states' integration into world society predict variations in the acculturation of states, and powerful states are often late adopters in particular issue areas (Goodman and Jinks 2004: 653–54). Adoption of structures and norms does not necessarily lead to concrete implementation, however, and persistent "decoupling" between norms and practices is most likely when states copy an internationally legitimated model that does not serve local interests (Goodman and Jinks 2004: 649, 651, 670).

This socialization theory is consistent with national judicial behaviors including the (a) prolific degree of transnational judicial activity among national courts in Europe, where countries are regionally integrated within two highly institutionalized legal regimes (Blackburn and Polakiewicz 2001; Slaughter and Burke-White 2006: 332; Stone Sweet and Keller 2008); (b) comparatively intense transnational judicial activity among national courts in countries with newly adopted constitutions or charters of rights, where states seek to demonstrate their membership in a "constitutional club" that departs from a past reliance on parliamentary sovereignty or a prior illiberal regime (e.g., Canada, Israel, New Zealand, South Africa and Argentina) (Benvenisti 2008; Carnota 2010); (c) the relative reluctance of the U.S. Supreme Court to engage in transnational judicial dialogue, particularly in the post–Cold War era, given its long constitutional traditions, exceptionalist self-understanding, and hegemonic power (O'Brien 2010: 9; Banner, Miller, and Provine 2010: 38; Whytock 2010; Sloss *et al.* 2011a); (d) the propensity of the U.S. Supreme Court to attend only to other democratic states when it invokes any foreign sources (Slaughter 1995: 524; O'Brien 2010; Sloss *et al.* 2011a); and (e) the greater resilience against abuse of emergency powers in the post-9/11 world in states whose national constitutional traditions were intricately linked to the postwar international human rights movement, in comparison to states with exceptionalist visions of their constitutional traditions (Scheppele, forthcoming). Moreover, the disproportionate angst that modest U.S. Supreme Court references to international and foreign sources have inspired (Martinez 2003: 479) suggests that threats to national identity and perception of the relative place of the United States in the world are the real source of opposition (Tushnet 2011; Waters 2011). And, finally, Goodman and Jinks (forthcoming) argue that the Supreme Court's habit of invoking foreign and international sources to identify typical practice reflects acculturation.

B. *Liberal Accounts*

Liberal international relations theories highlight the importance of domestic regime type in explaining states' interactions with one another and international institutions. Democratic states do not wage war against each other (Doyle 1986) and are more likely to honor the international human rights commitments that they make (Moravcsik 1995; Neumayer 2005; Simmons 2009; Hafner-Burton and Tsutsui 2007). The courts of democratic states are also more likely to interact with and take account of one anothers' decisions (Slaughter 1995). According to liberal theorists, these distinctive behaviors result from common normative commitments to the rule of law and trust in reciprocal treatment by democracies. An active civil society and effective domestic legal institutions constitute crucial mechanisms to hold democratic regimes accountable to their legal commitments (Moravcsik 1995; Simmons 2009). More recently established democracies are most willing to bind themselves to international human rights institutions, given their interest in democratic consolidation. Meanwhile, more long-standing democracies are more hesitant to accept human rights commitments, given their greater confidence in the durability of their domestic institutions, and may even align with illiberal regimes in their refusal to submit to international enforcement (Moravcsik 2000).

This liberal theorizing is consistent with evidence on the behavior of national courts. Democracies constitute all of the significant participants in judicial globalization, and recently established democracies, such as South Africa, or recently constitutionalized democracies, such as Canada, represent the most enthusiastic participants in the transnational judicial dialogue on human rights issues. By contrast, high courts of more established liberal regimes have disappointed transnationalists lately by adopting more dualist approaches toward international law: the U.S. Supreme Court generally and specifically in its *Medellin* case, the German Constitutional Court in the aftermath of reunification, and the ECJ in its recent *Kadi* case. With one of the world's longest established constitutional democracies, the United States would be among the least likely states to prioritize international human rights law over domestic civil rights law. Germany and the ECJ are particularly illustrative, given shifts in their behavior over time. Transnationalists praise the dialogic approach adopted by the German Constitutional Court in the *Solange* cases of the early years of European integration (and relatively early years of postwar German democracy), but observers later expressed alarm at the court's post-reunification *Maastricht* decision (Boom 1995; Ruggiero 2002). Similarly, transnationalists praise the historically constitutionalist approach of the ECJ toward international law and decry its recent articulation of the primacy of European law over UN resolutions (Weiler 2008; De Búrca 2010). Yet, this evolution is consistent with liberal theory, in which courts that are increasingly confident in the legitimacy of their own legal system prioritize it over international regimes considered to have greater democratic deficits. Also consistent with this liberal interpretation would be the reluctance of courts in Denmark, Sweden, and the United Kingdom to apply EU law over conflicting national laws (Golub 1996; Chalmers 2000; Wind 2010). Along with international reputations for having strong commitments to the rule of law, these countries also have among the longest established democracies within the EU.

Meanwhile, portrayals of the United States as an outlying outlaw, given cases like *Medellin*, obscure an extraordinary development of international human rights law within the federal judiciary. The ATS grants federal courts jurisdiction over "any civil action by an alien for a tort only, committed in violation of the law of nations or a treaty of the United States." Beginning with the *Filartiga v. Pena-Irala* case in 1980,[5] which permitted a Paraguayan plaintiff to sue a Paraguayan defendant for human rights violations that occurred in Paraguay, many ATS suits seek enforcement of international human rights norms that limit how states treat individuals within their borders. ATS litigation has proved to be highly controversial. Skeptics may charge that ATS litigation continues to reflect parochialism, in that the enforcement of international law relies on domestic law (Ku 2010–11), or that it reflects hegemonic action, in that suits against U.S. officials have met with less success than those against foreign officials (Dodge 2011: 376). The ATS's extraterritorial reach for civil claims has been condemned by Germany, Switzerland, the U.K., and three judges of the International Court of Justice. Julian Ku chastises the ATS doctrine for drawing on

---

[5] 630 F .2d 876 (2d Cir. 1980).

federal common law to create civil liability for corporations, which is not established in international law sources (2010–11).[6] Yet, ATS cases put the United States at the "forefront of efforts to strengthen the rule of law in international as well as domestic affairs" (Burley 1989: 493) and constitute "the most significant example of the direct application of customary international law by federal courts during the second half of the twentieth century" (Dodge 2011: 373).

Indeed, the enforcement of human rights norms in ATS disputes constitutes part of a broader empirical reality that is consistent with liberal theory: the judiciaries within liberal democracies, including the United States, are the most active participants in enforcing a variety of treaty-based rights (Slaughter *et al.* 1998; Alter 1998; Conant 2002; Simmons 2009; Sloss 2009; Hollis 2011; Van Alstine 2011; Stephan 2011; Damrosch 2011), in interpreting domestic statutes to be consistent with international law (Lee and Sloss 2011; Michaels 2011*b*, 534; Sloss, Ramsey, and Dodge 2011*b*: 49–50; Waters 2011: 393–394), and in resolving disputes based on private law – the law of contracts, property, and torts – in ways that serve global governance (Geeroms 2004; Whytock 2009–10). The U.S. Supreme Court has acknowledged that "we cannot have trade and commerce in world markets and international waters exclusively on our terms, governed by our laws, and resolved in our courts," and U.S. courts are arguably at the vanguard in transnational civil litigation, offering more liberal standing, broader jurisdiction, and much larger punitive damage awards, all of which have made foreign courts more reluctant to enforce U.S. judgments than the reverse (Martinez 2003: 511). Finally, empirical research on the EU case supports liberal theory's emphasis on the centrality of the mobilization of civil society and effective legal structures in generating a stream of opportunities for judges to engage international law (Alter and Meunier 1994; Moravcsik 1995; Alter and Vargas 2000; Conant 2001, 2002; Simmons 2009).

Meanwhile, liberals would predict that efforts to import institutional frameworks without sufficient domestic institutionalization of the rule of law or without vigorous civil society activism will contribute to little practical progress in the application of international law by national courts (Simmons 2009). A variety of empirical studies support this claim: the Andean Tribunal of Justice (ATJ), a carbon copy of the ECJ, has not been able to foster the type of rich transnational judicial dialogue that developed in the EU, but has instead been occupied with narrow intellectual property claims that arise as national courts passively respond to agency requests for referrals for ATJ preliminary rulings (Alter and Helfer 2009). Liberals would not find this outcome surprising, given that members of the Andean Pact – Bolivia, Chile, Colombia, Ecuador, Peru, and Venezuela – are not among the world's more established liberal democracies. The extent to which the Argentine Supreme Court has invoked international human rights laws in recent decades correlates positively

---

[6] As this volume goes to press, the question of corporate liability under the ATS is pending before the U.S. Supreme Court.

with the extent to which it has operated within a genuinely liberal, democratic political regime (Carnota 2010). The poor quality of domestic legal institutions in new postcommunist EU member states corresponds with the failures of national courts to enforce EU laws (Falkner and Treib 2008), and civil society weakness in some southern EU member states, due to the legacy of prior authoritarian regimes, limits the extent to which national courts address clear deficiencies in compliance with EU law (Börzel 2006). Domestic war crimes trials in Bosnia, Croatia, and Serbia have failed to apply international norms fairly or consistently, reflecting serious deficiencies in the domestic rule of law and commitment to human rights in all three countries (Subotic 2009).

C. *Comparative Institutionalist Accounts*

Comparative institutionalist scholarship includes overlaps with liberal IR theory in emphasizing legal dynamics that occur in liberal democratic regimes, but tends to derive from more comparative approaches to law and politics, and it anticipates and justifies tremendous variation in the ways that national courts will interpret international law. For comparative institutionalists, the application of international (or foreign) law is not a simple mechanistic process, but requires thoughtful "translation" to make sense in a domestic context (Knop 1999–2000). The process of translation generates variations in meaning and application that may reflect long-standing domestic legal traditions and institutional capabilities. The resulting variations in domestic rulings can provide a source of instructive alternatives to help other domestic courts invoke international law sensibly (Knop 1999–2000: 533). Paul Stephan (1998–99) makes an even stronger case for the primacy of national solutions in arguing that efforts to seek international unification are futile; instead, he argues that businesses can contract which national legal system will be used to settle any future disputes, a solution that utilizes stable and well-developed national legal systems to facilitate international commerce instead of much more recent and ambiguous international conventions. In these accounts, legal uniformity is neither expected nor desired. Acknowledging the lack of a truly global moral consensus in many areas, Melissa Waters (2007) suggests an alternative normative justification for transnational judicial globalization that emphasizes the mediating role that national courts play. In her view, judicial interference in the political process is legitimate and democracy enhancing where courts protect discrete and insular minorities whose interests tend to be ignored by domestic majoritarian political processes. Rather than necessarily prioritizing international norms, however, Waters argues that courts must balance their consideration of international and domestic norms that promote conflicting social values, incorporating only those international norms that are specifically appropriate to the domestic context.

Others may value legal uniformity but prefer centralized litigation before international tribunals. In large regimes such as the World Trade Organization (WTO), "transferring interpretive authority from one [Appellate Body] in Geneva to the national judiciaries of over 150 WTO members would likely produce inconsistent judicial interpretations. Frequent disagreements are inevitable when hundreds of domestic courts are all independently empowered to identify the best readings of ambiguous treaty texts" (Dunoff 2008:15). Dunoff cautions that if private parties are empowered to enforce international norms in domestic courts, domestic litigation could substitute for international dispute resolution, private litigation could largely replace interstate litigation, and domestic courts could actively create international law with a local accent (Dunoff 2008). The first two dynamics have unambiguously characterized the legal systems of the EU and the Council of Europe's Convention. Must less research exists to establish the third dynamic conclusively, but the discussion of Knop and Waters above indicate its likelihood, and the following in-depth studies of the application of EU law by national courts support it.

The unprecedented volume of litigation based on international law in the EU and Council of Europe (Alter 2006: 26) has generated sustained scholarly attention to the relationship between European law and national courts. Institutionalist accounts attribute national judicial application of EU law to instrumental strategies of empowerment (Alter 1996, 2001; Nyikos 2000) or professional norms and practices unique to judiciaries (Ramos Rameu 2006). Karen Alter identified variations in national court cooperation in the "bureaucratic politics" or "inter-court competition" model, proposing that first-instance and intermediate appellate courts have the greatest incentives to send references to the ECJ for preliminary rulings (or to apply ECJ precedents) because the EU legal system genuinely empowers these courts. Alter expects that national supreme courts will initially send fewer references than their lower-court counterparts, with constitutional courts sending the fewest references of all. As lower courts seize the opportunity to send references to the ECJ (or apply ECJ precedent) to achieve legal outcomes that are impossible under national law, national supreme courts begin to send references in an effort to influence the direction of the ECJ's legal interpretation in ways that are more deferential to national legal traditions (Alter 1996, 2001). Empirical research demonstrates that national judges do this by including opinions with their references, while the ECJ tries to maintain legal consistency in its responses by redefining issues and adding or suppressing questions. Further evidence indicates that national judges will usually comply with the preliminary rulings that respond to their references, but they will also evade unwelcome decisions by re-referring issues or reinterpreting the facts of particular cases (Nyikos 2000).

Legal scholars have challenged this strategic account of judicial politics with an institutionalist "team model" of judicial behavior that assumes judges' primary motivations are functional and legalistic. Here, judges conceive of themselves as a team and are sensitive to the signals that other courts are sending about the appropriate application of EU law. As a result, higher courts should cite the ECJ more often, since they direct legal interpretation, and lower courts should cite the

ECJ regularly only after higher courts incorporate the ECJ into the "team" by acknowledging and following ECJ case law. Eventually, Ramos Rameu expects that courts with more experience with EU law should cite ECJ case law less often and also diverge from ECJ "precedent" more often because they need less guidance than courts with less experience (Ramos Rameu 2006). In sum, issues of legal certainty and knowledge, rather than political preferences and empowerment, explain judicial behavior in the team model.

Empirical research on the behavior of national courts suggests strong support for institutionalist expectations of diversity. First, national courts vary in their willingness to refer cases to the ECJ. Failure to make references in appropriate circumstances – when a court of last instance rules on an ambiguous issue of EU law – regularly occurs. The EU Commission anecdotally reports on cases in which national high courts refrain from making references that are obligatory, and, in one unusual incident, charged that Swedish courts systematically sent too few references (Conant 2002: 91; Wind 2010). The few in-depth inquiries into national referral patterns suggest that failure to refer is an important judicial source of noncompliance with EU law. One study of environmental disputes in the U.K. demonstrated that British judges refrained from sending references when they wanted to shield domestic policy from unwelcome ECJ interference (Golub 1996). Surveys and interviews investigating the Danish and Swedish judiciaries indicate that most judges in these countries consider themselves ignorant about EU law, do not think it is legitimate for judges to overturn national law for its incompatibility with EU law, and feel political pressure from superiors to refrain from sending references (Wind 2010). This research implies that national courts may generate a systematic, yet largely hidden, source of variation in the application of EU law.

Because only a tiny fraction of EU legal disputes involve references for preliminary rulings, national courts' application of EU law and its interpretations in ECJ case law are ultimately a more meaningful measure of the role of national judicial enforcement. Findings from the few in-depth case studies that consider national judicial behavior outside the context of references for preliminary rulings uncover substantial diversity. A study of all reported U.K. national court judgments on EU law from 1973 to 1998 found that judges (a) typically apply EU provisions without addressing the status of incompatible national provisions and (b) had only considered the issue of whether national legislation needed to be overturned in two cases (Chalmers 2000).

The propensity of national courts to interpret EU treaties, regulations, and directives without any explicit reliance on ECJ case law, coupled with the need for more judicial training in EU law, generate wide discrepancies in interpretation (Conant 2002: 81–84). For example, courts in France and Germany denied EU migrants access to employment as educators when they independently interpreted EU law in the years before the ECJ ruled that the free movement of workers applied to education. German courts continued to rule against EU migrants even after the ECJ had specifically ruled that student teaching in Germany must be open to non-nationals (Conant 2002: 173). The practice of lower federal courts in the United States interpreting international treaties is similarly mixed and fails to accord with Supreme Court precedent as well (Stephan 2002: 345; Martinez 2003: 512).

A study testing a random sample of 475 Spanish court decisions that apply or cite EU law from 1986 until 2000 generates findings about the application of EU law by national courts that are consistent with institutionalist accounts. For instance, Spanish judges were 11 percent more likely to apply ECJ case law when there were reinforcing signals from other national courts, and they were 41 percent less likely to apply ECJ decisions when there were contradictory signals from other national courts, indicating that judges will tend to give national case law precedence if it conflicts with ECJ doctrines (Ramos Romeu 2006: 412). Spanish courts were also 15 percent less likely to apply ECJ judgments when the government was a party to the case, suggesting that these courts defer to national political concerns. Moreover, the Spanish Supreme Court and Constitutional Court are 28 percent less likely to cite the ECJ and 22 percent less likely to apply ECJ case law than other Spanish courts (Ramos Romeu 2006: 413–15), which parallels the behavior of many courts of last instance. Finally, while citation of ECJ case law has historically been low in Spanish courts, it declined further after fifteen years of membership (Ramos Rameu 2006: 409, 418), suggesting that legal interpretation across member states can be expected to diverge more over time.

Empirical inquiry into the "law in action" finds that judicial applications of international law are also insufficient to promote adherence to international legal norms. Case studies in a number of different policy areas demonstrate that innovative ECJ interpretation does not induce automatic, broad-based application of legal obligations. Member states most commonly comply with the specific terms of a judgment as it relates to the parties to the litigation and subsequently ignore the implications that the judicial interpretation may have for the universe of similarly situated parties. Active legal and political mobilization is usually necessary to override this tendency for "contained compliance" (Conant 2002). For example, ECJ case law that developed the mutual recognition doctrine did not lead to any policy changes. Instead, parties had to litigate case-by-case to apply the doctrine to 115 different products prior to the passage of the Single European Act. It took the Commission's advocacy and the mobilization of business and civil society groups to promote widespread adoption of the ECJ's new approach (Alter and Meunier 1994). Case studies tracing the impact of ECJ rulings that implied the need for reforms in telecommunications, electricity, air transport, public sector employment, and social benefits involve a similar dynamic, in which the implicit requirements of ECJ interpretation remained dormant for long periods until institutional and societal actors mobilized to demand major changes to legislation and practice (Conant 2002, 2003, 2004).

Similar tendencies can be seen in the United States. For example, several WTO dispute panels have held that a U.S. practice called "zeroing" violates WTO obligations (Dunoff, 2008). In response, the United States recalculated duties for the specific goods at issue in the WTO dispute, but did not apply the WTO ruling more generally and continued to use the discredited "zeroing" methodology with respect to other goods. Repeated efforts to get domestic courts to extend the logic of the ruling to similarly situated litigants proved unsuccessful. Only after several years and multiple defeats at the WTO did the United States move away from use of the zeroing methodology in certain phases of antidumping determinations.

D. *Realist Accounts*

Realists' enduring skepticism about the impact and independence of international tribunals means that national courts will be the only actors able to apply international law authoritatively (Stephan 2002: 335–38; Posner 2009: 130–49), and realists follow most comparative institutionalists in theorizing and finding diversity in the application of international law by national courts. For realists, however, this pattern results from constellations of national interest and power. Jack Goldsmith and Eric Posner integrate realist IR theory and institutionalist game theory to develop a realist theory of the application of customary international law. They argue that behaviors associated with customary international law reflect either a coincidence of interest or coercion (Goldsmith and Posner 2005).

Goldsmith and Posner find that many changes in state practices are consistent with changes to nations' interests and relative power in the international system (2005). With respect to judicial application, Goldsmith and Posner argue that courts take cues from the political branches about the content of customary international law, obey informal instructions when explicit direction is not available, or are deputized to apply the law in accordance with the national interest. They find that "biased national court interpretation of international law is a well-known phenomenon" (Goldsmith and Posner 1999: 1169). In analyzing the postwar customary international law of human rights, they find an enormous gap between what the law requires and the actual behavior of states, which is supported by extensive scholarship on the impact of human rights treaties (Hathaway 2001–02; Neumayer 2005; Hafner-Burton, Tsutsui, and Meyer 2008; Hafner-Burton and Tsutsui 2007.

Another IR theory with a foundation in the realist focus on the distribution of international power is the "second image reversed." This approach inverts liberal IR theory's argument that domestic regime type is a *cause* of peaceful interactions in international politics and asks if domestic structures and institutions are a *consequence* of a state's relative position in international politics (Gourevitch 1978). A second image reversed approach to the interpretation of international law by national courts generates a number of expectations: (a) national courts of powerful states will often find the application of much international law to serve their interests, given that they are primarily responsible for determining its content; (b) national courts of weaker states may take the greatest pains to apply international law to avoid damaging retaliation by more powerful states; and (c) national courts of the most powerful states will be most likely to ignore international law that generates costs if applied in a consistently principled manner, which is an inverse application of the coercion logic, in which no one is available to coerce the most powerful states into applying law consistently.

Doctrinal accounts of the application of international law by U.S. courts often mention and reject the expectations of the second image reversed approach. Yet, general empirical patterns discussed in previous sections are strikingly consistent with the core expectations of the second image reversed approach, particularly when a long-term historical exploration of the U.S. case is considered. The application of international law by national courts in the early, weak United States looks strikingly similar to the obedient application of international law by small states today (Simmons 2009: 130; Hollis 2011; Bederman 2011; Lee and Sloss 2011; Sloss *et al.* 2011*b*). More inconsistent and restrictive applications of international law become prevalent only by the early twentieth century, as the United States emerged as a great power, and then again after its victory in World War II established its status as one of two superpowers. Finally, its decisions become most dismissive of international law (e.g., *Medellin*) in an era of unparalleled U.S. military hegemony (Sloss *et al.* 2011*a*). Within the EU, the national courts that have been feistiest about accepting EU supremacy are also its larger, more dominant states (Alter 2001). Meanwhile, the most persistent partners in building the EU legal system, interacting with the ECJ, and applying EU law are smaller states that benefit the most from economic integration, such as the Netherlands (Slaughter et al. 1998, Stone Sweet and Brunell 1998).

Eyal Benvenisti's attribution of the growing willingness of national courts to invoke international law in recent decades to factors that mitigate the traditional anarchic environment of international politics supports second image reversed claims that features of the international system determine domestic outcomes. Specifically, the European integration process that produced the Single Market and European Union explains the leading role that national courts in Europe have played in judicial globalization (Benvenisti 1993). Benvenisti further attributes the growing willingness of many national courts to invoke their own interpretations of international law in recent decades to the effort of national judiciaries to reassert domestic influence over processes of globalization that are beyond the control of national executives in most states. The apparently more frequent use of international law by courts from states in Europe, as well as Canada, South Africa, New Zealand, and Israel, compared with less activity by courts in the United States, is consistent with the idea that smaller states have more difficulty resisting the global pressures that diminish domestic democratic autonomy and individual rights protection. In developing countries, the growing use of progressive interpretations of international law as a means to protect the environment or promote health is viewed as part of an effort to combat the powers that multinational corporations exert in negotiations with state officials over economic access and intellectual property rights (Benvenisti 2008). In contrast to transnationalist justifications for judicial globalization as a check on executive power, this account ultimately justifies the transnational judicial activity within realist terms: the courts are acting to serve a national interest that executives are otherwise powerless to pursue.

Here, judicial coordination across borders can be important to serve national interests and avoid negative consequences in areas such as asylum policy and the environment, where comparatively better rights protections could motivate destabilizing inflows of refugees or where comparatively stricter environmental protections could lead to capital flight. Strong domestic political pressures can override the impulse for cooperation, resulting in "defections" that threaten a united judicial front. The refusal of French and German courts to follow the lead of other European courts in the asylum area provides support for the realist conclusion that "interjudicial cooperation is a strategy of choice, pursued purely for parochial ends" (Benvenisti 2008: 269). Two prime sources of conflicts include national court competition with international tribunals and North–South divides between courts in advanced economies and emergent powers such as Brazil, China, India, and Russia (Benvenisti and Downs 2009).

III. CONCLUSION: GAPS IN THE LITERATURE AND AGENDA FOR FUTURE RESEARCH

National courts are the most prolific interpreters of international law, and they may also be the most innovative interpreters of international law, but scholars must engage in more systematic empirical exploration of domestic case law before they might confirm this possibility. Christopher Whytock observes that we still know very little about how domestic courts apply international law, why they apply law the way that they do, and how their decisions affect transnational activity. To address this gap, scholars must examine not only judicial doctrine but also the law in action, and explore the shadow of the law outside the courtroom (2009–10: 115). The contributions discussed in this chapter indicate that theorizing has outpaced systematic empirical testing. Evidence available in doctrinal accounts by legal scholars and empirical studies by political scientists can often be interpreted to confirm more than one theoretical approach.

As a result, an important next step is to design methodologically rigorous empirical studies to test existing theoretical propositions. Too much of the existing empirical research on national courts' application of international law is purely doctrinal or remains fairly anecdotal, focused exclusively on instances of cooperation, and idiosyncratically organized to explore one country with little effort to make findings comparable across cases. Systematic comparative research on the application of international law by national courts is challenging because it requires fluency in multiple languages, training in both legal analysis and social science methodologies, and, therefore, a team of researchers committed to testing the same sets of hypotheses with the same types of data. Comparable data on national case law are particularly challenging to collect since the legal systems of larger states generate millions of decisions a year, only a fraction of which are archived in electronic databases. Electronic databases vary in the extent to which they cover court decisions at different levels of the judiciary and allow for analytical legal basis searching that enables researchers to isolate cases engaging particular areas of law, yet electronic databases are also the only efficient means of searching and analyzing entire categories of law. Much existing research concentrates on the usual suspects of the United States, Germany, and the United Kingdom. Small states tend to receive very little attention and get included primarily in large-*n* quantitative studies, although Australia, Canada, the Nordic states, South Africa, and a handful of newer postcommunist member states have attracted relatively more attention than others. Much less research exists on the application of international law by lower courts everywhere despite their importance on the "front lines of transnational litigation" (Whytock 2009–10: 117). Survey research akin to the studies of the Swedish and Danish judiciaries and their attitudes toward EU law could be very fruitfully pursued all over the EU and wider world of constitutional democracies. The application of international law by illiberal states is another gap that might be pursued by liberal theorists to contrast more clearly how democracy matters. Given the central role of mobilization in many accounts of the law in action, and in activating judicial activity more generally, the activities of organized civil society deserve much greater scholarly attention as well. In the EU setting, the adjudication of the vast majority of EU law by national courts justifies a much greater focus on this activity, rather than the patterns of national court references to the ECJ for preliminary rulings, which has been the primary focus of political science scholarship.

REFERENCES

Aceves, William (2007). "Conclusion," in *The Anatomy of Torture* (Leiden/Boston: Martinus Nijhoff Publishers), pp. 159–83.

Aleinikoff, Alexander (2004). "International Law, Sovereignty, and American Constitutionalism," *American Journal of International Law*, Vol. 98, No. 1, pp. 91–108.

Alford, Roger (2004). "Misusing International Sources to Interpret the Constitution," *American Journal of International Law*, Vol. 98, No. 1, pp. 57–69.

Alter, Karen J. (1996). "The European Court's Political Power," *West European Politics (WEP)*, Vol. 19, No. 3, pp. 458–87.

_____ (1998). "Who Are the Masters of the Treaty?," *International Organization*, Vol. 52, No. 1, 121–47.

_____ (2001). *Establishing the Supremacy of European Law* (Oxford: Oxford University Press).

———— (2006). "Private Litigants and the New International Courts," *Comparative Political Studies*, Vol. 39, No. 1, pp. 22–49.

Alter, Karen J., and Laurence Helfer (2009). "The Andean Tribunal of Justice and Its Inter-locutors," *New York University Journal of International Law and Politics*, Vol. 41, No. 4, pp. 871–930.

Alter, Karen J., and Sophie Meunier (1994). "Judicial Politics in the European Community," *Comparative Political Studies*, Vol. 39, No. 4, pp. 535–61.

Alter, Karen J., and Jeanette Vargas (2000). "Explaining Variation in the Use of European Litigation Strategies," *Comparative Political Studies*, Vol. 33, No. 4, pp. 452–82.

Altschuller, Sarah, Amy Lehr, and Andrew Ormsond (2011). "Corporate Social Responsibility," *International Lawyer*, Vol. 45, No. 1, pp. 179–90.

Banner, Francine, Ken Miller, and Doris Marie Provine (2010). "Foreign Law in American Jurisprudence," in Donald Jackson, Michael Tolley, and Mary Volcansek (eds.), *Globaliz-ing Justice* (Albany: State University of New York Press), pp. 27–43.

Bederman, David (2011). "Customary International Law in the Supreme Court, 1861–1900," in David Sloss, Michael Ramsey, and William Dodge (eds.), *International Law in the U.S. Supreme Court* (New York: Cambridge University Press), pp. 89–123.

Bellia Jr., Anthony J., and Bradford R Clark (2011). "The Alien Tort Statute and the Law of Nations," *University of Chicago Law Review*, Vol. 78, No. 2, pp. 445–552.

Benvenisti, Eyal (1993). "Judicial Misgivings Regarding the Application of International Law," *European Journal of International Law*, Vol. 4, No. 2, pp. 159–83.

———— (2008). "Reclaiming Democracy," *American Journal of International Law*, Vol. 102, No. 2, pp. 241–74.

Benvenisti, Eyal, and George Downs (2009). "National Courts, Domestic Democracy, and the Evolution of International Law," *European Journal of International Law*, Vol. 20, No. 1, pp. 59–72.

Blackburn, Robert, and Jörg Polakiewicz (2001) (eds.). *Fundamental Rights in Europe* (New York: Oxford University Press).

Boom, Steve (1995). "The European Union after the Maastricht Decision," *American Journal of Comparative Law*, Vol. 43, No. 2, pp. 177–226.

Börzel, Tanja (2006). "Participation through Law Enforcement," *Comparative Political Stud-ies*, Vol. 39, No. 1, pp. 128–52.

Bradley, Curtis (2001). "The Costs of International Human Rights Litigation," *Chicago Journal of International Law*, Vol. 2, No. 2, pp. 457–73.

Bradley, Curtis, and Jack Goldsmith (1997a). "Customary International Law as Federal Com-mon Law," *Harvard Law Review*, Vol. 110, No. 4, pp. 815–76.

Bradley, Curtis, and Jack Goldsmith (1997b). "The Current Illegitimacy of International Human Rights Litigation," *Fordham Law Review*, Vol. 66, No. 2, pp. 319–70.

Burley, Anne-Marie (1989). "The Alien Tort Statute and the Judiciary Act of 1789" *American Journal of International Law*, Vol. 83, No. 3, pp. 461–93.

Burley, Anne-Marie, and Walter Mattli (1993). "Europe before the Court," *International Organization*," Vol. 47, No. 1, pp. 41–76.

Buxbaum, Hannah (2005–2006). "Transnational Regulatory Litigation," *Virginia Journal of International Law*, Vol. 46, No. 2, pp. 251–318.

Carnota, Walter F. (2010). "Judicial Globalization," in Donald Jackson, Michael Tolley, and Mary Volcansek (eds.), *Globalizing Justice* (Albany: State University of New York Press), pp. 255–66.

Chalmers, Damian (2000). "The Much Ado about Judicial Politics in the United Kingdom." Jean Monnet Working Paper No. 1/100 (Cambridge, MA: Harvard University).

Cleveland, Sarah (2006). "Our International Constitution," *Yale Journal of International Law*, Vol. 31, No. 1, pp. 1–125.

Conant, Lisa (2001). "Europeanization and the Courts," in Maria Green Cowles, James Caporaso, and Thomas Risse (eds.), *Transforming Europe* (Ithaca, NY: Cornell University Press), pp. 97–115.

_____ (2002). *Justice Contained* (Ithaca, NY: Cornell University Press).

_____ (2003). "Europe's No Fly Zone?," in Tanja Börzel and Rachel Cichowski (eds.), *The State of the European Union* (Oxford, UK: Oxford University Press), pp. 235–254.

_____ (2004). "Contested Boundaries," in Joel Migdal (ed.), *Boundaries and Belonging* (New York: Cambridge University Press), pp. 284–317.

Conforti, Benedetto, and Francioni, Francesco (1997) (eds.). *Enforcing International Human Rights in Domestic Courts* (Cambridge, MA: Nijhoff).

Damrosch, Lori (2011). "Medellin and Sanchez Llamas," in David Sloss, Michael Ramsey, and William Dodge (eds.), *International Law in the U.S. Supreme Court* (New York: Cambridge University Press), pp. 451–64.

de Búrca, Gráinne (2010). "The European Court of Justice and the International Legal Order after *Kadi*," *Harvard International Law Journal*, Vol. 51, No. 1, pp. 1–49.

Dodge, William (2011). "Customary International Law in the Supreme Court, 1946–2000," in David Sloss, Michael Ramsey, and William Dodge (eds.), *International Law in the U.S. Supreme Court* (New York: Cambridge University Press), pp. 353–79.

Doyle, Michael (1986). "Liberalism and World Politics." *American Political Science Review*, Vol. 80, No. 4, pp. 1151–69.

Dunoff, Jeffrey (2008). "Less Than Zero," *Loyola University Chicago International Law Review*, Vol. 6, No. 1, pp. 279–310.

Falk, Richard (1964). *The Role of Domestic Courts in the International Legal Order*. (Syracuse, NY: Syracuse University Press).

Falkner, Gerda, and Oliver Treib (2008). "Three Worlds of Compliance or Four?," *Journal of Common Market Studies*, Vol. 46, No. 2, pp. 293–313.

Flaherty, Martin (2006). "Judicial Globalization in the Service of Self-Government," *Ethics & International Affairs*, Vol. 20, No. 4, pp. 477–541.

Franck, Thomas, and Fox, Gregory (1996) (eds.). *International Law Decisions in National Courts* (Irvington, NY: Transnational).

Geeroms, Sofie (2004). *Foreign Law in Civil Litigation* (New York: Oxford University Press).

Goldsmith, Jack L. (1997) "Federal Courts, Foreign Affairs, and Federalism," *Virginia Law Review*, Vol. 83, No. 8, pp. 1617–715.

Goldsmith, Jack L., and Eric A. Posner (1999). "A Theory of Customary International Law," *University of Chicago Law Review*, Vol. 66, No. 4, pp. 1113–77.

_____ (2005). *The Limits of International Law* (New York: Oxford University Press).

Golub, Jonathan (1996). "The Politics of Judicial Discretion," *West European Politics*, Vol. 19, No. 2, pp. 360–85.

Goodman, Ryan, and Derek Jinks (2004). "How to Influence States," *Duke Law Journal*, Vol. 54, No. 3, pp. 622–703.

_____ (forthcoming). *Socializing States: Promoting Human Rights through International Law* (New York: Oxford University Press).

Gourevitch, Peter (1978). "The Second Image Reversed," *International Organization*, Vol. 32, No. 4, pp. 881–912.

Hafner-Burton, Emilie, and Kiyoteru Tsutsui (2007). "Justice Lost!" *Journal of Peace Research*, Vol. 44, No. 4, pp. 407–25.

Hafner-Burton, Emilie, and Kiyoteru Tsutsui, and John Meyer (2008). "International Human Rights Law and the Politics of Legitimation," *International Sociology*, Vol. 23, No. 1, pp. 115–41.

Hathaway, Oona (2001–02). "Do Human Rights Treaties Make a Difference?" *Yale Law Journal*, Vol. 111, No. 8, pp. 1935–2042.

Hofstötter, Bernhard (2005). *Non-compliance of National Courts* (The Hague: Asser).

Hollis, Duncan (2011). "Treaties in the Supreme Court, 1861–1900," in David Sloss, Michael Ramsey, and William Dodge (2011) (eds.), *International Law in the U.S. Supreme Court* (New York: Cambridge University Press), pp. 55–88.

Hunt, Murray (1997). *Using Human Rights Law in English Courts* (Oxford, UK: Hart).

Keohane, Robert (1998–1999). "When Does International Law Come Home?" *Houston Law Review*, Vol. 35, No. 3, pp. 699–713.

Keohane, Robert, Andrew Moravcsik, and Anne-Marie Slaughter (2000). "Legalized Dispute Resolution," *International Organization*, Vol. 54, No. 3, pp. 457–88.

Kirby, Michael (2005–2006). "International Law-The Impact on National Constitutions," *American University International Review*, Vol. 21, No. 3, pp. 328–64.

Knop, Karen. (2000). "Here and There," New York *University Journal of International Law and Politics*, Vol. 32, No. 2, pp. 501–35.

Koh, Harold (1991). "Transnational Public Law Litigation," *The Yale Law Journal*, Vol. 100, No. 8, pp. 2347–2402.

———— (1997a). "How Is International Human Rights Law Enforced?," *Indiana Law Journal*, Vol. 74, No. 4, pp. 1397–1417.

———— (1997b). "Why Do Nations Obey International Law?," *The Yale Law Journal*, Vol. 106, No. 8, pp. 2599–2659.

———— (1998). "1998 Frankel Lecture," *Houston Law Review*, Vol. 35, No. 3, pp. 623–81.

———— (2004). "International Law as Part of Our Law," *American Journal of International Law*, Vol. 98, No. 1, pp. 43–57.

Ku, Julian (2010–11). "The Curious Case of Corporate Liability under the Alien Tort Statute," *Virginia Journal of International Law*, Vol. 51, No. 2, pp. 353–96.

Lee, Thomas, and David Sloss (2011). "International Law as an Interpretive Tool in the Supreme Court, 1861–1900," in David Sloss, Michael Ramsey, and William Dodge (eds.), *International Law in the U.S. Supreme Court* (New York: Cambridge University Press), pp. 124–63.

Mattli, Walter, and Anne-Marie Slaughter (1998). "Revisiting the European Court of Justice," *International Organization*, Vol. 52, No. 1, pp. 177–209.

Martinez, Jenny (2003). "Towards an International Judicial System," *Stanford Law Review*, Vol. 56, No. 2, pp. 429–529.

McGinnis, John (2006). "Foreign to Our Constitution," *Northwestern University Law Review*, Vol. 100, No. 1, pp. 303–29.

Michaels, Ralf (2011a). "Global Problems in Domestic Courts," in Morly Frishman *et al.* (eds.), *The Law of the Future and the Future of Law* (Oslo: Torkel Opsahi Academic E Publisher, FICHL Publication Series No. 11), pp. 167–77.

———— (2011b). "Empagran's Empire," in David Sloss, Michael Ramsey, and William Dodge (2011) (eds.), *International Law in the U.S. Supreme Court: Continuity and Change* (New York: Cambridge University Press), pp. 533–46.

Moravcsik, Andrew (1994). "Why the European Union Strengthens the State," Working Paper Series No. 52 (Center for European Studies, Harvard University).

———— (1995). "Explaining International Human Rights Regimes," *European Journal of International Relations*, Vol. 1, No. 2, pp. 157–189.

_____ (2000). "The Origins of Human Rights Regimes," *International Organization*, Vol. 54, No. 2, pp. 217–252.

Neuman, Gerald (2004). "The Uses of International Law in Constitutional Interpretation," *American Journal of International Law*, Vol. 98, No. 1, pp. 82–90.

Neumayer, Eric (2005). "Do International Human Rights Treaties Improve Respect for Human Rights?," *Journal of Conflict Resolution*, Vol. 49, No. 6, pp. 925–53.

Newman, Abraham, and David Zaring (2013). "Regulatory Networks: Power, Legitimacy, and Compliance," in Jeffrey L. Dunoff and Mark A. Pollack (eds.), *Interdisciplinary Perspectives on International Law and International Relations: The State of the Art* (New York: Cambridge University Press), pp. 244–65.

Nollkaemper, André (2011). *National Courts and the International Rule of Law* (Oxford: Oxford University Press).

Nyikos, Stacy (2000). *The European Courts and National Courts*, University of Virginia Ph.D. thesis.

Nzelibe, Jide. (2003–04). "The Uniqueness of Foreign Affairs," *Iowa Law Review*, Vol. 89, No. 3, pp. 941–1009.

O'Brien, David (2010). "The U.S. Supreme Court's Use of Comparative Law in the Construction of Civil Rights," in Donald Jackson, Michael Tolley, and Mary Volcansek (eds.), *Globalizing Justice* (Albany: State University of New York Press), pp. 7–25.

Posner, Eric A. (2009). *The Perils of Global Legalism* (Chicago: University of Chicago Press).

Posner, Eric A., and Cass Sunstein (2007), "Chevronizing Foreign Relations Law," *Yale Law Journal*, Vol. 116, No. 6, pp. 1170–1228.

Ramos Romeu, Francisco (2006). "Law and Politics in the Application of EC Law," *Common Market Law Review* Vol. 43, No. 2, pp. 395–421.

Ramsey, Michael (2004). "International Materials and Domestic Rights," *American Journal of International Law*, Vol. 98, No. 1, pp. 69–82.

Rasmussen, Hjalte (1986). *On Law and Policy in the European Court of Justice* (Dordrecht, NL: Martinus Nijhoff Publishers).

Ruggiero Cristina (2002). "The European Court of Justice and the German Constitutional Court," *Studies in Law, Politics, and Society*, Vol. 24, No. 1, pp. 51–80.

Scheppele, Kim (forthcoming). *The International State of Emergency: The Rise of Global Security Law* (Cambridge, MA: Harvard University Press).

Simmons, Beth A. (2009). *Mobilizing for Human Rights* (New York: Cambridge University Press).

Slaughter, Anne-Marie (1995). "International Law in a World of Liberal States," *European Journal of International Law*, Vol. 6, No. 4, pp. 503–38.

_____ (1997). "The Real New World Order," *Foreign Affairs* Vol. 76, No. 5, pp. 183–97.

_____ (1999–2000). "Judicial Globalization," *Virginia Journal of International Law*, Vol. 40, No. 4, pp. 1103–24.

_____ (2003). "A Global Community of Courts," *Harvard International Law Journal*, Vol. 44, No. 1, pp. 191–219.

_____ (2004). *A New World Order* (Princeton, NJ: Princeton University Press).

Slaughter, Anne-Marie, Alec Stone Sweet, and Joseph Weiler (1998) (eds.). *The European Court and the National Courts – Doctrine and Jurisprudence* (Oxford: Hart).

Slaughter, Anne-Marie, and William Burke-White (2006). "The Future of International Law is Domestic," *Harvard International Law Journal*, Vol. 47, No. 2, pp. 327–52.

Sloss, David (2009) (ed.). *The Role of Domestic Courts in Treaty Enforcement* (Cambridge: Cambridge University Press).

Sloss, David, Michael Ramsey, and William Dodge (2011a) (eds.). *International Law in the U.S. Supreme Court* (New York: Cambridge University Press).

Sloss, David, Michael Ramsey, and William Dodge (2011b). "International Law in the Supreme Court to 1860," in David Sloss, Michael Ramsey, and William Dodge (2011) (eds.), *International Law in the U.S. Supreme Court* (New York: Cambridge University Press), pp. 7–51.

Stephan, Paul B. (1998–99). "The Futility of Unification and Harmonization in International Commercial Law," *Virginia Journal of International Law*, Vol. 39, No. 3, pp. 743–98.

——— (2002). "Courts, Tribunals, and Legal Unification," *Chicago Journal of International Law* Vol. 3, No. 2, pp. 333–52.

——— (2011). "Treaties in the Supreme Court, 1946–2000," in David Sloss, Michael Ramsey, and William Dodge (2011) (eds.). *International Law in the U.S. Supreme Court* (New York: Cambridge University Press), pp. 317–52.

Stone Sweet, Alec, and Thomas Brunell (1998). "Constructing a Supranational Constitution," *American Political Science Review*, Vol. 92, No. 1, pp. 63–81.

Stone Sweet, Alec, and Helen Keller (2008) (eds.). *A Europe of Rights* (New York: Oxford University Press).

Subotic, Jelena (2009). *Hijacked Justice* (Ithaca, NY: Cornell University Press).

Tushnet, Mark (2011). "International Law and Constitutional Interpretation in the Twenty-First Century," in David Sloss, Michael Ramsey, and William Dodge (eds.), *International Law in the U.S. Supreme Court* (New York: Cambridge University Press), pp. 507–17.

Van Alstine, Michael (2011). "International Law as an Interpretive Tool in the Supreme Court, 1946–2000," in David Sloss, Michael Ramsey, and William Dodge (2011) (eds.), *International Law in the U.S. Supreme Court* (New York: Cambridge University Press), pp. 380–415.

——— (2011). "Treaties in the Supreme Court, 1901–1945," in David Sloss, Michael Ramsey, and William Dodge (2011) (eds.), *International Law in the U.S. Supreme Court* (New York: Cambridge University Press), pp. 191–224.

Waters, Melissa (2007). "Normativity in the 'New' Schools," *Yale Journal of International Law*, Vol. 32, No. 2, pp. 455–84.

——— (2011). "International Law as an Interpretive Tool in the Supreme Court, 1946–2000," in David Sloss, Michael Ramsey, and William Dodge (2011) (eds.), *International Law in the U.S. Supreme Court* (New York: Cambridge University Press), pp. 380–415.

Weiler, J.H.H. (2008). "Editorial: *Kadi* – 'Europe's Medellín?," *European Journal of International Law*, Vol. 19, No. 5, 895–96.

Weisburd, Mark (2005–06). "Using International Law to Interpret National Constitutions – Conceptual Problems," *American University International Law Review*, Vol. 21, No. 3, pp. 365–77.

Whytock, Christopher (2009–2010). "Domestic Courts and Global Governance," *Tulane Law Review*, Vol. 84, No. 1, pp. 67–123.

——— (2010). "Foreign Laws in Domestic Courts," in Donald Jackson, Michael Tolley, and Mary Volcansek (eds.), *Globalizing Justice* (Albany: State University of New York Press), pp. 45–63.

420 *Lisa Conant*

Wind, Marlene (2010). "The Nordics, the EU, and Reluctance towards Supranational Judicial Review," *Journal of Common Market Studies*, Vol. 48, No. 4, pp. 1039–1063.

Young, Ernest (2001–02). "Sorting Out the Debate over Customary International Law," *Virginia Journal of International Law*, Vol. 42, No. 2, pp. 365–511.

———— (2005). "Foreign Law and the Denominator Problem," *Harvard Law Review*, Vol. 119, No. 1, pp. 148–67.

17

International Judicial Independence

Erik Voeten

Judicial independence strikes at the heart of what is different about a world with international courts (ICs). International courts have issued more than thirty thousand legally binding judgments (Alter 2013). Yet, if international judges were simply "diplomats in robes," then these judgments would be unlikely to result in noticeable changes in the policies and practices of states, even if compliance were perfect.

There is a scholarly consensus that most international courts enjoy a degree of autonomy within a defined sphere. The literature refers to this alternately as "constrained independence" (Helfer and Slaughter 2005), "bounded discretion" (Ginsburg 2005), or the "strategic space" (Steinberg 2004) within which international judges can freely operate. There is, however, little agreement on who or what defines the bounds of this sphere or how wide it is or should be. Some argue that the effective control that states exercise over judges is so minute that international judges should properly be considered "trustees" (Majone 2001; Alter 2008). Others question the degree to which ICs do or should enjoy independence (Posner and Yoo 2005; Carrubba, Gabel, and Hankla 2008). Moreover, there are theoretical debates about why ICs acquired the independence that they did.

This chapter provides an overview of what we know about international judicial independence. Rather than offering a summary of individual contributions, I discuss what I think of as the state-of-the-art answers to some important substantive questions about international judicial independence. Although I utilize examples from specific courts and tribunals, my focus is on the general phenomenon of international judicial independence.

First, what is international judicial independence? Judicial independence refers to the set of institutional and other factors that, to a lesser or greater extent, allows

I gratefully acknowledge suggestions and comments from Karen Alter, Cesare Romano, and the partic␣ipants at the Temple workshop, especially the many detailed suggestions from Jeffrey Dunoff and Mark Pollack.

judges autonomy from the preferences of other political actors when these judges issue legal opinions. How judges will use this autonomy is a separate question. Second, why do some ICs have a great deal of independence while others do not? Viable theories of judicial independence should not be based on assumptions that judges are ontologically inclined to favor greater separation from states, whereas states have opposite inclinations. Instead, I emphasize the answers offered by two groups of theories: sociological-institutionalist (or neofunctionalist) and rationalist-institutionalist (or principal–agent) approaches. Third, what do we know about the degree to which governments can use control mechanisms to influence judges? Here, I discuss the various challenges to empirically studying judicial independence. Finally, does judicial independence increase the effectiveness of ICs? This latter section highlights fears that the judicialization of politics is met by an increased politicization of the judiciary.

I. WHAT IS JUDICIAL INDEPENDENCE?

Consistent with Romano (1999), I define international judicial bodies as institutions that are permanent, are established by an international legal instrument, rely on international law for resolving cases, follow fixed rules of procedure, and issue legally binding judgments. I generally refer to these bodies as international courts. Exceptions are the temporary criminal tribunals for Yugoslavia (International Criminal Tribunal for Former Yugoslavia, the ICTY) and Rwanda (International Criminal Tribunal for Rwanda, the ICTR). Although these bodies are not permanent, I include these tribunals in the discussion.

The common element in all definitions of judicial independence is that it allows judges to develop legal opinions unconstrained by the preferences of other actors.[1] This does not mean that an independent judge "simply applies the law." In many cases, there is no such thing as straightforwardly applying settled law to specific circumstances. Independent judges apply the law as they see fit. Judges may well be influenced by their own judicial philosophies, cultural biases, or ideological blinders. Yet, an independent judge is at liberty to ignore the preferences and biases of outsiders.

The first question to ask is: "From whom are or should the judges be independent?" The literature is almost exclusively concerned about the degree to which ICs are influenced by governments. To the extent that the purpose of international law is to distinguish itself from interstate diplomacy, this is justified. Yet, international judges may be influenced by other actors. For example, nongovernmental organizations (NGOs) promote the cause of international criminal tribunals by lobbying governments and intergovernmental organizations for renewed financing,

---

[1] See, for example, article 1.1 of *The Burgh House Principles on the Independence of the International Judiciary* (International Law Association 2004): "The court and the judges shall exercise their functions free from direct or indirect interference or influence by any person or entity."

extension of deadlines, and other support (Danner and Voeten 2010). These same NGOs advocate particular interpretations of war crimes law and issue press releases demanding convictions or prosecutions (Danner 2006). This results in a potential threat to judicial independence that has received little attention (Danner 2003), perhaps because scholars perceive it as more innocuous than government influence or because both international law (IL) and political science have traditionally been state-centric disciplines.

Concerns about independence may also arise from a judge's past actions. For example, a judge on the Sierra Leone Court was disqualified for statements made outside the courtroom, and Israel (unsuccessfully) sought to disqualify an International Court of Justice (ICJ) judge for prior involvement in the Israeli-Palestinian conflict (Shany and Horovitz 2008). Similar issues arise on arbitral tribunals, where law firms repeatedly seek to appoint the same arbitrator, raising concerns that these arbitrators may become beholden to law firms that are repeat players.[2]

Yet, most operationalizations of judicial independence emphasize the institutional separation between governments and international judges. As Curtis Bradley and Judith Kelley (2008: 120) put it:

> Independence [. . .] depends on the control mechanisms that a state has over the decision-making body through its representation on the body, the body's rules and procedures, other institutional features such as oversight mechanisms, the permanence of the delegation, and authority over finances.

The literature highlights a range of potential *ex post* and *ex ante* control mechanisms that governments could potentially employ to influence judges (see Helfer [2006], for a useful overview). Judicial independence is enhanced when governments have fewer opportunities to affect the selection and tenure of judges, when judges have more legal discretion, and when judges have more control over material and human resources (Keohane, Moravcsik, and Slaughter 2000: 459–60). Independence may also be affected by the extent to which states indirectly or directly participate in proceedings, such as through third-party intervention or the appointments of ad hoc (impermanent) national judges (Posner and Yoo 2005). Others add that judicial independence increases when governments have less control over the docket of ICs, for example, by granting courts compulsory jurisdiction and allowing unfiltered access to private actors and/or supranational enforcement agencies (Alter 2006). Finally, governments can constrain ICs by (implicitly) threatening to override or ignore court decisions or even by threatening to exit the jurisdiction of a court (Carrubba *et al.* 2008). Institutional provisions that make noncompliance, override, and exit more difficult can thus enhance the independence of a court.

---

[2] For example, *Opic Karimun Corp. v. Bolivarian Republic of Venezuela*, ICSID Case No. ARB/10/14 (pending) and *Universal Compression International Holdings, S.L.U. v. Bolivarian Republic of Venezuela*, ICSID Case No. ARB/10/9 (pending).

A downside of focusing exclusively on formal institutional guarantees is that it ignores differences between de jure and de facto judicial independence. Studies of domestic judicial independence have found small correlations between formal institutional provisions and the degree to which judges are perceived as independent by experts (Feld and Voigt 2003). Although I am not aware of similar work in the international arena, the findings would likely be the same. There are many institutional carbon copies of the European Court of Justice (ECJ) that clearly do not enjoy similar levels of de facto judicial independence (Alter 2010). Conversely, some courts, like the Inter-American Court for Human Rights (IACtHR), that appear institutionally dependent, act "as if" they are rather independent (Neuman 2008).

It is thus imperative to avoid conflating institutional safeguards with behavioral output. Institutional control mechanisms *could* affect judicial behavior, but the extent to which they do is a matter of theoretical and empirical debate. First, independence does not necessarily imply that judges display impartiality or neutrality in their rulings.[3] The extent to which a court is (perceived as) biased may be a function of its independence from governments, but it need not be. For example, the sources of (alleged) bias could be cultural or linked to the professional backgrounds or predispositions of judges (Voeten 2008). Or governments could perceive courts as biased because the institutional design differs from those embedded in their own legal system (Mitchell and Powell 2011). Thus, even de facto autonomous judges could be biased. This also points to the need to carefully disentangle the question of whether a judge is independent from the question or whether a judge is making decisions based on the types of considerations we may believe judges ought to entertain – primarily their understanding of the facts and the law. Judges could decide cases based on irrelevant considerations, such as their political views or the time since lunch (Danziger, Levav, and Avnaim-Pesso 2011), absent outside interference. An independent judge is thus not by definition a good judge; although good judges tend to be independent.

Second, independence should be distinguished from effectiveness (Staton and Moore 2011). Indeed, there are fierce debates about the extent to which judicial independence makes ICs more or less effective. Much of the literature maintains that independence is the key to the legitimacy and effectiveness of ICs (Helfer and Slaughter 2005). Yet, some argue that the weakness of political controls makes states more likely to avoid ICs or disregard their decisions, potentially condemning courts to irrelevance (Posner and Yoo 2005). There is room for a middle ground in which there is a politically optimal level of judicial independence, which varies depending on the political context in which courts operate. The conclusion returns to these debates.

---

[3] See Haftel and Thompson (2006) for a different view in which neutrality is part of the definition of independence.

Given the difficulty of measuring de facto judicial independence, hypotheses about the behavioral consequences of specific (combinations of) control mechanisms lend themselves better to empirical testing than do hypotheses about the effects of judicial independence per se. There are also good policy reasons for such a focus: it is the control mechanisms that we can manipulate, not "judicial independence." Before delving deeper into the behavioral consequences of individual control mechanisms, it is useful to ponder why some ICs do or do not appear to have a great deal of independence.

II. WHY (NO) JUDICIAL INDEPENDENCE?

Much of the early literature conceptualized the problem of international judicial independence as a contest between judges interested in expanding the reach of their court and states eager to rein them in. This literature assumed that judges were always interested in attracting more cases, expanding their jurisdiction, and interpreting treaties broadly. States, conversely, wanted none of that. Different authors declared different winners, but the devotion to these assumptions (either implicitly or explicitly) was virtually universal.

Recent research and events have made these assumptions untenable. We now know that judges vary considerably in the degree to which they prefer their court to act independently from the raison d'état. The clearest quantitative evidence comes from the European Court of Human Rights (ECtHR), where votes are observed (Voeten 2007, 2008), but there is also evidence from the ECJ (Malecki 2009) and qualitative evidence from other courts (Terris, Romano, and Swiggart 2007; Alter and Helfer 2010). At least in the ECtHR, this variation among judges is correlated to variation in the preferences of the governments that appointed them, suggesting that some governments prefer more activist courts (Voeten 2007).

Even stronger evidence for the latter proposition is that governments with great regularity voluntarily design, join, and reform ICs with institutional guarantees for judicial independence. Even after years of experience with a supposedly activist ECJ, European Union (EU) member states ratified the Lisbon treaty, which delegates more authority to interpret human rights provisions. They also designed a new patent court.[4] Hundreds of legally binding findings that states violated the European Convention on Human Rights did not stop Council of Europe member states from designing (1994) and quickly ratifying (by 1998) Protocol XI, which made the ECtHR's compulsory jurisdiction and individual appeal mandatory, made the ECtHR a permanent court, and eliminated a body that filtered case applications (Drzemczewski 1995). States willingly exchanged the General Agreement on Tariffs and Trade's (GATT's) highly dependent dispute resolution mechanism for the World Trade Organization's (WTO's) much more independent body. They also

---

[4] Note that the ECJ has found that the proposed patent court is in violation of EU law.

created the International Criminal Court (ICC), which does not only have strong institutional guarantees for judicial independence but also features an independent prosecutor.

To be sure, not all governments eagerly embraced these developments, and there are substantive areas of international politics and regions of the world where ICs with high levels of judicial independence have barely made a dent (Kingsbury 2012). Moreover, all ICs continue to have control mechanisms that offer governments at least the theoretical possibility to influence judicial behavior. Yet, to make any sense of these developments in the 1990s and 2000s, it must be true that at least some governments at some times believe that delegating authority to an independent IC suits their interests just fine.

Two groups of social science theories explain why ICs do or do not obtain judicial independence. The first set of theories draws from sociological-institutionalism and neofunctionalism. The second set draws from rational choice institutionalism and principal–agent theory.

A. *Neofunctionalism, Sociological-Institutionalism, and Constructivism*

Neofunctionalist, sociological-institutionalist, and constructivist theories highlight that international courts can expand their autonomy from governments by building alliances with substate and supranational actors, most notably national courts, civil society actors, and supranational bureaucracies. This perspective was developed in the context of the ECJ (Mancini 1989; Weiler 1991; Burley and Mattli 1993; Alter 1998; Mattli and Slaughter 1998; Stone Sweet and Brunell 1998). The ECJ made its various constituencies aware of the opportunities that were entailed in the European Community's legal system. These constituencies included individual litigants, national courts, NGOs, and the European Commission. In turn, these constituents used the ECJ for their own purposes but also strengthened the Court by increasingly relying on it. In addition to the role of substate, transnational, and supranational actors, some of these approaches also stressed that the ECJ became more impervious to political interference by the "shield of domestic norms of rule of law and judicial independence" (Mattli and Slaughter 1998: 181). Thus, these approaches maintain that independent domestic courts and strong domestic civil societies in the member states of those courts are key elements to ensuring judicial independence at the international level.

Alter and Helfer (2010) further elaborate this model in a comparative study of two institutionally similar courts: the ECJ and the Andean Tribunal of Justice.[5] They argue that ICs are more likely to act autonomously from states when they obtain "nurturing" from substate interlocutors, such as government officials, advocacy

---

[5] Their dependent variable is expansionist law-making by the court, but their perspective has implications for independence as well.

networks, national judges, and administrative agencies. When these substate actors are sufficiently powerful and supportive, an IC is more likely to exert its authority at the expense of state discretion. The interaction between ICs and substate actors, especially NGOs, is also highlighted in the literature on international human rights courts (e.g., Cichowski 2010). Somewhat lacking in this literature is an examination of the role of business communities in this process, although it is implied in some neofunctionalist treatments of the ECJ (Stone Sweet and Brunell 1998).

Another extension is the focus on transnational networks of judges, governments, and nongovernmental actors in shaping constituencies for independent ICs. The law literature particularly highlights the transnational networks of judges who influence each other (Slaughter 1994, 2003, 2004; Koh 2004). Transjudicial communication aids the professionalization of judges and helps socialize them into valuing judicial independence. It also helps international and national judges build alliances that can be used to strengthen their respective positions. Such alliances could strengthen the position of international judges, vis-à-vis governments.

Often, but not always, the neofunctionalist and sociological-institutionalist (or constructivist[6]) approaches go together. The neofunctionalist label is used primarily in the context of EU studies. Neofunctionalists stress that international institutions are created as solutions to particular problems, something that constructivists or other theorists applying sociological theories do not always accept (Barnett and Finnemore 2004). Instead, constructivists highlight that international or domestic norms can influence states to create and accept independent ICs (Goodman and Jinks 2004). Similarly, judges can be socialized to value norms of judicial independence. Internalization of such norms may shield judges from bending to governmental pressures. Conversely, social norms play a less prominent role in neofunctionalism, although many self-identified neofunctionalist writers incorporate claims about norms.

The two approaches converge on the argument that the main constraints on an international court come not from member governments but from pressures to maintain legitimacy with non-state constituencies and incentives to demonstrate legal consistency. The latter is a clear driving force for greater judicial independence. Pressures to satisfy substate, transnational, or supranational actors could be a threat to judicial independence. After all, these actors may have particular preferences over legal interpretations that could shape the behavior of ICs. Nevertheless, given that the literature is almost exclusively concerned with independence from states, this issue is rarely examined in these terms.

---

[6] I prefer the label *sociological-institutionalism* because it is essentially an attempt to apply institutional and organizational theories from sociology to the study of international courts, as opposed to rational choice institutionalism, which applies political economy perspectives. Moreover, not all authors in this tradition identify themselves as belonging to the constructivist international relations tradition.

Member state preferences feature lightly in both approaches. Neofunctionalists stress that demands for some form of international court tend to be driven by transnational (economic) exchanges (Stone Sweet and Brunell 1998). Sociological approaches highlight that states that have strong domestic adherence to the rule of law are more likely to delegate authority to ICs (Kelley 2007). Yet, once a court is created, member state preferences recede to the background. Member states can inform court rulings by assisting judges in making better legal judgments. Yet, there are no explicit theoretical mechanisms that explain why judicial interpretations should cater to the wishes of member states, although some scholars argue that the mechanisms highlighted by principal–agent theory operate under some circumstances.[7] I now turn to that theoretical framework.

B. *Principal–Agent Theory and Rational Choice Institutionalism*

A second set of theories argue that the independence of international courts is a direct function of the contract (treaty) that governments (the principals) agree on when they delegate authority to an IC (the agent) (e.g., Pollack 1997; Moravcsik 2000). Any treaty is almost inevitably incomplete. An IC can fill in the gaps by resolving disputes between parties over the application of treaty provisions and by interpreting treaty provisions that are unclear (Guzman 2008). This informational rationale provides an argument for why courts should be independent: in order to incentivize judges, it may be advantageous to grant judges some independence.

A stronger (and more common) case for judicial independence is that it helps solve both domestic and international commitment problems. Treaties are generally commitments to policy reform. Yet, both domestic and international actors may be uncertain whether such commitments will be followed up by true reform. Delegation to an independent court increases the credibility of that commitment. It may thereby allow more cooperation than would be otherwise possible. The credibility of the commitment that states make is only increased if the delegation is meaningful and if there are nontrivial exit costs. Indeed, the logic of this argument stipulates that there are benefits to incurring sovereignty costs.

For example, delegating authority to an independent court increases the credibility of the commitment by the powerful that they will not exploit their more vulnerable counterparts in a cooperative agreement. The more independent a court is, the less likely its decisions cater to the wishes of powerful states. Consequentially, less powerful states should insist on greater independence at the design stage. This makes an independent court useful in order to persuade the less powerful to cooperate in the first place.

---

[7] For example, Alter (2010, 2013) argues that courts that primarily engage in dispute settlement and administrative review have a principal–agent relationship with states, whereas courts that primarily engage in enforcement and constitutional review activities are characterized by a trustee relationship.

Others focus on how international judicial independence increases the credibility of domestic policy reforms. For example, new democracies may signal that they are committed to upholding human rights by ratifying a human rights treaty. They could increase the credibility of that commitment by delegating authority to an independent regional court (Moravcsik 2000). This also has an international dimension: it may increase the perception of others that these governments are committed to a regional integration effort and perhaps make actors more likely to make long-term investments (Farber 2002).

Similarly, the ICC may serve as a way for governments engaged in civil conflicts to make commitments to ratchet down violence and start peaceful negotiations (Simmons and Danner 2010). The ECJ may help reassure EU states that the costly domestic policy reforms they implement are also implemented by other states, thus allowing them to reap the benefits of policy coordination. Delegation to an independent investment tribunal could spur foreign direct investment (Allee and Peinhardt 2011). Governments also use judgments by independent international tribunals to explain to their domestic publics why they have to maintain an unpopular policy (Reinhardt 2002), thus potentially alleviating fears that cooperation will stop due to domestic opposition.

Thus, an independent court may confer benefits on a state even if it occasionally rules against that state. Consequentially, if powerful states comply with a court ruling while expressing their displeasure, then this does not necessarily mean that the state wished that the court were less independent. The occasional cost of judicial independence may be worth the benefits of sustaining cooperative agreements or the enhanced perceived commitment to domestic policy reform. If there were no cost associated with delegating authority, then states could not reap the gains of delegation.

Yet, both principal–agent and legal theorists also argue that states generally design some control mechanisms in treaties that introduce some limits to judicial independence (Cogan 2008). Most principal–agent approaches assume that some conflict of interests exists between the principals (usually, although not necessarily, states) and the agents (judges). Without any control mechanisms, the agents could impose policy adjustments on states whose costs well exceed the informational and credibility benefits of an independent court. Thus, states tend to ensure that at least "fire-alarm" controls are built into a treaty, which can be triggered if judges exceed the bounds of their delegated authority. Obviously, the stronger the control mechanisms, the less credible the commitment. Politically optimal treaties weigh the benefits of increased commitment against the anticipated losses in policy autonomy.

C. *Differences and Similarities between the Two Approaches*

The two theoretical approaches emphasize different actors and mechanisms, but they are not always inconsistent with one another. For instance, it is plausible to devise a theory in which the initial act of delegation is motivated primarily by the desire of governments to make credible commitments, whereas the operation of the court is shaped by dynamics stressed by neofunctionalists. At the same time, we should not overstate the complementarity of the approaches. Neofunctionalists may contend that they never said that state interests do not matter, just as principal–agent theorists can declare the compatibility of their approach with non-state interlocutors. Yet, emphasis is important.

First, if the design of independent judicial institutions were primarily driven by member states' desires to make credible commitments, then the explanation for why judicial independence exists is "intergovernmentalist" (to borrow another term from EU scholarship). That is, what really matters are the grand bargains between states (treaties), not the actions of judges or supranational bureaucracies. One could argue that substate and supranational actors define the need for governments to make credible commitments in the first place by bringing human rights or international norms onto the agenda. This does not contradict liberal intergovernmentalism, which argues that the preferences of states are shaped by the preferences of domestic and transnational social actors concerning the management of interdependence (Moravcsik 2013). A distinct neofunctionalist argument is that international judges themselves strategically construct their independence through *Marbury v. Madison* type rulings (e.g., Alter 2006). In principal–agent theory, judges may have considerable independence to interpret treaties, but they cannot themselves redefine the terms of their contract. Some rational choice models stipulate how courts can enhance their authority by strategically earning the trust of a government's public (Carrubba 2009). Such models defy easy labeling, in that they highlight the centrality of the initial act of delegation while acknowledging that endogenous change can occur afterward.[8]

Second, neofunctionalists assign little causal importance to formal institutional control mechanisms. Some scholars conclude that delegation and abdication are equivalent (Majone 2001; Alter 2008). By contrast, principal–agent theorists argue that governments will use the available formal institutional control mechanisms to influence judicial behavior. This is an empirical question and the topic of the next section.

III. DO GOVERNMENTS INFLUENCE JUDICIAL BEHAVIOR?

To what extent do the institutional mechanisms designed to shield judges from government influence do so successfully? Alternatively, to what extent do the institutional mechanisms that are supposed to grant governments some influence over judicial behavior indeed have that effect? Scholars with realist inclinations are

---

[8] A limitation is obviously that these models would have to contain an argument explaining why rational states could not foresee this development.

skeptical that formal institutions can protect judges from political influence. They argue that, given the anarchical nature of the international system, international law works only if it fits the purposes of powerful states (Goldsmith and Posner 2005). If judges go against these wishes, they risk being punished or ignored.

Conversely, neofunctionalists are skeptical that even formal control mechanisms give states much power. These scholars claim that tools such as appointments, third-party observations, or threats of override and noncompliance are rarely credible means of influencing judges (e.g., Alter 2008; Stone Sweet and Brunell 2012). By contrast, rational-institutionalists argue that the degree of government influence is a direct function of institutional design. Where judges are well insulated, government influence should be minimal, but governments will and can use control mechanisms to shape how international judges behave.

Evaluating these alternative approaches requires us to engage a complex counterfactual: does observed court behavior differ from what it would have been if the preferences of political actors were inconsequential? We could overestimate government influence if the revealed preferences of governments happened to coincide with what the law demands. Alternatively, we may underestimate the influence of governments if judges anticipate how governments would respond if judges applied the law as they saw it. For example, the observation that the WTO's Appellate Body (AB) is restrictive in incorporating broader public international law may be attributable to expectations about government responses. Or, it could reflect a genuine belief among AB members that these general principles of international law ought not to be used when interpreting the WTO law (Pauwelyn 2001). The latter interpretation would be consistent with the sociological approach, whereas the former would reflect a principal–agent logic. Empirically, they are difficult to disentangle.

A starting point for any analysis is a precise theoretical statement of how governments can affect something that judges want. I organize the discussion based on the three most common types of arguments: that governments can affect the careers of judges, that governments affect the policy implications of judicial decisions through noncompliance or override, and that governments can affect the support for the legitimacy of the institutions judges serve on.

A. Appointments and Careers

The first set of control mechanisms presumes that judges, like everyone else, care about their careers (Posner 1993). The assumption is not that their only concern is career advancement but that they are sensitive to personal success and that governments have a decisive say in this (Voeten 2009). First, governments can select judges whom they expect to make decisions that match perceived government interests. This type of selection is common in many (although not all) advanced democracies and, presumably, in less liberal states. The international judicial appointment process is widely considered to be highly political (Mackenzie and Sands 2003). For example, governments more favorably disposed toward European integration appointed more activist judges on the ECtHR (Voeten 2007). Governments carefully interviewed candidates for the WTO's AB with an eye to ensuring that the candidate's interpretation of the law matched theirs (Steinberg 2004; Elsig and Pollack 2011). International Court of Justice judges appear to vote in ways that resemble the interests of the country from which they originate (Posner and de Figueiredo 2005).

An obvious limitation of the selection mechanism is that governments have imperfect *ex ante* information about how judges will behave while on the bench, although they may be able to make reasonable inferences from past behavior, interviews, or the political and professional backgrounds of prospective international judges. Another common objection is that it is difficult to stack an international court with like-minded judges, given that the appointment process involves multiple governments. This is true, but only because governments have heterogenous preferences over how independent they would like a court to be. There is no coordination problem. If all governments truly wished the ECJ to become less activist, it would be individually rational for each government to appoint a conservative diplomat. That is, the optimal appointment strategy for each government is to pick its most favored candidate, regardless of what other governments do. The exceptions are ICs in which judicial candidates are elected by majority vote, such as on the ICC and ICJ (i.e., not one-state-one-judge), or where candidates are subject to the approval of key member states (as in the WTO). In the former case, there is some evidence that international norms as to what an appropriate international criminal judge should be are important (Danner and Voeten 2010). In the latter case, the de facto veto power of the EU and the United States likely keeps some adventurous judges from being considered for the WTO's AB (Elsig and Pollack 2011).

Although there is ample evidence that politics shapes the appointment process, it is less clear that this affects judicial independence per se. The appointment process is highly political in many countries, with courts that are widely perceived as independent, including in the United States. A normative advantage of a political appointment process is that it makes general tendencies in judicial behavior responsive to (democratic) politics. These accountability advantages accrue to the extent that partisan politics shapes the appointment process. That is, the ideological views of the winners of elections get greater representation on the courts than those of the losers. Normatively, the law literature is troubled by such appointments because they do not always advance the most qualified candidates for international judgeships.[9] Threats to judicial independence are more severe when governments stack the courts with diplomats prone to protect national interests. The evidence suggests that both types of political appointments occur, although the partisan variant

---

[9] The most systematic empirical overview that examines the characteristics of international judges across courts is Terris *et al.* (2007).

appears more common than the diplomatic appointment (Voeten 2009). At the same time, as credible commitment theories suggest, some governments have incentives to deliberately appoint judges who are likely to display an independent attitude (Voeten 2007).

Second, governments may use (threats of) *ex post* sanctions and rewards. This is a more serious threat to judicial independence. It implies that governments can influence judges to make their preferred choice on specific cases. The most obvious "carrot" is reappointment. For example, ECtHR judges have six-year renewable terms. There is some evidence that judges who reach the mandatory retirement age when their terms expire are more willing to find violations against their own governments (Voeten 2008). Terris, Romano, and Swiggart (2007: 125) quote an ECJ judge who has precisely that fear if dissents were allowed:

> You would have the situation where judges start writing opinions before their mandate expires or before they are asked to resign. Whatever you do then is wrong: if you go against the government because now you are just doing it in order to show that you're independent. And if you go for the government, it's because you want to be reappointed. It opens up all these sorts of nasty speculations.

There are also some isolated examples of judges who have been fired for voting against their governments, although most cases of nonrenewal appear motivated by partisan politics or poor performance (Voeten 2009). There are also anecdotes that incurring the wrath of powerful states may shorten the career of judges, such as the speculation that the United States helped ensure that ICJ judge Christopher Weeramantry (Sri Lanka) was not reelected following his opinion in the *Nuclear Weapons* case.

Regardless of reappointment, international judicial careers depend heavily (although not exclusively) on government recommendations. Judges frequently move across ICs (Terris *et al.* 2007) or return to prestigious national posts. Thus, even in the absence of reappointment concerns, career incentives could motivate judges. Precisely how this plays out depends on government preferences. In order to be nominated for prestigious appointments, a judge from one country will need to demonstrate her independence from the raison d'état, whereas a judge from another country has incentives to behave in the opposite manner.

Nongovernmental organizations widely lament the degree to which politics impede the installment of international judges. They advocate, with some success, reform of such procedures (Interights 2003). For example, the ECtHR will move from six-year renewable terms to nine-year nonrenewable terms. Many of the newest courts deviate from the one-state-one-judge principle and/or the right of governments to pick the national who will serve on the court. Some courts use competitive elections, whereas others use independent selection committees (Voeten 2009).

On the one hand, this suggests that government control over the career opportunities of international judges is perceived to be a genuine threat to judicial independence. On the other hand, the occasional successes of NGOs validate the insights that transnational networks and the norms they advance carry weight. Moreover, while there is certainly evidence that the appointment and reappointment process is political and shapes judicial behavior to some degree, the size of the effects found in the literature so far is modest (Voeten 2008).

B. *The Implementation of Judgments*

A second set of control mechanisms focuses on the notion that judges care about the implications of their decisions. This does not mean that judges are simply "legislators in robes," as some political scientists assume. Rather, among the many motivations that judges have is that they would generally like to see that their judgments are implemented. Moreover, it assumes that governments can influence the consequences of decisions because they control implementation or because they can use legislative override. Legislative override is not always credible as it often requires unanimous consent of treaty parties. Indeed, it may be too hard to overturn the implications of international court decisions. As a WTO AB judge puts it: "Normally, in constitutional systems around the world, there is somebody who can correct the judges. In Geneva, that is not possible" (quoted in Terris *et al.* 2007: 128).

In some cases, override is easier. For example, the North American Free Trade Agreement parties can issue an interpretation of the treaty that may be binding on tribunals, even in pending cases.[10] This situation is somewhat unusual, however. For most IC judgments, the threat of legislative override is small.

All courts rely on states to implement their decisions. At the WTO, states may accept retaliatory sanctions rather than implement the policy remedies demanded by panel rulings. This is consistent with the WTO regime, but the Dispute Settlement Understanding suggests a preference that states to remove or amend those measures found to be WTO-inconsistent (Jackson 2004). Even if formal override is impossible, states can sometimes use their power to effectively persuade a panel to alter its previous decisions. For example, the WTO's AB retreated from its decision to accept amicus briefs from NGOs after considerable outcry from states (Dunoff 2004).

International criminal tribunals depend on states to capture indicted war criminals (Meron 2005). For ICJ rulings to be effective, states have to continue to accept its compulsory jurisdiction and, more important, implement its decisions. Compliance with ICJ decisions is relatively high, but imperfect (Paulson 2004). As it is with the ECtHR and IACtHR, partial compliance appears to be commonplace (Von Staden 2009; Hillebrecht 2010; Hawkins and Jacoby 2011). Even the ECJ, which is embedded in the strongest supranational organization, is not immune to issues of noncompliance. About one out of every eight infringement judgments required at

---

[10] See *ADF Group v. United States of American*, 18 ICSID Rev. 195 (2003).

least a second ruling because states did not comply with the first (Börzel, Hofmann, and Panke 2009).

A debate in the pages of the *American Political Science Review* illustrates the difficulties of evaluating claims about the effects of (threats of) noncompliance on judicial behavior. In a 2008 article, Clifford James Carrubba, Matthew Gabel, and Charles Hankla (CGH) found that the ECJ is significantly more likely to find in favor of a plaintiff the more that third-party (government) observations favor the plaintiff. CGH interpret this as evidence that the threat of legislative override affects ECJ behavior. Moreover, there is an additional effect of third-party observations when a government is a litigant. CGH argue that the ECJ depends on third-party enforcement of its decisions. Government litigation supported by many other governments makes such third-party enforcement more credible. This suggests that the ECJ takes the likelihood of compliance into account when ruling against a plaintiff.

In a response article, Alec Stone Sweet and Thomas Brunell (2012) reanalyze CGH's data and conclude that, "neofunctionalism wins in a landslide." They find that legislative override is not a credible threat. There are no qualitative examples of legislative override in CGH's data. Moreover, there are no cases in which government observations approach unanimity, the threshold for legislative override in virtually all the cases in the data. Stone Sweet and Brunell also observe that, on average, member state observations tend to favor the European Commission as frequently as the plaintiff (i.e., states frequently file in favor of more active enforcement). Stone Sweet and Brunell interpret the correlation between member state observations and ECJ rulings as evidence that the Court exercises "majoritarian activism." This refers to the tendency of the ECJ to rule against a plaintiff when its policies are out of sync with regulations in place in a majority of the other EU states (Maduro 1998). In this conceptualization, the ECJ acts as an agent of the majority of EU states when the majority cannot pass its preferred policies and regulations through the regular channels.

Although Stone Sweet and Brunell (2012) make a strong case on override, the argument with regard to compliance is less easily settled. For example, it is not entirely clear what would motivate independent judges to assume the role of "majoritarian activist."[11] It could be that the judges see member state observations as simple pieces of information that they deem relevant because they conceive of EU law as a living instrument that should be interpreted in light of developing practices and norms. Yet, it is also consistent with a model in which judges are swayed by

---

[11] Note also that government observations rarely constitute a majority of member states. So, the criticism that they leverage against CGH's override mechanism also applies to the majoritarian activism story. Moreover, observations are not equivalent to notifications that states have similar policies (which are collected by the Court through other means).

the revealed preferences of member states because they fear noncompliance.[12] This observational equivalence illustrates the point made at the beginning of this section about the difficulties of establishing the counterfactual.

C. *Institutional Support and Legitimacy*

A third argument is that judges care about the legitimacy of and support for the institution on which they serve. Governments can affect this by withholding funds or other support. They may also explicitly delegitimize the court or court decisions. This is a more general version of the argument in the previous subsection. Here, judges are not just concerned with the immediate consequences of their decisions but whether decisions undermine diffuse support for a court. Ultimately, a lack of diffuse support can also undermine the ability of courts to enforce compliance with decisions or extend their authority.

The literature suggests that (international) courts build up legitimacy by balancing the need to hand down legally consistent opinions with the need to hand down opinions that are implemented (Kelemen 2001; Carrubba 2005; Vanberg 2005; Staton and Vanberg 2008; Dothan 2011). Courts lose legitimacy when they hand down opinions that are routinely or openly ignored. Yet, they also lose legitimacy when they hand down opinions that blatantly defy the law that the court is charged to interpret or that otherwise upset the broader membership of the court.

For example, Smith (2003) argues that the WTO's AB encourages participation of states as third parties not just because it is concerned about noncompliance but also because it desires information on how a decision will be received by the WTO membership as a whole. Similarly, Busch and Pelc (2010) find that WTO panels invoke judicial economy to politically appease the wider WTO membership and not just to gain the litigants' compliance in the case at hand.

There is at least suggestive evidence that other courts are similarly sensitive to the revealed preferences of member states. For example, the ECtHR's Grand Chamber recently reversed an earlier decision by its Second Chamber that Italy's policy of hanging crucifixes in classrooms was a violation of the ECHR. An unprecedented number of states joined Italy in its appeal as third parties. Most of these third-party states did not have similar laws as Italy but objected to the activism the Court exhibited in this ruling. The notion that courts need to maintain the diffuse support of member states to remain effective is an alternative explanation for CGH's findings

---

[12] Although the European legal system does not formally recognize the principle of *stare decisis*, ECJ decisions set informal precedents and can thus have consequences for third-party states. If large numbers of states object, judges may fear that states will not implement the decisions or will otherwise undermine the court. Conversely, if large numbers of states support a prospective finding, the likelihood of compliance is high as states may engage in third-party enforcement. Alternatively, if the majority of states disapprove of the ECJ's decision, it may lose diffuse support, as discussed in the next subsection.

and is consistent with the observation of majoritarian activism, although it does not follow directly from neofunctionalism.

Neofunctionalists and sociological-institutionalists generally agree that ICs rely on legitimacy to achieve their goals. However, they emphasize that courts do so not just by catering to the wishes of member states but also by building up support from domestic publics and substate actors (Cichowski 2004; Alter and Helfer 2010). For example, Cavallaro and Brewer (2008) argue that the ability of the IACHR to effectively compel compliance depends on media attention and domestic public support for their decisions. This may travel to other courts. For example, the British media vigorously attacked the ECtHR for finding that a law that prohibits prisoners from voting violates the ECHR.[13] This put enormous pressure on British politicians. The U.K. House of Commons voted to extend the ban with a 212-vote majority, in open defiance of the Court's judgment.[14]

Research into the behavioral consequences of concerns about diffuse public support is common in the study of domestic courts, especially the U.S. Supreme Court. For example, evidence indicates that public discontent creates an incentive for the Court to exercise self-restraint (Clark 2009). Relatively few studies examine this question in a systematic, empirical way for ICs. Studies in the mid-1990s found that the ECJ was too obscure to build much public support and that few people were willing to accept controversial decisions (Caldeira and Gibson 1995; Gibson and Caldeira 1995, 1998).

There is considerable room for further empirical work that analyzes the relationship between IC decisions and diffuse support among states, non-state actors, and the public.

D. *Summary*

The increase in the number of IC decisions has been met by an increase in the number of studies that examine whether these decisions were shaped by political actors. Nevertheless, there are still many unexplored areas. In particular, there is considerable room for more systematic, empirical, quantitative, and qualitative research into how courts build up diffuse support from member states, NGOs, and domestic publics.

There is a danger that this empirical work will be overly focused on the "agent–trustee" debate. Both terms have connotations that easily lend themselves to straw-men constructions. The term "agent" is sometimes portrayed as equivalent with "diplomat in robes," even if principal–agent theories stipulate that judges have

---

[13] For example, the *Daily Mail* (Slack 2011) published a piece questioning the competence of each individual ECtHR judge.

[14] The likely consequence of consistent noncompliance is extensive lawsuits by British prisoners, forcing the U.K. government to pay monetary compensation to prisoners.

constrained independence. Conversely, the term "trustee" can be interpreted as meaning that judges operate in splendid isolation, even if the theories on which the trustee claim is based hinge on the social and political context in which courts operate. There is no evidence that international judges operate "as if" they were diplomats, and there is plenty of evidence that judges are acutely aware of the political context in which they operate. This makes the straw-men versions of either side of the agent–trustee dichotomy easy to falsify.

A more productive avenue for empirical research is to focus on theoretically motivated questions about the effects of specific institutional features on judicial behavior. These questions should not just emphasize the agent–trustee spectrum but also the relationship between judicial independence and effectiveness. This is the topic of the final section.

IV. CONCLUSION: DOES JUDICIAL INDEPENDENCE INCREASE EFFECTIVENESS?

Judicial independence is frequently cited as a necessary condition for the effectiveness of ICs (Helfer and Slaughter 1997; Keohane et al. 2000). If governments establish ICs to make credible commitments, then they want these courts to be independent. A court that would simply cater to the wishes of governments would not enhance the credibility of any commitment and thus would not serve the purposes of governments. Moreover, sociological institutionalists add that the normative appeal of judicial independence enhances the legitimacy of courts.

By contrast, Posner and Yoo (2005) are more skeptical of the value of independent ICs. They acknowledge that independent courts offer benefits by providing a more consistent jurisprudence and avoiding the transaction costs of constructing ad hoc tribunals. Yet, they argue that the costs often outweigh these benefits. In particular, judges might decide cases in a manner that is inconsistent with states' interests. This may lead states to ignore or defy ICs. Posner and Yoo (2005) are also skeptical that formal guarantees of independence actually make courts impartial. For example, Posner claims that states stopped using the ICJ largely because the judges did not apply the law impartially (Posner 2006). Posner and Yoo (2005) find that, outside the European context, independent ICs are not generally more effective.

A growing literature suggests that there may be politically optimal levels of judicial independence. These arguments accept that courts require a certain level of independence in order to be effective in settling disputes and applying law. Yet, they also argue that there can be such a thing as too much judicial independence or, more generally, overlegalization in international politics. For example, Helfer (2002) has argued that human rights law can become overlegalized, using the exit of three Caribbean states from the IACHR regime over a death penalty ruling as an example. The IACHR has been accused of too independently interpreting international law in ways that are out of touch with the preferences of regional actors, thus undermining the effectiveness of the inter-American human rights system (Neuman 2008).

Formal models have shown how strong ICs can induce parties to reveal less information in pretrial bargaining, reduce the probability of pretrial settlement, and lead to dangerous brinkmanship (Gilligan, Johns, and Rosendorff 2010). Consequentially, independent courts can be particularly harmful in situations of uncertainty or incomplete information. Other models stress that politically optimal levels of judicial independence depend on the heterogeneity in the preferences of the relevant actors (Hanssen 2004).

Cogan (2008) has argued that the limited power of control mechanisms hinders ICs but that the solution is not more state control but more competition among ICs. Presumably, this would keep in check the desire of ICs to expand their mandates by offering states the option to forum shop. Effectively, however, this would amount to more state control as it allows them to check their venues strategically (Busch 2007).

What these arguments have in common is their agreement that there is such a thing as an IC that is too independent. If politics becomes overly judicialized, the politicization of the judiciary likely follows (Ferejohn 2002). Both theoretical and empirical work should further explore the determinants of politically optimal levels of international judicial independence.

REFERENCES

Allee, Todd, and Clint Peinhardt (2011). "Contingent Credibility: The Impact of Investment Treaty Violations on Foreign Direct Investment," *International Organization*, Vol. 65, No. 3, pp. 401–32.

Alter, Karen J. (1998) "Who Are the Masters of the Treaty? European Governments and the European Court of Justice," *International Organization*, Vol. 52, No. 1, pp. 125–52.

(2006). "Private Litigants and the New International Courts," *Comparative Political Studies*, Vol. 39, No. 1, pp. 22–49.

—————— (2008). "Agents or Trustees? International Courts in Their Political Context," *European Journal of International Relations*, Vol. 14, No. 1, pp. 33–63.

—————— (2010). "Tipping the Balance: International Courts and the Construction of International and Domestic Politics," Working Paper No. 10–003 (Northwestern University Buffett Center for International and Comparative Studies).

—————— (2013). "The Multiple Roles of International Courts and Tribunals: Enforcement, Dispute Settlement, Constitutional and Administrative Review," in Jeffrey L. Dunoff and Mark A. Pollack (eds.), *Interdisciplinary Perspectives on International Law and International Relations: The State of the Art* (New York: Cambridge University Press), pp. 345–70.

Alter, Karen J., and Laurence R. Helfer (2010). "Nature or Nurture? Judicial Lawmaking in the European Court of Justice and the Andean Tribunal of Justice," *International Organization*, Vol. 64, No. 4, pp. 563–92.

Barnett, Michael, and Martha Finnemore (2004). *Rules for the World: International Organizations in Global Politics* (Ithaca, NY: Cornell University Press).

Börzel, Tanja A., Tobias Hofmann, and Diana Panke (2009). "Opinions, Referrals, and Judgments. Analyzing Longitudinal Patterns of Non-compliance," Berlin Working Paper on

European Integration No. 13 (Berlin: Freie Universität Berlin, Berlin Centre for European Integration).

Bradley, Curtis A., and Judith G. Kelley (2008). "The Concept of International Delegation," *Law and Contemporary Problems*, Vol. 71, No. 1, pp. 1–36.

Burley, Anne-Marie, and Walter Mattli (1993). "Europe before the Court" A Political Theory of Legal Integration," *International Organization*, Vol. 47, No. 1, pp. 41–76.

Busch, Marc L. (2007). "Overlapping Institutions, Forum Shopping, and Dispute Settlement in International Trade," *International Organization*, Vol. 61, No. 4, pp. 735–61.

Busch, Marc L., and Krzysztof J. Pelc (2010). "The Politics of Judicial Economy at the World Trade Organization," *International Organization*, Vol. 64, No. 2, pp. 257–79.

Caldeira, Gregory A., and James L. Gibson (1995). "The Legitimacy of the Court of Justice in the European Union: Models of Institutional Support," *American Political Science Review*, Vol. 89, No. 2, pp. 356–76.

Carrubba, Clifford James (2005). "Courts and Compliance in International Regulatory Regimes," *Journal of Politics*, Vol. 6, No. 3, pp. 669–89.

_____ (2009). "A Model of the Endogenous Development of Judicial Institutions in Federal and International Systems," *The Journal of Politics*, Vol. 71, No. 1, pp. 55–69.

Carrubba, Clifford J., Matthew Gabel, and Charles Hankla (2008). "Judicial Behavior under Political Constraints: Evidence from the European Court of Justice," *American Political Science Review*, Vol. 102, No. 4, pp. 435–52.

Cavallaro, James L., and Stephanie Erin Brewer (2008). "Reevaluating Regional Human Rights Litigation in the Twenty-First Century: The Case of the Inter-American Court," *American Journal of International Law*, Vol. 102, No. 4, pp. 768–827.

Cichowski, Rachel A. (2004). "Women's Rights, the European Court and Supranational Constitutionalism," *Law and Society Review*, Vol. 38, No. 3, pp. 489–512.

Cichowski, Rachel A. (2010). "International Courts and Democracy," Paper prepared for presentation at the Center for Research on International and Global Studies Research Seminar, May 21, 2010 (Irvine: University of California, Irvine).

Clark, Tom S. (2009). "The Separation of Powers, Court Curbing, and Judicial Legitimacy," *American Journal of Political Science*, Vol. 53, No. 4, pp. 971–89.

Cogan, Jacob Katz (2008). "Competition and Control in International Adjudication," *Virginia Journal of International Law*, Vol. 48, No. 2, pp. 411–50.

Danner, Allison Marston (2003). "Enhancing the Legitimacy and Accountability of Prosecutorial Discretion at the International Criminal Court," *American Journal of International Law*, Vol. 97, No. 3, pp. 510–52.

_____ 2006. "When Courts Make Law: How the International Criminal Tribunals Recast the Laws of War," *Vanderbilt Law Review*, Vol. 59, No. 1, pp. 1–65.

Danner, Allison, and Erik Voeten (2010). "Who Is Running the International Criminal Justice System?," in Deborah D. Avant, Martha Finnemore, and Susan K. Sell (eds.), *Who Governs the Globe?* (Cambridge: Cambridge University Press), pp. 35–71.

Danziger, Shai, Jonathan Levav, and Liora Avnaim-Pesso (2011). "Extraneous factors in judicial decisions," *Proceedings of the National Academy of Science*, Vol. 108, No. 17, pp. 6889–92.

Dothan, Shai (2011). "Judicial Tactics on the European Court of Human Rights," *Chicago Journal of International Law*, Vol. 12, No. 1, pp. 115–42.

Drzemczewski, Andrew (1995). "A Major Overhaul of the European Human Rights Convention Control Mechanism: Protocol No. 11," in *Collected Courses of the Academy of European Law, The Protection of Human Rights in Europe*, Vol. VI, Book 2 (Dordrecht: Kluwer Law International), pp. 121–244.

Dunoff, Jeffrey L. (2004). "Public Participation in the Trade Regime: Of Litigation, Frustration, Agitation and Legitimation," *Rutgers Law Review*, Vol. 56, No. 4, pp. 961–70.

Elsig, Manfred, and Mark A. Pollack (2011). "Agents, Trustees, and International Courts: Nomination and Appointment of Judicial Candidates in the WTO Appellate Body," Paper prepared for presentation at the 4th Annual Conference on the Political Economy of International Organizations (Zurich).

Farber, Daniel A. 2002. "Rights as Signals," *Journal of Legal Studies*, Vol. 31, No. 1, pp. 83–98.

Feld, Lars P., and Stefan Voigt (2003). "Economic Growth and Judicial Independence: Cross-Country Evidence Using a New Set of Indicators," *European Journal of Political Economy*," Vol. 19, No. 3, 497–527.

Ferejohn, John (2002). "Judicializing Politics, Politicizing Law," *Law and Contemporary Problems*, Vol. 65, No. 3, pp. 41–68.

Gibson, James L., and Gregory A. Caldeira (1995). "The Legitimacy of Transnational Legal Institutions: Compliance, Support, and the European Court of Justice," *American Journal of Political Science*, Vol. 39, No. 2, pp. 459–89.

———— (1998). "Changes in the Legitimacy of the European Court of Justice: A Post-Maastricht Analysis," *British Journal of Political Science*, Vol. 28, No. 1, pp. 63–91.

Gilligan, Michael, Leslie Johns, and B. Peter Rosendorff (2010). "Strengthening International Courts and the Early Settlement of Disputes," *Journal of Conflict Resolution*, Vol. 54, No. 1, pp. 5–38.

Ginsburg, Tom (2005). "Bounded Discretion in International Judicial Lawmaking," *Virginia Journal of International Law*, Vol. 45, No. 3, pp. 631–74.

Goldsmith, Jack L. and Eric A. Posner (2005). *The Limits of International Law* (New York: Oxford University Press).

Goodman, Ryan, and Derek Jinks (2004). "How to Influence States: Socialization and International Human Rights Law," *Duke Law Journal*, Vol. 54, No. 3, pp. 621–704.

Guzman, Andrew T. (2008). *How International Law Works: A Rational Choice Theory* (New York: Oxford University Press).

Hafner-Burton, Emilie M., David G. Victor, and Yonatan Lupu (2011). "Political Science Research on International Law: The State of the Field," *American Journal of International Law*, Vol. 106, No. 1, pp. 1–46.

Haftel, Yoram Z., and Alexander Thompson (2006). "The Independence of International Organizations: Concept and Applications," *Journal of Conflict Resolution*, Vol. 50, No. 2, pp. 253–75.

Hanssen, F. Andrew (2004). "Is There a Politically Optimal Level of Judicial Independence?," *American Economic Review*, Vol. 94, No, 3, pp. 712–29.

Hawkins, Darren, and Wade Jacoby (2010). "Partial Complaince: A Comparision of the European and Inter-American Courts of Human Rights," *Journal of International Law and International Relations*, Vol. 6, No. 1, pp. 35–85.

Helfer, Laurence R. (2002). "Overlegalizing Human Rights: International Relations Theory and the Commonwealth Caribbean Backlash against Human Rights Regimes," *Columbia Law Review*, Vol. 102, No. 7, pp. 1832–911.

———— (2006). "Why States Create International Tribunals: A Theory of Constrained Independence," in Stefan Voigt, Max Albert, and Dieter Schmidtchen (eds.), *International Conflict Resolution* (Tubingen: Mort Siebeck), pp. 255–76.

Helfer, Laurence R., and Anne-Marie Slaughter (1997). "Toward a Theory of Effective Supranational Adjudication," *The Yale Law Journal*, Vol. 107, No. 2, pp. 273–391.

———— (2005). "Why States Create International Tribunals: A Response to Professors Posner and Yoo," *California Law Review*, Vol. 93, No. 3, pp. 889–956.

Hillebrecht, Courtney (2010). "The European Court of Human Rights, Domestic Politics and the Ties That Bind: Explaining Compliance with International Human Rights Tribunals," Paper presented at the Annual Meeting of the International Studies Association, New Orleans, LA, February 2010.

Ikenberry, G. John (2001). *After Victory: Institutions, Strategic Restraint, and the Rebuilding of Order after Major Wars* (Princeton, NJ: Princeton University Press).

Interights (2003). *Judicial Independence: Law and Practice of Appointments to the European Court of Human Rights*, available at http://www.interights.org/document/142/index.html.

International Law Association (2004). *The Burgh House Principles on the Independence of the International Judiciary*, Study Group on the Practice and Procedures of International Courts and Tribunals (London: International Law Association).

Jackson, John H. (2004). "International Law Status of WTO Dispute Settlement Reports: Obligation to Comply or Option to 'Buy Out'?" *American Journal of International Law*, Vol. 98, No.1, pp. 109–25.

Kelemen, R. Daniel (2001). "The Limits of Judicial Power: Trade-Environment Disputes in the GATT/WTO and the EU," *Comparative Political Studies*, Vol. 34, No. 6, pp. 622–50.

Kelley, Judith (2007). "Who Keeps International Commitments and Why? The International Criminal Court and Bilateral Nonsurrender Agreements," *American Political Science Review*, Vol. 101, No. 3, pp. 573–89.

Keohane, Robert O., Andrew Moravcsik, and Anne-Marie Slaughter (2000). "Legalized Dispute Resolution: Interstate and Transnational," *International Organization*, Vol. 54, No. 3, pp. 457–88.

Kingsbury, Benedict (2012). "International Courts: Uneven Judicialization in Global Order," in James Crawford and Martti Koskenniemi (eds.), *Cambridge Companion to International Law* (Cambridge: Cambridge University Press), pp. 203–27.

Koh, Harold Hongju (2004). "International Law as Part of Our Law," *American Journal of International Law*, Vol. 98, No. 1, pp. 43–57.

Mackenzie, Ruth, and Philippe Sands (2003). "International Courts and Tribunals and the Independence of the International Judge," *Harvard International Law Journal*, Vol. 44, No. 1, pp. 271–85.

Maduro, Miguel Poiares (1998). *We the Court: The European Court of Justice and the European Economic Constitution* (Oxford: Hart Publishing).

Majone, Giandomenico (2001). "Two Logics of Delegation: Agency and Fiduciary Relations in EU Governance," *European Union Politics*, Vol. 2, No. 1, pp. 103–22.

Malecki, Michael (2009). "The Politics of Constitutional Review: Evidence from the European Court of Justice," Paper presented at the Annual Meeting of the American Political Science Association.

Mancini, G. Federico (1989). "The Making of a Constitution for Europe," *Common Market Law Review*, Vol. 26, No. 4, pp. 595–614.

Mattli, Walter, and Anne-Marie Slaughter (1998). "Law and Politics in the European Union: A Reply to Garrett," *International Organization*, Vol. 49, No. 1, pp. 183–90.

Meron, Theodor (2005). "Judicial Independence and Impartiality in International Criminal Tribunals," *The American Journal of International Law*, Vol. 99, No. 2, pp. 359–69.

Mitchell, Sara McLaughlin, and Emilia Justyna Powell (2011). *Domestic Law Goes Global: Legal Traditions and International Courts* (Cambridge: Cambridge University Press).

Moravcsik, Andrew (2000). "The Origins of Human Rights Regimes: Democratic Delegation in Postwar Europe," *International Organization*, Vol. 54, No. 2, pp. 217–52.

——— (2013). "Liberal Theories of International Law," in Jeffrey L. Dunoff and Mark A. Pollack (eds.), *Interdisciplinary Perspectives on International Law and International Relations: The State of the Art* (New York: Cambridge University Press), pp. 83–118.

Neuman, Gerald L. (2008). "Import, Export, and Regional Consent in the Inter-American Court of Human Rights," *European Journal of International Law*, Vol. 19, No. 1, pp. 101–23.

Paulson, Colter (2004). "Compliance with Final Judgments of the International Court of Justice since 1987," *American Journal of International Law*, Vol. 98, No. 3, pp. 434–61.

Pauwelyn, Joost (2001). "The Role of Public International Law in the WTO: How Far Can We Go?," *American Journal of International Law*, Vol. 95, No. 3, pp. 535–78.

Pollack, Mark A. (1997). "Delegation, Agency, and Agenda Setting in the European Community," *International Organization*, Vol. 51, No. 1, pp. 99–134.

Posner, Eric A. (2006). "The Decline of the International Court of Justice," in Stefan Voigt, Max Albert, and Dieter Schmidtchen (eds.), *International Conflict Resolution* (Tübingen: Mohr Siebeck), pp. 111–42.

Posner, Eric A., and Miguel F. P. de Figueiredo (2005). "Is the International Court of Justice Biased?," *Journal of Legal Studies*, Vol. 34, No. 2, pp. 599–630.

Posner, Eric A., and John C. Yoo (2005). "Judicial Independence in International Tribunals," *California Law Review*, Vol. 93, No. 1, pp. 1–74.

Posner, Richard A. (1993). "What Do Judges and Justices Maximze? (The Same Thing Everybody Else Does)," *Supreme Court Economic Review*, Vol. 3, pp. 1–41.

Reinhardt, Eric (2002). "Tying Hands without a Rope: Rational Domestic Response to International Institutional Constraints," in Daniel W. Drezner (ed.), *Locating the Proper Authorities: The Interaction of Domestic and International Institutions* (Ann Arbor: University of Michigan Press), pp. 77–104.

Romano, Cesare P. R. (1999). "The Proliferation of International Judicial Bodies: The Pieces of the Puzzle," *New York University Journal of International Law and Politics*, Vol. 31, No. 4, pp. 709–51.

Shany, Yuval, and Sigall Horovitz (2008). "Judicial Independence in The Hague and Freetown: A Tale of Two Cities," *Leiden Journal of International Law*, Vol. 21, No. 1, pp. 113–29.

Simmons, Beth A., and Allision Danner (2010). "Credible Commitments and the International Criminal Court," *International Organization*, Vol. 64, No. 2, pp. 225–56.

Slack, James (2011). "Named and Shamed: The European Human Rights Judges Wrecking British Law," *Daily Mail, Mail Online*, February 5.

Slaughter, Anne-Marie (1994). "A Typology of Transjudicial Communication," *University of Richmond Law Review*, Vol. 29, No. 1, pp. 99–138.

——— (2003). "A Global Community of Courts," *Harvard International Law Journal*, Vol. 44, No. 1, pp. 191–220.

——— (2004). *A New World Order* (Princeton, NJ: Princeton University Press).

Smith, James McCall (2003). "WTO Dispute Settlement: The Politics of Procedure in Appellate Body Rulings," *World Trade Review*, Vol. 2, No. 1, pp. 65–100.

Staton, Jeffrey K., and Georg Vanberg (2008). "The Value of Vagueness: Delegation, Defiance, and Judicial Opinions," *American Journal of Political Science*, Vol. 52, No. 3, pp. 504–19.

Staton, Jeffrey K., and Will H. Moore (2011). "Judicial Power in Domestic and International Politics," *International Organization*, Vol. 65, No. 3, pp. 553–87.

Steinberg, Richard H. (2004). "Judicial Lawmaking at the WTO: Discursive, Constitutional, and Political Constraints," *American Journal of International Law*, Vol. 98, No. 2, pp. 247–75.

Stone Sweet, Alec, and Thomas Brunell (1998). "Constructing a Supranational Constitution: Dispute Resolution and Governance in the European Community," *American Political Science Review*, Vol. 92, No. 1, pp. 63–81.

_____ (2012). "The European Court of Justice, State Non-compliance, and the Politics of Override: Reply to Carruba, Gabel, and Hankla," *American Political Science Review*, Vol. 106, No. 1, pp. 204-13.

Terris, Daniel, Cesare P. R. Romano, and Leigh Swigart (2007). *The International Judge: An Introduction to the Men and Women Who Decide the World's Cases* (Lebanon, NH: Brandeis University Press).

Vanberg, Georg (2005). *The Politics of Constitutional Review in Germany* (New York: Cambridge University Press).

Voeten, Erik (2007). "The Politics of International Judicial Appointments: Evidence from the European Court of Human Rights," *International Organization*, Vol. 61, No. 4, pp. 669–701.

_____ (2008). "The Impartiality of International Judges: Evidence from the European Court of Human Rights," *American Political Science Review*, Vol. 102, No. 4, pp. 417–33.

_____ (2009). "The Politics of International Judicial Appointments," *Chicago Journal of International Law*, Vol. 9, No. 2, pp. 387–406.

Von Staden, Andreas (2009). *Shaping Human Rights Policy in Liberal Democracies: Assessing and Explaining Compliance with the Judgments of the European Court of Human Rights*, Princeton University, Princeton, NJ, Ph.D. dissertation.

Weiler, J. H. H. (1991). "The Transformation of Europe," *Yale Law Journal*, Vol. 100, No. 8, pp. 2403–83.

18

The Politics of Treaty Interpretation:

Variations and Explanations across International Tribunals

Joost Pauwelyn and Manfred Elsig

International tribunals rely on interpretation of legal texts as a crucial tool in adjudication. What is puzzling is the wide variation we observe in treaty interpretation by international tribunals across policy areas and over time. The international relations (IR) literature has largely overlooked the factors that explain the extent and scope of treaty interpretation. Although there is an extensive normative literature in international law (IL) as to the right way to interpret, empirical work still lacks mid-range theories to account for the observed variance of behavior across international tribunals. This chapter tries to fill this gap by providing a conceptual toolkit inspired by IL and IR theories to approach the various types of interpretation (*interpretation choices*) and underlying explanations (demand-side *interpretation space* and supply-side *interpretation incentives*).

In IL scholarship, attention has focused on the normative question of how treaties should be interpreted, especially with reference to the Vienna Convention on the Law of Treaties (VCLT) referring, in turn, to text, context, object and purpose, and preparatory works of a treaty (Gardiner 2008; Van Damme 2009). These Vienna Convention rules apply, in principle, to all international tribunals, irrespective of their institutional setup, subject matter, or geographical scope. Divergence between international tribunals in the practical application of these rules of treaty interpretation has been pointed out (Weiler 2010). Yet, categorizing where exactly international tribunals have diverged in their approach and, especially, thinking about what factors might explain these differences, has received little or no attention. Instead, divergence has been labeled as an incorrect application of the Vienna Convention rules or proof that these rules are outdated or should not fully apply to a particular tribunal (Klabbers 2010: 33). This chapter leaves the normative issue aside and focuses on

We wish to thank Jeff Dunoff, Mark Pollack, Tonya Putnam, and other participants at the Temple University Interdisciplinary Research Group Workshop for comments on an earlier draft, and Susan Kaplan and Facundo Perez Aznar for research assistance.

the descriptive and conceptual aspects: what is it that international tribunals actually do, and how could this behavior be explained, first, within the same tribunal operating over time and, second, across tribunals operating in different contexts or regimes?

In current IR scholarship, research has paid attention to the role of international tribunals (e.g., in the broader "legalization" debate or as agents vs. trustees) and to the design of dispute settlement mechanisms in international agreements (Koremenos 2007; Alter 2008a; Koremenos and Betz 2013; Voeten 2013). Other studies have addressed the effects of proliferation of international tribunals and forum-shopping (Drezner 2006; Busch 2007). In addition, most of the commitment literature in IR focuses on the question why states sign or ratify international agreements, and what factors explain the degree of implementation of or compliance with international agreements. Yet, what has been largely overlooked is the stage between commitment (consent) and compliance, more specifically, the process by which commitments are interpreted in the first place. Although many actors in the realm of international politics may eventually influence the way treaty obligations are interpreted (in particular, treaty parties themselves), the key institutions (and usually the last resort) engaging in this process are increasingly international tribunals (Romano 2007). These tribunals are called on to engage in an interpretation precisely because member states or other actors that may have standing cannot agree among themselves on a way to read the commitments.

This chapter attempts to push the conceptual borders across both fields. After defining and discussing the increased importance of treaty interpretation (Part I), we describe the five interpretation choices that international tribunals most commonly make (Part II). We then offer a framework that may explain these choices (Part III). We provide illustrative examples to tease out our explanatory framework, but do not engage in proper empirical testing. At this stage, our goal is merely to demonstrate that tribunals have a varying degree of interpretation space within which they must select between different interpretative techniques. Understanding these techniques and the factors that may explain their adoption can, in turn, provide useful insights into the operation, role, and optimal design of international tribunals.

I. DEFINITION AND IMPORTANCE OF TREATY INTERPRETATION

For present purposes, treaty interpretation is the activity through which international tribunals give meaning to a treaty in the context of a particular case or fact pattern. Interpreting legal texts is what courts do. International tribunals are no exception. Whereas domestic courts most commonly interpret and apply contracts, statutes, or constitutions, international tribunals most commonly interpret and apply treaties. In most cases, international tribunals must interpret treaties to decide whether or not a party is complying with the treaty. If breach is found, treaty interpretation intervenes at a crucial stage between commitment and compliance.

Although international tribunals have existed for more than a century, the question of treaty interpretation has never attracted as much attention as it does today. We see three main reasons for this: the fragmentation, frequency, and peculiar nature of treaties.

First, much of today's hype around treaty interpretation is due to the proliferation or, as others put it, fragmentation, of international treaties and tribunals (Pauwelyn 2003). Seen from this fragmentation angle, treaty interpretation can be part of the *problem*. Different tribunals may interpret the same rules differently, each having their own guiding objective, underlying value system, and interpretative community, thereby contributing to the cacophony of fragmentation (Crema 2010). However, treaty interpretation can also be part of the *solution* to fragmentation. Treaty interpretation may offer shared hermeneutics in search of a more systemic integration of diverse treaties and tribunals and inject a degree of coherence into the fragmented landscape of international law (Bianchi 2010).

Second, from a more practical perspective, with more tribunals in place, the question of how tribunals interpret treaties has moved from a largely normative, academic debate to a day-to-day activity of deciding real cases, which are subsequently closely scrutinized by a variety of affected actors beyond the state parties themselves. In less than twenty years, both the numbers of international tribunals and the number of cases they are asked to decide have dramatically increased.

Third, the question of how international tribunals interpret poses a particular paradox compared to domestic legal systems. Treaties tend to be more incomplete contracts than national texts because of high transaction costs and future uncertainties (Allott 1999). This is especially the case for multilateral treaties (many parties must agree on one single text, often left deliberately vague and translated into multiple languages), as well as for treaties between countries with highly diverse interests and backgrounds (leaving even the most basic notions or terms open to disagreement or different interpretations). Since more questions are left open (Voeten 2008), choice of interpretative method becomes more important. At the same time, since treaties are concluded between sovereign states, treaty parties remain, for the same reasons that explain treaty ambiguity (party consent, diversity of interests), wary of delegating discretionary power to international tribunals (sensitivity of treaties). As a result, international tribunals must interpret more (treaties as incomplete contracts), but, in doing so, are also under closer scrutiny (treaties as contracts between sovereign states). Making this combination even more difficult is a third element: the rigidity of treaties once they are enacted. Whereas parliaments can correct domestic courts, in most cases, by simple majority, "legislative correction" of international tribunals by treaty makers is subject to the consent rule. This means that all parties to the treaty, including the party that benefited from the "wrong interpretation" by the tribunal, must agree to change that interpretation or adapt the treaty to keep it up to date. Thus, the rigidity of treaties makes judicial interpretation even more important. This triple interaction could be referred to as the "paradox of international adjudication":

more demand for treaty interpretation, given ambiguity and rigidity of treaties, yet *less supply* of treaty interpretation, given the reluctance of states and (more often than not) tribunals to deal judicially with highly contested questions between sovereign states (sensitivity of treaties).

International law does offer "general rules" for interpreting treaties. These rules are set out in Articles 31 to 33 of the VCLT and reflect customary international law binding on all states. The VCLT offers two main principles. The first is that treaties must be interpreted in "good faith," in accordance with the "ordinary meaning" of the "terms" or text of the treaty, in their "context," and in light of the treaty's "object and purpose."[1] This summing up of text, context, and purpose is described as a holistic, nonhierarchical exercise, albeit one that starts with the text of the treaty (Abi-Saab 2010). The VCLT's second main principle is that the "preparatory work of the treaty and the circumstances of its conclusion" are only secondary sources of interpretation to confirm meaning established under the first principle or in case the meaning of the treaty remains unclear or leads to an absurd result.[2]

As general rules, these VCLT rules apply to all treaties, irrespective of the subject matter, goal, or number of parties to the treaty. If states so wish, they can contract out of these general rules by including specific rules in a particular treaty. If no special rules are provided (which is the case for most treaties), the general VCLT rules apply. This said, there is general agreement that the application of these VCLT rules, in any particular case, leaves ample scope for maneuver and allows different tribunals to prioritize different interpretative methods or elements (e.g., text, context, or purpose). Indeed, the VCLT rules themselves are a result of negotiations and are ridden with ambiguities. Therefore, when, for example, a World Trade Organization (WTO) panel must interpret a WTO treaty provision it is, in effect, giving meaning to one incomplete contract (the WTO treaty) using another incomplete contract (the VCLT) as guidance.

In addition, the VCLT rules, although generally applicable, are not necessarily exhaustive, and other additional principles or guidelines may exist or can develop as part of customary international law or within specific treaty regimes. This gives international tribunals additional flexibility.

International law scholars have been debating for decades which interpretative method is most appropriate, with some agreeing with the VCLT rules and others vehemently opposing them (McDougal 1967). Our goal is not to add to this debate by arguing that one or another technique is normatively better. Instead, we want to enter the "black box" of judicial discretion left to international tribunals when they apply the VCLT rules. When exercising the wiggle room available to them under the VCLT, what directions have courts taken, and how do these directions differ over time and among different international tribunals? To the extent that we see variation, what factors may explain it?

---

[1] Vienna Convention on the Law of Treaties, 1153 U.N.T.S. 331 (1969).
[2] Ibid., art. 32.

As to the importance of treaty interpretation, two caveats apply. First, our claim is not that treaty interpretation is always the crucial factor in the outcome of disputes. In some cases, the tribunal's establishment of the facts rather than the law is more important. Second, although we believe that a tribunal's stated method of interpretation influences outcomes (especially where a court's discretion is bound by a particular method selected by earlier courts), we do acknowledge that, in some cases, a tribunal's interpretative method may be little more than an *ex post* justification or "façade" for an outcome reached on other grounds (Lauterpacht 1949). In these cases, the impact of the five interpretation choices we identify below is undoubtedly diminished. Yet, even (and perhaps especially) in these cases, our explanatory framework (Part III) remains important: the factors we identify there are exactly the types of "other grounds" (in this case, grounds other than methods of legal interpretation) that may explain a tribunal's decision. The discussions and deliberations among tribunal members take place out of the public eye. This is a strategic advantage that court members are well aware of and want to preserve. They may (or may not) want to provide specific clues in an attempt to sustain their informational advantage. They might at times leave observers and scholars in the dark about their true intentions. Therefore, paradoxical situations can evolve. For instance, judicial agents anticipate that "poorly justified decisions tend not to have extensive impact" (Ferejohn 2002: 54). Therefore, they may abstain from explaining to the public how their decision was driven by interpretation. This makes the task of systematizing and analyzing treaty interpretations more complex than many other types of policy outcomes. This said, even where a stated interpretative choice is merely a façade, it remains worthy of study "since at the very least it represents an effort at self-conscious public justification" that "enables us to understand what are regarded as satisfactory and publicly acknowledgeable grounds for decision making" (Bankowski *et al.* 1991: 17).

II. INTERPRETATION CHOICES

How should the International Court of Justice (ICJ) interpret Costa Rica's right to free navigation on the San Juan River "*con objetos de comercio?*"[3] For Nicaragua, which was taxing Costa Rican tourists on the river, these Spanish terms in an 1858 treaty between the two countries are limited to free transport of *goods*.[4] In contrast, for Costa Rica, which has a booming tourist industry, "*con objetos de comercio*" covers the free transport of both goods and passengers, *including tourists*.[5] Similarly, when the WTO treaty states that import duties to offset subsidies provided in the country of production must be imposed "in the *appropriate* amounts in each case," does this prohibit the imposition of such duties together with duties to offset

---

[3] Dispute Regarding Navigational and Related Rights (*Costa Rica v. Nicaragua*), 2009 I.C.J. 213 (13 July).
[4] Ibid.
[5] Ibid.

dumping? Finally, where a provision is silent on the question, does the International Criminal Tribunal for the Former Yugoslavia (ICTY) have jurisdiction over offenses committed in *internal* armed conflict or only those committed in *international* armed conflict? The above examples indicate how common and important questions of treaty interpretation before international tribunals can be. Opt for one interpretation, and the claimant wins; opt for the other, and the defending country or person is left untouched.

How then do international tribunals make their choice? As noted above, the VCLT rules do impose a general framework, but within this framework, a certain degree of discretion remains. Here, we offer a taxonomy of the most important and most commonly discussed choices of interpretation techniques that tribunals must select from. Obviously, this is not by any means an exhaustive list. We have only picked a limited number of variations, focusing on the major, commonly practiced and discussed ways of interpreting treaty texts. Although there may be overlaps and interactions (as discussed below), these five variables generally operate independently so that, technically, tribunals may have five different choices to make.

Once the main strands or variations in treaty interpretation are identified, a serious problem arises when it comes to identifying an international tribunal using one or the other technique. Although some tribunals have been more consistent than others, in many cases, the same tribunal may stress one technique in one case, but another in the next. Also, within the same tribunal, one judge may push for one technique, whereas another judge goes for an opposing method. As a result, there may be as many interpretative choices as there are cases to decide. This said, certain generalizations can be made. When we do so here, we will base these generalizations on the dominant views of scholars rather than make our own claims. Most courts have central tendencies and generally prefer certain types of interpretation over others. However, variation can also be observed over time; for example, comparing early cases of the WTO Appellate Body (AB) with cases decided fifteen years after its creation. Finally, the same tribunal may opt for one method when it comes to one set of cases, but select another method for other types of disputes: think of the European Court of Human Rights (ECtHR) interpreting torture cases differently than cases on freedom of speech (Letsas 2010: 510), or the ICJ using different methods of interpretation for unilateral declarations or United Nations (UN) Security Council Resolutions than for interpretation of treaties (Gordon 1965; Orakhelashvili 2008).

A. The Dominant Hermeneutic: Text, Party Intent, or Underlying Objective?

The first distinguishing feature we observe relates to the guiding principle or substantive benchmark that a tribunal sets for itself when giving meaning to a treaty. Three broad types of dominant hermeneutic can be detected: in case of doubt, will the tribunal rely primarily on: (a) the text of the treaty, (b) the intent of the parties to the treaty, or (c) the underlying objective that the treaty seeks to attain? As noted earlier, the VCLT refers, in one way or another, to all three elements. When applying VCLT rules, however, a tribunal can be guided more by one element (say, text) than the other (for example, objective).

Most interpreters agree that the task bestowed on them is to give effect to the intentions of the parties. In this sense, tribunals are the agents of the state-parties (principals) who created the tribunal. The next question is where a tribunal must look to find this intention of the parties. The first approach is to say that the best and most objective expression of intent can be found in the treaty text itself (Fachiri 1929). The second approach is to argue that text is but one element and that the interpreter needs to dig deeper to uncover the actual, subjective intentions of the parties, for example, by looking at the preparatory works of a treaty (Lauterpacht 1950; McDougal, Lasswell, and Miller 1967). The third approach is to focus not so much on the raw text of the treaty or the subjective intentions of the drafters themselves, but on the underlying objectives these drafters were attempting to achieve – the so-called teleological approach (Letsas 2010: 512). Thus, a tribunal's guiding star or dominant hermeneutic can be text, party intent, or objective.

The differences between these three approaches are not trivial. A textual approach will give meaning to words, for example, by looking these words up in a dictionary and trying to give the words, as they are used in a particular context, their "ordinary meaning." In so doing, the interpreter will tend to refer to common understandings among a relatively broad group of people (e.g., those reading and understanding English). In contrast, if party intent is a tribunal's guiding star, the interpretative community tends to be narrowed down to the more limited group of drafters actually involved in the treaty-making process. This subjectivity – referring, for example, to shared expectations or values of the drafters (rather than the meaning of words) – has been said to (further) open the door for judges to yield to the preferences of the most powerful actors involved. For example, relying on the negotiation history of the WTO treaty is likely to yield more statements by the United States, the European Union (EU), or Canada, than those that reflect the views of Malawi or Paraguay, let alone Oman or Taiwan, which only joined the WTO after its establishment. Finally, if a tribunal's guiding star is the underlying objective of the treaty, interpretation can take account of a broader interpretative community, beyond the original state parties as such, and rapidly becomes value based (e.g., in favor of the protection of human rights, investors, or free trade). Meaning is then given to the treaty with less reference to the linguistic meaning of words or subjective intent of the drafters and more with the spirit of the treaty in mind, in an attempt to give maximum effect to the treaty's underlying normative values. As pointed out above, such value-based interpretation is probably the interpretative method that risks the most fragmentation or conflict between tribunals. If investment tribunals interpret pro investors; human rights tribunals interpret *pro homine*, and WTO tribunals interpret pro traders, the risk of inconsistent outcomes is higher.

International tribunals that have commonly been placed in the textual school are the WTO's AB, the ICJ, and the International Criminal Court (ICC). One member of the AB, who also served as a judge on the ICTY and the ICJ, went so far as to call the AB an *"obsédé textuel"* (Abi-Saab 2010: 106). An ICC observer (Grover 2010: 557) stated,

> If legality is recognized as the guiding principle for interpreting crimes in the Court's jurisdiction [see Article 22.2 of the ICC Statute providing that the definition of a crime "shall be strictly construed"], it would require the textual approach to prevail over competing intent as well as object and purpose based approaches.

Although the dominant hermeneutic of the ICJ is less outspoken, the conventional view is that, if anything, the ICJ's method of interpretation is more textual than intent- or objective-based. One author concluded, for example, that "the [ICJ] usually gives excessive primacy to the textual element without combining it with other elements of the general rule" (Romani 2007: 156).

Examples of tribunals that follow party intent as their dominant hermeneutic are more difficult to find, if only because the VCLT explicitly demoted preparatory works to the class of secondary sources. One example is General Agreement on Tariffs and Trade (GATT) panels, which operated before the establishment of the WTO in 1995. As Howse describes, "Traditionally, under GATT, resort to the *travaux* constituted a pervasive and largely uncontroversial interpretative practice" (Howse 2000: 57). Confirming the existence of a relatively small interpretative community, centered on the subjective intentions of the original GATT drafters, acceptance of a GATT panel ruling was a function of "a ruling's consistency with the general consensus among the trade policy élite" (Howse 2000: 57). Indeed, it is this subjective interpretation, with reference to preparatory works, that led the drafters of the WTO treaty (which succeeded the GATT) to explicitly include a reference to VCLT rules of interpretation. This was done to steer WTO panels toward a more "objective," text-based interpretation (Kuijper 1994). Arbitration is another example in which frequent reference is made to the intentions of the parties, including investor–state arbitration, where the principle of "party autonomy" is pervasive (especially in commercial arbitration) (Schreuer 2010: 138).

Finally, examples of international tribunals that have favored a teleological approach are the European Court of Justice (Lenaerts 2007), European and Inter-American Courts of Human Rights (Letsas 2010: 512; Lixinski 2010: 588), the International Criminal Tribunals for Yugoslavia and Rwanda (Swart 2010: 770; Schabas 2003), and, albeit to a lesser extent, investor – state arbitration (Fauchald 2008: 316; Schreuer 2010: 131).

B. *Timing: Original or Evolutionary Interpretation?*

A second, major interpretative choice that international tribunals face relates to timing. When the ICJ interprets the term "commerce" in the 1858 treaty between

Costa Rica and Nicaragua referred to earlier, does it take the meaning of that word in 1858, when the treaty was concluded, or its meaning in 2009, when the ICJ had to interpret the treaty?[6] If 1858 is chosen, Costa Rica's claim for free navigation of tourists would probably be rejected because, at that time, there were no tourists on the river. If 2009 is picked, Costa Rica most likely wins. Similarly, when the AB must give meaning to the words "exhaustible natural resources" (which can be protected by trade restrictive measures under GATT Article XX), is it to pick the prevailing meaning in 1947 (when the GATT was concluded) or that in 1998, when it decided the famous *US–Shrimp* (*Shrimp*) dispute?[7] In 1947, when the terms were written, drafters had minerals in mind (whose exportation could be restricted to conserve "exhaustible natural resources"). In 1996, when the *Shrimp* dispute arose, the United States imposed an import ban to protected endangered sea turtles that, in its eyes, were also "exhaustible natural resources."[8]

The above-explained VCLT rules are silent on this question of timing. Unlike the first variation discussed earlier – focused on *what* it is that the tribunal takes as its guiding star (text, intent, or purpose) – this second variation asks at what point in time or *when* the interpretation must take place: contemporaneous with the date of conclusion of the treaty (original interpretation), or evolving over time and set at the time of deciding a dispute (evolutionary interpretation).

Much like the first variation (*what*), this second variation (*when*) has major consequences. If an evolutionary interpretation is chosen, Costa Rica wins the ICJ case; in the WTO dispute, the United States can rely on an exception. The importance of this interpretative choice is further highlighted by what we referred to earlier as the rigidity of treaties. Given the consent rule, treaties can normally only be amended or adjusted to new developments if all parties to the treaty so agree. As a result, the more parties to a treaty, the more difficult it becomes for treaty makers to adjust it. This puts the burden on an international tribunal to either do this "legislative updating" itself or to refuse to do so but risk becoming less relevant as an adjudicator.

Examples of tribunals taking an evolutionary approach and interpreting treaties as "living instruments" are the AB (Van Damme 2009) and the Inter-American and European Courts of Human Rights (which commonly apply moral and societal views of the day updated since the conclusion of their respective treaties, be it on questions of abortion, divorce, or homosexuality) (Letsas 2010: 527). Examples of evolutionary interpretation can also be found in investor–state arbitration (Schill 2010). In contrast, international tribunals opting for a static or original approach are the International Criminal Court (which can only hold someone responsible

---

[6] Dispute Regarding Navigational and Related Rights (*Costa Rica v. Nicaragua*), 2009 I.C.J. 213 (13 July).

[7] United States – Import Prohibition of Certain Shrimp and Shrimp Products, WT/DS58/AB/R (Oct. 12, 1998).

[8] Ibid.

if the conduct constituted a crime at the time it took place, not with reference to the date of the tribunal's decision) (Grover 2010; Okowa 2010: 351), so-called Claims Tribunals set up to decide on reparation claims in the context of particular past events (Caron 2006: 404–05), and, at least to some extent, GATT panels (focused on the intention of the drafters as expressed in 1947) (Howse 2000). The ICJ, in contrast, falls somewhere in between, at times taking an evolutionary approach (as in the *Costa Rica v. Nicaragua* case discussed earlier[9]), while in other cases opting for a static or original interpretation. To decide on which approach to take in a particular case, the ICJ examines the implied intentions of the parties to the treaty, finding that they can be presumed to have chosen an evolutionary approach if they have used "generic terms" and concluded the treaty for an indefinite period of time (Milanovic 2009).

When this second, time-related variation (original vs. evolutionary) is put together with the first, benchmark-related variation (text, intent, purpose), it is clear that any tribunal can select its own particular combination. Confirming that the two sets of variations do deal with different questions, a tribunal can be textual and evolutionary (such as the WTO), but also textual and originalist (such as the ICJ in some cases). A tribunal whose dominant hermeneutic is party intent is more likely to be originalist (looking for the subjective intent and meaning in the minds of the drafters when the treaty was concluded, as was arguably the case with GATT panels), but can also be evolutionary (if party intent indicates that the parties wanted treaty terms to evolve over time, as in some of the cases decided by the ICJ). This said, a tribunal that has as its guiding star the underlying objective of the treaty (teleological interpretation) is likely to update its interpretation of the treaty with reference to new developments. In that sense, teleological and evolutionary interpretations go hand in hand.

C. *Activism: Work-to-Rule or Gap-Filling Approach?*

A third fundamental variation we observe is between tribunals that take a deferential, strict constructionist or work-to-rule approach, and tribunals taking a more activist, gap-filling approach. Although some overlap exists, this third variation is fundamentally different from the first (text, intent, or purpose-based interpretation). Whereas the first variation relates to what the tribunal sets as its guiding star or dominant hermeneutic (does it look at the text, try to uncover party intent, or is it guided by the underling purpose of the treaty?), this third variation says something about how the tribunal construes its own role or function, irrespective of what it has chosen as its guiding principle. Is the function of the tribunal to apply only what the treaty (text, intent, or purpose) provides for, or is it the task of the tribunal also to push the

---

[9] Dispute Regarding Navigational and Related Rights (*Costa Rica v. Nicaragua*), 2009 I.C.J. 213 (13 July).

envelope and complete the contract where appropriate or fill gaps in the treaty as they are discovered in the judicial process?

The work-to-rule approach tends to favor defendants, as tribunals defer to the sovereignty or presumed innocence of the party whose obligations are assessed. In case of doubt, the tribunal will find no obligation. Where the treaty does not (explicitly) cover a matter, the tribunal will find no violation. In contrast, where a tribunal is ready to fill gaps, even if the treaty does not explicitly regulate a question, the tribunal (based on text, intent, or purpose) will construe an applicable rule. Such gap-filling can work either way (in favor of the defendant or of the complainant). What matters is that tribunals take on a role which, according to some, ought to be reserved to the legislator. According to others, gap-filling is exactly what courts must do, functioning as antimajoritarian devices to guarantee individual rights against government (including majority-approved) abuse. Looked at from a different angle, the spectrum of activism of tribunals has, at one extreme, work-to-rule tribunals that are simply obedient agents, completely differential to the views and action of the treaty makers. At the other extreme, we find activist, gap-filling courts that are quite "self-confident" agents operating largely independently of the parties that made the treaty and established the tribunal.

It is notoriously difficult to determine the level of activism of a court. Obviously, parties whose preferred interpretation was rejected by a tribunal tend to argue that the tribunal got it wrong and that it engaged in impermissible activism. The other side, of course, will take the view that the tribunal's interpretation is exactly what the parties intended and that no judicial activism took place. This said, and at the risk, once again, of making overly general conclusions, the following tribunals are often described as activist or gap-filling: the European Court of Justice (Rasmussen 1986) and European and Inter-American Courts of Human Rights (Letsas 2010: 518). Because of its Statute, the ICC, in contrast, is, at least at this early stage, best qualified as a deferential or work-to-rule tribunal (Grover 2010: 556). Other courts are more difficult to classify. Although the AB was generally described as cautious and deferential in its early years (Howse 2000), in more recent years, it has taken a more activist stance (Steinberg 2004). Similarly, whereas the ICJ in its earlier case law often took a deferential or pro-sovereignty approach, it has recently opted for a more neutral assessment (interpreting treaties neither restrictively nor expansively) (Milanovic 2009). When it comes to investor – state arbitrations, the substantive principles involved are few and broadly defined (e.g., obligation to offer "fair and equitable treatment") so that some degree of gap-filling is inevitable. At the same time, few, if any, cases can be pointed to where tribunals engaged in gap-filling beyond the principles provided for in the treaty. Whereas some tribunals have taken a deferential stance in favor of host countries others a more activist approach in favor of investors, the most recent trend is for tribunals (very much like the ICJ) to take a neutral position (no presumptions either way) (Roberts 2010).

D. *Case-by-Case Analysis or Rule of Precedent?*

A fourth important variable we observe is the extent to which a tribunal decides every case de novo, without reference to previously decided disputes or, instead, relies on precedent, accepting earlier decisions either as legally binding or persuasive guidance. In a case-by-case approach, earlier interpretations do not bind or guide a tribunal, and every dispute is decided afresh on its own merits. This means that the parties are fully in control and need not worry about precedents. It also means that there is no (or less) need to get involved in other disputes as third parties so as to avoid or steer precedents that may one day affect one's own case. Where weight is given to precedent, in contrast, a normative regime develops that is composed not only of the treaty as such but also of previously decided cases (in the ECJ context, referred to as the *acquis communautaire*).

Although judicial decisions are referred to as one of the (secondary) sources of international law in the ICJ Statute, the VCLT rules are silent on the interpretative role of earlier judicial decisions. Only one international tribunal that we know of (Caribbean Court of Justice) follows a rule of legally binding precedent. Still, most other tribunals, to some extent, do refer to and rely on earlier decisions (by the same or another tribunal) (Jacob 2011). For some international tribunals, the weight to be given to earlier decisions is explicitly provided for.[10] In other cases, reliance on precedent developed de facto. Fauchald (2008) finds, for example, that 92 of 98 investor – state tribunals (that is, 94 percent of cases between 1998 and 2006) refer to prior awards. At the same time, he does add that, "the extent to which ICSID tribunals in general felt free to criticize and deviate from the findings in previous case law was remarkable" (Ibid.: 338). In other words, there is a difference between referring to precedent and generally feeling bound by it, as in the ICJ (Ginsburg 2005: 5; Rosenne 2006: 1555) and even more so in the WTO (David 2009), and referring to earlier decisions and then going your own way (as is commonly the case for investor – state arbitrations or as often happened in the GATT).

A further distinction that can be made is between reference back to cases decided earlier by the same tribunal (e.g., the ICJ referring to an earlier ICJ judgment) or to a higher court within the same system (e.g., a WTO panel referring to an earlier AB ruling), as opposed to one tribunal making reference to another tribunal in an entirely different system or regime (say, the ICTY or the AB referring to the ICJ or vice versa). Although there is no formal hierarchy between international tribunals, de facto, judgments by the ICJ ("the principal judicial organ of the UN") are quite often referred to by specialized tribunals (Rosenne 2006: 1555). Interestingly, however, in more recent times, the reverse has also been happening: the ICJ referring back, for example, to an earlier AB report or ruling by the ICTY or the International Criminal Tribunal for Rwanda (ICTR) (Payne 2010).

---

[10] Rome Statute of the International Criminal Court, Art. 21.2, 2187 U.N.T.S. 3 (1998).

E. Linkage: Self-Contained or Systemic Interpretation?

The fifth, and final, interpretative choice relates to how international tribunals position themselves in relation to the outside world, in particular, their linkage to other treaties and tribunals. Some tribunals construe their universe as a self-contained regime that is purely inward-looking. In the process of treaty interpretation, they limit themselves to the four corners of their constitutive treaty and the legal instruments enacted within their regime. Pre-1995 GATT panels, for example, limited themselves to the GATT and only in exceptional circumstances did they refer to general international law (including, for that matter, the VCLT) or branches of international law other than trade law (e.g., international environmental agreements) (Howse 2000). In addition, self-contained tribunals will not normally refer to rulings of other international tribunals.

In contrast, other international tribunals are outward-looking and interpret their constitutive treaties with reference to general international law and other treaties. In so doing, they strive for a systemic interpretation that attempts to reconcile different treaties and read international law as a coherent system of law (rather than a collection of self-contained regimes). Whereas the GATT was largely inward-looking, one of the major transformations that occurred with the establishment of the WTO was the openness of the AB to other rules of international law. Moving away from what it called "clinical isolation," the AB has gradually construed the WTO treaty in the broader context of other treaties and general international law. In so doing, the AB has referred not only to VCLT rules and general international law principles on burden of proof, proportionality, or state attribution, but also to environmental agreements, customs classification treaties, and regional trade agreements (Pauwelyn 2003). Indeed, when it comes to VCLT rules, more than any international tribunal (and certainly more so than the ICJ), the AB has, in almost every case, explicitly referred to them. In addition, more than any other court, it applies VCLT rules to the letter, in many cases going through each and every element or interpretative guideline referenced in the VCLT (Abi-Saab 2010). More recently, however, this formalistic trend has declined, and the AB has reduced its formal attachment to each of the steps of treaty interpretation in the VCLT (Van Damme 2009).

The ICJ, in contrast, as a court of general jurisdiction (states can, technically, send cases to it on any subject matter), has from the start been more outward-looking. At the same time, when it comes to explicitly referring to VCLT rules on treaty interpretation, the ICJ was, somewhat paradoxically, one of the last tribunals to do so (Torres-Bernárdez 1998: 722). Nor has the ICJ traditionally spent a lot of time explaining its interpretative approach or gone through the VCLT steps of treaty interpretation in any great detail. A recent trend has been detected, however, in which the ICJ refers more explicitly and in more detail to VCLT rules (Gardiner 2008: 14).

Investment tribunals generally have broad powers in terms of the law they can apply to resolve a dispute (domestic law, the bilateral investment treaty that grants them jurisdiction, and other rules of international law). Somewhat surprisingly, in the process of treaty interpretation, investment tribunals have been reluctant to refer to outside treaties (Hirsch 2009) (more so, for example, than the AB, even though the WTO treaty does not explicitly incorporate other international law as part of the applicable law to resolve WTO disputes). Moreover, only recently have investment tribunals started to explicitly and commonly refer to VCLT rules on interpretation (Gardiner 2008). Investment tribunals also increasingly refer to Permanent Court of International Justice (PCIJ) and ICJ rulings (Fauchald 2008: 343), while at the same time expressing a general reluctance to incorporate ideas of international trade law or WTO jurisprudence (although that trend may be changing) (DiMascio and Pauwelyn 2008).

The European Court of Human Rights, although it does not often refer to VCLT rules when it interprets (Letsas 2010: 513) (as noted above, it pursues more of a tele- ological interpretation), has resolutely chosen to take an outward-looking, systemic approach to interpretation. In so doing, it construes the European Convention on Human Rights (ECHR) with reference to general international law as well as to other treaties. A similar approach is taken by the Inter-American Court of Human Rights (IACHR) (Lixinski 2010: 603). The ECJ is a special case in this respect, especially as it is gradually coming closer to being a domestic rather than a truly international tribunal. Some authors, however, have described an evolution within the ECJ from being a court relatively open to other international law to one that is increasingly closed (Kuijper and Bronckers 2005).

A different type of outreach or linkage in which variance between tribunals can be detected relates to the extent to which tribunals refer to academic writings in the process of giving meaning to a treaty. This may come as a surprise to other academics, but under international law "the teachings of the most highly qualified publicists" are considered as a supplementary source of international law.[11] At the same time, very much like precedent, VCLT rules do not make any reference to academic writings as an interpretative tool. In the WTO, for example, notwithstanding the increasing number of academics focusing on WTO law, panels, and, even less so, the AB, hardly ever refer to academic writings. If they do so, it is, most likely to be a reference to relatively old publications on general international law and not to writings on GATT or WTO law (Van Damme 2009). In addition, even the parties to a WTO dispute hardly ever refer to the multitude of academic studies on WTO law.

In contrast, and like most of the variance described above, notwithstanding the fact that the same VCLT rules generally apply, investment tribunals frequently refer to publicists (in Fauchald's study [2008: 352], publicists were cited in seventy-three out of ninety-eight decisions examined). When it comes to the PCIJ/ICJ, one of its most

---

[11] Statute of the International Court of Justice, art. 38.1, 33 U.N.T.S. 993.

astute observers writes, "both Courts are very reticent in direct citation of named publicists in support of any proposition of law." However, "[w]ritings of publicists and of members of the Court are frequently quoted in pleadings, and in individual and dissenting opinions" (Rosenne 2006: 1558).

The five interpretation choices discussed above, with illustrative examples of variance between international tribunals, are summarized in Table 18.1.

III. EXPLAINING VARIATION IN INTERPRETATION

Above, we presented our conceptualization of five types of interpretation. We now turn to explanations. Why is it, for example, that an international tribunal opts for evolutionary rather than original interpretation? How can we explain that GATT panels focused on party intent (including the *travaux préparatoires* of GATT) and were largely inward-looking, work-to-rule agents, whereas the AB focuses on text and adopts an outward-looking, systemic method of interpretation? In this section, we develop an initial framework of analysis. We suggest that variation of interpretative methods across tribunals is not randomly distributed. Members of tribunals do not toss a coin to decide which approach to take. We realize that the factors we list here are not exhaustive and sometimes overlap. Still, we believe that the framework captures the essential drivers and offers a useful way to distinguish between them.

We suggest that *interpretation choice* is a result of the interaction of two key variables: (a) the demand-side *interpretation space* that is made available to a tribunal and (b) the supply-side *interpretation incentives*, defined as intrinsic motivations of a tribunal's members when operating within this space. Interpretation space, in turn, is defined by degree of contract incompleteness and principals' ability to overcome collective action problems. Interpretation incentives, finally, are conditioned by institutional factors and existing norms. Figure 18.1 provides an overview of the causal setup of our framework.

A. *Interpretation Space*

The starting point for treaty interpretation is the demand side, in particular, the interests of states as principals. These interests (and their impact) are reflected in the degree of contract incompleteness and states' ability to act collectively.

1. Contract Incompleteness

The literature on incomplete contracts defines interpretation as part of a tribunal's contribution toward maximizing *ex post* contract performance. How much a tribunal is asked to interpret is defined by (a) the degree of guidance established in the contract (interpretative aids, how to deal with uncertainty) and (b) the clarity and precision of obligations (little ambiguity requires less interpretation).

TABLE 18.1. *Overview of interpretation choices*

Interpretative choice	Options	Examples
Dominant hermeneutic	**Text**: linguistic meaning; relatively broad interpretative community **Intent**: more subjective; closer community of drafters **Objective**: value-driven; prone to fragmentation	**Text**: AB, ICC, ICJ **Intent**: GATT panels, ad hoc arbitration **Objective**: ECJ, ECtHR, IACHR, ICTY, ICTR
Timing	**Original**: meaning at the time the treaty was concluded (static, frozen in time) **Evolutionary**: meaning at the time the dispute is decided (dynamic, evolves with new developments); addresses problem of treaty rigidity	**Original**: ICC, Retrospective Claims Tribunals, GATT panels **In between**: ICJ **Evolutionary**: AB, ECtHR, IACHR, ECJ
Activism	**Work-to-rule**: deferential, strict constructionist often in favor of defendant; tribunals as work to rule agents **Gap-filling**: legislative function; tribunals as self-confident agents completing the contract	**Work to rule**: ICC, GATT, early AB **Gap-filling**: ECJ, ECtHR, IACHR, later AB
Precedent	**Case-by-case**: no or less weight given to earlier rulings; settles dispute between the parties only; little or no impact on third parties **Precedent**: earlier rulings complement normative framework; third parties are affected; de facto binding	**Case-by-case**: GATT (to some extent), investor–state arbitration **Precedent**: Caribbean Court of Justice, ECJ, AB, ICJ, ECtHR, IACHR
Linkage	**Self-contained**: inward-looking; reference to own legal instruments only; prone to fragmentation **Systemic**: outward-looking; links to general international law (including VCLT) and other treaties and tribunals; academic writings	**Self-contained**: GATT panels (more recently), ECJ **Systemic**: ICJ, AB (more recently), investor–state arbitration, ECtHR, IACHR

As to overall guidance, for some international tribunals (e.g., the ICC or WTO) the treaty stipulates explicit rules on how to interpret. This offers a first important means for treaty drafters to influence interpretation space; by stipulating precise interpretation rules, drafters can guide treaty interpretation. The strict constructionist guidance in Article 22 of the ICC Statute is said to be a response to the

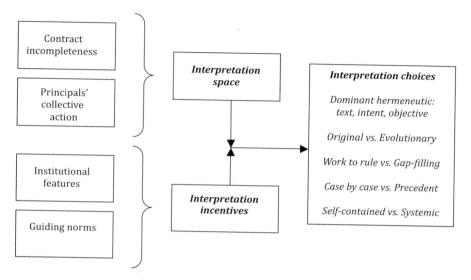

FIGURE 18.1. General Framework for Explaining Interpretation.

"perceived liberal interpretive reasoning of the ad hoc [ICTY and ICTR] tribunals" (Grover 2010: 553). The direction in the WTO Dispute Settlement Understanding to follow the "customary rules of interpretation of public international law," that is, VCLT rules, was provided to change certain interpretative practices of GATT panels. Unlike GATT panel practice, these VCLT rules put text before *travaux préparatoires* and call on an interpreter to give meaning in the context of the broader field of international law. By contrast with the ICC and WTO examples, however, most tribunals (and especially ad hoc tribunals) lack any explicit guidance (e.g., investor – state arbitrations).

In terms of clarity and precision of obligations (the second factor in contract incompleteness), we may witness important differences between treaties. Some treaties can set out very precise rules (e.g., tariff reductions in trade agreements). Others (such as human rights or investment agreements) may be limited to general principles or standards. Similarly, some treaties are more akin to contracts concluded at arm's length (so that the intentions of the parties may be an appropriate benchmark for interpretation). Others are more like legislative or even constitutional documents (where reliance on a broader interpretative community and treaty objectives may be more appropriate) (Weiler 2008). The more general the obligation, the more demand for interpretation in *ex post* contract performance. If normative prescriptions resemble rules (say, a maximum customs duty of 5 percent on a given product), then we expect less need for interpretation. If prescriptions are in the form of standards (say, no inhumane punishment or unfair treatment of investors), states increase the degree of delegation to international tribunals (Abbott *et al.* 2000). The use of generic terms increases incompleteness and pushes international tribunals to adopt an evolutionary rather than an original interpretation. Because treaty terms are ambiguous, and generic treaty terms often remain in place, unamended for decades, international tribunals (e.g., the AB, the ECtHR/IACHR and, increasingly, the ICJ) are inclined to update the treaty through evolutionary interpretation. Treaty incompleteness, both at origin and increasing over time, can also explain a tribunal's interpretative choice on the activism scale discussed above (work-to-rule vs. gap-filling); the more incomplete a treaty is, the bigger the mandate or temptation to fill gaps. The ECJ (Arnull 2006: 621), ECtHR, and the IACHR (Lixinski 2010: 589) have, for example, been relatively activist, not because of some dark conspiracy among judges, but because of the inherent vagueness and nature of their constituent treaties.

2. Principals' Collective Action

We suggest four specific factors that reflect or determine collective action on the principals' side: function, saliency, competition, and control.

First, the interests of principals can be captured by the expectations of the function of a tribunal. These range from making credible commitments (Helfer and Slaughter 2005), addressing reneging or opportunistic behavior (Alter 2008*b*), and resolving disputes efficiently, to constraining powerful states (Grant and Keohane 2005), avoiding escalation (Davis 2011), representing powerful states in *ex post* contract performance (Posner and Yoo 2005), and ensuring constitutional checks and balances, including against majoritarian decisions (McGinnis and Movsesian 2000). One and the same tribunal may contribute to several of these functions. Principals' interests as to the exact function of the tribunal, in turn, determine interpretation space. For example, ad hoc tribunals deciding on past events, whose core function is to settle specific claims or disputes (retrospective tribunals with a fixed docket), have less interpretation space than, for example, the ECtHR or AB whose function is (also) to clarify agreements and develop predictable rules with a much longer time horizon (prospective tribunals with an open-ended docket). We also expect retrospective tribunals with a fixed docket to be more inclined to opt for an original interpretation (so as to ensure equal treatment of all claims), whereas prospective tribunals with an open-ended docket will be more likely to interpret treaties in an evolutionary manner (so as to update the treaty to reflect new developments over time). Finally, where a core function of the international tribunal is to develop a consistent and predictable set of rules (as in the WTO), the tribunal will be more inclined to give weight to precedent rather than to decide each case de novo.

Second, whether principals' interests translate into influence depends on the extent to which principals and the broader community care about the outcomes of courts (saliency). If there is low saliency, courts get more interpretation space. In the EU, for example, scholars have demonstrated that the activism of the ECJ was largely unexpected. Over time, however, as member states became aware of the nature and stakes of ECJ activism, they increased their efforts to influence, and in some cases overturn, unwelcome judicial decisions (Mattli and Slaughter 1998). Low saliency may also explain some of the activist pro-trade decisions made by early GATT panels, given that, in its early decades, GATT was seen as a largely technical, customs-only organization, hardly reaching the political headlines. Similarly, activism detected in certain (early) investor – state arbitrations may be explained by low saliency—that is, the fact that some of these early cases were decided behind closed doors and litigated between technical experts, with higher-level officials and the public not being "in the loop." The same can be said about the ICTY/ICTR (attracting little attention from principals) compared to the ICC (higher saliency, partly because of *ex post* awareness of the impact of ICTY/ICTR activity).

Third, competition between principals affects collective action. From the principal – agent literature, we have learned that the existence of multiple principals affects the overall discretion of the agents (or interpretation space in our case) (Nielson and Tierney 2003). If divergence of interests among principals increases, new autonomy will open up for judicial agents, or, as John Ferejohn put it, "Courts and agencies are capable of independent or autonomous action where the constitutional legislature is too fragmented to react" (2002: 63). This is a crucial insight that may explain the AB's more recent activism. Whereas at the time of its creation in 1994, the WTO was dominated by a handful of countries (especially the EU and the United States), in more recent years, multiple powerful actors have emerged (including China, Brazil, India, and South Africa). This interest divergence increases the interpretation space and, in turn, enables the AB to be more activist, knowing that its rulings may upset some powerful countries but please others. Steinberg (2004: 275) argues that

> WTO dispute settlement could assume a new form as a result of fundamental changes in the political environment, such as the dispersion of power at the WTO or a divergence of interests of powerful states. If either shift were to occur, the strategic space for judicial lawmaking at the WTO would expand, as it would become more difficult to establish and sustain the political cooperation necessary to check or correct [AB] action.

Fourth, collective action depends on control. Principals have different sets of *ex ante* and *ex post* control tools by which they can influence interpretation space. *Ex ante* control predominantly functions through the selection of judicial agents. There is no lifetime appointment in international tribunals. Appointments vary between fixed terms for standing bodies (with the possibility of renewal and with or without a compulsory retirement age) and ad hoc short-term appointments (e.g., for GATT or WTO panels and investor – state arbitrations). Where adjudicators are appointed ad hoc, we expect them to be under closer control by the parties (their interpretation space shrinks) and, hence they are more likely to opt for party intent as the dominant hermeneutic and adopt a more deferential, less activist approach. Fixed-term appointments, on the other hand, would lead to the opposite conjecture. Appointments also differ as a function of the composition of tribunals. Attention (politicization) tends to be less in the case of a representative court (e.g., ECJ and ECtHR, where all members can nominate a judge, and other parties tend merely to rubber stamp each other's nomination) (Voeten 2007, 2008) than with a selective court (seats are limited and all parties have a say on all selections, as for the AB and, somewhat less so, the ICJ) (Elsig and Pollack, forthcoming). *Ex ante* control may change over time. In the WTO, its members, in the face of a more activist AB, seek to enhance control through the selection process (Elsig and Pollack, forthcoming). In investor–state arbitrations, where each party appoints one of the three arbitrators, the divide between investor-appointed and state-appointed adjudicators has widened. Arbitrators increasingly belong in one or the other camp and are appointed accordingly, with certain expectations as to interpretative choice and outcome. In many cases, this constellation gives the deciding vote to the neutrally appointed president of the tribunal and, in turn, increases the tension and control over presidential appointments.

Ex post control relates to whether principals can overturn rulings through negotiations, sanction agents by not reappointing them, or disregard rulings. Given the rule of state consent, legislative correction of treaties by principals is very difficult. This rigidity of treaties increases the general law-making power of courts (Ginsburg 2005: 37–8) and makes evolutionary and gap-filling approaches more likely, a tendency that may increase as time passes, and "the 'blanks' between negotiated agreements and current policy issues grow ever bigger" (Levy 2011: 50). In terms of reappointment, we expect tribunals in which judges are appointed for one term only (especially, a relatively long term) to be less controlled and more activist interpreters (Ehlermann 2002). *Ex post* control increases where (especially younger) judges can or must seek reappointment (possible once, for a second four-year term, in the AB; twice, for an additional term of nine years each, at the ICJ). This, in turn, can be expected to limit interpretation space. In terms of disregarding rulings as a form of *ex post* control, where the cost of exit is high, countries will tolerate adverse rulings. Yet, at some point, a line can be crossed where, for example, the benefits of WTO membership no longer outweigh a certain amount or degree of adverse AB rulings (Helfer 2002). Risk of exit limits interpretation space and should temper activism.

Rhetorical control by principals over tribunals (Steinberg 2004; Helfer and Slaughter 2005) is more subtle and informal, such as discussion and possible criticism of AB rulings by WTO members in monitoring bodies such as the WTO's Dispute Settlement Body (DSB). Although AB rulings are automatically adopted, such discussion filters through to the AB and has, in some cases, influenced and tempered AB activism, as when the AB opened proceedings to *amicus curiae*, a decision that it subsequently, for all practical purposes, reversed after heavy criticism at the DSB.

From the above, we generally expect that the greater the interpretation space – all other factors being constant – the more an international tribunal will engage in activist and expansive types of interpretation, in particular witnessed through completing the contract (filling gaps), adopting an evolutionary approach, and experimenting with setting precedents.

B. Interpretation Incentives

The motivations of tribunal members determine how the above-defined interpretation space is used. These intrinsic incentives are causally determined in our framework by two sets of factors: first, institutional factors and second, dominating norms. These supply-side factors (interpretation incentives) interact with the demand-side factors (interpretation space) to influence choice of interpretive strategy.

1. Institutional Features

We differentiate three institutional features: a tribunal's lifespan, the composition of its constituency, and institutional competition.

Tribunal's lifespan. We suggest that whether a tribunal is established as a permanent institution or is created ad hoc (to be distinguished from how individual tribunal members are appointed) strongly determines the motivation of tribunal members. Creating a permanent institution suggests that creators substantially support a tribunal and intend to engage in long-term cooperation with other participating countries. Not surprisingly, most standing bodies are created in the context of regional political integration. Normative support of strong principals for a standing tribunal also affects the way judicial agents read their mandate. Similarly, judges develop a more long-term vision. In addition, standing bodies profit from more professional support through established secretariats. Permanent courts are confronted with a stream of cases and are characterized by constant interaction (and learning and adaptation). Taken together, these features allow them to develop more systematic approaches to interpretation (opening up to other fields of international law), including, over time, more focus on evolutionary interpretation and using precedent to build case law coherence. Ad hoc arbitrators, by contrast, look at interpretation more on a case-by-case basis. Not only is principals' support limited, but also the lack of long-term cooperation inhibits the development of systematic approaches to interpretation, leading to more attention to parties' intent and originalist and self-contained interpretation.

The composition of constituency. This institutional factor pertains to the question of who has standing, as well as the type of actors that are involved or affected by the work of the tribunal. A tribunal's motivations are shaped by the number of actors involved directly or indirectly in its proceedings. Where a tribunal operates only to solve a dispute between two parties (without affecting other actors), the tribunal will be inclined to focus on party intent, to reject precedent, and to take a more deferential approach to interpretation (as in commercial arbitration and, to a lesser extent, investor–state arbitration). In contrast, where a tribunal's constituency or audience goes beyond the governments that set up the tribunal (e.g., private traders or investors, or individual victims of human rights violations), we expect the tribunal's motivations to differ and to lead more easily to a teleological or more activist interpretation that refers back to earlier case law and draws guidance from a larger interpretative community.

Empirical evidence on the ECJ and the Andean Court of Justice shows that, in particular, permanent courts attempt to work with lower-level institutions (e.g., national courts) and private actors that pursue similar interests (Alter and Helfer 2010). Where private parties have standing, given the absence of intergovernmental gatekeeping determining which cases will be brought, courts feel inclined to interpret rules more in light of individual rights than state-based rights, in turn encouraging other private actors to file or to support the court by following precedents. Private standing will drive courts to test more activist types of interpretation, seeking support for its evolving case law beyond principals. This may explain some of the activism of, for example, the ECtHR, the IACHR, and the ECJ (as well as, less frequently, investor–state arbitrations).

Institutional competition. A specific institutional feature is the presence or absence of alternative courts to which parties may turn. Institutional competition (other courts or other dispute resolution possibilities) allows states to strategically forum-shop to choose the court where they anticipate rulings to be closest to their own preferences (Busch 2007). Therefore, institutional competition may weaken the discretion of judicial agents as they anticipate costs related to forum-shopping. Competition may also come from specialized fields where no tribunals exist (such as international environmental law) but over which a general court (e.g., the ICJ) wants to keep control. Judicial competition, when it comes to interpretation, can also explain why certain tribunals (including the AB but also the ICJ) have taken a more systemic approach to interpretation. Rather than look inward and construe one's treaty as a self-contained regime, a tribunal that faces competition, especially from specialized courts, may be inclined to engage with other fields of law and establish connections to previously neglected regimes. This is what we observe at the ICJ, which is engaging more actively with international environmental law, human rights law, and even trade and investment law. That in the *LaGrand*[12] case, the ICJ finally held that its provisional measures are legally binding has also been explained with reference to a perceived competition with the International Tribunal on the Law of the Sea (ITLOS), whose provisional measures are unquestionably binding. Competition from other courts and tribunals (ICJ, but also the North American Free Trade Agreement, investor–state arbitration, and ITLOS) may also (partly) explain the AB's increasingly systemic approach to treaty interpretation. In this sense, the proliferation of tribunals may motivate judges to use more systemic interpretation.

---

[12] LaGrand Case (*Germany v. United States of America*), 1999 I.C.J.9 (March 3).

2. Norms

A second set of factors that impact supply-side interpretation incentives relate to norms and principles. Tribunal members may have, or may develop, different personal visions of the right role of the court (e.g., more or less deference to the political branch) (Gibson 2006: 518), or their precise mandate, or the role of international law (in newly created and/or weak countries, for example, international law is more likely to be viewed as supreme). Motivations of judicial agents are also shaped by past experience and individual characteristics that may include ideological and political attitudes (conservative judges, for example, are more likely to defer to national sovereignty and thereby are less likely to engage in strong activism) (Segal and Spaeth 1993). In the following, we focus on three norm-type factors that influence the supply side of interpretation: legitimacy, interpretative community, and legal tradition.

Legitimacy. Tribunals only function well if their rulings are widely accepted and implemented. As international law lacks domestic-type enforcement mechanisms, it relies heavily on its decisions being seen as fair and legitimate. This specific compliance pull is pivotal to international tribunals. In this respect, we suggest that young tribunals (such as the early AB) that have not yet established a reputation as a legitimate platform are more reluctant to engage in activist or evolutionary types of interpretation, which might easily invite criticism. By contrast, older and established tribunals (such as the more recent AB) have more wiggle room. Early case law of the AB was also characterized by AB members clearly indicating the interpretative steps (e.g., in relation to sequencing the various steps in the VCLT) as a way to counter potential criticism for lack of coherence (Weiler 2001). Another legitimacy gap may come from the public impression that a tribunal is established by powerful actors and only rules in favor of these actors. In the scenario of courts facing significant criticism from domestic audiences that they have an in-built bias, courts will carefully draft their arguments as a signaling tool to build their overall legitimacy. Therefore, if tribunals are young and face "bias" concerns, they may act more timidly than tribunals that are well established and face fewer legitimacy concerns. The designers of the AB, as well as its first seven members, were well aware of their difficult task; they saw in the AB "a young plant that needed protection" (Elsig and Pollack, forthcoming).

Interpretative community. Norms on how to interpret international law may develop differently from one issue area to another. In particular, in some policy domains, there exist shared concepts or closely knit epistemic or interpretative communities (such as in the field of human rights or early GATT), whereas, in other fields, disagreements over the meaning of concepts are dominant (e.g., in general international law disputes before the ICJ and, increasingly, trade disputes before the WTO). Shared concepts are often driven by norm entrepreneurs in the creation and diffusion of certain concepts (Keck and Sikkink 1998). Generalist courts (such as the ICJ) may be driven less by value-based interpretations than specialist courts (such as the ECtHR or GATT). Over time, shared concepts may develop that may substantially differ from one issue area to another. In those cases, interpretation choices can be issue- or field-specific. The more concepts are shared within an issue area, the more entrepreneurial the tribunal may act, for example, by adopting a teleological interpretation based on the underlying goals and values shared by the interpretative community in question. We should, in that scenario, witness a preference for gap-filling, evolutionary interpretation, and attempts to set precedents. In the context of conflicting concepts (as is often the case, for example, in ICJ disputes), tribunals should be more inclined to operate as work-to-rule agents and abstain from completing the analysis on behalf of principals.

Legal tradition. A particular aspect that may affect treaty interpretation is whether tribunal members (or courts as a whole) are driven by either civil law or common law traditions. This matters in particular when one type dominates over the other. Judicial agents in the civil law tradition are more likely to engage in gap-filling, privileging an evolutionary reading, and attempt to build a coherent legal system. Scholars in the tradition of common law, however, will be more likely to abstain from gap-filling and focus on designers' intentions. In term of hermeneutics, they are more likely to rely on textual rather than teleological interpretations (Lasser 2004; Arnull 2006: 612). Normative commitments may also derive from a judge's conception of the proper form of argument and persuasion. The ECJ's style of reasoning (and much of that court's success) has, for example, been described as formalist and separate from politics, in line with the generally formalist legal culture of Europe (Shapiro 2002). Other legal traditions that may influence interpretation incentives are, in the context of investor–state arbitration, tribunal members with a commercial law background as compared to those with a public international law background (Hirsch 2009). The former are more inclined to focus on party intention and to settle the dispute between the parties rather than create precedent. Public international lawyers, in contrast, have a tendency to opt for a more textual and systemic interpretation with a role for precedent, reading investment treaties in the light of other rules of international law (Laird 2009: 153).

IV. CONCLUSION

This chapter offers a taxonomy of treaty interpretation observed in international courts and tribunals. It lays out five major *interpretation choices* focused on dominant hermeneutic, timing, activism, precedent, and linkage. In addition, the chapter attempts to fill a gap in the literature by formulating a framework to analyze the observed variation across tribunals. We propose two major factors: demand-side interpretation space and supply-side interpretation incentives. We argue that the greater the interpretation space – which, in turn, is determined by contract incompleteness and principals' ability to take collective action – the more likely tribunals are to use expansive strategies. This should be reflected in particular in teleological, evolutionary, and gap-filling interpretation techniques. However, this interpretation space interacts with a crucial second factor: a tribunal's motivation (interpretation incentives). We have listed institutional factors and norm-type factors that condition a tribunal's motivation. These supply-side incentives may, in turn, steer the tribunal toward more or less expansive strategies. At this stage, we only provide examples to illustrate our framework. The next step would be to explore in greater detail the interaction effects between interpretation space and interpretation incentives to offer more specific hypotheses to be tested empirically.

We conclude this chapter with a final observation. Although debates about treaty interpretation predominantly are about the use of dominant hermeneutics, at this stage, our explanatory variables provide little leverage to capture the fine differences between text, intent, and objective. Our – inductively developed – hunch is that the type of hermeneutics is not the best proxy for understanding the intentions or motivations of international tribunals. A tribunal can, at times, use a textual approach for the same (strict or expansive) purpose it could use an intent-type approach. Therefore, systematically suggesting causal arguments when it comes to the dominant hermeneutic seems a difficult task because the same type of hermeneutic can be used for different objectives.

REFERENCES

Abbott, Kenneth W., Robert O. Keohane, Andrew Moravcsik, Anne-Marie Slaughter, and Duncan Snidal (2000). "The Concept of Legalization," *International Organization*, Vol. 54, No. 3, pp. 401–19.

Abi-Saab, Georges (2010). "The Appellate Body and Treaty Interpretation," in Malgosia Fitzmaurice, Olufemi Elias, and Panos Merkouris (eds.), *Treaty Interpretation and the Vienna Convention on the Law of Treaties: 30 Years on* (Leiden: Martinus Nijhoff), pp. 99–109.

Allott, Philip (1999). "The Concept of International Law," *European Journal of International Law*, Vol. 10, No. 1, pp. 31–50.

Alter, Karen J. (2008a). "Agents or Trustees? International Courts in Their Political Context," *European Journal of International Relations*, Vol. 14, No. 1, pp. 33–63.

——— (2008b). "Delegating to International Courts: Self-Binding vs. Other-Binding Delegation," *Law and Contemporary Problems*, Vol. 71, No. 1, pp. 37–76.

Alter, Karen J., and Laurence R. Helfer (2010). "Nature or Nurture? Judicial Lawmaking in the European Court of Justice and the Andean Tribunal of Justice," *International Organization*, Vol. 64, No. 4, pp. 563–92.

Arnull, Anthony (2006). *The European Union and Its Court of Justice*, 2nd ed. (Oxford: Oxford University Press).

Bankowski, Zeno, Neil MacCormick, Robert S. Summers, and Jerzy Wroblewski (1991). "On Method and Methodology," in D. Neil MacCormick and Robert S. Summers (eds.), *Interpreting Statutes: A Comparative Study* (Brookfield, VT: Dartmouth Press), pp. 9–28.

Bianchi, Andrea (2010). "Textual Interpretation and (International) Law Reading: The Myth of (In)determinacy and the Genealogy of Meaning," in Pieter H. F. Bekker, Rudolf Dolzer, and Michael Waibel (eds.), *Making Transnational Law Work in the Global Economy: Essays in Honour of Detlev Vagts* (Cambridge: Cambridge University Press), pp. 34–55.

Busch, Marc L. (2007). "Overlapping Institutions, Forum Shopping, and Dispute Settlement in International Trade," *International Organization*, Vol. 61, No. 4, pp. 735–61.

Caron, David D. (2006). "Towards a Political Theory of International Courts and Tribunals," *Berkeley Journal of International Law*, Vol. 24, No. 2, pp. 401–22.

Crema, Luigi (2010). "Disappearance and New Sightings of Restrictive Interpretation(s)," *European Journal of International Law*, Vol. 21, No. 3, pp. 681–700.

David, Felix (2009). "The Role of Precedent in the WTO-New Horizons?," Working Paper No. 2009–12 (Maastricht: Maastricht University Faculty of Law, Institute for Globalisation and International Regulation).

Davis, Christina L. (2011). "WTO Adjudication as a Tool for Conflict Management," Paper presented at the 4th Annual Conference on the Political Economy of International Organizations, Zurich.

DiMascio, Nicholas, and Joost Pauwelyn (2008). "Non-discrimination in Trade and Investment Treaties: Worlds Apart or Two Sides of the Same Coin?," *American Journal of International Law*, Vol. 102, No. 1, pp. 48–89.

Drezner, Daniel (2006). "The Viscosity of Global Governance: When Is Forum-Shopping Expensive?," Paper presented at the Annual Meeting of the American Political Science Association, Philadelphia, PA.

Ehlermann, Claus-Dieter (2002). "Six Years on the Bench of the 'World Trade Court': Some Personal Experiences as Member of the Appellate Body of the World Trade Organization," *Journal of World Trade*, Vol. 36, No. 4, pp. 605–39.

Elsig, Manfred, and Mark A. Pollack (forthcoming). "Agents, Trustees, and International Courts: Nomination and Appointment of Judicial Candidates in the WTO Appellate Body," *European Journal of International Relations*.

Fachiri, Alexander P. (1929). "Interpretation of Treaties," *American Journal of International Law*, Vol. 23, No. 4, pp. 745–52.

Fauchald, Ole Kristian (2008). "The Legal Reasoning of ICSID Tribunals – an Empirical Analysis," *European Journal of International Law*, Vol. 19, No. 2, pp. 301–64.

Ferejohn, John (2002). "Judicializing Politics, Politicizing Law," *Law and Contemporary Problems*, Vol. 65, No. 3, pp. 41–68.

Gardiner, Richard (2008). *Treaty Interpretation* (Oxford: Oxford University Press).

Gibson, James L. (2006). "Judicial Institutions," in R. A. W. Rhodes, Sarah A. Binder, and Bert A. Rockman (eds.), *The Oxford Handbook of Political Institutions* (Oxford: Oxford University Press), pp. 514–34.

Ginsburg, Tom (2005). "International Judicial Lawmaking," in Stefan Voigt, Max Albert, and Dieter Schmidtchen (eds.), *International Conflict Resolution* (Ochsenfurt-Hohestadt: Mohr Siebeck), pp. 155–82.

Gordon, Edward (1965). "The World Court and the Interpretation of Constitutive Treaties: Some Observations on the Development of an International Constitutional Law," *American Journal of International Law*, Vol. 59, No. 4, pp. 794–833.

Grant, Ruth W., and Robert O. Keohane (2005). "Accountability and Abuses of Power in World Politics," *American Political Science Review*, Vol. 99, No. 1, pp. 29–43.

Grover, Leena (2010). "A Call to Arms: Fundamental Dilemmas Confronting the Interpretation of Crimes in the Rome Statute of the International Criminal Court," *European Journal of International Law*, Vol. 21, No. 3, pp. 543–83.

Helfer, Laurence R. (2002). "Overlegalizing Human Rights: International Relations Theory and the Commonwealth Caribbean Backlash against Human Rights Regimes," *Columbia Law Review*, Vol. 102, No. 7, pp. 1832–911.

Helfer, Laurence R., and Anne-Marie Slaughter (2005). "Why States Create International Tribunals: A Response to Professors Posner and Yoo," *California Law Review*, Vol. 93, No. 3, pp. 899–956.

Hirsch, Moshe (2009). "Investment Tribunals and Human Rights: Divergent Paths," in Pierre-Marie Dupuy, Francesco Francioni, and Ernst-Ulrich Petersmann (eds.), *Human Rights in International Investment Law and Arbitration* (Oxford: Oxford University Press), pp. 97–114.

Howse, Robert (2000). "Adjudicative Legitimacy and Treaty Interpretation in International Trade Law: The Early Years of the WTO," in J. H. H. Weiler (ed.), *The EU, the WTO and the NAFTA: Towards a Common Law of International Trade?* (Oxford: Oxford University Press), pp. 35–70.

Jacob, Marc (2011). "Precedents: Lawmaking through International Adjudication," *German Law Journal*, Vol. 12, No. 5, pp. 1005–32.

Keck, Margaret E., and Kathryn Sikkink (1998). *Activists beyond Borders: Advocacy Networks in International Politics* (Ithaca, NY: Cornell University Press).

Klabbers, Jan (2010). "Virtuous Interpretation," in Malgosia Fitzmaurice, Olufemi Elias, and Panos Merkouris (eds.), *Treaty Interpretation and the Vienna Convention on the Law of Treaties: 30 Years on* (Leiden: Martinus Nijhoff), pp. 17–37.

Koremenos, Barbara (2007). "If Only Half of International Agreements Have Dispute Resolution Provisions, Which Half Needs Explaining,"? *Journal of Legal Studies*, Vol. 36, No. 1, pp. 189–212.

Koremenos, Barbara, and Timm Betz (2013). "The Design of Dispute Settlement Procedures in International Agreements," in Jeffrey L. Dunoff and Mark A. Pollack (eds.), *Interdisciplinary Perspectives on International Law and International Relations: The State of the Art* (New York: Cambridge University Press), pp. 371–93.

Kuijper, Pieter Jan (1994). "The Law of GATT as a Special Field of International Law: Ignorance, Further Refinement or Self-Contained System of International Law?," *Netherlands Yearbook of International Law*, Vol. 25, No. 1, pp. 227–57.

Kuijper, Pieter Jan, and Marco Bronckers (2005). "WTO Law in the European Court of Justice," *Common Market Law Review*, Vol. 42, No. 5, pp. 1313–55.

Laird, Ian (2009). "Interpretation in International Investment Arbitration – Through the Looking Glass," in Jacques Werner and Arif Hyder Ali (eds.), *A Liber Amicorum: Thomas Wälde – Law beyond Conventional Thought* (London: Cameron May), pp. 151–64.

Lasser, Mitchel de S. O. L'E. (2004). *Judicial Deliberations: A Comparative Analysis of Judicial Transparency and Legitimacy* (Oxford: Oxford University Press).

Lauterpacht, Hersch (1949). "Restrictive Interpretation and the Principle of Effectiveness in the Interpretation of Treaties," *British Yearbook of International Law*, Vol. 26, pp. 48–85.

——— (1950). "De l'Interprétation des Traités: Rapport," *Annuaire de l'Institut du Droit International*, Vol. 43, No. 2, pp. 366–460.

Lenaerts, Koen (2007). "Interpretation and the Court of Justice: A Basis for Comparative Reflection," *The International Lawyer*, Vol. 41, No. 4, pp. 1011–32.

Letsas, George (2010). "Strasbourg's Interpretive Ethic: Lessons for the International Lawyer," *European Journal of International Law*, Vol. 21, No. 3, pp. 509–41.

Levy, Philip I. (2011). "Doha Round: Keep Moving Forward or Fall Down," in Richard Baldwin and Simon Evenett (eds.), *Why World Leaders Must Resist the False Promise of Another Doha Delay* (London: Centre for Economic Policy Research), pp. 47–52.

Lixinski, Lucas (2010). "Treaty Interpretation by the Inter-American Court of Human Rights: Expansionism at the Service of the Unity of International Law," *European Journal of International Law*, Vol. 21, No. 3, pp. 585–604.

Mattli, Walter, and Anne-Marie Slaughter (1998). "Revisiting the European Court of Justice," *International Organization*, Vol. 52, No. 1, pp. 177–209.

McDougal, Myres S. (1967). "The International Law Commission's Draft Articles upon Interpretation: Textuality *Redivivus*," *American Journal of International Law*, Vol. 61, No. 4, pp. 992–1000.

McDougal, Myres S., Harold D. Lasswell, and James C. Miller (1967). *The Interpretation of International Agreements and World Public Order: Principles of Content and Procedure* (New Haven, CT: Yale University Press).

McGinnis, John O., and Mark L. Movsesian (2000). "The World Trade Constitution," *Harvard Law Review*, Vol. 114, No. 2, pp. 511–605.

Milanovic, Marko (2009). "The ICJ and Evolutionary Treaty Interpretation," *Blog of the European Journal of International Law: EJIL: Talk!*, 14 July, available at http://www.ejiltalk.org/the-icj-and-evolutionary-treaty-interpretation/

Nielson, Daniel L., and Michael J. Tierney (2003). "Delegation to International Organizations: Agency Theory and World Bank Environmental Reform," *International Organization*, Vol. 57, No. 2, pp. 241–76.

Okowa, Phoebe (2010). "Interpreting Constitutive Instruments of International Criminal Tribunals: Reflections on the Special Court for Sierra Leone," in Malgosia Fitzmaurice, Olufemi Elias, and Panos Merkouris (eds.), *Treaty Interpretation and the Vienna Convention on the Law of Treaties: 30 Years on* (Leiden: Martinus Nijhoff), pp. 333–55.

Orakhelashvili, Alexander (2008). *The Interpretation of Acts and Rules in Public International Law* (Oxford: Oxford University Press).

Pauwelyn, Joost (2003). *Conflict of Norms in Public International Law: How WTO Law Relates to Other Rules of International Law* (Cambridge: Cambridge University Press).

Payne, Cymie R. (2010). "Pulp Mills on the River Uruguay: The International Court of Justice Recognizes Environmental Impact Assessment as a Duty under International Law," *American Society of International Law Insight*, Vol. 14, No. 9, available at http://www.asil.org/insights100422.cfm .

Posner, Eric A., and John C. Yoo (2005). "Judicial Independence in International Tribunals," *California Law Review*, Vol. 93, No. 1, pp. 1–74.

Rasmussen, Hjalte (1986). *On Law and Policy in the European Court of Justice: A Comparative Study in Judicial Policymaking* (Dordrecht: Martinus Nijhoff).

Roberts, Anthea (2010). "Power and Persuasion in Investment Treaty Interpretation: The Dual Role of States," *American Journal of International Law*, Vol. 104, No. 2, pp. 179–225.

Romani, Carlos Fernández De Casadevante (2007). *Sovereignty and Interpretation of International Norms* (Heidelberg: Springer).

Romano, Cesare P. R. (2007). "The Shift from the Consensual to the Compulsory Paradigm in International Adjudication: Elements for a Theory of Consent," *New York University Journal of International Law and Politics*, Vol. 39, No. 4, pp. 791–872.

Rosenne, Shabtai (2006). *The Law and Practice of the International Court, 1920–2005: Procedure*, Vol. III, 4th ed. (Leiden: Martinus Nijhoff).

Schabas, William A. (2003). "Interpreting the Statutes of the Ad Hoc Tribunals," in Lal Chand Vohrah *et al.* (eds.), *Man's Inhumanity to Man: Essays on International Law in Honour of Antonio Cassese* (The Hague: Kluwer Law International), pp. 847–88.

Schill, Stephan W. (2010). "Glamis Gold, Ltd. v. United States," *American Journal of International Law*, Vol. 104, No. 2, pp. 253–59.

Schreuer, Christoph (2010). "Diversity and Harmonization of Treaty Interpretation in Investment Arbitration," in Malgosia Fitzmaurice, Olufemi Elias, and Panos Merkouris (eds.),

Treaty Interpretation and the Vienna Convention on the Law of Treaties: 30 Years on (Leiden: Martinus Nijhoff), pp. 129–51.

Segal, Jeffrey A., and Harold J. Spaeth (1993). *The Supreme Court and the Attitudinal Model* (New York: Cambridge University Press).

Shapiro, Martin (2002). "The Success of Judicial Review and Democracy," in Martin Shapiro and Alec Stone Sweet (eds.), *On Law, Politics, and Judicialization* (Oxford: Oxford University Press), pp. 149–83.

Steinberg, Richard H. (2004). "Judicial Lawmaking at the WTO: Discursive, Constitutional, and Political Constraints," *American Journal of International Law*, Vol. 98, No. 2, pp. 247–75.

Swart, Mia (2010). "Is There a Text in This Court? The Purposive Method of Interpretation and the Ad Hoc Tribunals," *Zeitschrift für Ausländisches Öffentliches Recht und Völkerrecht*, Vol. 70, No. 4, pp. 767–87.

Torres-Bernárdez, Santiago (1998). "Interpretation of Treaties by the International Court of Justice following the Adoption of the 1969 Vienna Convention on the Law of Treaties," in Gerhard Hafner *et al.* (eds.), *Liber Amicorum: Professor Ignaz Seidl-Hohenveldern: In Honour of His 80th Birthday* (The Hague: Kluwer Law International), pp. 721–48.

Van Damme, Isabelle (2009). *Treaty Interpretation by the WTO Appellate Body* (Oxford: Oxford University Press).

Voeten, Erik (2007). "The Politics of International Judicial Appointments: Evidence from the European Court of Human Rights," *International Organization*, Vol. 61, No. 4, pp. 669–701.

—— (2008). "The Impartiality of International Judges: Evidence from the European Court of Human Rights," *American Political Science Review*, Vol. 102, No. 4, pp. 417–33.

—— (2013). "International Judicial Independence," in Jeffrey L. Dunoff and Mark A. Pollack (eds.), *Interdisciplinary Perspectives on International Law and International Relations: The State of the Art* (New York: Cambridge University Press), pp. 421–44.

Weiler, J. H. H. (2001). "The Rule of Lawyers and the Ethos of Diplomats: Reflections on the Internal and External Legitimacy of WTO Dispute Settlement," *Journal of World Trade*, Vol. 35, No. 2, pp. 191–207.

—— (2008). "Prolegomena to a Meso-theory of Treaty Interpretation at the Turn of the Century," draft available at www.iilj.org/courses/documents/2008Colloquium.Session5.Weiler .pdf.

—— (2010). "The Interpretation of Treaties – a Re-examination, Preface," *European Journal of International Law*, Vol. 21, No. 3, p. 507.

PART V

Enforcement, Compliance, and Effectiveness

19

The Engines of Compliance

Jana von Stein

Compliance with international law (IL) has long puzzled scholars and policy-makers. For decades, debates centered around the question of whether IL was even law at all, given its lack of an overarching enforcer (Morgenthau 1948; Hart 1961).[1] Later, international relations (IR) scholars showed that international *cooperation*[2] was not only possible and sustainable, but also common (Axelrod 1984; Axelrod and Keohane 1986). Around the same time, Henkin (1979: 47) famously stated, "it is probably the case that *almost all nations observe almost all principles of international law and almost all of their obligations almost all of the time*" (italics in original).[3] But, by and large, most scholars agreed that it was puzzling – even surprising – that states ever abided by their international legal commitments (Keohane 1984: 99; Franck 1988: 705).

Why do – and don't – states comply with international rules? If we *do* observe compliance, what does this tell us about laws' usefulness as a tool for effecting real changes in how governments treat their citizens, whether they defend their partners when war breaks out, how they apply antidumping measures, and whether they curb pollution? International law scholars have long been interested in compliance. Political scientists have considered compliance with international law puzzling for decades, if not longer, but even ten years ago these questions rarely received in-depth attention in the literature. This has changed dramatically. Across both fields, scholars are interested in how governments use laws to structure their relations with one another, and why, if at all, governments abide by those rules.

This chapter takes stock of the key debates and findings in the compliance literature, with particular attention paid to what we have learned in the past decade or

---

[1] See D'Amato (1985) for an overview.
[2] See Martin (2013) for an insightful discussion of the difference between cooperation, compliance, and effectiveness.
[3] See also Fisher 1981.

so. Following Keohane (1997), I divide the literature into two main groups – instrumentalist and normative – based on the mechanism(s) thought to drive compliance. It would be tempting to categorize the first set of arguments as "IR" and the second as "IL," but this would be inaccurate. A number of international law scholars are concerned with the material costs of adhering to agreements. A number of international relations scholars care about norms, identity, and legitimacy. It would also be tempting to think that these mechanisms are mutually exclusive. In reality, the mechanisms are permeable in places, and not always mutually exclusive.

Throughout, I draw examples from the qualitative and the quantitative literatures, although the emphasis lies more heavily on the latter. Previous reviews provide good overviews of earlier, predominantly qualitative, literatures (Kingsbury 1998; Raustiala and Slaughter 2002; Simmons 1998, 2010). One of the most dramatic evolutions in the compliance literature over the past decade has been the introduction of quantitative analysis. Statistics are now commonplace in the IR literature and increasingly common in the IL literature. In this optic, in addition to considering what new questions the literature is tackling, I discuss the benefits and drawbacks of this "quantification" of the study of international law.

I define *compliance* as the degree to which state behavior conforms to what an agreement prescribes or proscribes (Young 1979: 104). Importantly, (non)compliance is a spectrum, not a dichotomy. I limit the study to first-order compliance (adherence to rules), setting aside second-order compliance (adherence to rulings). I focus on *written* international law,[4] such as treaties, memoranda of understanding, and the like. My motivation is chiefly practical: this is the focus of most compliance literature. Custom and, more controversially, soft law, are other sources of international law. Later, I consider why compliance scholarship has not explored these as extensively and what might be gained in doing so.[5]

I. INSTRUMENTALIST APPROACHES

For scholars with an instrumentalist orientation, the puzzle starts with the observation that no overarching power exists to enforce international law. If no higher authority exists, why should we ever observe compliance? For some, any compliance we observe is coincidence; states abide because it is in their immediate interest to do so (Morgenthau 1948; Mearsheimer 1994–95). Most agreements simply articulate identical or complementary interests, and those that do not are unlikely to last. But if states would do the same in any event, why bother writing agreements down? If states have identical interests, the desired outcome can be achieved with no

---

[4] I do not include written instruments that create private international law, which governs relations between private persons or firms in more than one state.

[5] I also avoid, wherever possible, the term "enforcement." International law scholars and political scientists tend to use the term slightly differently, so I use a different terminology in order to prevent confusion.

communication whatsoever. If states have complementary interests, they can simply agree informally (Keohane 1984). In neither case is a formal arrangement needed. Surely, international agreements must do more than simply spell out identical or complementary interests; otherwise, it is hard to understand why they exist.

A. *(International) Inducements*

Adherence may be important enough to a (group of) state(s) that it is willing to pay the cost of inducing others to comply. These inducements might be positive, such as increased aid, trade concessions, and cooperation in other issue areas, or they might include punishments, such as economic sanctions, development assistance cuts, and – rarely – military intervention. Linkage is a common means of getting states to comply. Some issues are linkable because they are substantively related and affect each other. But this need not be the case: sanctions linkage, in particular, is a way to apply the engines of compliance from one issue area to another, presumably more intractable, area (Leebron 2002). Hafner-Burton (2005, 2009) argues that Western states can compel others to respect human rights by explicitly tying these to trade concessions in preferential trade agreements. Even governments that are perfectly happy to abuse their citizens can be "forced to be good" when the continuation of trade concessions depends on their respect for human rights.

Issue linkage is also about expanding the set of possible inducements that can be used to sustain compliance, which ties directly into ideas of "issue barter" (Leebron 2002: 12–13).[6] For example, Poast (2012) notes that a number of military alliances, almost all asymmetric, include trade provisions. These enhance compliance by increasing the costs of reneging; if the stronger state decides not to defend its ally, it will lose the trade concessions. Poast finds not only that trade provisions make states more willing to respect their alliance commitments, but also that these make alliances more credible.

International inducements are typically decentralized and based on self-help, placing the right to punish/reward in the hands of the (potential) victim and/or the powerful. Consequently, application can be uneven. Grave transgressions may attract no response, whereas minor noncompliance may be met with severe sanctions. The strong are also more likely to escape reprisals – and to administer them. International inducements, then, may have much more to do with national interests and the distribution of power than anything else (Morgenthau 1948; Goldsmith and Posner 2005).

At the same time, smaller states and actors other than states can and have punished noncompliers. Lebovic and Voeten (2009) find that the World Bank reduces aid to

---

[6] For some, this takes us into the territory of reciprocity, where governments make concessions on one front in exchange for concessions on another front. I prefer to keep these distinct, such that reciprocity is truly about meeting one behavior with the same behavior.

countries when the (now defunct) United Nations (UN) Human Rights Commission has explicitly criticized noncompliance with human rights standards. Coordination of multilateral efforts can be difficult, however (Martin 2000). Key actors might disagree on whether it is worthwhile to punish noncompliance. Alternatively, punishment or rewards might be in the collective interest of all, but each member faces incentives to free-ride. This often leads to an undersupply of multilateral inducements to comply (Barrett 2007).

Moreover, international inducements are not always renegotiation-proof. If a punishment (or a reward) is too costly to dispense, and the agreement is not self-enforcing, parties cannot credibly commit to imposing it (Barrett 2007). This is particularly acute in multilateral contexts (Guzman 2008: 66–68). Moreover, the *political* costs of punishing noncompliance can make sanctioning particularly costly: coercive sanctions can lead nontargeted states to feel threatened and to question the sanctioner's motives. However, international organizations can help lower the costs of punishing noncompliance by clarifying ambiguous rules, providing transparency and monitoring, and supplying information about powerful states' intentions (Thompson 2009, 2013).

B. *Reciprocity*

Scholars have long understood reciprocity to be an engine of *cooperation* (Schachter 1991). Axelrod (1984) demonstrates that, even when parties have an immediate incentive to defect, tit-for-tat strategies can effectively promote cooperation by establishing a direct connection between an actor's present behavior and expected future payoffs. Applying this premise to compliance specifically, the mechanism is as follows: if both parties gain from mutual compliance and will reciprocate noncompliance by reneging, the threat of reversion to the no-agreement status quo prevents either party from reneging in the first instance (Guzman 2008). The shadow of the future is critical; if it is not sufficiently long, a feud of reciprocal noncompliance begins and the shadow of the future "burns up."

Many conditions must hold for reciprocity to ensure mutual compliance. Most obviously, reciprocal noncompliance must harm the party that is tempted to renege. This is rarely the case for human rights agreements (HRAs) (Hafner-Burton 2005). In contrast, reciprocity often suffices to ensure compliance with agreements covering war conduct or trade, since bad behavior creates cross-national externalities, and retaliation can be targeted. Morrow (2007) finds that mutual ratification of the laws of war produces fewer violations of these principles through joint deterrence. Tit-for-tat can be a double-edged sword, however: if one party reneges, compliance breaks down more quickly because reciprocity is more effective when both parties have ratified.

It must also be clear whether a violation has happened (or not). This is particularly true for reciprocity because of the possibility of "spirals" of noncompliance. Although states often debate whether noncompliance has actually occurred, it is much easier to detect violations when the government is the only plausible actor. When individuals play an important role, this is harder. Morrow (2007), for instance, finds that when individual soldiers commit violations, making it unclear whether noncompliance was intentional, punishment through reciprocity is more difficult.

Finally, it is not always possible to limit the "punishment" to the violator. This is a common problem for international environmental agreements (Barrett 2007). Consider greenhouse gas emissions. The punishment of reciprocal noncompliance cannot be targeted only at states that are breaking their commitments. As a result, the threat of increased emissions is not harmful enough to convince the tempted party to respect its obligations (Barrett 2007; Guzman 2008). Even a series of bilateral accords would not do the job in most cases.

C. Reputation

Henkin (1979: 52) noted decades ago that "[e]very nation's foreign policy depends substantially . . . on maintaining the expectation that it will live up to international mores and obligations." Why might a reputation for honoring legal commitments matter? For some, the answer is that states inherently value a reputation for respecting international law. I discuss this perspective later in this chapter. For others, the answer is that reputation can have real material consequences. A reputation for keeping promises can make it easier for governments to secure cooperation more broadly. Conversely, a reputation for unreliability may hinder cooperation because promises appear noncredible (Keohane 1984; Guzman 2008). Reputation is important for predicting future behavior, not for punishing past actions (Brewster 2009).

Scholars have focused chiefly on the ways in which noncompliance endangers cooperation in the future or in other issue areas. Gibler (2008) argues that if reputation matters, it should be easier for governments that keep their promises to conclude agreements down the line. He finds that states that honor alliance commitments are more likely to create alliances in the future. Simmons (2000) argues that governments comply with Article VIII of the International Monetary Fund (IMF) Treaty because they want *market actors* to perceive them as trustworthy in their commitments to protect property rights in the future. A reputation for law-governed behavior can be useful for reassuring market actors about willingness to maintain the same policies down the road.

Whether noncompliance in one area affects a state's reputation in other issue areas seems to be a subject of greater debate. The Swedish government may not infer from Saudi Arabia's failure to abide by its HRA obligations that it is an unreliable World Trade Organization (WTO) partner. The reason, Downs and Jones (2002) argue, is that the sources of compliance costs are unrelated. To the extent that governments are able to "compartmentalize" their reputations (Fisher 1981: 130), reputation may not travel well across issue areas. Guzman (2008: 100–06) disagrees, arguing that although states undoubtedly have multiple reputations, these are often interrelated (Chayes and Chayes 1993). Noncompliance in one area might tell a state's partners something about its attitudes toward the law more generally. It also conveys information about a government's underlying willingness to sacrifice long-term for short-term gains.

An example of issue area reputational linkage can be found in Moore (2003), who argues that when a state reneges on an HRA commitment, investors become less willing to invest because they conclude that the state is not willing to restrain the present use of power in the interest of long-term benefits. The act of breaking a promise is key and involves actors in one area inferring untrustworthiness from behavior in another. Tomz's (2011) survey offers a novel approach to gauging cross-issue reputational spillovers. Respondents were more likely to believe that states were pursuing nuclear weapons if they frequently violated their economic agreements. If presented with a state that always complied with its economic agreements, respondents were more willing to believe that ratification of the Nuclear Non-Proliferation Treaty "mattered" (i.e., that a ratifier was less likely to be pursing nuclear weapons than was a nonratifier). This effect was much weaker if respondents were presented with a state that violated its economic agreements.

Concerns about reputation, however, might not always weigh in favor of obeying the law. Governments might instead want a reputation for being tough, defending allies, or protecting their interests (Keohane 1997). If these conflict, governments may decide not to comply. In the late 1990s, for example, the United States seemed to have gained additional leverage from refusing to fulfill its UN financial obligations, rather than losing influence as a result of a damaged reputation (Keohane 1997). Moreover, the existence of frequent leadership turnover calls into question the idea, or at least narrows the scope of the argument, that reputational concerns drive states to compliance. States usually continue well into the foreseeable future; governments change. As Brewster (2009, 2013) notes, some governments do not bear the full brunt of reputational costs because they are in office for a limited time. Particularly when the political party at the helm changes, reputations do not necessarily carry over. In the case of the Bush administration's treatment of detainees, international audiences expected that the Obama administration would behave differently. As a result, the reputational costs to the United States as a whole were probably relatively low (Brewster 2009).

Testing reputational theories is challenging. Existing evidence is mostly anecdotal and is limited by endogeneity problems (Gibler 2008; Tomz 2011). The measures that scholars use often pick up on so many other mechanisms that it is difficult to say with much certainty that reputation is the driving factor. Tomz's (2008, 2011) work, which relies on surveys, experiments, and elite interviews, provides the most sophisticated effort to date. The challenge for this research, of course, is external validity. Citizens and leaders seem to care about the state's reputation for compliance. But how do they weigh these against competing objectives, and how do these preferences translate into policy and practice?

D. Domestic Institutions and Politics

Important sources of compliance lie inside the state. In general, scholars focus on the effects of courts, elections, and legislatures (and their interplay). Slaughter (1995) laid much of the groundwork for a dialogue between IL and IR scholars on the effect of domestic courts, arguing that the judicial systems of liberal states enhance compliance in at least three respects. Individuals are able to mount legal challenges against their governments. Citizens enjoy a number of individual rights, which serve as tools with which to make their case in court. Independent courts can review government (in)action and deem it inconsistent with existing law. In the realm of human rights, Simmons (2009) also points out that even if litigation is unsuccessful, it can empower citizens to think, talk, and struggle over new rights that become part of the national dialogue and future political change.

Others take insight from the literature on leader punishment and international cooperation/conflict (McGillivray and Smith 2000), arguing that because competitive elections provide a relatively costless means for citizens to "punish" leaders who renege on commitments, democratic leaders have stronger incentives to comply in the first place.[7] Political accountability forces leaders to be more vigilant about breaking international promises for at least two reasons. First, it forces a tighter alignment of citizen preferences and policy. Setting aside (for now) the question of what groups in society *want*, political accountability forces leaders to be more concerned about whether noncompliance will cost them the support of citizens who benefit from the particular treaty or from the state's compliance with international law more broadly (Trachtman 2010).[8] Second, breaking rules can reflect poorly from a valence perspective, activating even groups that have no interest in international law but are concerned about competence more generally (Leeds 2003).

Putnam's (1988) now-canonical "logic of two-level games" spurred a large literature on how legislative constraints affect states' ability to conclude international agreements and sustain cooperation (Milner 1997; Mansfield, Milner, and Rosendorff 2000; Martin 2000). Legislatures can frustrate compliance in a variety of ways. They can delay or refuse to pass implementing legislation. They can refuse to shift budgetary resources needed to come into compliance. These *ex post* mechanisms of legislative control force executives to take legislators' preferences into account in the negotiation phase, particularly for agreements that require formal legislative ratification. This makes negotiations more complex, but it is also an asset

---

[7] See also Schachter (1991).

[8] Moreover, Trachtman (2010) argues that when noncompliance is reciprocal, it can attract the ire of additional domestic groups (i.e., those that suffer from the partner state's retaliation).

because it makes the agreements reached through this fractious bargaining process more credible (Martin 2000).

Scholars have often relied on one measure – democracy – to test arguments about the impact of independent courts, elections, and legislative constraints. There is some evidence to support the claim that democracies abide by their international legal commitments more than nondemocracies: they are more reliable alliance partners (Leeds 2003); they are, with some exceptions, more likely to comply with the HRAs they have ratified (Hathaway 2002; Neumayer 2005); they take their obligations under the laws of war more seriously (Morrow 2007); and they reach deeper trade cooperation (Mansfield *et al.* 2000). But there are also many null or negative findings. Democracies are no more likely to abide by their obligations under Article VIII of the IMF Treaty (Simmons 2000); they are less likely to intervene to protect their allies in time of war (Gartzke and Gleditsch 2004).

There are at least two ways to make sense of these mixed findings. One interpretation is chiefly about data; the lack of consensus may simply reflect the bluntness of the measures used. The often-used Polity "democracy" data are a useful starting point, but they do little to gauge specific mechanisms and are particularly problematic for getting at judicial independence (Powell and Staton 2009). Especially with recent waves of democratization, it is clear that the "liberal democracy," with strong and independent courts, competitive elections, and constraints on the executive, is not the only possible constellation of institutions. Recently, scholars have begun "unpacking" mechanisms (Powell and Staton 2009; Conrad, forthcoming; Conrad and Ritter 2012; von Stein 2012), but data availability continues to be a challenge.

A second reason for these mixed findings is that, with further scrutiny, it is clear that there are many contingencies and even countervailing pressures. Courts have complex doctrines detailing when treaties may or may not be invoked in domestic litigation (Dunoff, Ratner, and Wippman 2010).[9] Hence, courts may choose, or be obligated, not to order other domestic actors to comply with international legal obligations. Some scholars and practitioners worry that law from international sources can, in fact, pose a real danger to principles of democratic self-governance.[10] Research on countries with some liberal democratic institutions, but not others, is particularly useful, since it allows some parsing out of mechanisms. Conrad (forthcoming) focuses on the divergent incentives that domestic institutions create for dictators' compliance with the Convention Against Torture. When these leaders face a relatively independent judiciary, she finds that the prospect of enforcement tugs toward compliance; however, political leaders anticipate this and, so, are less likely to ratify in the first place.

---

[9] See also *Medellin v. Texas*, 52 US 491 (2008).
[10] These concerns are often rooted in larger jurisprudential debates about the nature and sources of law, particularly the extent to which law is properly understood as an expression of self-governance or a check/restraint on democracy. (C.f., Bradley 2003, as well as Justice Scalia's concurrence in *Sosa v. Alvarez-Machain*, 542 US 692 (2004).)

Elections do not necessarily induce greater rates of compliance either. This relationship depends critically on what voters want and on who carries political leverage and informational advantages (Dai 2006). Gartzke and Gleditsch (2004) argue that if a treaty is unpopular domestically, democratic leaders will find it *more* difficult to disregard public sentiment because of the problem of cycling. Opening up competition, even when elections are not fully free and fair, can create anticompliance incentives as well. As Conrad (forthcoming) demonstrates, dictators of countries where some political opposition is allowed have incentives to engage in repression, as "too much" dissent can lead to overthrow.

Finally, although legislative–executive relations can enhance the credibility of promises in some circumstances (Setear 2002), they might frustrate compliance as well. U.S. compliance with adverse WTO rulings is usually good when the executive can implement changes unilaterally. When the matter requires congressional involvement, however, noncompliance often drags on, unless and until inaction would result in sanctions on U.S. exports (Davey 2006). It is well known that legislative veto players make policy reversal more difficult (Tsebelis 2002). If a state is already abiding by the rules, this may be good news for compliance. If it is not, this may be bad news for compliance. Börzel, Hofmann, and Panke (2012), for instance, find that states with more veto players remain noncompliant much longer because it is more difficult for them to pass the necessary domestic legislation to come into compliance with European Union (EU) law.

II. NORMATIVE APPROACHES

Thus far, I have focused on interest-driven compliance. This provides an incomplete view of the literature. For some scholars, noncompliance should be viewed chiefly as a problem of management. Others argue that ideas and norms are critical to understanding compliance. Still others emphasize the importance of fairness and legitimacy. These perspectives are rather diverse, but they are united in the view that compliance with international legal rules is not primarily motivated by states' concerns about *ex post* costs.

A. *Compliance as a Problem of Management*

States are under no legal obligation to join any treaty; thus, they are bound only to treaty norms to which they consent. This is one of the most fundamental principles of international law. For Chayes and Chayes (1991, 1993), the implication is that governments generally only take on obligations that are in their interest, an idea that resonates well with instrumentalist views. Here is where the divergences begin, first about the "baseline" of state incentives. Instrumentalists typically assume that, in the absence of constraints, governments will cheat. The starting point for managerialists is quite the opposite: governments have a general propensity to keep their international promises (Chayes and Chayes 1993). The care that states take when negotiating and entering into agreements is evidence that they have a strong underlying sense of obligation to comply. What is more, constantly recalculating the costs and benefits of compliance is onerous. In a context of limited resources, following an established rule is typically more efficient and, therefore, the default option. Finally, norms are important: the sense of legal obligation that comes with joining a treaty regime pushes states to comply unless there are strong reasons not to do so.

Why, then, do states sometimes violate international rules? Drawing from various international environmental regimes, Raustiala and Victor (1998) conclude that noncompliance is rarely a willful and calculated act. Instead, it results from inadequate planning, agreement ambiguities, capacity limitations, and significant changes over time. In this context, it is not difficult to understand why managerialists are skeptical of mechanisms that drive up the costs of noncompliance. Punitive sanctions are difficult to mobilize and therefore only practically available in special circumstances. In support of this idea, Chayes and Chayes (1991) note that even when violations are unambiguous, reprisal is rare. Even when sanctions are mobilized, they are often inefficient and are sometimes counterproductive (Chayes and Chayes 1993; Young 1994). Retaliation can be particularly problematic when violations are chiefly a problem of capacity, for then they simply exacerbate the conditions that led to noncompliance.

For managerialists, the better path to compliance lies in more transparent agreement design, dispute resolution, and technical and financial assistance (Chayes and Chayes 1991, 1993; Young 1994; Brown Weiss and Jacobson 1998). In a preliminary analysis of more than 100 treaties, Chayes and Chayes (1991) find that agreements rarely provide for formal punitive sanctions. What is more, when treaties do include dispute resolution provisions, these focus more on negotiation than on what to do when negotiations break down. Instead, treaties emphasize technology transfer and technical assistance (the Montreal Protocol is a good example) and do not condition these on compliance. Among the authors discussed here, Haas (1989) is perhaps the one who most clearly relies on both managerialist and norm-driven arguments. He argues that epistemic communities of ecologists and marine scientists involved in the Mediterranean Action Plan provided crucial technical expertise. But they also contributed to the regime's success by defining many of the terms of the debate and by articulating a persuasive argument about the need to take action.

Mitchell's (1994) study of intentional oil pollution at sea offers an interesting comparison of two very different compliance systems. One required tanker owners to install expensive equipment by specific dates. The other established pollution limits. The first system made violations more transparent in a variety of ways, which ultimately led to much higher compliance than did the second regime. Although managerialists have often been critical of efforts to "punish" noncompliance, Mitchell (1994) emphasizes that equipment standards, by enhancing transparency, can also make monitoring and sanctioning more efficient. This resonates with instrumentalist accounts (Abbott and Snidal 2000).

Some argue that management and raising the *ex post* costs of noncompliance are reinforcing, not competing, approaches (Danish 1997; Tallberg 2002; Thompson 2013). Many cases of noncompliance with EU law, Tallberg (2002) argues, result from capacity limitations. But there are also plenty of instances where states fail to abide by EU law because they face incentives to defect, often because of interest group pressures. The EU's compliance system relies on mechanisms to improve capacity *and* on mechanisms that detect and, when necessary, "punish" violations. Börzel, Hofmann, and Panke's (2012) quantitative analyses of noncompliance with EU law strongly support the idea that both mechanisms are at play.

Few would question that capacity matters for compliance. That said, it is probably no coincidence that managerialist arguments have gained the most traction in areas where scientific and/or technological expertise are crucial. If we look to other issue areas, managerialism seems to give us less purchase. Expertise and capacity are undoubtedly part of the story. But it is not hard to find examples where governments have willfully decided not to comply, having carefully considered the costs and benefits.[11] In trade affairs, the 2002 U.S. steel tariffs are but one example. In the human rights arena, examples abound; governments regularly violate the HRAs to which they are parties. Management or expertise cannot prevent or solve these problems. Changing the leader's cost–benefit calculus – whether with carrots or sticks – has been found to work in some cases (Hafner-Burton 2005; Simmons 2009). Recent developments, such as the creation of the WTO's dispute settlement mechanism, also suggest that, although understanding (how to use) rules is important, the possibility of *ex post* punishment is also key.

Another critique comes from Downs, Rocke, and Barsoom (1996), who argue that there are serious inference problems in the managerialist logic. Managerialists view the relatively good compliance and the rarity of penalizing institutions as good news for cooperation. Downs *et al.* argue that these observations may instead indicate that states are avoiding deep cooperation because they cannot develop the punishment mechanisms necessary to sustain it. The managerial school's findings may simply tell us that states are only committing to agreements that require minor departures from what they would have done in the absence of an agreement. I return to this question later in the chapter.

B. *Norms and Identity*

Others focus on the role of norms and identity. Rarely does this literature deny the importance of cost–benefit considerations. However, these scholars emphasize that

---

[11] Conversely (and perhaps more difficult to track because these are the "dogs that didn't bark"), countries regularly debate the pros and cons of following the rules, and comply.

norms and identity often reshape and/or carry greater weight than these costs (Jepperson, Wendt, and Katzenstein 1996; Koh 1997). A key concept is internalization: the point at which a norm is so deeply ingrained that it can be "taken for granted." This is the end stage of many accounts, but the mechanisms that motivate this process are many.[12]

Koh (1997, 1998) emphasizes transnational legal processes. This typically starts with an international actor(s), A, inciting an interaction with another actor(s), B, in an international legal forum. This forces an interpretation of the global norm that applies to that situation. Importantly, the transaction creates a legal rule that guides subsequent interactions. Over time, this process reshapes B's interests and identities, and leads it to internalize the norms into domestic policy, law, and social practice. At this point, B "obeys" – an act that carries greater significance than compliance because it is based on B's sense of *obligation* (Koh 1997, 1998).

Constructivist IR scholars often focus on socialization, a process by which beliefs about right and wrong become norms (Finnemore and Sikkink 1998), which in turn reshape state identities, interests, and behavior (Risse and Sikkink 1999).[13] The culmination is norm internalization – but how do states get there? Johnston (2001) argues that the microprocesses fall chiefly into two categories: persuasion and social influence.

Persuasion is about changing minds and attitudes in the absence of overt coercion (Johnston 2001: 496). Pro-compliance groups increase their persuasive appeal by framing issues so that they resonate with accepted norms and/or evoke strong feelings (Keck and Sikkink 1998). Argumentation is important. For instance, constructivists point out that governments often ratify HRAs even when they do not genuinely intend to comply (Finnemore and Sikkink 1998). Once tactical concessions such as these are in place, however, the "logic of arguing" takes over. Governments argue with their critics, making argumentative concessions and specifying their justifications. Domestic opposition groups and transnational advocacy networks take these justifications seriously and start a sincere dialogue about how to stop abuses. Continued dialogue and institutional reform often lead to compliance and norm internalization, although Risse and Sikkink (1999) are clear that the process moves in fits and starts and may fail. Thomas (2001), for instance, argues that Eastern Bloc countries ratified the Helsinki Final Act believing they could gain legitimacy without having to follow through with compliance. But ratification had unintended consequences. The repeated invocation of, and mobilization around, these norms are credited with helping to undermine Communist rule in the Soviet bloc and pave the way for transition to democracy.

---

[12] As Keohane (1997) notes, some (Kratochwil and Ruggie 1986) are dubious of this causal way of looking at things. I return to this question later.

[13] I set aside the question of how principled beliefs become norms, as it does not pertain directly to compliance and internalization.

Whereas successful persuasion results in compliance and internalization, successful social influence often results in compliance without internalization (Johnston 2001). Governments care about the perceptions of other states and of advocacy networks. The possibility of social rewards and social punishments often motivates them to abide by rules. Finnemore and Sikkink (1998) emphasize three motivations. Governments want to look legitimate in the eyes of peers, which also affects their domestic legitimacy. What is more, governments want to "belong" to some desirable reference group. Finally, leaders want to enhance national (and personal) esteem; they want others to like them, and they want to feel good about themselves. The threat of social punishments – shaming, exclusion, dissonance from taking actions inconsistent with identity, and the like – also looms (Johnston 2001). International conferences play a role in these processes by providing new information and diffusing new norms (Haas 2002).

Acculturation – adopting the behaviors of a reference group – is a similar process (Goodman and Jinks 2004). Cognitive and social pressures, like those discussed above, push states to follow rules. Acculturation, however, places greater emphasis on the disconnect that can emerge between practices and beliefs. Acculturation does not require state A to view the reference group's rule as legitimate. It only requires that state A, which cares about how it is perceived, understand that the reference group values the rule. It is the social structure rather than the content of the rule that matters for compliance (Goodman and Jinks 2004). This can lead to a situation in which states adopt an internationally legitimated model that does not fit their local needs, resulting in a "decoupling" of values from action like that described in Hafner-Burton and Tsutsui (2005).

Critics of the literature on norms and identity raise several objections. Some of the literature discussed above maps attributes of individuals – discomfort, a desire to conform, esteem – onto states, which is an uncomfortable fit. States do not have feelings. Leaders do, but this begs more questions. How can we know what leaders feel? How do leaders' feelings translate into policy? Moreover, much of this literature focuses on "successful" cases. We know less about partially successful or unsuccessful outcomes. As a result, this literature is subject to the endogeneity problems discussed elsewhere in this chapter. Finally, although much of this research has made greater efforts to specify under what conditions norms and identity matter, it is still difficult to validate empirically (Keohane 1997). Kelley's (2007) study of the International Criminal Court (ICC) and bilateral nonsurrender agreements[14] offers one of the most sophisticated "large-N" efforts to assess the impact of norms and identity. She argues that affinity for the court itself and the *pacta sunt servanda* principle motivated many not to undercut their ICC commitments. She finds that democracies, states that identified as the strongest ICC supporters, and rule of law states are less prone to

[14] Kelley (2007) understands the signing of these agreements as a type of noncompliance with the Rome Statute, although there is some debate about whether this is technically the case.

sign these agreements. It is unclear whether these variables really gauge norm-based processes, however. Others have used these same measures to test instrumentalist mechanisms (Morrow 2007; Simmons 2000, 2009). Until we have variables that allow the parsing out of different mechanisms, it will be difficult to make much headway in pitting theories against each other.

C. *Legitimacy and Fairness*

Others argue that legitimacy and fairness are key to understanding compliance. For Franck (1988), a rule is legitimate when the individuals it addresses believe that it has come into existence and is applied in accordance with right process. This consists of four elements. First, the law clearly communicates which behaviors are permitted and which are not. Second, the rule communicates authority via symbolic rituals and other formalities. Third, the law relates to other rules in the system in a principled manner; like cases receive the same treatment. Fourth, the rule is not made in an ad hoc fashion, but rather through procedures that an organized community accepts (Franck 1988: 752). When a law fulfills these criteria, it exerts a "compliance pull" independent of the material conditions that affect state practice.

Critics charge that in holding legitimacy, rather than justice, as the chief goal, Franck (1988) favors procedural regularity and adherence to rules even if they are immoral or unjust (Tesón 1992). Franck's (1995) subsequent work is in part an effort to address this question (Koh 1997). A rule's fairness, he argues, depends on two factors. First, the substantive element: a rule is fair if it meets parties' expectations of justifiable costs and benefits. Second, the procedural component: a rule is fair if it is legitimate (as defined above). These elements are often in tension, but "fairness is the rubric under which this tension is discursively managed" (Franck 1995: 7). Here, Franck emphasizes discourse, reasoning, and renegotiation, practices that are reminiscent of those emphasized in the constructivist IR work discussed earlier. However, Franck places greater emphasis on process than on persuasion; the back-and-forth involved in discussion and debate lead us to fairer rules and decisions, which in turn elicit better compliance.

These arguments about the impact of legitimacy and fairness on compliance leave several questions open. Legitimacy is difficult to gauge independently of the compliance it is meant to explain (Bodansky 2013). A rule's "compliance pull" is its index of legitimacy (Franck 1988), but legitimacy also explains "compliance pull," making the reasoning circular (Keohane 1997). Moreover, it is not entirely clear *why* and *how* the discursive process that underlies the fairness mechanism makes rules more obligatory (Koh 1997). Empirical testing – by whatever method – proves very difficult. Finally, Franck's arguments beg the question: if legitimacy and fairness lead to compliance, why do governments not always create "legitimate" and "fair" agreements?

III. ADDITIONAL QUESTIONS: SOME OLD, SOME NEW

A. *Endogeneity and Selection*

As discussed earlier, scholars like Downs, Rocke, and Barsoom (1996) argue that compliance does not, by itself, demonstrate that international law imposes meaningful restraints on state behavior. States may simply be creating and committing to agreements that require minor departures from what they would have done in the absence of an agreement. This has important implications for how we study the impact of rules on state behavior. Any theory of compliance must recognize that institutional design is at least in part endogenous: states are only likely to invest time and resources in agreements with which they have *some* interest in complying. Answering the question "why do states comply?" requires that we also understand why states join in the first place (von Stein 2005). These insights have important implications for how we conduct empirical compliance research. Medical researchers can randomly assign treatments and hence can make inferences by comparing "treated" and "untreated" groups. Of course, states do not randomly select into international agreements, and researchers cannot randomly assign that "treatment." Simply comparing ratifiers' and nonratifiers' compliance does not tell us whether we can attribute differences to the agreement's effect.

These concerns have led quantitative researchers to use increasingly sophisticated methods to control for endogeneity. This represents an important improvement over previous work, which either ignored the problem or attempted to control for it in ways that were often inadequate. Unfortunately, there is little agreement on which statistical technique is most appropriate.[15] Ideally, theory would tell us which approach is appropriate, the quantitative analyses would provide clues, and results would not vary substantially depending on the technique employed. This seems to be more the exception than the rule in treaty compliance research at present.

There are many critiques and questions to raise here. One important question for scholars like Downs, Rocke, and Barsoom (1996) is, if treaties simply embody behaviors in which states were already planning to engage, why ever bother to create or ratify treaties? Imagining for a moment that this extreme version is true for all states, all the time, treaties still fulfill important purposes. Simply having a clear definition of what constitutes (non)compliance can be useful (Morrow 2002). This is particularly true in highly technical areas, where much of the battle lies in articulating a common standard and ensuring that all parties understand it. Moreover, treaties can serve an important "screening" function, separating states willing to uphold the standard from

---

[15] Some use Heckman-style techniques (von Stein 2005; Mitchell and Hensel 2007; Conrad and Ritter 2012). Others employ propensity score matching (Simmons and Hopkins 2005; Grieco *et al.* 2009). Still others use an instrumental variables approach (Morrow 2007; Simmons 2009; von Stein 2012).

those that are not (Morrow 2002; von Stein 2005). Screening, of course, can happen because of *ex ante* or *ex post* costs, as game theorists have long understood.[16] The idea behind screening via *ex ante* costs is straightforward. If the process of becoming a party is onerous enough, or if membership is extended only to states that have convincingly demonstrated their ability to meet the agreement's terms, then only compliant "types" ratify. Being a member is useful because, for instance, it conveys valuable information about type to other actors – states, markets, domestic groups, and others. The EU's stringent accession process is an example (albeit a murky one because it also includes managerial-type mechanisms such as preaccession assistance) and is embedded in a much broader set of institutions.

To argue that endogeneity is a problem, of course, is not tantamount to saying that it tells the whole story. States are typically motivated by various factors when deciding whether to join international agreements. What is more, governments are, to at least some degree, behind a veil of ignorance when they negotiate and ratify treaties (Keohane 1997). It is impossible for them to fully anticipate the range of challenges that can arise and undermine compliance. Although it is true that governments often hedge against these uncertainties via escape clauses and other flexibility provisions (Helfer 2013), not all treaties contain these mechanisms.

If the treaty does not include flexibility provisions, what happens when compliance is more difficult than expected? Exit is possible, but it does not happen all that often.[17] One interesting approach involves looking at cases in which the ratifying government had pro-compliance preferences, but the new government does not.[18] Does it nonetheless comply? Grieco, Gelpi, and Warren (2009) find that partisan shifts to the left lead to more current account restrictions and hence noncompliance with Article VIII of the IMF Treaty. Nonetheless, having committed does appear to impose some constraint: faced with a shift to the left, signatories engage in fewer restrictions than do nonsignatories. In contrast, although not specifically looking at partisan change, von Stein (2005) uses a different statistical technique but finds little evidence that Article VIII constrains. The question of method continues to be crucial.

Another approach involves looking at situations in which states ratify with little or no intention of complying. HRAs are particularly interesting in this context. There is considerable evidence that, for states with well-functioning domestic mechanisms to help ensure compliance, ratification is largely endogenous (Hathaway 2007; von Stein 2012) and imposes little additional constraint on state behavior (Hill 2010). However, HRAs also have many "insincere ratifiers" – countries that commit with little intention of complying (Hafner-Burton 2005; Simmons 2009). This can be quite

[16] "Screening" and "signaling" are often used interchangeably in the literature. See Stiglitz and Weiss (1989) for a discussion of the differences.
[17] Helfer (2005) finds that states exit multilateral treaties about 5 percent of the time. This is clear evidence that exit is not as exceedingly rare as the common wisdom held. That said, it is still relatively uncommon.
[18] See also Nzelibe (2011) for a fascinating take on related questions.

useful from a research design perspective, as it (potentially) allows us to "avoid" the endogeneity problem. Simmons (2009) and Smith (2012) offer interesting findings about the conditions under which even insincere ratifiers will find themselves compelled to make meaningful changes.

B. *Definitions of Compliance*

Following much of the literature, I have used a particular definition of compliance: *conformity to rules*. This approach faces at least two criticisms. One comes from Kingsbury (1998), who argues that the concept of compliance depends on one's theory of law. My definition is appropriate if we view law as rules intended to regulate behavior. But, if we have a process-based theory, which sees law as something that creates and shapes identities and social relations, this definition does not work. *Attitudinal* alignment becomes a core area of interest. What is more, we cannot understand how international law operates without understanding how it comes about and how it shapes identities (Brunnée and Toope 2010). We should instead be examining what really makes international law "matter": intent and internal motivation (Howse and Teitel 2010). Because rules are constitutive and not just regulative, it is impossible to separate them from behavior or to make causal statements about the two (Kratochwil and Ruggie 1986).

A second criticism suggests that a focus on compliance is itself misguided. In focusing on compliance, scholars have mistakenly ascribed state behavior to institutional participation.[19] In addition, they have underestimated the impact of institutions on states that, despite making improvements, are not fully compliant. Instead, we should be interested in effectiveness (the extent to which a treaty solves the problem that led to its formation) and implementation (efforts to administer policy directives) (Young 1994; Brown Weiss and Jacobson 1998; Martin 2013).[20] This critique has at least two important implications. First, we need to think in a more considered fashion about the counterfactuals, which also involves careful assessment of what the treaty is intended to accomplish.[21] Second, and put (overly) simply, quantitative-oriented scholars at very least need to rethink their dependent variable.[22]

---

[19] This concern is precisely what motivated scholars like Downs *et al.* (1996) and von Stein (2005) to emphasize the importance of understanding the basis of institutional participation.

[20] Looking at implementation, for instance, the passage of domestic laws, makes good sense for countries like the United States, where this step is often necessary to give a treaty effect. But in monist systems, this step often is not necessary. In the latter situation, it would be erroneous to conclude that failure to pass implementing legislation is (necessarily) equivalent to a treaty having no effect. Conversely, passing implementing legislation does not always imply improvements in practice; putting laws on the books is a step in the right direction, but they must also be applied.

[21] This opens up some difficult questions. Some treaties aim to stop a process that is under way rather than to decrease current levels. In that case, we might consider looking at predicted outcomes. This involves making a number of assumptions, which, of course, raises more questions.

[22] The international environmental literature has grappled with these kinds of questions fairly extensively. See, for example, Young (1994), Raustiala and Victor (1998), and Victor *et al.* 1998.

The problem may not, however, be as grave as Martin (2013) suggests. On the theoretical side, much of the literature, while using the language of compliance, is interested in effects. This may largely be a problem of carelessness in vocabulary, not theory. On the empirical side, Martin's is an important point, but I would caution against throwing the baby out with the bathwater. Suppose we are interested in the effects of a treaty requiring each state to emit no more than some target level of a pollutant. State B is far above target (and therefore noncompliant[23]), but we suspect that the treaty has affected its practice, as we observe that it has significantly cut its pollution since ratification and in relation to nonratifiers. To get at effectiveness, as Martin (2013) defines it, we need to know what constitutes "solving" the problem. How would we do this? We might consider the problem "solved" when countries entirely stop emitting the pollutant. Alternatively, we might look to the treaty and think that reaching the target counts as "solving" the problem. Either way, we go back down the road of taking conformity to rules into account, even if we calculate the outcome variable somewhat differently.[24]

Another approach involves looking at behavioral change, $\frac{pollution_t}{pollution_{t-1}}$ or some variant. This does not gauge effectiveness as Martin defines it (above), although in my view it is potentially quite a useful approach.[25] However, it has limitations (as will, most likely, any measure we try to develop). Suppose that, because of some factor(s) that preceded ratification – a greening of domestic politics, a disaster involving the pollutant – state C has reduced its pollution to the point of being well below target. If we look at behavioral change, we will likely overstate the treaty's impact, since C's pollution was already on the road to being below target. Indeed, this may be why C wanted to create a treaty in the first place. One way around this problem, although imperfect, would involve excluding or "capping" countries once they reach the target, which takes us back down the road of bringing compliance into the equation.

Although there are good reasons to be concerned that looking solely at compliance is leading us to miss important causal impacts, once we go about the hard work of developing alternate measures, it is difficult and probably not wise to avoid the question of conformity to rules. Compliance, far from being orthogonal to understanding causal effects, is an important component of measures that we might develop.

---

[23] The term "compliance" is not technically appropriate for nonparties. If need be, one could instead use the terms "compliant behavior" or "conformity to what the treaty prescribes or proscribes."

[24] For instance, we might calculate a "progress toward target" variable. This might look something like $\frac{\text{pollution in year of ratification} - \text{pollution}_t}{\text{pollution in year of ratification} - \text{target}}$ (note that target is part of the calculation). Ideally, of course, the problem is "solved" when the pollutant's adverse effects no longer exist. There are many reasons why this is a problematic way to of looking at things.

[25] See Martin (2013) for a critique of looking at change as a gauge of effectiveness.

C. *Quantification*

Empirically, we now know a great deal more about compliance than we did just a decade ago. Throughout this process, scholars have made choices about which questions and research tools to privilege. One example of this is the "quantification" of the study of international law, a trend that is evident throughout this chapter. This move has been beneficial in many ways. The use of time-series-cross-national data has made it possible to move beyond the idiosyncrasies of a particular time period or country to make more generalizable assessments of how international law works. In some cases, data have allowed comparisons across agreements and issue areas, a task that is typically more difficult in a case study. Cutting-edge statistical techniques have made it possible to grapple with difficult questions of endogeneity, although this debate is far from resolved.

At the same time, the quantification of the study of IL has perils. We gain the ability to make general statements, but lose the richness of understanding one gets from homing in on one country or a few cases. Case studies are crucial complements in this regard. Moreover, existing measures are often unable to distinguish between different mechanisms. This is an important challenge for future research. The growth of quantitative research has not – for the time being, anyhow – generated consensus on most questions of interest to scholars of international law. Findings often vary by agreement, issue area, and/or methodology. Variability in findings, of course, can be of great interest. Now, the solution is *not* to add more agreements on an agreement-by-agreement basis. Rather, we need to think more critically about causal processes and conditionalities, and to make comparisons across time, country, *and* agreement.

IV. CONCLUSION

IL and IR scholars are talking to each other with much greater frequency now than they were even a decade ago. They are asking many of the same questions, sharing theoretical approaches, and using many of the same empirical methodologies. As a result, we know much more about why states abide by international legal commitments. We know, for instance, that it is *not* the case that almost all states respect their obligations almost all the time (Henkin 1979: 47). In some cases, compliance is dismal; in others, it is quite good. In many situations, we now know, various pieces must fall into place if treaties are to have meaningful impacts. This chapter has provided an overview of the main arguments and explanations at play in these debates.

Looking forward, a few points are worth mentioning. First, less formal institutions, especially customary IL, have received virtually no attention in the IR literature. For many IR scholars, unwritten law derived through practice feels slippery. But customary *matters* to legal practitioners and scholars. Are we missing important parts of law by focusing almost exclusively on written agreements? Second, scholars need to develop ways to parse out different mechanisms that are currently captured by the same variables. This means carefully considering what other observable implications follow from our theories. Third, and related, there is great promise in looking at how countries that are not "liberal democracies" behave. Finally, it is worthwhile to start looking at the causal impact of international law through a different lens, which could, for instance, involve studying changes in practice or implementation. In my view, compliance is a critical component of this effort.

REFERENCES

Abbott, Kenneth W., and Duncan Snidal (2000). "Hard and Soft Law in International Governance." *International Organization*, Vol. 54, No. 3, pp. 421–56.
Axelrod, Robert (1984). *The Evolution of Cooperation* (New York: Basic Books).
Axelrod, Robert, and Robert O. Keohane (1986). "Achieving Cooperation under Anarchy: Strategies and Institutions," in Kenneth A. Oye (ed.), *Cooperation under Anarchy* (Princeton, NJ: Princeton University Press), pp. 226–54.
Barrett, Scott (2007). *Why Cooperate? The Incentive to Supply Global Public Goods* (Oxford: Oxford University Press).
Bodansky, Daniel (2013). "Legitimacy: Concepts and Conceptions/Normative and Descriptive," in Jeffrey L. Dunoff and Mark A. Pollack (eds.), *Interdisciplinary Perspectives on International Law and International Relations: The State of the Art* (New York: Cambridge University Press), pp. 321–41.
Börzel, Tanja A., Tobias Hofmann, and Diana Panke (2012). "Caving In or Sitting It Out? *Longitudinal* Patterns of Non-compliance in the European Union," *Journal of European Public Policy*, Vol. 19, No. 4, pp. 454–71.
Bradley, Curtis A. (2003). "International Delegations, the Structural Constitution, and Non-Self-Execution," *Stanford Law Review*, Vol. 55, No. 5, pp. 1557–96.
Brewster, Rachel (2009). "Unpacking the State's Reputation," *Harvard International Law Journal*, Vol. 50, No. 2, pp. 231–69.
———— (2013). "Reputation in International Relations and International Law Theory," in Jeffrey L. Dunoff and Mark A. Pollack (eds.), *Interdisciplinary Perspectives on International Law and International Relations: The State of the Art* (New York: Cambridge University Press), pp. 524–43.
Brown Weiss, Edith, and Harold K. Jacobson (1998) (eds.). *Engaging Countries: Strengthening Compliance with International Environmental Accords* (Cambridge, MA: MIT Press).
Brunnée, Jutta, and Stephen J. Toope (2010). *Legitimacy and Legality in International Law: An Interactional Account* (Cambridge: Cambridge University Press).
Chayes, Abram, and Antonia Handler Chayes (1991). "Compliance without Enforcement: State Behavior under Regulatory Treaties," *Negotiation Journal*, Vol. 7, No. 3, pp. 311–30.
———— (1993). "On Compliance," *International Organization*, Vol. 47, No. 2, pp. 175–205.
Conrad, Courtenay (forthcoming). "Divergent Incentives for Dictators: Domestic Institutions and (International Promises Not to) Torture," *Journal of Conflict Resolution*.
Conrad, Courtenay, and Emily Hencken Ritter (2012). "Treaties, Tenure, and Torture: The Conflicting Domestic Effects of International Law." Available at http://bama.ua.edu/~eritter/treaties.pdf.
Dai, Xinyuan (2006). "The Conditional Nature of Democratic Compliance," *Journal of Conflict Resolution*, Vol. 50, No. 5, pp. 690–713.

D'Amato, Anthony (1985). "Is International Law Really 'Law'?," *Northwestern University Law Review*, Vol. 79, No. 5 & 6, pp. 1293–314.

Danish, Kyle (1997). "Management vs. enforcement: The new debate on promoting treaty compliance," *Virginia Journal of International Law*, Vol. 37, No. 4, pp. 789–819.

Davey, William J. (2006). "The WTO: Looking Forward," *Journal of International Economic Law*, Vol. 9, No. 1, pp. 3–29.

Downs, George W., and Michael A. Jones (2002). "Reputation, Compliance, and International Law," *Journal of Legal Studies*, Vol. 31, No. 1, Part 2, pp. S95–S114.

Downs, George W., and David M. Rocke (1995). *Optimal Imperfection? Domestic Uncertainty and Institutions in International Relations* (Princeton, NJ: Princeton University Press).

Downs, George W., David M. Rocke, and Peter N. Barsoom (1996). "Is the Good News about Compliance Good News about Cooperation?," *International Organization*, Vol. 50, No. 3, pp. 379–406.

Dunoff, Jeffrey, Steven R. Ratner, and David Wippman (2010). *International Law: Norms, Actors, Process: A Problem-Oriented Approach*, 3rd ed. (New York: Aspen Publishers).

Finnemore, Martha, and Kathryn Sikkink (1998). "International Norm Dynamics and Political Change," *International Organization*, Vol. 52, No. 4, pp. 887–917.

Fisher, Roger (1981). *Improving Compliance with International Law* (Charlottesville: University of Virginia Press).

Franck, Thomas M. (1988). "Legitimacy in the International System," *American Journal of International Law*, Vol. 82, No. 4, pp. 705–59.

———— (1995). *Fairness in International Law and Institutions* (New York: Oxford University Press).

Gartzke, Erik, and Kristian Skrede Gleditsch (2004). "Why Democracies May Actually Be Less Reliable Allies," *American Journal of Political Science*, Vol. 48, No. 4, pp. 775–95.

Gibler, Douglas M. (2008). "The Costs of Reneging: Reputation and Alliance Formation," *Journal of Conflict Resolution*, Vol. 52, No. 3, pp. 426–54.

Goldsmith, Jack L., and Eric A. Posner (2005). *The Limits of International Law* (New York: Oxford University Press).

Goodman, Ryan, and Derek Jinks (2004). "How to Influence States: Socialization and International Human Rights Law," *Duke Law Journal*, Vol. 54, No. 3, pp. 621–703.

Grieco, Joseph M., Christopher F. Gelpi, and T. Camber Warren (2009). "When Preferences and Commitments Collide: The Effect of Relative Partisan Shifts on International Treaty Compliance," *International Organization*, Vol. 63, No. 2, pp. 341–55.

Guzman, Andrew T. (2008). *How International Law Works: A Rational Choice Theory* (New York: Oxford University Press).

Haas, Peter M. (1989). "Do Regimes Matter? Epistemic Communities and Mediterranean Pollution Control," *International Organization*, Vol. 43, No. 3, pp. 377–403.

———— (2002). "UN Conferences and Constructivist Governance of the Environment," *Global Governance*, Vol. 8, No. 1, pp. 73–91.

Hafner-Burton, Emilie M. (2005). "Trading Human Rights: How Preferential Trading Agreements Influence Government Repression," *International Organization*, Vol. 59, No. 3, pp. 593–629.

———— (2009). *Forced to Be Good: Why Trade Agreements Boost Human Rights* (Ithaca, NY: Cornell University Press).

Hafner-Burton, Emilie, and Kiyoteru Tsutsui (2005). "Human Rights in a Globalizing World: The Paradox of Empty Promises," *American Journal of Sociology*, Vol. 110, No. 5, pp. 1373–411.

Hart, H. L. A. (1961). *The Concept of Law* (New York: Oxford University Press).

Hathaway, Oona A. (2002). "Do Human Rights Treaties Make a Difference?," *Yale Law Journal*, Vol. 111, No. 8, pp. 1935–2042.

―――― (2007). "Why Do Countries Commit to Human Rights Treaties?," *Journal of Conflict Resolution*, Vol. 51, No. 4, pp. 588–621.

Helfer, Laurence R. (2005). "Exiting Treaties," *Virginia Law Review*, Vol. 91, No. 7, pp. 1579–648.

―――― (2013). "Flexibility in International Agreements," in Jeffrey L. Dunoff and Mark A. Pollack (eds.), *Interdisciplinary Perspectives on International Law and International Relations: The State of the Art* (New York: Cambridge University Press), pp. 175–96.

Henkin, Louis (1979). *How Nations Behave: Law and Foreign Policy*, 2nd ed. (New York: Columbia University Press).

Hill, Daniel (2010). "Estimating the Effects of Human Rights Treaties on State Behavior," *Journal of Politics*, Vol. 72, No. 4, pp. 1161–74.

Howse, Robert, and Ruti Teitel (2010). "Beyond Compliance: Rethinking Why International Law Really Matters," *Global Policy*, Vol. 1, No. 2, pp. 127–36.

Jepperson, Ronald L., Alexander Wendt, and Peter J. Katzenstein (1996). "Norms, Identity, and Culture in National Security," in Peter J. Katzenstein (ed.), *The Culture of National Security: Norms and Identity in World Politics* (New York: Columbia University Press), pp. 33–75.

Johnston, Alastair Iain (2001). "Treating International Institutions as Social Environments," *International Studies Quarterly*, Vol. 45, No. 4, pp. 487–515.

Keck, Margaret E., and Kathryn Sikkink (1998). *Activists beyond Borders. Transnational Networks in International Politics* (Ithaca, NY: Cornell University Press).

Kelley, Judith (2007). "Who Keeps International Commitments and Why? The International Criminal Court and Bilateral Nonsurrender Agreements," *American Political Science Review*, Vol. 101, No. 3, pp. 573–89.

Keohane, Robert O. (1984). *After Hegemony: Cooperation and Discord in the World Political Economy* (Princeton, NJ: Princeton University Press).

―――― (1997). "International Relations and International Law: Two Optics," *Harvard International Law Journal*, Vol. 38, No. 2, pp. 487–502.

Kingsbury, Benedict (1998). "The Concept of Compliance as a Function of Competing Conceptions of International Law," *Michigan Journal of International Law*, Vol. 19, No. 2, pp. 345–72.

Koh, Harold Hongju (1997). "Why Do Nations Obey International Law?," *Yale Law Journal*, Vol. 106, No. 8, pp. 2599–659.

―――― (1998). "Bringing International Law Home," *Houston Law Review*, Vol. 35, No. 3, pp. 623–81.

Kratochwil, Friedrich, and John Gerard Ruggie (1986). "International Organization: A State of the Art on an Art of the State," *International Organization*, Vol. 40, No. 4, pp. 753–75.

Lebovic, James H., and Erik Voeten (2009). "The Cost of Shame: International Organizations and Foreign Aid in the Punishing of Human Rights Violators," *Journal of Peace Research*, Vol. 46, No. 1, pp. 79–97.

Leebron, David W. (2002). "Linkages," *American Journal of International Law*, Vol. 96, No. 1, pp. 5–27.

Leeds, Brett Ashley (2003). "Alliance Reliability in Times of War: Explaining State Decisions to Violate Treaties," *International Organization*, Vol. 57, No. 4, pp. 801–27.

Mansfield, Edward D., Helen V. Milner, and B. Peter Rosendorff (2000). "Free to Trade: Democracies, Autocracies, and International Trade," *The American Political Science Review*, Vol. 94, No. 2, pp. 305–21.

Marshall, Monty G., Ted Robert Gurr, and Keith Jaggers (2010). Polity IV Project: Political Regime Characteristics and Transitions, 1800–2009: Dataset Users' Manual (Vienna, VA: Center for Systemic Peace).

Martin, Lisa L. (2000). *Democratic Commitments: Legislatures and International Cooperation* (Princeton, NJ: Princeton University Press).

——— (2013). "Against Compliance," in Jeffrey L. Dunoff and Mark A. Pollack (eds.), *Interdisciplinary Perspectives on International Law and International Relations: The State of the Art* (New York: Cambridge University Press), pp. 591–610.

McGillivray, Fiona, and Alastair Smith (2000). "Trust and Cooperation through Agent-Specific Punishments," *International Organization*, Vol. 54, No. 4, pp. 809–24.

Mearsheimer, John J. (1994–95). "The False Promise of International Institutions," *International Security*, Vol. 19, No. 3, pp. 5–49.

Milner, Helen V. (1997). *Interests, Institutions, and Information: Domestic Politics and International Relations* (Princeton, NJ: Princeton University Press).

Mitchell, Ronald B. (1994). "Regime Design Matters: Intentional Oil Pollution and Treaty Compliance," *International Organization*, Vol. 48, No. 3, pp. 425–58.

Mitchell, Sara McLaughlin, and Paul R. Hensel (2007). "International Institutions and Compliance with Agreements," *American Journal of Political Science*, Vol. 51, No. 4, pp. 721–37.

Moore, David H. (2003). "A Signaling Theory of Human Rights Compliance," *Northwestern University Law Review*, Vol. 97, No. 2, pp. 879–910.

Morgenthau, Hans (1948). *Politics among Nations: The Struggle for Power and Peace* (New York: McGraw-Hill).

Morrow, James D. (2002). "The Laws of War, Common Conjectures, and Legal Systems in International Politics" *Journal of Legal Studies*, Vol. 31, No. S1, pp. S41–S60.

——— (2007). "When Do States Follow the Laws of War?," *American Political Science Review*, Vol. 101, No. 3, pp. 559–72.

Neumayer, Eric (2005). "Do International Human Rights Treaties Improve Respect for Human Rights?," *Journal of Conflict Resolution*, Vol. 49, No. 6, pp. 925–53.

Nzelibe, Jide (2011). "Strategic Globalization: International Law as an Extension of Domestic Political Conflict," *Northwestern University Law Review*, Vol. 105, No. 2, pp. 635–88.

Poast, Paul (2012). "Can Issue Linkage Improve Treaty Credibility? Buffer State Alliances as a 'Hard Case,'" Forthcoming, *Journal of Conflict Resolution*. Available at http://www(?PMU?).paulpoast.com/#/research/4553371618.

Powell, Emilia Justyna, and Jeffrey K. Staton (2009). "Domestic Judicial Institutions and Human Rights Treaty Violation," *International Studies Quarterly*, Vol. 53, No. 1, pp. 149–74.

Putnam, Robert D. (1988). "Diplomacy and Domestic Politics: The Logic of Two-Level Games," *International Organization*, Vol. 42, No. 3, pp. 427–60.

Raustiala, Kal, and Anne-Marie Slaughter (2002). "International Law, International Relations, and Compliance," in Walter Carlsnaes, Thomas Risse, and Beth A. Simmons (eds.), *Handbook of International Relations* (London: Sage), pp. 538–58.

Raustiala, Kal, and David G. Victor (1998). "Conclusions," in David G. Victor, Kal Raustiala, and Eugene B. Skolnikoff (eds.), *The Implementation and Effectiveness of International*

Environmental Commitments: Theory and Practice (Cambridge, MA: MIT Press), pp. 659–708.

Risse, Thomas, and Kathryn Sikkink (1999). "The Socialization of International Human Rights Norms into Domestic Practices: Introduction," in Thomas Risse, Stephen C. Ropp, and Kathryn Sikkink (eds.), *The Power of Human Rights: International Norms and Domestic Change* (Cambridge: Cambridge University Press), pp. 1–38.

Schachter, Oscar (1991). *International Law in Theory and Practice* (Dordrecht: Martinus Nijhoff Press).

Setear, John K. (2002). "The President's Rational Choice of a Treaty's Preratification Pathway: Article II, Congressional-Executive Agreement, or Executive Agreement?" *Journal of Legal Studies*, Vol. 31, No. 1, pp. S5–S31.

Simmons, Beth A. (1998). "Compliance with International Agreements," *Annual Review of Political Science*, Vol. 1, pp. 75–93.

_____ (2000). "International Law and State Behavior: Commitment and Compliance in International Monetary Affairs," *American Political Science Review*, Vol. 94, No. 4, pp. 819–35.

_____ (2009). *Mobilizing for Human Rights: International Law in Domestic Politics* (New York: Cambridge University Press).

_____ (2010). "Treaty Compliance and Violation," *Annual Review of Political Science*, Vol. 13, pp. 273–96.

Simmons, Beth A., and Daniel J. Hopkins (2005). "The Constraining Power of International Treaties: Theory and Methods," *American Political Science Review*, Vol. 99, No. 4, pp. 623–31.

Slaughter, Anne-Marie (1995). "International Law in a World of Liberal States," *European Journal of International Law*, Vol. 6, No. 4, pp. 503–38.

Smith, Heather (2012). *Insincere Commitments: Human Rights Treaties, Abusive States, and Citizen Activism* (Washington, DC: Georgetown University Press).

Stiglitz, Joseph, and Andrew Weiss (1989). "Sorting Out the Differences between Screening and Signalling Models," in Michael Dempster (ed.), *Papers in Commemoration of the Economic Theory Seminar at Oxford University* (Oxford: Oxford University Press).

Tallberg, Jonas (2002). "Paths to Compliance: Enforcement, Management, and the European Union," *International Organization*, Vol. 56, No. 3, pp. 609–43.

Tesón, Fernando R. (1992). "The Kantian Theory of International Law," *Columbia Law Review*, Vol. 92, No. 1, pp. 53–102.

Thomas, Daniel C. (2001). *The Helsinki Effect: International Norms, Human Rights, and the Demise of Communism* (Princeton, NJ: Princeton University Press).

Thompson, Alexander (2009). "The Rational Enforcement of International Law: Solving the Sanctioners' Dilemma," *International Theory*, Vol. 1, No. 2, pp. 307–21.

_____ (2013). "Coercive Enforcement in International Law," in Jeffrey L. Dunoff and Mark A. Pollack (eds.), *Interdisciplinary Perspectives on International Law and International Relations: The State of the Art* (New York: Cambridge University Press), pp. 502–23.

Tomz, Michael (2008). "Reputation and the Effect of International Law on Preferences and Beliefs," Working Paper (Stanford, CA: Stanford University). Available at http://www.stanford.edu/~tomz/working/Tomz-IntlLaw-2008-02-11a.pdf.

_____ (2011). "Reputation Spillovers in International Relations," Paper presented at the annual conference of the Midwest Political Science Association, Chicago, IL.

Trachtman, Joel P. (2010). "International Law and Domestic Political Coalitions: The Grand Theory of Compliance with International Law," *Chicago Journal of International Law*, Vol. 11, No. 1, pp. 127–58.

Tsebelis, George (2002). *Veto Players: How Political Institutions Work* (Princeton, NJ: Princeton University Press).

Victor, David G., Kal Raustiala, and Eugene B. Skolnikoff (1998) (eds.) *The Implementation and Effectiveness of International Environmental Commitments: Theory and Practice.* (Cambridge, MA: MIT Press).

von Stein, Jana (2005). "Do Treaties Constrain or Screen? Selection Bias and Treaty Compliance," *American Political Science Review*, Vol. 99, No. 4, pp. 611–22.

———— (2012). "Making Promises, Keeping Promises: Democracy, Ratification, and Compliance in International Human Rights Law," Working Paper (Ann Arbor: University of Michigan, Dept. of Political Science & Center for Political Studies). Available at http://www-personal.umich.edu/~janavs/research.html.

Young, Oran R. (1979). *Compliance and Public Authority: A Theory with International Applications* (Baltimore, MD: Johns Hopkins Press).

———— (1994). *International Governance: Protecting the Environment in a Stateless Society* (Ithaca, NY: Cornell University Press).

20

Coercive Enforcement of International Law

Alexander Thompson

Questions surrounding the enforcement of international legal rules – whether it exists, how it operates, and how effective it is – have implications for important debates in the fields of international law (IL) and international relations (IR). Legal theorists have pondered for centuries whether the existence of robust enforcement is a necessary condition for international law to be considered "law" in a meaningful sense. Skeptics in both fields argue that the lack of a centralized enforcement mechanism renders international law epiphenomenal to state interests and relative power considerations (Mearsheimer 2001; Goldsmith and Posner 2005). This critique has been applied most vehemently to the use of force: critics claim that it is not adequately regulated by international law, or worse, that military interventions are often conducted for political reasons but in the guise of legal enforcement (Hoffmann 1961; Glennon 2001).

Scholars with a more expansive appreciation for international law point to a wider range of incentives to comply, both internal and external to the state, but most nevertheless recognize the importance of enforcement in some form. Although Louis Henkin argues that states are motivated by a "culture of compliance" with international law, he also recognizes that "external inducements" – retaliation and sanctions by other states – play a crucial role in promoting compliant behavior (Henkin 1995: 50–51). Mary Ellen O'Connell is equally optimistic about compliance but nevertheless stresses the value of enforcement: "So long as sanctions exist and support widespread law compliance, international law is a legal system worthy of the name" (2008: 369). Because the stakes are so high, theoretically and in the real world of international affairs, it is important to develop an accurate sense of how enforcement operates and how it relates to compliance behavior.

For valuable comments, the author thanks Jeff Dunoff, Mark Pollack, Lori Damrosch, and participants in the International Law/International Relations Interdisciplinary Research Group workshop at Temple University.

Although I begin with a general discussion of enforcement in international law, my primary focus is on *coercive* enforcement, which I define as the actual or threatened imposition of costs on a perceived violator of international law for the purpose of promoting compliance. The most obvious costs are material, as with economic sanctions or the use of force, but they need not be – states can use purely diplomatic means and can apply various forms of social pressure and shaming to punish violations. It should be noted that coercive enforcement is used to promote compliance in a broad sense; although the action might be intended to reverse or prevent a specific violation, it might also have the more diffuse goals of convincing a violator to comply in the future or of deterring third parties from breaking the law. In other words, by demonstrating that there is a price to be paid for noncompliance, punishing a violator might be useful as an act of enforcement even if compliance does not result in the case at hand.[1]

My focus on coercive enforcement points me in the direction of "horizontal" actions of enforcement, where states target other states. I devote less attention to domestic avenues of legal enforcement, an important topic that is covered in the literature and elsewhere in this volume.[2] As a self-help approach to addressing violations of the law, coercive enforcement is a strategic and ultimately political phenomenon.[3] Partly for this reason, it is an ideal subject for those interested in exploring the intersection of IL and IR, with great potential for achieving the conceptual and empirical value-added called for by Dunoff and Pollack in their introductory chapter. Political scientists and legal scholars have much to learn from each other when it comes to enforcement and, indeed, there is already some useful dialogue between the disciplines.

This chapter takes stock of existing scholarship and explores elements of enforcement research that span the two disciplines. The next section discusses the variety of enforcement mechanisms in international law, noting that they are ultimately decentralized in nature and rely on self-help measures taken by states themselves. I then discuss scholarly views on how important a role enforcement plays in international law, including the prominent debate surrounding the "management" and "enforcement" approaches. I argue that this distinction breaks down in practice, both because these tools can be used in tandem and because institutional setting and design are important factors for managing decentralized enforcement. A fourth

---

[1] For example, when the United States used the WTO's dispute settlement mechanism to successfully challenge the EU's import restrictions on genetically modified foods, this was part of a broader strategy to convince developing countries not to impose similar rules (Stewart 2009: 9–10). Nossal (1989) argues that economic sanctions are often used to punish a violator rather than reverse its noncompliance.

[2] There is a substantial literature on the "vertical" enforcement of international law through domestic legal systems (see Koh 1999; Hathaway 2005; Conant 2013; and Trachtman 2013).

[3] As one legal scholar notes, in light of the marked decentralization of international enforcement, bringing a political and strategic perspective to bear on these questions is especially helpful (Setear 1997: 3–4).

section considers the incentives to act from the perspective of a potential enforcer, outlining the main obstacles in terms of costs but also the potential and often overlooked benefits to a state willing to take on the responsibility of enforcement. The concluding section presents three overlapping questions that deserve more attention in the literature and that could form the basis of a promising research agenda at the intersection of IR and IL: (a) How does power shape international enforcement? (b) What is the role of non-state actors in promoting enforcement? And, (c) How can institutional design contribute to effective enforcement?

I. THE DECENTRALIZED NATURE OF INTERNATIONAL ENFORCEMENT

Hans Kelsen (1942) famously described the international legal order as a "primitive" one, lacking a sanctioning authority distinct from the parties involved. This is consistent with the mainstream IR view that the international system is anarchic insofar as it lacks coercive institutions above the level of states (Waltz 1979). That international law lacks *centralized* enforcement institutions does not, however, imply that enforcement is nonexistent. As one prominent legal scholar explains, "the absence of these institutions does not mean that international law isn't really law; rather, it simply means that international law is enforced in a different way" (D'Amato 1987: 24–25). The main mechanisms of enforcement are decentralized ones, based on the actions of states themselves.

This perspective might seem outdated given the proliferation of international tribunals and other judicial institutions since the end of the Cold War (Romano 1999; Oellers-Frahm 2001; Goldstone and Smith 2009; Pauwelyn and Elsig 2013), some of which possess substantial independence from states (Alter 2008; Voeten 2013). This is part of a general trend toward the increased legalization of world politics (Goldstein *et al.* 2001), including delegation to international organizations (IOs) with sometimes unexpected power (Barnett and Finnemore 2004; Hawkins *et al.* 2006; Bradley and Kelley 2008). However, supranational enforcement authority is still rare and relatively weak. The International Court of Justice lacks compulsory jurisdiction and is increasingly underutilized for high-stakes disputes (Satzer 2007). Except in cases of self-defense, enforcement via the use of force can be authorized only by the Security Council, a body that resolves disputes based ultimately on political rather than legal considerations (Cronin-Furman 2005: 441; Voeten 2001) and lacks independent enforcement capacity. The International Criminal Court (ICC) is independent in novel ways but still depends on states to execute arrest warrants, provide evidence, and enforce sentences (Kirsch 2007). Even the World Trade Organization's (WTO) dispute settlement mechanism, notable for its high level of legalization, still must rely on states to conduct the actual enforcement in the form of trade retaliation.

Regional courts have the potential to contribute to more effective supranational adjudication and enforcement, as the European case demonstrates (Helfer and Slaughter 1997). In practice, however, the proliferation of international judicial and quasi-judicial bodies can complicate the legal aspects of compliance and enforcement. To begin with, when IOs issue recommendations in response to a violation, these recommendations vary in their degree of authority and bindingness, and it is not always clear whether they have a justifying effect on subsequent sanctions (Frowein 1987: 69–71). When international tribunals overlap in terms of the legal rules they address, in the absence of a clear division of labor or hierarchy, the resulting "diversity in international law" may complicate rather than clarify the interpretation of compliance and enforcement activities and their relationship to legal norms (Charney 1999: 707; Dupuy 1999: 792).[4] Moreover, when states are able to forum shop among multiple institutions and to invoke different sets of rules to justify their behavior, they are much less constrained and have more room to engage in self-interested action (Drezner 2009; Shaffer and Pollack 2010). For these reasons, we should not automatically associate the expansion of global governance institutions in general, and more legalized international courts in particular, with a more hierarchical or rule-oriented enforcement regime for international law.

In the end, as Joyner (1995: 265) notes, "Enforcement measures will continue to be implemented and coordinated principally by individual governments, rather than wielded as instruments of some supranational policy authority." In other words, most of the relevant enforcement mechanisms in international law are *decentralized* ones, conducted by states themselves and operating according to the logic of self-help. These decentralized actions are nevertheless conducted in the shadow of law and institutions that constrain and facilitate enforcement behavior, a point developed below.

Decentralized or horizontal enforcement comes in a variety of forms. It can be *bilateral*, in the form of retaliation by one state against another that has either violated a bilateral treaty or violated a more general law that primarily affects the one state. These cases are the most common and straightforward, since the state imposing costs has the most at stake and a built-in incentive to act. An aggrieved state can respond by suspending its own performance of treaty obligations, severing diplomatic ties, withdrawing aid, imposing economic sanctions, or inflicting social costs on the offender through strategies of pressure and shaming (Hafner-Burton 2008; Donno 2010; Posner 2002). Although there are legal rules governing these actions – it is "not 'lawless' in the sense that anything goes" (O'Connell 2008: 264) – the relevant law has many gray areas and is subject to abuse, especially when it comes to the issue of "countermeasures" and "reprisals" (acts that are normally illegal but which might be rendered legal as a response to a violation of the law).[5]

---

4 It is partly for this reason that my definition of coercive enforcement focuses on a "perceived violation" of international law. Because there are often competing claims of fact and competing interpretations of law, in most cases we lack a single, authoritative determination that a breach has (or has not) taken place (see Brewster 2009: 1139–41 and Elsig and Pauwelyn 2013).

5 On the law of *countermeasures*, *reprisals*, and *sanctions*, and its shortcomings, see White and Abass (2006), Noortmann (2005), and Alland (2002). According to Schachter (1995: 185), "few areas of international law are in need of greater clarification."

Enforcement can also be *collective* when a violation affects the international community more broadly (Frowein 1987). Collective enforcement, often authorized
by an IO, can be truly multilateral, when multiple states impose costs on a target
together. Examples are the imposition of sanctions on apartheid South Africa, Security Council–approved sanctions against weapons proliferators (Damrosch 2002),
and the authorization of force against Iraq after its invasion of Kuwait (Thompson
2009a). True collective enforcement is relatively rare in practice, however. Even
when a coalition is formed, most sanctions episodes involve one or a small number
of leading "senders" who initiate enforcement actions and bear the brunt of the
costs (Martin 1992). Similarly, when the Security Council authorizes member states
to intervene militarily, often the resulting action is conducted unilaterally or by a
small coalition led by a powerful member (Koskenniemi 1996: 461). The "peace
enforcement" missions in Haiti (led by the United States), the Ivory Coast (led by
France), and East Timor (led by Australia) are examples, as is the recent and more
militarized intervention in Libya (led by a small number of North Atlantic Treaty
Organization [NATO] countries). The senders of coercion in these cases are theoretically defending the rights of other members of the international community,
along with their own.

Although bilateral means of enforcement will always play a prominent role in
international law, there is no question that collective enforcement is on the rise. The
Security Council has become much more active in its enforcement role since the
end of the Cold War: whereas only a handful of Chapter VII resolutions were passed
during the entire Cold War era, more than 400 have been passed since. This form
of collective enforcement has become routine, with more than half of all Council
resolutions now invoking Chapter VII (Johansson 2009). Many of these resolutions
authorize economic sanctions of one form or another, with the result that collective economic sanctions are now a very common form of enforcement (Damrosch
et al. 2009: 539–41). The Security Council has begun to use its enforcement power to
address an ever-expanding range of issues, including humanitarian crises, civil wars,
and terrorism (Matheson 2006), which has led some critics to complain of over-
reaching (Talmon 2005). These United Nations (UN)-based activities have been
complemented in recent years by increasingly active regional organizations, like
NATO, the Economic Community of West African States (ECOWAS), and the
African Union, which sometimes act on their own but often implement UN-based
enforcement measures (Coleman 2007). There are more forums than ever for states
that wish to enforce collectively and with the backing of an IO, rather than rely on
traditional bilateral mechanisms.

II. ENFORCEMENT VERSUS MANAGEMENT?

Assessing whether enforcement exists and how it operates is separate from the question of how much it matters. Some scholars argue that a focus on enforcement

distracts from other, potentially more important sources of compliant behavior. For those who adopt a norm-based perspective on international law, compliance follows naturally from an internalized sense that rules are legitimate; law exerts its own "compliance pull" (Franck 1990; Koh 1997). Studies of domestic law do indeed find that individuals obey because they view rules as legitimate, not necessarily because they fear punishment (Tyler 2006). In this view of law, violations are deterred more by informal social mechanisms than by government-imposed sanctions (Ellickson 1991).

In the IR field, this perspective is echoed by social constructivist scholars who focus on internalized norms and social pressure as motivations for state behavior (Finnemore and Sikkink 1998; Wendt 1999; Johnston 2001). Empirical studies show that states are indeed sensitive to international norms, even in the competitive realm of security affairs (e.g., Tannenwald 2007), although these arguments generally are not applied to the influence of *legal* norms per se. An exception is Kelley's (2007) study of the ICC. She finds that many states refused to sign the bilateral immunity agreements proffered by Washington, which have the effect of undermining the authority of the ICC and the spirit of the Rome Statute, even though doing so was potentially costly. Bayram (2011) also finds that political elites and ordinary citizens are often motivated by a sense of obligation to international law.

What norm-based scholars in IL and IR have in common is that they emphasize the legitimacy of law and the sense of obligation that derives from it (Finnemore and Toope 2000). Formal enforcement mechanisms are less important from this perspective because the expectation is that states have a baseline propensity to comply.

Building from this view, Chayes and Chayes (1995) offer a "managerial" theory of compliance with international law. Managerialists, in both IR and IL, maintain that most cases of noncompliance occur not because of intentional cheating but for more benign reasons, such as ambiguity in the rules, a lack of capacity on the part of governments that makes implementation difficult, or delays in adjusting policies to conform with new international rules. The best way to promote compliance is, therefore, to design more effective regimes and to provide mechanisms for assistance and problem solving (Young 1994; Chayes and Chayes 1995; Brown Weiss and Jacobson 1998; Stinnett *et al.* 2011). This approach is often coupled with the observation that an "acceptable" level of compliance – rather than perfect compliance – is sufficient for the smooth functioning of the international legal system (Chayes and Chayes 1993: 197–204; Diehl and Ku 2010: 58–59). The implication of these arguments is that noncompliance should be treated as a problem to be managed and should not be met primarily with coercion or punishment.

Others counter with the view that enforcement is indeed necessary for compliance. Adopting a purely instrumental perspective, they argue that international law and international cooperation generally are not likely to produce significant changes in state behavior without the threat of enforcement to deter noncompliance (Downs, Rocke, and Barsoom 1996). As the requirements of compliance become more onerous, the threat of enforcement must become commensurately more serious. Consistent with this logic, empirical studies have found that "deep" and "complex" cooperation problems – requiring significant change in behavior and incentives to defect – are associated with more robust monitoring and enforcement mechanisms (Downs 1998; Koremenos 2007). Realists agree that enforcement – in the form of a materially costly consequence – is necessary for compliance, but doubt that these institutional solutions can induce compliance when it matters most. For important issues, the most likely source of enforcement is powerful states and their ability to punish violators (or reward compliers) (Morgenthau 1985; Goldsmith and Posner 2005). To the extent that international institutions play a role in inducing compliance, they must be backed up by a powerful state (Waltz 1979: 88). What unites the enforcement school is the belief that meaningful compliance is not likely unless violations are met with a consequential cost.

The management and enforcement perspectives both make an important contribution to the compliance debate. There is a tendency, however, to overlook the extent to which these arguments are complementary. Enforcement is indeed an important ingredient for promoting compliance, yet we should not point to the lack of robust, centralized mechanisms of enforcement and conclude that it is therefore absent. Most enforcement is horizontal, as noted in the previous section, and its effectiveness is partly a function of institutions and their design, which can either facilitate or hinder the decentralized sanctioning of violators. Enforcement, in other words, must be managed.

The first component of "managing enforcement" concerns the way in which violations are approached. The enforcement school assumes that violations occur as a result of cheating, whereas managerialists see noncompliance as largely unintentional. This stark dichotomy, which implies very different responses to noncompliance, is less useful in practice. The motivation behind noncompliance is often difficult to discern and, in any case, most instances of noncompliance occur for a combination of reasons. This explains why so many regimes in fact combine a management approach to noncompliance with an enforcement approach. In the ozone regime, the Montreal Protocol establishes a procedure for working with noncompliant parties to develop a "compliance plan," but the same parties are simultaneously barred from receiving funding from the Global Environment Facility until their compliance plan is approved (Raustiala 2000: 418–20). The most extensive study along these lines is by Jonas Tallberg (2002), who discusses the complex and multilevel compliance system of the European Union (EU), which includes elements of both management and enforcement. He argues that these strategies are "complementary and mutually reinforcing" (Tallberg 2002: 610) in the European context, and he makes a compelling argument that combining them is the best way to induce compliance.

One possibility is that management and enforcement can be combined in a system of "graduated sanctions," an approach advocated by Elinor Ostrom (1990) for managing common-pool resources. As she notes, it may be optimal to punish a first-time violator with a "modest sanction" at first, to remind him that he is being monitored and to see whether this succeeds in inducing compliance. This strategy might help to screen real cheaters, who will continue to break the rules, from unintentional violators (Verdier 2009). It also has the advantage of being less costly to the sanctioners if more modest efforts produce results. In the case of repeated or egregious violations, the punishment can be escalated appropriately.

We see precisely this sort of graduated compliance system in the climate regime. The parties to the Kyoto Protocol established (with the 2001 Marrakesh Accord) a Compliance Committee that is divided into two branches, an enforcement branch and a facilitative branch. "As their names suggest, the facilitative branch aims to provide advice and assistance to Parties in order to promote compliance, whereas the enforcement branch has the responsibility to determine consequences for Parties not meeting their commitments" (UNFCCC 2012). If the management efforts of the facilitative branch are unsuccessful, its members can refer the case to their enforcement colleagues. The result is an unusually elaborate compliance mechanism that relies on a sequenced approach from management to enforcement (Brunnée 2003).

The second component of "managing enforcement" concerns the institutional setting. Notwithstanding the premise that enforcement of international law is fundamentally decentralized, it is often conducted in the "shadow" of relevant institutions. The costs – and thus the likelihood and effectiveness – of enforcement are affected by the design of the rules being defended and by the institutional setting within which coercion takes place.

Some international legal rules are more conducive to enforcement than others. In general, a more legitimate and fair process for creating rules will also produce more defensible rules (Franck 1995), which, in turn, can be enforced at a lower cost. The design of rules matters a great deal as well. By requiring highly observable behavior, for example, an international agreement makes the detection of violations much easier and thereby facilitates enforcement actions. One example is requiring antipollution technologies that are highly visible, rather than regulating the polluting behavior itself (Mitchell 1994; Urpelainen 2010). A lesson here is that many of the same design features that scholars have emphasized for promoting compliance are also virtuous in the event of noncompliance.

The institutional setting of enforcement matters as well. Institutions are a potentially valuable source of information and coordination when it comes to noncompliance and enforcement, even if they lack independent enforcement capacity. First, they provide clarification when rules are ambiguous and resolve conflicts of interpretation (Helfer and Slaughter 2005: 923). Second, by providing transparency and monitoring, institutions help identify behavior as noncompliant (Chayes and Chayes 1995; Mitchell 1998). For example, election monitors from the Organization for Security and Cooperation in Europe supply information that helps to trigger sanctions against norm-violating governments (Donno 2010). Third, institutions help supply information on the motivations of states that interact within and through them, thereby clarifying whether the enforcing state is acting in defense of international rules or more aggressively (Thompson 2006). All of these functions increase the probability that noncompliance will be met with enforcement actions.

Of course, not all institutions are equally effective in this regard. In general, highly legalized and independent institutions are viewed more credibly when it comes to clarifying rules, finding facts, and endorsing sanctions against a violator (Abbott and Snidal 2000: 427; Smith 2000: 138; Guzman 2008: 52). Nevertheless, we know that even modest centralized information provision by an informal institution can fundamentally alter the cooperative incentives of actors and promote exchange (Milgrom, North, and Weingast 1990). Although they are not backed up by enforcement power, the clear statements provided by WTO panel rulings cast a shadow that strengthens the position of those who challenge unfair practices (Busch and Reinhardt 2000). Even international bodies with no judicial authority can promote peer pressure and sanctions simply by publicizing and assessing state behavior (Helfer and Slaughter 2005), an argument made in studies of the UN-based human rights committees (Buergenthal 2006) and the WTO's Trade Policy Review Mechanism (Qureshi 1995). The process by which an institution considers responses to noncompliance is also important. For example, UN-authorized sanctions that derive from a legitimate and law-based process are more often effective than are sanctions viewed as politically motivated (Joyner 1995: 266).

Enforcement and management cannot be separated in practice. Indeed, even those who downplay the importance of coercive enforcement nevertheless concede that cost-imposing by other states, individually or collectively, is sometimes necessary to promote compliance (Henkin 1995: 50–51; Franck 2002). At the same time, those who emphasize enforcement as a necessary ingredient for compliance tend to overlook the importance of the rules and institutions that define compliance and cast a shadow over any enforcement actions. The viability of enforcement, in other words, is partly a matter of management and design.

III. ENFORCEMENT INCENTIVES

The decentralized nature of international law implies that it must be largely self-enforcing (Koremenos, Lipson, and Snidal 2004; Barrett 2004; Scott and Stephan 2004), either because states have an incentive to comply in the first place or because they have an incentive to impose costs on violators (i.e., to engage in enforcement). Although there is a vast and productive literature, spanning the IR and IL fields, on the conditions under which states comply with international law,[6] much less attention has been focused on the incentives of states to supply enforcement. This is

---

[6] For overviews see Raustiala and Slaughter (2002), Simmons (2010), and von Stein (2010). For a discussion of empirical evidence and methodological issues in this literature, see von Stein (2013).

surprising, since the viability of international law's decentralized system of enforcement depends on these incentives.

Effective enforcement confronts the fundamental problem that enforcement actions are almost always costly to the sender. Guzman (2008: 48), for example, doubts whether retaliatory sanctions can be an effective means of inducing compliance because the costs to the sender are often prohibitive. This matters because, in theory, a potential enforcer will not act if the costs of enforcing are higher than the benefits of inducing compliance by the target (I relax this assumption below). Indeed, under these circumstances, the coercive threat should not be credible. This problem is exacerbated in the multilateral context, where free-rider incentives make individual states even less likely to bear the burden of enforcement. While all states stand to gain from compliance – punishment is a public good for the community (Elster 1989: 41) – only those that sanction bear the cost, creating a collective action problem. Elsewhere I refer to this as the "sanctioners' dilemma" (Thompson 2009*b*).

Although the material costs of engaging in enforcement are an obvious concern for the sender, the potential *political* costs are an equally important consideration. When states engage in coercive actions, perceptions matter; other members of the community (beyond the target) may feel threatened and may ascribe a variety of motives to the behavior. As Hedley Bull (1977: 69) notes, "Because of the low degree of consensus or solidarity among states, actions which the state committing them sees as self-help or rule-enforcement are frequently not viewed as such by international society at large." The sender, therefore, must convince other states that its actions are a form of enforcement in defense of legal rules rather than an aggressive pursuit of more selfish goals. Reaching a consensus on whether enforcement is justified in a given case is problematic because almost every situation is ambiguous in terms of the facts, the law, or both. A state that resorts to self-help enforcement measures can almost always be accused of doing so too quickly – without sufficient resort to negotiation or arbitration – or with disproportionate measures. In some cases, each side can invoke conflicting principles of international law (Noortmann 2005). If rules or behavior are unclear, the target can argue that no violation has taken place (Guzman 2008: 93–100). Finally, states might have different interpretations of how legally binding a rule is, with the sender claiming that enforcement is justified by a violation of hard law and the target claiming that the rule was of a softer variety that should not trigger enforcement. If the sender cannot convince the international community that it is engaged in justified enforcement, other states can respond by imposing a variety of costs, including opposition to the policy itself, reciprocal noncompliance in other shared regimes, and various forms of "soft" balancing, such as those imposed on the United States after its 2003 invasion of Iraq (Walt 2005; Thompson 2009*a*).

The costs of enforcement are not always high, however. If the enforcer is much more powerful than the noncompliant state, the material costs might be insignificant.

Multilateral burden sharing, in the form of collective sanctions or a military coalition, can also bring the material costs of coercion down. Some means of enforcement are inherently less costly. In particular, an appealing feature of diplomatic responses and strategies of shaming and ostracism is that they entail very low costs for the sender (Rasmussen 1996). Finally, enforcement is less politically fraught when the target has clearly violated international law. As noted in the previous section, international courts and organizations can help in this regard by clarifying rules, identifying noncompliance, and endorsing enforcement actions.[7]

Although the literature tends to emphasize the costs of engaging in enforcement activities, we should also consider more fully the benefits that can accrue to the sender and thereby make enforcement more likely. To begin with, there are indeed times when individual states, usually powerful ones with a stake in maintaining the status quo, have an incentive to unilaterally provide a public good to the international community. As Snidal (1985: 581) notes, "This outcome will be most likely when some single state, the hegemonic power, is sufficiently large relative to the others that it will capture a share of the benefit of the public good larger than the entire cost of providing it." This argument is usually applied to the provision of economic and security stability, and such stability often includes the enforcement of legal rules.

The possibility that the benefits of compliance will offset the costs of enforcement appears more plausible if we consider the potential long-term benefits of enforcing compliance. What if the game is repeated? Keohane (1984) argues that states obey regime rules because regimes are so difficult to create and replace; thus, noncompliance risks dissolving the entire regime and sacrificing the long-term benefits it provides. The same logic can be applied to enforcement. In a repeated game, even where agents change their partners over time and with only modest assumptions about information, "community enforcement" can be sustained. In other words, even agents that care only about their own utility and do not care about a rule for its own sake have an incentive to punish those that violate social rules, for fear that violations will spread and cooperation will break down (Kandori 1992). When a potential enforcer contemplates taking action, it thus takes into account the long-term benefits supplied by the relevant international law, not just the benefits of compliance in the case at hand. Along these lines, a further advantage of enforcement is to signal that the rule in question is worth defending. Active enforcement is one means by which states can demonstrate their belief in the importance and bindingness of international law (O'Connell 2008: 10).

Another factor to consider is the reputation benefit of sanctioning a law violator. Many of the arguments about the reputational incentives to comply (see Brewster

---

[7] There is, however, a potential danger for a sender of attempting to reduce its costs too much. Committing to a costly policy, such as self-damaging economic sanctions, can serve as a credible signal that a state is serious and will not back down, thereby increasing its leverage (Damrosch 1994).

2013) can be extended to the question of enforcement. States have and value many reputations beyond that for compliance, including a reputation for defending one's interests and for toughness in the face of challengers. Indeed, it might be in an actor's interest to pay the price of confronting even a relatively unthreatening challenger if doing so deters future challengers; this is the logic of the "chain store paradox" in economics (Kreps and Wilson 1982). For example, Alt, Calvert and Humes (1988) argue that a hegemonic state may have an incentive to engage in costly coercive actions as an investment in its reputation for toughness, one that makes coercion cheaper in the future. The power of the reputation logic in the context of enforcement is that, by punishing a violator, a state can at once boost its benevolent reputation as a defender of international law and its "less savory" (Keohane 1997: 497) reputation for being tough and assertive. Supplying enforcement is one of the rare cases in which these seemingly divergent reputational incentives are not in conflict. Johns (2012) raises the further possibility that states have an incentive to develop a reputation not just for defending their own rights but also for supplying third-party enforcement to other victims. Doing so increases the chance that others will come to their own defense.

Given the conventional wisdom that peer enforcement is often prohibitively costly, this review of enforcement incentives paints a surprisingly promising picture for the viability of decentralized enforcement. Even if we maintain relatively narrow assumptions about self-interested behavior, we see that states can indeed be motivated to supply costly enforcement actions. If we assume that states care intrinsically about upholding international law as a system of community norms, the space for peer-to-peer enforcement widens even further. A considerable literature in the social sciences shows that humans can effectively regulate community norms through third-party punishment under a wide range of conditions. Even when they are not the victims, individuals "are willing to punish others at a cost to themselves to prevent unfair outcomes or to sanction unfair behavior" (Fehr and Fischbacher 2003: 785; see also Sigmund 2007). A crucial implication is that rules that carry normative weight, and especially those embedded in a well-defined social community, are more likely to elicit robust decentralized enforcement, although these mechanisms normally operate with much less force at the international level.

IV. EXTENDING ENFORCEMENT RESEARCH: POWER, ACTORS, AND DESIGN

This overview of enforcement questions and research points to several areas of overlapping interest between IR and IL scholars and suggests some themes that merit further investigation. In this concluding section, I highlight three areas of potentially fruitful research and exchange between the two fields, focusing on the role of power, the importance of non-state actors, and questions of institutional design. Each has both normative and positive implications for our understanding of coercive enforcement in international law.

A. *Power and Enforcement*

Realists have long pointed out that powerful states are doubly advantaged when it comes to the enforcement of international law: they are well positioned to engage in enforcement and to resist enforcement efforts of others. In Morgenthau's (1985: 312) formulation, the international system of law enforcement "makes it easy for the strong both to violate the law and to enforce it, and consequently puts the rights of the weak in jeopardy." The most dramatic examples are in security affairs, where great powers intervene to protect international law (and their own interests) but are difficult to stop or punish when they violate the law themselves. Glennon (2003) points to the U.S. invasion of Iraq as a recent and prominent example.

Although the role of power seems most obvious in military-security settings, power and distributive concerns shape enforcement in a variety of issue areas and sometimes in subtle ways. One impact of globalization has been to create complicated and overlapping regulatory rules and institutions, a setting that allows large states to take advantage of their superior capacity and multiple sources of leverage, both formal and informal (Benvenisti and Downs 2007; Stone 2011), and to forum shop among regimes as a matter of convenience (Shaffer and Pollack 2010: 738). Even when dispute settlement procedures have been established to level the playing field, as in the case of the WTO, weak states often lack the resources and expertise to effectively defend their rights (Shaffer 2006; Kim 2008), and larger economies have a decided advantage when it comes to implementing sanctions and other remedies (Brewster 2009). This suggests a need for more research on whether increased institutionalization does indeed create more rule-oriented rather than power-oriented environments for compliance and enforcement.

The most profound disparities may come well before the enforcement stage, when rules and institutions are being designed in the first place. Large states have used their bargaining power to push for new rules that reflect their interests in areas such as trade, finance, and Internet governance (Steinberg 2002; Drezner 2007). This allows them subsequently to defend their interests in the guise of innocently enforcing international law. The UN Security Council offers perhaps the best example of how powerful states use their ability to shape rules to promote self-interested enforcement. The United States and the other Permanent Five members have increasingly used Chapter VII resolutions to establish sweeping and legally binding new rules in areas such as terrorism (Resolution 1373) and weapons proliferation (Resolution 1540) – in effect, using the Council's enforcement authority to legislate (Talmon 2005). Once established, these resolutions can be used to justify a variety of enforcement measures consistent with the goals of the resolution. For example, Resolution 1540 has been used by the United States to justify its ambitious Proliferation Security Initiative, which otherwise involves actions of questionable legality.

These examples remind us that power considerations are never lurking far behind when it comes to the enforcement of international law. IL and IR scholars should continue to explore these issues, and their positive and normative implications, keeping in mind that power is often exercised in indirect and informal ways that are difficult to detect.

B. *Domestic and Transnational Actors*

Scholars of IR and IL have focused increased attention on non-state actors, both domestic and transnational, and many of the resulting insights have implications for the question of enforcement. For example, we should expect domestic politics to shape the incentives of a government contemplating enforcement (Trachtman 2013). Just as governments sometimes face domestic pressure to ratify agreements and to comply with international law (Haftel and Thompson, forthcoming; Dai 2007), they also face pressure to enforce rules that affect important domestic constituents. What Miles Kahler (2000: 675) refers to as domestic "compliance constituencies" encourage their own government's compliance but also "encourage imposition of sanctions on other governments that violate legal commitments." Public opinion can have the same pro-enforcement effect (Joyner 1995: 265; Whang 2011). These factors create a positive political benefit for a sender if it sanctions a noncompliant state.[8]

Non-state actors can also pressure governments directly and thereby perform an enforcement role themselves. Transnational advocacy groups use various strategies to raise the political costs for a government violating international norms (Keck and Sikkink 1998). Domestic actors seeking to pressure their government to comply can also use international legal rules to strengthen their political and legal strategies at home, as Alter (2000) shows in the EU context. This can produce short-term victories but also long-term changes. For example, the spread of international human rights law and the advent of the ICC have shifted domestic political and legal debates within countries in a more pro-rights direction (McCormak 2008; Simmons 2009). Incorporating non-state actors into the study of international enforcement is especially important since some issue areas are governed to a significant degree by networks of private actors rather than by states (Büthe and Mattli 2011). The enforcement question here is whether and how these private actors can develop mechanisms of self-regulation that deter noncompliance.

The study of international enforcement will inevitably move in the direction of two-level analysis and considerations of private authority to understand the many

---

[8] At the same time, of course, domestic politics sometimes contribute to the intransigence of a target state, as in the case of economic sanctions that trigger a "rally 'round the flag" response. In their study of WTO disputes over genetically modified foods, Pollack and Shaffer (2009) show that entrenched political interests and public opinion may prevent compliance or settlement of disputes even when a robust enforcement mechanism is in place.

mechanisms and actors involved. An important question for scholars to consider is whether these private actors are complementing the traditional role of states or drawing power away from them. In either case, we should also ask whether the non-state enforcement of international law is more efficient or more desirable from a normative standpoint.

C. *The Design of Law and Institutions*

How can international law and its attendant institutions be designed to more effectively promote enforcement and compliance? Increasing the robustness of international courts and dispute settlement mechanisms is one possibility, but often legalization is not a politically viable strategy due to sovereignty concerns. Existing studies in political science and law show that high levels of legalization may not be necessary if monitoring and compliance institutions are designed to match the problem at hand, to provide credible information that governments lack, or to strategically link issues (Ostrom 1990; Helfer and Slaughter 2005; Hafner-Burton 2009; Jojarth 2009; Donno 2010). The viability of enforcement may also have more to do with the legitimacy of institutions and underlying rules than with the presence of robust enforcement institutions. Violations of rules that match prevailing social norms trigger a wider variety of sanctions, formal and informal (Ellickson 1991; Posner 2002), and legitimate institutions are more authoritative and less dependent on the threat of punishment to be effective (Hurd 2007; Dickson, Gordon, and Huber 2009). This suggests that fairness and impartiality in the production of rules and IO decisions can promote more efficient enforcement.

Well-designed institutions should go beyond traditional tools of statecraft to capture the widest range possible of enforcement actors and mechanisms – public and private, formal and informal. Exploring the optimal mixture of these mechanisms is an important area of research (Scott and Stephan 2006; Brewster 2013). Transnational dispute resolution mechanisms – those that give direct access to private parties – are less influenced by state interests and tend to empower a wider range of actors, including nongovernmental organizations (NGOs) and domestic courts (Keohane, Moravcsik, and Slaughter 2000). Hawkins (2008) shows that when IOs provide access to NGOs, this helps facilitate enforcement of human rights norms. Studies of institutional design should thus focus on the increasing variety of actors and mechanisms that can be leveraged to promote decentralized enforcement.

This discussion suggests a multidisciplinary research agenda that goes beyond the hard law–soft law distinction to ask how international law and institutions can be designed to increase the likelihood of enforcement. Ideally, enforcement should rely on powerful states when they have incentives to provide public goods, but should also rely on other actors to supply a range of enforcement mechanisms when doing so is more efficient or when the influence of powerful states is undesirable from a distributive perspective.

REFERENCES

Abbott, Kenneth W., and Duncan Snidal (2000). "Hard and Soft Law in International Governance," *International Organization*, Vol. 54, No. 3, pp. 421–56.

Alland, Denis (2002). "Countermeasures of General Interest," *European Journal of International Law*, Vol. 13, No. 5, pp. 1221–39.

Alt, James E., Randall L. Calvert, and Brian D. Humes (1988). "Reputation and Hegemonic Stability: A Game-Theoretic Analysis," *American Political Science Review*, Vol. 82, No. 2, pp. 445–66.

Alter, Karen J. (2000). "The European Legal System and Domestic Policy: Spillover or Backlash?", *International Organization*, Vol. 54, No. 3, pp. 489–518.

———— (2008). "Agents or Trustees? International Courts in their Political Context," *European Journal of International Relations*, Vol. 14, No. 1, pp. 33–63.

Barnett, Michael, and Martha Finnemore (2004). *Rules for the World: International Organizations in Global Politics* (Ithaca, NY: Cornell University Press).

Barrett, Scott (2004). "Self-Enforcing International Environmental Agreements," *Oxford Economic Papers*, Vol. 46, pp. 878–94.

Bayram, A. Burcu (2011). *How International Law Obligates: International Identity, Legal Obligation, and Compliance in World Politics*, Ohio State University, Ph.D. thesis.

Benvenisti, Eyal, and George W. Downs (2007). "The Empire's New Clothes: Political Economy and the Fragmentation of International Law," *Stanford Law Review*, Vol. 60, No. 2, pp. 595–631.

Bradley, Curtis, and Judith Kelley (2008). "The Concept of International Delegation," *Law and Contemporary Problems*, Vol. 71, No. 1, pp. 1–39.

Brewster, Rachel (2009). "Shadow Unilateralism: Enforcing International Trade Law at the WTO," *University of Pennsylvania Journal of International Law*, Vol. 30, No. 4, pp. 1133–46.

———— (2013). "Reputation in International Relations and International Law Theory," in Jeffrey L. Dunoff and Mark A. Pollack (eds.), *Interdisciplinary Perspectives on International Law and International Relations: The State of the Art* (New York: Cambridge University Press), pp. 524–43.

Brown Weiss, Edith, and Harold K. Jacobson (1998). *Engaging Countries: Strengthening Compliance with International Environmental Accords* (Cambridge, MA: MIT Press).

Brunnée, Jutta (2003). "The Kyoto Protocol: Testing Ground for Compliance Theories?," *ZaöRV*, Vol. 63, No. 2, pp. 255–80.

Buergenthal, Thomas (2006). "The Evolving Human Rights System," *American Journal of International Law*, Vol. 100, No. 4, pp. 783–807.

Bull, Hedley (1977). *The Anarchical Society: A Study of Order in World Politics* (New York: Columbia University Press).

Busch, Marc L., and Eric Reinhardt (2000). "Bargaining in the Shadow of the Law: Early Settlement in GATT/WTO Disputes," *Fordham International Law Journal*, Vol. 24, No. 1, pp. 158–72.

Büthe, Tim, and Walter Mattli (2011). *The New Global Rulers: The Privatization of Regulation in the World Economy* (Princeton, NJ: Princeton University Press).

Charney, Jonathan I. (1999). "The Impact on the International Legal System of the Growth of International Courts and Tribunals," *New York University Journal of International Law & Politics*, Vol. 31, No. 4, pp. 697–708.

Chayes, Abram, and Antonia Handler Chayes (1993). "On Compliance," *International Organization*, Vol. 47, No. 2, pp. 175–205.

_____ (1995). *The New Sovereignty: Compliance with International Regulatory Agreements* (Cambridge, MA: Harvard University Press).

Coleman, Katharina P. (2007). *International Organisations and Peace Enforcement* (New York: Cambridge University Press).

Conant, Lisa (2013). "Whose Agents? The Interpretation of International Law in National Courts," in Jeffrey L. Dunoff and Mark A. Pollack (eds.), *Interdisciplinary Perspectives on International Law and International Relations: The State of the Art* (New York: Cambridge University Press), pp. 394–420.

Cronin-Furman, Kathleen R. (2005). "The International Court of Justice and the United Nations Security Council: Rethinking a Complicated Relationship," *Columbia Law Review*, Vol. 106, No. 2, pp. 435–63.

Dai, Xinyuan (2007). *International Institutions and National Policies* (New York: Cambridge University Press).

D'Amato, Anthony (1987). *International Law: Process and Prospect* (New York: Transnational).

Damrosch, Lori F. (1994). "The Collective Enforcement of International Norms through Economic Sanctions," *Ethics and International Affairs*, Vol. 8, No. 1, pp. 59–75.

_____ (2002). "The Permanent Five as Enforcers of Controls on Weapons of Mass Destruction: Building on the Iraq 'Precedent'?" *European Journal of International Law*, Vol. 13, No. 1, pp. 305–21.

Damrosch, Lori F., Louis Henkin, Sean D. Murphy, and Hans Smit (2009) (eds.). *International Law: Cases and Materials*, 5th ed. (St. Paul, MN: West).

Dickson, Eric S., Sanford C. Gordon, and Gregory A. Huber (2009). "Enforcement and Compliance in an Uncertain World: An Experimental Investigation," *Journal of Politics*, Vol. 71, No. 4, pp. 1357–78.

Diehl, Paul F., and Charlotte Ku (2010). *The Dynamics of International Law* (New York: Cambridge University Press).

Donno, Daniela (2010). "Who Is Punished? Regional Intergovernmental Organizations and the Enforcement of Democratic Norms," *International Organization*, Vol. 64, No. 4, pp. 593–625.

Downs, George W. (1998). "Enforcement and the Evolution of Cooperation," *Michigan Journal of International Law*, Vol. 19, No. 2, pp. 319–44.

Downs, George W., David M. Rocke, and Peter N. Barsoon (1996). "Is the Good News about Compliance Good News about Cooperation?," *International Organization*, Vol. 50, pp. 379–406.

Drezner, Daniel W. (2007). *All Politics Is Global: Explaining International Regulatory Regimes* (Princeton, NJ: Princeton: Princeton University Press).

_____ (2009). "The Power and Peril of International Regime Complexity," *Perspectives on Politics*, Vol. 7, No. 1, pp. 65–70.

Dupuy, Pierre-Marie (1999). "The Danger of Fragmentation or Unification of the International Legal System and the International Court of Justice," *International Law and Politics*, Vol. 31, No. 4, pp. 791–807.

Ellickson, Robert C. (1991). *Order without Law: How Neighbors Settle Disputes* (Cambridge, MA: Harvard University Press).

Elster, Jon (1989). *The Cement of Society* (New York: Cambridge University Press).

Fehr, Ernst, and Urs Fischbacher (2003). "The Nature of Human Altruism," *Nature*, Vol. 425, pp. 785–91.

Finnemore, Martha, and Kathryn Sikkink (1998). "International Norm Dynamics and Political Change," *International Organization*, Vol. 52, No. 4, pp. 887–917.

Finnemore, Martha, and Stephen J. Toope (2000). "Alternatives to 'Legalization': Richer Views of Law and Politics," *International Organization*, Vol. 55, No. 3, pp. 743–58.

Franck, Thomas M. (1990). *The Power of Legitimacy among Nations* (New York: Oxford University Press).

———— (1995). *Fairness in International Law and Institutions* (New York: Oxford University Press).

———— (2002). "Inspections and Their Enforcement: A Modest Proposal," *American Journal of International Law*, Vol. 96, No. 4, pp. 899–900.

Frowein, Jochen Abr. (1987). "Collective Enforcement of International Obligations," *ZaöRV*, Vol. 47, No. 1, pp. 67–79.

Glennon, Michael J. (2001). *Limits of Law, Prerogatives of Power* (New York: Palgrave).

———— (2003). "Why the Security Council Failed," *Foreign Affairs*, Vol. 82, No. 3, pp. 16–35.

Goldsmith, Jack L., and Eric A. Posner (2005). *The Limits of International Law* (New York: Oxford University Press).

Goldstein, Judith L., Miles Kahler, Robert O. Keohane, and Anne-Marie Slaugther (2001) (eds.). *Legalization in World Politics* (Cambridge, MA: MIT Press).

Goldstone, Richard J., and Adam M. Smith (2009). *International Judicial Institutions* (New York: Routledge).

Guzman, Andrew T. (2008). *How International Law Works: A Rational Choice Theory* (New York: Oxford University Press).

Hafner-Burton, Emilie M. (2009). *Forced to Be Good: Why Trade Agreements Boost Human Rights* (Ithaca, NY: Cornell University Press).

———— (2008). "Sticks and Stones: Naming and Shaming the Human Rights Enforcement Problem," *International Organization*, Vol. 62, No. 4, pp. 689–716.

Haftel, Yoram Z., and Alexander Thompson (forthcoming). "Delayed Ratification: The Domestic Fate of Bilateral Investment Treaties," *International Organization*.

Hathaway, Oona A. (2005). "Between Power and Principle," *University of Chicago Law Review*, Vol. 71, No. 2, pp. 469–536.

Hawkins, Darren G. (2008). "Protecting Democracy in Europe and the Americas," *International Organization*, Vol. 62, No. 3, pp. 373–403.

Hawkins, Darren G., David A. Lake, Daniel L. Nielson, and Michael J. Tierney (2006) (eds.). *Delegation and Agency in International Organizations* (New York: Cambridge University Press).

Helfer, Laurence R., and Anne-Marie Slaughter (1997). "Toward a Theory of Effective Supra-national Adjudication," *Yale Law Journal*, Vol. 107, No. 2, pp. 273–391.

———— (2005). "Why States Create International Tribunals," *California Law Review*, Vol. 93, No. 3, pp. 899–956.

Henkin, Louis (1995). *International Law: Politics and Values* (Boston, MA: Martinus Nijhoff).

Hoffmann, Stanley (1961). "International Systems and International Law," *World Politics*, Vol. 14, No. 1, pp. 205–37.

Hurd, Ian (2007). *After Anarchy: Legitimacy and Power in the United Nations Security Council* (Princeton, NJ: Princeton University Press).

Johansson, Patrik (2009). "The Humdrum Use of Ultimate Authority: Defining and Analysing Chapter VII Resolutions," *Nordic Journal of International Law*, Vol. 78, No. 3, pp. 309–42.

Johns, Leslie (2012). "Courts as Coordinators: Endogenous Enforcement and Jurisdiction in International Adjudication," *Journal of Conflict Resolution*, Vol. 56, No. 2, pp. 257–89.

Johnston, Alastair Iain (2001). "Treating International Institutions as Social Environments," *International Studies Quarterly*, Vol. 45, No. 3, pp. 487–515.

Jojarth, Christine (2009). *Crime, War, and Global Trafficking: Designing International Cooperation* (New York: Cambridge University Press).

Joyner, Christopher C. (1995). "Collective Sanctions as Peaceful Coercion: Lessons from the United Nations Experience," *Australian Yearbook of International Law*, Vol. 16, pp. 241–70.

Kahler, Miles (2000). "Conclusion: The Causes and Consequences of Legalization," *International Organization*, Vol. 54, No. 3, pp. 661–83.

Kandori, Michihiro (1992). "Social Norms and Community Enforcement," *Review of Economic Studies*, Vol. 59, No. 1, pp. 63–80.

Keck, Margaret E., and Kathryn Sikkink (1998). *Activists beyond Borders* (Ithaca, NY: Cornell University Press).

Kelley, Judith (2007). "Who Keeps International Commitments and Why? The International Criminal Court and Bilateral Non-surrender Agreements," *American Political Science Review*, Vol. 101, No. 3, pp. 573–89.

Kelsen, Hans (1942). *Law and Peace in International Relations* (Cambridge, MA: Harvard University Press).

Keohane, Robert O. (1984). *After Hegemony: Cooperation and Discord in the World Political Economy* (Princeton, NJ: Princeton University Press).

——— (1997). "International Relations and International Law: Two Optics," *Harvard International Law Journal*, Vol. 38, No. 2, pp. 487–502.

Keohane, Robert O., Andrew Moravcsik, and Anne-Marie Slaughter (2000). "Legalized Dispute Resolution: Interstate and Transnational," *International Organization*, Vol. 54, No. 3, pp. 457–88.

Kim, Moonhawk (2008). "Costly Procedures: Divergent Effects of Legalization in the GATT/WTO Dispute Settlement Procedures," *International Studies Quarterly*, Vol. 52, No. 3, pp. 657–86.

Kirsch, Philippe (2007). "The Role of the International Criminal Court in Enforcing International Criminal Law," *American University International Law Review*, Vol. 22, No. 4, pp. 539–47.

Koh, Harold Hongju (1997). "Why Do Nations Obey International Law?," *Yale Law Journal*, Vol. 106, pp. 2598–659.

——— (1999). "How Is International Human Rights Law Enforced?," *Indiana Law Journal*, Vol. 74, No. 4, pp. 1397–417.

Koremenos, Barbara (2007). "If Only Half of International Agreements Have Dispute Resolution Provisions, Which Half Needs Explaining?" *Journal of Legal Studies*, Vol. 36, No. 1, pp. 189–212.

Koremenos, Barbara, Charles Lipson, and Duncan Snidal (eds.) (2004). *The Rational Design of International Institutions* (New York: Cambridge University Press).

Koskenniemi, Martti (1996). "The Place of Law in Collective Security," *Michigan Journal of International Law*, Vol. 17, No. 2, pp. 455–90.

Kreps, David M., and Robert Wilson (1982). "Reputation and Imperfect Information," *Journal of Economic Theory*, Vol. 27, pp. 253–79.

Martin, Lisa L. (1992). *Coercive Cooperation: Explaining Multilateral Economic Sanctions* (Princeton, NJ: Princeton University Press).

Matheson, Michael J. (2006). *Council Unbound: The Growth of UN Decision Making on Conflict and Postconflict Issues after the Cold War* (Washington, DC: U.S. Institute of Peace).

McCormak, Tim (2008). "The Contribution of the International Criminal Court to Increasing Respect for International Humanitarian Law," *University of Tasmania Law Review*, Vol. 27, No. 1, pp. 22–46.

Mearsheimer, John J. (2001). *The Tragedy of Great Power Politics* (New York: Norton).

Milgrom, Paul R., Douglass C. North, and Barry R. Weingast (1990). "The Role of Institutions in the Revival of Trade: The Law Merchant, Private Judges, and the Champagne Fairs," *Economics and Politics*, Vol. 2, No. 1, pp. 1–23.

Mitchell, Ronald B. (1994). *Intentional Oil Pollution at Sea: Environmental Policy and Treaty Compliance* (Cambridge, MA: MIT Press).

——— (1998). "Sources of Transparency: Information Systems in International Regimes," *International Studies Quarterly*, Vol. 42, No. 1, pp. 109–30.

Morgenthau, Hans J. (1985). *Politics among Nations*, 6th ed. (New York: Alfred A. Knopf).

Noortmann, Math (2005). *Enforcing International Law: From Self-Help to Self-Contained Regimes* (Burlington, VT: Ashgate).

Nossal, Kim Richard (1989). "International Sanctions as International Punishment," *International Organization*, Vol. 43, No. 2, pp. 301–22.

O'Connell, Mary Ellen (2008). *The Power and Purpose of International Law* (New York: Oxford University Press).

Oellers-Frahm, Karin (2001). "Multiplication of International Courts and Tribunals and Conflicting Jurisdiction – Problems and Possible Solutions," *Max Planck Yearbook of United Nations Law*, Vol. 5, pp. 67–104.

Ostrom, Elinor (1990). *Governing the Commons* (New York: Cambridge University Press).

Pauwelyn, Joost, and Manfred Elsig (2013). "The Politics of Treaty Interpretation: Variations and Explanations across International Tribunals," in Jeffrey L. Dunoff and Mark A. Pollack (eds.), *Interdisciplinary Perspectives on International Law and International Relations: The State of the Art* (New York: Cambridge University Press), pp. 445–73.

Pollack, Mark A., and Gregory C. Shaffer (2009). *When Cooperation Fails: The International Law and Politics of Genetically Modified Foods* (New York: Oxford University Press).

Posner, Eric A. (2002). *Law and Social Norms* (Cambridge, MA: Harvard University Press).

Qureshi, A.H. (1995). "Some Lessons from Developing Countries' Trade Policy Reviews in the GATT Framework: An Enforcement Perspective," *The World Economy*, Vol. 18, No. 3, pp. 489–503.

Rasmusen, Eric (1996). "Stigma and Self-fulfilling Expectation of Criminality," *Journal of Law and Economics*, Vol. 39, No. 2, pp. 519–43.

Raustiala, Kal (2000). "Compliance and Effectiveness in International Regulatory Cooperation," *Case Western Reserve Journal of International Law*, Vol. 32, No. 3, pp. 387–440.

Raustiala, Kal, and Anne-Marie Slaughter (2002). "International Law, International Relations and Compliance," in Walter Carlsnaes, Thomas Risse, and Beth A. Simmons (eds.), *Handbook of International Relations* (London: Sage Publications), pp. 538–58.

Romano, Cesare P. R. (1999). "The Proliferation of International Judicial Bodies: The Pieces of the Puzzle," *New York University Journal of International Politics & Law*, Vol. 31, No. 4, pp. 709–51.

Satzer, Janina (2007). "Explaining the Decreased Use of International Courts – the Case of the ICJ," *Review of Law and Economics*, Vol. 3, No. 1, pp. 11–36.

Schachter, Oscar (1995). *International Law in Theory and Practice* (Boston, MA: Martinus Nijhoff).

Scott, Robert E., and Paul B. Stephan (2004). "Self-Enforcing International Agreements and the Limits of Coercion," *Wisconsin Law Review*, No. 2, pp. 551–630.

——— (2006). *The Limits of Leviathan: Contract Theory and the Enforcement of International Law* (New York: Cambridge University Press).

Setear, John K. (1997). "Responses to Breach of a Treaty and Rationalist International Relations Theory," *Virginia Law Review*, Vol. 83, No. 1, pp. 1–126.

Shaffer, Gregory C. (2006). "The Challenges of WTO Law: Strategies for Developing Country Adaptation," *World Trade Review*, Vol. 5, No.2, pp. 177–98.

Shaffer, Gregory C., and Mark A. Pollack (2010). "Hard vs. Soft Law: Alternatives, Complements, and Antagonists in International Governance," *Minnesota Law Review*, Vol. 94, No. 3, pp. 706–99.

Sigmund, Karl (2007). "Punish or Perish? Retaliation and Collaboration among Humans," *Trends in Ecology and Evolution*, Vol. 22, No. 11, pp. 593–600.

Simmons, Beth A. (2009). *Mobilizing for Human Rights: International Law in Domestic Politics* (New York: Cambridge University Press).

———— (2010). "Treaty Compliance and Violation," *Annual Review of Political Science*, Vol. 13, pp. 273–296.

Smith, James McCall (2000). "The Politics of Dispute Settlement Design: Explaining Legalism in Regional Trade Pacts," *International Organization*, Vol. 54, No. 1, pp. 137–80.

Snidal, Duncan (1985). "The Limits of Hegemonic Stability Theory," *International Organization*, Vol. 39, No. 4, pp. 579–614.

Steinberg, Richard (2002). "In the Shadow of Law or Power? Consensus-Based Bargaining and Outcomes in the GATT/WTO," *International Organization*, Vol. 56, No. 2, pp. 339–74.

Stewart, Richard B. (2009). "GMO Trade Regulation and Developing Countries," NYU Public Law and Legal Theory Working Papers 165 (NYU School of Law).

Stinnett, Douglas, Bryan R. Early, Cale Horne, and Johannes Karreth (2011). "Complying by Denying: Explaining Why States Develop Nonproliferation Export Controls," *International Studies Perspectives*, Vol. 12, No. 3, pp. 308–26.

Stone, Randall (2011). *Controlling Institutions: International Organizations in the Global Economy* (New York: Cambridge University Press).

Tallberg, Jonas (2002). "Paths to Compliance: Enforcement, Management, and the European Union," *International Organization*, Vol. 56, No. 3, pp. 609–43.

Talmon, Stefan (2005). "The Security Council as World Legislature," *American Journal of International Law*, Vol. 99, No. 1, pp. 175–93.

Tannenwald, Nina (2007). *The Nuclear Taboo* (New York: Cambridge University Press).

Thompson, Alexander (2006). "Coercion through IOs: The Security Council and the Logic of Information Transmission," *International Organization*, Vol. 60, No. 1, pp. 1–34.

———— (2009a). *Channels of Power: The UN Security Council and U.S. Statecraft in Iraq* (Ithaca, NY: Cornell University Press).

———— (2009b). "The Rational Enforcement of International Law: Solving the Sanctioners' Dilemma," *International Theory*, Vol. 1, No. 2, pp. 307–21.

Trachtman, Joel P. (2013). "Open Economy Law," in Jeffrey L. Dunoff and Mark A. Pollack (eds.), *Interdisciplinary Perspectives on International Law and International Relations: The State of the Art* (New York: Cambridge University Press), pp. 544–67.

Tyler, Tom R. (2006). *Why People Obey the Law* (Princeton, NJ: Princeton University Press).

UNFCCC (2012). "An Introduction to the Kyoto Protocol Compliance Mechanism," available at http://unfccc.int/kyoto_protocol/compliance/items/3024.php.

Urpelainen, Johannes (2010). "Enforcing International Environmental Cooperation: Technological Standards Can Help," *Review of International Organizations*, Vol. 5, No. 4, pp. 475–96.

Verdier, Daniel (2009). "Sanctions as Revelation Regimes," *Review of Economic Design*, Vol. 13, No. 3, pp. 251–78.

Voeten, Erik (2001). "Outside Options and the Logic of Security Council Action," *American Political Science Review*, Vol. 95, No. 4, pp. 845–58.

——— (2013). "International Judicial Independence," in Jeffrey L. Dunoff and Mark A. Pollack (eds.), *Interdisciplinary Perspectives on International Law and International Relations: The State of the Art* (New York: Cambridge University Press), pp. 421–44.

von Stein, Jana (2010). "International Law: Understanding Compliance and Enforcement," in Robert A. Denemark (ed.), *The International Studies Encyclopedia* (Oxford: Wiley-Blackwell).

von Stein, Jana (2013). "The Engines of Compliance," in Jeffrey L. Dunoff and Mark A. Pollack (eds.), *Interdisciplinary Perspectives on International Law and International Relations: The State of the Art* (New York: Cambridge University Press), pp. 477–501.

Walt, Stephen M. (2005). *Taming American Power* (New York: W. W. Norton).

Waltz, Kenneth N. (1979). *Theory of International Politics* (New York: McGraw-Hill).

Wendt, Alexander (1999). *Social Theory of International Politics* (New York: Cambridge University Press).

Whang, Taehee (2011). "Playing to the Home Crowd: Symbolic Use of Economic Sanctions in the United States," *International Studies Quarterly*, Vol. 55, No. 3, pp. 787–801.

White, Nigel, and Ademola Abass (2006). "Countermeasures and Sanctions," in Malcolm D. Evans (ed.), *International Law*, 2nd ed. (Oxford: Oxford University Press), pp. 509–32.

Young, Oran (1994). *International Governance: Protecting the Environment in a Stateless Society* (Ithaca, NY: Cornell University Press).

Reputation in International Relations and International Law Theory

Rachel Brewster

The anarchic nature of the international system is a theme that informs both international law (IL) and international relations (IR) scholarship. Without a centralized governing body to enforce agreements, states that contract at the international level are constantly aware of the possibility of defection. Within international relations, this focus on anarchy has made several scholars pessimistic about the possibility of cooperative activities. Postwar realists emphasized that states can always discard their obligations, whether legal or political, and, therefore, other states cannot put their faith in international agreements (Morgenthau 1978). To the extent that states were forming international institutions and making international obligations, these were likely to be a ratification of the results of power politics and sustainable only as long as the distribution of power remained unchanged (Mearsheimer 1994–95; Waltz 2000).

Against this backdrop of skepticism, regime theorists in the 1980s began to argue that the anarchical nature of the international system was not necessarily a bar to cooperative interactions. They claimed that the increasing number of international institutions in the global system "mattered" to state behavior. The institutions' rules were constraining state behavior, at least in areas of "low politics," and the institutions were surprisingly stable in the face of shifts in power between states (Axelrod 1984; Keohane 1984; Oye 1996). These theorists largely explained the creation of international institutions and the subsequent compliance with the institutions' rules through a combination of states' needs to overcome collective action problems and concern with their reputations. Keohane (1984: 105) argued that the possible exclusion from international regimes provided states with an incentive to abide by existing international agreements, which can overwhelm the immediate benefits of defection. Early approaches did not differentiate between legal and nonlegal obligation, but later work in political science explored the varying reputational effects of formal and informal obligations (Lipson 1991; Abbott and Snidal 2000).

More recent IR theory focuses greater attention on the question of how international regimes influence state behavior, rather than whether it is possible for regimes to influence state behavior (Mitchell 1994; Simmons 2000). This shift in the debate represents an acceptance by modern IR theorists that international cooperation is not only possible but is an important part of global interactions. Yet, there remains some skepticism about how pervasive cooperation is. Grieco (1988) argues that relative gains concerns inhibit states' interests in cooperation. Downs, Rocke, and Barsoom (1996) challenge the idea that high rates of compliance with international agreements are indicative of significant levels of cooperation. Others examine whether seemingly cooperative agreements are actually coercive (Gruber 2000). Nonetheless, reputation remains an important causal mechanism in the political science literature on compliance (Simmons 2000, 2010; Tomz 2007).

In some ways, international law scholars start their analysis from a different baseline. Although international legal scholars are highly aware that the international system lacks a centralized enforcement system, legal academics have historically understood the rates of compliance with international agreements to be very high (Henkin 1968). And, although there are debates about why rates of compliance are high – whether it is because the rules are viewed as legitimate (Frank 1990), in the state's interest (Chayes and Chayes 1993), or part of transnational legal process (Koh 1997) – this common understanding has generally made legal scholars more optimistic about the possible influence of international institutions on state behavior. For instance, legal scholars tend to ask why the international system does not have more international courts (Guzman 2002), rather than whether it is possible for dispute settlement systems to improve compliance (Kono 2007; Thompson 2009). This difference should not be overstated. Still, it does indicate that the two disciplines use different points of departure.

When IL and IR scholars began to collaborate, the idea of reputation as a causal mechanism was one of the first ideas that both disciplines could recognize as common ground. Abbott (1989, 69–70), in his *Modern International Relations Theory: A Prospectus for International Lawyers*, focused on the importance of incomplete information in various strategic games and the function of reputation in providing this information. Other scholars working in the area of IL/IR have similarly focused on reputation as a source of compliance with international agreements (Goldsmith and Posner 2005; Hathaway 2005; Raustiala 2005; Guzman 2008).

This chapter reviews the concept of reputation as it currently exists in joint IL/IR research projects and surveys critiques of reputation as a causal mechanism in compliance. This chapter also lays out those areas where greater research is needed to theoretically understand and empirically test the influence of reputational concerns. The chapter concludes by considering how the effects of reputational concerns on compliance may be sharpened or dulled by increased formal dispute resolution institutions.

I. A REPUTATION FOR "COOPERATIVENESS"

Reputation is thought to influence state decision-making because it can expand or diminish the state's opportunities for beneficial cooperative activity. The logic runs along the following lines: governments are interested in forming international agreements that offer benefits to the state and look for treaty partners that could also benefit from cooperation. The fact that a treaty is in a potential partner-state's interests does not assure compliance with the agreement's rules. If the underlying strategic situation is a prisoner's dilemma–type game, then the state may have an interest in choosing cooperation over the status quo because the gains to the state that result from cooperation are greater than those that would accrue to the state in a world without the international agreement. However, the state will nonetheless have an incentive to defect from the agreement because the state will gain the most if it defects while others comply (Axelrod 1984). All parties understand the underlying strategic situation and its implication that cooperation is beneficial but that obstacles to cooperation persist: a state may announce that it plans to abide by the treaty's terms, but will the state be able to resist the temptation to cheat on the agreement at a later date? As a result, states are careful in selecting treaty partners.

One source of information of a state's likely behavior is the history of its past actions. If a state has cheated on treaties in the past, then that state may be likely to do so in the future. The audience does not need to understand the domestic reason for the cheating to form an opinion about the state. The cause can vary from a scofflaw dictatorial ruler to a gridlocked separation of powers system that makes passing the necessary implementing legislation difficult. Such additional information may be useful, but is not strictly necessary for a state to develop a reputation. The audience can use its knowledge of the state's reputation when deciding whether to include it in a particular treaty agreement. A state with a poor reputation may be completely excluded. When such a state is included in the treaty negotiations, its reputation may remain relevant in the negotiations of a reciprocal concessions treaty regime (Guzman 2008). For instance, if State A abides by its trade concessions 90 percent of the time while State B does so 80 percent of the time, trade concessions by State A will be discounted less than those from State B, all else being equal. Thus, a state's past reputation can affect the "price" of treaty concessions in current negotiations.

If a member of the audience has complete information regarding a state's course of action or the probability that a state will take various policy actions, then reputation becomes irrelevant. In such a case, the audience member does not need the additional information that reputation provides and will rationally ignore it. In international relations, audience members rarely, if ever, have complete information on a state's future actions. Thus, reputation is widely believed to be relevant in a broad variety of settings. The informational point, however, remains important. First, to the extent that a state's past actions cease to be predictive of its future actions, for example, because of a change in leadership or in the form of government, then the state's reputation is either discounted or ceases to be pertinent. Second, reputational analysis is not a sanctioning system, and the inclusion of reputation into the audience's analysis is not costly (it is in the audience's interest to incorporate the information that it has about a state to the point where information-related search costs equal the expected benefits of greater information), whereas imposing sanctions often is (Guzman 2008). Third, the audience is not actively trying to reward or punish a state for its past acts in considering the state's reputation. Past bad (or good) acts that the audience considers irrelevant to a state's future behavior, whether toward cooperation in general or toward a specific treaty regime, are not incorporated into reputational analysis.

II. HOW THE AUDIENCE'S VIEWS LEAD TO GREATER COMPLIANCE

Because reputation is thought to be relevant to a state's future set of potential cooperative ventures, the loss of reputation can deter states from violating international agreements. As with most deterrence mechanisms, the restraint on behavior occurs primarily in the mind of the principal (here, the state considering the possibly uncooperative action). The principal considers undertaking an action that violates an international rule, or that it suspects the audience would consider to be a violation of an international rule. The principal then performs an analysis concerning the audience's likely reaction. This analysis begins with a determination of the probability that observers will view the action as a violation of the relevant legal rule. The action may be kept covert, such that the audience never discovers it, or the principal may be able to convince the audience (or some percentage of the audience) that the action is consistent with the legal rule. Naturally, since the audience is not a homogenous group, there can be a diverse range of interpretations of the act.

The principal will gauge the likely range of reactions to its action, then assess how these reactions will influence its set of related future interactions. In order to do this, the principal must first calculate what impact the audience's reactions will have on its future interactions within the relevant issue area. For instance, if the action involves a breach of a security agreement, the greatest effects will be felt in the area of security cooperation. Yet, the reputational effects of a breach may, to a lesser degree, extend to other areas as well (Guzman 2008). For example, the breach of the security agreement may also decrease the principal's access to trade agreements, although not as much as a violation of a trade agreement would. The principal will factor these costs into its analysis and discount the total costs depending on how far in the future the potential cooperation is likely to occur. These reputational costs are then weighed along with other costs, such as reciprocal noncompliance by other states or negative market reactions, against the benefits of deviating from the international rules.

Reputational analysis can also be important to the principal's calculus if a public act of international law compliance can improve the principal's reputation and enhance its future cooperative ventures. Although violations of the rule can lower the state's reputation from the status quo, public acts of compliance can improve the state's reputation. The critical baseline for this analysis is the audience's current expectations regarding the state's actions (Tomz 2007; Guzman 2008). Both the potential costs of lowering the state's reputation and the potential benefits of improving its reputation depend on the state's existing reputation. States with particularly poor reputations may only suffer small additional losses from a violation of international rules, but may see significant gains for public acts of compliance. Along the same lines, states with sterling reputations may suffer large losses from public acts of violation, but gain little from continued compliance.

III. WHAT COOPERATIVE REPUTATION DOES NOT MEAN

A reputation for cooperativeness is only one of several reputations that a state can maintain. The IL/IR literature focuses on this reputation because it is thought to correlate with a state's desirability as a treaty partner. Yet, a state may wish to cultivate other reputations that are not necessarily compatible with cooperativeness.

The first of these is a reputation that is particularly important to security studies in IR: the state's "toughness" or "resolve." Security studies in IR have long been focused on a state's willingness to bear costs to reach a security goal. Conceptions of a state's power focus not only on a state's financial and military resources, but also on the state's willingness to expend these resources when challenged. The state's resolve is a form of reputation: a belief among members of the international community that the state is willing to absorb losses to obtain or retain strategic goals (Levy 1987). If rivals believe that the state has a high level of resolve, then these rivals will assume their actions are less likely to be successful and will therefore challenge the state less frequently. As a consequence, governments may be willing to expend a level of resources that is disproportionate to the strategic importance of the dispute in isolation, in order to establish the state's general level of toughness and deter future disputes. As Thomas Schelling (1967: 124–25) argued, "Few parts of the world are intrinsically worth the risk of serious war by themselves, especially when taken slice by slice, but defending them or running risks to protect them may preserve one's commitments to action in other parts of the world and at later times. . . . [A state's 'face'] is a country's reputation for action, the expectations other countries have about its behavior. We lost thirty thousand dead in Korea to save face for the United States and the United Nations, not to save South Korea for the South Koreans, and it was undoubtedly worth it." A reputation for resolve is an asset, but not one that is necessarily perfectly compatible with a reputation for abiding by international law obligations. For instance, in domestic civil wars, governments may attempt to demonstrate their resolve in crushing rebel movements by engaging in actions that are prohibited under the Geneva Conventions, such as the killing of civilians (Walter 2009: 148–53).

Alternatively, a government may wish to have a reputation for good policy or for concern for humanitarian goals. Such a concern for the state's global standing is also a form of reputation that is of concern to IL scholars in particular. Harold Koh has frequently argued that taking community-oriented international actions benefits the United States and other democratic nations, because these actions improve the state's reputation in world affairs and provide democratic states with greater soft power to influence and persuade other governments (Koh 2003: 1500–01).

Although this type of reputation may have a significant overlap with a reputation for cooperativeness, the fit is not perfect. One potential point of tension is the decision to sign onto a treaty regime where the state expects it may face difficulty coming into compliance with all of the treaty's terms. A state interested in maximizing its global standing may join a great number of treaties to demonstrate its support for a developing norm even while recognizing that its current national policies are not entirely consistent with that norm. For instance, the United States has refused to ratify several widely adopted international agreements, including the Convention Against Landmines and the Kyoto Protocol to the United Nations (UN) Climate Convention. Arguably one of the easiest ways for the United States to raise its popular reputation abroad, and its global standing, would be to join these agreements. But joining these agreements would not necessarily aid the United States' reputation for abiding by compliance. The state's reputation for compliance may, in fact, decrease – even as its global standing increases as a result of endorsing the new norm –; if it is unable to pass the requisite domestic legislation, such as national laws regulating the production of greenhouse gases, to abide by the treaties' terms.

In some circumstances, a state's global standing and its reputation for compliance with international rules run in opposite directions. The phrase "illegal but legitimate" highlights the gap between actions that are widely understood to be good policy and actions that are legally permissible. This phrase became prominent after an independent panel of international lawyers reviewed the appropriateness of the North American Treaty Organization (NATO) bombing of Serbia in 1999. The UN Charter requires that any use of force against another state other than self-defense receive the prior approval of the UN Security Council. The NATO nations sought such approval but never requested a formal vote on the resolution because of a threatened Russian veto. NATO justified its use of force as necessary to prevent further ethnic cleansing in the Former Yugoslavia. The panel of independent international lawyers report pinpoints the tension that can exist between a reputation for compliance and one for global standing. The panel acknowledged that the action was illegal under international law – a clear violation of the UN Charter restriction on the use of force – yet, the action was widely viewed as a legitimate use of force in support of the policy goal of preventing further ethnic cleansing. The NATO nations' willingness to use force most likely raised the nations' global standing as good actors even while the action violated core international rules.

Commentators who attempt to develop a general theory of reputation must separate out these tensions. Simply saying that a state adopts a policy to improve its "reputation" is not particularly helpful in predicting what course of action that state will take. A state can have an interest in having a strong reputation for resolve, compliance, and good policy actions, but these reputational concerns can push the state in different directions. This chapter defines reputation to mean the state's reputation for compliance with international law, as the IL/IR compliance literature does (Downs and Jones 2002; Guzman 2008). This is the convention in the literature because scholars generally assume that compliance with treaty agreements is highly correlated with desirability as a treaty partner. This assumption is itself questionable because formally legal measures may be viewed as uncooperative (Brewster 2009). For instance, a government that withdraws from a treaty may be acting in a manner that is completely legal, and yet this action may make the government a poor treaty partner because it indicates unreliability (Helfer 2005). Nonetheless, this chapter adopts the compliance/cooperativeness meaning of reputation because it is the standard definition in the literature and thus provides a basis from which to review existing studies.

IV. EMPIRICAL ANALYSIS OF REPUTATIONAL EFFECTS

Empirical studies of whether a state's concern with its "cooperative" reputation has effects on state behavior have mixed results. Simmons (2000: 829–32) finds that states that voluntarily accepted additional legal obligations to refrain from imposing capital restrictions were more likely to do so than states that did not have such a legal obligation. Simmons' study attributes unexplained differences between the behavior of states that have taken on legal obligations, as compared to states that have not done so, to reputational concerns. Kono (2007: 757) finds that trade agreements that include a third-party dispute resolution system have higher levels of compliance than trade agreements that do not include dispute resolution, and attributes this difference, in part, to heightened reputational concerns. These studies indicate that legal obligations and institutions have an effect on compliance, although they raise attribution questions concerning whether the unexplained difference is due to the influence of law or to intrinsic differences between the states that have chosen to adopt the legal obligation or institutional design feature (Simmons and Hopkins 2005; von Stein 2005).

Tomz (2007) finds that the state's reputation for repaying sovereign debt has a causal role in determining the discount rate on government bonds. Tomz's findings demonstrate that reputation has an effect in issue-specific areas. These findings are suggestive to international law, but are not necessarily evidence that violations of international law carry negative effects: the study does not attempt to distinguish between the reputational effects of the state's poor behavior (they are a bad credit risk) and the reputational effects of the state's lack of respect for law (the breach of the contract). Also outside of the international law arena, Walter (2009) finds that governments with more domestic separatist groups will resist military challenges (by any of the domestic groups) in order to build a reputation for toughness and that this reputation can be effective in deterring separatist group challenges. Similarly, Sartori (2005) finds that states with a reputation for honesty deter international challenges. However, not all empirical studies of reputational concerns find that the state's (or other principal's) reputation influences audience behavior (Fearon 1994), or that reputational concerns influence the state's behavior (von Stein 2005).

To date, there have not been systemic empirical studies of whether the state's reputation influences a state's opportunities to join treaty regimes, either within a particular regime's issue area or outside of it. Nor are there empirical studies of whether a reputation for compliance affects the value of a state's concessions in treaty negotiations.

V. CRITIQUES OF AND COMPLICATIONS TO THE REPUTATION MODEL

A number of scholars have critiqued the use of reputational analysis, and several key questions regarding reputation's role in promoting compliance with international law warrant further scholarly exploration. This section reviews some of these critiques and identifies several promising areas for future research.

A. Decision Biases in the Formation of Reputation

Reputation is fundamentally an issue of perception (Mercer 1996). Individuals will bring to their analysis of reputation different biases that will influence their judgments. The ability of a decision-maker in a home government to put himself into the mind-set of a foreign actor, or even a domestic actor, can be limited. In some issue areas, the task may be relatively easy – for example, a matter of asking if the state paid its sovereign debt—in others, it may be more difficult and involve a question such as whether a military intervention is justifiable on humanitarian grounds. As a consequence, the growing literature in decision theory seems highly relevant to understanding how reputations are formed and how they influence international relations (Jervis 1976; Kahneman and Tversky 1979; Jolls 1998; Sunstein and Thaler 2003).

There are several points in the reputational analysis process at which the decision biases of the analyst (a member of the audience interpreting the event in question) influence the analysis. First, the analyst must decide what actually occurred in the event in question. The international system is noisy, and even factual claims about the relevant action can be contestable, leading different analysts in the audience to reach different conclusions. This can be both an advantage and a disadvantage to the acting state, since the state can attempt to control the narrative of what events transpired, either honestly or falsely, and thereby cast its actions in a more positive light. The audience may be skeptical of the home state's narrative, even when it is honest, and accept a different narrative. This pattern also applies to state secrets: the acting state may attempt to prevent the audience from ever discovering that an event has occurred, but will attach some probability to the secret being discovered and publicized. In addition, the international audience knows that states keep secrets, and this contributes to the audience's skepticism of the acting state's narrative.

Second, analysts may disagree about how to interpret the relevant event. Most of the rules of international law are not subject to dispute resolution, and governments are left to their own judgments concerning whether a violation of international law has occurred. Treaties can be quite ambiguous (Chayes and Chayes 1993), and thus different analysts may have varying interpretations of what international law requires. When analysts believe that a violation has occurred, there may still be disagreement over how serious the breach is and what the appropriate remedy would be.

Finally, analysts may disagree about why the breach occurred. Mercer (1996) provides a broad critique of the conception of reputation as a psychological construct. Mercer emphasizes that reputational assessments have both characteristic and situational components. To the extent that the audience believes that the state's actions were dictated by situational exigencies – that is, that the state had little choice but to take the course of action it followed – then the action is not relevant to the state's reputation because it provides little information about what the state would do if it had discretion regarding policy choice. If the audience believes that the state had policy freedom, then the act is relevant to reputational analysis because it speaks to the character of the state. The audience's perception of whether the actions are situation-driven or characteristic depends on the observers' decision bias. Mercer argues that this systematically adds a pessimism distortion: an observer is likely to view an ally's action supporting an alliance as situational, but an adversary's action supporting a competing alliance as characteristic. Regardless of whether one agrees with this analysis of how decision biases influence the reputational analysis, Mercer is certainly correct in that reputation is a very perception-based concept and that psychological decision biases will influence the analysis, perhaps in systematic and predictable ways.

B. *The Scope of Reputation*

Reputation is thought to be useful as information regarding the state's likely future course of action. Because reputation is taken more seriously as a causal mechanism than as a predictor of future actions, one of the key issues to resolve is *what* the principal has a reputation for. George Downs and Michael Jones (2002) argue that information in one issue area is not necessarily useful for predicting state action in others. They maintain that a state's defection from a treaty signals that the relevant compliance costs have surpassed the state's benefits from that treaty. This information should lead other states to expect similar defections *only if* the source of higher compliance costs impacts other agreements *and* if other agreements are of equal or lesser value to the defecting state. For instance, if the United States blocks the entry of Japanese goods into its market during a recession, in violation of a trade agreement, what does this information relay about the United States' likely compliance with other agreements? A recession might not make the United States any more likely to violate a military alliance or environmental agreement if it does not similarly raise the costs of complying with the agreement. In addition, the costs of compliance might not be high enough to make the United States violate a trade agreement with the European Union (EU).

More broadly, compliance with international rules is a function of domestic support for the goals of the treaty regimes, as well as respect for international legal obligations (Brewster 2009; Simmons 2010). Treaties are policy outcomes as well as legal agreements. Noncompliance might not signal a general lack of respect for legal rules, but could instead indicate a shift in the policy goals of the state. In such cases, the likelihood of compliance might increase for some agreements and decrease for others.

Understanding how the audience views a violation of international law is critical when discussing the enforcement of agreements where there is not significant intra-issue enforcement, such as in human rights. For instance, let us say that a government that violates a human rights treaty *only* suffers a reputational loss in the human rights issue area. This is not much of a deterrent because the government would continue to be invited to join trade agreements, security treaties, and other cooperative ventures – just not human rights treaties. Reputation *must* be bundled across issue areas for it to be an important cause of compliance with a wide range of agreements. Downs and Jones (2002) argue that reputation is not bundled in this way, and thus conclude that reputation cannot sustain compliance with all international rules. Of course, reputational information from one issue area can carry over to another issue area in a discounted fashion (Guzman 2008).

The key issue, then, is to theorize about how and when information will transfer across issue areas to determine whether reputational concerns are sufficient to sustain compliance with international rules generally. Such a theory is important, not only to human rights agreements but also to environmental public goods agreements, where intra-issue reciprocity is not effective because the violator cannot be excluded from its use of the public good. For example, the problem of global climate change involves a public good: all states share the atmosphere, and pollution from any one state affects global levels of greenhouse gases. Whether reputational concerns can be an effective means of enforcing some future agreement on global warming depends on understanding whether, and if so, how, reputation crosses issue areas in the audience's perception.

C. To Whom Does Reputation Attach?

One of the most difficult questions in reputational analysis is the issue of to whom the relevant reputation attaches. This question applies not only to the reputational analysis of the state – for example, the analysis of a government acting on behalf of the state – but also to the analysis of the audience, and whether the audience attaches the relevant reputation to the state, to the government, or to some other actor. Even if we limit the question to whether reputation attaches to the "state" (the ongoing political entity) or the "government" (the current person or persons making decisions for the state), or both, the analysis can quickly become complicated.

There are at least two key issues here. The first is identification of the reputational costs and benefits to the government acting for the state. Governments might not fully internalize reputational costs to the state. That is, the reputational costs to the government of a breach of international law might be significantly less than the reputational costs to the state. Yet, when we are discussing the government's incentive to comply with international law, it is the government's reputational analysis that is relevant to the compliance calculus. The second issue is what the reputational costs to the *state* are. Even if the current government does internalize reputational costs to the state in its decision making, these costs might be low if the audience expects the behavior of the state to change with a new government. Reputation is taken to provide information about the state's future actions, and the violations of the last government might not be particularly good indicators of the new government's behavior.

1. How Does the Government Internalize the State's Reputation?

The idea that a state is an individual or a black box is obviously a fiction, but it can be hard to determine who the state is once we depart from that fiction. The state is a collection of people, traditions, government processes, political parties, and individual leaders. International law scholarship has tended to view the state as a territorial entity and thus view the "country" as having a reputation, much like an individual would. This view of the state as a unitary entity encompasses the idea that the state is the same "person" over time, even though almost all observers would agree that the governments of states change along many dimensions and that the state cannot control its reputation in the same way that an individual can. Both of these ideas are problematic when we consider the government's motivation to comply with international law.

Governments do not fully or consistently internalize the costs of an action to the state. Although the state, as a country, will last into the indefinite future, the government making the decisions will almost always have *shorter and varying* time horizons (Brewster 2009). For instance, Walter (2009) finds that governments with shorter tenures in power are less likely to invest in a reputation for resolve and will thus deter fewer challenges. In addition, within a government's lifecycle, the government may care about the state's reputation (or the government's own reputation) to differing degrees. Governments coming to the end of their terms may be less concerned with reputation than governments just beginning their tenure in power. As a consequence, reputation is not a constant that can be calculated as part of the state's cost–benefit analysis. The state may very well have a reputation, but this does not mean that the government fully internalizes the costs (or benefits) of an action to the state's reputation or that the government will place a consistent value on the state's reputation throughout its term in power.

In addition, governments do not always have the capacity to control the state's reputation. In many circumstances, the state's reputation is unrelated to the current government's actions. If the reputation of the state is based on the structure of its governmental system, the characteristics of its population, or its history, then current government leaders may have few tools with which to change the state's reputation. Thus, the fact that the state's reputation is relevant to the audience will not necessarily mean that reputational concerns will influence present government leaders.

2. The Audience's Perception of the Relevant Reputation Actor

States are not static. Even though the state may continue to exist with the same legal status for years, the state's goals, or its preferred means of achieving those goals, can change radically. Indeed, American interventions in Afghanistan and Iraq were premised on the idea that changing the regime in power would result in radically different policy preferences for the state. When a new government comes to power, the audience will discount the predictive value of the last government's actions. The differences in successive governments can be relatively minor – for example, the transition from Margaret Thatcher to John Major in the United Kingdom – or of great significance – for example, the transition from the Shah to the Ayatollah Khomeini in Iran. These are differences of degree, not of category. There will always be *some* discount of the state's past actions when a new government comes to power.

This point is relevant not only for determining the expected costs of a reputational loss, but also for analyzing a government's decision to improve its reputation. For instance, in Tomz's (2007) study of sovereign debt, the fact that states regularly underwent changes in government was critical to his analysis of reputational change. Unlike traditional models, in which the state is considered to be the same "person" across governments, Tomz assumes that the audience (in that case, potential buyers of sovereign debt) realizes that governments change and that each successive government can have different preferences for repaying the state's debt. Without such an assumption, the state can develop a reputation as a type (here, a "stalwart" or a "lemon") that, over time, is very difficult for the government to alter. Thus, the stalwart can default on debt to little reputational effect, and the lemon has no incentive to invest in improving its reputation. Far from having a unitary view of the state, Tomz's empirical work demonstrates that sovereign debt investors are highly responsive to changes in governments in determining the "state's reputation."

Understanding how the audience's view of state reputation changes, or whether the state is even the relevant reputational actor, is thus highly relevant to compliance studies. Depending on the issue area, the audience's evaluation of a state's reputation may be highly dependent on the current government or current political conditions. This is important, because if the expectations of the audience change when a new administration comes into power or when political conditions change, then the reputational costs to the state of violating international law, as well as to the current government, may not be very high.

D. *The Limits of Reputation Where There Are Power Disparities*

There are reasons to question whether reputation is, in fact, an effective mechanism for encouraging compliance in the face of significant power disparities. Reputation works through exclusion: the state with a poor reputation is either excluded from deals, or it is charged a high price of admission (for instance, its concessions are worth less than other states' concessions because the expected level of compliance with the agreement is lower). In the prisoner's dilemma game, each state is modeled as being equally powerful; in contrast, in the international system, state power varies tremendously. Thus, exclusion or a higher price of admission will not be an effective strategy against every state. For states with the capacity to be a bully – that is, states that cannot effectively be excluded because of their importance to the cooperative activity – reputational sanctions may simply not work particularly well.

A state with significant power in some issue area, say, trade, can be next to impossible to exclude from an agreement even if its record of compliance is less than sterling. For instance, the United States and the EU are necessary partners for any global trade deal. Even if the United States and the EU have less than stellar records for compliance with the World Trade Organization (WTO) rules, the possibility of excluding them is simply unrealistic. In fact, these governments establish the most important terms of a given trade agreement, rather than taking worse terms because of their poorer reputation.

Furthermore, it is not obvious that a good reputation for compliance in the issue area of trade is ideal for the state. The rationalist international law literature assumes that states want a cooperative reputation because this maximizes the states' gains. But does a good reputation always lead to the greatest future gains? In the prisoner's dilemma, states are able to maximize their gains by agreeing to cooperate. But, in many international trade situations, a reputation for being a bully can be beneficial because it may allow a government to credibly demand a larger share of the joint gains. As Robert Keohane has noted, states might just as well prefer to have a reputation as a bully or as being willing to violate international rules as they would having a reputation for being cooperative (Keohane 1997: 496–99).

Although this might seem to be a conflation of two different types of reputation – one for resolve and one for cooperativeness – this reasoning speaks to the rationale for why states are thought to want a reputation for cooperativeness; namely, the opportunity to participate in mutually beneficial agreements. In the mutually beneficial prisoner's dilemma game (or any other cooperative game), the payoffs of the game are set. Yet, in international relations, states can change the payoffs of cooperative activity. For instance, if there are possible gains from cooperation, the division of the gains accruing from the agreement will have distributional implications (Krasner 1991).

When negotiating a treaty, it is generally accepted that a state can negotiate a larger share of the gains from an agreement if it has a reputation for not backing down. Treaty negotiations can resemble a coordination game in which the players want to coordinate their action, but often have opposing preferences for which action to pursue. In a coordination game, the state's share of the joint gains can depend on how credibly it can insist on getting its preferred outcome.

Some may dismiss this concern as a matter of timing. That is, states might want a tough reputation when bargaining for an agreement, but then want a cooperative reputation once the agreement is sealed. However, having a tough reputation even after an agreement is struck can produce gains for the state. Treaties are always susceptible to renegotiation. If one party can credibly threaten to exit from a treaty regime unless the changes it desires are made, even if these changes involve short-term losses to both parties, then that party is more likely to have its demands met.

For instance, in 1965, the French government wanted to stop the implementation of super-majority voting in the European Economic Community (EEC). The members of the EEC had agreed in 1958 to transition to super-majority voting in eight years, but at year seven, the French government was not ready to accept this treaty provision. The French government threatened to not participate in EEC decision making (the "empty chair" crisis), effectively withdrawing from the agreement unless its demand that each nation retain a veto over community decisions was met. If France carried through with its threat, it would have hurt itself as well as other EEC states (Lindberg 1965: 61). The other members of the EEC backed down in the Luxembourg Compromise, which extended the national veto of community decisions for the next seventeen years. Similarly, in 1953, the United States used the threat of withdrawal from the General Agreement on Tariffs and Trade (GATT) as a bargaining chip (Jackson 1969: 548). The United States requested a waiver on agricultural goods, and the other parties to the GATT refused. It was only after the United States threatened to withdraw from the organization that the waiver was approved.

Having a tough reputation can be particularly effective in improving a state's gains in customary international law. Unlike treaty law, customary international law is the result of state practice rather than negotiations. A primary means of changing customary international law is for a state to violate the existing rule and try to change other states' practices to conform to the violating state's practice. In the short term, the violating state might suffer a loss. But the state might achieve greater gains if it has a reputation for sticking with its violation of customary law until other states adopt its proposed change to the rule. Here, again, having a good reputation for compliance with international law does not necessarily maximize the state's future gains.

In short, states might be rewarded – not punished – for noncompliance with current agreements. Governments are not locked into the payoffs of any one game. When engaging with other states, the government can consider the gains to changing the distribution of the benefits (through threatened or actual defection), as well as the gains of continuing to cooperate within the current treaty or customary international law structure. These competing considerations indicate that a simple strategy of always wanting to be viewed as law-abiding is not necessarily the best way for a state to maximize its gains.

E. *Interactions between Dispute Resolution and Reputation*

Finally, there needs to be greater attention paid to the interaction between dispute resolution and perceptions of the state's cooperativeness. The dominant idea appears to be that dispute resolution works in multiple ways to increase the constraint of international rules on state behavior. First, a dispute resolution system can provide authoritative definitions of relevant international law requirements and apply these rules to the issue in dispute (Kono 2007). This limits the state's freedom of action by decreasing the state's ability to dispute what the relevant rule is or how it applies to the specific circumstances. Second, a dispute resolution system can clarify the situations under which other states should be permitted to use formal sanctions. This should increase the use of decentralized sanctions because it solves the "sanctioners' dilemma," or the potential negative reputational ramifications to sanctioning states that can result from inappropriate application of sanctions (Thompson 2009: 307). Third, in addition to whatever formal sanction is forthcoming from a dispute resolution system, a government will face higher reputational costs for noncompliance under a dispute resolution system because its violation will be publicized to the international audience (Helfer and Slaughter 1997; Guzman 2002; Schwartz and Sykes 2002).

Although dispute resolution may increase the reputational costs of treaty violation, it is also possible that dispute resolution may decrease these costs by altering the audience's, or some portion of the audience's, beliefs about what defines "cooperative" behavior (Brewster 2012). Here, it is useful to draw a distinction between a breach and a violation of a treaty. As I use the terms, a *breach* refers to a deviation from the substantive terms of a treaty: an action that is contrary to the first-order rules of an agreement is a breach. Breaches can be resolved within the treaty's framework through dispute resolution and remedies. A *violation* of a treaty is a deviation from the dispute resolution rules: an action that is contrary to the treaty's second-order rules. Using these definitions, a state can breach a treaty (that is, deviate from its substantive rules) without violating the treaty (deviating from its second-order rules). Any time a state breaches a treaty's substantive terms, it can stay within the treaty's framework (not violate the treaty) by accepting the jurisdiction of the dispute resolution system and complying with the remedy.

Dispute resolution can, in some cases, be designed to manage departures from the regime's substantive obligations while maintaining the regime's cooperative equilibrium (Rosendorf 2005; Johns 2011). In doing so, dispute resolution can normalize violations of the regime's substantive rules by providing a framework whereby governments can "pay" for breaches by complying with the treaty's remedy regime. So long as the government does not violate the regime's framework rules – that is, the obligation to pay for breaches – the government can demonstrate that it is not in violation of the broader treaty regime and maintain it reputation for being cooperative.

Although the idea that the use of formal remedies may decrease the reputational costs of breach may sound counterintuitive, there is an increasingly robust literature on how imposing formal sanctions can "crowd out" informal sanctions, such as reputation. Bruno Frey and others have demonstrated that the addition of formal remedies can lead the audience to rely on these remedies exclusively, and thereby decrease the use of informal remedies, such as reputation and reciprocity (Huang and Wu 1994; Frey and Oberholzer-Gee 1997; Bohnet, Frey, and Huck 2001). For instance, adding a monetary reward for an activity can reduce a population's willingness to engage in the activity (Frey and Oberholzer-Gee 1997). This is true with regards to monetary punishments as well. Even if there are very few formal consequences to breach (as there have traditionally been in international law), the addition of a formal punishment can decrease compliance with the rule rather than raise it (Gneezy and Rustichini 2000). Robert Scott and Paul Stephan (2006) similarly discuss how formal court systems can "crowd out" informal cooperative norms. They argue that once individuals are engaged in formal dispute resolution, they are less constrained by background norms of fairness and reciprocity.

Formal remedies can crowd out reputational costs by redefining what cooperative action is. If the audience views a treaty as having remedies to price for noncompliance – paying the remedy as an acceptable alternative to abiding by substantive rules – then there is a real reputational difference between breach and violation (Cooter 1984). Breaches may not be preferred, but remedies provide a means for states to demonstrate that they are continuing to be cooperative with the treaty agreement. Indeed, the audience may view remedies – and states' option to pay the remedy instead of obeying the substantive treaty rule – as part of the political equilibrium that the treaty embodies. Thus, much of the reputational effect of dispute resolution may not come from the finding or publicity of breach, but instead from the state's response to that finding. In the international system, compliance with remedy regimes (like compliance with substantive rules) is essentially voluntary. As such, compliance with the treaty's dispute resolution system is a costly signal that allows the state to demonstrate its commitment to the treaty's goals and its willingness to comply with the broader treaty regime.

Relating this discussion back to institutional design, the form of an international regime frames the parties' understanding of how the regime will function. The framing of the institution and the role that dispute resolution plays within the institution are important to the international audience's (and the home government's) beliefs about what actions are indicative of noncooperative behavior. Creating a formal dispute resolution system can redefine cooperative behavior and potentially facilitate breach. Just as a dispute settlement can resolve the sanctioners' dilemma, dispute resolution institutions normalize breach by defining the type of government action that counts as a breach and setting a "price" for such violations (Brewster 2012). Dispute resolution can thereby be a mechanism of escape as well as enforcement, managing departures from the regime's substantive obligations yet keeping states within the cooperative framework of the agreement.

The possible interactions between dispute settlement and reputational concerns are particularly pertinent when designing international institutions. For instance, most remedy regimes are designed to establish a certain level of compliance. The designers of a regime understand that member governments may deviate from the regime's substantive rules at some point in the future, and negotiators may not wish to deter all of these possible deviations. In establishing the regime's remedy rules, negotiators can attempt to establish a level of penalty that approximates the negotiating parties' view of when deviations should be permitted. Understanding whether the formal sanctions will work to supplement reputational losses, or will instead undermine reputational losses, is thus critical to optimal remedy design.

VI. CONCLUSION

There is consensus among IL/IR scholars that reputation is a motive for compliance with international law. The importance of reputation is particularly emphasized by scholars in the rationalist tradition, who view governments as acting based on an explicit cost–benefit basis. Reputational concerns are thought to be particularly important because they can make cooperative activity sustainable even without a centralized enforcement system. The causal logic runs along the following lines: governments have reputations that extend into the indefinite future and potentially apply across issue areas. They care about their reputations because they are engaged in cooperative activities with other actors, and continued interaction depends, at least in part, on having a good reputation for cooperation. As a consequence, governments consider reputational loss due to noncompliance with international law as one that is balanced against the possible benefits of violations. Reputational concerns make governments more likely to comply with international law because a bad reputation leads to less cooperative opportunities in the future.

As this chapter details, the reputational narrative becomes more complicated if we abstract away the simple model of unitary states cooperating in a full-information environment. Reputational concerns do not become insignificant, but the causal role of reputation in promoting compliance with international law becomes less certain. A number of factors can attenuate the link between the state's reputation and government decision-making, including how reputation crosses issue areas and to whom the state's reputation attaches. This chapter also highlights the importance of the audience's perception to reputation. Cognitive biases among the audience and the target can substantially alter the reputation analysis but have not received significant scholarly attention. In addition, commentators need a greater appreciation of how institutions, including dispute resolution systems and formal remedy rules, can influence the audience's views of what cooperative activity entails.

REFERENCES

Abbott, Kenneth W. (1989). "Modern International Relations Theory: A Prospectus for International Lawyers," *Yale Journal of International Law*, Vol. 14, No. 2, pp. 335–411.

Abbott, Kenneth W., and Duncan Snidal (2000). "Hard and Soft Law in International Governance," *International Organization*, Vol. 54, No. 3, pp. 421–56.

Axelrod, Robert (1984). *The Evolution of Cooperation* (New York: Basic Books).

Bohnet, Iris, Bruno S. Frey, and Steffen Huck (2001). "More Order with Less Law: On Contract Enforcement, Trust, and Crowding," *American Political Science Review*, Vol. 95, No. 1, pp. 131–44.

Brewster, Rachel (2009). "Unpacking the State's Reputation," *Harvard International Law Journal*, Vol. 50, No. 2, pp. 231–69.

——— (2012). "Pricing Compliance: When Formal Remedies Displace Reputational Sanctions," draft.

Chayes, Abram, and Antonia Handler Chayes (1993). "On Compliance," *International Organization*, Vol. 47, No. 2, pp. 175–205.

Cooter, Robert (1984). "Prices and Sanctions," *Columbia Law Review*, Vol. 84, No. 6, pp. 1523–60.

Downs, George W., and Michael Jones (2002). "Reputation, Compliance, and International Law," *Journal of Legal Studies*, Vol. 33, No. S1, pp. S95–S114.

Downs, George W., David Rocke, and Peter Barsoom (1996). "Is the Good News about Compliance Good News about Cooperation?," *International Organization*, Vol. 50, No. 3, pp. 379–406.

Fearon James D. (1994). "Signaling versus the Balance of Power and Interests: An Empirical Test of a Crisis Bargaining Model," *Journal of Conflict Resolution*, Vol. 38, No. 2, pp. 236–69.

Frank, Thomas M. (1990). *The Power of Legitimacy among Nations* (New York: Oxford University Press).

Frey, Bruno S., and Felix Oberholzer-Gee (1997). "The Costs of Price Incentives: An Empirical Analysis of Motivation Crowding Out," *American Economic Review*, Vol. 87, No. 4, pp. 746–55.

Gneezy, Uri, and Aldo Rustichini (2000). "A Fine Is a Price," *Journal of Legal Studies*, Vol. 29, No. 1, pp. 1–17.

Goldsmith, Jack L., and Eric A. Posner (2005). *The Limits of International Law* (New York: Oxford University Press).

Grieco, Joseph M. (1988). "Anarchy and the Limits of Cooperation: A Realist Critique of the Newest Liberal Institutionalism," *International Organization*, Vol. 42, No. 3, pp. 485–507.

Gruber, Lloyd (2000). *Ruling the World: Power Politics and the Rise of Supranational Institutions* (Princeton NJ: Princeton University Press).

Guzman, Andrew T. (2002). "The Cost of Credibility: Explaining Resistance to Interstate Dispute Resolution Mechanisms," *Journal of Legal Studies*, Vol. 31, No. 2, pp. 303–26.

_____ (2008). *How International Law Works: A Rational Choice Theory* (New York: Oxford University Press).

Hathaway, Oona (2005). "Between Power and Principle: An Integrated Theory of International Law," *University of Chicago Law Review*, Vol. 72, No. 2, pp. 469–536.

Helfer, Laurence R. (2005). "Exiting Treaties," *Virginia Law Review*, Vol. 91, No. 7, pp. 1579–1648.

Helfer, Laurence R., and Anne-Marie Slaughter (1997). "Towards A Theory of Supranational Adjudication," *Yale Law Journal*, Vol. 107, No. 2, pp. 273–391.

Henkin, Louis (1968). *How Nations Behave* (New York: Columbia University Press).

Huang, Peter H., and H. M. Wu (1994). "More Order without More Law: A Theory of Social Norms and Organizational Cultures," *Journal of Law, Economics, & Organization*, Vol. 20, No. 2, pp. 390–406.

Jackson, John H. (1969). *World Trade and the Law of GATT* (Indianapolis, IN: Bobbs-Merrill).

Jervis, Robert (1976). *Perception and Misperception in International Politics* (Princeton, NJ: Princeton University Press).

Johns, Leslie (2011). "Depth versus Rigidity in the Design of International Trade Agreements," Working Paper. Available at http://www.sscnet.ucla.edu/polisci/faculty/ljohns/DvR_120123 .pdf.

Jolls, Christine (1998). "Behavioral Economics Analysis of Redistributive Legal Rules," *Vanderbilt Law Review*, Vol. 51, pp. 1653–78.

Kahneman, Daniel, and Amos Tversky (1979). "Prospect Theory: An Analysis of Decision under Risk," *Econometrica*, Vol. 47, No. 2, pp. 263–92.

Keohane, Robert O. (1984). *After Hegemony: Cooperation and Discord in the World Political Economy* (Princeton, NJ: Princeton University Press).

_____ (1997). "International Relations and International Law: Two Optics," *Harvard Journal of International Law*, Vol. 38, No. 2, pp. 487–502.

Koh, Harold H. (1997). "Transnational Legal Process," *Nebraska Law Review*, Vol. 75, No. 1, pp. 181–207.

_____ (2003). "On American Exceptionalism," *Stanford Law Review*, Vol. 55, No. 5, pp. 1479–1527.

Kono, Daniel Y. (2007). "Making Anarchy Work: International Legal Institutions and Trade Cooperation," *Journal of Politics*, Vol. 69, No. 3, pp. 746–59.

Krasner, Stephen D. (1991). "Global Communications and National Power: Life on the Pareto Frontier," *World Politics*, Vol. 43, No. 3, pp. 336–66.

Levy, Jack S. (1987). "Declining Power and the Preventive Motivation for War," *World Politics*, Vol. 40, No. 1, pp. 82–107.

Lindberg, Leon N. (1965). "Decision Making and Integration in the European Community," *International Organization*, Vol. 19, No. 1, pp. 56–80.

Lipson, Charles (1991). "Why Are Some Agreements Informal?," *International Organization*, Vol. 45, No. 4, pp. 495–538.

Mearsheimer, John (1994–95). "The False Promise of International Institutions," *International Security*, Vol. 19, No. 3, pp. 5–26.

Mercer, Johnathan (1996). *Reputation and International Politics* (Ithaca, NY: Cornell University Press).

Mitchell, Ronald B. (1994). *International Oil Pollution at Sea: Environmental Policy and Treaty Compliance* (Cambridge, MA: MIT Press).

Morgenthau, Hans J. (1978). *Politics among Nations: The Struggle for Power and Peace*, 5th ed. (New York: Knopf).

Oye, Kenneth (1996). "Explaining Cooperation under Anarchy: Hypothesis and Strategies" in Kenneth Oye (ed.), *Cooperation under Anarchy* (Princeton, NJ: Princeton University Press), pp. 1–24.

Raustiala, Kal (2005). "Form and Substance in International Agreements," *American Journal of International Law*, Vol. 99, No. 3, pp. 581–614.

Rosendorff, B. Peter (2005). "Stability and Rigidity: Politics and Design of the WTO's Dispute Settlement Procedure," *American Political Science Review*, Vol. 99, No. 3, pp. 389–400.

Sartori, Anne E. (2005). *Deterrence by Diplomacy* (Princeton, NJ: Princeton University Press).

Schelling, Thomas C. (1967). *Arms and Influence* (New Haven, CT: Yale University Press).

Schwartz, Warren F., and Alan O. Sykes (2002). "The Economic Structure of Renegotiation and Dispute Resolution in the World Trade Organization," *Journal of Legal Studies*, Vol. 31, No. S1, pp. S179–S204.

Scott, Robert, and Paul Stephan (2006). *The Limits of Leviathan: Contract Theory and the Enforcement of International Law* (New York: Cambridge University Press).

Simmons, Beth A. (2000). "International Law and State Behavior: Commitment and Compliance in International Monetary Affairs," *American Political Science Review*, Vol. 94, No. 4, pp. 819–35.

——— (2010). "Treaty Compliance and Violation," *Annual Review Political Science*, Vol. 13, pp. 273–96.

Simmons, Beth A., and Daniel J. Hopkins (2005). "The Constraining Power of International Treaties: Theory and Methods," *American Political Science Review*, Vol. 99, No. 4, pp. 623–31.

Sunstein, Cass R., and Richard H. Thaler (2003). "Libertarian Paternalism Is Not an Oxymoron," *University of Chicago Law* Review, Vol. 70, No. 4, pp. 1159–1202.

Thompson, Alexander (2009). "The Rational Enforcement of International Law: Solving the Sanctioners' Dilemma," *International Theory*, Vol. 1, No. 2, pp. 307–21.

Tomz, Michael (2007). *Reputation and International Cooperation: Sovereign Debt across Three Centuries* (Princeton, NJ: Princeton University Press).

von Stein, Jana (2005). "Do Treaties Constrain or Screen? Selection Bias and Treaty Compliance," *American Political Science Review*, Vol. 99, No. 4, pp. 611–22.

Walter, Barbara F. (2009). *Reputation and Civil War: Why Separatist Conflicts Are So Violent* (New York: Cambridge University Press).

Waltz, Kenneth N. (2000). "Structural Realism after the Cold War," *International Security*, Vol. 25, No. 1, pp. 5–41.

22

Open Economy Law

Joel P. Trachtman

Applied to relations between nations, [the] bureaucratic
politics model directs attention to intra-national games,
the overlap of which constitutes international relations.

Graham Allison (1971: 149)

Within international relations (IR) scholarship, the field of "open economy politics"
(Lake 2009)[1] refers to a body of scholarship that has been emerging for the past
forty years and that seeks to understand the impact of domestic politics on international politics and the impact of international politics on domestic politics. One
foundational premise of this field of study is that domestic politics and law play
an important role in causing international political and legal dynamics, and that
international political and legal dynamics play an important role in determining
domestic politics and law. Thus, an examination of international political and legal
dynamics alone would often miss an important part of the picture, and an examination of domestic law and politics alone would also, only somewhat less often, miss
an important part of the picture.

The study of international politics and law is less important for an understanding
of domestic politics than vice versa simply because of the fact of subsidiarity: international politics and law generally plays a subsidiary role to domestic politics and
law. That is, states enter the market of international relations when they can obtain
policy outcomes better by doing so than by not doing so. Some actions are best
taken domestically, without any international political or legal extension, whereas
all international political or legal actions are extensions of some domestic policy. In
this sense, as the late Congressman Tip O'Neill suggested, all politics is domestic.

---

[1] For the defining review paper, see Lake (2009). The term "open economy politics" is an homage to
the field of "open economy macroeconomics," which recognized that the macroeconomic policy of
a particular state could only be understood in an international setting.

However, under globalization, politics is increasingly also global (Drezner 2007). Given the understanding that domestic politics and international politics are significantly interdependent, any study of the relationship between international politics and international law must examine the domestic political and legal dimension.

In his seminal article, *The Second Image Reversed: The International Sources of Domestic Politics*, Peter Gourevitch (1978) develops the implications of the fact that the international system can affect the structure of domestic politics. This is the *second image* (an image of the impact of domestic politics on international relations) reversed.[2] In his leading article, *Diplomacy and Domestic Politics: The Logic of Two-Level Games*, Robert Putnam (1988) focuses attention on the role of international pressure – foreign demands – in inducing domestic political change. Putnam saw that both the second-image approach (focusing on domestic causes of international relations) and the *second-image reversed* approach (focusing on international causes of domestic political phenomena) were inadequate by themselves. He claimed that:

> A more adequate account of the domestic determinants of foreign policy and international relations must stress *politics:* parties, social classes, interest groups (both economic and noneconomic), legislators, and even public opinion and elections, not simply executive officials and institutional arrangements. (Putnam 1988)

International relations and international law (IL) form a mechanism by which, as Graham Allison suggests in the quote at the beginning of this chapter, the domestic politics of different states may be linked, modifying the otherwise applicable political equilibrium in different states. The interaction of states matters for domestic politics, and is, in fact, simply an extension of domestic politics. It is an extension that constitutes limited functional cross-national political equilibria and, in effect, communities. Examining international law and politics in this way suggests a range of questions and topics for research.

In Part I of this chapter, I review the theoretical and empirical literature on the relationship between domestic politics and international law, focusing on the two critical moments of consent (adherence) to an international legal obligation and compliance with that obligation. I divide the literature among arguments focusing on several types of causal factors: (a) domestic structure; (b) public law litigation and civil society action; (c) ideas, acculturation, and managerial factors; and (d) domestic interests and partisan politics. It is easy to see that more than one, and perhaps all, of these types of causal factor will be at play in any given circumstance. But I argue that these different causal factors have different roles and operate in different ways.

In Part II, I develop a model of adherence and compliance that highlights domestic interests, or preferences. Although recognizing that the other potential causal

---

[2] Kenneth Waltz (1959) developed the idea of three images. The first image examines the role of individuals in international relations. The second focuses on the effects of domestic politics on international relations, whereas the third focuses on the effects of the international system on international relations.

factors may indeed have power, I make the simplifying assumption, consistent with preference-based economic theory, that preferences will generally play a greater role in determining adherence and compliance than (a) structural factors, managerial factors, public law litigation, and civil society action, which relate to how preferences are expressed, and (b) ideas and acculturation, which determine what preferences are held. My model highlights preferences and assumes that preferences determine the kinds of commitments that a state will seek or accept in international relations and will also determine whether a state will comply with its international commitments. Importantly, the possibility for reciprocal international contracting may induce lobbies that are interested in foreign actions to lend their political support to a domestic action that will be the quid pro quo for the foreign action. That is, international reciprocity provides a link between domestic politics in one country and domestic politics in another country, and it also provides an additional vector that can transform the balance of political power in each country.

I. CAUSAL FACTOR CANDIDATES

A number of factors within the domestic politico-legal sphere may cause states to adhere to, and to comply with, international law. It is unlikely that any monocausal explanation would be broadly successful, and this field would benefit from empirical evaluation of the relative causal power of different factors. The literature has focused on the following categories of causal factors: domestic structure; domestic litigation and interest groups; ideas, acculturation, and managerial factors; and domestic interests. I discuss each of these briefly, and then focus on domestic interests, simply because I speculate that a preference-based explanation of entry into and compliance with law will generally provide the greatest causal power. My speculation is supported by a broad consensus in social science that preferences have great (although definitely not exclusive) causal power. However, this is not based on systematic empirical validation, and I would expect other causal factors to be important in most circumstances.

A. Domestic Structure

Helen Milner and Peter Rosendorff (1997), following Putnam, develop a model of a two-level game. Their model emphasizes the effects of government structure. The factors on which they focus are the degree of divided government (i.e., between legislature and executive) and the asymmetric distribution of information within the domestic system. These factors are not concerned, as the present chapter is, with the constellation of lobbying interests and their relative power. Milner and Rosendorff assume a polyarchic state – a nonhierarchical state in which aggregate preferences arise from a political process. The actors that they examine are the domestic executive, the domestic legislature, domestic interest groups, and a unitary foreign government.

Interestingly, Milner and Rosendorffs separation between the domestic executive and the domestic legislature requires an assumption of differential interest group influence on the executive compared to the legislature, or of structural factors that cause the executive and the legislature to have a different interest. The Grossman and Helpman model discussed below, on the other hand, assumes a unified government, or government branches with identical interests, but focuses attention on diverse interests of interest groups, with those interest groups influencing policy through contributions. On the other hand, Milner and Rosendorff focus on domestic information asymmetries and examine interest groups as "endorsers" – as agents able to overcome information asymmetries through their knowledge and action.

The liberal theory of international politics and of IL, as revised and developed by Andrew Moravcsik (1997) and Anne-Marie Slaughter (1995), includes the argument that the structure of liberal states causes them to behave differently in international relations compared to nonliberal states. In particular, the liberal states theory highlighted the empirical observation that democracies seem to go to war with each other less often than nondemocracies and drew the inference that the liberal structure of democratic states reduces the likelihood of entry into war with other (Doyle 1983). Slaughter (1995) proposes other hypotheses about the legal relations among liberal states and between liberal and nonliberal states.

More specifically, a number of scholars have evaluated claims that democracies behave differently from nondemocracies. This goes beyond "democratic peace" claims to include claims that democracies are more committed to international environmental protection (Neumayer 2002) and claims that democracies are less likely to comply with Article VIII of the International Monetary Fund Articles of Agreement (Simmons 2000).

Rachel Brewster (2004) examines the domestic politics of treaty making, arguing that the structure of domestic foreign relations law must be considered in assessing the demand by states for international treaties. The specific structural features that she highlights include the power of the president in the United States to control the treaty-making process, the differences in requirements for approval of treaties compared to ordinary legislation, and the more subtle factors that cause treaties to be relatively entrenched.

Jide Nzelibe (2011) argues that international law can be understood as a tool of partisan politics, and that by entering into certain commitments, incumbent governments attempt to limit future options in a way that will advance their partisan fortunes. Note that this is not an argument about particular policies or lobbies, but about the broader competition between political parties. His approach assumes that some parties build reputations for addressing certain issues better than others and use international legal commitments to lock in policy on those issues, thus narrowing the scope of future policy. He gives the example that "a right-leaning government may support an international trade agreement that reduces tariff barriers not only because of policy preferences, but also because such an agreement is likely to undercut the ability of a future left-leaning government to reward its loyal trade union constituencies" (Nzelibe 2011).

B. *Public Law Litigation and Civil Society Action*

There is no doubt that, in certain contexts, the effects of international law on domestic politics take place through the channel of domestic public law litigation or through civil society action. Beth Simmons (2009), in her comprehensive study of the effects of international human rights law, rejects the causal effect in that context of reputation, retaliation, or reciprocity, arguing instead that international human rights law has its effect purely through domestic mechanisms, including changes in elite agendas, public law litigation, and civil society action. This does not answer the question of why states desire other states to enter into human rights treaties, or why states agree to do so, but it does provide an important analysis and empirical validation of the proposition that international human rights treaties can produce behavioral effects through these channels.

Anne van Aaken (2009) suggests greater attention to the utility of private rights of action, as well as other private sector mechanisms, in enforcing international law more broadly. In this regard, she follows some of the recommendations of the transnational legal process school, as articulated by Harold Koh (1991, 1997, 2005). Koh suggests that transnational public law litigation can "provoke judicial articulation of a *norm* of transnational law, with an eye toward using that declaration to promote a political settlement in which both governmental and nongovernmental entities will participate" (Koh 1991: 2349, emphasis in original). A growing literature has sought to assess the benefits and detriments of private rights of action. Joel Trachtman and Philip Moremen evaluated the possible utility of private rights of action in connection with trade law (Trachtman and Moreman 2003). Alan Sykes (2005) compared private rights of action in connection with investment law to private rights of action in connection with trade law.

A number of other scholars have criticized the role of courts in international relations, focusing on the U.S. context. Daniel Abebe and Eric Posner (2011) argue that the belief that greater judicial involvement in foreign relations would curb executive abuses and promote adherence rests on implausible assumptions about the incentives and capacities of courts. They criticize those, such as Derek Jinks and Neal Katyal (2007), who argue for reduced judicial deference to the U.S. executive.

C. *Ideas, Acculturation, and Managerial Factors*

Constructivist theories focus on the role of ideas and on the social construction of meaning as an influence on behavior. Social practices and interaction may change ideas and may therefore change behavior. To some degree, constructivism may be reconciled with a rationalist approach that would accept malleable preferences and the importance of nonmaterial preferences.

One influential school of thought, led by Harold Koh (2005, 2007), suggests that international law and institutions may play a role in inducing changes in state preferences through "norm internalization." A sociological extension of this school, led by Ryan Goodman and Derek Jinks (2003, 2004, 2005), utilizes sociological tools to examine the role of international law in an acculturation process. Each of these schools is described in more detail below.

Harold Koh has developed a constructivist approach to international law that focuses on the extent to which repeated interactions in legal process result in the internalization of international legal rules.

> As governmental and non-governmental actors repeatedly interact within the transnational legal process, they generate and interpret international legal norms and then seek to internalize those norms domestically. To the extent that these norms are successfully internalized, they become future determinants of why nations obey. The international society theorists seem to recognize that this process occurs, but have given little close study to the "transmission belt," whereby norms created by international society infiltrate into *domestic* society. (Koh 1997: 2651)

For Koh, the key factor is repeated participation in the international legal process. This, however, is hardly theoretically satisfying, as repeated interaction with duplicity or hostility would not necessarily change anyone's ideas or their incentives to comply. Nor would it necessarily overcome strong incentives to defect.

However, one may agree with Koh that this type of internalization process could occur and that it could have some effects. The interesting question, still unanswered, is the relative strength of this mechanism, compared to other mechanisms that induce compliance. A rationalist theory would be able to accept this constructivist insight as a model of one way in which preferences may be not static but malleable: individuals' ideas about who they are, what their roles are, and what they want may change. But, as Koh recognizes, this is only one type of explanation of compliance with international law. The preference-based approach that I articulate below is capacious enough to include changing preferences over time, but contextualizes this phenomenon within a broader model.

Ryan Goodman and Derek Jinks have proposed acculturation as a distinct causal mechanism in connection with compliance (2003, 2004, 2005). By acculturation, they mean the process by which actors assimilate beliefs and behavioral patterns of their culture. Acculturation is driven by identification with a reference group that generates cognitive and social pressures to conform with its behavioral expectations (Goodman and Jinks 2008: 726). Goodman and Jinks argue that neither coercion-based nor persuasion-based accounts of the influence of international law are sufficient to explain the pattern of isomorphism and decoupling that is observed among states. "Isomorphism" refers to a tendency of states to have similar structures and commitments, whereas "decoupling" refers to repeated departures from this similarity.

> Structural similarity exceeds that which might be explained by reference to the material incentives of target states, and yet persistent decoupling strongly suggests an "incomplete internalization" inconsistent with persuasion-based explanations. The upshot is that coercion and persuasion-based accounts, however indispensable for a comprehensive theory of global social influence, require supplementation. The resultant, more comprehensive theory of global social influence further suggests several regime design principles that might guide the fashioning of more effective human rights law and institutions. (Goodman and Jinks 2008: 727)

The managerial theory of compliance, developed by Abram and Antonia Chayes (1993, 1995), focuses on a specific set of domestic determinants of compliance. However, the one domestic determinant of compliance that this chapter highlights – the possibility of gain by domestic coalitions – is excluded from the determinants that form the core of their theory. The managerial approach explicitly rejects a focus on "a narrow set of externally defined 'interests' " (Chayes and Chayes 1993: 178). A focus on interests implies a focus on sanctions as a basis for enforcement:

> Because these [sanctions] are costly, difficult to mobilize, and of doubtful efficacy, they are infrequently used in practice. Meanwhile, analytic attention is diverted from a wide range of institutional and political mechanisms that in practice bear the burden of efforts to enhance treaty compliance. (Ibid.)

First, from the fact that states have presumably consented to the relevant international legal rule in order to be bound, the managerial approach infers that states are disposed to comply with the rule. This factor arises from a concern for efficiency and recognizes that the domestic cost–benefit analysis that gives rise to entry into an international legal commitment is costly and would not ordinarily be repeated continuously. This gives rise to a presumption of continued compliance. Of course, one response is that much depends on the extent to which the domestic cost–benefit analysis may change. Another response is that the cost–benefit analysis that gives rise to entry into the treaty may not support compliance with the treaty (Chayes and Chayes 1993: 184). In a sense, this determinant suggests that the international legal rule was unnecessary: that the state would have complied without the added influence of international law. This has been a basis for criticism of the Chayes approach (Downs, Rocke, and Barsoom 1996).

Second, assuming that states erect a bureaucratic mechanism to comply with the relevant rule, it is bureaucratically difficult to reverse course and determine not to comply. The domestic bureaucracy created in order to manage compliance may itself "lobby" for compliance in order to preserve its role.

Third, in a constructivist vein, states are disposed to comply out of a sense of obligation that is induced by virtue of the international legal rule. Furthermore, Chayes and Chayes suggest that much of the noncompliance that we see can be explained by managerial factors, rather than by interest-based rationalist accounts. In particular, they argue that most noncompliance is the result of (a) ambiguity and indeterminacy of treaty language, (b) limitations on the capacity of parties to carry out their undertakings, and (c) the temporal dimension of the social and economic changes contemplated by regulatory treaties (Chayes and Chayes 1993: 188). The "temporal dimension" is intended to refer to lags in compliance that Chayes and Chayes argue are anticipated when states enter treaties. However, many modern treaties contain transition periods that allow states to avoid this type of formal noncompliance.

Although the factors adduced by the managerial school no doubt have some relevance, a theory such as that developed in this chapter, which ascribes noncompliance to purposive political decisions to defect, would take account of the types of noncompliance that causes the greatest concern: cases where states intend to breach international law.

D. *Domestic Interests and Partisan Politics*

The liberal theory of international relations, as revised and developed by Andrew Moravcsik (1997), calls attention to the domestic sources of international relations preferences. Thus, "the demands of individuals and societal groups are treated as analytically prior to politics" (Moravcsik 1997: 517). Liberal theory focuses on preferences of states resulting from the aggregation of individual preferences by the state's political mechanisms. Governments then act purposively in world politics on the basis of these preferences. Thus, preferences are the cause of state behavior within a world system that provides constraints based on other states' preferences.

States are dynamic systems, with individuals and groups of individuals vying with one another for influence. To the extent that these systems are assumed to be closed, it may be appropriate to expect a fairly stable equilibrium among these individuals and groups. Coalition politics may be relatively stable, with change occurring based on demographic, technological, ideational, or other factors that disrupt the equilibrium. The market of international relations, in which states seek modifications of the behavior of other states, provides an additional, dynamic source of stimuli that may disrupt otherwise extant national political equilibria. On the other hand, as the market of international relations becomes deeper and more efficient, it will increasingly be a part of a normal national equilibrium.

Thus, while, as Putnam explains, "it is fruitless to debate whether domestic politics really determine international relations, or the reverse" (Putnam 1988: 427), the relationship between domestic politics and international relations has a particular directional structure. Liberal theory envisions states entering the "market" of international relations to satisfy preferences.[3] The "market" is a constraint: all preferences cannot be satisfied. Similarly, a nonmonopolist/monopsonist corporation entering the market cannot determine alone the price at which it sells and buys. And, as this chapter argues, the state is a dynamic aggregator of individual, group, and coalition preferences. Methodological individualism begins with individual preferences and moves up the vertical ladder of hierarchy according to the principle of subsidiarity in order to better satisfy those preferences.

Much of the rationalist literature developing the relationship between domestic politics and international relations focuses on international relations writ large, rather than international law in particular. Although some of this literature makes a turn toward international law, where it does so, its focus is often on "cooperation" in the form of adherence to rules, rather than the later, and more critical, moment of compliance with rules.[4] However, whether a counterparty is expected to comply will often determine the willingness of a state to adhere.

Putnam's two-level game theory suggests that the role of the national government in international relations is to mediate between two separate "games," the international game and the domestic game: "The unusual complexity of this two-level game is that moves that are rational for a player at one board (such as raising energy prices, conceding territory, or limiting auto imports) may be impolitic for that same player at the other board" (Putnam 1988: 434).

Although this provides important insights, especially as to the position of government officials caught in between, another perspective might suggest that there is no real conflict between these games. Rather, opportunities in the international game shape the strategy for maximizing an aggregate basket of preferences in the domestic game. The state is always maximizing its preferences under constraint. It is as erroneous to say that there is an inconsistency between the international and the domestic as it is to say that a corporation, entering the market, is in conflict with the market. It seeks the benefits of the market, in terms of the ability to purchase and to sell (Trachtman 2008). The corporation must decide whether to make or to buy – whether to be satisfied with internal production – or whether to contract with others. It only contracts to buy where this is superior to making. Similarly, in Coasean terms, where outsiders impose an externality on the corporation, the corporation only contracts with the outsider when it achieves a better outcome than acting on its own. Putnam sees the opportunity for national gain in the market of international relations as the exception, rather than the rule: "On occasion, however, clever players will spot a move on one board that will trigger realignments on other boards, enabling them to achieve otherwise unattainable objectives" (Putnam 1988: 434).

---

[3] See, for example, Dunoff and Trachtman (1999) (analogizing the "market of international relations" to the market of goods, except that states trade in units of power).

[4] But see Dai (2005, 2007) (developing a model of compliance, discussed below).

Putnam is right in his core insight that, if we examine the domestic game, we may find that there is an opportunity for a domestic equilibrium that would not exist except for the existence of the international game (what Putnam refers to as a "synergistic linkage") (Putnam 1988: 447–48). This is not the exception, however, but the rule in international cooperation and international law. As Jongryn Mo (1994) points out, domestic bargaining is endogenous to international cooperation – it is affected by opportunities for international cooperation. Domestic bargaining is constrained by the range of international opportunities, wherever the international opportunities allow a superior outcome compared to a purely domestic equilibrium. We must assume that international cooperation will only be efficient, and will only ensue, where it allows a superior aggregate outcome, either from a public choice or from a public interest standpoint.

It is important to focus on the role of realignments on the domestic board: on the fact that entry into, and compliance with, international law is *always* motivated by either the prospect of change in domestic coalitions that the new international law causes or by the prospect of avoiding unattractive change from an existing beneficial coalition. If there were no modification of domestic coalitions, there would be no purpose for the international law – once it is accepted that compliance is always a domestic political decision, the international law will only be effective if it modifies domestic politics.

Mo (1994) formalizes and extends Putnam's conjecture that greater domestic constraints can be a bargaining advantage in international negotiations. This conjecture seems dependent on a particular definition of the state's preferences and on a particular definition of advantage. That is, constraint can only be seen as an advantage if constraint is separated, and understood to be independent, from the state's actual preferences. However, it is difficult to understand how this type of artificial constraint could arise.

Putnam seems to assume that the state's true preferences are distinct from those expressed in domestic politics, and so it can be an advantage in achieving the true preferences if the constraint, which is visible and credible to counterparties in international negotiations, causes them to give up more of the surplus from an agreement than they otherwise would. This concept of constraint as advantage would be more logical if the constraint were a false constraint, or a false negotiating signal.

Otherwise, domestic constraint can be better understood simply in terms of domestic preferences, and the power that domestic constraint confers is simply the power of the negotiation concept of BATNA: the "best alternative to a negotiated agreement." This "power" is actually the simple fact that when the surplus generated by a negotiated agreement is less than that generated by an alternative unilateral action, we can expect the actor to choose the alternative unilateral action.

Mo develops a formal model of the interplay between domestic and international bargaining. He examines the context in which the negotiator has preferences different from those of her domestic constituents: the case of conflicting domestic interests. Although Mo's model, like Putnam's, focuses on adherence rather than compliance, his model could be extended by adding a compliance phase.

Mo's model has two stages: proposal and ratification. Mo represents domestic politics as the process of forming a viable coalition.

> The model presented is also an example of a nested game. We can think of international bargaining as consisting of domestic and international games that are played simultaneously. In the domestic game, the incentives of groups trying to form a domestic coalition are structured by the international game. Because groups need to make a proposal attractive to the foreign country, their incentives in choosing domestic coalition partners thus do not depend exclusively on domestic considerations (Mo 1994: 406).

Mo's model also provides that each group prefers to receive the benefits of an agreement earlier, rather than later, making it costly to cause delay by proposing unacceptable terms. However, the higher the discount factor – meaning the more that the group values future benefits – the more willing it is to adopt a strategy of waiting for a better offer. Mo accounts for this with the concept of a "continuation value," which is the discounted value of the expected outcome in continuing play *after rejection* of the current proposal (Mo 1994: 410). Players are expected to compare the continuation value to the value of the proposal and choose the greater.

Mo's model depicts a bargaining game of alternating offers between two countries. Each country has three lobbies (including as one "lobby" the government), and each country can only make an international agreement if two of the three lobbies agree. The foreign country will seek to provide concessions that will be marginally sufficient to induce a marginally sufficient number of the domestic country's lobbies to accept its proposal. Domestic lobbies left out of the coalition are assumed to receive no benefits.

Note, however, that the assumed foreign country strategy may be counterproductive at a compliance stage. If the foreign country offers concessions calculated to be just sufficient to induce marginally sufficient political support, then small shifts in lobby preferences may result in insufficient political support for compliance. So, depending on the incremental force of lobbies whose support increases upon adherence (which may include the government, international lawyers, and even other domestic players whose lobbying power is increased by the benefits they obtain from entry into the agreement), a foreign country strategy to ensure compliance would focus on concessions sufficient to induce marginally sufficient support for future compliance, not adherence.

This review of relevant literature has shown a variety of candidate causal factors relating to the determination by a state to adhere to or to comply with international law. These candidate causal factors are domestic structure; public law litigation and civil society action; ideas, acculturation, and managerial factors; and domestic interests. Although it is easy to see that any particular event of adherence or compliance would implicate more than one – and possibly all – of these factors, it is also possible to contextualize and interrelate these factors. A preference-based model can understand domestic structures, public law litigation, managerial factors, and partisan politics as mechanisms that will determine the relative influence of particular types of preferences, whereas ideas and acculturation can be understood as mechanisms that can change preferences. In Part II, I explore a model that highlights preferences as the basis for adherence to and compliance with international law.

II. A MODEL OF ADHERENCE TO AND COMPLIANCE WITH INTERNATIONAL LAW

In this part,[5] I begin to develop a model of adherence to and compliance with international law, focusing on domestic lobbying and voting based on preferences as the causal factors. This approach is based, in part, on the Grossman-Helpman political support model designed for use in connection with international trade negotiations (Grossman and Helpman 1995: 678). In that model, incumbent governments are assumed to seek to maximize a political support function. This political support function is assumed to have two components. First, organized interest groups are assumed to make political contributions that can assist in reelection, thus providing an incentive for governments to implement policies that enhance organized interest group welfare. Second, voters are assumed to respond in their voting behavior to their own welfare, and so one can expect some incentive to implement policies that enhance voter welfare.[6] The government then sets its policy to aggregate a weighted sum of total contributions and aggregate social welfare. Politicians thus seek to please the "winning" lobbies and the electorate as a whole.

I adapt the Grossman-Helpman model of the lobbying process as follows: each lobby, representing a particular policy decision in connection with international law (whether for or against the adherence or compliance decision), confronts the government with a contribution schedule. The contribution schedule arrays contributions against policy decisions. The government then sets a policy and collects from each lobby the appropriate contribution. "An equilibrium is a set of contribution schedules such that each lobby's schedule maximizes the aggregate utility of the lobby's members, taking as given the schedules of the other lobby groups" (Grossman and Helpman 1994: 836). This model has the structure of a common agency problem: a situation in which several principals seek to influence the behavior of a single agent. "The government here serves as an agent for the various (and conflicting) special interest groups, while bearing a cost for implementing an inefficient policy that stems from its accountability to the general electorate" (Grossman and Helpman 1994).

---

[5] For a more extensive exposition, see Trachtman (2010).
[6] It may also be that politicians are civic-minded, resulting in precisely the same motivation, assuming that the voter's utility is actually congruent with the politician's civic vision.

Here, for simplicity, I do not examine the distinction or the strategic relationship between legislatures and executives; I aggregate these components of government. I am interested here in focusing attention not on the governmental processes or the structure of government, but on the constellation of political support. The lobbies make implicit offers relating prospective contributions to the policies of the government.

The Grossman-Helpman model is designed to explain the effectiveness of lobbying in regard to trade policy, and specifically, tariffs and subsidies (Grossman and Helpman 1994: 834). Individual preferences over protectionism are assumed to arise from their sector-specific endowments. Following Mancur Olson (1965), there are some owners of factors of production who are able to organize, and some who are unable to do so. The unorganized owners of factors of production do not make contributions, and so lack this type of influence over policy. I assume that each lobby structures its contribution schedule to maximize the total welfare of its members. Like Grossman and Helpman (1994: 838), I am first "interested in the political equilibrium of a two-stage noncooperative game, in which the lobbies simultaneously choose their political contribution schedules in the first stage and the government sets policy in the second."

In *The Politics of Free Trade Agreements*, Grossman and Helpman (1995) extend their 1994 model to examine the conditions under which two states might agree to a free trade agreement. This model uses assumptions about the welfare effects of trade liberalization and addresses adherence rather than compliance. Therefore, this extended model is not directly adaptable to a general international law model of compliance. However, it provides a good basis for a broader model of adherence and can be extended to analyze compliance.

Grossman and Helpman (1995: 668–70) assume that the status quo prior to an international agreement is itself a domestic political equilibrium in each state. This assumption seems appropriate. Thus, the opportunity for an international agreement can be understood as an exogenous shock to the existing domestic equilibrium. The opportunity for an international agreement changes the relative prices. In the trade context, the possibility for foreign compliance with a commitment to liberalize makes the price of domestic protectionism higher by engaging the concerns of domestic producers for export.

In the trade context where Grossman and Helpman develop their model, it is possible to assume that specific industry groups, or lobbies, have specific types of interests in trade policy. In the broader international law context, lobby interests will be more diverse, and preferences cannot be assumed to be confined to narrow wealth gains. However, there may be industry groups, ethnic groups, or other groups that have narrower interests.

Although, in the Grossman-Helpman model, lobbies make their contributions contingent on trade policy, we may generalize to assume that lobbies make their contributions contingent on international legal policy. For example, within domestic societies, there will be a lobby group that is interested in increased human rights in other states. Although this interest may be explained in terms of preferences, the types of preferences involved will depend on the particular legal rule involved, and this type of interest cannot be compared directly with other types of interests that may be measured in monetary terms. Nor are we able to make any assumptions about the utility function of any particular group. Rather, the only assumption that seems defensible is that each international law rule will harm some groups and help some other groups. However, one type of lobby generally appears to be in favor of international legal adherence and compliance.[7] That type of lobby is exemplified, in the United States by the members of the American Society of International Law (ASIL). I will discuss this type of lobby in greater detail below.

It is important to recognize that, in this political Pareto efficiency-based model, "compliance can be rational even if the country as a whole pays for it more than benefits from it" (Dai 2007). And the converse is true: compliance may be irrational, in the sense that it is not supported by sufficient political force, even if the country as a whole benefits from it more than it pays. However, if public welfare is included in the government's utility function (as in the Grossman-Helpman model) through the mechanism of voting, then international legal rules that increase public welfare are more likely to meet with both adherence and compliance.

A. Depth and the Adherence–Compliance Lag

The question regarding compliance is thus: conditional upon entry into an international legal rule at an initial time (t_1), what are the circumstances under which a particular country will comply with that legal rule at a later time (t_2)? I also assume that domestic politics change, in an "obsolescing bargains" (Vernon 1971: 46–53) sense (Maggi and Rodríguez-Clare 1998). Thus, the coalition that supports adherence at t_1 may not have the same structure or magnitude, and may not even support compliance, at t_2.

I assume an international legal rule with some "depth" in the sense described in the legalization literature: the rule requires behavior that would not occur without the added inducement that arises from operation of the rule (Downs *et al.* 1996; Goldstein *et al.* 2001). In our context, the domestic political process by itself and without any effect of international law would not decide to conform national behavior to the rule. This is a slightly different issue from the question, addressed, for example, by Grossman and Helpman, of whether the domestic political process would decide to adhere to an international agreement. It is possible that *adherence* to an international agreement would be supported purely by domestic political forces, whereas *compliance* with the same agreement would require the

---

[7] Of course, there will be exceptions. For example, some rules of international law may be found to be objectionable by some portion of the membership of the ASIL.

additional effect of international law. Indeed, domestic adherence under "depth" for the adhering state would presumably be conditioned on an expectation of foreign compliance, depending on the magnitude of other, nonreciprocal incentives for compliance.

I further assume that, in order for any state to decide to comply with an international legal rule, there must be a coalition of domestic lobbies strong enough to determine national behavior. This assumption can survive the diversity of national politics: it is not necessary to have a dominant interest group-based politics, such as that of the United States, for this type of model to apply. Even autocracies involve sensitivity to political support, although the relative importance of political support compared to government policy may differ markedly. Furthermore, decision-making may, in some circumstances, take place in arenas that are insulated from interest group politics, and even from executive policy. This is the case with international legal rules that have direct effect, in which the decision is delegated exclusively to courts. I focus on lobbies more broadly, recognizing that other mechanisms, such as courts, may play the critical role in compliance (Van Aaken 2009).

B. *Information Problems with Adherence and Compliance*

Xinyuan Dai has developed a model of compliance with international law, incorporating both electoral leverage and informational advantage as sources of influence for a domestic lobby (2005: 363). Dai models a government's compliance decision in the context of competing domestic lobbies. She emphasizes the information problem whereby lobbies cannot observe the government's action directly. The accuracy of the lobbies' inference about the government's action "depends on how much information they have about the policy process and how much resources they invest in monitoring the governmental action" (Dai 2005: 365). Dai thus develops a model in which a government's compliance decision is determined by both the electoral leverage of the domestic lobby and the domestic lobby's informational position.

In Dai's model, interest groups differ in (a) their preferences regarding compliance – for example, one group may prefer a low compliance level, while the other prefers a high compliance level – and (b) their informational endowments. She models informational endowments as a separate variable, even though it might be that information endowments vary with the magnitude of preferences. Her main concern is that interest groups do not perfectly observe compliance *efforts* (Dai 2005: 368, 384). However, we might speculate that in many international law areas, interest groups would perfectly observe *compliance itself*.

Although recognizing the importance of Dai's reference to each lobby's informational advantage as a source of influence, I make the simplifying assumption that the informational advantage is either included in the measure of political strength or is co-variable with the magnitude of political strength or preferences, and, therefore,

I do not account separately for informational advantage. Furthermore, although Dai's approach assumes that lobbies have difficulty in assessing the degree of effort expended by government to comply, I focus on actual measures of compliance rather than efforts toward compliance, and assume that actual compliance is easier to measure than efforts. This will not always be true, but it seems to be a reasonable simplification. In appropriate circumstances, separate accounting for information would be important.

As might be expected, because it is built into Dai's model, Dai finds that where the group that favors compliance has greater electoral leverage and monitoring ability, compliance increases (Dai 2005: 364). Conversely, where the group that favors violation has greater leverage and monitoring ability, compliance decreases. Of course, because aggregate social welfare is included in the equation, these differences in leverage and monitoring ability are not necessarily by themselves determinative, and the model does not tell us how to quantify the contributions of these different factors. Furthermore, as Dai points out, the value to the incumbent of reelection, and his or her discount factor, will affect the incumbent's susceptibility to influence by lobbies (Dai 2005: 374).

C. Reciprocity

A number of scholars have examined reciprocity, or retaliation, as a means of inducing compliance with international law (Keohane 2005; Guzman 2008). This theoretical approach is elegant and compelling: states comply with international law in order to induce other states to comply, or in order to induce other states to continue to refrain from retaliation. In Keohane's "specific reciprocity" (as opposed to diffuse reciprocity) sense, there is little difference between reciprocity and retaliation (Keohane 1986: 4).

Most work in this area has arisen from a growing rationalist debate regarding compliance with customary international law (Guzman 2002; Swaine 2002; Verdier 2002; Goldsmith and Posner 2005; Norman and Trachtman 2005). Norman and Trachtman (2005: 548), for example, developed a repeated multilateral prisoners' dilemma model of formation of and compliance with customary international law. Norman and Trachtman highlighted some of the characteristics of different states' domestic politics that might affect their level of patience and their resulting propensity to accept and comply with rules of customary international law. (In custom, the adherence and compliance phases may be less distinct than in treaty.) However, they did not analyze the decision-making process within states or the lobbying game within states. Other rationalist approaches focusing on retaliation are characterized by the same limitation.

A good example of the type of specific reciprocity and engagement of domestic interests that benefits from reciprocity comes from the trade context. As discussed by Grossman and Helpman (1995: 687) exporters are a domestic constituency interested in foreign liberalization. Therefore, exporters are concerned with domestic compliance with liberalization commitments in order to ensure against reciprocal punishment in the form of protectionism abroad.

It is important to note that reciprocity may be complex: it is not necessarily tit-for-tat, in which each state promises the same performance (Putnam 1988: 446–47). Indeed, the possibility for complex barter or package deals increases the set of possible transactions. On the other hand, uncertainty as to which commitments the counterparty will suspend in response to a violation would limit the likelihood that the domestic lobby concerned with those commitments will lobby for compliance. There may be a collective action problem among possible lobbies. One way to reduce the effects of this collective action problem would be to designate in advance, and specifically, the type of retaliatory action that the counter-party will take.[8]

D. *Role of the Pro-International Law Lobby*

A lobby that focuses on promoting the use of international law (a *pro-international law lobby* or PILL) can be included in a model of the domestic politics of international law in the same way that other lobbies are included. It may be motivated by an expectation that more international law will bring more power and income to international lawyers. This could not only cause the PILL to argue for more international law, but also cause it to argue for more compliance, as more compliance would be expected to evidence the importance of international law. Evidence for the importance of international law, in turn, would add to the prestige and income of international lawyers. Furthermore, more compliance with international law might result in more international law, further benefiting the PILL. It is in connection with the PILL – and with the government as a "lobby" itself, as described below – that the constructivist model may have the greatest power: ideas and engagement may support compliance through the PILL and the government.

The PILL may, alternatively or in addition, be motivated by altruism, including a general idea that international law provides broad benefits, and, in this sense, it might be included in constructivist or sociological models. Importantly, this public welfare position may be held both by the PILL and by government officials. The PILL may seek to educate government officials as to the public welfare effects of compliance with international law. The altruistic position might be based on facts or based on beliefs. In a more recent World Public Opinion survey (2009), respondents in 17 of 21 countries placed compliance with international law above national interest.

It is important to note that there may also be an anti-international law lobby.[9] To the extent that such a lobby exists, its effects can be netted against the PILL, and to

---

[8] This would be one benefit of the type of "contingent liberalization commitments" suggested by Robert Lawrence (2003) as a structure for remedies in the trade context.

[9] Consider Spiro (2000).

should avoid easy hypotheses linking the institutional form of the organization (as opposed to its identity or setting) to the sort of legal argumentation it will use. Even courts, limited to making legal arguments in a public setting, have ways of adjusting the amount, directness, and tone of their opinions. Tribunals may be bold, detailed, and comprehensive, but they may equally avoid issues and even turn away cases, depending on the parties, issues at stake, and their sense of their appropriate role. One important implication of this study is that each organization should be prepared to examine these parameters, including through scrutiny of its own identity, just as the ICRC has. For instance, an NGO may discover that its strategies emphasizing law talk (including stretches of the law well beyond *lex lata*) require adjustment.

These very choices show that the invocation of international law (and, *a fortiori*, its public invocation) does not represent the exclusive or even dominant method for seeking law compliance. If we assume actors' persuasion strategies are rational and based on what works, then we can say that achieving *compliance with law* does not necessitate – or even argue for – a conversation *laden with law*. Legal argumentation might assist the task, but it can equally undermine it. As Harold Koh has pointed out (1997: 2600–01), the relationship between norms and behavior that matches those norms forms a spectrum from (a) coincidence, or matching by chance, to (b) conformity, or matching only when convenient and with little sense of obligation, to (c) compliance, matching to gain incentives or avoid punishment, to (d) obedience, matching due to a target's internal acceptance of the norm as part of its value system.[8] Obedience could entail an internal acceptance of the content of the norm, or, as H. L. A. Hart preferred, an internal acceptance of the bindingness of the norm (Hart 1961: 112–14).

Although Koh considers obedience the highest form of respect for law (1997: 2645), the modes of argumentation adopted by institutions seeking to promote law show that they are more than willing to settle for compliance,[9] given the hurdles to obedience. That is, the choices that persuading entities make regarding the modes of legal argumentation are *choices about how to achieve behavior consistent with the law* – about respect for law in the broadest sense of the term. They are not seeking to persuade a target to internalize a norm, although they are not opposed to it when that is feasible. Although scholars can usefully identify reasons why entities may follow legal norms, the mode of argumentation adopted by a persuading entity is based on a much more basic question – how will its use of the law promote compliance in this case, given this dispute, these actors, this setting, and the persuading institution's identity?

This conclusion about the limitations of a focus on obedience is consistent with other theoretical insights about the influence of law on behavior. International relations scholars recognize that obedience is too much to expect of states and other

---

[8] Koh relies on Kelman (1958), although Kelman defined his terms somewhat differently.
[9] My use of the term *compliance* includes Koh's conformity.

actors, as well as hard to observe or measure. Institutionalist scholars, for their part, do not regard obedience or internalization as essential to effective regimes. And the literature on socialization identifies distinct processes of social influence aimed at conformity and compliance (Johnston 2001: 499). In the domestic context, Raz (1990: 178–82) has pointed out that the best law can really expect of individuals is compliance in the sense used by Koh (although Raz uses the term "conformity" for the same idea).

Indeed, as the ICRC demonstrates, even institutions that place a priority on – indeed, that make one of their defining missions – the implementation of specific bodies of international law are prepared to forego obedience for compliance. For them, avoidance of law talk can be just another means to that end. If a state or armed group observes the rules because it has become convinced of the advantages of observance, rather than accepted the rule in its heart, the ICRC is prepared to call its work a success. Moreover, even those groups that adopt a wholly differ-ent modus operandi on legal argumentation, such as large international human rights NGOs with their public, detailed, direct, and confrontational approach, seem prepared, at least based on my interactions with them, to settle for compliance. Unlike the ICRC, they believe that such law talk is necessary or the best path to compliance, as well as central to their identity – but they, too, do not insist on obedience.

For lawyers, a persuasive process oriented toward compliance might represent a poor substitute for the rule of law. From the perspective of improving behavior, internal acceptance of the rule, either its substance or its bindingness, should remain the long-term goal. The ICRC recognizes this aim through work on implementation of law (e.g., the need for armed forces and groups to develop codes of conduct with teeth). With internalization, entities seeking respect for rules avoid repeatedly engag-ing with the same targets. In addition, for standards whose customary international law status is questioned, obedience, in the sense of acceptance of the rule because it is law, adds that magical ingredient – *opinio juris* – that turns practice into custom. Even consistent compliance falls short in this sense.

Yet, in the end, international lawyers should not object to compliance compared to obedience. In the case of IHL, given the obstacles to internalization during armed conflict, the gravity of the violations and thus the urgency of terminating them, and the actors with whom ICRC delegates interact – not typically lawyers in foreign ministries or legislatures – compliance sounds hard enough. Beyond the ICRC, Raz's insight regarding the realistic goals of a legal system seems even more compelling at the international level; and sophisticated international actors comprehend that their goal of furthering law compliance can be undercut if they make the target's legal obligations too prominent during the persuasion process. Legal scholars obsessed with the ideal of internalization are missing the true picture of advocacy in the international arena, where actors concerned with norms argue – and settle – for action merely in conformity with them.

REFERENCES

Abbott, Kenneth W., Robert O. Keohane., Andrew Moravcsik, Anne-Marie Slaughter, and Duncan Snidal (2000). "The Concept of Legalization," *International Organization*, Vol. 54, No. 3, pp. 401–19.

Abbott, Kenneth W., and Duncan Snidal (2013). "Law, Legalization and Politics: An Agenda for the Next Generation of IL/IR Scholars," in Jeffrey L. Dunoff and Mark A. Pollack (eds.), *Interdisciplinary Perspectives on International Law and International Relations: The State of the Art* (New York: Cambridge University Press), pp. 33–56.

Alvarez, Jose E. (2001). "Do Liberal States Behave Better? A Critique of Slaughter's Liberal Theory," *European Journal of International Law*, Vol. 12, No. 2, pp. 183–246.

Bangerter, Olivier (2008). "The ICRC and Non-State Armed Groups," in Geneva Call (ed.), *Exploring Criteria & Conditions for Engaging Armed Non-state Actors to Respect Humanitarian Law & Human Rights Law* (Geneva: Geneva Call), pp. 74–85.

Barnett, Michael (2009). "Evolution without Progress? Humanitarianism in a World of Hurt," *International Organization*, Vol. 63, No. 4, pp. 621–63.

Bellal, Annyssa, and Stuart Casey-Maslen (2010). "Ownership of Norms by Non-state Actors: Policies and Programs: A Review of Practice" (unpublished paper of the Geneva Academy of International Humanitarian Law and Human Rights).

Brunnée, Jutta, and Stephen J. Toope (2010). *Legitimacy and Legality in International Law: An Interactional Account* (Cambridge: Cambridge University Press, 2010).

——— (2013). "Constructivism and International Law," in Jeffrey L. Dunoff and Mark A. Pollack (eds.), *Interdisciplinary Perspectives on International Law and International Relations: The State of the Art* (New York: Cambridge University Press), pp. 119–45.

Carruthers, Bruce G., and Terrence Halliday (2006). "Negotiating Globalization: Global Scripts and Intermediation in the Construction of Asian Insolvency Regimes," *Law and Social Inquiry*, Vol. 31, No. 3, pp. 521–84.

Chaiken, Shelly, Wendy Wood, and Alice H. Eagley (1996). "Principles of Persuasion," in E. Tory Higgins and Arie W. Kruglanski (eds.), *Social Psychology: Handbook of Basic Principles* (New York: Guilford Press), pp. 702–44.

Chayes, Abram, and Antonia Handler Chayes (1995). *The New Sovereignty: Compliance with International Regulatory Agreements* (Cambridge, MA: Harvard University Press).

Checkel, Jeffrey T. (2001). "Why Comply? Social Learning and European Identity Change," *International Organization*, Vol. 55, No. 3, pp. 553–88.

Deitelhoff, Nicole (2009). "The Discursive Process of Legalization: Charting Islands of Persuasion in the ICC Case," *International Organization*, Vol. 63, No. 1, pp. 33–65.

Franck, Thomas M. (1990). *The Power of Legitimacy among Nations* (New York: Oxford University Press).

Finnemore, Martha, and Kathryn Sikkink (1998). "International Norm Dynamics and Political Change," *International Organization*, Vol. 52, No. 4, pp. 887–917.

Geneva Call (2010). *Non-state Actor Mine Action and Compliance to the Deed of Commitment Banning Anti-personnel Landmines: January 2008 – June 2010* (Geneva: Geneva Call).

Gibson, Dirk Cameron (1991). *The Role of Communication in the Practice of Law* (Lanham, MD: University Press of America).

Goodman, Ryan, and Derek Jinks (2004). "How to Influence States: Socialization and International Human Rights Law," *Duke Law Journal*, Vol. 54, No. 3, pp. 621–703.

Grobe, Christian (2010). "The Power of Words: Argumentative Persuasion in International Negotiations," *European Journal of International Relations*, Vol. 16, No. 1, pp. 5–29.

Gross, Oren, and Fionnuala Ní Aoláin (2006). *Law in Times of Crisis: Emergency Powers in Theory and Practice* (New York: Cambridge University Press).

Guzman, Andrew T. (2008). *How International Law Works: A Rational Choice Theory* (New York: Oxford University Press).

Hart, H. L. A. (1961). *The Concept of Law* (New York: Oxford University Press).

Hawkins, Darren (2004). "Explaining Costly International Institutions: Persuasion and Enforceable Human Rights Norms," *International Studies Quarterly*, Vol. 48, No. 4, pp. 779–804

Higgins, Rosalyn (1970). "The Place of International Law in the Settlement of Disputes by the Security Council," *American Journal of International Law*, Vol. 64, No. 1, pp. 1–18.

Hohfeld, Wesley Newcomb (1919). *Fundamental Legal Conceptions as Applied in Judicial Reasoning and Other Legal Essays* (New Haven, CT: Yale University Press).

ICRC (2004). "What Is the ICRC's role in Ensuring Respect for Humanitarian Law?," available at http://icrc.org/web/eng/siteengo.nsf/htmlall/5kzmkm?opendocument.

———— (2005). "Action by the International Committee of the Red Cross in the Event of Violations of International Humanitarian Law or of Other Fundamental Rules Protecting Persons in Situations of Violence," reprinted in *International Review of the Red Cross*, Vol. 87, No. 858, pp. 393–400.

———— (2006). "Case No. 142, ICRC, Iran/Iraq Memoranda," reprinted in Marco Sassòli and Antoine A. Bouvier (eds.), *How Does Law Protect in War?: Cases, Documents and Teaching Materials on Contemporary Practice in International Humanitarian Law*, 2nd ed. (Geneva: ICRC), pp. 1529–40.

———— (2008). "Increasing Respect for International Humanitarian Law in Non-international Armed Conflicts" (Geneva: ICRC), available at http://www.icrc.org/eng/assets/files/other/icrc_002_0923.pdf.

———— (2009a). "Gaza: ICRC Demands Urgent Access to Wounded as Israeli Army Fails to Assist Wounded Palestinians," available at http://www.icrc.org/eng/resources/documents/news-release/palestine-news-080109.htm.

———— (2009b). "US Detention Related to the Fight against Terrorism – the Role of the ICRC," available at http://www.icrc.org/eng/resources/documents/misc/united-states-detention-240209.htm.

———— (2009c). "Sri Lanka: ICRC Makes Urgent Appeal for Wounded to be Given Medical Care," available at http://www.icrc.org/eng/resources/documents/news-release/sri-lanka-news-180509.htm.

———— (2009d). "Armed Groups and the ICRC: A Challenging but Necessary Dialogue" (on file with author).

Johnston, Alastair Iain (2001). "Treating International Institutions as Social Environments," *International Studies Quarterly*, Vol. 45, No. 4, pp. 487–515.

Johnstone, Ian (2008). "Legislation and Adjudication in the UN Security Council: Bringing Down the Deliberative Deficit," *American Journal of International Law*, Vol. 102, No. 2, pp. 275–308.

———— (2011). *The Power of Deliberation: International Law, Politics and Organizations* (New York: Oxford University Press).

Kellenberger, Jakob (2004). "Speaking Out or Remaining Silent in Humanitarian Work," *International Review of the Red Cross*, Vol. 86, No. 855, pp. 593–609.

Kelman, Herbert C. (1958). "Compliance, Identification, and Internalization: Three Processes of Attitude Change," *Journal of Conflict Resolution*, Vol. 2, No. 1, pp. 51–60.

Keohane, Robert O. (1984). *After Hegemony: Cooperation and Discord in the World Political Economy* (Princeton, NJ: Princeton University Press).

——— (1997). "International Relations and International Law: Two Optics," *Harvard International Law Journal*, Vol. 38, No. 2, pp. 487–502.

Koh, Harold Hongju (1997). "Why Do Nations Obey International Law?" *Yale Law Journal*, Vol. 106, No. 8, pp. 2599–659.

——— (1998). "Bringing International Law Home," *Houston Law Review*, Vol. 35, No. 3, pp. 623–81.

Kratochwil, Friedrich (1989). *Rules, Norms, and Decisions: On the Conditions of Practical and Legal Reasoning in International Relations and Domestic Affairs* (Cambridge: Cambridge University Press).

Lutz, Ellen, and Kathryn Sikkink (2001). "International Human Rights Law in Practice: The Justice Cascade: The Evolution and Impact of Foreign Human Rights Trials in Latin America," *Chicago Journal of International Law*, Vol. 2, No. 1, pp. 1–33.

McDougal, Myres S., and W. Michael Reisman (1981). "The Prescribing Function in the World Constitutive Process: How International Law Is Made," in Myres S. McDougal and W. Michael Reisman (eds.), *International Law Essays: A Supplement to International Law in Contemporary Perspective* (Mineola, NY: Foundation Press), pp. 355–80.

Melzer, Nils (2008). "Interpretive Guidance on the Notion of Direct Participation in Hostilities under International Humanitarian Law," *International Review of the Red Cross*, Vol. 90, No. 872, pp. 991–1047.

Nash, Kate (2009). *The Cultural Politics of Human Rights: Comparing the US and UK* (Cambridge: Cambridge University Press).

Nollkaemper, André (1992). "On the Effectiveness of International Rules," *Acta Politica*, Vol. 27, No. 1, pp. 49–70.

Payne, Rodger A. (2001). "Persuasion, Frames and Norm Construction," *European Journal of International Relations*, Vol. 7, No. 1, pp. 37–61.

Pfanner, Toni (2009). "Various Mechanisms and Approaches for Implementing International Humanitarian Law and Protecting and Assisting War Victims," *International Review of the Red Cross*, Vol. 91, No. 874, pp. 279–328.

Ratner, Steven R. (2000). "Does International Law Matter in Preventing Ethnic Conflict?," *New York University Journal of International Law and Politics*, Vol. 32, No. 3, pp. 591–698.

——— (2001). "Corporations and Human Rights: A Theory of Responsibility," *Yale Law Journal*, Vol. 111, No. 3, pp. 443–545.

——— (2007). "Business," in Daniel Bodansky, Jutta Brunnée, and Ellen Hey (eds.), *Oxford Handbook of International Environmental Law* (New York: Oxford University Press), pp. 807–28.

——— (2011). "Law Promotion beyond Law Talk: The Red Cross, Persuasion, and the Laws of War," *European Journal of International Law*, Vol. 22, No. 2, pp. 459–506.

Raz, Joseph (1990). *Practical Reason and Norms* (New York: Oxford University Press).

Reinard, John C. (2002). "Persuasion in the Legal Setting," in James Price Dillard and Michael Pfau (eds.), *The Persuasion Handbook: Developments in Theory and Practice* (Thousand Oaks, CA: Sage Publications), pp. 543–604.

Reisman, W. Michael (1981). "International Lawmaking: A Process of Communication," *American Society of International Law Proceedings*, Vol. 75, pp. 101–20.

——— (1992). "The Concept and Functions of Soft Law in International Politics," in Emmanuel G. Bello and Prince Bola A. Ajibola (eds.), *Essays in Honor of Judge Taslim Olawale Elias*, Vol. 1, Contemporary International Law and Human Rights (London: Martinus Nijhoff Publisher), pp. 135–44.

Rieke, Richard D., Malcolm O. Sillars, and Tarla Rai Peterson (2009). *Argumentation and Critical Decision Making*, 7th ed. (Boston: Pearson/Allyn and Bacon).

Risse, Thomas (2000). "'Let's Argue!': Communicative Action in World Politics," *International Organization*, Vol. 54, No. 1, pp. 1–39.

Ruggie, John Gerard (1998). "What Makes the World Hang Together? Neo-Utilitarianism and the Social Constructivist Challenge," *International Organization*, Vol. 52, No. 4, pp. 855–85.

Schimmelfennig, Frank (2001). "The Community Trap: Liberal Norms, Rhetorical Action, and the Eastern Enlargement of the European Union," *International Organization*, Vol. 55, No. 1, pp. 47–80.

Simmons, Beth A. (2009). *Mobilizing for Human Rights: International Law in Domestic Politics* (New York: Cambridge University Press).

Slaughter, Anne-Marie (1995). "International Law in a World of Liberal States," *European Journal of International Law*, Vol. 6, No. 4, pp. 503–38.

24

Against Compliance

Lisa L. Martin

International institutions and organizations influence state behavior and policy.[1] However, the nature of this influence, its extent, and the conditions under which it is most evident are not fully specified and are the subject of much empirical research. One challenge in this empirical exploration has been identifying appropriate outcome variables with which to measure institutional effects. As I argue below, much of the literature, in both political science and international legal studies, has settled on compliance as a dependent variable. The concept of compliance may have certain advantages, such as the relatively systematic and accessible collection of data on patterns of compliance.

However, compliance is a legal concept that is unusually ill-suited to the central social-scientific pursuit: the identification and measurement of causal effects. Identification of the causal effect of an institution requires asking a counterfactual: how would state behavior have varied in the absence of the institution?[2] In most instances, asking about compliance provides no leverage on this question. Compliance is a concept of obvious and inherent interest to lawyers and legal scholars, whose normative focus involves enhancing degrees of compliance. As such, data on compliance are abundantly available. However, political scientists using such data as a proxy for institutional effects make errors of both omission and commission – mistakenly

My thanks go to Inken von Borzyskowski for providing excellent research assistance, and to comments from numerous audiences, including the International Relations Colloquium at the University of Wisconsin–Madison. I especially appreciate comments on a very early draft from David A. Singer.

[1] Following Mearsheimer (1994/95: 8), I understand an international institution to be "a set of rules that stipulate the ways in which states should cooperate and compete with each other." This sparse definition is consistent with the standard usage in political science and economics. International organizations are formalized interstate bodies that oversee these sets of rules. In legal scholarship, what I call "organizations" are sometimes referred to as "institutions," perhaps leading to some confusion. When I refer to compliance with institutions, I understand this as identical to compliance with sets of rules.

[2] For a similar argument, see Raustiala (2000: 388).

attributing state behavior to institutional participation, and underestimating the influence of institutions on states that are not "in compliance." This is a dilemma that cannot be addressed by more careful treatment of compliance; it can only be addressed by dropping compliance as a central concept in the study of institutional effects.

I begin this chapter by summarizing some of the major work in international relations (IR) on compliance with the rules specified by international institutions. I then turn to a review of work on compliance by legal scholars, primarily with the aim of clarifying the conceptualization of compliance. The third section of this chapter elaborates my critique of the use of compliance as an outcome variable by political scientists. I conclude by drawing lessons for the study of institutional effects.

I. COMPLIANCE IN POLITICAL SCIENCE (INTERNATIONAL RELATIONS)

Much scholarship on the role of international institutions and organizations in world politics has examined the effects of institutions on state policies and behavior, and a substantial portion has focused on whether and when states comply with the rules and norms of the institutions that they choose to join. In this section, I examine and summarize both classics in the study of compliance and the best newer work by political scientists on state compliance with international institutions and agreements.

One of the most widely cited articles in the study of compliance is Abram Chayes and Antonia Chayes' classic, "On Compliance" (Chayes and Chayes 1993). In this article, Chayes and Chayes set forth what has become known as the "managerial" view of compliance. Their view identifies deeply with the legal tradition, supporting Louis Henkin's (1979) supposition that most states comply with their international legal obligations, most of the time. Although Chayes and Chayes do specify a number of general factors that could lead states to comply, their interest is not in explaining variation in patterns of compliance based on institutional or state incentives. Instead, their pressing questions focus on those who have crafted agreements with which states do not comply. Why did drafters of agreements misestimate the capacity or willingness of governments to behave in certain ways? Could support for parties to an agreement enhance their capacity for compliance? Could agreements be recrafted so that compliance becomes less problematic?

Downs, Rocke, and Barsoom (1996) soon published a powerful rejoinder to the managerial perspective. They argued, from a rationalist perspective, that the managerial perspective misunderstood the actual role of international agreements. Compliance (as I also argue) is not of particular interest. States might only sign onto those agreements that they would find easy to adopt. International cooperation would then be shallow. Compliance, as an outcome measure, suffers from severe selection bias effects; international cooperation is likely just shallow cooperation. I agree with parts of Downs, Rocke, and Barsoom's critique, but want to take it further. All international cooperation is probably not shallow; some is quite deep. My claim, in contrast to Downs, Rocke, and Barsoom, is that we cannot possibly assess the depth (or shallowness) of international cooperation if we rely on compliance as a valid measure of outcomes.

Works on compliance in international politics by political scientists, represented by the prominent publications summarized below, roughly fall into three general categories. One body of work uses the language of compliance, but in the operationalization of it disregards legal judgments and ends up measuring cooperation or domestic policy change rather than compliance. A second set accepts the legal conceptualization and operationalization of compliance, but conflates it with the political concept of cooperation. A third category takes the legal concept of compliance seriously, accepts the judgment of legal scholars about who is in compliance, and goes on to persuasively demonstrate the factors that give rise to patterns of compliance. I argue later in this chapter that these lessons about compliance, unfortunately, tell us little about the causal impact of international institutions or agreements.

Beth Simmons' (2009) thorough and persuasive account of the impact of international human rights law on domestic politics illustrates a common treatment of compliance by political scientists. Simmons studies a range of important international human rights laws: civil rights such as religious freedom, women's rights, protection against torture, and children's rights. Throughout, she asks two sets of questions: when do states ratify international human rights agreements? And when do they comply with them? Her measure of compliance, however, is not based on a legal reading of what would constitute full or partial compliance. As Simmons (2009: 19) argues: "Although I often use the language of compliance, this part [of the book] is about behavioral or institutional changes ... whether or not that behavior constitutes full legal compliance with every aspect of the treaty."

Simmons' justifications for measuring behavioral change rather than technical compliance are compelling. First, she argues that improvement in human rights practices is of substantive interest regardless of legal judgments about compliance. Second, she points out that authoritative judgments about compliance are typically absent unless a "courtlike determination" has occurred (Simmons 2009: 19). Additionally, parties to agreements often recognize numerous paths to compliance, and legal treatment of various loopholes in treaties makes assessing compliance difficult. Given these impediments to the actual operationalization of compliance, Simmons instead studies something of far more interest to social scientists: the conditional impact of treaties on state behavior. However, this series of judgments yields an important question: why use the language of compliance if that is not in fact the behavior under inspection?

Simmons finds that human rights agreements typically have a conditional impact on behavior and that they have in some situations been instrumental in encouraging governments to improve their human rights records. Although analyses of the unconditional effects of agreements often find that they have no effect, or even a negative effect, once selection effects, provisions for lags, and control variables are taken into account, the positive effects of human rights commitments emerge. In general, the effects are conditional on two domestic factors: mobilization of domestic groups and a relatively independent court system. In some instances, she also finds that the effects are most pronounced in states undergoing democratic transitions.

Although there is a fair amount of consistency in Simmons' results, there is also some important variation, and substantial variation in the statistical specifications that lead to her results. For example, the lag structure used varies from model to model, without a substantive rationale for such variation. Substantively, in considering civil rights, she finds that the causal story underlying changes in the use of the death penalty is quite different from other civil rights, such as the right to fair trials. In the case of most civil rights, the causal mechanism involves mobilized groups that are able to use the legitimacy and framing effects of international commitments along with litigation to push forward changes in policies. In contrast, in the case of the death penalty, Simmons concludes that governments more often take the lead in eliminating the death penalty, with domestic support following rather than leading government actions. For this issue, the evidence suggests that any apparent causal effect of signing an anti-death penalty agreement is more likely a selection effect, as governments that have become skeptical of the death penalty and intend to reduce their reliance on it sign the agreement. This finding is in contrast to the positive causal effects of other civil rights agreements that Simmons identifies.

In her analysis of women's rights, Simmons similarly finds persuasive conditional effects of signing the Convention on Elimination of Discrimination Against Women (CEDAW). Transitional governments, especially those that have in place adequately independent court systems, have shown the greatest degree of change in practices. This effect is also greater for countries that are more secular (less religious). Similar effects appear in her analysis of the Convention on the Rights of Children, although again the substantive and statistical significance of the results, and the statistical specification of the models, varies quite a bit across specific issues.

One of Simmons' more intriguing chapters involves the Convention Against Torture (CAT). Previous analyses, such as Oona Hathaway's (2002), had suggested the troubling result that, if anything, signing the CAT led to increased use of torture by governments. Simmons again finds that the effect of signing the CAT is conditional. For established democracies, which for the most part do not utilize torture, signing the CAT makes no difference. However, for transitional democracies with a somewhat independent judiciary, a CAT ratification can lead to substantial improvement in practices.

It is useful to compare Simmons' results to those of James Vreeland, whose work may have been published too late to be cited by Simmons. Vreeland (2008) similarly looks for a conditional effect of the CAT, but uses a different measure of regime type. Rather than differentiating transitional democracies, he distinguishes among democracies, dictatorships with no organized opposition, and competitive dictatorships (those in which an organized opposition exists, although it may be repressed). Using this categorization, Vreeland finds that a CAT signature has a modest positive impact for democracies. It is difficult to discern an impact in the most repressive dictatorships, since they rely on torture and intimidation to maintain their rule and can use refusal to sign the CAT as a signal to any potential rivals that they will be treated harshly. However, for competitive dictatorships, the negative relationship that Hathaway identified reemerges. These governments, under pressure from an organized opposition and wanting some veneer of representative legitimacy, do sign the CAT. However, because, in practice, these governments are not interested in ceding power, they continue to use repressive measures, including torture. Thus, when looking at competitive dictatorships, Vreeland finds that those that sign the CAT are more likely to use torture. Resolving any conflict between this result and Simmons' findings is an important subject for future research – at what point does a transition toward democracy result in improved, rather than deteriorating, respect for human rights agreements?

Simmons' broad-ranging, painstaking collection of data and analysis provides vital clues about the conditions under which governments that sign and ratify human rights agreements go on to improve their human rights practices. Through a mobilization mechanism, treaties cause behavioral change. From a conceptual perspective, however, it is not clear what the discussion of compliance adds to this persuasive analysis of the causal effects of agreements. As Simmons notes, she eschews any attempt to determine whether observed behavior is compliant in a legal sense. An intriguing distinction between the theoretical and empirical chapters of her book becomes evident. In the introduction, theoretical discussion, and conclusion, questions of compliance are front and center. For example, Simmons (2009: 355) sums up the mechanisms she finds as about "compliance pressure" and describes treaties as "a nudge toward compliance." She argues that "domestic groups demand compliance" (Simmons 2009: 364). In contrast, in the empirical chapters, the term "compliance" is barely mentioned; instead, the discussion is about behavioral change. This inconsistency creates a certain lack of conceptual clarity and raises the question of whether the compliance theoretical framework provides any additional insights.

One of Simmons' central conclusions is that domestic groups demand compliance. Her studies of CEDAW and of the CAT include qualitative evidence that allows us to gain some insight as to whether groups have sincere demands for compliance. In her study of CEDAW, Simmons focuses on Japanese employment policy and reproductive rights in Colombia; in her study of the CAT, she examines its effects in Chile and in Israel. These case studies provide valuable evidence to support her quantitative results, in that the mobilization of domestic groups and their access to independent courts are essential parts of the story.

However, it is difficult to discern much evidence that domestic lobby groups have genuine demands for compliance. That is, groups seem to be uninterested in whether government policy is compliant or not. They care about substantive outcomes – elimination of discrimination in the workplace, access to contraceptives, trial of those who have committed atrocities, humane treatment of prisoners. Ratified treaties prove valuable tools in pursuing these goals, as they create greater legitimacy for groups' agendas and mechanisms to place pressure on courts, legislatures, and executives. But the use of compliance language by domestic pressure groups seems purely strategic – that is, they care about policies and substantive outcomes, not whether governments are technically in compliance or not.

In contrast, some domestic officials do seem to care about compliance per se. For example, on signing CEDAW the Japanese Ministry of Labor set about determining the minimum conditions for compliance (Simmons 2009: 238). The Japanese Diet also conducted debates about what would constitute minimally acceptable compliance. In contrast, the lobby groups that Simmons highlights in these four case studies clearly see discussions of compliance as merely a tool to pressure their governments to change behavior, rather than seeing compliance as a goal in and of itself. That is, while domestic interest groups may publicly demand compliance, for them, compliance is primarily a strategy used to push governments toward desired substantive outcomes. Characterizing these groups as caring deeply about compliance thus seems quite misleading and adds little to our understanding of causal mechanisms.

Beyond Simmons' magisterial work, two other notable pieces that discuss compliance but actually measure cooperation or other changes in state behavior are worth mentioning. Judith Kelley (2007) considers bilateral nonsurrender agreements. The United States has pressured members of the International Criminal Court (ICC) to sign bilateral nonsurrender agreements, which would prevent the surrender of U.S. nationals to the ICC. Kelley asks which states have signed these agreements. U.S. power explains part of the pattern, in that states that are more dependent on the United States are more likely to sign these agreements. However, domestic respect for the rule of law also matters. Kelley concludes that state preferences are at least in part normative. In her analysis, Kelley uses the legal literature on compliance as a frame, suggesting that compliance with the ICC implies refusal to sign a nonsurrender agreement. In legal terms, this analysis would likely be questionable, as states could sign such agreements while remaining in technical compliance. A more straightforward – and in terms of understanding patterns of state behavior, more interesting – interpretation of Kelley's results would be that domestic practice with respect for the rule of law causes governments to become more reluctant to sign nonsurrender agreements.

James Morrow (2007) considers states' compliance with the laws of war. He begins with the observation that states' compliance with the laws of war is mixed. Statistical analysis reveals that democracies that have ratified the relevant treaties are more likely to comply, but nondemocracies that have ratified are not. In addition, reciprocity matters: if both warring parties have ratified, compliance increases. Morrow (2007: 561) concludes that "[c]ompliance becomes problematic when a state at war has not signaled its acceptance of the relevant treaty through ratification or if the prescribed behavior is not an equilibrium."

Morrow (2007: 562) measures compliance along four dimensions: the magnitude of violations, the frequency of violations, the role of central political or military authority in the conduct of violations, and the clarity of violations. He then collapses these measures to create a four-category ordinal scale of the level of compliance. "[T]he data are not based on a precise legal analysis of whether particular acts constitute violation of the treaty in question. The legal status of some acts are contested, particularly when questions of military necessity and proportionality arise. Instead, the codings capture whether the broad pattern of acts by a warring party are consistent with the standards of the relevant treaty" (Morrow 2007: 563). As these comments indicate, Morrow is not interested in whether state behavior meets any particular legal definition of compliance. Instead, he uses criteria specified in treaties as defining a standard of behavior, and then asks to what extent state behavior meets this standard, regardless of whether a state has committed itself legally to observing that standard. Morrow's analysis provides compelling evidence about the factors that lead states to respect the laws of war. It is highly misleading, however, to consider his work as being about compliance in any sense, as he applies the same standards to both states that have and that have not ratified the treaty. Labeling a state that has not ratified a treaty and that is not meeting the treaty's standards as "out of compliance" does not do much to further our understanding of either compliance or institutional effects.

The category of work just reviewed has the virtue of being clear about using changes in state behavior as a dependent variable, although they misleadingly label this variable "compliance." The second body of work on compliance has less clarity about the distinction between the concepts of cooperation and compliance. Gerda Falkner *et al.* (2005) use transposition of European Union (EU) social directives as an indicator of compliance. Contributors to the volume find that national preferences and ideology affect the speed of transposition, but that the overall picture is "untidy." For example, they conclude that "[n]o causal condition pre-supposed by existing theories is able to explain our empirical observations" (Falkner *et al.* 2005: 317). In response to this finding, the authors conclude that causal analysis is not possible and instead develop a typology of "three worlds of compliance": law observance, domestic politics, and neglect. In this instance, although the volume includes much rich, insightful knowledge of EU social policy, this research has unfortunately little impact on our understanding of either compliance with EU policy or of determinants of changes in member states' social policies, in large part because compliance and policy change are poorly conceptualized and poorly articulated.

Xinyuan Dai (2007) elaborates a "domestic constituency" mechanism of compliance with international environmental, human rights, economics, and security agreements, and focuses on states' "compliance strategies." She finds that compliance is more likely when domestic constituencies put pressure on governments to change policies, and she provides the most extensive empirical evidence on this question with respect to a particular environmental issue, sulfur emissions. Dai provides a formal model of government policy, in which governments are responsive to interest groups and, in some circumstances, electoral pressures. The more that interest groups are able to influence governments and desire policy change, the more likely governments are to adopt new policy.

One question that this analysis begs is whether states have "compliance strategies" or, more directly, strategies about substantive policies. That is, when governments make decisions about whether to change their environmental policies to meet international standards, to what extent are these decisions framed as strategies for compliance? Or, do they focus more on the substance of policy, its attendant costs and benefits, including, of course, any possible costs of failing to change policy to meet international standards? Dai's model presents groups with ideal points with respect to particular policies and provides a rigorous theoretical analysis of how the interaction of these groups and governments leads to policy change. However, the discussion that surrounds this model consistently uses the term "compliance," although international institutions and possible penalties for noncompliance do not enter the model. That is, Dai assumes that desires for compliance can be conflated with desires for particular policy outcomes, when in fact these may be two independent dimensions. Do domestic constituencies care about compliance per se, or about substantive policies? Overall, Dai's intriguing analysis may have resulted in more definitive and influential findings if it did not use the language of compliance, but instead asked more directly about the causal impact of international environmental agreements on state behavior, as in fact her central model does.

A third body of work by political scientists on compliance is more conceptually coherent and consistent, as it accepts the legal definition and measurement of compliance and asks about the conditions that give rise to higher rates of compliance. Although much of this work is rigorous and persuasive about the factors that are conducive to compliance – and therefore likely of interest to legal scholars – these authors do not go far in addressing the more pressing social-scientific question of the causal impact of international agreements and institutions.

One prominent example is the debate between Beth Simmons and Jana von Stein on whether International Monetary Fund (IMF) members comply with the IMF's Article VIII, which requires members to avoid restrictions on their current accounts and discriminatory currency practices. Simmons (2000) hypothesizes that compliance with Article VIII will be highest when it is relatively easy, as, for example, when underlying economic conditions facilitate compliance. Not surprisingly, she finds support for this hypothesis; but one might infer from this result that Article VIII itself is not having much impact, as these countries may have followed the easy course even in the absence of this institutional commitment. And, indeed, this is close to the argument that von Stein (2005) makes in her rejoinder. Controlling for selection into IMF Article VIII, von Stein finds that compliant behavior is determined by underlying propensities, and she concludes that "international legal commitment" has little independent constraining power. Her overall conclusion in this piece, therefore, is that the causal effect of institutions is zero.

However, this may be an incorrect inference, in that the selection process into Article VIII could be acting as a screening device, as von Stein suggests. If this screening device is effective, it could allow states to reveal their types and facilitate cooperation that would not otherwise occur. The fact that institutions effectively screen is not enough, in itself, to imply that they have no causal effect. Instead, the implication of this line of analysis is that we need to distinguish between screening (or signaling) and commitment effects, which result from different mechanisms, give rise to different patterns of cooperation, and may require different models of causal inference to measure.[3]

Other political scientists studying compliance have focused on other areas within international political economy (IPE). Tim Büthe and Helen Milner (2008) focus on how membership in trade institutions sends signals about compliance propensities. They find that World Trade Organization (WTO) and preferential trading agreements (PTA) membership lead to higher foreign direct investment (FDI) for developing countries. Büthe and Milner argue that higher FDI flows result because commitment to multilateral trade institutions leads to dissemination of information about states' likelihood of compliance. They assume reciprocal compliance as the enforcement mechanism, which raises the question of whether reciprocity works on the basis of legal compliance or actual policies implemented. Similarly, one might wonder whether the information these trade institutions disseminate is about compliance per se, or about the substance of the policies that member states adopt. The question of whether information about compliance or about the substance of policies matters is potentially an interesting one for future research, but it does point to the importance of distinguishing between the legal concept of compliance and more substantive measures of state policies.

Moving beyond IPE, other political scientists have considered compliance in other settings. Sara McLaughlin Mitchell and Paul Hensel (2007) study compliance with agreements to settle territorial claims. They find that the involvement of international institutions increases rates of compliance, and that binding enforcement is the most effective. McLaughlin Mitchell and Hensel (2007: 721) equate compliance with "interstate cooperation." In this particular case, since agreements to settle territorial claims require specific behavioral changes by all parties, the elision of compliance and cooperation may be justified, although it is also possible that by accepting the International Correlates of War's coding of compliance as a measure of cooperation, the authors miss institutional effects that are not captured by the relatively narrow compliance measure. One possible weakness in the authors' causal story is that they

---

[3] Von Stein (2013) reflects on her earlier results and comes to a conclusion much like the one I propose here.

do not consider the endogenicity of the terms of a settlement and how compliance might be related to these terms.

Some political scientists have considered issues of compliance more generally, rather than with respect to specific institutions or agreements. In an edited volume, Michael Zürn and Christian Joerges (2005) discuss general compliance problems in "post-nationalist Europe." Their major conclusion is that "[w]hile institutions that build on the logic of rational institutionalism and legalization can elicit sufficiently high rates of overall compliance, legitimacy is decisive for effectively handling compliance problems" (Zürn and Joerges 2005: 183). In contrast, Todd Sandler (2007) provides a theory of treaty "adherence" from a purely rationalist perspective. His argument is that, in a strategic framework, the expected net gains of a treaty explain whether states will comply.

Political scientists have thus made substantial contributions to the study of compliance with international institutions and agreements, and the volume of work in this vein is increasing rapidly. The question these writings raise, and which I elaborate below, revolves around whether studies of compliance tell us much, if anything, about the causal effect of institutions. In some cases, this work has given insight into causal effects, but that is largely because those authors are studying cooperation while misleadingly labeling it compliance. In other cases, the terms cooperation and compliance are used interchangeably, leading to substantial conceptual confusion, or authors are indeed studying compliance in a straightforward manner, but leaving open many questions about causal impacts. In the next section, I provide a selective and critical review of work on compliance by international legal scholars.

II. COMPLIANCE IN INTERNATIONAL LEGAL STUDIES

In this section, I provide a brief summary of major works on the study of compliance by legal scholars. This section has two main purposes: to clarify the concept and definition of compliance, and to differentiate the legal study of compliance from the role it has assumed in political science. International legal scholars tend to be more careful and explicit in their definition of compliance than political scientists have been. To a striking extent, legal scholars seem to be more sensitive to the distinction between compliance and institutional effects than most political scientists have been.

One of the most useful definitions of compliance in this literature reads as follows:

Compliance needs to be distinguished from the concepts of implementation and effectiveness. Unlike those two concepts, compliance focuses neither on the effort to administer authoritatively public policy directives and the changes they undergo during this administrative process (implementation) nor on the efficacy of a given regulation to solve the political problem that preceded its formulation (effectiveness). .... *Assessing compliance is restricted to the description of the discrepancy between the (legal) text of the regulation and the actions and behaviors of its addressees*. Perfect compliance, imperfect implementation and zero effectiveness therefore are not necessarily mutually exclusive. (Neyer and Wolf 2005: 41–42, emphasis added)[4]

Compliance should be distinguished from the political concept of cooperation. As initially defined by Robert O. Keohane (1984), and as the term is now generally used, international cooperation is defined as mutual policy adjustment. As Neyer and Wolf make clear in the definition of compliance presented above, it is possible for a state to comply but not cooperate (in that it undertakes no policy adjustment). It is also possible for a state to cooperate but not to comply (in that the degree of policy adjustment falls short of what is required by the terms of a treaty). In the discussion above of the political science literature on compliance, we found conflation between the concepts of compliance and cooperation to be common. At times, this conflation has led to the mistaken implication that findings about compliance tell us something about patterns of international cooperation. At other times, it has led to studies of cooperation that are mistakenly labeled as being about compliance. And finally, at times, it has led to little but confusion and the inability to identify systematic patterns of behavior.

Although Chayes and Chayes drew the attention of political scientists to the work of legal scholars on compliance, other legal scholars were at the time also producing substantial accounts of compliance that have not had as much impact on political science. Thomas Franck (1988, 1990) focused attention on the importance of legitimacy in producing compliant state behavior. Franck considers the sources of the legitimacy of a rule, identifying textual determinacy, symbolic validation, coherence, and adherence as especially important. From the perspective of identifying causal effects, Franck's account is problematic in that "adherence" is a source of legitimacy as well as an effect; there is a certain inevitable circularity in this argument. His concern is with a strictly legal definition of compliance, and thus does not raise questions of effectiveness or causal impact, as more recent studies have.

Harold Koh (1997) considers the interaction of "internationalization" and compliance. His major argument centers on the internalization of norms. When states internalize international norms, these norms become incorporated into domestic legal systems, as well as value systems more generally. This incorporation, in turn, enhances compliance. Koh thus specifies one particular pathway to compliance. Both Franck and Koh, as legal scholars, are primarily interested in the process by which law is generated and interpreted. However, they do not specify causal claims that could readily be subject to empirical investigation, perhaps limiting their impact on those with a more social-scientific focus.[5]

---

[4] Neyer and Wolf build on earlier conceptual work by Raustiala and Slaughter (2002). Shelton (2000) draws attention to the difficulties of defining and measuring compliance.

[5] Robert Keohane (1998) provides an extended critique of the argument of Franck and Koh, as well as of other international legal scholars of the time.

Andrew Guzman (2008), writing as a legal scholar but integrating insights from political science, directly addresses the dilemma of discussing both compliance and the "effectiveness" of international law. He argues that compliance relies on three "Rs": reputation, reciprocity, and retaliation.[6] Guzman accurately argues that determining the effect of international law requires far more than the famous observation that most states comply most of the time. Instead, "[i]t is necessary to determine if and when international law changes the behavior of states" (Guzman 2008: 22).

Guzman then equates the observed changes induced by international law in state behavior with institutional "effectiveness" (note that his definition of effectiveness differs from that of Neyer and Wolf), and he recognizes the empirical challenges associated with inferring institutional effects from observed state behavior. However, he goes on to argue that effectiveness should be understood as "improved compliance" or the encouragement of compliance, and specifies such statements as being about the impact of rules on the level of compliance. "That is, [such statements] are considering how the rate of compliance is affected, which is, of course, the same as asking if the rule in question is effective" (Guzman 2008: 23). Throughout the book, Guzman is unable to systematically maintain the distinction between compliance and effectiveness, and his theoretical and empirical discussion conflates the two.

Guzman's summary of the reputational, reciprocal, and retaliatory mechanisms for compliance with international law accurately portrays the standard political science wisdom about how these mechanisms operate. However, he is unable to systematically maintain the distinction between compliance and effectiveness. Thus, for example, his chapter 3 provides a solid account of how potential loss of reputation could lead states to comply with international commitments even when they are inconvenient in the short term. However, this discussion suffers from three notable weaknesses. First, it is not evident how the reputational mechanism would work for states that were already "in compliance" before they made any explicit commitment. Second, Guzman does not address how a reputational mechanism could be effective when what constitutes compliance in any given instance is legally ambiguous, as is typically the case. Finally, and most important from the perspective of my argument, in this discussion, he drops the emphasis on effectiveness that he promises earlier in the book. That is, his discussion of reputation provides some insights into why a state might comply under some circumstances and when compliance is less likely. But he does not develop the connection between decisions to comply and whether the institution is actually causing change in state behaviors, leaving the issue of institutions' causal effect (or "effectiveness") unaddressed. Unfortunately, the same critique applies to Guzman's discussions of reciprocity and retaliation, so that this elegantly argued book by a prominent legal scholar ultimately fails to answer the question it sets up for itself: how international law works.

---

[6] See Brewster (2013) for a broader review of the role of reputation in international relations and international law.

While Guzman's book on compliance is highly prominent in this field, other authors writing recently for law journals have also tacked the issue of compliance. George Downs and Michael Jones (2002) argue that the costs of compliance "invariably" fluctuate. Stochastic costs of compliance will complicate the reputational mechanism of enforcement, as states will inevitably develop multiple reputations. Reputations, defined as "compliance strategies" (Downs and Jones 2002: S98), will not carry across agreements as effectively as they would if the costs of compliance were stable. Downs and Jones (2002: S108) argue that reputations will only carry over to other agreements of lesser value and where compliance costs are correlated. This argument leads to a prediction of higher levels of compliance by newly established states as they work to establish reputations, in anticipation of higher value agreements in the future.

Colter Paulson (2004) examines compliance with the decisions of the International Court of Justice (ICJ). He focuses on final judgments of the ICJ between 1987 and 2002, of which there were fourteen. He finds that in no circumstances did any of these judgments lead to direct defiance; in nine of these cases, compliance appears to have been very good. In five of the cases, however, compliance was less than complete, as parties dragged their feet or attempted to find loopholes in the Court's judgment. These five cases all involved disputed land boundaries, suggesting that this type of issue (similar to that studied by McLaughlin Mitchell and Hensel, discussed above) proves particularly intractable (Paulson 2004: 457). Paulson, in contrast to some political scientists writing on related subjects, is careful to note that his findings about compliance tell us little if anything about the effectiveness of the ICJ in settling disputes. For example, as is typically the case in studying courts, most cases are settled well before the final judgment stage. In these cases, the Court presumably had an impact on the settlement of the dispute – see McLaughlin Mitchell and Hensel – but this effect cannot be identified by looking at compliance with final judgments.

In his survey of the literature on compliance with environmental treaties, Raustiala (2000: 397) likewise notes that one cannot draw conclusions about compliance from data on state behavior, or vice versa. In examining issues such as marine pollution in the North Sea or the Convention on Long Range Transboundary Air Pollution, he draws one particularly intriguing implication of the distinction between compliance and effectiveness, namely, that nonbinding agreements may lead to more behavioral change than legally binding agreements, even though compliance is not at stake when agreements are nonbinding. One reason for this is that nonbinding agreements can avoid the "lowest common denominator" problem, in which governments that anticipate an agreement to be binding will lobby hard to have its standards set low (Raustiala 2000, 425). As Downs, Rocke, and Barsoom (1996) argued earlier, binding agreements may turn out to be shallow ones; agreements that allow more flexibility may actually have greater causal effects.[7]

---

[7] See also Gilligan (2004), on the potential for agreements that are not one-size-fits-all to have larger effects on international cooperation.

Oona Hathaway (2003), in a precursor to Simmons' work on human rights agreements, looks at human rights treaties. She criticizes existing work for looking only at compliance with these treaties, without considering motivations to join them. She argues that by neglecting these possible selection effects, previous studies have misspecified the effects of treaties. "A country considering whether to join a treaty compares its current practices with those required of it under the treaty. If the country's practices are already consistent with the requirements of the treaty, committing to the treaty entails only de minimus administrative costs.... The less a country's practices diverge from the requirements of the treaty, the lower the cost of compliance with the terms of the treaty and hence the greater the likelihood that a country will join" (Hathaway 2003: 10).

Hathaway (2003: 13) argues that compliance costs are also a function of the expectation that a country will actually comply, in that countries that have no intention of complying do not anticipate any real costs. Although Hathaway offers many useful insights, by focusing on compliance rather than actual policies, her analysis becomes unnecessarily complex and predictions unclear. For example: "Countries with better human rights practices should be more reluctant to commit to human rights treaties than otherwise expected, and countries with poor human rights practices should be less reluctant to do so than otherwise expected" (Hathaway 2003: 15). This is a difficult sentence to parse, or to determine what its empirical implications might be. What does "otherwise expected" mean in this context? How could we know what was "otherwise expected" in a way precise enough to allow for any empirical testing?

Laurence Helfer (2005) offers a conceptual critique of the legal literature on compliance and some data to illustrate his central points. Setting up compliance as a dichotomous choice between honoring or violating a treaty's obligations is inaccurate, he argues, because states often have a third option: treaty exit. If procedures for withdrawal are followed, the state is not in breach of the treaty and so reciprocal acts of noncompliance are not allowed under international law. That is, if a treaty provides for legal withdrawal from its provisions, and a state follows such provisions, it is not meeting the standard of behavior specified in the treaty, but is still legally in compliance. Thus, "exit enables a state to cease cooperation with other treaty parties while avoiding or at least reducing opportunities to be penalized for noncompliance" (Helfer 2005: 1589).

Such conceptual concerns might be dismissed if few treaties contained withdrawal provisions, or if few states availed themselves of such provisions. However, Helfer's data show that, in fact, the use of such provisions is frequent and widespread. His figure 1 (Helfer 2005: 1603) shows data on total denunciations and withdrawals from multilateral treaties from 1945 to 2004. During this period, he identifies more than 1,500 such cases. Helfer's work is important in making the crucial point that defection from treaties or other agreements and legal noncompliance cannot be understood as identical (Helfer 2005: 1613).

In comparing the legal literature on compliance to the literature in political science, it is evident that legal scholars have devoted more time to the conceptualization and definition of compliance. They have also begun to draw on the data and methods of political science for more systematic analysis of the causes of compliance. Yet, to the extent that these scholars aim to make a contribution to the political science literature, it seems evident that lack of conceptual clarity about the differences among compliance, cooperation, effectiveness, and related terms undermines most efforts. The next sections build on the work discussed in both fields to offer an elaborated critique of the social-scientific study of compliance as a means of assessing institutional effects, and to begin offering some alternative ways to proceed.

III. CRITIQUE

Why have political scientists adopted the legal concept of compliance as an interesting measure of outcomes? Although it is impossible to provide a definitive answer to this question, I would suggest that the relatively easy availability of data on compliance has pushed political scientists to adopt it as a dependent variable. Unfortunately, in nearly all cases, studying patterns of compliance tells us nothing about the causal effect of institutions, which is reputedly the goal of social-scientific research. The concept of compliance is orthogonal to the concept of causal effect; relying on compliance measures as an indicator of institutional effects has unfortunately caused the field to veer off in less-than-productive directions. Compliance is a legal concept, developed by lawyers and legal scholars to assess the degree of conformity between legal requirements and the actions of those subject to those requirements. The legal community is necessarily focused on regulation and related compliance. A major focus of legal discourse and practice relates to the process of determining who may be noncompliant and the measures that may then follow.

But what could studying compliance potentially tell us about the question of more interest to social scientists: institutions causal effects? A causal effect is stated as a counterfactual: how does state behavior in the presence of an institution differ from the behavior that would have occurred in the absence of the institution? The question of compliance is entirely distinct from the question of institutional effect. As Raustiala (2000: 388) noted, in arguing that it would be more fruitful to study effectiveness than compliance, it is entirely possible to have low compliance but a substantial causal effect, or high compliance and a negligible institutional effect. Compliance with treaties can often be "inadvertent, coincidental, or an artifact . . ." (Raustiala 2000: 391).

To illustrate this claim, consider two cases of states entering an institution regulating the emission of pollutants. State A has strong environmental leanings and has already taken extensive steps to limit emissions prior to entering the institution. In fact, the institution's requirements are less stringent than those State A has already adopted. In this case, State A would be fully "in compliance," but the institution arguably would have no causal effect; instead, State A's strong environmental record is likely entirely attributable to its own proclivities. State B, in contrast, has a poor environmental record when it joins the institution. The institution provides knowledge and capacity, and, in response, State B modestly improves its performance on the emissions indicators. However, it still falls short of institutional requirements. If compliance were measured dichotomously, State B would be found out of compliance. If compliance were measured in more continuous terms, State B may be coded as being in partial compliance. However, the institution in the case of State B has had a substantial causal effect, in spite of the lack of full compliance. In both cases – State A and State B – relying on compliance as a measure of institutional effects would seriously mislead those interested in determining the institution's causal effect or in understanding patterns of international cooperation.

To some extent, the way that compliance has entered the IR literature is a cautionary tale about the risks associated with celebrating interdisciplinarity without careful attention to the different demands and purposes of various disciplines. States have policies – they pollute, reduce pollution, trade, obstruct trade, protect human rights, violate human rights, and so on. They do not necessarily have a strategy about whether or not to comply; that is, state policies are not obviously or primarily "compliance policies." Our understanding of the causal effects of institutions and agreements will be much stronger if we focus directly on substantive policies rather than compliance strategies. Operationalizing state policy as the degree of compliance implicitly assumes that the agreements have a causal effect, when, in fact, states could be technically "in compliance" without actually paying any attention to the agreement or having made a decision "to comply." One weakness of thinking about policy as compliance is, therefore, that it assumes what we wish instead to test; namely, whether agreements cause changes in state actions.

When determining the effect of institutions on policies, social scientists should focus on variation in substantive policies. When a state joins an institution, or when an institution develops new rules, do that state's policies change? And can the change in policies reasonably be attributed to the institution? If not, it is difficult to argue that the institution had any causal effect. Compliance and causal effect are independent concepts that do not necessarily covary. Social scientists who adopt the legal concept of compliance and assume that it allows us to identify the causal effect of institutions are making a logical error, unless a series of stringent underlying assumptions are met. Thus far, empirical studies of compliance have not generally recognized the distinction between compliance and causal effect, and have not examined whether the necessary conditions to infer one from the other are met.

This conflation of two very different concepts, and the dangers of inferring causal effect from observed compliance, is not merely an abstract concern. It has confounded many otherwise serious empirical studies of institutional effects. Take, for instance, Edith Brown Weiss' and Harold Jacobson's (1998) excellent edited collection of studies of international environmental agreements. This wide-ranging and exhaustive study provides a great deal of information about how environmental agreements are implemented. However, one of its major findings is that those states most likely to be "in compliance" are those whose policies met the agreements' provisions before the agreements were even in place. In these cases, the causal effect of the agreements is prima facie zero. In other words, in its focus on "strengthening compliance" this major (and costly-to-execute) study missed an opportunity to learn about the causal effect of environmental agreements. Although this is a particularly stark example of the dangers of relying on the legal concept of compliance for causal inference, the same underlying dilemmas and unexamined assumptions affect all social-scientific studies of institutional effects that use compliance as a dependent variable.

IV. CONCLUSION

What does this review of scholarly work on compliance with international institutions suggest? Primarily, that those studying the effect of institutions should choose alternative measures of outcomes, staying away from a discussion of compliance as a measure of interest. Positively, what steps do political scientists need to take to more accurately assess the causal effect of institutions on state policy and behavior?

Some political scientists, aware of the difficulty of inferring causal effects from compliance records, have confronted the problem through mechanisms such as the inclusion of carefully chosen control variables, sophisticated statistical specifications, and so on. However, I would argue that none of these measures is adequate or even appropriate. Rather than starting with measures of compliance and attempting to modify them to the task of measuring causal effects, social scientists should begin with measures that are more appropriately conceptualized and designed to elicit more valid inferences. Taking this path requires both direct measurement of the policies that states implement and careful attention to counterfactuals through statistical and/or qualitative analysis.

One example of a recent book that, in essence, asks the same questions as Simmons or Guzman, but without the conceptual apparatus of legal compliance, is Emilie Hafner-Burton's (2009) examination of the impact of trade agreements on human rights practices. Hafner-Burton begins by noting that many PTAs have begun writing human rights provisions into their treaties. However, the approach that PTAs use has varied. Some rely on only soft measures, using socialization mechanisms to influence members' human rights practices. Others rely on harder enforcement provisions. Using statistical techniques similar to those that Simmons uses, but without framing the discussion in terms of compliance, Hafner-Burton conclusively demonstrates that only PTAs with harder provisions have been effective in inducing behavioral change.

Rather than starting with measures of compliance and attempting to modify them to the task of measuring causal effects, social scientists should begin with measures that are more appropriately conceptualized and designed to elicit more valid inferences, as Hafner-Burton does. Taking this path requires both direct measurement of the policies that states implement and careful attention to counterfactuals through statistical and/or qualitative analysis.[8]

Overall, this review of recent empirical work on compliance reveals some promising work as well as conceptual weaknesses, while suggesting Raustiala's (2000: 388) conclusion from over a decade ago that the "prevailing analytical focus on compliance is often misplaced and even counterproductive" remains apt. Legal scholars writing on compliance have typically understood the crucial distinctions between compliance and institutional effectiveness, although to the extent that these scholars draw on theories from political science, this clarity unfortunately is lost. Political scientists studying compliance tend to fall into three different categories: those who use the language of compliance but actually provide careful studies of behavioral change or cooperation; those who conflate the concepts of compliance and cooperation; and those who provide careful studies of compliance but who fail to illuminate the causal effects of institutions and agreements. If political scientists' primary goal in studying international institutions and agreements is to discern their causal effects, using the language and conceptual apparatus of compliance is an inappropriate starting point. As Raustiala noted, this emphasis has led to misallocation of research resources. A more productive turn would be to move away from studies of compliance to more standard social-scientific mechanisms for establishing counterfactuals and identifying causal effects.

REFERENCES

Brewster, Rachel (2013). "Reputation in International Relations and International Law Theory," in Jeffrey L. Dunoff and Mark A. Pollack (eds.), *Interdisciplinary Perspectives on International Law and International Relations: The State of the Art* (New York: Cambridge University Press), pp. 524–43.

Brown Weiss, Edith, and Harold K. Jacobson (1998) (eds.). *Engaging Countries: Strengthening Compliance with International Environmental Accords* (Cambridge, MA: MIT Press).

Büthe, Tim, and Helen V. Milner (2008). "The Politics of Foreign Direct Investment into Developing Countries: Increasing FDI through International Trade Agreements?, " *American Journal of Political Science*, Vol. 52, No. 4, pp. 741–62.

Chayes, Abram, and Antonia Handler Chayes (1993). "On Compliance," *International Organization*, Vol. 47, No. 2, pp. 175–205.

Dai, Xinyuan (2007). *International Institutions and National Policies* (New York: Cambridge University Press).

[8] Techniques being developed by Kosuke Imai and his colleagues may prove valuable in offering more precise identification of the causal effects of international agreements and institutions (see Imai, Keele, and Tingley, 2009).

Downs, George W., and Michael A. Jones (2002). "Reputation, Compliance, and International Law," *Journal of Legal Studies*, Vol. 31, No. 1, pt. 2, pp. S95–S114.

Downs, George W., David M. Rocke, and Peter N. Barsoom (1996). "Is the Good News about Compliance Good News about Cooperation?," *International Organization*, Vol. 50, No. 3, pp. 379–406.

Falkner, Gerda, Oliver Treib, Miriam Hartlapp, and Simone Leiber (2005). *Complying with Europe: EU Harmonisation and Soft Law in the Member States* (New York: Cambridge University Press).

Franck, Thomas (1990). *The Power of Legitimacy among Nations* (New York: Oxford University Press).

—— (1988). "Legitimacy in the International System," *American Journal of International Law*, Vol. 82, No. 4, pp. 705–59.

Gilligan, Michael J. (2004). "Is There a Broader-Deeper Tradeoff in International Multilateral Agreements?," *International Organization*, Vol. 58, No. 3, pp. 459–84.

Guzman, Andrew T. (2001). "International Law: A Compliance Based Theory," *California Law Review*, Vol. 90, No. 6, pp. 1823–88.

—— (2008). *How International Law Works: A Rational Choice Theory* (New York: Oxford University Press).

Hafner-Burton, Emilie M. (2009). *Forced to Be Good: Why Trade Agreements Boost Human Rights* (Ithaca, NY: Cornell University Press).

Hathaway, Oona A. (2003). "The Cost of Commitment," *Stanford Law Review*, Vol. 55, No. 5, pp. 1821–62.

—— (2002). "Do Human Rights Treaties Make a Difference?," *Yale Law Journal*, Vol. 111, No. 8, pp. 1935–2042.

Helfer, Laurence R. (2005). "Exiting Treaties," *Virginia Law Review*, Vol. 91, No. 7, pp. 1579–1648.

Henkin, Louis (1979). *How Nations Behave: Law and Foreign Policy*, 2nd ed. (New York: Columbia University Press).

Imai, Kosuke, Luke Keele, and Dustin Tingley (2009). "A General Approach to Causal Mediation Analysis," unpublished manuscript, Princeton University.

Kelley, Judith (2007). "Who Keeps International Commitments and Why? The International Criminal Court and Bilateral Nonsurrender Agreements," *American Political Science Review*, Vol. 101, No. 3, pp. 573–89.

Keohane, Robert O. (1998). "When Does International Law Come Home?," *Houston Law Review*, Vol. 35, No. 3, pp. 699–714.

—— (1984). *After Hegemony* (Princeton, NJ: Princeton University Press).

Koh, Harold (1997). "Why Do Nations Obey International Law?," *Yale Law Journal*, Vol. 106. No. 8, pp. 2599–659.

McLaughlin Mitchell, Sara, and Paul R. Hensel (2007). "International Institutions and Compliance with Agreements," *American Journal of Political Science*, Vol. 51, No. 4, pp. 721–37.

Mearsheimer, John J. (1994/95). "The False Promise of International Institutions," *International Security*, Vol. 19, No. 3, pp. 5–49.

Morrow, James (2007). "When Do States Follow the Laws of War?," *American Political Science Review*, Vol. 101, No. 3, pp. 559–72.

Neyer, Jürgen, and Dieter Wolf (2005). "The Analysis of Compliance with International Rules: Definitions, Variables, and Methodology," in Michael Zürn and Cjristian Joerges (eds.), *Law and Governance in Postnational Europe: Compliance beyond the Nation-State* (Cambridge: Cambridge University Press), pp. 40–64.

Paulson, Colter (2004). "Compliance with Final Judgments of the International Court of Justice since 1987," *American Journal of International Law*, Vol. 98, No. 3, pp. 434–61.

Raustiala, Kal (2000). "Compliance and Effectiveness in International Regulatory Cooperation," *Case Western Journal of International Law*, Vol. 32, No. 2, pp. 387–440.

Raustiala, Kal, and Slaughter, Anne-Marie (2002). "International Law, International Relations and Compliance," in Walter Carlsnaes, Thomas Risse, and Beth A. Simmons (eds.), *Handbook of International Relations* (Thousand Oaks, CA: Sage), pp. 538–58.

Sandler, Todd (2007). "Treaties: Strategic Considerations," *University of Illinois Law Review*, Vol. 2008, No. 1, pp. 155–80.

Shelton, Dinah (2000) (ed.). *Commitment and Compliance: The Role of Non-binding Norms in the International Legal System* (Oxford: Oxford University Press).

Simmons, Beth A. (1998). "Compliance with International Agreements," *Annual Review of Political Science*, Vol. 1, pp. 75–93.

———— (2000). "International Law and State Behavior: Commitment and Compliance in International Monetary Affairs," *American Political Science Review*, Vol. 94, No. 4, pp. 819–35.

———— (2009). *Mobilizing for Human Rights: International Law in Domestic Politics* (New York: Cambridge University Press).

von Stein, Jana (2005). "Do Treaties Constrain or Screen? Selection Bias and Treaty Compliance," *American Political Science Review*. Vol. 99, No. 4, pp. 611–22.

———— (2013). "The Engines of Compliance," in Jeffrey L. Dunoff and Mark A. Pollack (eds.), *Interdisciplinary Perspectives on International Law and International Relations: The State of the Art* (New York: Cambridge University Press), pp. 477–501.

Vreeland, James Raymond (2008). "Political Institutions and Human Rights: Why Dictatorships Enter into the United Nations Convention against Torture," *International Organization*, Vol. 62, No. 1, pp. 65–101.

Zürn, Michael, and Christian Joerges (2005) (eds.). *Law and Governance in Postnational Europe: Compliance beyond the Nation-State* (Cambridge: Cambridge University Press).

Conclusions

25

International Law and International Relations Theory:

Twenty Years Later

Anne-Marie Slaughter

Turning the pages back two decades to confront my hopes and claims as a younger scholar is an interesting and slightly scary prospect. Jeffrey Dunoff and Mark Pollack have been kind enough to refer to *International Law and International Relations Theory: A Dual Agenda* (Slaughter Burley 1993), as one of the "canonical" calls for interdisciplinary scholarship, alongside Kenneth Abbott's *Modern International Relations Theory: A Prospectus for International Lawyers* (published four years earlier, in 1989). As the proud possessor of a newly minted DPhil in international relations (IR) from Oxford, the writing of which was spent mostly at Harvard absorbing more social scientific American approaches to the discipline, and two years of law teaching, I perceived a more vibrant and interesting set of debates taking place among IR scholars than among my international law (IL) colleagues. At the same time, I knew that those debates raised many issues familiar to international lawyers. I envisioned a series of conferences that would bring together scholars from both disciplines working on common problems, as occurred in the work presented in a special symposium issue of *International Organization* devoted to "Legalization and World Politics" and other conferences hosted both at law schools and by political science scholars like Robert Keohane at Duke and Beth Simmons at Harvard. Indeed, perhaps the best evidence of at least the partial convergence of parts of both disciplines is that virtually all the participants in this volume know one another and one another's work.

The essays in this volume, as the editors point out, reflect multiple strands of IL/IR work. Pieces like Laurence R. Helfer's chapter on "Flexibility in International Agreements" (2013, Chapter 7, this volume) and Karen Alter's chapter on "The Multiple Roles of International Courts and Tribunals" (2013, Chapter 14, this volume) are archetypes of different kinds of interdisciplinary work. Helfer, an international lawyer with a public policy degree, takes a subject that is of interest to international lawyers, political scientists, and practicing regime designers: what degree of flexibility, with regard to withdrawal provisions, is optimal for effective international agreements? He draws on a wide range of empirical and theoretical studies by both political scientists and international lawyers to bring the disciplines together in a search for systematic answers to this basic question. This type of work allows scholars from both disciplines to draw on a wider range of sources and intellectual perspectives to ask questions and generate insights on an issue that would not necessarily occur to a scholar working in only in IR or IL.

On the other hand, Alter, a political scientist who has spent a great deal of time with lawyers, looks at legal institutions as political actors and thereby investigates dimensions of their behavior that lawyers are actively discouraged from examining lest it undermine their authority as agents of the law. She studies the activities of international courts and tribunals "in the round," looking at the different types of cases that they hear, including categories of cases that international lawyers would not typically think are relevant. For instance, she analyzes the role of international courts in the function of "administrative review," reviewing the actions of administrative actors in cases brought by private litigants typically working within the regime that established the international court or tribunal in question. She is able to show how even these kinds of cases actually play an important role in what she calls the "uneven construction of an international rule of law." Her training as a political scientist allows her to see the importance of features of the international judicial landscape that classically trained international lawyers might be inclined to overlook.

In addition, the increasing specialization of both IR and IL means that more and more of the best work is being done in teams. Over the same past two decades, public international law has splintered into international human rights law, international environmental law, international criminal law, international humanitarian law, international litigation, international arbitration, international trade, and international investment – each of which can now merit its own course. Most of these subjects were covered in a week or so as part of the general public international law course in the 1980s; some, like international criminal law and international environmental law, did not exist. Political scientists have moved from a general division between international security and international political economy to subfields focusing on traditional state-to-state security issues; transnational security issues (from terrorism to climate change); international trade, finance, and investment; international institutions and governance; and international development issues. The best way to knit these various specialized bodies of knowledge together in the service of advancing knowledge on a broader set of puzzles or subjects is to collaborate, which is one reason Abbott and Snidal have generated a rich stream of articles, or indeed, as evidenced by the collaboration between Dunoff and Pollack that led to this volume.

I. A DETOUR INTO FOREIGN POLICY AND GOVERNMENT SERVICE

My own professional trajectory has taken me in a different direction, first to a School of Public and International Affairs with faculty from ten different disciplines, ranging from history to astrophysics, and then to the State Department for two years as the Director of Policy Planning. In answering the invariable question about the difference between academia and government, I laugh that never a day went by when I did not hear the word "academic" used as a synonym for "irrelevant." The intellectual pedigree of many of the ideas under discussion, however, told a very different story. The "canonical" demonstration of the relevance of IR scholarship to foreign policy is the way in which empirical evidence of "the democratic peace" shaped foreign policy thinking in both the Clinton and the George W. Bush administrations. But I saw many more nuanced examples.

To begin with, as many government officials are as aware of Snyder and Mansfield's work (Mansfield and Snyder 2005) showing that democratizing states are more likely to go to war than other states as they are of the original democratic peace findings. In other cases, my fellow officials were conscious of arguments for the effectiveness of institutions like the International Criminal Court that depend on the impact of the Court in shifting the balance of power in domestic politics toward groups that favor domestic prosecution of war criminals. In analyzing bilateral relations with China, everyone around the table, whether they knew it or not, typically proceeded from the assumption of the basic security dilemma first labeled by Robert Jervis (1978). And, in debating the value of pursuing a value-based international order and integrating rising nations into that order, many officials had internalized John Ikenberry's arguments about the specifically liberal nature of the current international order (2011) as well as Robert Keohane's institutionalist rationale for international institutions generally as providers of information and reducers of transaction costs (1984).

At the same time, following in the footsteps of countless government officials before me, I saw plenty of instances where international law helped guide policy choices. The most obvious example during the Obama administration was the continual resort to the United Nations (UN) Security Council to muster multilateral support for actions ranging from sanctions on North Korea and Iran to pressure on the Ivory Coast to airstrikes on Libya. Equally important was a focus on regional organizations such as the Organization of American States in trying to address the coup in Honduras, the African Union in addressing the coup in the Ivory Coast, and the Arab League and Gulf Cooperation Council in authorizing a no-fly zone in Libya and increasing sanctions on and human rights monitors in Syria. Moreover, the Obama administration focused intensively on the need to create institutions where the existing regime landscape was inadequate. The two most important items on this agenda were the transition for most purposes from the G-8 to the G-20 *as a leaders' group* (the G-20 had previously met only as a group of finance ministers) and the establishment of the East Asia Summit as the premiere trans-Pacific institution to address security issues.

Theoreticians of every stripe will find evidence to support their preferred causal narratives. Realists can point to the obvious shift in attitudes toward international rules and institutions as the United States moved from superpower in the 1990s and early 2000s to overstretched international debtor in a world of rising powers. As soon as the precedents the United States was setting looked as if they could credibly be applied to the benefit of other nations with divergent interests, both the Pentagon and the State Department found common cause in a grand strategy of building "an international order based upon rights and responsibilities."[1] Far better to resolve boundary issues in the South China Sea multilaterally according to agreed-upon rules of the game than unilaterally by the strongest nation. And, far better to have an International Monetary Fund that accords a greater share of voting authority to China and South Korea than to risk the establishment of an Asian Monetary Fund with its own rules.[2] Even better to amend the supposedly unamendable UN Charter to change the membership of the UN Security Council than risk growing impatience with and disregard for the judgments of an institution established by the victors of a war won in the middle of the last century.[3]

But Institutionalists have plenty of evidence on their side as well. One of the key reasons for focusing on building or strengthening institutions in Asia was the difficulty of trying to address multiple issues through bilateral, trilateral, and quadrilateral diplomacy. The transaction costs of negotiating with tens of nations on scores of issues ranging from piracy to trafficking in women to nuclear nonproliferation are ever present and ever higher. Fear of misinformation and resulting crises that could spiral out of control was another factor, just as predicted. Moreover, government officials often began with analyses of the underlying convergence of state interests, even if such analyses were not described in those terms. Plenty of bureaucrats argued against the expansion of the G-8 into the G-20 on the grounds that the G-20 would never, due to a fundamental divergence of interests, be able to address a wide range of issues that the G-8 had routinely put on its agenda.

And, of course, these were only the first round of choices. Questions such as whether to create formal or informal institutions arose frequently. Consider the decision to establish the Global Counterterrorism Forum (GCTF), which was launched in September 2011 by Secretary Clinton and Turkish Foreign Minister Davutoglu, with foreign ministers and senior representatives of twenty-seven other countries and the European Union (EU) on the margins of the UN General Assembly. The GCTF is a classic government network, described as an "informal, multilateral body" bringing together national counterterrorism officials to "meet with their counterparts . . . to share counterterrorism experiences, expertise, strategies, capacity needs,

---

[1] National Security Strategy of the United States, May 2010, available at http://www.whitehouse.gov/sites/default/files/rss_viewer/national_security_strategy.pdf, p. 3.

[2] Sandrine Rastello, "IMF Approves China as Third-Biggest Power, Weakening Influence of Europe," Bloomberg, November 5, 2010, available at http://www.bloomberg.com/news/2010-11-06/imf-approves-china-as-third-biggest-power-weakening-influence-of-europe.html.

[3] BBC News, "Obama Backs India on Permanent UN Security Council Seat," November 8, 2010, available at http://www.bbc.co.uk/news/world-south-asia-11711007.

and capacity-building programs."[4] Its model was the Financial Action Task Force (FATF), which was established by the G-7 in 1989 as the Financial Action Task Force on Money-Laundering and was designed to bring government experts together to share best practices and make recommendations for a government plan of action. The UN already has an UN Office on Drugs and Crime (UNODC), which was established in 1997 to "assist Member States in their struggle against illicit drugs, crime and terrorism."[5] The decision whether to build up UNODC as opposed to establishing a new informal institution turned on various considerations well established in the institutionalist literature, such as the need for speed, flexibility, and selective membership versus legitimacy, legal authority, economy of institutions, and global reach.

Liberals could point to the shift in the administration's foreign policy agenda after the mid-term elections of 2010, particularly the focus on getting the free-trade agreements with Colombia, Panama, and South Korea through the Senate, something that the Obama administration was able to do only when its party was relatively weaker and thus anti-free-trade groups in the Democratic party were more willing to follow or less able to obstruct the White House lead. Or, consider the fate of the President's inaugural pledge to close the prison for terrorist detainees at Guantánamo Bay within one year, a move that was clearly in the foreign policy interests of the United States but was repeatedly and successfully blocked by Republicans and some Democrats manipulating domestic constituencies afraid of holding terrorists within the United States. More generally, I almost never participated in a foreign policy meeting at top levels where domestic political considerations were not an important factor.

Finally, Constructivists could find many places where officials who felt themselves to be custodians of the values and the vision that the Obama presidency stood for did battle with self-described Realists focusing on a much more instrumentalist calculation of U.S. interests. Diplomatic historians and political scientists will mine the papers of the Obama administration (or perhaps the e-mails) to recount the story of the U.S. response to the uprisings across the Arab world. That story is still unfolding as of this writing, but it is evident that those uprisings are likely to bring governments into power much less amenable to U.S. interests in Israeli security, steady oil production, counterterrorism, and regional stability, a fact not lost on the White House. Yet, President Obama announced in May 2011 that the United States would stand for a set of core principles in the region, including opposition to the use of violence and repression against the people of the region and support for a set of universal rights. Realists can argue that the United States is just choosing long-term over short-term interests, because the status quo of stability through repression

---

4 U.S. Department of State, Office of the Spokesperson, Global Counterterrorism Forum, Fact Sheet, Washington, DC, September 9, 2011, available at http://www.state.gov/r/pa/prs/ps/2011/09/172010.htm.

5 United Nations Office on Drugs and Crime, "About UNODC," available at http://www.unodc.org/unodc/en/about-unodc/index.html?ref=menutop.

cannot be maintained, but Constructivists will find plenty of evidence that, even absent that argument, many in the White House – indeed the President himself – could not bring themselves to stand with Middle East governments against their people "because that is simply *not who we are.*"

II. AN IL/IR AGENDA LOOKING FORWARD

Based on my government experience, if I were to sit down today to revise A *Dual Agenda* for the next decade, I would focus on a very different set of issues. Interestingly, as I will address further below, these are issues that at least initially fall much more within the traditional domain of legal scholars than of their IR colleagues.

A. Humanity Law

First is the definition and delimitation of an entire new legal domain that draws together the many different ways that individuals are now direct subjects of international law, both as subjects of protection and bearers of obligation. States have long taken on obligations to foreign individuals within their territories or jurisdiction under international law, from providing immunity to the diplomats of other nations to guaranteeing specific tax treatment to foreign investors. In the twentieth century, states took on obligations to their own people through international human rights treaties, meaning that individuals had direct rights under international law against their governments. In the late twentieth century, individual government officials accepted direct obligations under international criminal law not to commit genocide, crimes against humanity, grave and systematic war crimes, or ethnic cleansing against their own people. Thus, the leader of a country can negotiate as the head of state with other states with regard to a cross-border conflict and simultaneously be the target of an international criminal investigation, as Sudanese President Omer al-Bashir has demonstrated.

From another perspective, states are increasingly declaring war on individuals who can simultaneously be prosecuted in national courts subject to domestic criminal law. A member of al Qaeda can plot a terrorist attack on the United States and be arrested and tried in U.S. federal court. Such is the case of Umar Farouk Abdulmutallab, the Nigerian who tried to detonate explosives in his underwear on an in-bound flight to Detroit. Alternatively, a member of al Qaeda can plot against the United States and be killed in a drone attack, which the United States justifies on the grounds that it is at war with al Qaeda, even in countries such as Yemen and Pakistan, where U.S. ground troops are not otherwise engaged. Finally, prisoners who have been captured in the context of a military conflict, such as the prisoners held at Guantánamo Bay who were captured by U.S. troops on the ground in Afghanistan are being treated *neither* as prisoners of war under the Geneva Conventions nor as criminals under U.S. law.

What are the unifying principles that draw these different categories of cases together under a common body of law? Alternatively, if each category is to be treated as the extension of an existing body of law, such as humanitarian law or domestic criminal law, how do we justify the differential treatment in each category? Ruti Teitel has taken on this task in her brilliant new book *Humanity's Law* (2011), in which she argues that the "law of humanity" is a framework that spans the law of war, human rights law, and international criminal law. In a less theoretical vein, legal adviser Harold Koh tackled some of the same issues in his speech to the American Society of International Law in 2010, in which he addressed what he called "the law of 9/11: detentions, use of force, and prosecutions."[6]

Looking forward, these breaks and eddies in traditional legal domains will gradually build into waves that will sweep away existing boundaries of doctrine and establish new ones. The interpretation of these mounting trends should also encompass popular writing about globalization, where pundits such as Thomas Friedman have been arguing for over a decade that the twenty-first century is the era of "superempowered individuals," whereby individuals can exercise the same kind of power that once only states could muster (Friedman 1999: 14–15). Osama bin Laden is the example that jumps most readily to mind, but Bill Gates and Warren Buffett also fit this category. If global rules regulate individuals, corporations, foundations, nongovernmental organizations (NGOs), and other social actors, as well as states, does the category of "international law," whether public or private, make any sense? Perhaps we are moving toward intergovernmental law (regulating relations between governments) and global law (regulating all nongovernmental actors acting across borders)? Remember that the term and the contemporary concept of "international law" is barely 150 years old; it grew out of the era when national identities and state identities were becoming coterminous, and it can disappear just as quickly as globalization create multiple global identities.

B. *Private Actors, Public Purpose*

A second category of issues that needs careful examination and hard thinking revolves around public–private partnerships (PPPs) and the notion of government as a platform for convening and connecting public to private actors and private actors to one another. Multisector partnerships are a natural trend in an era not only of constrained government resources but also of a growing awareness of the limits of government, corporate, or civic expertise with regard to complex multidisciplinary problems. Public–private partnerships offer at least a theoretical way out.

The Obama National Security Strategy mentions PPPs more than thirty times. Over the past three years, both the White House and the State Department have set

---

[6] Harold Koh, "The Obama Administration and International Law," speech at the Annual Meeting of the American Society of International Law, March 25, 2010, available at http://www.state.gov/s/l/releases/remarks/139119.htm.

up offices to reach out to the private sector. Notable successes include the Global Clean Cookstove Alliance, which brings together more than 175 government agencies, corporations, NGOs, and foundations around the world to secure the adoption of 100 million clean cook-stoves by 2020, thereby reducing carbon emissions, improving the health of tens of millions of families, and increasing the security of millions of women. Another notable initiative has been the Partners for a New Beginning (PNB), a collaboration created after President Obama's speech in Cairo between the State Department, the Aspen Institute, and scores of corporations, foundations, and universities in the United States, Algeria, Egypt, Indonesia, Morocco, Pakistan, the Palestinian Territories, Tunisia, and Turkey. In barely over a year, the PNB has supported more than seventy projects connected with science and technology, economic opportunity, and education.[7]

The political argument for PPPs is that they stretch scarce government resources and ensure that they leverage other contributions of money, expertise, and other in-kind resources. The initial emphasis on PPPs came from the Reinventing Government initiative under the Clinton administration, but the George W. Bush administration was also enthusiastic. Equally important is the effectiveness argument: these alliances are better at taking advantage of local knowledge in developing countries and at pooling and learning from the experience of many diverse actors. And the energy, innovation, and capacity in the private sector, both corporate and civic, are a vital foreign policy resource.

Finally, the kinds of global problems we face – proliferation of nuclear weapons, global terrorist and criminal networks, climate change, global pandemics, fragile states, resource scarcity (water, oil, minerals), civil conflict – cannot be solved by governments alone, much less by governments increasingly strapped for funds. Governments will be in the business of negotiating agreements, resolving crises, and solving problems with one another for a long time to come, but top-down efforts cannot stimulate the widespread behavioral change that is required to address social and economic challenges. Those changes are most effectively motivated from the bottom up, through many different initiatives that come from individuals determined to improve their health, water and energy usage, education, and security.[8]

For the moment, government rhetoric on PPPs still exceeds the reality. A particular problem is that the federal government is still badly set up to engage corporations. A recent Center for Strategic and International Studies report on PPPs points out a number of operational problems due to government rules and multiple instances

---

[7] PNB, Partners for A New Beginning, *Status Report: A Year of Impact through Partnership*, September 2011, available at http://www.aspeninstitute.org/publications/partners-new-beginning-2011-status-report.

[8] Former Army Colonel Richard Holshek has written persuasively on this score; see http://www.huffingtonpost.com/christopher-holshek/the-power-of-both_b_864645.html.

when the right government hand did not know what the left was doing.[9] One consumer products company reports being approached by six different parts of the government, including parts of the same agency, to join in the same partnership. Another is the fundamental difficulty of genuinely aligning the corporate, public, and civic interests. All participants love the veneer of "partnership," but what does it actually mean? Glossy brochures with intertwined logos? Or a corporation willing to accept a lower profit margin for the sake of a public health campaign? Or governments more willing to be held to account by NGOs monitoring their compliance with an agreed set of international obligations?

Government in these contexts is acting as a partner and a platform rather than as a single and independent agent in international affairs. What is its liability for the consequences of a PPP that produces defective products? That causes environmental damage? Or that simply does not deliver on its promises? Are there contractual arrangements? In a PPP that has local chapters, what happens if some members of those local chapters turn out to have affiliations with terrorist groups or drug traffickers or sexual exploitation rings? The State Department is required to do due diligence on all prospective partnerships, but mistakes happen and partners are often not what they seem to be. Equally important, what is the responsibility and liability of corporations and civic organizations who join specific partnerships or broader collaborative networks? And, is there a way to treat broad networks, such as the Global Alliance for Vaccination and Immunization (GAVI) as international "persons" or subjects of international law? Are they a kind of international actor? A kind of institution? The overall point is that we will be seeing more and more hybrid actors in the international system, coalitions of individuals and institutions from the private, public, and civic sectors, and we need to conceptualize their identities and the space they will operate in.

C. *Liberty and Security in Virtual Space*

On February 15, 2011, Secretary of State Hillary Clinton gave her second speech on Internet freedom. In her words:

> The Internet has become the public space of the 21st century – the world's town square, classroom, marketplace, coffeehouse, and nightclub. We all shape and are shaped by what happens there, all 2 billion of us and counting. And that presents a challenge. To maintain an Internet that delivers the greatest possible benefits to the world, we need to have a serious conversation about the principles that will guide us, what rules exist and should not exist and why, what behaviors should be encouraged or discouraged and how (Clinton 2011).

---

[9] "Seizing the Opportunity in Public–Private Partnerships," available at http://csis.org/publication/seizing-opportunity-public-private-partnerships.

Her challenge is a profound one. How can the United States and other nations develop rules and principles that will prohibit governments from shutting down political opposition through a combination of Internet monitoring and censorship while simultaneously allowing governments to protect their people from terrorist attacks and criminal violence of all kinds through Internet monitoring and data-mining? Is it legal and legitimate for a government to send a ship to anchor just outside another nation's territorial waters to provide servers and other electronic assistance to protesters battling their government in the name of universal human rights?

Within one country, can a government shut down the Internet in its own territory if it chooses to? In her first Internet speech in January 2010, Secretary Clinton declared that the "freedom to connect" was a fundamental human right, an extension of the basic rights of freedom of speech and assembly in the Internet age.[10] The declaration of such a right by the U.S. Secretary of State would constitute one possible indicator of *opinion juris* under customary international law, but hardly makes it so as a matter of general international law. Is the freedom to connect an inherent part of the universally recognized freedom of speech? Or does it need to be established as a twenty-first-century human right?

Yet another cluster of issues concerns the liability of corporations and their governments for making technology that citizens can use to communicate but that governments can equally use to spy on those citizens and shut down their communication. A body of international rules has been developed to govern such liabilities in the context of the manufacture of nuclear fuel and equipment, but not for electronic communications and interception technology. Criminalization of such manufacture and export is a matter first of domestic law, but it could also have implications for international human rights law.

III. ENTER THE LAWYERS

The issues raised above are, in the first instance, more questions for lawyers than for political scientists, questions that lawyers will have to answer using the traditional tools of the legal trade: analogy, precedent, categorization, recategorization, rupture, and reconceptualization. When an individual should be treated as a criminal, an unlawful combatant, or a lawful combatant is a classic legal question. Empirically, the individual in question is a person who kills some number of other people, both civilians and military. What to call that person and what consequences to attach to his behavior is a function of some combination of existing law, policy, politics, and social and moral values. Similarly, when a state should be treated like an abstract legal entity with special protections and when it should be treated like an individual participant in a market; when state leaders are entitled to the legal immunities

---

[10] Hillary Rodham Clinton, "Remarks on Internet Freedom," available at http://www.state.gov/secretary/rm/2010/01/135519.htm.

of their office; and what liabilities attach to "hosting," "convening," "connecting," or "partnering" functions that involve both public and private actors are all legal questions to be answered based on different combinations of the same grounds. Different lawyers will also come up with different answers, as will politicians and, ultimately, judges.

It is quite possible, in the process, that the lawyers, legislators, and judges will turn to empirical studies to answer a question or bolster an argument. A cross-national and cross-temporal study showing that treating terrorists as "combatants" rather than "criminals," subjecting them to military rather than criminal law, helped make them martyrs in their communities and aided terrorist groups in their recruitment efforts, for instance, would be very useful in helping lawyers determine what impact different legal categorizations might have on the policy goal of fighting terrorism. Empirical evidence with regard to the deterrent effect of international indictments and/or prosecutions would be similarly helpful in analyzing the policy impact of deciding that a UN Security Council resolution invoking the responsibility to protect as justification for taking action within a country should trigger a request to the International Criminal Court to investigate the conduct of that country's leaders.

But when the legal dust settles, the landscape of international relations will be altered in ways that will have a direct impact on IR scholars. In the first place, the lawyers will be deconstructing Waltz's classic distinguishing of man, the state, and war (2001). If the behavior of individual leaders against their own people becomes grounds for the international use of force under the responsibility to protect doctrine, as happened in Libya, what does that mean for structural realist theories of power politics? When will it make sense to treat governments as unitary agents for their states and when as individual agents directly responsible for their actions? If individual leaders are aware of and are deterred by international criminal liability, how does that affect balance of power calculations, an assessment of the desirability of institutions, or responses to domestic constituencies? Alternatively, can current theories of interstate war account for decisions to target individuals? Can deterrence work in that context?

Second, how should IR scholars think about states that are self-consciously transforming themselves into "platforms" for partnerships between different parts of the state – different agencies, parts of agencies, and subnational governments – and non-state actors? Is the state an agent or principal in these interactions? More fundamentally, is the state the actor worth studying? The categories that the lawyers construct, and the resulting responsibilities and liabilities, will bear on the social scientists' answer to this question.

Third, the extent to which the law chooses to merge physical and virtual space has enormous implications for whether IR scholars choose to study state action in virtual space (cyber war, cyber espionage, censorship, spreading false information and assuming false identities, etc.) the same way that they study state action on the high seas or in space. If the lawyers determine that cyberspace is not a global commons but rather "created" space that depends on the physical location of servers within the territorial boundaries of sovereign nations, then it becomes very difficult to conceptualize states acting "within" space that they, in fact, create and can shut down at any moment. On the other hand, a legal determination that rights and freedoms in virtual space are an inherent outgrowth of those same rights and freedoms in physical space will be a determination that virtual space is an unalterable extension of physical space. Obviously, legal categories do not necessarily change the way computer scientists, terrorist networks, and political activists think about cyberspace, but they certainly shape the thinking of government actors, from soldiers to diplomats to telecommunications regulators. The actions of those governments are, in turn, the subject of empirical and theoretical work in IR.

The deeper point flows from law's character as a "professional" as well as academic discipline. What legal scholars think and write can directly shape the field that they study; academic writings in law can become law and thus then shape the future study and practice of law. That reality also inevitably shapes the world that IR scholars study as well. All of which means that IR scholars need to know much more about how law is in fact made and what their international legal colleagues are doing not as IL/IR experts but as legal scholars.

Finally, law is also inescapably normative. Many of the critics of IL/IR scholarship accuse it of seeking to erase the normative dimension of international law, but in my view, it is precisely the contrast *between* IL and the empirical discipline of IR that brings out law's normative character. IL/IR scholars have to cross the empirical/normative boundary all the time, understanding how both theoretical and empirical scholarship in IR can inform law but never replace it. Indeed, both legal theorists and doctrinal scholars must be constantly aware of how their normative precommitments inform their scholarship, whether or not they are being explicitly normative. There, too, they have something to teach their IR colleagues, many of whom are far less conscious of the inevitable influence of their normative biases.

In sum, twenty years on, I remain committed to the intellectual and practical intersection and even integration of IL and IR scholarship and practice. But I am less starry-eyed about the intellectual hegemony of IR scholarship; much of it has become narrower and narrower and obsessed with methodological questions that often seem to ignore the poor quality of the data in the first place. Yet, at its best, as practiced by many of the contributors to this volume, the study of the politics of the international system still has much to contribute to the study of the law that both reflects and regulates those politics. At the same time, I have a greater appreciation for the role of international law, or perhaps I should say the different categories of global law, in shaping international reality, and for the normative and conceptual core of the legal discipline. Above all, given the expansion of human knowledge and the relentless march of specialization, I am deeply encouraged by the many younger scholars who choose to pursue degrees in both IR and IL and thus to understand not only the scholarship but also the deep habits of mind and mindsets of both disciplines.

A volume like this one could not have been assembled twenty years ago. Twenty years from now, I hope that it will no longer be necessary to take stock of IL/IR scholarship as a particular strand of work in both disciplines. May it become an integral part of all efforts both to understand the world and to make it a better place.

REFERENCES

Abbott, Kenneth W. (1989). "Modern International Relations Theory: A Prospectus for International Lawyers," *Yale Journal of International Law*, Vol. 14, p. 335.

Alter, Karen J. (2013). "The Multiple Roles of International Courts and Tribunals: Enforcement, Dispute Settlement, Constitutional and Administrative Review," in Jeffrey L. Dunoff and Mark A. Pollack (eds.), *Interdisciplinary Perspectives on International Law and International Relations: The State of the Art* (New York: Cambridge University Press), pp. 345–70.

Clinton, Hillary R. (2011). "Internet Rights and Wrongs: Choices and Challenges in a Networked World," speech given at George Washington University, Washington, DC, February 15, 2011. Transcript available at: http://www.state.gov/secretary/rm/2011/02/156619.htm

Dunoff, Jeffrey L., and Mark A. Pollack (2013). "International Law and International Relations: Introducing an Interdisciplinary Dialogue," in Jeffrey L. Dunoff and Mark A. Pollack (eds.), *Interdisciplinary Perspectives on International Law and International Relations: The State of the Art* (New York: Cambridge University Press), pp. 3–32.

Friedman, Thomas L. (1999). *The Lexus and the Olive Tree: Understanding Globalization* (New York: Anchor Books).

Helfer, Laurence R. (2013). "Flexibility in International Agreements," in Jeffrey L. Dunoff and Mark A. Pollack (eds.), *Interdisciplinary Perspectives on International Law and International Relations: The State of the Art* (New York: Cambridge University Press), pp. 175–96.

Ikenberry, G. John (2011). *Liberal Leviathan: The Origins, Crisis, and Transformation of the American World Order* (Princeton, NJ: Princeton University Press).

Jervis, Robert (1978). "Cooperation under the Security Dilemma," *World Politics*, Vol. 30, No. 2, pp. 167–214.

Keohane, Robert O. (1984). *After Hegemony: Cooperation and Discord in the World Political Economy* (Princeton, NJ: Princeton University Press).

Mansfield, Edward D., and Jack Snyder (2005). *Electing to Fight: Why Emerging Democracies Go to War* (Cambridge, MA: MIT Press).

Slaughter Burley, Anne-Marie (1993). "International Law and International Relations Theory: A Dual Agenda," *The American Journal of International Law*, Vol. 87, No. 2, pp. 205–39.

Teitel, Ruti G. (2011). *Humanity's Law* (New York: Oxford University Press).

Waltz, Kenneth (2011). *Man, the State, and War: A Theoretical Analysis*, rev. ed. (New York: Columbia University Press).

26

Reviewing Two Decades of IL/IR Scholarship:

What We've Learned, What's Next

Jeffrey L. Dunoff and Mark A. Pollack

After two decades, and twenty-five chapters, of international law and international relations (IL/IR) scholarship, where do we stand? More specifically, what are the value-added insights of IL/IR relative to the extant scholarship in IL and IR taken separately, what are the weaknesses or lacunae in the literature, and what productive research agenda lies ahead? In this concluding chapter, we begin to outline preliminary answers to these questions.

The chapter is organized in five parts. Following this introduction, the first three sections address the volume's core thematic issues, asking what IL/IR has taught us about the making, interpretation of, and compliance with international law. In each area, we demonstrate that IL/IR scholarship has generated substantial theoretical insight and empirical knowledge about international law. However, in each case, this same scholarship has exhibited blind spots and gaps that can, and should, be addressed in a new generation of IL/IR scholarship that draws in a more balanced way on insights and methods from both disciplines.

In the fourth section, we turn to theory, summarizing not only what our four "theory chapters" have argued about the strengths and weaknesses of each theory, but also to what extent, and how, each of the four primary IR theories (institutionalism, liberalism, constructivism, and realism) has informed the substantive scholarship reviewed in the other, thematic chapters of the volume. Since its institutionalist origins, IL/IR scholarship has undergone a substantial theoretical diversification, drawing – albeit unevenly – from all four traditions of IR theory. Indeed, each theory has generated specific and useful insights, with institutional theory emphasizing factors such as the strategic structure of cooperation problems and the potential impact of institutions in facilitating cooperation; liberal theory emphasizing the significance of domestic law and politics in shaping not only state preferences but also subsequent workings and dynamic development of the international legal system; constructivism emphasizing the importance of norms and identity, and the constitutive effects of international law on states; and realism continuing to emphasize the importance of distributive conflict and state power as fundamental shapers of international law.

The theoretical pluralism of the past two decades of scholarship, we argue in the final section, has been productive, moving IL/IR past its institutionalist roots and generating important new insights. These advances suggest two general conclusions. First, IL/IR scholars should avoid the winner-take-all confrontations among the four "isms" that have occupied some IR scholars, and instead adopt an eclectic or "tool-kit" approach, drawing insights from multiple bodies of theory as a function of their specific research questions. Second, future IL/IR scholarship should seek a greater balance in the intellectual terms of trade between the two disciplines – not for its own sake, but because international legal theory and scholarship contains underutilized conceptual approaches and tools that can further enrich and deepen our understanding of the causes and consequences of the legalization of international affairs.

I. MAKING INTERNATIONAL LAW

Prior to the rise of IL/IR scholarship, IR and IL scholars were both interested in, but took very different approaches to, the issue of international law-making, with minimal overlap between them. On the IR side, realists argued that international law reflected the preferences of the most powerful states, yet this assertion was not generally followed up with rigorous empirical work to test that claim. Institutionalist theorists, by contrast, were interested in how international institutions might help states cooperate, but these studies were theoretically preliminary, relying primarily on basic prisoners' dilemma and collective action models, and largely abstracting away from the specifically legal features of international institutions. By contrast, liberal theories emphasizing state-society relations were in their infancy, as were constructivist theories emphasizing the expressive nature and constitutive power of international legal norms.

On the international law side, positivist legal scholars focused largely on *sources* of international law, but legal scholars in the New Haven and International Legal Process schools examined in greater detail the *processes* through which states negotiated international treaties, as well as the ways in which customary international law was created through an ongoing dialectic of claim and counter-claim by international legal actors. Furthermore, New Haven School scholars in particular responded to realist IR theory by paying close attention to the particular role of great powers, such as the United States, in the process of international law-making, while critical legal studies scholars sought to identify the hidden power structures embedded in international legal norms.

From this baseline, the IL/IR scholarship reviewed in this volume has contributed to our understanding of law-making in five major areas, which we label *design, distribution and power, new actors, regime complexity and legal fragmentation,* and *normative questions* about legitimacy and accountability. Let us say a few words about each.

Perhaps the most striking feature of IL/IR scholarship over the past decade has been the common focus of both law and political science scholars on issues of legal and institutional *design*. Prior to the most recent wave of scholarship informed by the "rational design" project (Koremenos, Lipson, and Snidal 2001), design issues had been of primary interest to legal scholars in specific issue areas, such as debates among trade law scholars over the continued efficacy of the World Trade Organization's (WTO) practice of decision-making by consensus (e.g., Ehlermann and Ehring 2005). By contrast, legal scholars in the New Haven and International Legal Process schools had drawn scholarly attention away from international legal rules toward legal processes (Slaughter Burley 1993), while IR regime theorists had deliberately downplayed formal rules and institutions in favor of a broader conception of regimes that included implicit norms and principles (Krasner 1982) and intersubjectively shared understandings (Kratochwil and Ruggie 1986). As the chapters by Barbara Koremenos (2013; Chapter 3), Barbara Koremenos and Timm Betz (2013; Chapter 15), Laurence R. Helfer (2013; Chapter 7), and Gregory Shaffer and Mark A. Pollack (2013; Chapter 8) all demonstrate, however, scholars from both disciplines have increasingly sought to not only classify but also explain broad patterns in legal and institutional design choices across multiple issue areas. Beginning with Charles Lipson's (1991) influential work on the choice of informal and formal rules, Abbott and Snidal (2000) and others (Shelton 2004; Shaffer and Pollack 2010) explored why, and under what conditions, states and other actors might opt for nonbinding, soft-law provisions. With the rational design volume (Koremenos *et al.* 2001) came a full-blown research program that sought to explain a multitude of design choices (in the original formulation, membership, scope, centralization, control and flexibility) with reference to a set of environmental variables (distribution problems, enforcement problems, number, and various types of uncertainty). One of the most fruitful streams of scholarship to come out of this project has explored the design of various flexibility mechanisms, such as safeguard clauses, exit clauses, limited duration clauses, and reservations, each of which has been shown to vary systematically in terms of their design and the conditions under which they are selected (Helfer 2013; Koremenos 2013; Koremenos and Betz 2013). A closely related literature has adopted the language of principal–agent analysis to understand the design and independence of international organizations, including international courts and tribunals (Voeten 2013; Koremenos and Betz 2013). Such questions had long been of interest to legal scholars, who, however, rarely utilized rich theoretical frameworks to analyze state choices, but had been largely ignored by political science scholars with a realist-induced disinterest in the details of formal international organizations. The rational design approach therefore represents, in our view, one of the most fruitful intersections and interactions of IR and IL scholars reviewed in this volume.

Notwithstanding its significant strengths, the rational design approach has had its share of critics, who argue that the rational design framework reduced international design choices to a set of correlations between a set of environmental independent variables and another set of institutional design variables – thereby black-boxing both the *process* of law-making and the role of *power* therein. One traditional focus of realist political science work, for example, was its close attention to the role of power, and in particular of the great powers, in international law-making, since the terms of any international agreement were likely to have distributive implications among the participants, and states with greater power resources were likely to achieve outcomes that came closest to their own preferences (Morgenthau 1948; Krasner 1991). The rational design approach drew in part from realist theory in its explicit consideration of distributive conflict as a potential determinant of institutional design choices, but arguably paid insufficient attention to state power its initial formulations, where it did not appear as an explicit explanatory variable (Duffield 2003). More recent work in this tradition, however, has sought to reintroduce the role of power (e.g., Koremenos and Betz 2013). These welcome developments speak to the common interest in power among IR scholars, as well as among New Haven and critical legal scholars in law.

A third element of the recent IL/IR literature also concerns process, specifically the rise of *new actors* in international law-making (as well as in the later stages of interpretation, enforcement, and compliance). Although both systemic IR theory and positivist legal theory share a common focus on states as the primary makers and subjects of international law, the chapters by Ian Johnstone (Chapter 11), Peter J. Spiro (Chapter 9), and Abraham L. Newman and David Zaring (Chapter 10) in this volume make clear that states are no longer – if indeed they ever were – alone in the making of international law. In his theoretically and empirically rich chapter, Johnstone (2013, Chapter 11) analyzes the various ways that international organizations – acting in some cases as subsets of the entire membership, in some cases through secretariats with delegated powers – engage in meaningful international legislation, adopting binding international rules, in some cases without the explicit consent of their states parties. Spiro's (2013) chapter directs our attention to another set of non-state actors, namely, nongovernmental organizations (NGOs), which he shows to be increasingly active and influential participants in international law-making, both as advocates or lobbyists targeting state negotiators, and in some instances as direct participants in international law-making. The rise of non-state actors like NGOs and private firms becomes even more important if we extend our analysis beyond traditional treaty negotiations to the full web of what Abbott and Snidal (2009) call "regulatory standard-setting" schemes, in which international norms are established by various combinations of public (state) and private (firm and NGO) actors. Finally, although the state remains a key actor, it increasingly acts in nontraditional ways. Newman and Zaring (2013) summarize a growing literature on the phenomenon of international law-making (and implementation) by transgovernmental networks of traditionally domestic national regulators. Neither the concept nor the reality of transgovernmental regulatory networks is new (see, e.g., Keohane and Nye 1974), yet recent decades have witnessed a sharp rise in the incidence and activity of such networks, and Newman and Zaring make a strong case for the coincidence of interests and the complementarity of insights generated by political science and legal scholars on this question.

A fourth vital area of scholarly activity relates to what political scientists call *regime complexity* (Raustiala and Victor 2004; Alter and Meunier 2009) and what legal scholars term *legal fragmentation* (Koskenniemi and Leino 2002). As reviewed by Kal Raustiala (2013) in Chapter 12 of this volume, these twin literatures point to a fundamentally important development, namely, the emergence of increasingly dense, overlapping, and nonhierarchically arranged international legal regimes in issue areas such as international trade, environmental protection, human rights, and so on. By and large, legal scholarship on this question has focused in particular on the dilemmas that fragmentation poses for legal interpretation in an increasingly plural international legal order. In such a setting, scholars have advanced different approaches to resolve inconsistent or conflicting norms found in different regimes, ranging from "conflicts of law" approaches (Pauwelyn 2003) to more ambitious calls for a constitutionalized legal order (Dunoff and Trachtman 2009) or for pluralist dialogues among overlapping normative communities, courts, and tribunals (Berman 2007). Although legal scholars have focused most of their attention on the interpretation stage, by contrast, nearly all of the interdisciplinary IL/IR literature has focused on the implications of regime complexity at the law-making stage, where strategic states (and other actors) are seen to engage in "strategic inconsistency" (Raustiala and Victor 2004), "regime shifting" (Helfer 2004), and "forum shopping" (Jupille and Snidal 2006) to advance their interests and secure the adoption of favorable rules and judgments amidst the proliferation of international legal institutions. The preliminary findings of this literature, Raustiala (2013) notes, are not reassuring for the rule of international law, with many scholars concluding that a proliferation of international legal regimes empowers already powerful states with the legal and diplomatic sophistication to engage in strategic forum shopping across issue areas. Nevertheless, other analysts like Helfer (2004) argue that regime complexity can also empower weak states to challenge hegemonic rules and norms, and the relationship between power and proliferation remains open to further systematic empirical study.

Fifth and finally, as Daniel Bodansky (2013) argues in his contribution to this volume (Chapter 13), the dramatic growth in the volume, scope, and invasiveness of international law has produced a vigorous debate on normative questions, including most strikingly over the *legitimacy* of international law-making. This debate first flowered in the exceptionally institutionalized legal order of the European Union (EU), which has been denounced for a democratic deficit (e.g., Hix 2008; for a defense, see Moravcsik 2002), but has since spread, with issues of democratic accountability at the heart of much of the U.S. "sovereigntist" (Spiro 2000) critique of international law and institutions (e.g., Goldsmith and Posner 2005). Recent work – including not least Bodansky's careful taxonomic discussion in this volume – has helped to clarify frequently confused meanings of legitimacy (e.g., normative vs. sociological, input vs. output) and to put forward new and novel proposals that seek to enhance the legitimacy of international governance through greater democratic accountability (e.g., Hix 2008), more systematic international administrative law (Kingsbury, Krisch, and Stewart 2005), and more deliberative supranational decision making (Joerges 2001; Johnstone 2011).

Nevertheless, although we can identify a substantial number of value-added concepts and empirical findings in the IL/IR literature on law-making, we can also find substantial blind spots and gaps. We have already suggested that the sharp focus on questions of design has reduced scholars' attention to issues of process and power, although we see these omissions being slowly and sporadically addressed in recent years. A related concern is the relative inattention to the actual *use* of international legal provisions, such as safeguard, exit, and dispute settlement clauses, beyond the initial design phase. Much of the early rational design literature rested on a sometimes unstated assumption that legal provisions were actually employed by states in the ways posited by rational design models. Helfer's (2013) careful analysis of the use of safeguard and exit clauses in this volume (Chapter 7) suggests that these assumptions may be ill-founded, raising the prospect of a *post hoc, ergo propter hoc* fallacy in which the choice or design of an institution is wrongly attributed to its eventual function, which may have been unintended by the designers. Koremenos and Betz (2013), by contrast, confront the relatively infrequent use of formal dispute settlement mechanisms, but argue that such infrequent use is consistent with a rational design model, in which the adoption of robust dispute settlement provisions may screen out potential violators, and signatories may resolve their disputes bilaterally in the shadow of litigation. Clearly, the transition from "design" to "use" remains an important challenge to IL/IR scholarship in the years to come.

Another manifest weakness of the IL/IR literature has been the persistent neglect, until very recently, of customary international law-making. Ironically, legal scholars in the New Haven School had long noted the intensely political nature of customary international law-making, characterized by Myres McDougal in 1955 as "a process of continuous interaction, of continuous demand and response" by affected nations (McDougal 1955; see also Reisman 2003), whereas political scientists generally adopted a formalist approach, effectively equating international law with the text of international treaties! IL/IR scholars have now begun to analyze customary international law, including recent efforts informed by game theory, seeking to model and empirically analyze how states interact and jockey for advantage in the making (Swaine 2002; Norman and Trachtman 2005) and codification of customary international law (Meyer 2012).

Of course, international law is made and spreads through other methods as well, and a small number of constructivist scholars are starting to study the processes whereby international legal norms are generated and diffused (see, e.g., Johnstone 2011). Indeed, Johnstone (2013) argues compellingly that both IL and IR conceptions of law-making have been too narrow and formalistic, and that many other activities normally classed as interpretation or implementation generate "normative ripples" and in practice also "make law."

A final potential weakness of the IL/IR literature on law-making, depending on one's perspective, has been its strong emphasis on rationalist and instrumentalist accounts of legal norms. Although both legal scholars and constructivists in IR have long argued that international law can serve an expressive function (Dunoff and Trachtman 1999) and reflect community values, constructivist scholars have, in practice, focused much of their empirical attention on the stages of legal interpretation and compliance, to which we now turn.

II. INTERPRETING

By contrast with international law-making, which has long been of interest to both legal and political science scholars, the question of legal interpretation has been the subject of intense interest among legal scholars and, until recently, neglected by political science scholars. International lawyers have devoted substantial attention to the rules and methods of treaty interpretation, with particular focus on the Vienna Convention on the Law of Treaties, which provides that treaties "shall be interpreted in good faith in accordance with the ordinary meaning to be given to the terms of the treaty in their context and in the light of its object and purpose." International courts and scholars have debated the relative weight to be given to factors such as the intent of the treaty's parties, the significance of *travaux préparatoires*, the importance of subsequent practice, whether the same interpretative approach is appropriate for all treaties, and the legitimacy of functional or teleological approaches to interpretation.

With the rise of an IL/IR approach, the long neglect by IR scholars of the interpretation function has come to an end, and recent scholarship has illuminated – albeit selectively – four significant questions or themes: (a) the design of dispute settlement bodies; (b) judicial behavior, with an emphasis on judicial independence; (c) patterns of state behavior with respect to international litigation; and (d) the dynamic evolution of dispute settlement systems over time. IL/IR approaches are not without their blind spots and lacunae, to which we will turn presently, but let us first consider these four distinctive IL/IR contributions.[1]

---

[1] Note that, in many of these areas, there are antecedents in IL, but the IL/IR work adds a richer and more systematic empiricism and substantial methodological sophistication. Thus, international lawyers have long been concerned about, say, judicial independence (see Brown Weiss 1987), but generally have not engaged in the careful coding and sophisticated statistical analysis found in much IL/IR work. Similarly, when lawyers focus on the design of dispute settlement bodies, they often focus on jurisdictional provisions, evidentiary rules, and available remedies, as opposed to the broader issues of institutional architecture addressed in IL/IR writings.

First, in keeping with the increasing focus on rational design, a handful of scholars, represented in this volume by Koremenos and Betz (2013), have sought systematically to understand and explain the design of international dispute settlement bodies. This is not, of course, an entirely new subject, as legal scholars had long devoted significant attention to the charters and other design features of individual courts such as the International Court of Justice (ICJ), the European Court of Justice (ECJ), and the WTO Dispute Settlement Body. In general, however, IL/IR scholarship has sought not only to analyze and critique the design of individual courts and tribunals, but also to classify and explain broad patterns in international dispute settlement systems. For example, Keohane, Moravcsik, and Slaughter (2000) provided an influential analytical framework that classified various international dispute settlement mechanisms along three dimensions – access, independence, and embeddedness – characterizing courts that were low in all three dimensions as "interstate" courts and those that were high as "transnational" courts. Such differences in design, they argued, largely determine how frequently and by whom courts were used, whether those courts provide for the credible and neutral adjudication of disputes, and whether the resulting decisions would have immediate effects in the legal orders of their member states. Karen J. Alter's (2013) contribution to this volume (Chapter 14) offers an alternative classification of international courts in terms of the functions they perform. Other recent work goes further still, seeking to explain the conditions under which states design particular types of dispute settlement bodies. In the most extensive such study, Koremenos (2007) and Koremenos and Betz (2013) adapt the rational design research project to the study of dispute settlement systems, demonstrating that international dispute settlement systems vary dramatically across regions and across issue areas. Koremenos and Betz hypothesize that states systematically adopt dispute settlement mechanisms, as well as particular types of dispute settlement (informal vs. formal, arbitration vs. adjudication, etc.), in response to particular types of cooperation problems, including enforcement problems, commitment problems, and uncertainty, and they find considerable support for these hypotheses in their empirical analysis.

A large and well-developed second strand of IL/IR scholarship has focused on explaining the nature, extent, and determinants of international judicial behavior and independence. The focus here has been on characterizing and explaining the voting behavior of international judges, often with an eye to establishing the extent and the determinants of their independence from the states that appoint them to their positions. Although a few legal studies had problematized and studied the independence of specific international courts (e.g., Weiss 1987), IL/IR scholarship has systematized such analysis, defining judicial independence clearly and providing comprehensive theoretical frameworks identifying a wide range of potential control mechanisms available to states (Pollack 2003; Voeten 2013), as well as other legal and political sources of influence (Helfer 2006) over international judicial behavior. Just as significantly, this research agenda has given rise to a spate of qualitative and quantitative empirical work seeking to establish, despite considerable method-ological challenges, the nature and sources of judicial independence in the ECJ (cf. Carrubba, Gabel, and Hankla 2008; Stone Sweet and Brunell 1998, 2012), the European Court of Human Rights (ECtHR) (Voeten 2008), the ICJ (Posner and Figueiredo 2005), and the WTO Appellate Body (Elsig and Pollack, forthcoming), among others. Controversies remain within this literature, but the focus of anal-ysis has increasingly moved from broad questions of whether international courts are entirely dependent or epiphenomenal at one extreme or entirely independent trustees at the other extreme, to more fine-grained analysis of the effects of judicial appointment and reappointment practices, the ease or difficulty of legislative over-ruling, and the prospect of state noncompliance as potential sources of influence over international courts. Interestingly, Erik Voeten's chapter (Chapter 17) suggests that, in addition to studying judicial independence as a dependent variable, schol-ars increasingly ask whether judicial independence as an independent variable may help to explain other phenomena, including the effectiveness of international courts (cf. Helfer and Slaughter 2005; Posner and Yoo 2005). This research, in turn, raises the intriguing concept of *optimal judicialization*. In an influential paper, Helfer (2002) asks whether international human rights law has become "overlegalized," prompting a backlash against such treaties by Caribbean nations, and similar con-cerns have been raised in the trade context by Goldstein and Martin (2000), Hudec (1999), and Dunoff (1999), each of whom has warned of the potential overrigidity of dispute settlement and limitations of courts in addressing highly politicized disputes. Voeten (2013) concludes that identifying optimal levels of judicialization represents one of the frontier subjects for future IL/IR research.

A third major contribution of IL/IR scholarship, less frequently discussed but of equal interest, has been to problematize, theorize, and study empirically patterns of state behavior as litigants in international dispute settlement. In both political science and law, international court rulings are frequently examined, as are subsequent acts of compliance or defiance by states, with less attention devoted to state behavior preceding the initiation of litigation. As Todd Allee (2004: 3) notes, the "decision to sue" is an important and understudied question, of interest not only for its own sake but because the cases that actually reach international courts constitute a small – and potentially biased – subset of the universe of international legal disputes. Hence, the behavior of litigants may shape international jurisprudence as decisively as the preferences of international judges or their member state principals.

Fortunately, recent IL/IR scholarship has begun to address this question across a number of issue areas. In one study of international territorial disputes, for example, Allee and Huth hypothesize that states are most likely to refer international disputes to judicial settlement when the domestic audience costs of making significant political concessions are high. In such settings, they argue, international judicial rulings can provide "political cover" for domestically unpopular decisions, and their analysis of nearly 1,500 territorial disputes provides support for the claim that "state leaders opt for legal dispute resolution when they are highly accountable to domestic political opposition, as well as when the dispute is highly salient to domestic audiences" (Allee and Huth 2006: 219). This study supports the liberal theoretical view that state behavior with respect to international litigation is driven in large part by domestic politics and domestic political institutions (Dunoff 1998; Shaffer 2003). Other work, particularly on state behavior in WTO dispute settlement, points to other potential influences on state litigation behavior, including state power (Horn and Mavroidis 2007), actor estimates of the probability of winning (Allee 2004), regime type (Busch 2000), and previous litigation experience (Davis and Bermeo 2009). In a similar vein, students of the ECJ, investment arbitrations, and other fora that grant access to individuals have extended this research by studying the behavior of such litigants, noting systematic differences in the behavior of "one-shot" and "repeat players" (Conant 2002), as well as differences across more or less liberal domestic political systems (Alter and Helfer 2010).

Fourth, and most tentatively, IL/IR scholars have begun to develop and test hypotheses on the conditions under which, and the ways in which, international dispute settlement systems develop dynamically over time. IL/IR scholars have suggested that transnational dispute settlement systems, characterized by high levels of access, independence, and embeddedness, should show greater dynamism over time, as individuals (not subject to governmental gatekeeping) bring cases that are likely to be decided independently and enforced through domestic legal systems, creating a feedback loop of ever more developed law and ever-growing caseloads (see also Helfer and Slaughter 1997; Stone Sweet and Brunell 1998; Keohane *et al.* 2000). Indeed, Andrew Moravcsik's (2013) chapter in this volume (Chapter 4) suggests that the explanation of dynamic development of dispute settlement regimes is one of the signature contributions of liberal theory to the study of international law.

Despite these substantial contributions, much of the IL/IR scholarship arguably suffers from a systematic bias in favor of certain research questions and empirical subjects, while ignoring others. We limit ourselves here to three such omissions.

First, much of the literature reviewed in this volume suffers from an *overemphasis on international courts*, as opposed to other actors engaged in the interpretation of international law. Such a focus is understandable, given the dramatic increase in the number and activity of such courts over the past two decades. However, the universe of actors engaged in legal interpretation is far broader than that of international courts (Romano 2011), including a large number of international arbitration systems, intergovernmental and expert human rights commissions, international environmental compliance systems, and WTO committees at the international level, and national governments and national courts at the domestic level. Political scientists have, for example, largely ignored the workings of international arbitration schemes, although a spate of recent scholarship on investor–state arbitration demonstrates the promise of interdisciplinary scholarship in understanding the decisions by states to accept arbitration, the subsequent behavior of arbitrators, and the apparent backlash against arbitral decisions by states (see, e.g., Alvarez 2011; Roberts 2013). Similarly, IL/IR scholars have focused growing attention on the powerful ECtHR, but have devoted little or no study to international human rights interpretation bodies, including the expert Human Rights Committee that has issued controversial interpretations of provisions of the International Convention on Civil and Political Rights, and the intergovernmental United Nations (UN) Human Rights Council (and its predecessor, the Commission on Human Rights), which has attracted the ire of the United States and other Western countries for its allegedly biased interpretation and application of international human rights law. In addition, a large number of scholars study patterns of litigation and judicial behavior in the WTO dispute settlement system, but far fewer have examined the resolution of disputes in WTO intergovernmental bodies such as the Sanitary and Phytosanitary Committee, or how the North American Free Trade Agreement (NAFTA) parties can issue authoritative interpretations of NAFTA treaty provisions. These nonjudicial bodies would seem a natural object of study for IR scholars, but they have thus far been studied primarily by sociologically and empirically oriented international lawyers (Dunoff 2006; Lang and Scott 2009). A pioneering IL/IR study in this regard is Steven Ratner's (2013) chapter in this volume (Chapter 23), which explores the conditions under which international actors such as the International Committee of the Red Cross are likely to invoke and employ legal arguments in their interactions with states and other combatants.

The focus on *international* courts has similarly led to an underemphasis on the roles of *domestic* courts in interpreting international law. The lawyers and IR scholars who study national courts have tended to focus either on European or U.S. courts, as Lisa Conant notes in her contribution (2013, Chapter 16). EU scholarship has been in the forefront here, with a large and sophisticated law-and-politics literature studying both qualitatively and quantitatively the reception of EU law by national courts, and the subsequent judicial interactions or dialogues between national and European courts. These works have analyzed not only doctrinal developments but also the strategic interactions between domestic lower courts, high courts, and the ECJ, and the strategies employed by national courts to limit or "contain" the impacts of EU law in domestic settings (see, e.g., Burley and Mattli 1993; Weiler 1994; Alter 2001; Conant 2002). By contrast, the literature on international law in U.S. courts has thus far been largely doctrinal and jurisprudential, focusing the status of different forms of IL as domestic law, the incorporation of customary international law by courts, and the self-executing or non–self-executing character of international treaties. Much of this U.S. literature has been overtly normative in orientation, with little or no effort to identify causal factors that influence patterns of judicial interpretation. For this reason, we would argue, the comparative social-scientific study of international legal interpretation by national courts, in the United States and elsewhere, represents a promising area for future IL/IR research.

Moreover, on the domestic plane (as on the international plane), most legal interpretation takes place outside of courts. Legislatures enact statutes, and executives implement the law, against the backdrop of a state's international legal obligations. But this activity has largely fallen outside the purview of IL/IR scholarship. To be sure, some work by lawyers in the international legal process and New Haven schools (Chayes 1974; Reisman 1990) examine how international law is interpreted by and shapes the behavior of leaders and officials in the United States and other governments. This work has no precise counterpart in today's scholarship, although the literature on compliance with and internationalization of international law, reviewed below, addresses related questions.

A second limit of existing IL/IR scholarship in this area is its almost exclusive emphasis on judicial *behavior* and its relative neglect of *legal interpretation* per se. With its increasingly extensive use of quantitative methods to detect patterns of international judicial decision-making, as well as correlations between judicial rulings and other factors, much of the existing literature reduces judicial rulings to a single dimension; namely, whether a court ruled for or against any given state on a particular issue. The results of these studies have been valuable, demonstrating the ability of at least certain courts to rule against the interests of powerful states, as well as identifying some important predictors of judicial behavior (Voeten 2013). Yet, in so doing, most of the IL/IR literature ignores other aspects of judicial interpretation, including questions of the principles used to guide interpretation, the formal or informal use of precedent, the nature of legal arguments, and more. A notable exception to this trend is Joost Pauwelyn and Manfred Elsig's (2013) chapter in this volume (Chapter 18), which is exceptional in combining a legal scholar's attention to interpretive strategies with a social-scientific effort to both classify interpretive strategies and explain why courts and judges might adopt one or another of those strategies. Pauwelyn and Elsig emphasize that their approach is exploratory, but it represents the promise of a research agenda that brings together the lawyer's attention to doctrine and discourse with the political scientist's effort to explain broad patterns of and variations in behavior.

A third and related limitation of existing IL/IR scholarship has been its nearly exclusive *emphasis on the dispute settlement function of courts, at the expense of other functions.* Although courts do unquestionably play an important role in settling legal disputes among parties to international agreements, Alter (2013) rightly points out that courts also serve other functions, including what she calls enforcement, administrative review, and constitutional review. Perhaps most important, when international courts interpret law, they elaborate, develop, and necessarily create new law. As Lauterpacht (1933) noted, "in interpreting and applying concrete legal rules the Court does not act as an automatic slot-machine. . . . It exercises in each case a creative activity, having as its background the entirety of international law and the necessities of the international community. The distinction between the making of law by judges and by the legislature is upon analysis one of degree . . . judicial activity is nothing else than legislation in concreto. . . . " In this sense, legal interpretation is a far broader concept than dispute settlement, which describes only one function of international courts, and IL/IR scholars can fruitfully study international courts as law-makers.

Finally, dispute settlement takes in far more than the judicial role played by courts and arbitrators, in many cases comprising complex systems for bringing disputes, holding consultations, settling disputes diplomatically, selecting among possible dispute-settlement forums, building legal and administrative capacity, selecting remedies, and so on. The methodological challenges of studying dispute settlement outside the judicial arena are substantial, given the nontransparent nature of these processes, but a small number of IL/IR scholars have begun to study both dispute-settlement and enforcement systems in their entirety – which takes us to our next topic of compliance, enforcement, and effectiveness.

III. COMPLIANCE

The subject of compliance with international law was long neglected by both IL and IR scholars. Among IL scholars, there has been widespread acceptance, and almost ritual incantation, of Louis Henkin's (1979: 47) famous claim that "almost all nations observe almost all principles of international law and almost all of their obligations almost all the time." Against this intellectual background, only a handful of legal scholars sought to engage in any systematic analysis of state compliance with international law prior to the 1990s. International relations scholars similarly slighted the subject of legal compliance until recently, assuming that law per se had no independent causal influence on state behavior, with compliance attributed largely to states' instrumental calculation of their own interests, as well as to the shallowness of most international agreements (Downs, Rocke, and Barsoom 1996).

During the course of the 1990s, scholars from both disciplines finally put issues of compliance front and center, resulting in the famous "management versus enforcement debate," which pitted a team of international legal scholars (Chayes and Chayes 1993, 1995) against skeptical political scientists (Downs *et al.* 1996). Abram and Antonia Chayes set forth a "managerial" theory of compliance premised on the assumption that states have a propensity to comply with their legal obligations. They argued that most cases of noncompliance are inadvertent and result from ambiguous treaty language, low national capacity, or unavoidable time lags between commitment and compliance. The managerial school argues that sanctions are less useful than noncoercive managerial strategies in promoting compliance. Downs, Rocke, and Barsoom, by contrast, argued that high levels of compliance with treaty norms simply reveal the "shallowness" of many international agreements. They claimed that as regimes deepen and the gains from cooperation grow, so too do the incentives to defect. Thus, deeper agreements require correspondingly harder enforcement mechanisms.

A common perception among political scientists is that the management versus enforcement debate was essentially "won" by the enforcement side, which demonstrated the limited usefulness of management techniques in precisely those situations in which compliance was most problematic – as well as the naïveté of IL scholars. As Alexander Thompson (2013) argues in his contribution to this volume (Chapter 20), however, the "debate" formulation of the literature creates a tendency "to overlook the extent to which these arguments are complementary," as well as the phased use of both management and enforcement mechanisms in many areas of international law (cf. Tallberg 2002). For this reason, the debate between the management and enforcement schools, and the implication that one must choose between the insights of legal and political science scholars, is a false one.

Building on these early studies, IL/IR scholars have launched an intensive research program into the extent, the causal mechanisms, and correlates of state compliance with international law across a wide range of issue areas. This literature, reviewed by the contributors to Part V of this volume, has made three signal contributions: a *conceptual contribution*, clarifying the meaning of compliance and its relation to other concepts such as enforcement and effectiveness; a *theoretical contribution*, in which various authors have identified numerous potential causal mechanisms that might explain compliance with international law; and a *methodological contribution*, in which scholars have attempted to both measure and explain compliance with international law, both qualitatively and quantitatively, while controlling for competing explanations and, in particular, for the problem of endogeneity and selection effects. We consider each, very briefly, in turn.

First, with respect to conceptual issues, Raustiala and Slaughter (2001) did much to clear the intellectual underbrush by distinguishing among a number of related and sometimes confused concepts, including compliance, implementation, enforcement, and effectiveness (cf. von Stein 2013; Martin 2013). The most commonly used term in the literature, *compliance*, is typically defined, as Jana von Stein (2013) does in her contribution to this volume (Chapter 19), as "the degree to which state behavior conforms to what an agreement prescribes or proscribes."[2] So defined, the question of compliance is conceptually separable from that of implementation (defined in terms of state efforts to administer policy directives) and effectiveness (the extent to which a treaty solves the problem that led to its formation). Indeed, as a number of scholars have now pointed out, states may comply with (shallow) international agreements without engaging in any form of implementation, and without producing any effect with respect to the aims of the agreements. Conversely, states may undertake significant efforts to implement deep and demanding international

---

[2] Von Stein also offers another important distinction, between first-order compliance (adherence to rules) and second-order compliance (adherence to rulings of international judicial bodies), which emerges as vital in Brewster's (2013) analysis of the relationship between international dispute settlement and state reputation.

agreements, resulting in effective efforts to address the stated problem, but fall short of full compliance (cf. Raustiala and Slaughter 2001; von Stein 2013; Martin 2013).

Recent scholarship in both international relations and international law has underlined the significance of this distinction. In her contribution to this volume, for example, Lisa L. Martin (Chapter 24) claims that political scientists have – in their effort to engage in interdisciplinary work – paid too much attention to the legal concept of compliance and, as a result, have paid insufficient attention to international law's effectiveness. She therefore argues "against compliance" as the primary focus of study. Interestingly, Robert Howse and Ruti Teitel (2010) have recently offered a similar critique from a legal perspective, arguing that international law matters in a variety of ways – shifting decision-making authority from some actors to others, setting benchmarks for private as well as state action, shaping the interpretation of domestic law, and providing categories through which actors see the world – which are not captured by a simple focus on compliance as the correspondence of state behavior and rules. For this reason, Howse and Teitel argue that we must look "beyond compliance" at the other potential effects of international law on states and non-state actors. Like von Stein, in her excellent introduction to Section V of the volume, we take these cautionary messages seriously and note the dangers of conflating compliance with other concepts, such as implementation and effectiveness, yet we also agree that compliance remains an important subject of study in and of itself – and one to which recent IL/IR scholarship has made major contributions.

In theoretical terms, the primary contribution of recent scholarship at the intersection of law and political science has been to move beyond broad debates about management and enforcement to much more nuanced and fine-grained examinations of the potential *causal mechanisms* whereby international law may induce compliance.

Von Stein (2013, Chapter 19) provides a comprehensive review of these mechanisms, which she divides into instrumentalist and normative categories. Instrumentalist mechanisms comport largely with the assumptions and predictions of rational choice theory, and include international inducements, retaliation, reciprocity, reputation, and the strategic actions of domestic actors and institutions. Normative mechanisms, in contrast, induce compliance through processes that are not primarily driven "by states' concerns about *ex post* costs"; examples here include mechanisms emphasizing expertise and capacity-building, the impact of law on norms and identity, and issues of legitimacy and fairness.

In this volume, the chapters by Thompson (2013, Chapter 20), Brewster (2013, Chapter 21), Ratner (2013, Chapter 23), and Trachtman (2013, Chapter 22) explore a number of these various mechanisms in greater depth, noting the promise and the problems associated with each. Simplifying considerably, we can say that each of these chapters addresses a mechanism that is distinct to one of the four great theoretical families of realism (enforcement, Thompson), institutionalism (reputation, Brewster), constructivism (persuasion, Ratner), and liberalism (domestic law and politics, Trachtman).

Thompson's chapter on enforcement (Chapter 20) begins with an excellent discussion of the false choice between management and enforcement, and an argument that most international agreements represent a hybrid of the two approaches. Nevertheless, he argues, decentralized enforcement of international law *is* problematic, presenting a "sanctioners' dilemma" to any state that would seek to enforce international law in the face of violations. The costs, he argues, are multiple, including not simply the material (military or economic) costs associated with enforcement actions, but also the political costs associated with establishing and defending the claim that one's actions are in fact un-self-interested enforcement actions and not self-interested opportunism. Despite these substantial obstacles, Thompson argues, international legal institutions can ameliorate the sanctioners' dilemma by minimizing collective action problems (e.g., through multilateral sanctions against violators) and by interpreting and applying the law authoritatively to individual cases (e.g., international court rulings or UN Security Council Resolutions) in ways that reduce the political costs to a state seeking to enforce the law. These institutional functions do not vitiate the sanctioners' dilemma and they do not render IL an Austinian world in which law is a general command issued by a sovereign and inevitably backed by sanctions, but they do make enforcement more likely, albeit selectively and under specified conditions, and hence constitute an important potential mechanism for enhancing compliance with international law.

Among institutionalist scholars, much of the incentive for states to comply with international law revolves around what Guzman (2008) has labeled the "three R's": retaliation, reciprocity, and reputation. In her chapter, Rachel Brewster (Chapter 21) unpacks the concept of reputation, demonstrating that the role of reputation in international law compliance rests on a series of often unexamined assumptions, each of which is potentially problematic. Put simply, reputational accounts rest on the assumption that violations of international law lead states to develop reputations as unreliable partners, and hence are costly to states beyond the immediate context of a particular breach, giving states a long-term interest in establishing reputations for reliable compliance with their agreements. Such a reputational mechanism may be undermined, however, to the extent that a reputation for noncompliance in one area fails to "travel" to other areas, or to the extent that reputations inhere in individual governments rather than states, or to the extent that states seek reputations for characteristics such as toughness rather than for compliance. Brewster concludes her chapter with an interesting and original insight; namely, that the establishment of a dispute settlement mechanism may *undermine* a reputational compliance mechanism, insofar as states might violate their original commitment (hence, first-order noncompliance), but salvage their reputations by complying with any potential adverse judgments (second-order compliance). Brewster's excellent theoretical exploration of the issues serves to highlight the need for empirical work on this, and other, mechanisms of IL compliance.

Constructivist scholarship, and a related literature in international law, has identified other potential compliance mechanisms, which fall broadly under von Stein's "non-instrumental rubric," including Koh's (1997) theory of legal internalization, Goodman and Jinks' (2004) concept of acculturation, and multiple theories of persuasion. In each of these studies, scholars have identified the potential for normative and social processes leading to the internalization of and compliance with international legal (and nonlegal) norms, although here again we find a dearth of empirical works demonstrating such processes at work and the conditions under which they do so.[3] Ratner's chapter in this volume (Chapter 23) does not seek to capture internalization or persuasion of state actors, but breaks new ground in understanding the complex calculations of normatively driven actors seeking to promote state compliance with international law. Perhaps his most striking finding is that actors promoting compliance carefully modulate the nature of their arguments to resonate with the interests and perspectives of their targets, and that – contrary to much constructivist thinking, which considers internalized obedience to be the highest and most effective form of respect for law – principled actors are often "prepared to forego obedience for compliance" (Ratner 2013).

Liberal theories, finally, overlap with many constructivist accounts in their emphasis on domestic political and legal processes, and in their conviction, in von Stein's (2013) words, that, "important sources of compliance lie inside the state." Joel P. Trachtman (2013) identifies four distinct causal factors or mechanisms at the domestic level that that might drive internalization of and compliance with international law: domestic structure; public law litigation and civil society action; ideas, acculturation, and managerial factors; and domestic interests and partisan politics. Trachtman then puts forward his own, broadly rationalist, theory, which highlights the importance of preferences of domestic actors, which are more complex, and contingent, than existing theories suggest.

In theoretical terms, therefore, we have a variety of perspectives, from political science as well as law, that have identified a variety of potential causal mechanisms, and, in nearly every case, we have emphasized the need for more empirical research. Indeed, this focus on empirical analysis, and the increasing sophistication of empirical and especially quantitative compliance studies is the third and final contribution – but also a major limitation – of recent IL/IR scholarship. As von Stein (2013) points out, the past decade alone has witnessed a dramatic increase in the number and sophistication of compliance studies in international law, in areas such

---

[3] Simmons' (2009) study of compliance with human rights treaties presents both qualitative and quantitative evidence of domestic internalization, which she shows (vindicating Keohane [1998]) varies across domestic regime types. Simmons' causal mechanisms, however, focus on the resources that IL provides to specific domestic actors (what Kahler [2000] called "compliance constituencies"), and not on persuasion or socialization mechanisms.

as human rights law (Hathaway 2002, 2003; Goodman and Jinks 2003; Hafner-Burton 2005; Simmons 2009), international criminal law (Kelley 2007), and international humanitarian law (Valentino, Huth, and Croco 2006; Morrow 2007). Furthermore, much of this new scholarship is sensitive to and attempts to control for problems of endogeneity and selection effects, whereby international treaties may act to screen states rather than to constrain them (von Stein 2005, 2013; Simmons and Hopkins 2005; Koremenos and Betz 2013).

Perhaps the most striking weakness in the burgeoning compliance literature is the *mismatch between the central theoretical contribution of IL/IR scholarship, namely the specification of diverse causal mechanisms, and the primary methodological contribution, which has been what von Stein (2013) calls the quantification of compliance studies, which excels in establishing correlations among variables but not at illuminating causal mechanisms.*[4] The solution to this mismatch, obvious in principle if extraordinarily challenging in practice, is for scholars to engage in multimethod research, combining large-*n* studies of compliance among large numbers of states with in-depth case study analysis allowing scholars to identify and trace complex causal mechanisms in action. Beth Simmons' *Mobilizing for Human Rights* (2009) represents the most successful such effort to date, but more such work is needed to establish whether, and under what conditions, the many hypothesized mechanisms for international law compliance actually explain observed behavior.

IV. THEORY

Finally, we return to theory and, in particular, to the four theoretical approaches reviewed in Part II of this volume. We argued in the introduction that IL/IR scholarship consists in large part of the application of IR theory to the subject matter of IL, and one major development of the last two decades has been the successive enlargement of the body of relevant theories from rational institutionalism (Abbott 1999; Koremenos 2013) to liberalism (Slaughter Burley 1993; Moravcsik 2013), constructivism (Kratochvil 1989; Brunnée and Toope 2010, 2013), and finally coming full circle to realism (Steinberg 2013). A full analysis of each theory is beyond the scope of this chapter, so we limit ourselves here to some brief observations about the extent to which, and the ways in which, each theory has been invoked in the substantive chapters of the volume.

Institutionalism has, from Abbott's (1989) prospectus to the present day, been at the center of IL/IR scholarship, and the influence of rational choice institutionalist approaches is both asserted in Koremenos' (2013) chapter and demonstrated in the

---

[4] In addition, although von Stein does not emphasize this point in her chapter, the vast majority of quantitative compliance studies operationalize "international law" as the body of treaties ratified by a given state, thereby ignoring both customary international law as well as the possibility that widely accepted international legal norms might exert a normative impact even on states that had failed to ratify them.

substantive chapters of the volume. With respect to law-making, classical regime theory and game-theoretic models have been influential from the beginning, and have been incorporated into the rational design literature, with its emphasis on what has been variously called situation structure (Hasenclaver, Mayer, and Rittberger 1997), problem structure (Hafner-Burton, Victor, and Lupu 2012), or the nature of the cooperation problem (Koremenos *et al.* 2001; Koremenos 2013). This influence is most evident in the study of flexibility provisions, the design of dispute resolution, the choice of hard and soft law, and the workings of regime complexes (Helfer 2013; Koremenos and Betz 2013; Shaffer and Pollack 2013; and Raustiala 2013). Looking beyond law-making, rational institutionalism provides the groundwork for principal–agent theories of judicial delegation and independence which, despite their critics (Alter 2008), have proven influential in virtually all IL/IR analyses of international courts (Voeten 2013). Compliance studies also show the imprint of rational institutionalist thinking, providing the basis for the "enforcement" school of the 1990s, and for the articulation of a broad set of "instrumentalist" theories of compliance (von Stein 2013; Thompson 2013; Brewster 2013). Institutionalist analyses, by virtue of their state-centrism and their treatment of national preferences as exogenously given and fixed, have limitations, about which Koremenos' (2013) analysis is admirably frank; yet, by the same token, institutionalist analysis is arguably consistent in its basic assumptions with, and can therefore be synthesized with insights from, both realism and liberalism.

   The promise of liberal theory for the understanding of international law, and the common interest in domestic politics and state–society relations that it shares with IL approaches such as the New Haven School and International Legal Process, was pointed out early on by Slaughter Burley (1993) in her "dual agenda," and Moravcsik's (2013) contribution to this volume (Chapter 4) lays out a powerful manifesto for the approach, which he argues can illuminate not only the initial phases of preference formation and law-making, but also the workings of international judicial processes, the domestic politics of international legal compliance, and the dynamic evolution of legal and judicial processes over time. Looking across our surveys of the literature, we see that much of the IL/IR scholarship of the past two decades begins with state-centric, unitary rational actor assumptions, yet, in all three areas, we find growing bodies of scholarship that incorporate domestic or transnational state–society relations – including regime types, domestic interest groups, partisan competition, and political and legal institutions, among others – as important explanatory variables. Rational design studies of international law-making, for example, recognize the significance of domestic politics as a motivation for the adoption of flexibility mechanisms in international legal agreements (Koremenos 2013; Helfer 2013). Indeed, there now seems to be enough evidence across enough types of flexibility mechanisms to suggest a general hypothesis that *flexibility provisions are particularly appealing to, and most likely to be used by, particular types of regimes, namely democratic, rule-of-law systems that take their international legal responsibilities, and the legal rights of their citizens, most seriously* (Neumayer 2007; Helfer 2013). Other works reviewed in this volume seek explicitly to disaggregate the state as an actor in international law-making (Newman and Zaring 2013) or to incorporate non-state actors as direct participants in law-making (Spiro 2013; Johnstone 2013; Shaffer and Pollack 2013).

Moving beyond this initial law-making or design stage, the substantive chapters in this volume support Moravcsik's claim that the importance of domestic state–society relations also extends to the interpretation and compliance stages. Although the traditional view of international litigation in both IL and IR was clearly statist, recent scholarship focuses on the significance of domestic interest groups and domestic audience costs in shaping state decisions to litigate (see, e.g., Shaffer 2003; Allee and Huth 2006) in interstate courts, as well as the pattern of litigation by individual litigants in transnational courts (e.g., Stone Sweet and Brunell 1998; Conant 2002). Liberal claims and hypotheses also feature prominently in the compliance literature, which has paid increasing attention to the significance of domestic factors such as regime type (Slaughter 2000), domestic interest groups and "compliance constituencies" (Kahler 2000; Trachtman 2013), and partisan competition (Grieco, Gelpi, and Warren 2009) for international legal compliance. Most generally, we see a tendency for state-centric analysis in both IL and IR to be supplemented (if not supplanted) by state–society analysis – a trend that we expect to continue in the years to come.

Constructivist theory, reviewed in this volume by Jutta Brunnée and Stephen Toope (Chapter 5), is distinguished from the previous two theories by the rejection of rationalist assumptions and the common focus on "the role that culture, ideas, institutions, discourse, and social norms play in shaping identity and influencing behaviour" (Brunnée and Toope 2013: 121). Although IR constructivists have only recently turned their attention to the study and specific features of international *legal* norms (Finnemore 2000), the focus on the power of norms and their ability to define appropriate behavior and even "constitute" actors makes constructivism an appealing and accessible theory for many international legal theorists. Constructivism has also demonstrated a greater sensitivity to the nature of law as a realm "characterized by an institutionally autonomous, distinctive discourse that draws on a pre-existing set of norms and practices of justification, and which delegitimizes the raw pursuit of power and self-interest" (Brunnée and Toope 2013: 127; c.f. Reus-Smit 2004; Johnstone 2011). In terms of the scholarship reviewed in this volume, it appears that the bulk of the admittedly very recent constructivist scholarship on international law is concentrated in the study of compliance, where constructivist scholars in both disciplines have identified a variety of "noninstrumental" causal mechanisms, including Franck's (1990) concept of "compliance pull" of legitimate legal norms; Brunnée and Toope's (2010) related conception of "interactional international law" arising out of ongoing practices that generate "fidelity to the rule of law" in international affairs; Harold Koh's (1997, 1998) transnational legal process theory of international legal internalization and obedience; and Goodman and Jinks' (2004) concept of national acculturation to international norms and rules. By contrast, it appears that constructivist scholarship has made less of an impact into the literatures on international law-making and interpretation – although we hasten to add that constructivist ideas about the expressive characteristics of law and the workings of "norm cascades" offer useful frameworks for thinking about the making and development of customary as well as treaty law, while the constructivist focus on discourse offers a distinctive window into international legal interpretation and courts that has so far been slighted in favor of a more narrow instrumentalist focus on judicial behavior. Our expectation is, therefore, that constructivist scholars will in the years to come focus more explicitly on the specific features of international legal norms, and on all stages of the international legal process.

Realism, finally, is invoked relatively rarely in much of the literature reviewed in this volume, and then – as Richard Steinberg (2013) points out in his provocative review (Chapter 6) – largely as a foil against which to argue for the significance of international law. Realist theory, in our view, shares a number of common assumptions with institutionalism, including the centrality of states and their interests or preferences, but what constitutes the distinctiveness of realism as a project is its focus on the role of distributive conflict and, above all, power in international politics and law. To be sure, realism does not "own" the concept of power, and realists may in fact utilize a relatively narrow, purely materialist conception of power (Barnett and Duvall 2005) – yet, it does seem to us, as to Steinberg, that much of the early institutionalist, liberal, and constructivist literature understated the importance of state power as an explanatory variable in the making, interpretation, and enforcement of international law. Much of the IL/IR literature, for example, relies heavily on the application of a single game-theoretic model, that of the prisoner's dilemma, which assumes away distributive conflict and leaves no room for state power to influence cooperative outcomes (Krasner 1991). Similarly, rational design models, from the beginning, incorporated the possibility of distributive conflict, but the initial formulation of the research program (Koremenos *et al.* 2001) failed to include state power as an explanatory variable. Happily, as Steinberg notes in his discussion of "hybrid" approaches, IL and IR scholars from other theoretical traditions have increasingly moved to incorporate power into their theoretical and empirical analyses – in the process, not only rectifying the oversight but also bringing new insights into the sources and working of power. To take only a few examples, rational design scholars like Koremenos and Betz (2013) have incorporated power differentials among the parties to an agreement as a explanatory variable in their empirical work, asking whether great contrasts in power correlate with particular design features. Others have examined how powerful states can exert influence even in formally egalitarian institutional settings like the WTO (Steinberg 2002), or more generally how powerful states take advantage of informal norms to protect their interests in the face of formal legal rules designed in large part to protect the weak (Steinberg 2002; Stone 2011). The issue of power has also emerged as central in the debate over regime complexity and legal fragmentation, with a growing number of scholars claiming that the proliferation of legal regimes has operated to the benefit of powerful states. Students of international dispute settlement have similarly moved to incorporate power into their analyses, demonstrating the importance and the limits of power as a variable in explaining the behavior of states as litigants before international courts (Davis and Bermeo 2009; Shaffer and Melélendez-Ortiz 2010), and/or the pattern of concessions offered by strong and weak states in such disputes (Busch and Reinhardt 2003). Finally, it is worth noting, critical constructivists and critical legal studies scholars have employed notions of what Barnett and Duvall call "structural" or "productive" power, identifying the relations of power underlying the basic constitutive norms of the international legal order (Sinclair 2010; Brunnée and Toope 2013).

V. CONCLUSION: AN ECLECTIC, AND INTERDISCIPLINARY, AGENDA FOR FUTURE RESEARCH

In the previous section, we argued that all four of the major traditions of IR theory have made substantial conceptual contributions to the IL/IR literature of the past two decades, albeit with emphases in different areas of empirical analysis. We close the chapter with two final observations about the state of the field and the agenda for future research, the first about the rising incidence and importance of theoretical eclecticism among IR scholars, and the second about the desirability of rebalancing the terms of trade to draw more on the strengths and contributions of legal scholars to address some of the lacunae and blind spots identified in the IL/IR literature to date.

On the first issue, as editors, we took an early decision to start the volume with statements from four leading scholars on what we took to be the most active and productive schools of thought in IR theory as applied to IL. Some participants in the project noted that this organization threatened to reignite the so-called "isms war" decried by David Lake (2011) and many others, and suggested that we abandon the analyses of institutionalist, liberal, constructivist, and realist thought. At one workshop, one participant suggested provocatively that we replace these four chapters with analyses of the four causal mechanisms – institutions and information, domestic politics, norms, and power – associated with each of these schools of thought. Although we were tempted to do away with the "isms" in this way, we ultimately decided against doing so, for three reasons. First, as a matter of disciplinary history, theory development takes place largely within individual research programs, and all four programs have been developed self-consciously by scholars over the past two decades in ways that we wanted to capture, analyze, and present to our readers. Second, we were, and remain, wary of attempting any grand synthesis of the four theories, which are based on some overlapping but other very different basic assumptions, such that any effort at unification could lead to an incoherent muddle. Third and finally, efforts at unification seldom take place on neutral terms, implicitly privileging either the theoretical or the epistemological views of some theoretical approaches over others (Nau 2011). In the same vein, it seemed to us that any effort to reduce the four theories to specific causal mechanisms implicitly committed our contributors to a positivist epistemology that is broadly, but not universally, shared among scholars in the four schools.[5] For all these reasons, we have retained in Part II of the volume an "ism"-centered approach, with our four contributors articulating what we consider to be the definitive statements of each theory, including its strengths, its weaknesses, and its applications thus far to the study of international law.

That said, however, our organizational choices for the volume should not be interpreted as an endorsement of a gladiatorial and unproductive "isms war." Although we strongly suspect that theoretical development advances most effectively in the nursery of individual research programs, we also agree with the growing number of scholars who advocate pragmatic, eclectic theoretical approaches to the problem-driven empirical research that increasingly dominates IL/IR scholarship (see, e.g., Fearon and Wendt 2002; Katzenstein and Sil 2008; Dunoff and Pollack 2013, Chapter 1). And, indeed, this is the direction that we detect in the contemporary IL/IR scholarship reviewed in this volume. To take just a few examples, Ian Johnstone's contribution to the volume (Chapter 11) examines the phenomenon of law-making by international organizations (IOs), presenting the diversity of IO practices and then providing three theoretical lenses or "cuts" at the question, comparing a rationalist approach with two distinct varieties of constructivist theory. Rather than choosing and insisting on the superiority of a particular "ism," Johnstone explores the implications and the specific insights of each theory for his question. Another compelling effort comes from Koremenos and Betz (Chapter 15), who seek to understand the design of international dispute resolution systems. The authors derive much of their analytic and research design choices from the rational design research program, yet, in their empirical analysis, they make an explicit and serious effort to integrate into their empirical analysis other variables such as domestic regime type and state power, traditionally associated with the liberal and realist research programs, respectively. Koremenos and Betz thereby provide an exemplar of the type of pragmatic, eclectic, "tool-kit" approach called for by reformers in the IR field. Indeed, even our four "theory" authors, nominally the guardians of the "isms," all make an effort to acknowledge the limitations of their respective approaches, the points of tangency or compatibility with other research programs, and the potential for what Steinberg calls "hybrid" approaches. Indeed, we would argue, the promise of such problem-driven, theoretically eclectic research is amply demonstrated in the substantive chapters in Parts III, IV, and V of this volume.

---

[5] A significant minority of constructivist scholars, for example, take a post-positivist, critical approach; see Brunnée and Toope (2013). Furthermore, the question of epistemological commitments becomes even more problematic when we expand our consideration beyond IR theory to international legal theory, as we do presently.

Despite our general optimism about the state of the field, we have identified systematic and persistent lacunae in the literature, and we would suggest, in conclusion, that much of this blindness can be attributed to the grossly unbalanced disciplinary terms of trade between political science and law that we identified in the introduction to this volume.[6] As we have seen, the canonical works in the IL/IR tradition have largely advocated the application of IR as a *discipline* to IL as a *subject* – in the process ignoring or devaluing the contributions of international legal theory and methods. To the extent that IR scholars consider IL theory at all, it is primarily to dismiss it as unhelpful, because it is considered to be either unduly narrow in its focus on the language of international legal instruments, politically naïve in devoting substantial attention to unenforceable legal rules but failing adequately to account for power, or methodologically suspect, as legal writings are often normative but rarely (or inadequately) positivist.

Ironically, by ignoring what lawyers know about how law international operates, IR scholars themselves may unwittingly fall prey to a type of formalism that is insufficiently attentive to the practical realities of how the international legal order works. For example, as we have seen, contemporary IR accounts of international law-making are dominated by a rational design approach that focuses almost exclusively on treaties and formal institutions. This approach has generated important insights, but has drawn attention away from the processes of law-making, including the means by which states wield power in treaty negotiations; overlooks important law-making fora, such as the push and shove of customary international law formation; and elides the varied roles of non-state actors in emerging soft-law processes. Similarly, IR analyses of international legal interpretation focus almost exclusively on international courts, misleadingly overlooking the numerous other sites where interpretation and application occurs, including committees, councils, and other subsidiary treaty bodies. Such studies also tend to reduce international judicial behavior to a single dimension of dispute settlement – does the court rule for or against state *x*? – and ignore the role of courts in shaping the development of international law over time. Finally, IR studies of compliance typically assume that legal texts are unambiguous and that international law's effects are most relevantly measured in terms of state behavior that is (or is not) consistent with the terms of international agreements. But this formalist view of international law fails to account for the wide variety of ways in which, and the processes through which, international law influences both states and non-state actors. As a result, much – although by no means all – of IL/IR scholarship presents an incomplete or even a distorted picture of IL and its effects on states and the international order.

Happily, IR scholars can remedy these defects by drawing – pragmatically and selectively – on the theoretical frameworks and empirical analyses of their

---

[6] The following paragraphs draw in part from our extended analysis of international legal thought in Dunoff and Pollack (2012).

counterparts in law. The insights of the New Haven School of international legal theory, for example, are seldom referenced in IL/IR research, and the epistemology of that school's practitioners is likely to be perceived as dubious by positivist IR scholars; yet, New Haven School and international legal process scholars have long since focused analytic attention on issues, such as the uses of state power in treaty-making and the claims and counterclaims of customary international law-making, that constitute some of the most persistent blind spots in the IL/IR literature thus far. Although a comprehensive review of international legal theory is beyond the scope of this chapter, it is worth noting that all international legal theory is not, as it is often depicted in IR circles, monolithic, formalistic, doctrinal, and normative. Indeed, international legal theory is as diverse an intellectual marketplace as IR theory, with positivist scholarship existing alongside New Haven and international legal process approaches; "new stream" or critical approaches, including critical legal studies, feminist theory, and third-world approaches; rationalist theories drawing from economics as well as IR; and other contemporary approaches such as global administrative law, global constitutionalism, and global pluralism, all of which combine analytical, normative, and empirical aims and insights.[7]

These diverse bodies of international legal theory represent an untapped resource, capable of illuminating the blind spots in existing IL/IR research. Thus, for example, in their contribution to this volume, Kenneth Abbott and Duncan Snidal (Chapter 2) illustrate how insights from both disciplines can be used to develop a theory of the dynamics of legalization. Similarly, Anne-Marie Slaughter, in the previous chapter, argues that many of the emerging issues in the international legal order will call upon the specific skills and insights of international lawyers, and a number of our contributors have made analogous claims with respect to their specific topics (e.g., Brunnée and Toope 2013, Chapter 5; Johnstone 2013, Chapter 11; Spiro 2013, Chapter 9; Bodansky 2013, Chapter 13). We agree, and by way of example would highlight four sets of insights – what we call process, power, pluralism, and normativity – that international legal scholarship may contribute to the future development of IL/IR scholarship.

With respect to *process*, Slaughter has noted that a shift from understanding law as rules to an emphasis on law as process was a central analytic move in postwar international legal thought (Slaughter Burley 1993). Process-based approaches offer IR scholars new ways of thinking, and new questions to ask, about international legal rules and institutions. Consider, for example, the WTO's highly legalized dispute settlement mechanism, which has attracted substantial attention from both IR and international law scholars. International relations writings tend to focus on issues like which parties participate as complainants and respondents, what types of cases settle before panel reports are issued, what types of issues get litigated, and

---

7 For a brief primer on these and other approaches, see Dunoff and Pollack (2012); cf. Ratner and Slaughter (1999).

which actors benefit from WTO dispute settlement (e.g., Busch and Reinhardt 2002; Guzman and Simmons 2005). However, the impressive advances in this scholarship teach us little about numerous other critical issues, such as why particular parties file certain cases, what theories they choose to litigate and which they abandon, why disputes are resolved on one ground rather than another, and why decisions are articulated in broad or narrow terms. Process-based inquiries that explore, for example, rules on who has standing to bring claims, which actors are allowed to participate, the role of precedent, the function of judicial economy, and in what order the panels are to address multiple claims, can provide substantial purchase on questions of interest to IR scholars, including who participates in WTO proceedings and who prevails. More generally, we concur with Thompson's (2010) and Koremenos' (2013) claim that institutional design approaches should be supplemented by approaches that reintroduce, theorize, and test hypotheses about international legal processes, and, in doing so, IL/IR scholars can and should be attentive to the work of international legal scholars who have both theorized and empirically analyzed such processes.

Power is, of course, a central concern of political scientists. Realists, institutionalists, liberals, and constructivists might not agree on much, but all agree that power matters – although what exactly power consists of remains elusive and contested. International relations scholarship often presumes that legal writings pay insufficient attention to the role of power in international affairs. In fact, however, virtually all of the leading schools of international legal thought foreground the importance of power in international legal affairs. For example, the concept of power is integral to the New Haven School's conception of international law; for this approach, law is a process of *authoritative decision-making* grounded in *effective power*. According to leading New Haven scholars, lawyers should analyze power by examining "[t]he ways in which resources (material and symbolic) are manipulated, or the *strategies* used by different participants, involve the management of resources aimed at optimizing preferred outcomes. Strategic modes are considered along a persuasive-coercive continuum. They include diplomatic, propagandistic, economic, and military techniques in varying ensembles" (Reisman, Wiessner, and Willard 2007: 578). Note here the emphasis, not just on power as a set of capabilities, but also on the "strategies" and "techniques" whereby states employ different power resources in international legal fora – an approach that contemporary IR theory, with its emphasis on correlational (and often statistical) analysis, has largely lost. Power is likewise central to the other schools surveyed above. Thus, for example, critical approaches to IL emphasize how power manifests itself in substantive treaty and customary rules, in procedural mechanisms, and in institutional designs. Moreover, many of the critical schools foreground not only state power, but also the power of privileged groups, and identify how that power is inscribed into the fabric of international law. In this sense, critical legal approaches share common ground with Gramscian and other critical IR approaches, in which international law represents a dominant, naturalized discourse that constitutes actors and renders some options legitimate or unthinkable, without any overt exercise of power (Barnett and Duvall 2005).

A third potential insight of international legal theory is its distinctive take on the phenomenon of international legal *pluralism*. Although a growing number of IR scholars have now explored what they refer to as "regime complexity" (Raustiala and Victor 2004; Alter and Meunier 2009), much of this literature has focused narrowly on the strategic use of multiple fora by state actors through strategies of forum shopping and regime shifting. Legal scholars, however, have arguably taken a more comprehensive approach, analyzing with considerable success the impact of legal fragmentation or pluralism on the integrity of the international legal order, as well as the dilemmas posed for international tribunals called on to adjudicate in the presence of multiple bodies of law (International Law Commission 2006; Dunoff 2012). Such choices, moreover, are not merely technical or doctrinal questions, for the choice of norms and the strategies adopted for reconciling overlapping legal claims and orders have important distributive implications that should be of interest to IR scholars – yet they can only be adequately understood through a mastery of the "internalist" logic of international legal discourse.

Finally, as we noted in the introduction to this volume, legal scholarship is profoundly concerned with what we have called the *normativity* of law, understood as a sense of obligation said to inhere in law independent of its content or consequences. Although one might argue that the normativity of law is partly captured in IR through the widespread adoption of the "obligation" dimension of the legalization framework (Abbott *et al.* 2000), international legal scholars generally consider this dimension to be undertheorized and narrowly associated with the purely formal question of legal bindingness (Finnemore and Toope 2001). The issue of law's normativity also figures as a moral question that cuts across disciplinary lines. In stark contrast with instrumentalist, IR-influenced perspectives holding that "international legality does not impose any moral obligations" (Goldsmith and Posner 2005: 197), many international lawyers are committed to the idea (Koskenniemi 1990: 8) that:

> Law should be applied regardless of the political preference of legal subjects. It should not just reflect what states do but should be critical of state policy. In particular, it should be applicable even against a state which opposes its application to itself. . . . [L]egal rules whose content or application depends on the will of the legal subject for whom they are valid, are not proper legal rules at all but apologies for the legal subject's political interest.

Although international legal theory's normativity has traditionally rendered it less useful to IR scholars, recent developments in IR heighten the opportunities for dialogue with normative legal scholarship. Within IR, Steve Smith (1992) argues that the end of the Cold War coincided with the end of what he calls "forty-years detour," in which normative ethical concerns had largely been driven out of mainstream IR scholarship. The field has only recently begun to recover from this detour and has rediscovered normative international political theory. This new "ethics and IR" literature addresses many themes that implicitly or explicitly implicate law, such as the justice of the international economic order (largely codified in international law and institutions) and the balance between state sovereignty and human rights, but the distinctly legal components of these issues, and the long discussions in the legal community over them, are largely ignored.[8] In these, and other normative debates that receive attention from IR scholars, there is an as yet unexploited opportunity for dialogue and debate between IL scholars and ethics and IR scholars.

To be clear, our call here is not for a perfect "balance" between IL and IR scholarship, either for its own sake or to soothe the egos of neglected legal scholars. When we highlighted the asymmetry in the interdisciplinary "terms of trade" at the opening workshop of this project, one of our discussants, Beth Simmons, replied with a simple question: "So what?" Disciplinary balance, she argued, is not an end in itself, but should be pursued only to the extent that it generates theoretical insights or hypotheses about topics that IL/IR scholars care about. We agree with this view, and our call is therefore not for token inclusion of IL approaches, but rather for an interdisciplinary version of the pragmatic, analytically eclectic, tool-kit approach increasingly advocated within IR. Just as an exclusive focus on a particular "ism" can lead scholars to a narrow research agenda that ignores potentially significant causal variables, or indeed entire avenues of research, a nearly exclusive focus on IR theory already has produced an IL/IR scholarship that, for all its insights, is characterized by the large and persistent blind spots identified above. A more "balanced" IL/IR research program along the lines suggested here would be one that brought in IL as well as IR theory and methods as appropriate to the individual scholar's research question; but it would, by the same token, be one in which research questions themselves would be broadened and enriched, such that the next two decades of IL/IR scholarship will not only generate more confident answers to existing questions, but ask new questions and address new challenges that contemporary scholars have only begun to consider.

REFERENCES

Abbott, Kenneth W. (1989). "Modern International Relations Theory: A Prospectus for International Lawyers," *Yale Journal of International Law*, Vol. 14, No. 2, pp. 335–411.
Abbott, Kenneth W., and Duncan Snidal (2000). "Hard and Soft Law in International Governance," *International Organization*, Vol. 54, No. 3, pp. 421–56.
————— (2009). "The Governance Triangle: Regulatory Standards, Institutions and the Shadow of the State," in Walter Mattli and Ngaire Woods (eds.), *The Politics of Global Regulation* (Princeton, NJ: Princeton University Press), pp. 44–88.

---

[8] See, e.g., *Ethics and International Affairs*, a journal established in 1987 and now in its twenty-fifth year of publication.

――――― (2013). "Law, Legalization and Politics: An Agenda for the Next Generation of IL/IR Scholars," in Jeffrey L. Dunoff and Mark A. Pollack (eds.), *Interdisciplinary Perspectives on International Law and International Relations: The State of the Art* (New York: Cambridge University Press), pp. 33–56.

Allee, Todd L. (2004). "Legal Incentives and Domestic Rewards: The Selection of Trade Disputes for GATT/WTO Dispute Resolution," unpublished paper.

Allee, Todd L., and Paul K. Huth (2006). "Legitimizing Dispute Settlement: International Adjudication as Domestic Political Cover," *American Political Science Review*, Vol. 100, No. 2, pp. 219–34.

Alter, Karen J. (2001). *Establishing the Supremacy of European Law: The Making of an International Rule of Law in Europe* (New York: Oxford University Press).

――――― (2008). "Agents or Trustees? International Courts in Their Political Context," *European Journal of International Relations*, Vol. 14, No. 1, pp. 33–63.

――――― (2013). "The Multiple Roles of International Courts and Tribunals: Enforcement, Dispute Settlement, Constitutional and Administrative Review," in Jeffrey L. Dunoff and Mark A. Pollack (eds.), *Interdisciplinary Perspectives on International Law and International Relations: The State of the Art* (New York: Cambridge University Press), pp. 345–70.

Alter, Karen J., and Laurence R. Helfer (2010). "Nature or Nurture? Judicial Lawmaking in the European Court of Justice and the Andean Tribunal of Justice," *International Organization*, Vol. 64, No. 4, pp. 563–92.

Alter, Karen J., and Sophie Meunier (2009). "The Politics of International Regime Complexity," *Perspectives on Politics*, Vol. 7, No. 1, pp. 13–24.

Alvarez, Jose E. (2011). "The Return of the State," *Minnesota Journal of International Law*, Vol. 20, No. 2, pp. 223–64.

Barnett, Michael, and Raymond Duvall (2005) (eds.). *Power in Global Governance* (New York: Cambridge University Press).

Berman, Paul Schiff (2007). "Global Legal Pluralism," *Southern California Law Review*, Vol. 80, No. 6, pp. 1155–238.

Bodansky, Daniel (2013). "Legitimacy: Concepts and Conceptions/Normative and Descriptive," in Jeffrey L. Dunoff and Mark A. Pollack (eds.), *Interdisciplinary Perspectives on International Law and International Relations: The State of the Art* (New York: Cambridge University Press), pp. 321–41.

Brewster, Rachel (2013). "Reputation in International Relations and International Law Theory," in Jeffrey L. Dunoff and Mark A. Pollack (eds.), *Interdisciplinary Perspectives on International Law and International Relations: The State of the Art* (New York: Cambridge University Press), pp. 524–43.

Brown Weiss, Edith (1987). "Judicial Independence and Impartiality: A Preliminary Inquiry," in Lori Damrosch (ed.), *The International Court of Justice at a Crossroads* (Dobbs Ferry, NY: Transnational Publishers).

Brunnée, Jutta, and Stephen J. Toope (2010). *Legitimacy and Legality in International Law: An Interactional Account* (Cambridge: Cambridge University Press).

――――― (2013). "Constructivism and International Law," in Jeffrey L. Dunoff and Mark A. Pollack (eds.), *Interdisciplinary Perspectives on International Law and International Relations: The State of the Art* (New York: Cambridge University Press), pp. 119–45.

Burley, Anne-Marie, and Walter Mattli (1993). "Europe before the Court: A Political Theory of European Integration," *International Organization*, Vol. 47, No. 1, pp. 41–76.

Busch, Marc L. (2000). "Democracy, Consultation, and the Paneling of Disputes under GATT," *Journal of Conflict Resolution*, Vol. 44, No. 4, pp. 425–46.

Busch, Marc L., and Eric Reinhardt (2002). "Testing International Trade Law: Empirical Studies of GATT/WTO Dispute Settlement," in Daniel M. Kennedy and James D. Southwick (eds.), *The Political Economy of International Trade Law: Essays in Honor of Robert Hudec* (New York: Cambridge University Press).

——— (2003). "Developing Countries and GATT/WTO Dispute Settlement," *Journal of World Trade*, Vol. 37, No. 4, pp. 719–35.

Carrubba, Clifford, Mathew Gabel, and Charles Hankla (2008). "Judicial Behavior under Political Constraints: Evidence from the European Court of Justice," *American Political Science Review*, Vol. 102, No. 4, pp. 435–52.

Chayes, Abram (1974). *The Cuban Missile Crisis: International Crises and the Role of Law* (New York: Oxford University Press).

Chayes, Abram, and Antonia Handler Chayes (1993). "On Compliance," *International Organization*, Vol. 47, No. 2, pp. 175–205.

——— (1995). *The New Sovereignty: Compliance with International Regulatory Agreements* (Cambridge: Harvard University Press).

Conant, Lisa (2002). *Justice Contained: Law and Politics in the European Union* (Ithaca, NY: Cornell University Press).

——— (2013). "Whose Agents? The Interpretation of International Law in National Courts," in Jeffrey L. Dunoff and Mark A. Pollack (eds.), *Interdisciplinary Perspectives on International Law and International Relations: The State of the Art* (New York: Cambridge University Press), pp. 394–420.

Davis, Christina L., and Sarah Blodgett Bermeo (2009). "Who Files? Developing Country Participation in GATT/WTO Adjudication," *Journal of Politics*, Vol. 71, No. 3, pp. 1033–1049.

Downs, George, David M. Rocke, and Peter Barsoom (1996). "Is the Good News about Compliance Good News about Cooperation?," *International Organization*, Vol. 50, No. 3, pp. 379–406.

Duffield, John S. (2003). "The Limits of 'Rational Design,'" *International Organization*, Vol. 57, No. 2, pp. 411–30.

Dunoff, Jeffrey L. (1998). "The Misguided Debate over NGO Participation at the WTO," *Journal of International Economic Law*, Vol. 1, No. 3, pp. 433–56.

——— (1999). "The Death of the Trade Regime," *European Journal of International Law*, Vol. 10, No. 4, pp. 733–62.

——— (2006). "Lotus Eaters: Reflections on the Varietals Dispute, the SPS Agreement and WTO Dispute Resolution," in George A. Bermann and Petros Mavroidis (eds.), *Trade and Human Health and Safety* (New York: Cambridge University Press), pp. 153–89.

——— (2012). "A New Approach to Regime Interaction," in Margaret Young (ed.), *Regime Interaction in International Law: Facing Fragmentation* (Cambridge: Cambridge University Press), pp. 136–74.

Dunoff, Jeffrey L., and Mark A. Pollack (2012). "What Can International Relations Learn from International Law?" (April 9, 2012). Temple University Legal Studies Research Paper No. 2012-14. Available at SSRN: http://ssrn.com/abstract=2037299 or http://dx.doi.org/10.2139/ssrn.2037299.

——— (2013). "International Law and International Relations: Introducing an Interdisciplinary Dialogue," in Jeffrey L. Dunoff and Mark A. Pollack (eds.), *Interdisciplinary Perspectives on International Law and International Relations: The State of the Art* (New York: Cambridge University Press), pp. 3–32.

Dunoff, Jeffrey L., and Joel P. Trachtman (1999). "Economic Analysis of International Law," *Yale Journal of International Law*, Vol. 24, No. 1, pp. 1–59.

Ehlermann, Claus-Dieter, and Lothar Ehring (2005). "Decision-Making in the World Trade Organization," *Journal of International Economic Law*, Vol. 8, No. 1, pp. 51–75.

Elsig, Manfred, and Mark A. Pollack (forthcoming). "Agents, Trustees, and International Courts: Nomination and Appointment of Judicial Candidates in the WTO Appellate Body," *European Journal of International Relations*.

Fearon, James D., and Alexander Wendt (2002). "Rationalism and Constructivism in International Relations Theory," in Walter Carlsnaes Thomas Risse, and Beth Simmons (eds.), *Handbook of International Relations Theory* (London: Sage Publications), pp. 52–72

Finnemore, Martha (2000). "Are Legal Norms Distinctive?," *New York University Journal of International Law & Politics*, Vol. 32, No. 3, pp. 699–705.

Finnemore, Martha, and Stephen J. Toope (2001). "Alternatives to 'Legalization': Richer Views of Law and Politics," *International Organization*, Vol. 55, No. 3, pp. 743–58.

Franck, Thomas M. (1990). *The Power of Legitimacy among Nations* (New York: Oxford University Press).

Goldsmith, Jack L., and Eric A. Posner (2005). *The Limits of International Law* (New York: Oxford University Press).

Goldstein, Judith, and Lisa L. Martin (2000). "Legalization, Trade Liberalization, and Domestic Constituents: A Cautionary Note," *International Organization*, Vol. 54, No. 3, pp. 603–32.

Goodman, Ryan, and Derek Jinks (2003). "Measuring the Effects of Human Rights Treaties," *European Journal of International Law*, Vol. 14, No. 1, pp. 171–83.

_____ (2004). "How to Influence States: Socialization and International Human Rights Law," *Duke Law Journal*, Vol. 54, No. 3, pp. 621–703.

Grieco, Joseph M., Christopher F. Gelpi, and T. Camber Warren (2009). "When Preferences and Commitments Collide: The Effect of Relative Partisan Shifts on International Treaty Compliance," *International Organization*, Vol. 63, No. 2, pp. 341–55.

Guzman, Andrew T. (2008). *How International Law Works: A Rational Choice Theory* (New York: Oxford University Press).

Guzman, Andrew T., and Beth A. Simmons (2005). "Power Plays and Capacity Constraints: The Selection of Defendants in World Trade Organization Disputes," *Journal of Legal Studies*, Vol. 34, No. 2, pp. 557–98.

Hafner-Burton, Emilie M. (2005). "Trading Human Rights: How Preferential Trade Agreements Influence Government Repression," *International Organization*, Vol. 59, No. 3, pp. 593–629.

Hafner-Burton, Emilie M., David G. Victor, and Yonatan Lupu (2012). "Political Science Research on International Law: The State of the Field," *American Journal of International Law*, Vol. 106, No. 1, p. 47–97.

Hasenclever, Andreas, Peter Mayer, and Volker Rittberger (1997). *Theories of International Regimes* (Cambridge: Cambridge University Press).

Hathaway, Oona (2002). "Do Human Rights Treaties Make a Difference?," *Yale Law Journal*, Vol. 111, No. 8, pp. 1935–2042.

_____ (2003). "Testing Conventional Wisdom," *European Journal of International Law*, Vol. 13, No. 1, pp. 185–200.

Helfer, Laurence R. (2002). "International Relations Theory and the Commonwealth Caribbean Backlash against Human Rights Regimes," *Columbia Law Review*, Vol. 102, No. 7, pp. 1832–1911.

_____ (2004). "Regime Shifting: The TRIPs Agreement and New Dynamics of International Intellectual Property Lawmaking," *Yale Journal of International Law*, Vol. 29, No. 1, pp. 1–83.

_____ (2006). "Why States Create International Tribunals: A Theory of Constrained Inde-pendence," in Stefan Voight, Max Albert, and Dieter Schmidtchen (eds.), *International Conflict Resolution* (Tuebingen: Mohn Siebeck), pp. 255–76.

_____ (2013). "Flexibility in International Agreements," in Jeffrey L. Dunoff and Mark A. Pollack (eds.), *Interdisciplinary Perspectives on International Law and International Relations: The State of the Art* (New York: Cambridge University Press), pp. 175–96.

Helfer, Laurence R., and Anne-Marie Slaughter (1997). "Toward a Theory of Effective Supra-national Adjudication," *Yale Law Journal*, Vol. 107, No. 2, pp. 273–392.

_____ (2005). "Why States Create International Tribunals: A Response to Professors Posner and Yoo," *California Law Review*, Vol. 93, No. 3, pp. 899–956.

Henkin, Louis (1979). *How Nations Behave: Law and Foreign Policy* (New York: Columbia University Press).

Hix, Simon (2008). *What's Wrong with the European Union and How to Fix It* (Cambridge: Polity Press).

Horn, Henrik, and Petros C. Mavroidis (2007). "International Trade: Dispute Settlement," in Andrew T. Guzman and Alan O. Sykes (eds.), *Research Handbook in International Economic Law* (Cheltenham: Edward Elgar), pp. 177–210.

Howse, Robert, and Ruti Teitel (2010). "Beyond Compliance: Rethinking Why International Law Really Matters," *Global Policy*, Vol. 1, No. 2, pp. 127–36.

Hudec, Robert E. (1999). "The New WTO Dispute Settlement Procedure: An Overview of the First Three Years," *Minnesota Journal of Global Trade*, Vol. 8, No. 1, pp. 1–50.

International Law Commission (2006). "Fragmentation of International Law: Difficulties Aris-ing from the Diversification and Expansion of International Law," UN Doc. A/CN.4/L.682.

Joerges, Christian (2001). "Deliberative Supranationalism – a Defence," *European Integration online Papers (EIoP)*, Vol. 5, No. 8, available at http://eiop.or.at/eiop/texte/2001–008a.htm, accessed on April 2, 2012.

Johnstone, Ian (2011). *The Power of Deliberation: International Law, Politics and Organization* (New York: Oxford University Press).

_____ (2013). "Lawmaking by International Organizations: Perspectives from IL/IR The-ory," in Jeffrey L. Dunoff and Mark A. Pollack (eds.), *Interdisciplinary Perspectives on International Law and International Relations: The State of the Art* (New York: Cambridge University Press), pp. 266–92.

Jupille, Joseph, and Duncan Snidal (2006). "The Choice of International Institutions: Coop-eration, Alternatives, Strategies" (unpublished manuscript).

Kahler, Miles (2000). "Conclusion: The Causes and Consequences of Legalization," *International Organization*, Vol. 54, No. 3, pp. 661–83.

Katzenstein, Peter J., and Rudra Sil (2008). "Eclectic Theorizing in the Study and Practice of International Relations," in Christian Reus-Smit and Duncan Snidal (eds.), *The Oxford Handbook of International Relations* (Oxford: Oxford University Press), pp. 109–30.

Kelley, Judith (2007). "Who Keeps International Commitments and Why? The Interna-tional Criminal Court and Bilateral Nonsurrender Agreements," *American Political Science Review*, Vol. 101, No. 3, pp. 573–89.

Keohane, Robert O. (1998). "When Does International Law Come Home?" *Houston Law Review*, Vol. 35, No. 3, pp. 699–713.

Keohane, Robert O., Andrew Moravcsik, and Anne-Marie Slaughter (2000). "Legalized Dis-pute Resolution: Interstate and Transnational," *International Organization*, Vol. 54, No. 3, pp. 457–88.

Keohane, Robert O., and Joseph S. Nye, Jr. (1974). "Transgovernmental Relations and Inter-national Organizations," *World Politics*, Vol. 27, No. 1, pp. 39–62.

Kingsbury, Benedict, Nico Krisch, and Richard B. Stewart (2005). "The Emergence of Global Administrative Law," _Law and Contemporary Problems_, Vol. 68, Nos. 3 & 4, pp. 15–61.

Koh, Harold Hongju (1997). "Why Do Nations Obey International Law?," _Yale Law Journal_, Vol. 106, No. 8, pp. 2599–659.

———— (1998). "Bringing International Law Home," _Houston Law Review_, Vol. 35, No. 3, pp. 623–81.

Koremenos, Barbara (2007). "If Only Half of International Agreements Have Dispute Resolution Provisions, Which Half Needs Explaining?," _Journal of Legal Studies_, Vol. 36, No. 1, pp. 189–212.

———— (2013). "Institutionalism and International Law," in Jeffrey L. Dunoff and Mark A. Pollack (eds.), _Interdisciplinary Perspectives on International Law and International Relations: The State of the Art_ (New York: Cambridge University Press), pp. 59–82.

Koremenos, Barbara, and Timm Betz (2013). "The Design of Dispute Settlement Procedures in International Agreements," in Jeffrey L. Dunoff and Mark A. Pollack (eds.), _Interdisciplinary Perspectives on International Law and International Relations: The State of the Art_ (New York: Cambridge University Press), pp. 371–93.

Koremenos, Barbara, Charles Lipson, and Duncan Snidal (2001). "The Rational Design of International Institutions," _International Organization_, Vol. 55, No. 4, pp. 761–99.

Koskenniemi, Martti (1990). "The Politics of International Law," _European Journal of International Law_, Vol. 1, No. 1, pp. 4–32.

Koskenniemi, Martti, and Paivi Leino (2002). "Fragmentation of International Law? Postmodern Anxieties," _Leiden Journal of International Law_, Vol. 15, No. 3, pp. 553–79.

Krasner, Stephen D. (1982). "Structural Causes and Regime Consequences: Regimes as Intervening Variables," _International Organization_, Vol. 36, No. 2, pp. 186–205.

———— (1991). "Global Communications and National Power: Life on the Pareto Frontier," _World Politics_, Vol. 43, No. 3, pp. 336–66.

Kratochwil, Friedrich V. (1989). _Rules, Norms and Decisions: On the Conditions of Practical and Legal Reasoning in International Relations and Domestic Affairs_ (Cambridge: Cambridge University Press).

Kratochwil, Friedrich V., and John Gerard Ruggie (1986). "International Organization: A State of the Art on an Art of the State," _International Organization_, Vol. 40, No. 4, pp. 753–75.

Lake, David A. (2011). "Why 'isms' Are Evil: Theory, Epistemology, and Academic Sects as Impediments to Understanding and Progress," _International Studies Quarterly_, Vol. 55, No. 2, pp. 465–80.

Lang, Andrew, and Joanne Scott (2009). "The Hidden World of WTO Governance," _European Journal of International Law_, Vol. 20, No. 3, pp. 575–614.

Lauterpacht, Hersch (1933). _The Function of Law in the International Community_ (Oxford: Oxford University Press).

Lipson, Charles (1991). "Why Are Some International Agreements Informal?," _International Organization_, Vol. 45, No. 4, pp. 495–538.

Martin, Lisa L. (2013). "Against Compliance," in Jeffrey L. Dunoff and Mark A. Pollack (eds.), _Interdisciplinary Perspectives on International Law and International Relations: The State of the Art_ (New York: Cambridge University Press), pp. 591–610.

McDougal, Myres S. (1955). "The Hydrogen Bomb Tests and the International Law of the Sea," _American Journal of International Law_, Vol. 49, No. 3, pp. 356–61.

Meyer, Timothy L. (2012). "Codifying Custom," _University of Pennsylvania Law Review_, Vol. 160, No. 4, pp. 995–1069.

Moravcsik, Andrew (2002). "In Defense of the Democratic Deficit: Reassessing Legitimacy in the European Union," *Journal of Common Market Studies*, Vol. 40, No. 4, pp. 603–24.

———— (2013). "Liberal Theories of International Law," in Jeffrey L. Dunoff and Mark A. Pollack (eds.), *Interdisciplinary Perspectives on International Law and International Relations: The State of the Art* (New York: Cambridge University Press), pp. 83–118.

Morgenthau, Hans (1948). *Politics among Nations: The Struggle for Power and Peace* (New York: Knopf).

Morrow, James D. (2007). "When Do States Follow the Laws of War?," *American Political Science Review*, Vol. 101, No. 3, pp. 559–72.

Nau, Henry R. (2011). "No Alternative to 'isms,'" *International Studies Quarterly*, Vol. 55, No. 2, pp. 487–91.

Neumayer, Eric (2007). "Qualified Ratification: Explaining Reservations to International Human Rights Treaties," *Journal of Legal Studies*, Vol. 36, No. 2, pp. 397–430.

Newman, Abraham, and David Zaring (2013). "Regulatory Networks: Power, Legitimacy, and Compliance," in Jeffrey L. Dunoff and Mark A. Pollack (eds.), *Interdisciplinary Perspectives on International Law and International Relations: The State of the Art* (New York: Cambridge University Press), pp. 244–65.

Norman, George, and Joel P. Trachtman (2005). "The Customary International Law Game," *American Journal of International Law*, Vol. 99, No. 3, pp. 541–80.

Pauwelyn, Joost (2003). *Conflict of Norms in Public International Law: How WTO Law Relates to Other Rules of International Law* (Cambridge: Cambridge University Press).

Pauwelyn, Joost, and Manfred Elsig (2013). "The Politics of Treaty Interpretation: Variations and Explanations across International Tribunals," in Jeffrey L. Dunoff and Mark A. Pollack (eds.), *Interdisciplinary Perspectives on International Law and International Relations: The State of the Art* (New York: Cambridge University Press), pp. 445–73.

Pollack, Mark A. (2003). *The Engines of European Integration: Delegation, Agency and Agenda Setting in the EU* (New York: Oxford University Press).

Posner, Eric A., and Miguel de Figueiredo (2005). "Is the International Court of Justice Biased?," *Journal of Legal Studies*, Vol. 34, No. 2, pp. 599–630.

Posner, Eric A., and John C. Yoo (2005). "Judicial Independence in International Tribunals," *California Law Review*, Vol. 93, No. 1, pp. 1–74.

Ratner, Steven R. (2013). "Persuading to Comply: On the Deployment and Avoidance of Legal Argumentation," in Jeffrey L. Dunoff and Mark A. Pollack (eds.), *Interdisciplinary Perspectives on International Law and International Relations: The State of the Art* (New York: Cambridge University Press), pp. 568–90.

Ratner, Steven R., and Anne-Marie Slaughter (1999). "Appraising the Methods of International Law: A Prospectus for Readers," *American Journal of International Law*, Vol. 93, No. 2, pp. 291–423.

Raustiala, Kal (2013). "Institutional Proliferation and the International Legal Order," in Jeffrey L. Dunoff and Mark A. Pollack (eds.), *Interdisciplinary Perspectives on International Law and International Relations: The State of the Art* (New York: Cambridge University Press), pp. 293–320.

Raustiala, Kal, and Anne-Marie Slaughter (2001). "International Law, International Relations and Compliance," in Walter Carlsnaes, Thomas Risse, and Beth A. Simmons (eds.), *Handbook of International Relations* (London: Sage Publications), pp. 538–58.

Raustiala, Kal, and David G. Victor (2004). "The Regime Complex for Plant Genetic Resources," *International Organization*, Vol. 58, No. 2, pp. 277–309.

Reisman, W. Michael (1990). "Necessary and Proper: Executive Competence to Interpret Treaties," *Yale Journal of International Law*, Vol. 15, No. 2, pp. 316–30.

――― (2003). "Assessing Claims to Revise the Laws of War," *American Journal of International Law*, Vol. 97, No. 1, pp. 82–90.

Reisman, W. Michael, Siegfried Wiessner, and Andrew R. Willard (2007). "The New Haven School: A Brief Introduction," *Yale Journal of International Law*, Vol. 32, No. 2, pp. 575–82.

Reus-Smit, Christian (2004). *The Politics of International Law* (Cambridge: Cambridge University Press).

Roberts, Anthea (2013). "Clash of Paradigms: Actors and Analogies Shaping the Investment Treaty System," *American Journal of International Law*, Vol. 107, No. 1.

Romano, Cesare P. R. (2011). "A Taxonomy of International Rule of Law Institutions," *Journal of International Dispute Settlement*, Vol. 2, No. 1, pp. 241–77.

Shaffer, Gregory C. (2003). *Defending Interests: Public-Private Partnerships in WTO Litigation* (Washington, DC: Brookings).

Shaffer, Gregory C., and Ricardo Meléndez-Ortiz (2010) (eds.). *Dispute Settlement at the WTO: The Developing Country Experience* (Cambridge: Cambridge University Press).

Shaffer, Gregory C., and Mark A. Pollack (2010). "Hard vs. Soft Law: Alternatives, Complements, and Antagonists in International Governance," *Minnesota Law Review*, Vol. 75, No. 3, pp. 706–99.

――― (2013). "Hard Law and Soft Law," in Jeffrey L. Dunoff and Mark A. Pollack (eds.), *Interdisciplinary Perspectives on International Law and International Relations: The State of the Art* (New York: Cambridge University Press), pp. 197–222.

Shelton, Dinah (2000)(ed.). *Commitment and Compliance: The Role of Non-binding Norms in the International Legal System* (New York: Oxford University Press).

Simmons, Beth A. (2009). *Mobilizing for Human Rights: International Law in Domestic Politics* (New York: Cambridge University Press).

Simmons, Beth A., and Daniel J. Hopkins (2005). "The Constraining Power of International Treaties: Theory and Methodology," *American Political Science Review*, Vol. 99, No. 4, pp. 623–31.

Sinclair, Adriana (2010). *International Relations Theory and International Law: A Critical Approach* (Cambridge: Cambridge University Press).

Slaughter Burley, Anne-Marie (1993). "International Law and International Relations Theory: A Dual Agenda," *American Journal of International Law*, Vol. 87, No. 2, pp. 205–39.

Slaughter, Anne-Marie (2000). "A Liberal Theory of International Law," *Proceedings of the American Society of International Law*, Vol. 94, pp. 240–48.

――― (2013). "International Law and International Relations Theory: Twenty Years Later," in Jeffrey L. Dunoff and Mark A. Pollack (eds.), *Interdisciplinary Perspectives on International Law and International Relations: The State of the Art* (New York: Cambridge University Press), pp. 613–25.

Smith, Steve (1992). "The Forty Years' Detour: The Resurgence of Normative Theory in International Relations," *Millennium*, Vol. 21, No. 3, pp. 489–506.

Spiro, Peter J. (2000). "The New Sovereigntists: American Exceptionalism and Its False Prophets," *Foreign Affairs*, Vol. 79, No. 6, pp. 9–16.

――― (2013). "Nongovernmental Organizations in International Relations (Theory)," in Jeffrey L. Dunoff and Mark A. Pollack (eds.), *Interdisciplinary Perspectives on International Law and International Relations: The State of the Art* (New York: Cambridge University Press), pp. 223–43.

Steinberg, Richard H. (2002). "In the Shadow of Law or Power? Consensus-Based Bargaining and Outcomes in the GATT/WTO," *International Organization*, Vol. 56, No. 2, pp. 339–74.

――― (2013). "Wanted – Dead or Alive: Realist Approaches to International Law," in Jeffrey L. Dunoff and Mark A. Pollack (eds.), *Interdisciplinary Perspectives on International Law and International Relations: The State of the Art* (New York: Cambridge University Press), pp. 146–72.

Stone, Randall (2011). *Controlling Institutions: International Organizations and the Global Economy* (New York: Cambridge University Press).

Stone Sweet, Alec and Thomas Brunell (1998). "Constructing a Supranational Constitution: Dispute Resolution and Governance in the European Community," *American Political Science Review*, Vol. 92, No. 1, pp. 63–81.

——— (2012). "The European Court of Justice, State Noncompliance, and the Politics of Override," *American Political Science Review*, Vol. 106, No. 1, pp. 204–13.

Swaine, Edward T. (2002). "Rational Custom," *Duke Law Journal*, Vol. 52, No. 3, pp. 559–627.

Tallberg, Jonas (2002). "Paths to Compliance: Enforcement, Management and the European Union," *International Organization*, Vol. 56, No. 3, pp. 609–43.

Thompson, Alexander (2010). "Rational Design in Motion: Uncertainty and Flexibility in the Global Climate Regime," *European Journal of International Relations*, Vol. 16, No. 2, pp. 269–296.

——— (2013). "Coercive Enforcement in International Law," in Jeffrey L. Dunoff and Mark A. Pollack (eds.), *Interdisciplinary Perspectives on International Law and International Relations: The State of the Art* (New York: Cambridge University Press), pp. 502–23.

Trachtman, Joel P. (2013). "Open Economy Law," in Jeffrey L. Dunoff and Mark A. Pollack (eds.), *Interdisciplinary Perspectives on International Law and International Relations: The State of the Art* (New York: Cambridge University Press), pp. 544–67.

Valentino, Benjamin, Paul Huth, and Sarah Croco (2006). "Covenants without the Sword: International Law and the Protection of Civilians in Times of War," *World Politics*, Vol. 58, No. 3, pp. 339–76.

Voeten, Erik (2008). "The Impartiality of International Judges: Evidence from the European Court of Human Rights," *American Political Science Review*, Vol. 102, No. 4, pp. 417–33.

——— (2013). "International Judicial Independence," in Jeffrey L. Dunoff and Mark A. Pollack (eds.), *Interdisciplinary Perspectives on International Law and International Relations: The State of the Art* (New York: Cambridge University Press), pp. 421–44.

von Stein, Jana (2005). "Do Treaties Constrain or Screen? Selection Bias and Treaty Compliance," *American Political Science Review*, Vol. 99, No. 4, pp. 611–22.

——— (2013). "The Engines of Compliance," in Jeffrey L. Dunoff and Mark A. Pollack (eds.), *Interdisciplinary Perspectives on International Law and International Relations: The State of the Art* (New York: Cambridge University Press), pp. 477–501.

Weiler, Joseph H. H. (1994). "A Quiet Revolution: The European Court of Justice and Its Interlocutors," *Comparative Political Studies*, Vol. 26, No. 4, pp. 510–34.

Index

Abbott, Kenneth, 3, 8, 10, 13, 20, 21, 40, 45, 86, 129, 199–204, 208, 213, 217, 226, 236–237, 371, 525, 613–614, 626–629, 643, 650
accountability, 108, 227, 233, 240, 255, 258, 267, 280, 284, 322, 324, 331–332, 333, 335, 336, 399, 401, 432, 483, 555, 572, 628, 630–631
  See also legitimacy
acculturation, 12, 43, 100, 133, 199, 280, 403–404, 489, 545–546, 548–549, 554–555, 564, 570, 642, 646
  See also compliance
acquis communautaire, 456
  See also European Union
adhere. *See* treaties
Adler, Emanuel, 124, 135
administrative law, 246, 255–257, 260, 267, 283–285, 330–332, 345, 631
  See also global administrative law
administrative review, 24, 345, 350, 352–353, 355, 356, 357, 359, 360, 362–365, 366, 428, 614, 637
Afghanistan, 533, 618
Africa, 294, 347, 348
African Commission on Human and Peoples' Rights, 233
African Union, 351, 506
agent. *See* principal-agent analysis
agreements. *See* treaties
agriculture, 89, 94, 99, 305
  Consultative Group on International Agricultural Research (CGIAR), 300
al Qaeda, 618
Alford, Roger, 399
Algeria, 620
Alien Tort Statute (ATS), 235, 401, 405–406
Allee, Todd, 634

alliances, 65, 151, 152, 159, 161, 239, 426–427, 479, 481, 484, 532, 533, 620
  See also military alliances
Alt, James, 513
Alter, Karen, 24, 73, 74, 102, 103, 278, 397, 408, 426, 515, 613–614, 633, 637
Alvarez, José, 269
amendment. *See* treaties
American Convention on Human Rights, 386
American Society of International Law, 215, 557, 619
analytic eclecticism, 155
analytical positivism, 125
anarchy, 12, 14, 63, 77, 524
Andean Pact, 103, 406
  See also Andean Tribunal of Justice, international courts
Andean Tribunal of Justice (ATJ), 347, 348, 349, 353, 355, 360, 364, 365, 366, 406, 426
  preliminary rulings, 360, 363, 403, 406, 414
  See also international courts
antibribery convention. *See* Organization for Economic Cooperation and Development
antitrust, 244, 252
Arab League, 615
arbitration, 9, 95, 354, 371, 375, 376, 379, 380, 382, 383, 384, 385, 386, 452, 453, 455, 456, 460, 463, 464, 465, 468, 511, 614, 633, 635
arms control, 50, 93, 137, 182, 183, 215, 296
Asia-Pacific Economic Cooperation (APEC), 301
Association of Small Island States (AOSIS), 231
Association of Southeast Asian Nations (ASEAN), 347, 355, 364, 366
audience costs, 203, 634, 645
Austin, John, 18–19, 126, 160, 641